THE NEW
AMERICAN
VOTER

THE NEW AMERICAN VOTER

★　★　★

WARREN E. MILLER

J. MERRILL SHANKS

Harvard University Press

Cambridge, Massachusetts

London, England　1996

Library of Congress Cataloging-in-Publication Data

Miller, Warren E. (Warren Edward), 1924–
    The new American voter / Warren E. Miller and J. Merrill Shanks.
        p. cm.
    Includes bibliographical references and index.
    ISBN 0-674-60840-2 (alk. paper).
    ISBN 0-674-60841-0 (pbk.: alk. paper)
    1. Elections—United States.   I. Shanks, J. Merrill.   II. Title.
JK1976.M55 1996
324.973—dc20
96-8079

To Angus Campbell,
without whom none of this would have happened

Preface

In this book we discuss evidence from recent U.S. presidential elections concerning a comprehensive set of explanations for electoral choices made by individual citizens. Those explanations concern the decision to vote or abstain as well as the choice, for voters, among major candidates for President. Since the publication of *The American Voter* in 1960, the electoral field has considered a remarkable array of competing and complementary explanations for these basic questions. This diversity of explanatory perspectives is a consequence of the continuing eclecticism of students of electoral behavior, who have adopted—or modified—fragments of substantive theory, holistic methodological approaches, analytic techniques, and empirical generalizations from many different disciplines and philosophical traditions. Theories based on group identification and influence, rational choice, developmental psychology, and socialization have all made their contributions, as have the conventional wisdom of political participants and the observations of media commentators. These varied sources of information and insight, however, have neither rested on nor produced an integrated or unified body of theory from which specific hypotheses can be derived. One of the primary purposes of this book is to present an overall framework which can be used to assess and compare explanatory ideas based on different theoretical or conceptual foundations. In some instances, our analyses will suggest that several different competing explanations may all be "correct," based on our use of a multiple-stage model that considers different types of explanations for different stages in the evolution of electoral decisions.

More than three decades have passed since the publication of *The*

American Voter, and forty years since the studies of the elections of 1952 and 1956 on which it was based. During that period, academic analyses of U.S. presidential elections have produced a wide variety of insights into the origins of voters' decisions. These diverse conclusions have been based on a growing body of survey data and analytic procedures that did not exist in the 1950s. Most of the electoral studies that have been published during this period, however, have focused on specific electoral explanations or hypotheses, rather than attempting a comprehensive accounting like that in *The American Voter;* nor have they suggested the ways in which a wide variety of alternative explanations may fit together.

Given the substantial period of time that has elapsed since *The American Voter* was published, we have taken another look at many, but not all, of the questions addressed in that book. Some of our conclusions represent a restatement or clarification of general conclusions presented in *The American Voter,* while others present somewhat different conclusions for more recent elections based on survey measures that did not exist when the earlier book was being prepared. We have preserved, however, the original book's emphasis on the way in which multiple explanations may be combined in an overall explanatory framework.

The American Voter presented a perspective that sketched a provisional location for various determinants of the vote decision in what was described as a "funnel of causality." In this scheme, one began the analysis of electoral behavior with the acts to be understood—the citizens' decisions (a) to vote or not to vote, and (b) to choose among candidates for election. After identifying the immediate or proximate antecedents of electoral decisions, one could then trace back to the sources or origins of those proximate causes of the vote.

At one point in the planning of the present book, we had decided to give systematic if not exhaustive attention to "the causes of the causes" by, wherever possible, tracing out the antecedents of causal elements involved in the vote decision, even if they added little to our direct comprehension of the vote. We abandoned this goal when it became apparent that the adequacy of such analysis would vary tremendously across the many different elements included to explain the vote, and that it would be virtually impossible to maintain a coherent focus on our major goal while extending the inquiry to a host of secondary objectives.

Out of the tradition of *The American Voter,* a number of useful propositions have emerged. Some causative factors have been designated as *long-term,* stable factors influencing the vote decisions but, at least in the short run, not influenced by the process of deciding. Other factors have been seen as *short-term,* shaped by an interaction of election campaign events with the long-term elements. Although seldom presented as explicit elements in the funnel of causality, other seemingly necessary contributions to more complete explanation have been added from time to time—analyses from the media of mass communication, the specification of conditions for evaluation that are fixed by the economic and social context of the election, general orientations to the social, economic, and political values of the society, theories of attribution, and distinctions between cognitive and affective components of attitudes and beliefs.

This book is perhaps as notable for that which it does not attempt as for that to which it aspires. We do not present a unified, integrated general theory of voting behavior which might pull thirty years of accumulated fragments of insight and understanding together into a single body of knowledge. We do note, more or less in passing, occasions on which interrelated generalizations form islands of coherent theory in a sea of empirical evidence. Bringing theoretical order to all of the bits and pieces is a task for another book. For now, we are attempting to lay out one set of rules by which we may assess the relative contribution of each fragment to the ultimate electoral outcome which rests on the two fundamental decisions: should I vote, and (if so) for whom? This kind of assessment is a necessary first stage in the transition from empirical generalization to theoretical development. We pursue the task of clarifying possible linkages in a comprehensive explanatory structure by employing an analytic scheme which limits the credit given to each factor to its "unique" contribution to the vote. The same scheme suggests some of the contributions of antecedent factors as well as the mediating processes by which a given element is subsequently translated into the vote.

This scheme ultimately tests a great many potential explanations of voter turnout and vote choice for which relevant data have been collected. Inevitably, given the original vision of an infinite expansion of multiple origins for each of the proximate causes of the vote, the sequence of analytic procedures is guided by the skeleton of a complex causal structure. In some instances the skeleton has connecting tissues which provide a partial—even a substantial—description or explanation of both the origins *and* the consequences of an element that is embedded in the midst of a larger explanatory structure. In other instances, however, we learn little about the origins of a given factor and are left perplexed about the processes by which it contributes to the voting decision. This is so because the potential components of a structure that would probe the origins as well as the consequences of an explanatory factor are available for analysis *only* because they themselves have been thought to be related to the vote decision. Put somewhat differently, no variable has been included in our analysis because it was thought to be part of the explanation for some other intersection of "causes."

At this point we should re-emphasize the haphazard manner in which the evolving content of the National Election Studies has, over the years, satisfied various needs of a relatively complete causal structure for "explaining the vote." The specification of the questions to be asked in each of the quadrennial NES inquiries has not proceeded by deduction from a single theoretical framework. Rather it has proceeded by fits and starts, by fad and fancy. In some instances, anomalies resulting from a disjuncture of theory and fact have prompted hypothesis building and testing. Thus, the frequent failure or inability to document the translation of voters' apparent economic self-interest into rational electoral choices eventually produced the concept of socio-tropic voting as an alternative to egocentric motivation. In other instances, with the temporal extension of the NES time series, emerging patterns of empirical regularity have prompted the exploration of theories of generational differences to explain differences between later cohorts and their earlier predecessors. Or, with increasing frequency, the importation of new analytic methodologies has suggested the fallibility of prior substantive conclusions. Thus the introduction of simultaneous equation models and two-stage least squares has led to arguments over whether a presumed stable, long-term factor such as party identification stands outside the short-term changes which precede an election or, instead, should be properly conceived as thoroughly endogenous to short-term forces which produce the vote decision.

The scholars charged with maintaining the content of the American election study time series through succeeding elections have been representatives of a relatively closely knit, interactive community of researchers—including the authors of this book. Nevertheless, changes in explanatory outlook have been encouraged. As a result of turnover in the personnel designing successive studies, criticism sought from abroad from review panels, and responses to new contributions to the professional literature, the array of factors shaping the content of the current National Election Studies has produced great variation in the substantive analytic themes that can be examined, election by election. From our perspective, each succeeding data collection in the NES series has been richer and more inclusive than its predecessor. The continued growth in the substantive scope of this data base has added to the need for an analytic mode with which to address a veritable host of potential explanations of electoral decisions.

In recent years, our analytic goal has been to keep pace with the proliferation and enrichment of study content. To that end we have employed a multi-stage, bloc recursive model to arrange a variety of putative causes or explanations in a single, cumulative descriptive array. This analytic model has emerged as we have tried to clarify our thinking about causality and causal sequence.

The structure of the model is shaped by our attempt to exploit and make explicit the "logic of causal analysis" for the analysis of survey data, as introduced by Paul F. Lazarsfeld, elaborated by Morris Rosenberg, and summarized and extended by James Davis in *The Logic of Causal Order* (1985). The logic accommodates the idea of multiple causes of phenomena, and our implementation of the logic ultimately turns to analytic procedures based on the machinery of multiple regression. The logic of causal analysis is totally free of substantive theoretical content. It does not rest on the postulates of rational choice theory nor any other theory. Nor does it arise from empirical generalizations about the nature of attitudes, beliefs, values, and behaviors in general, or about economic, social, or psychological phenomena in particular. The essence of the logic of causal order is a simple formal statement of conditions under which a chain of inferences about the causes of some ultimate dependent variable (such as the vote) seems plausible. Our emphasis on the plausibility of assumptions about causal relationships has moved us away from being satisfied with descriptions of co-variation that are not interpreted in the context of explicit temporal order.

From some perspectives, the logic of causal analysis as we employ it may seem primitive or simplistic. It has a strong deterministic flavor, derived from the presumption that if we take enough factors into account we *can,* indeed, achieve a satisfactorily complete rendering of the origins and consequences of a behavioral act. It is not intended to produce theory rather than empirical generalization, but it can readily accommodate theoretical interpretation after the fact. The erection of explanations may come after the fact, and the analytic product may be used to confirm theoretical propositions already in existence, as well as suggesting new substantive hypotheses. In our minds, however, the strength of this approach lies in its contribution to the interpretation, or the meaningfulness, of complex, interrelated structures of empirical generalization.

Throughout our study of American voting behavior, we have been impressed with the usefulness of many of the perspectives that guided the original version of *The American Voter.* True, we have turned sharply away from the original emphasis on Levinian field theory, but we have a renewed interest in many of the elements that led to the concept of the "funnel of causality." Indeed, the fundamental logic of elaboration in the analysis of survey data formalizes the implicit relationships embedded in the funnel and is central to our present work and to our attempt to achieve at least a partial untangling of causal relationships that are defined in terms of a temporal dimension.

The American Voter simplified the temporal theme inherent in the funnel metaphor and avoided searching for first causes by settling for the distinction between long-term and short-term factors influencing the vote. We have explicitly introduced more temporal variation with a scheme of six stages in our hierarchical, causal structure. But we have often avoided the search for a proliferation of origins by settling, as did *The American Voter,* for historical roles that could be assigned to persistent predispositions.

This restatement of a one-time orthodoxy is impelled by a number of considerations. We think it is important to know which, if any, aspects of a given vote decision, or election outcome, were in place because of long-term factors held in common with other, adjoining decisions or elections, and which factors were produced by the immediate context of the particular decision, or election. With every change of government the argument rages, and new policies are shaped by conclusions about the electoral role played by the performance of the previous administration, by the issues made salient by a new domestic or international context, or by the evident contrasts in the personal attributes of the candidates exposed by the campaign. In particular, as a prominent sub-theme, we think that sorting out the contribution of the voters' policy-related preferences and their evaluations of retrospective or prospective performances is essential to a politically useful reconstruction of the election outcome.

The logical imperative invoked by the search for a general reference point for comparing elections does not mean that such a reference point exists. However, it is our belief that many such reference points do exist to guide the comparative study of voting behavior. Our basic model for the study of change in human behavior, the so-called generational persistence model of societal change, presumes that great openness to change among the young is gradually replaced by stability in the persistence of early orientations. We see individual maturation leading to various sets of values, beliefs, attitudes, and behavioral patterns that are more or less stable. In our formulation we have labeled the stable orientations "predispositions" to suggest that they subsequently guide, or determine, individuals' responses to the changing environment around them. Were the predispositions fixed and immutable, they would be the basis for a deterministic view of the individual's world. Were they completely open to change, prior knowledge about them would not be useful in the delineation of causal structures.

On a different level, if the systematic study of voting behavior is to be faithful to the processes that produce the behavior, the sequence of events that make up the process should be reflected in the structure of the analysis. But, as the metaphor of the funnel implies, there is no single starting point for any behavior that is the result of multiple causes. However, insofar as party identifications (and a limited number of other predispositions) summarize a multiplicity of historical causes, they do provide a means of bounding our curiosities about antecedents.

We are quite aware of how little we have done so far to test some of these causal perspectives. We have identified one predisposition, party identification, that has been subjected to relatively intensive scrutiny over the years, and we often refer to a second, and less well documented, predisposition based on ideological self-placement. The operational label for that concept indicates that our understanding of it is incomplete: should it be called ideological identification, or is it simply a self-classification with few affective overtones and only limited connotations of a personal sense of self? We have given equally brief treatment to a battery of "policy-related predispositions" concerning specific areas, including egalitarianism, moral tolerance, and attitudes toward limited government. And yet we see these predispositions also as possible manifestations of learned readiness to respond in particular ways to various aspects of politics and political debate. We think they represent relatively enduring perspectives that are available to be engaged by political events and political actors and thereby provide the foundation for short-term evaluations, just as party identification does.

If the National Election Studies have enriched the concept of long-term forces by adding such predispositions as ideological self-placement, moral tolerance, and egalitarianism to party identification, our explicit use of the logic of elaboration has extended, if not enriched, the distinction between long-term and short-term forces. In our earlier work we distinguished among eight degrees of "long-termedness/short-termedness" in our multi-stage, bloc recursive model of the voter's decision (Shanks and Miller, 1991). There are problems with maintaining the credibility of such a highly differentiated explanatory structure while relying primarily on cross-section data, and therefore we have reduced the number of sequential stages that we distinguish to six. Nevertheless, the increase in differentiation (from the long-term/short-term nomenclature of *The American Voter*) calls for a new articulation of the meaning associated with temporal duration implied by the bounding concepts of long-term and short-term.

The problem is not entirely simple because our causal structure presumes that the real "forces" in a given election are created by the interaction of intra-psychic phenomena with the environment external to the voter. For example, party identification qualifies as a long-term force in the lexicon of American voting behavior in part because it is the most enduring and stable of the intra-psychic states that characterize individual voters. It is also true that the continuity of meaning is attributable to the persistence of the two-party system. As Converse argued in "Of Time and Partisan Stability" (1969), the disappearance of old parties and the rise of new ones causes disruptions that greatly modify any long-term nature of party identification. And the party identification of the young differs from that of the old precisely because it has not had

time to stabilize and acquire the pervasive relationship with other political attitudes that is characteristic of party identification in older
voters. Even though, on the average and across all age groups, party
identification is the most persistent and enduring of all political attitudes, its status as a long-term force varies with the age of the identifier—or with the length of the period of identification. Its relevance to
the vote decision depends on some blend of the emphasis given to
partisanship in the pre-election campaign with the circumstances of the
early political socialization of the voter.

A related point has to do with voters' preferences concerning current
policy issues. Policy preferences come and go as factors influencing the
vote, and some stay longer than others. How long preferences endure as
forces relevant to voters' choices among presidential candidates depends
in part on the political environment, on whether successive sets of
candidates focus on the same policy choices across two or more elections. And whether a given issue is emphasized in a succession of
campaigns depends in part on whether there is a continuing responsiveness to that issue on the part of the voters.

A classificatory dilemma can arise when short-term emphasis on a
particular campaign theme draws a response because of pre-existing
long-term predispositions. In this circumstance our inclination is to
credit the short-term stimulus as the more proximate cause. Attitudes
toward egalitarianism may qualify as stable, persistent long-term intra-
psychic forces—but they are not relevant to our understanding of the
vote unless short-term elements of the campaign, or relatively short-term
changes in the context of the election (for example, media emphasis on
the growing disparity of income distributions) give them salience and
relevance.

In any event, the use of the logic of elaboration in our analytic format
does not rest on resolving classificatory or definitional dilemmas. It does,
however, call for serious attention to developmental or causal sequence.
To continue with our example, general attitudes toward equality may
have no direct effect on the vote. But if such attitudes have a significant
total effect that is then mediated by various short-term policy preferences, we conclude that egalitarianism is a relevant factor essential to
our understanding of the decision-making process that produced the
vote. Our basic challenge is to formulate a causal sequence which gives
credit to longer-term forces with total effects while recognizing the

additional explanatory power associated with intervening shorter-term factors. If perceptions of candidate attributes appear to be affected because of prior policy-related preferences, the question is not so much the definitional distinction of long-term versus short-term but whether we have the sequence right.

This book would not have been possible without the series of national surveys that have been carried out by the National Election Studies in the Center for Political Studies at the University of Michigan. The NES studies, in turn, owe much to the many scholars who have contributed their ideas and efforts toward the enrichment of those studies. We would like to express our continuing appreciation for the financial support provided for the election studies by the National Science Foundation and for the expert assistance of the NES staff and the Inter-university Consortium for Political and Social Research, who have prepared and distributed the resulting data and documentation. In addition to the collection and preparation of the survey data used in this project, financial support for our own work has been provided by the Department of Political Science at Arizona State University, the Center for Political Studies at the University of Michigan, and both the Survey Research Center and the Department of Political Science at the University of California, Berkeley. The two of us, however, are responsible for all of the statistical results and substantive interpretations in this book, and therefore none of our conclusions should be attributed to the National Science Foundation, the National Election Studies, the Consortium, or our respective universities.

In addition, we would like to acknowledge the many contributions to this project made by Douglas Strand, who served as our principal graduate assistant throughout the preparation of this book. He implemented many different versions of the constructed measures and multivariate analyses that are discussed in Chapters 9 through 17, and he has been a frequent discussant and friendly critic for our evolving interpretations of the 1988 and 1992 elections. We are very grateful to Doug for the skill and patience he exhibited during the periods when we re-evaluated specific measures and analytic procedures, and for the many suggestions he made based on his own dissertation research.

We are also indebted to Joy Erickson of the Political Science Department at Arizona State University, who prepared the final drafts for all sections of the book and worked with us through many earlier versions and revisions. We also relied on Jesse Chanley, David Shafir, and Scott Thompson for the data tabulations associated with Chapters 3–9; and we benefited from the work of Pat Crittendon, whose well-honed editorial skills added to the readability of much of the book. We are likewise grateful to Deborah Putnam of the Computer-assisted Survey Methods Program at the University of California, Berkeley, who prepared draft versions for many chapters and dealt with our frequent revisions during the two-site preparation of this book.

Our collaboration in analyzing voting behavior in U.S. presidential elections dates from the summer of 1981 and produced a series of essays in the *British Journal of Political Science* before we began this book. We are grateful to the editors of the *British Journal* during that period, Ivor Crewe and Anthony King, for their encouragement and suggestions, and for their willingness to consider manuscripts that were much longer than normal journal articles. The flexibility of that format permitted us to develop many of the concepts and analytic strategies found in this book.

Since 1981 we have benefited from specific suggestions and criticisms from a large number of colleagues in the electoral field. Although it is impossible to identify all of them, we would like to acknowledge in particular the suggestions of Richard Brody, David Collier, Bob Luskin, Tom Mann, Herbert McClosky, Richard Niemi, Steven Rosenstone, Paul Sniderman, Laura Stoker, and Raymond Wolfinger. In addition, we received extensive comments, as well as informal suggestions, based on earlier drafts of these materials from Philip Converse, Ivor Crewe, Heinz Eulau, William Flanigan, Kent Jennings, John Kessel, and David Leege. Their detailed comments have been particularly helpful in our efforts to clarify the rationale and logic for our general approach to electoral explanation, but these colleagues are not responsible for any errors that may remain in our analytic procedures or substantive conclusions.

Finally, we would like to express our gratitude for the way in which our wives, Ruth Jones and Patricia Shanks, have coped with the intensity and duration of our collaboration, from the earlier *British Journal* phases of our work through the preparation of this manuscript. We greatly appreciate their patience and encouragement.

Contents

★ ★ ★

Tables and Figures

★ ★ ★

▪ Tables

▪ Figures

▪ Appendix Tables

PART I

INTRODUCTION AND HISTORICAL CONTEXT

Electoral Explanation and Survey Research: An Introduction to Substantive Objectives and Quantitative Methods

After each presidential election, a combination of scientific curiosity, widespread popular interest, and the need for interpretations that satisfy political partisanship invariably leads to competing interpretations of the election results. Such interpretations typically suggest somewhat different answers to the following recurring questions:

- Why did some citizens participate while others did not?
- Of those who did go to the polls, why did some vote for one candidate and some for another?
- Why did one candidate and not the other win? And why was the margin of victory so big (or small)?

Since the introduction of modern sampling and interviewing, one of the most prominent applications of survey research has been the description—and explanation—of voters' political choices.[1] The results of presidential elections matter a great deal to many citizens as well as to opposing candidates, parties, and allied groups. Because much is at stake, the opposing sides almost always emphasize different explanations for the most recent election outcome. The winning party typically claims a "mandate" to carry out the policies it has proposed, based on the public claim (if not private conviction) that the majority of voters have embraced those proposals as reasons for their choice. In contrast, the losing party often emphasizes the deficiencies of its candidate, uncontrollable external conditions, or the winning candidate's personal qualities—rather than the voters' rejection of that party and its policies.

3

The Republicans claimed, for example, that Ronald Reagan's and George Bush's victories in 1980, 1984, and 1988 were based on majority support for a strong defense, lower taxes, restraint if not reductions in programs for the disadvantaged, and rejection of Democratic social policies on topics such as abortion and affirmative action. Many Democrats interpreted the same elections in terms of Jimmy Carter's apparently ineffectual performance as president (in 1980), Reagan's skills as "the great communicator" (in 1984), and a strong economy (in both 1984 and 1988). In a similar fashion, Democrats often interpreted Bill Clinton's victory in 1992 in terms of popular rejection of the failed "Reaganomic" policies of the Bush administration and majority support for Clinton's proposals concerning welfare, health care, and education. Many Republicans interpreted the same election in terms of the recession that began in 1990, coupled with George Bush's weakness in arguing against Clinton's liberal positions. It is, of course, not only active partisans who provide such interpretations. Editors, reporters, political commentators—as well as political scientists—all offer interpretations of this order.

Because there are persistent differences in the interpretation of elections, substantial resources are regularly invested in the collection of survey data that can be used to explain current political circumstances in anticipation of a forthcoming election as well as the actual voting behavior of the electorate after an election has taken place. These data collections include frequent polls by Gallup, CBS/*New York Times,* and other media-based organizations, such as the Times-Mirror group; a large volume of private surveys conducted for parties and candidates; and a variety of university-based surveys whose primary purpose is basic or scholarly research.

This book is based entirely in the latter tradition of electoral surveys, in two respects. In the first place, the data for our analyses have been collected by the National Election Study (NES), the organization which continues the biennial election surveys that have been conducted by scholars at the University of Michigan since 1952 (Miller, 1994). The data are collected precisely because of scientific curiosity about the many facets of each election. Second, we regard the most frequently cited book based on the Michigan election surveys, *The American Voter,* as the primary reference point for our work. As suggested by its title, the current book represents a return to that classic report. The book has been powerfully shaped by the concepts and explanatory ideas in *The*

American Voter, but our conclusions are quite different from those that would have been produced by a straightforward replication. Like *The American Voter,* the present book presents a comprehensive approach to explaining electoral behavior in presidential elections, including explanations of electoral participation or turnout, individual vote choice, and the interpretation of election results. In pursuing these objectives we have considered a wide variety of alternative explanatory ideas, including most of those featured in *The American Voter.* Our overall model represents an attempt to clarify and extend that book's emphasis on the evolution of political attitudes over time. While focusing on recent elections, we have updated conclusions in the original work that are different in the current period, and we have identified several areas in which contemporary survey questions and analytic methods lead to significantly different conclusions.

Many of our analyses are devoted to the 1992 presidential election, with selected comparisons to the three preceding elections in the 1980s. We have concentrated on these recent elections because of their greater relevance for our understanding of contemporary politics, and because the NES surveys in those years contain the most comprehensive set of measures with which to test alternative explanatory ideas. However, we would not limit the application of our analytic scheme to the Reagan/Bush/Clinton era. Our analyses are based on an explanatory model and survey-based procedures that we recommend for any electoral context which calls for the evaluation of a comprehensive set of explanatory ideas. For that reason, our presentation will emphasize the rationale and logic behind our general approach to electoral explanation as well as our interpretation of both individual and aggregate decisions during the 1980s and 1990s.

The New American Voter is intended to be more than an exemplary analysis of the 1992 election. As the bibliographic references are intended to suggest, it is in some aspects an interim summation of four decades of research by scores of social scientists. Its predecessor volumes, *The Voter Decides* and *The American Voter,* established a research tradition that was continued by the original authors and provided a point of departure for many other students of voting behavior. A substantial fraction of their work is cited throughout this book. Any comparison of more recent work with *The American Voter* would also include a progress report on continuity and change in both research methodology and our understanding of mass political behavior. Our pursuit of all these objectives has been made possible because the Michigan election studies—the National Election Study since 1978—have provided survey data for all eleven presidential elections (as well as ten of the eleven off-year congressional elections) between 1952 and 1994. Insofar as this book is a reflection of the work of other scholars, it is so because since 1962 all of the NES data have been in the public domain and accessible through the Inter-University Consortium for Political and Social Research. The utilization of those resources by others has created a sub-field of the discipline of political science. Furthermore, it has enriched the work of colleagues in other disciplines far beyond the limits suggested by the works cited in the notes.

With the publication of *The American Voter* in 1960 the study of American electoral behavior became identified with the discipline of political science. Although the intellectual origins—if not roots—of electoral research are shared with sociology and social psychology, political science has provided the organizational locus for most of the scholars who make up the invisible college of students of voting for whom this volume has been assembled. Furthermore, this book is about voting—voting in national presidential elections in the United States. It necessarily touches on many topics, including attitude formation and change, the transmission of values, group identification, social connectedness, and the perceptions of other persons—but always and only because of their relevance for our attempts to understand better the individual's decision to vote, and for whom.

Beyond describing the generic nature of our approach to electoral explanation, we have been deliberately inclusive in conceptual or substantive terms. As outlined in the following paragraphs, the field of electoral analysis has been shaped by several different academic disciplines as well as by conflicting political perspectives. Because of that diversity, we have considered a wide variety of individual attributes of voters as potential partial explanations of individual voting behavior. The electoral field also includes several distinct approaches to the utilization of survey data for explanatory purposes. For that reason, this chapter and several that follow also include discussions of several methodological issues, each of which involves substantive (as well as technical) assumptions about the phenomena we are trying to explain, and each of which can make a substantial difference in subsequent interpretations of elections. The final pages of this chapter identify the sequence in which major topics are addressed in the rest of this book.

▪ Diversity in the Content of Potential Explanatory Variables[2]

In addition to politically motivated differences in electoral interpretations, conflicting conclusions about any specific election may be attributed to the remarkable variety of explanatory ideas or "themes" that have been suggested by several academic disciplines as well as politicians and journalists. It *is* easy for observers to disagree when they are trying to explain only one electoral decision and can select their preferred explanations from so many potential factors, issues, or considerations—all of which compete for explanatory credit in accounting for both individual and aggregate decisions in a given election campaign. In identifying some apparent causes as more important than others, electoral analysts rely on several different ways of classifying potential explanations, including distinctions between political versus non-political variables; opinions about parties versus issues versus candidates; short-term versus long-term forces; and issues that are defined in terms of conflict or consensus concerning basic governmental objectives.

Non-Political and Political Variables

One of the earliest—and most persistent—distinctions between alternative types of explanatory variables rests on the assumption that characteristics of voters which are not defined in "political" terms can nevertheless play an important role in influencing their electoral preferences and behavior. At various points, the electoral field has been described in terms of a competition between sociological explanations based on social or economic characteristics of the voters and psychological explanations based on their attitudes or opinions. In contemporary research, social or economic characteristics are usually included as explanatory variables. Even though such characteristics are technically exogenous to political or electoral preferences, they have an indirect impact through their influence on a variety of political attitudes which, in turn, determine the vote. Indeed, a cultural approach to electoral analysis gives primary emphasis to political perceptions and evaluations as they are captured by and reflected in the social and economic characteristics of the voter. They are the result of social and political experiences that define social location and cultural values. The most frequently used characteristics of this sort include voters' race or ethnicity, gender, age (or generation), religion, marital status, level of education, employment status, family income, social class, union membership, and the region of the country in which they live. Each of these variables represents a highly stable characteristic in the sense that voters' current "positions" on the variable were established long before the election, although the political effects of that characteristic may not have arisen until the current campaign. In general, highly stable variables of this sort usually become politically relevant when they serve as indicators of past political experiences that have left their mark on distinctive values or preferences that are then emphasized (or activated) in a given election campaign. Of course, such characteristics may also become directly relevant when they are central to specific campaign issues, as with religion in 1960 and 1992, or race in 1964.

Parties/Issues/Candidates

The most frequently used distinction among different types of explanatory variables concerns the *object* of the attitude involved—that is, voters' opinions about the parties, about governmental policies or conditions that are discussed during the campaign, or about personal characteristics of the candidates. No matter what other distinctions are employed, these traditional categories are reflected in most comprehensive explanations of the vote.[3] As with other distinctions between different types of explanatory variables, the primary motivation for this classification has been to assess the relative importance of these aspects of a given campaign.

Long-Term Predispositions and Short-Term Forces

The traditional classification of electoral explanations in terms of parties, issues, and candidates is hard to separate from the suggestion that some political opinions have a "long-term" influence on voters' decisions, while other opinions represent only "short-term" forces in the current campaign. To qualify as a long-term influence, a given characteristic must both be stable (or resistant to change from campaign-specific forces) and have a continuing impact on other partisan attitudes or the vote. In contrast, short-term forces in a given campaign can be based on either the temporary activation of stable predispositions or some unique (and therefore transient) aspect of the current campaign. Short-term forces need not have an impact on other forces that help shape the vote.

In principle, any characteristic that might be used to explain the vote can be placed on a continuum from extremely stable to highly volatile. On the basis of more than three decades of NES-related research, most analysts have concluded that the NES question concerning partisan identification represents the most stable of all political attitudes. Measures based on perceptions or evaluations of specific candidates represent the most volatile potential causes of the vote—and different groupings of issue-related opinions occupy intermediate, and sometimes somewhat uncertain, positions in this respect. As emphasized below, however, electoral analysts do not agree about the degree to which these three types of attitudes are influenced by other short-term forces in the current campaign—or by one another.

In the original version of *The American Voter,* the metaphor of a "funnel of causality" was introduced to portray two dimensions distinguishing causal factors from the vote. The concept was that of a host of historic "causes" converging, in the passage of time, to produce the vote at the small end of the funnel. The cross-section of the funnel portrayed relative proximity to the political core. The distance from the mouth of the funnel to its small end represented temporal distance from the vote. In the present volume we preserve both dimensions, but we recognize more differentiation among long-term and short-term factors than was made explicit in the original version. Explicit representation of the linkages between causal elements implicitly located near the outside of the funnel, at some conceptual remove from the political core, provides the sharpest contrast between the present book and *The American Voter.* In Chapters 9 and 10, for example, we connect voters' social and economic characteristics to their vote decisions through five presumably intermediate causal stages. The entire book is based on an explanatory structure that organizes all potentially relevant factors into a sequence of stages and a sequence of multivariate analyses for each of the stages.

Two Major Types of Issues

In landmark studies that defined the electoral field for several decades, researchers at both Columbia and Michigan suggested that campaign issues should be described in terms of two contrasting criteria for political evaluations.[4] Subsequently, the conceptual dichotomization of issue content has been described in various terms, including contrasting criteria based on *conflict* or *consensus* in the electorate concerning specific governmental objectives; candidates' *positions* on a given issue in contrast to their *style* (or *valence*); and voters' preferences concerning *policy* or their evaluations of candidate (or incumbent) *performance*. In our view, this family of similar distinctions may be clarified by noting that some positive or negative impressions of a candidate may be based on voters' beliefs that a controversial policy supported by that candidate is either *right* or *wrong*, while other impressions may be based on voters' perceptions of a candidate's or party's *success* or *failure* concerning the attainment of some consensual objective.

Contemporary analysts do not agree on the necessity of these distinctions. In our view, however, such distinctions are very important for understanding the origins and therefore the implications of election-induced changes in democratic governments when the nature of the electoral mandate is in question. In our previous work, we have emphasized the elements of *similarity* among various alternative distinctions between these two types of issues. As suggested by the subtitle of this book, however, we have reformulated our explanatory model in a way that emphasizes the *difference* between conflict and consensus concerning the purposes or objectives for governmental activities. Furthermore, as explained in Chapter 8, we recommend that the concept of "performance evaluation" be used sparingly in electoral explanation because of the ambiguities resulting from the variety of meanings associated with that expression.

Other Conceptual Distinctions

We have suggested only a few of the ways in which electoral analysts have classified and summarized the large number of political attitudes that may have influenced voter decisions in a specific election. To clarify the role played by different types of factors, electoral analysts have also suggested distinctions based on voters' economic interests (defined in terms of individual or group benefits), their evaluations of personal and national conditions, the degree of specificity or generality in their preferences, the degree to which policy preferences constitute hard or easy choices for voters, the degree to which preferences are based on ends rather than means, and the degree to which evaluations represent retrospective assessments of past performance in contrast to prospective expectations concerning the future.

In our previous essays on the 1980, 1984, and 1988 elections, we have presented results concerning many of these distinctions while analyzing different themes, and this book continues that tradition (Miller and Shanks, 1982; Shanks and Miller, 1990, 1991). We will identify all of the variables in our analysis with one or another of eight explanatory themes.

The eight themes begin with (1) stable social and economic characteristics of the voters. The list goes on to include (2) party identification, (3) various policy-related predispositions, and (4) current preferences on policy issues, as well as (5) perceptions of current conditions. We next separate evaluations into (6) retrospective evaluations of the incumbent President, (7) comparative evaluations of personal traits of the presidential candidates, and (8) prospective evaluations of both the political parties and the candidates. Finally, we note that any explanatory effort of this sort must consider the potentially confounding effects of explanatory variables that have been omitted (or badly represented) *and* are related to variables that have been included in the analysis. Because of the possibility of bias in our conclusions that might result simply from the omission of relevant variables, the analyses summarized in this book have included searches through a large set of potential explanatory variables, as well as explorations of alternative ways of representing their apparent effects. In numerous instances, the result has been to disclose evidence that an explanation or reason given for election results, as presented in the popular media, had, in fact, little or no apparent bearing on individual voters' decisions or on the election outcome.

Explanation of Individual versus Aggregate Decisions

Much of this book concentrates on the role played by specific types of variables (or explanatory themes) in determining *individual voter behavior.* It should be noted, however, that academic, journalistic, and political use of such explanations is often linked to a quite different—but related—analytic question about the aggregate result or outcome of the election. In particular, many observers of a given election want to understand why the victorious party won, and why its margin of victory was as big (or small) as it was. Because of that impulse, analysts often try to decompose the winner's plurality into a set of positive and negative components or sources which, in combination, appear to have produced the collective electoral decision. Unfortunately, the very real distinction between explanations of *individual* decisions and their summation in *aggregate* results is often lost in detailed discussions of the role played by alternative explanatory variables in any specific election—for example, the importance of economic conditions or of policy-related differences between the candidates. Electoral analysts should be certain that they are trying to answer the same question about a given election before trying to unravel any conflicts concerning the importance of various alternative explanations.

This distinction between the explanation of individual-based preferences (or individual choices) and the interpretation (or decomposition) of aggregate results has a long history in the electoral field. The rationale and procedures for assessing the importance of specific factors with respect to these two different aspects of a given campaign are discussed extensively in Part V of this book. At this point, we offer only the following observations:

- A variable or factor that plays a major role in determining individual choices may not necessarily make a significant contribution to the winning candidate's victory. This may be true *if* the distribution of voters' opinions with respect to that factor is "evenly balanced," so that neither candidate has an advantage in that area. Preferences concerning policy direction often have this quality, when opposing parties advocate policy alternatives about which voters are approximately evenly divided.
- Factors that play only a modest role in explaining individual differences in voting behavior may still make a major contribution to the aggregate result. Such a result occurs whenever an explanatory variable has a substantial effect, but is a variable on which opinions are skewed to favor one of the candidates. A clear example of this possibility can be seen in the 1980 electorate's nearly unanimous view that the national economy had gotten worse since the year before. Such a factor must exhibit some cross-sectional variation among voters for us

to estimate its contribution to the winner's plurality, but we shall examine evidence that suggests how highly skewed variables can play a much larger role in shaping the aggregate result than in explaining individual-based differences in vote choice.

▪ Volunteered Reasons and Structured Measures: Methodological and Substantive Issues

All techniques for interpreting the aggregate results of a single election are necessarily based on some kind of explanation at the individual level, and will be suspect insofar as that individual-level account is incorrect. In particular, interpretations of the outcome of an election may be subject to a pervasive controversy (discussed in several chapters of this book) over the validity of respondents' self-reports concerning the reasons or causes for their own vote preferences. Analysts who have confidence in the validity of voters' reports about the determinants of their own candidate preferences are likely to adopt a method for interpreting the aggregate result of a given election that is based on those self-reported reasons. Analysts who are not persuaded of the validity of self-reported causes must rely on some other, less direct, approach to explain both individual decisions and aggregate results. Although we will consider both bases for explanation at some length, in our analysis of the contributions to an election contest we have ultimately relied on indirect analytic techniques rather than accepting a direct explanation based on voters' proffered reasons for a candidate preference.

Most conflicts between alternative interpretations of the same election are assumed to be substantive, based on rival analysts' emphasis on different explanatory variables. Some differences in interpretations, however, can be traced to methodological or technical differences between analysts in the assumptions they have made about causation, measurement, and the effects of omitted (missing) variables. Thus, substantive issues are often confused with controversies concerning alternative methodological strategies for trying to explain any choice or behavior with survey data.

In *The American Voter,* each voter's decision was seen as determined by a "field of psychological forces" that was created by that person's reactions to the current campaign. Such forces were measured by categorizing responses to open-ended questions concerning those aspects of the candidates and parties which the voter "liked" and "disliked." In that approach, the relative importance of six different types of forces (for example, concerning domestic policy or group benefits) was assessed by describing the statistical connections between the vote and attitudinal components which summarized the psychological forces in each of the substantive areas. Each component variable was constructed by assigning a score which indicated the partisan direction of each response that could be classified in a given substantive area (for instance, domestic policy) and then calculating the sum of those signed (pro-Democratic or anti-Republican, pro-Republican or anti-Democratic) values.

It was acknowledged that many other characteristics of the voters (other than their campaign-specific partisan attitudes) might have an indirect impact on their choice by influencing some of those "likes" and "dislikes." *The American Voter* introduced the concept of the funnel of causality to suggest ways in which causally prior variables might have an indirect impact on the vote by influencing proximate psychological forces. However, party identification was the only such variable whose indirect as well as direct effects on the vote were examined in any detail. It was assumed that all of the statistical information needed to explain the vote could be captured in variables which represented attitudes that were highly proximate to voters' actual decisions based on their own reports concerning the nature of those psychological forces.

Some critics of *The American Voter,* however, were concerned about the possibility that its conclusions were misleading because of its conceptualization and measurement of the individual-level forces involved. In particular, advocates of "rational" or policy-based interpretations of voters' choices suggested that responses to open-ended questions did not accurately represent the impact of voters' policy-related attitudes on their vote preferences.

Beginning in the late 1960s, structured questions were introduced which described respondents' own preferences concerning specific policy alternatives *and* their perceptions of the candidates' positions concerning the same policies. Vote choices could then be explained in terms of a linear combination of variables that were defined in terms of "issue proximities." Each variable assessed the degree to which respondents saw their own preferences (on a given topic) as closer to the perceived position of one candidate or party than the other. After the 1972 Michigan study, analyses based on issue proximities became a standard, if not dominant, approach to explaining vote choice influenced by policy-related preferences. More recently, however, explanations based on proximities (and all other candidate evaluations) have been, in turn, severely criticized because of their vulnerability to reverse causation or feedback in which evaluations are the result and not the cause of the vote decision. Our discussion of these issues appears in Chapters 8 and 12 and in Appendix D (the methodological appendix).

Our own research has gradually moved away from explanatory models that rely on voters' explicit evaluations of the candidates and parties by concentrating on the total effects of variables that are presumably located further back in the funnel of causality. In particular, we have shifted our policy-related analyses away from issue proximities in favor of measures of voters' general predispositions and current preferences concerning policy direction—all of which are defined operationally by survey questions that make no reference to policy preferences of the candidates or the parties. In doing so, we forgo an individual-level description of the psychological processes that connect policy preferences to vote choice, but we also avoid drawing erroneous conclusions about the extent to which such connections are the true basis for those decisions rather than rationalizations.[5]

In general, we have assumed that the overall structure for the processes that culminate in the vote can be represented (and analyzed) as a sequence of six causal stages or blocs. Each of these stages contains those explanatory variables whose current values were acquired at approximately the same point in time, at least in comparison to the variables in other stages. In sequence, the explanatory variables we have assigned to each stage are defined in terms of (1) stable social and economic characteristics, (2) partisan identification *and* policy-related predispositions, (3) preferences concerning current policy issues *and* perceptions of current conditions, (4) explicit evaluations of the incumbent President, (5) evaluations of the candidates' personal qualities, and (6) prospective evaluations of the candidates and the parties.

On the basis of these six stages, we use a bloc recursive model to generate what we regard as conservative estimates of the total effects for specific variables in each stage. Our use of this multiple-stage and bloc recursive multivariate model is based on a growing conviction that, in contrast to variables based on analysis of issue proximities, respondents' own policy-related preferences and their perceptions of current personal or national conditions are *only moderately* affected by persuasion effects, based on influences *from the campaign* of the candidate they favor for other reasons or because of other factors. At the same time, it has become evident that all candidate evaluations (implicit in proximity measures) are subject to very substantial "projection" effects in which evaluations in one area are *affected by candidate preferences* which, in turn, were really based on other considerations. As emphasized at several points in this book, these assumptions should be challenged by subsequent research in a variety of ways, including tests of alternative formulations based on panel and experimental designs. In the meantime, our results should be viewed with an understanding of their dependence on the degree to which our assumptions are valid.

▪ Sequence of Major Questions in Subsequent Chapters

Our introduction to electoral explanation continues in Chapter 2, which reviews the social and political background for the presidential elections which took place between 1980 and 1992. That review begins with the major conflicts and failures of presidential administrations which pervaded U.S. presidential politics from the 1960s through the 1990s, and then summarizes the issues which have been featured in the 1980, 1984, 1988, and 1992 campaigns.

Our interest in electoral explanation includes the decision to vote (or participate) in presidential elections as well as the choice between major party candidates. Part II examines the individual-level factors which shape citizens' decisions to vote in U.S. presidential elections and presents a generational interpretation of the much-discussed decline in voter turnout between 1960 and 1988—as well as the recent increases in 1992 and 1994.

The task of distinguishing between voters and non-voters is a persistent and perplexing challenge for all political analysts. The clearest indicator that there is a problem is the discrepancy between official aggregate election statistics and the estimates based on individual reports collected in surveys. Invariably survey estimates, based on respondents' reports of their own behavior, suggest voting turnout rates that range from 15 to 20 percentage points *higher* than the rates derived from official statistics. At the same time, the discrepancy is very constant. As a consequence, NES estimates track with the ups and downs of aggregate figures, albeit at an inflated level. Nevertheless, the reconciliation of such disparate estimates has commanded the attention of the National Election Studies throughout the past thirty years. Although some visible portion of the discrepancy can be readily explained in terms of the definitions of the denominators used in calculating voting rates, the remainder—some 10 or 11 percent of any given sample—is usually attributed to over-reporting by survey respondents (Rosenstone and Hansen, 1993, p. 58).[6]

Attempts to reduce the magnitude of over-reporting have been pursued by a variety of experiments with the NES survey procedures.[7] These efforts have been almost totally unsuccessful, although there is suggestive evidence that regular or habitual voters are more inclined to misreport occasions in which they actually did not vote, and habitual non-voters are more likely to forget to report instances in which they did vote. In general, however, neither time lapse (between the date of an election and the date of the survey interview), memory failures (other than the suggestive evidence just mentioned), nor minimization of the social desirability of voting appear to do much to account for the persistent over-reporting of voting turnout.

Moreover, Appendix B, which presents tables showing voting within various social and economic categories of citizens, provides clear if implicit evidence of some *variability,* from election to election, in turnout within selected categories. We have concluded that the population of the United States includes a range of citizens extending from the regular voters ("I never miss an election even if I have to vote absentee") to the persistent non-voters who have never voted—and include some in between who are erratic, sometime-participants across any series of elections. We have also concluded from the NES validation effort that in any given election the non-voters who erroneously report that they voted are very similar to those who really did vote, whereas the acknowledged non-voters differ from the reported voters on many important dimensions. In Chapter 7, for example, we review data that illustrate how the party identifications of avowed non-voters are much more variable, from election to election, than the party identifications of declared voters.

Because of the frequency with which acknowledged non-voters and avowed voters differ in matters pertaining to vote choice, we came to an early decision to present *all* of the data relevant to electoral preferences and choice only for self-reported voters. Although in any given year the "voters" will inevitably include a minor fragment who were in fact non-voters, the latter numbers (as a fraction of all reported voters) are not large, and their attributes are sufficiently similar to those of the real voters to minimize mischaracterization of the voters. We believe that a pure separation of non-voters from voters would not visibly alter any of the conclusions we have drawn for any given election. Consequently, we are reasonably confident that our rhetoric, which often does not qualify the presumption that year in and year out there are habitual voters and habitual non-voters, does not run counter to empirical evidence, and the inclusion of some inflated self-reports of voting has had little or no impact on our substantive arguments.

As noted in the preceding review of alternative explanatory themes, personal identifications with the Republican or Democratic party are more stable than any other political variable and play a major role in shaping most other political attitudes as well as vote choice. The NES measure of Party Identification was featured in *The American Voter* and has been the focus of conflicting interpretations ever since. Because of those controversies, Part III is devoted to an analysis of the concept of long-term partisan identification and the several issues that have arisen concerning the NES questions involved in its measurement. In particular, Chapter 6 reviews both theory and data relevant to an understanding of the nature of party identification and its role in our approach to electoral explanation. Chapter 7 is devoted to an analysis of the aggregate changes in partisan identification that took place in the South in the 1960s and 1970s, and nationally in the 1980s, including differences between groups that are defined in terms of race, region, gender, and generation.

The next group of chapters (Part IV) examines a comprehensive set of explanatory ideas concerning the influence of different types of voters' characteristics on their final choice for President. As suggested above, we have classified the many factors or variables that might have played some role in shaping vote choice into a small number of explanatory principles or themes. Chapter 8 summarizes those explanatory themes, presents our multiple-stage model of the evolution of the vote decisions, and discusses our assumptions about the causal sequence in which voters acquired their current positions for each type of variable. That discussion also presents the rationale for all of our subsequent analytic procedures, including selected comparisons between results based on structured questions and the somewhat different conclusions suggested by voters' responses to the open-ended questions (producing the "likes and dislikes") used in *The American Voter.*

Specific explanatory themes are then covered in separate chapters, beginning with social and economic characteristics in Chapters 9 and 10. Subsequent chapters are devoted to partisan and policy-related predispositions (Chapter 11), current policy issues (Chapter 12), current national and personal conditions (Chapter 13), evaluations of the president regarding governmental "results" and prospective evaluations concerning the candidates and the parties (Chapter 14), and evaluations of the candidates' personal qualities (Chapter 15). Finally, Chapter 16 applies the same concepts and analytic procedures to the explanation of vote choice concerning a third-party candidate, based on the unusual success of Ross Perot in the 1992 election.

Our final section (Part V) is devoted to the larger interpretive questions concerning the importance of particular explanatory variables or theories in specific presidential elections—and to comparisons between elections that are defined in those terms. Chapter 17 reviews several different senses in which one factor may be more important than another in an electoral context, and alternative ways in which survey data may be used to support such conclusions. We then present our own approach to such comparisons in the 1992 election, based on the distinction between the relative importance of any given variable (or theme) in explaining differences between individual voters in their choice for President and the contribution of that factor to the aggregate results of that election. Chapter 17 applies those concepts and procedures to a comparison of the 1988 and 1992 presidential elections, and Chapter 18 reviews the continuing issues that should be considered in comparisons of this sort.

One of the distinguishing factors that separate books in the tradition of *The New American Voter* from other types of analyses of political behavior is a self-conscious commitment to sharing the evidence on which substantive conclusions are based. Most of our evidence consists of various statistical summaries of individual responses given in the thousands of NES interviews with members of the electorate. Those summaries provide the primary basis for our generalizations. Occasionally we will present individual responses to illustrate a point, but in general, equation-based coefficients provide the evidence to test our conclusions. Many sets of statistical results are presented in the course of the discussions in each chapter. We have also included four appendixes to the main body of the book. Some of these appendixes are devoted to technical discussions of measurement and analytic methodology, but others present supplementary data which readers may find useful in pursuing questions not elaborated in the text.[8]

2

Political Change in the United States: Historical Antecedents of the Reagan/Bush/Clinton Elections

This book focuses on the electorate's response to, and contribution to, the politics of the period that began with Ronald Reagan's defeat of Jimmy Carter in 1980 and ended in 1992 with Bill Clinton's victory over George Bush. Any understanding of that era must, however, include a recognition of the extent to which major political events in the immediately prior decades shaped the electorate of the 1980s and helped form its decisions in subsequent presidential elections.

A first and fundamental fact to note is that the composition of the post-war national electorate was literally transformed between the time of the Eisenhower elections (on which *The American Voter* was based) and the elections of the Reagan/Bush era. The first micro-analytic view of the national electorate was provided by the Michigan studies of the 1952 and 1956 elections.[1] Across the forty years separating those first national election studies from 1992, the composition of the eligible voting-age population underwent a massive social transformation, and, we believe, the political perspectives of the new electorate were powerfully shaped by a series of dramatic conflicts and failures in political leadership.

Change in the Composition of the Presidential Electorate

Setting aside for the moment the politically relevant events of the four decades separating 1952 from 1992, the changes in the sheer size and generational composition of the electorate are noteworthy in and of

21

themselves. First, the voting-age population increased in size by more than 80 percent. During this period, when the total number of citizens eligible to vote grew from 100 million to more than 180 million, well over 40 million of the 100 million members of the 1952 electorate died. Those 40 million were more than replaced by approximately 120 million citizens who came of voting age in the same interval. The demographic turnover in the composition of the electorate in the forty years between Eisenhower and Clinton was therefore substantial, although not complete. No more than 60 million of the 180 million members of the 1992 electorate were of voting age in 1952. Such individuals made up 60 percent of the 1952 electorate, but they constituted only one-third of the Bush-Clinton voting-age population. The other 120 million potential voters in 1992 had come of age in the interim; indeed, some 90 million were *born* in the years subsequent to the election of 1952.

If life in the United States had not included a host of momentous political events during those four decades, these simple facts of demographic change could have spoken rather unambiguously to a number of generic theoretical questions of interest to students of electoral behavior. As an electorate is further and further removed in time from a formative epoch—such as that of the Great Depression that bred the New Deal presidency of Franklin D. Roosevelt—what happens to political beliefs and values? How swiftly does the intergenerational transmission of party loyalties through the family weaken with the sheer passage of time? (Beck, 1976; Beck and Jennings, 1991). Are the personal traits of candidates more important when campaigns are removed from formative political events? Do party images that are developed during times of change inevitably decay, or are they sustained through the quadrennial repetition of traditional campaign slogans?

Generational Differences in Political Perspectives

Direct answers to these questions have been compromised by the turmoil that has engulfed national politics throughout much of the period since the 1950s. The following discussion, which recounts highlights of recent political history, has been included for only one purpose: to recall some of the major divisive or discouraging political events that *might* account for the strength of the anti-politics, anti-government sentiments that have been so prominent in national electoral politics in the 1990s. We believe that the voter sentiments involved in a series of taxpayer revolts, the drive for term limits, or the 1994 Republican conception of a revolutionary reduction in the role of the federal government may be only the most recent manifestation of a general rejection of partisan politics by young, newly eligible voters that began in the 1970s.

It is clear that the sense of confidence in the institutions of politics and government, shared by cohorts who could see the end of the Great Depression and the successful conclusion of World War II as triumphs of the American political system, was apparently not passed on to those who were to learn first hand about the shortcomings of the political system and the fallibility of national leaders in the years from Johnson to Bush.[2] As Wilson Carey McWilliams put it (albeit from a Democratic partisan's perspective):

> Until recently, memory was a Democratic fortress, recalling the Great Depression and World War II, the glory years of the Roosevelt era—and in the South, where memories faded more slowly than in the North, nursing the straight-ticket heritage of Reconstruction. Now those old remembrances are quieting into whispers, losing their connection to contemporary partisanship, especially since, wounded by change and the media, our political memory is growing shorter. . . . Increasingly, the focus of American political retrospection is Vietnam and the turbulence of the 1960s, permissive morality, stagflation, and the decline of America's imperium.[3]

In the next two sections of the book we will present and discuss evidence of differences among three generations of citizens—pre-New Deal, New Deal, and post-New Deal—that have been the source of some stability and much dramatic change in the long-term orientations of the national electorate between the 1950s and the 1990s. The changes were reflected in a steady decline in the aggregate turnout of voters between the Kennedy election in 1960 and the Bush election in 1988. During the same period, the incidence of party identification also declined across the nation, and there was a realignment of party identifications in the South that has profoundly influenced national politics and government. In accounting for changes in national voting rates and in the party identification of the citizenry we will rely heavily on an explanation that rests on the compositional change of the electorate as the post-New Deal cohorts, who came of age during the turmoil of the

1960s and 1970s, replaced a generation that had come of voting age *before* Franklin Roosevelt and the New Deal.

Such an uncomplicated explanation is credible only if the pre-New Deal and post-New Deal generations differed in appropriate ways, and if the New Deal generation made no net contribution to the aggregate national changes. It is not difficult to document precisely such generational differences, and we will do so. However, the generational compositional explanation of a changing electorate is very different from most of the explanations of participation and partisanship offered in the literature on electoral behavior. Moreover, some of the theoretical implications for our understanding of relevant phenomena are central to major controversies concerning electoral analysis that have persisted throughout the four decades. We will devote much discussion in Parts II and III to the most important aspects of the argument that differences among the generations, presumably based on their formative political experiences, are responsible for striking aggregate changes in turnout and party identification.

It is much more difficult to explain *why* the generations differed in the ways they did. Indeed, with a continuing focus on voting turnout, Part II concludes with a declaration of failure in our attempt to account for documented inter-generational differences in voting rates that suggest, in turn, that the disappearing pre-New Deal generation had been as different from the continuing New Deal generation as the New Dealers were different from the post-New Deal newcomers.

The purpose of this chapter is to make the argument that much of the change in the long-term orientations of the electorate may well have been a consequence of a succession of political shocks during the years in which the post-New Deal generation was coming of age. We make no attempt to explain the origin of differences in the political engagement of the New Deal and pre-New Deal cohorts. However, the inferences we draw about the impact of major conflicts and shortcomings in presidential leadership on post-New Deal cohorts during the 1970s and 1980s seem plausible as well as possible.

Nevertheless, we have no more than circumstantial evidence concerning the origins of these generational differences. We note, however, that the validity of any argument about the *causes* of the discontinuity between the post-New Deal generation and earlier political generations does not affect, in any direct sense, the validity of our conclusions about the *consequences* of generational turnover in the electorate between the 1950s and the 1990s. In the next five chapters we shall describe and document dramatic differences among those three generations. On the basis of this evidence, we feel that we understand the consequences of change in the generational composition of the electorate. We remain uncertain, however, about the causes of the differences between generations in the first place.[4]

▪ The Origins of Political Turmoil

Race-Related Issues

Early in his second term, in 1957, President Eisenhower, along with Governor Faubus of Arkansas, first gave Little Rock a prominent place in contemporary American politics with the conflict over racial segregation and integration in Little Rock Central High School. Their confrontation was scarcely the beginning of the struggle to change federally sanctioned policies of racial discrimination, but it did mark an early stage in national awareness of the emerging conflict about racial equality. That conflict moved to center stage within the decade, and it came to a climax—but not a conclusion—with the congressional passage of the Civil Rights Act and the Voting Rights Act in 1964 and 1965.

The social and political manifestations of adjusting to new national policies concerning racial equality included the "hot summers" of the late 1960s when, for many, the Civil Rights movement was associated with urban violence, rioting, looting, and arson in scores of cities across the country. The election of 1964 saw the surging mobilization of the Black vote and the beginning of a new era of Black political participation—both in the polling place and in candidacies for public office.[5] In the same year, the Goldwater "Southern Strategy" made evident the disagreement between national Democrats and national Republicans on questions of federal policy toward race.

In 1968 the intensity of racial emotions was symbolized and exacerbated by the assassination of the Black Civil Rights leader, the Reverend Martin Luther King, Jr. In that same year, Governor George Wallace and his American Independent Party mounted a third-party challenge. On the basis of fundamental disagreement with the new national Civil Rights policies, and impatient with Johnson's pursuit of the war in Vietnam,

Wallace ran as an unreconstructed segregationist who also epitomized the hawk in foreign policy. Four years later, with President Nixon and Vice President Agnew as their leaders, the Republicans again appealed to the anti-Black vote, albeit less directly, by promising "law and order" and less sympathy for the rights of the accused—a category with dispro-portionate numbers of Blacks.

With the candidacy and presidency of Jimmy Carter, a "peanut farmer" from Georgia who campaigned as a moderate, and with the emergence of Jesse Jackson as a national leader and spokesperson for the Black community, race-related issues took a somewhat less prominent or vis-ible form at the turn of the decade. But the hard reality of racial tensions was reinforced by the Reagan administration's critiques of affirmative action and "welfare queens" and the Bush campaign's ill-famed Willie Horton ad in the 1988 election.[6]

These paragraphs stop short of recounting even the most visible events in nearly five decades of race-related conflicts in American politics. Among other things, this summary fails to convey the enormity of the resultant changes in federal policies with regard to race. Throughout World War II, the national armed forces, commanded by Democratic Presidents Franklin D. Roosevelt and Harry S Truman and led by General Dwight D. Eisenhower, were racially segregated. That policy of racial segregation—if not the fact—was ended by Truman in 1948. President Eisenhower's intervention in Little Rock in 1957, nine years later, was particularly noteworthy in signaling the eventual end of federal govern-mental support for segregationist policies in the states.

The Counterculture and Vietnam

The Eisenhower presidency also inherited the phenomenon of McCar-thyism, which had its beginnings in the Truman administration. In the early 1950s, with the post–World War II Cold War as the backdrop, Senator Joseph McCarthy of Wisconsin had inaugurated a period of political repression using tactics that now bear his name. The beginnings of the Civil Rights movement, led by Black student sit-ins in the South, were the more remarkable because they marked the end of the period of public political quiescence and the start of an era of dissent and protest—activities that are now a part of everyday political discourse in the United States. The freedom to criticize, reject, disagree, and engage in open protest quickly spread beyond the Civil Rights movement into a more diffuse cultural protest with demands for change on a variety of other fronts. Music, modes of dress, literature, the use of drugs, and sexual mores were particularly salient, but many other domains of national life were affected by the "counterculture" of the 1960s and 1970s. It is impossible to assess the political impact of the counterculture and the Civil Rights movement, however, without acknowledging the enormous impact of the Vietnam War (Miller and Levitin, 1976; Koning, 1987; Stockton and Wayman, 1983).

The war began as a minor intervention under President Eisenhower at a time in which "propping up the dominoes" to prevent the Communist takeover of friendly countries shaped much of American foreign policy. For our purposes, it is not necessary to recount the escalating American involvement in the Vietnam War under the Democrats Kennedy and Johnson. It is important, however, to recall some indicators of the political fallout of that conflict.

By the mid- to late 1960s, the counterculture, the Civil Rights movement, and an anti-war movement had virtually merged. Politics and social protest had moved to the streets—and the fields—and "teach-ins" were in vogue on college campuses across the nation. Although Johnson was elected in 1964 as a worthy successor to Kennedy, and although he was hailed as the master planner for a "Great Society" to be built on Kennedy's "New Frontier," segments of his support quickly turned against him. The Vietnam War, which began as Eisenhower's intervention and grew under Kennedy (a distant complement to the Cuban missile crisis if not the Bay of Pigs), quickly became "Johnson's war." The youthful rallying cry, "Don't trust anyone over 30," was easily transformed into "Don't trust the establishment." The "free speech movement," first directed against the University of California administration and then against police and local authority figures in cities across the country, enlarged the freedom for voicing harsh criticism of national policy in Vietnam: "Hey, hey, LBJ, how many kids did you kill today?" Protest had become legitimate—indeed, it approached the status of being "trendy" in many circles—and mass demonstrations, including some in which Bill Clinton took part, grew in frequency and size.

Apart from public opinion polls, the New Hampshire primary in 1968 was the first electoral expression of mass voter concern over the Vietnam War. Another Senator McCarthy, this time Eugene McCarthy from Minnesota, had been championing opposition to the war, as had Robert Kennedy—the late John F. Kennedy's brother and U.S. Attorney General. McCarthy formally entered the New Hampshire primary in January 1968, and challenged President Johnson to respond. Johnson did so, but belatedly—too late to be anything other than a write-in candidate. Despite this handicap, as well as a late start with little campaigning, Johnson won. But McCarthy had so exceeded pre-election expectations that he won a major psychological and political victory over the sitting President.

Shortly after the New Hampshire primary, Johnson made political history with an unprecedented decision to abandon the presidency. He would fill out his term, but he would not run for re-election, ostensibly in order to increase the credibility and effectiveness of his continuing efforts to bring the Vietnam War to a successful conclusion.[7] In effect, however, Johnson resigned the presidency because he was convinced that he did not command enough popular support for the policies he intended to pursue. Shortly thereafter, and on the basis of Johnson's decision as well as an anti-war perception of the results of New Hampshire's primary, Robert Kennedy announced his own decision to become a candidate for the nomination. He joined the war issue with Eugene McCarthy and, with the candidacy of Wallace, made it a three-way race in the remaining primaries. An intense campaign ensued, until the assassination of Kennedy added to the political traumas of the year—and of the decade.

Johnson's Vice President, Hubert Humphrey, entered the presidential lists of 1968 without competing in a single primary election. In late summer, against the outraged opposition of the anti-war protesters, Humphrey was nominated as the Democratic establishment's candidate for the presidency. So violent was the protest that the Chicago convention site erupted in riots; tear gas laced with pot smoke and cries of police brutality were reminiscent of Civil Rights demonstrations and rock concerts gone awry. The protesters were mostly young, and for them the establishment was caricatured in the leadership of Chicago's longtime political boss, Mayor Richard Daley. Nevertheless, the impact of their outrage (and Humphrey's narrow defeat by Nixon in November) registered with the established Democratic party leadership.

By 1972, in an effort to open the process and give access to those who had lost the fight in 1968, the Democratic party introduced sweeping reforms into its nominating process. Quotas were established to ensure broadened participation of women, Black citizens, and the young, in proportion to their numbers in the population. The Democratic nominee in 1972 was another midwestern Senator, George McGovern of South Dakota. He had been co-chair of a Democratic commission created to change the nominating process, in part by encouraging more states to use primary elections in the selection of delegates to the ultimate nominating convention. McGovern accepted the nomination in Miami on behalf of his early version of a "rainbow coalition." Four years earlier Humphrey had been narrowly defeated by Nixon, Eisenhower's Vice President, thus ending a period of 36 years in which Democratic leadership represented continuity with the tradition of Roosevelt and the New Deal. In 1972 Nixon was re-elected in a landslide over McGovern, with a level of popular enthusiasm surpassing that registered for the war hero and incumbent President, Dwight Eisenhower, in 1956.

From Watergate to Irangate

Although the Nixon campaign was harsh and divisive and the McGovern campaign was unusually ineffective, there was little public warning that an additional calamity of an unexpected order was about to engulf the electorate. Two years into his second term, Nixon resigned the presidency in disgrace to avoid virtually certain impeachment. "Watergate" derived its name from a minor episode in a series of illegal acts carried out at the behest of President Nixon in an exaggerated effort to ensure his re-election. In this instance, it was Republican (instead of Democratic) partisans who were the disappointed victims of a failure in presidential leadership (after his Vice President, Spiro Agnew, had also been forced to resign in personal disgrace). Nixon's culpability provided the greatest shock to the nation, but the criminal convictions of a dozen or more of his closest associates in the Committee to Re-Elect the President (CREEP) emphasized additional weaknesses in the political process. Indeed, the national embarrassment was so widespread that Congress was moved to enact major reforms intended to reveal and contain if not control the role of money in electoral politics.

So pervasive was the lack of regard for national political leadership that a former governor of Georgia, running as an outsider who would "clean up the mess in Washington," was elected President in 1976.

Jimmy Carter was indeed an outsider as well as a comparative moderate in terms of ongoing conflicts over policy. Carter's lack of familiarity with the complexities of national government—in particular, his lack of appreciation of the central role of the political parties in the President's relationships with Congress, combined with unforeseen problems both in the domestic economy and in foreign policy—led to another "failed" presidency. Including the Ford interregnum (which in itself ended in the electoral defeat of a sitting, if unelected, President), Carter's defeat represented the fourth presidential failure in a row.[8]

With the election of Reagan in 1980, much of the political news from Washington was positive or encouraging. Presidential gaffes and mistakes did not dim the luster provided by a booming economy in the mid-1980s, although the apparent lack of consequence of well-publicized presidential missteps did earn Reagan the title of the "Teflon President." As time went on, however, the negative revelations came in waves—the Pentagon procurement scandals, the Housing and Urban Development scandals, the Environmental Protection Agency scandals, and charges of influence-peddling on the doorstep of the White House. There were innumerable revelations of corruption in the highest reaches of government, with unprecedented numbers of senior governmental officials convicted of criminal behavior and sent to prison—all on the heels of the Watergate conspirators a decade before.[9] In 1987 *Time* magazine concluded that Reagan had "forfeited, indeed squandered, his role as the nation's moral father." The end of the Reagan administration was further marred by the sensational revelations of the Iran-Contra affair, a series of events that continued to provide an irritation for Reagan's Vice President, George Bush, even as Bush was running for re-election as President six years later in 1992.

The Reagan Legacy

In highlighting the political events that set the stage for the election of 1992, it should be noted that several other policies of the Reagan years had begun to bear bitter fruit, even before the Bush victory in 1988. First, Reagan's thesis that one could increase governmental spending (for defense), reduce taxes, maintain the "social safety net," and at the same time not incur a deficit, was convincingly countered by a huge increase in the national debt. The immense size of the debt, and the seemingly irresistible pressure from annual national governmental deficits, did much to shape the politics of the Bush-Clinton years.

Second, and less obvious until the actual denouement, a general policy of governmental "deregulation" set the stage for large-scale fraud and catastrophic defaults within the nation's savings and loan industry. The "Keating Five" symbolized bipartisan governmental corruption and collusion with leaders of the nation's financial institutions. A sequence of events ensued that outraged the nation, seriously complicated the public's understanding of the nature of the national economy, and further blackened the reputation of national political leadership. These excesses of the 1980s also exacerbated the sense of relative deprivation of the middle-class and the poor, anticipating the next decade and the continued widening of the gap between the few who are very rich and the many who are poor.

Third, whether measured by the number of people living in poverty, the number of homeless, the rate of violent crime, public outbursts such as the riots in Los Angeles, national trends in educational testing results, or the onset of the AIDS epidemic, the quality of life in the United States had clearly degenerated for millions of people during the 1980s. In this same period, however, there was a commensurate or even larger improvement in the quality of life for others. By the turn of the decade, the polarization of economic and social experience, exacerbated by a widespread "tax revolt" of voters calling for retrenchment in governmental social programs, was not softened by the well-publicized national experience with the most extended, if not the most severe, recession in sixty years.

One apparent consequence of the excesses of the 1980s was a growing voters' revolt against incumbent officeholders. Regardless of its actual effectiveness, the "anti-incumbent" theme marked many campaigns, including those at the congressional level where populist fires were stoked by the media's coverage of the so-called "bank scandal" in the House of Representatives. Public indignation was such that more than a baker's dozen of proposals on state and local ballots to limit officeholders' terms of service were successful.

In short, for much of the four-decade period of interest to us, there was little good news and a great deal of very bad news about the performance of the federal government in Washington, as well as bitter conflict over foreign and domestic policy. To be sure, there were occasional "eras of good feeling." The Eisenhower years were a tranquil time if one were neither Black nor posted to Korea. And the spirit of Kennedy's Camelot and Johnson's Great Society marked a high point in national regard for politics and political institutions. But Nixon, Carter, and Reagan were each first elected on the failure of their predecessors, and two of the three, in turn, preceded Bush in overseeing the bad news that helped elect their successors.

▪ Political Generations and Mass Electoral Behavior

There is at least one large irony associated with the turmoil engendered by the Civil Rights movement, the counterculture, and protests against

Table 2.1 Distribution of the National Electorate by Political Generation

Political Generations: Defined by Year of First Eligibility to Vote for President	Election Year					
	1952	1956	1960	1964	1968	1972
Pre-New Deal						
1. Pre-1920	29.0 (514)	20.3 (354)	18.7 (364)	13.9 (217)	10.2 (158)	6.4 (172)
2. Republican Normalcy, 1920–1928	16.1 (286)	15.1 (263)	15.6 (305)	12.8 (200)	12.4 (192)	9.7 (260)
New Deal						
3. Roosevelt Era, 1932–1964	38.7 (687)	39.3 (684)	36.0 (702)	32.5 (509)	29.2 (453)	23.4 (629)
4. New Deal Consolidated, 1948–1964	16.1 (286)	25.3 (441)	29.7 (579)	40.9 (640)	41.0 (636)	35.4 (951)
Post-New Deal						
5. Years of Turmoil, 1968–1976	—	—	—	—	7.3 (113)	25.1 (676)
6. Reagan Era, 1980–1988	—	—	—	—	—	—
Total:	100%	100%	100%	100%	100%	100%
Number of Cases	(1899)	(1762)	(1954)	(1571)	(1557)	(2705)

— No cases in sample.

the war in Vietnam. The youthful cohorts who were in the vanguard of the Civil Rights movement and the protest against the war in Vietnam succeeded in changing important and longstanding policies of the national government, and they also challenged and changed the procedures for setting policy. Despite their substantial political victories, however, two decades later those same cohorts, the first set of cohorts in the post-New Deal generation (see Table 2.1), carried visible battle scars into the politics of the 1980s.

Although there were signs of change among them in 1992, they were still a generation that reflected the fact that many of their leaders became politically active "outside the system." In their early years, many of the post-New Deal additions to the electorate challenged governmental poli-

Table 2.1 (*continued*)

Political Generations: Defined by Year of First Eligibility to Vote for President	Election Year				
	1976	1980	1984	1988	1992
Pre-New Deal					
1. Pre-1920	4.0 (115)	2.0 (33)	.7 (15)	.5 (10)	—
2. Republican Normalcy, 1920–1928	8.8 (251)	5.5 (88)	4.9 (109)	2.5 (51)	.9 (23)
New Deal					
3. Roosevelt Era, 1932–1964	23.0 (657)	22.1 (357)	18.0 (402)	14.9 (304)	13.9 (345)
4. New Deal Consolidated, 1948–1964	30.5 (868)	28.4 (458)	25.7 (575)	24.5 (500)	24.0 (598)
Post-New Deal					
5. Years of Turmoil, 1968–1976	29.0 (826)	27.5 (444)	28.5 (638)	28.0 (570)	22.2 (551)
6. Reagan Era, 1980–1988	4.7 (135)	14.4 (232)	22.3 (498)	29.6 (602)	39.0 (970)
Total:	100%	100%	100%	100%	100%
Number of Cases	(2870)	(1614)	(2257)	(2040)	(2488)

— No cases in sample.

cies and did not always work patiently within the established party avenues of influence. Neither President Clinton nor Vice President Gore was a prominent leader of the Civil Rights or Vietnam protests, but they did participate. For many protesters, however, it was not enough to wait for election day to choose among the alternatives offered by the two parties. For the rank and file among their peers, particularly those who did not go on to college or who were not enrolled in the elite schools, political protest may not have been a high priority, but these same people, perhaps as a result of malfeasance by the government in Washington, were part of a steadily growing cadre of younger citizens who were less than enamored with governmental institutions.

The systematic inquiry into the behavior of political cohorts or generations has not been prominent in the contemporary study of American electoral behavior. We suspect that this was true in the early days of the micro-analysis of electoral behavior because of an essentially ahistorical interest in using new techniques to study the impact of new candidacies, new circumstances, and new issues in each election. It was also the case that conventional analytic approaches to the study of electoral behavior were established before the existence of data bases that would sustain micro-level longitudinal inquiries into generational politics.

Moreover, newer analytic technologies seldom emphasized that they resulted in descriptions of average citizens, or average voters, and often concealed circumstances in which the "average," whether represented as a proportion or as a regression coefficient, did not fit both Black and Caucasian, men and women, young and old, or rich and poor equally well. Even today social scientists are typically more interested in how the collective, that is, the national electorate, "changed its mind" between 1976 and 1980, or 1988 and 1992, than we are with the question of whether such changes might have different origins and meanings for some people than for others. Furthermore, when we do separate the young from the old, such inquiries usually examine the consequences of aging and the cross-sectional correlates of age rather than considering time-specific differences in the socializing experiences of different age cohorts or generations.

However, the reason why the years from 1968 to 1988 have not been treated as a defining political "period" probably had most to do with the failure to recognize a family of formative events that in combination could leave a decisive mark on an entire generation. In considering formative periods that left their mark on twentieth-century politics, there is widespread agreement that the Civil War of the previous century and the Great Depression of the 1930s were major contributors to electoral politics in the mid-twentieth century. We believe that the turmoil of the Johnson, Nixon, Carter, Reagan, and Bush years was more diffuse and chronologically dispersed but no less important as a watershed in national presidential politics.

The many years of conflict and disillusionment that set the stage for the elections of the Reagan/Bush/Clinton era did not, at the time, seem to be on a par with a Civil War or a Great Depression. This may be a result of the very recency of the events, as well as the fact that scholars and commentators have not set boundaries for the period or given it a generic name that unifies the events in a single theme. The events themselves, however, may have been more portentous than they seemed at the time because their impact (compared to that of the Depression of the 1930s) has been confused by the revolutionary changes in mass communications that built on an equally dramatic expansion in mass education, including a variety of "affirmative" governmental actions taken for women and ethnic minorities.

Of course, it may well be that only a few decades hence the post-New Deal generation will have lost its distinctiveness. In the meantime, in order to understand the elections of this period, we believe it is both useful and necessary to document generational differences as they were manifest in the politics of the 1980s. In analyzing the presidential elections of the period from 1980 to 1992, these same generational differences will play an important role in clarifying an era of apparent partisan dealignment, and in resolving the puzzle associated with persistently declining rates of voter turnout.

PART II

ELECTORAL PARTICIPATION

3

★ ★ ★ Voting Turnout in
Presidential Elections

The analysis of voting turnout in presidential elections has received much less attention than has the analysis of preferences or choice among voters. This difference may have persisted, at least in part, because comprehensive explanations of the difference between voters and non-voters have proved to be more difficult to develop. This difficulty, in turn, may be generally attributed to a certain asymmetry between the two groups. It is not hard to understand why most non-voters don't vote: they are uninterested, uninformed, and uninvolved. One might as well ask why people who have never watched a football game don't play football, or why those who have never heard an opera don't sing operatic arias. The real question is why so many uninterested, uninformed, and uninvolved citizens bother to vote. So far, political scientists have not been very successful in defining criteria that distinguish non-engaged voters from comparably non-engaged non-voters.

The problem of non-voting in presidential elections has received more attention in recent years because of a continued decline in turnout over three decades that was halted only in 1992. The popular press, in particular, has noted the decline and repeatedly expressed normative concerns about the implications of that decline for the continuing health of our democratic form of government. Not unreasonably, many observers have drawn the conclusion that reduced participation must mean increased apathy or alienation on the part of the electorate as a whole.[1]

The persistent downward trend in turnout is both unmistakable and a potential matter for concern. In 1960 only 63 percent of the American electorate of voting age actually voted. The proportion of voters then declined from this relatively low level in virtually every year for the next 28 years. In 1964 turnout was 62 percent; in 1968, 61 percent; and in 1972, following the enfranchisement of the 18-, 19-, and 20-year-olds, turnout dropped to 55 percent. The decline continued until the low point of 1988, when only slightly more than 50 percent of the potential electorate actually went to the polls.[2] We think that this decline can be explained, and that the details of that explanation constitute one consequence of the four decades of national political turmoil that were described in the last chapter. This explanation, moreover, does not accord with the more dramatic critiques of the presumed decline in the political quality of the citizenry; instead it gives us a broader understanding of the role of national political history in shaping the subsequent behavior of an electorate.

▪ The Puzzle of Declining Turnout

In 1978, Richard Brody approached the problem of declining turnout by identifying a puzzle warranting analytic attention: "the shrinking level of participation in American national elections confounds our expectations and is at odds with the explanations of turnout offered by available theories of political behavior" (Brody, 1978). Brody noted that what was then only a sixteen-year decline in turnout in presidential elections had occurred despite the relaxation of restrictions on suffrage, and, in particular, despite a sharp upturn in such relevant citizen resources as educational attainment. Ten years later, Cassell and Luskin reviewed much of the relevant professional literature of the 1980s and concluded that, despite a continuation of declining turnout and despite a spate of studies that purported to explain the continuing decline with one or another of a handful of variables, most of the decline remained unexplained (Cassell and Luskin, 1988).[3] Progress had been made in accounting for differences between voters and non-voters in any given year, but there had been no satisfactory accounting for the steady decline in turnout for presidential elections, which had dropped more than a fifth (13 percentage points out of 63) between the early 1950s and the late 1980s.

The Generational Explanation[4]

Our basic argument is relatively straightforward. By the late 1980s, all but the very youngest cohorts of the pre-New Deal political generation that came of voting age *prior* to the 1932 election of Roosevelt had disappeared. This disappearance was, of course, the inevitable consequence of human mortality. The fading size of the pre-New Deal generation, so noticeable by the 1960s, had actually begun with the election of 1952. By 1988 the pre-New Deal generation had been more than replaced by the post-New Deal generation that came into being in the midst of the turmoil following the Kennedy-Johnson era and the 1964 elections. As we noted in Chapter 2, the post-1964 generations provided substantial growth in the sheer size of the eligible electorate in the 1970s and 1980s, but they were dramatically less engaged by, and less likely to participate in, national politics than were their predecessors at the same stages of their adult lives.[5] Their turnout rates were dramatically lower than those of the generation made up of the New Deal cohorts whose first votes were cast between 1932 and 1964. Throughout the period from the 1950s to the late 1980s, the New Deal electors had turnout rates that were, in turn, slightly lower than those of the predecessor generation, but, far from participating in or contributing to the national decline of voting turnout, the New Deal generation actually may have *increased* their rate of voting over the three decades of national aggregate decline.

It was the gradual replacement of the habitual voters of the pre-New Deal generations with the non-voting post-New Deal cohorts that produced the thirty-year national decline in aggregate voter turnout from the early 1960s to the late 1980s. In the process of documenting this conclusion, an examination of the trajectories of stability and change within each of the three generations casts new light on conventional ways of understanding turnout. Indeed, the results of disaggregating the electorate by political cohorts prior to aggregating by generations contravene some of the standard explanations of the difference between voters and non-voters in single elections. Moreover, the disaggregation appropriately relocates those explanations in the historical context reviewed in the last chapter.

First let us consider the case of the pre-New Deal generation, the

oldest of the three. Even as they were declining both in raw numbers
and as a proportion of the electorate, their turnout rates were obviously
in decline; among non-Black electors, voting turnout dropped some 15
percentage points between the 1950s and the 1980s. Even though this
decline within the pre-New Deal generation became less and less politically important as their numbers dwindled, it is still an important
phenomenon that calls for explanation. As the current American electorate ages, with longer life expectancies for larger and larger numbers
of people, the political engagement and participation of older cohorts
will be more and more important politically as well as analytically.
Declining turnout among elderly voters warrants our serious attention;
however, the pre-New Deal generation is the *only* generation available
for our study that has recorded an actual decline in voting.

There has been no observable overall decline in voting in either of the
other two generations. Within the New Deal generation, turnout rates
in the 1980s scarcely differed from those of the 1950s. Across the nine
four-year cohorts that are included in that generation there are more
instances of apparent *increased* turnout than of decline. The result, for
our purposes, is to remove the entire generation, which made up 55
percent of the Eisenhower electorate and 38 percent of the Clinton electorate, from any explanation of the three-decade drop in voter turnout.

Whatever the explanation for changes in voting turnout among the
cohorts of the third, post-New Deal, generation, the net result between
1968 and 1988 was an increase, not a decrease, in voter turnout. This
was particularly true among those with some college education, who
constituted well over a majority of the post-New Deal generation by the
late 1980s. However, the level of voting among post-New Deal cohorts
was still so low in the period from 1980 to 1988 that they continued to
depress the national turnout averages.

▪ Period, Life Cycle, and Generational Influences

Before proceeding further, our approach to the analysis of change in rate
of voter turnout can be put in the theoretical terminology of standard
cohort analysis. We have just asserted the existence of generational
differences (*among* three generations), life cycle changes (*within* both
pre-New Deal and post-New Deal generations), and period effects (creating the distinctiveness of the post-New Deal cohorts without seriously

affecting their New Deal generation elders). And yet it is a truism for cohort analyses that, without side information, we have only two factors, age and time, with which to account directly for the independent consequences of these three different types of effects. According to conventional wisdom, the low turnout rate of the post-New Deal generation must be, at least in part, a consequence of their youthful age. However, although by definition they are younger than their New Deal counterparts, their politically formative years coincided with political events in a period that could have socialized them into anti-party, anti-establishment predispositions that militate against orthodox political engagement.

Is the low turnout of the post-New Deal generation a function of their stage in the life cycle, a consequence of a period effect, or both? And, just as one of the meanings of aging may be an increased resistance to change in one's outlook (or a decreased susceptibility to influence from the outside world), so the NES surveys may have caught the New Deal generation well after their patterns of behavior had been established, past the point when a period of turbulence in American domestic politics could have a negative impact on their propensity to vote. An established pattern of electoral behavior could account for their failure to reflect the shocks created by the Civil Rights movement and the Vietnam War; could it also account for an apparent lack of overt response to Watergate, Carter's Misery Index, and the Iran-Contra and Iraq-gate scandals? Why is there no period effect for the New Deal cohorts between 1964 and 1972, or 1972 and 1988? Is it possible that the turnout rates of all three generations were depressed throughout the period after 1960, but that the offsetting effect of the life cycle maintained a steady rate of voter turnout within the New Deal cohorts and provided the increase in turnout in the aging leading edge of the post-New Deal generation?

▪ The Analysis of Political Generations

Our interpretation of the decline in voter turnout between the 1950s and the 1980s follows from the generational persistence model of societal change introduced by Sears in 1981 (Sears, 1981; Kiesler, Morgan, and Oppenheimer, 1981). Our version of that model requires support for three hypotheses: (1) younger cohorts are particularly vulnerable to influence by historical events in their political environment; (2) older cohorts may entertain a "lifelong openness to change," but, in fact, reveal great stability in the persistence of earlier orientations; and (3) even in the face of large historical events, long-term societal change may occur largely as a consequence of generational replacement. This is not to deny that on an individual level, changes reflecting life-cycle stages occurred even as turnout was declining over a 30-year period; and it does not preclude the possibility of electorate-wide responses reflected in period effects in the same time span; but it does assert that the decline in voter turnout was largely a consequence of generational exchange in the composition of the electorate.[6]

▪ Cohorts and Generations

Others before us have established their own definitions of political generations. One recent specification of generational boundaries has been contributed by Paul R. Abramson, and we find it most congenial, differing only in detail from our own—and not surprisingly so inasmuch as we have used a common data base, the SRC/CPS/NES presidential election studies (Abramson, 1989).

Like Abramson, we began with an inspection of four-year cohorts, defining the cohorts by the years in which citizens were first old enough to vote for President. Our initial inquiry was focused on changes in the parameters of national partisanship. Separating self-reported voters from non-voters, the South from the non-South, and Black from non-Black, we studied various cohort scores for strength of partisanship, proportion of party identifiers, and balance of partisanship (Democrat-Republican) for the total eligible electorate. In our investigation we noted a set of apparently persistent discontinuities that suggested three sets of cohorts or political "generations."

Subsequently we have extended this inductive inquiry to other long-term variables that might strengthen our operational definition of the generations. In general, across a wide array of attitudinal and behavioral variables, the cohorts within each generation seem more like one another and less like those of adjoining generations. This is not only true for our present analysis of voter turnout but for our interest in the long-term partisan base for *voters'* presidential choices as well. Indeed, the definitions of the generational boundaries in our analysis of party identification are markedly sharper within the restricted population of voters than they are between the cohorts of the total voting-age population. Moreover, it should be noted that if our interest in generations were confined to voter turnout, without regard for partisanship, we might define post-New Deal cohorts as beginning with 1964 instead of 1968, and New Deal cohorts as including 1928. Such changes would sharpen generational differences in *turnout,* but they would blur differences in *party identification.* In any event, the all-purpose definitions we have chosen are only slightly less than optimal for our treatment of generational differences in both voter turnout and party identification.

The analyses that we now present therefore rest on a somewhat modified version of three political generations that were tentatively identified in an earlier work (Miller, 1991, 1992).[7] There is substantial congruence between our generational boundaries and a plausible description of distinctive political eras in twentieth-century America. The oldest generation, the pre-New Deal, is composed of eight cohorts available for study in the 1952 survey. The oldest of these cohorts entered the electorate shortly after the turn of the century; only minuscule sample representations of the youngest of the six remained for analysis in 1988, and they had virtually disappeared by 1992. The New Deal generation is composed of the nine cohorts who entered the electorate from 1932 through 1964; all nine cohorts are well represented in our data base, particularly from 1964 on. The post-New Deal generation is composed of seven cohorts in 1988 (counting the new entrants in 1972 as two cohorts because of the lowering of the voting age that year). It is the cohorts of this post-New Deal generation that came into the electorate as the turmoil and failures in leadership described in the last chapter were occurring.

▪ Compositional Change of the Electorate: A Context for Declining Turnout

The potential impact of past events on the living memory of the electorate is implicit in the relative speed and magnitude of turnover in the generational composition of the electorate. The transformation that has occurred during the past thirty years is portrayed in the sample estimates shown earlier in Table 2.1. As we have noted, the pre-New Deal cohorts whose first votes were cast *before* the Roosevelt era constituted about half of the Eisenhower electorate but had virtually disappeared from the electorate of the late 1980s. Citizens in the post-New Deal generation who came of age in the midst of the turmoil that came *after* the election of Lyndon Johnson made up well over half of the electorate that chose George Bush in 1988 and almost two-thirds of those eligible to participate in the Bush-Clinton contest in 1992.

Continuity through time was provided by the middle, New Deal generation who made up a third of the 1992 electorate. The two sets of New Deal cohorts depicted in Table 2.1 suffered relatively little in the way of life cycle mortality between 1952 and 1992; the very oldest of those who first voted for Franklin Roosevelt had aged from 41 in 1952 to 81 in 1992. Between 1964 and 1992, the decline in the proportion of the electorate contained in these New Deal generations is largely accounted for by the growth of the voting-age population in the United States, from 118 million to 183 million, over the same period. In their continuing presence as a generation completed by 1964 and almost fully represented throughout the 1980s, the cohorts of the New Deal era provide a crucial basis for evaluating the consequence of the generational replacement involving older and younger generations.[8]

▪ Non-Voting within Political Generations

In presenting evidence about differences in voting and non-voting among and within political generations, we will usually present data from four successive sets of elections rather than pursue a year-by-year analysis. The boundaries of these four election periods, as with the boundaries for our three generations, have been set to match what we think are separable political epochs that had somewhat different consequences for different segments of the electorate. The earlier epoch is defined by the elections of 1952, 1956, and 1960. We begin with 1952 only because it is the first year in the NES/CPS series of data collections, and we close the first epoch with 1960 because it provides the generally accepted high point of turnout (low point of non-voting) following World War II. Given the apparent absence of relevant change across the three elections, the data from the three NES presidential year studies have been combined, thereby increasing the stability of the generational estimates for the period of high turnout.

The second epoch is defined in Table 3.1 by the elections of 1964 and 1968. These elections mark the mobilization of the Black vote and the early stages of party realignment in the South. The third time period,

Table 3.1 Distribution of the National Electorate by Political Generation and Election Period

Political Generations: Defined by Year of First Eligibility to Vote for President	Election Periods				
	1952–56–60	1964–68	1972–76–80	1984–88	1992
Pre-New Deal: Pre-1920 to 1928	38 (2086)	25 (767)	13 (918)	4 (185)	1 (23)
New Deal: 1932 to 1964	62 (3379)	72 (2238)	55 (3920)	42 (1781)	38 (943)
Post-New Deal: 1968 to 1992	—	4 (113)	32 (2313)	54 (2308)	61 (1521)
Total: Number of Cases	100% (5615)	100% (3128)	100% (7189)	100% (4297)	100% (2488)

— No cases in sample.

1972–1976–1980, encompasses the low point in the national incidence of party identification—the period of so-called partisan dealignment. The elections of 1984 and 1988 reflect the impact of the Reagan years and mark the low point in turnout after the election of 1960. Although 1984 marked the first upturn in turnout since 1960, the election of 1988 marked the low point for the entire 36-year period.

Again, averaging the estimates across two or three elections provides an overall picture of the major periods in recent history during which the generational transformation in turnout had occurred. In selected instances we will refer to individual years, but, in general, our omission of reference to specific years will simply mean the omission of unremarkable trends that are highlighted by our emphasis on the broader periods.[9]

The examination of voting rates within the three political generations in each of our four time periods introduces the one dramatic fact that has been missing from most earlier analyses of declining turnout. During the interval of national aggregate decline, the *continuing* New Deal generation did not experience any drop in turnout. If anything, the New Dealers experienced a small *increase* in turnout. A substantial part of that overall increase can be attributed to the mobilization of the Black vote in the 1960s, but the upturn was also evident within the non-Black portion of the electorate.

The fact that the New Deal generation (making up some 60 percent of the electorate in the 1950s and about 40 percent in the 1980s) apparently did not contribute to the three-decade national decline in net aggregate turnout has many important implications. In the first place, it provides a point of departure for our thesis of a decline in turnout that rests on a compositional change in the electorate resulting from the generational exchange of the post-New Deal generation for the pre-New Deal generation. Of equal importance, the record of a steady level of turnout among New Dealers challenges many explanations by other scholars that presumably account for a decline in voting. Those explanations have included apparent evidence of diminished political and social involvement of potential voters, as well as a decline in political mobilization. The effects of these changes were presumably only partially offset by increases in years of formal education (and other personal resources such as those pertaining to income and occupation) and the relaxation of legal barriers to voting (Teixeira, 1992, p. 47; Rosenstone and Hansen, 1993, p. 215).

Within the New Deal generation, whose youngest members were over 40 years of age in 1952, there was obviously no change in education over the next 40 years. This leaves the relaxation of legal inhibitions to voting as a primary source of increased support for voter turnout. The Rosenstone-Hansen estimate that this would increase turnout (in the total electorate) by about two percentage points is of similar magnitude to the increase we shall document for the New Deal generation over the same 40-year span in question. This does nothing, of course, to account for the 13 percentage point *decline* across the total electorate.

In the next two chapters we will note evidence that neither party identification, social connectedness, nor political involvement appears to have had any appreciable net effect on changing turnout in the New Deal generation between the 1950s and the 1980s. We will not attempt to reconcile our view of this process with divergent views. It is possible that conflicting pressures of the kind noted by Teixeira and Rosenstone and Hansen simply had approximately offsetting weights within the New Deal generation. We think it more likely, however, that our more parsimonious explanation, derived from the generational persistence model of societal change, provides a satisfactory accounting for the observed behavior of all three generations and, therefore, for the changes in the national parameters concerning turnout.[10]

▪ Voting Turnout among Blacks

A review of national data separating Black and non-Black citizens is provided by Table 3.2, which shows that changing participation rates of Blacks do not constitute a major part of the general puzzle we are trying to solve. Their turnout rates *increased* over the full span of years, whether because of increases in personal resources, such as education, or in response to enhanced access to the polls as a result of the Civil Rights movement and federal civil rights legislation. The increase in Black voter turnout is most apparent within the continuing New Deal cohorts; non-voting was cut in half, down to about 30 percent in the 1980s, compared to 60 percent in the earlier epoch.

Nevertheless, a shadow of our basic puzzle is apparent in the New

Table 3.2 Self-reported Voting Among Blacks, 1952–1992

Political Generation	Election Year				
	1952	1956	1960	1964	1968
Pre-New Deal	36 (21/59)	29 (12/41)	53 (27/51)	58 (18/31)	75 (21/28)
New Deal	32 (31/96)	37 (38/104)	53 (54/102)	66 (77/116)	67 (67/100)
Post-New Deal	—	—	—	—	** (2/5)
Total Cases	(155)	(145)	(153)	(147)	(133)

Political Generation	Election Year					
	1972	1976	1980	1984	1988	1992
Pre-New Deal	58 (19/33)	67 (25/38)	** (3/7)	** (4/6)	** (1/3)	** (1/4)
New Deal	71 (90/127)	68 (72/106)	81 (70/87)	71 (62/88)	65 (49/76)	78 (71/91)
Post-New Deal	58 (33/57)	60 (45/75)	52 (37/71)	62 (72/117)	58 (79/137)	63 (123/195)
Total Cases	(217)	(218)	(165)	(211)	(216)	(290)

NOTE: Entry shows the percentage voting followed by the number reporting voting/total number of cases.
** Too few cases for estimation.
— No cases in sample.

Deal/post-New Deal generational comparisons in Table 3.2. As with the non-Blacks, the turnout rates within the younger generations were not as high in the 1980s as they were for the somewhat older, *less well educated* New Deal generation of Black citizens. Overall, about 60 percent of the younger generation reported voting, as against more than 70 percent of Blacks who were one generation older. However, in contrast to the pattern among non-Blacks, the younger, post-New Deal Black citizens had *higher* rates of participation in the 1980s than the earlier rates among the pre-New Deal generations that they were replacing. As a consequence of the difference between Black and non-Black patterns, we will limit our analysis to non-Black citizens as we pursue the puzzle of declining turnout.

▪ The Allocation of Credit for Change

Setting aside the octogenarians among our older pre–New Deal generation, who had been reduced to a tiny fraction of the non-Black electorate by the 1980s, we show in Table 3.3 a number of the consequences of replacing the disappearing pre–New Deal generations in the non-Black electorate with growing numbers of citizens who came of age after 1968. Insofar as the continuing, New Deal generation of non-Black electors reflected any change in turnout, they apparently *increased* their turnout; voting appeared to be up as much as five points, from a self-report of about 75 percent in the 1950s to at least 80 percent in the 1980s.[11] The aggregate decline in national turnout occurred, therefore, despite this intra-generational increase in voting (and the counterpart increase among Blacks). The national decline was largely a result of the non-Black electorate having replaced its oldest cohorts, those who had voted at an 80 percent level through the early 1960s. These older generations had been more than replaced with a host of new additions who voted at only a 65 percent rate in the 1980s.

However, as we suggested earlier, the full magnitude of the ultimate consequence of this generational replacement is not immediately obvious in Table 3.3. In accounting for aggregate trends that are accompanied by the continuing growth of a population, the impact of new additions to the population is determined both by their relative uniqueness vis-à-vis the remainder of the population (as revealed in Table 3.3), and by their sheer numbers—their size (not apparent in Table 3.3). The voting

Table 3.3 Self-reported Voting Among Non-Blacks, 1952–1992

Political Generation	Election Year				
	1952	1956	1960	1964	1968
Pre-New Deal	82 (544/667)	81 (468/576)	83 (476/575)	81 (281/348)	74 (205/279)
New Deal	76 (583/769)	73 (747/1021)	81 (888/1101)	79 (748/952)	80 (698/871)
Post-New Deal	—	—	—	—	57 (59/104)
Total Cases	(1436)	(1597)	(1676)	(1300)	(1254)

Political Generation	Election Year				
	1972	1976	1980	1984	1988	1992
Pre-New Deal	70 (230/331)	70 (185/265)	71 (66/93)	67 (60/90)	66 (31/47)	** (9/16)
New Deal	78 (940/1208)	80 (925/1168)	80 (498/622)	82 (637/774)	80 (514/641)	82 (613/745)
Post-New Deal	66 (341/514)	61 (439/715)	62 (325/522)	69 (609/888)	65 (558/864)	73 (858/1177)
Total Cases	(2053)	(2148)	(1237)	(1752)	(1552)	(1938)

NOTE: Unless noted otherwise, all subsequent tables will be for Non-Blacks.
Entry shows the percentage voting followed by the number reporting voting/total number of cases.
** Too few cases for estimation.
— No cases in sample.

rates of the departing cohorts were clearly different from those of the continuing generations (higher in the 1950s, lower in the 1980s), and the new generations were even more distinctive in their lower turnout rates throughout the 1970s and 1980s. But from 1972 onward the new cohorts were much larger than those they replaced (see Table 3.1).[12]

▪ Education and Turnout

In pursuing a resolution of Brody's puzzle, we next consider why the national decline in turnout took place in the face of a steady rise in educational attainment. An exploration of the non-Black electors makes clear that the generational differences in turnout existed *despite* the educational differences across generations.[13]

The need for a new perspective on changes in national turnout becomes even more apparent when we examine the changes that have occurred, generation by generation, to raise the national level of formal education. Although there is some ambiguity concerning the precise nature of the role of education in predisposing citizens to turn out and vote (Cassell, 1987; Luskin, 1987), our analysis provides strong confirmation of its underlying fundamental importance (Rosenstone and Wolfinger, 1980; Leighley, 1990; Rosenstone and Hansen, 1993). The role of education takes on an added significance as we note the striking generational differences in educational attainment.

With the end of World War II, the traditional American veneration of education was given new meaning through federal programs designed to increase veterans' educational opportunities. Among the many programs offered at various levels, provisions in the so-called G.I. Bill, offering college education to returning veterans, were unique. They enabled virtually everyone who had served in the armed forces (certainly every high school graduate) to be compensated with college enrollment for a period of time to match the length of service: for example, thirty-six months of military service provided thirty-six months of college—a full four years at nine months per school year.

By the 1960s the normal expectation for high school graduates to pursue college educations was producing a mass electorate with a level of education beyond the experience of any other society in modern history. Table 3.4 illustrates the extent to which the post-New Deal generation was the carrier of this legacy. Even an acute awareness of the steady national gains in education across recent years scarcely prepares one for the contrast between the educational levels of the disappearing cohorts and those of their replacements. In an age when at least some college education for everyone has become the norm, it is startling to note that more than half of the pre-New Deal generation (which constituted 40 percent of the total Eisenhower electorate) ended their education *without graduating* from high school.

The direct confrontation of the relationship between education and turnout among our different political generations produces a striking but thoroughly coherent array of information. The data presented in Table 3.5 support several corollaries of the thesis that declining turn-

Table 3.4 Educational Attainment[a] of Political Generations

| Political Generations | Years of Formal Education | | | | |
	0–11	12	13+	Total	N
Pre-New Deal					
1. Pre-1920	62%	28	10	100%	386
2. Republican Normalcy, 1920–1928	50%	35	15	100%	338
New Deal					
3. Roosevelt Era, 1932–1944	24%	54	22	100%	866
4. New Deal Consolidated, 1948–1964	8%	58	34	100%	488
Post-New Deal					
5. Years of Turmoil, 1968–1976	3%	41	56	100%	613
6. Reagan Era, 1980–1988	1%	59	40	100%	364

a. Measured for the third, fourth, and fifth generations in 1952, 1968, and 1988, respectively, when youngest member of generation was at least 30 years of age. The distribution for the Reagan Era generation reflects the fact that the generation was captured in the earliest phases of their political life cycle. The oldest was 26 years old in 1988; some of the youngest were still in high school. Given the continuing increase in the proportions of high school graduates who go on to college (for at least one year), the ultimate figures for the Reagan-Bush generation will doubtless surpass those for the generation of turmoil.

out can be attributed in large part to the replacement of the pre-New Deal generations by the post-New Deal cohorts. First, we can turn to the New Deal generation that anchors our comparisons among generations: within each of the three New Deal groups characterized by different educational backgrounds, members of the continuing New Deal generation scarcely changed their voting rate across four decades. Their turnout rates do not reveal much in the way of election-specific influences, and they certainly do not match any trend toward lower turnout over the forty-year interval. Once again, with an apparent small net *increase* within the college groups, if there is any trend among these cohorts it is in the direction of *increased* turnout in the Bush elections compared with those of the Eisenhower era. In general, however, across

Table 3.5 Self-reported Voting of Non-Blacks Within Political Generations, by Education

Years of Education	Political Generation	1952	1956	1960	1964	1968
0–11	Pre-New Deal	78 (374/478)	75 (288/382)	78 (301/387)	78 (175/224)	66 (123/187)
	New Deal	64 (235/366)	60 (236/396)	67 (268/401)	68 (218/322)	66 (177/269)
	Post-New Deal	—	—	—	—	** (4/18)
12	Pre-New Deal	89 (57/64)	93 (71/76)	96 (42/44)	84 (31/37)	** (19/21)
	New Deal	84 (138/165)	76 (198/261)	86 (250/292)	80 (205/255)	86 (181/211)
	Post-New Deal	—	—	—	—	** (11/21)
13+	Pre-New Deal	90 (111/123)	92 (104/113)	92 (132/143)	86 (73/85)	90 (62/69)
	New Deal	89 (210/237)	86 (313/364)	91 (370/408)	87 (323/371)	87 (340/391)
	Post-New Deal	—	—	—	—	68 (44/65)

Years of Education	Political Generation	1972	1976	1980	1984	1988	1992
0–11	Pre-New Deal	63 (141/223)	63 (100/159)	59 (30/51)	57 (29/51)	** (13/23)	** (1/5)
	New Deal	62 (260/419)	64 (224/350)	63 (110/176)	64 (134/211)	62 (110/178)	65 (133/205)
	Post-New Deal	41 (35/85)	28 (27/95)	27 (15/56)	35 (28/81)	30 (30/100)	27 (31/117)
12	Pre-New Deal	89 (31/35)	83 (33/40)	** (8/9)	** (8/11)	** (11/16)	** (4/5)
	New Deal	83 (232/279)	79 (194/245)	74 (72/97)	83 (116/140)	84 (171/204)	84 (220/261)
	Post-New Deal	55 (72/131)	49 (89/180)	49 (57/117)	52 (93/179)	51 (161/317)	64 (245/380)
13+	Pre-New Deal	79 (57/72)	81 (51/63)	84 (27/32)	84 (21/25)	** (7/8)	** (4/5)
	New Deal	88 (448/510)	89 (508/573)	91 (314/347)	91 (384/420)	91 (225/247)	94 (240/255)
	Post-New Deal	79 (234/297)	73 (324/441)	73 (253/349)	78 (487/626)	83 (359/434)	86 (562/656)

NOTE: The education variable is based on the NES Cumulative File education summary variable v140. The 0–11 (or less than high school) category consists of persons who have not received a high school diploma. The 12 (or high school) category consists of persons who have received a high school diploma and non-academic training. The 13+ (or more than high school) category consists of persons who have some college or a college degree.

Entry shows the percentage voting followed by the number reporting voting/total number of cases.

— No cases in sample.

** Too few cases for estimation.

a forty-year span of time, neither aging nor intervening period effects seem to have materially altered the rates of electoral participation within the non-Black New Deal cohorts.

However, still within the New Deal generations, differences in educational attainment are clearly associated with persistent differences in rates of voter turnout throughout those 40 years. More generally, shifting our analytic perspective from the question of stability of turnout over time to viewing the voting rates across the three levels of educational attainment within *each* generation, it is hard to imagine questioning the effect of education—be it direct or indirect—on turnout throughout the entire period.[14] The effect is modest within the pre-New Deal generation. Elsewhere, the apparent effect of education on turnout is of the same large magnitude across all the decades. Within the New Deal generation, those who had been exposed to some college education had an average voting turnout rate that was more than 25 percentage points higher than the rate for citizens who did not graduate from high school. Within the post-New Deal generation, the difference between the same pair of education groups averaged some 50 points.

Generational Differences in Turnout

The comparison of participation rates for the entering and departing generations is of direct relevance to our puzzle. Since it is those generations that are responsible for the change in aggregate national turnout figures, the generational comparisons of turnout *within* common educational backgrounds are the most revealing. It immediately becomes clear that generational differences in education have obscured the true magnitudes of the generational differences in turnout. Once we have taken into account the better education of the most recent political generations, as well as the lesser education of the oldest generations, we arrive at new estimates of generational differences and their impact on changes in the generational composition of the electorate.

Without taking education into account, the overall generational replacement difference in turnout rates for the oldest and youngest generations among non-Blacks was about 17 percentage points.[15] In Table 3.5, among those who had not graduated from high school, the difference was more than 45 points (77 to 31); among those with some college the "generational-exchange" difference was only 9 points (89 to 80).

Among the high school graduates the difference was another astronomical 40 points—a drop from an average voting rate of over 90 percent in 1952–1964 to only 50 percent voting in 1972–1988. As a consequence, the fact that the post-New Deal generations contain more than three times the proportion of college educated found in pre-New Deal ranks and only one-fourth as many who had not graduated from high school (see Table 3.3) is highly significant. Everything else being equal, the upgrading of educational attainment across the four decades separating 1988 from 1952 forestalled what could have been a cataclysmic drop in national voting turnout by the 1980s.

Exposure to college education clearly inhibited the overall drop in aggregate turnout between the middle generation and the younger cohorts of the post-New Deal group. Nevertheless, when we examine the contribution of education to voting turnout, we are reassured that more education did not, in some perverse way, lead to less turnout. Among the continuing cohorts present in both the 1950s and the 1980s, education continuously played a dominant role in shaping voter turnout. Our interest in accounting for generational differences in voting participation is simply sharpened by the discovery that for half of the electorate of the 1980s—those with no college education—there is a gap of more than 30 points between the older generation and the new.[16]

At this point in developing the generational persistence explanation of societal change in voter turnout, it is appropriate to display the raw data underlying the model, which we do in the tables shown in Appendix A. The display format is straightforward: Appendix A provides sample estimates of turnout within three education categories for each four-year cohort for each presidential election from 1952 to 1988. This means, of course, that estimates are often based on very small samples; we will shortly draw attention to summary estimates to illustrate the crucial generalization. It should be noted that the ability to observe the independent estimates of cohorts through time is more than simply a counterpart to longitudinal analyses that are based on comparisons of successive cross-section samples of a population. It is much more akin to an extended panel analysis in which the same individuals are followed through time. One can follow each cohort as it ages, and as, along with other cohorts, it is exposed to new historical events. This capacity affects our analysis in a number of ways. First, it permits us to seek out evidence of life cycle effects. By noting the turnout record of each cohort following its entry into the voting-age population, we can note the early adult life cycle effects on turnout. Similarly, the record of each cohort in its declining years reflects life cycle effects as life runs its course. In addition, the course of the intervening years is comparably charted in election-by-election detail.

▪ Life Cycle or Generational Differences in Voting Turnout

Each of the first three basic tables in Appendix A casts the same light on the conventional wisdom relating voter turnout to aging. Inspection of the election year columns in these tables conveys the pattern reported most often in the literature. Year after year the turnout rate appears to rise rapidly up to perhaps 35 to 45 years of age. The *rate* of increase then declines, but turnout apparently continues to go up until old age sets in. Finally, in the last decade of life, voting rates decline. In the typical multivariate equation used to explain turnout, this pattern is represented by two coefficients, for age and age squared. The first produces a positive coefficient indicating that, overall and on average, turnout increases with age. The second entry always produces a very small unstandardized coefficient, but it is virtually always statistically significant, and it always carries a negative sign which represents decreasing turnout among the very old.

The Early Years

Treating the basic data as records of cohort experiences through time suggests a dramatically different story. Instead of comparing *columns* of electors of different ages, signifying that they were comparably young at different times, we can follow *rows* of cohorts as they age through time. The cohort rows provide evidence that the early life cycle effects exist, but sharply modified from the usual discussions of age and voter turnout. First, evidence reflecting probable early life cycle effects is most uniform and persuasive for citizens who did not graduate from high school (see Tables A1, A2, and A3 in Appendix A). Among them, virtually every cohort entering the electorate between 1952 and 1968 showed an increase in turnout over the succeeding two or three elections. Among high school graduates, evidence of life cycle effects across the first three elections is missing in seven of the ten cohorts who had an opportunity to vote in at least three elections in the NES series. Only one cohort with college education clearly fits the early life cycle pattern (the cohort that entered in 1984), and most cohorts failed to show an increase in turnout at their second chance to vote. Thanks largely to the least well educated citizens, the generalization specifying early year life cycle effects is sustained, but the evidence overall is not impressive.

Second, the pattern of accelerating turnout (where it can be seen) is concentrated in the cohorts of the New Deal generation; it is notably absent in many sets of post-New Deal cohorts. As Figure 3.1 shows, no statement is possible about the older cohorts because our data base begins with 1952 and the youngest *pre*-New Deal cohorts entered the electorate more than twenty years earlier. As a consequence, we cannot assess changes in the early years of pre-New Deal turnout. Within the *post*-New Deal generation, the oldest three or four cohorts had an opportunity (three to six elections) to exhibit an early life cycle pattern of increasing turnout, but the actual record is mixed.

Among the college-educated post-New Deal cohorts, turnout rose from 1984 to 1988. Among the remainder, however, turnout dropped in their second election in 1984 and again in their third election in 1988.

For the cohorts of 1980 and 1984, the life cycle upturn that might be expected in the early stages of their political experience is largely missing for those citizens who had not attended so much as one year of college. We shall note in the next chapter that the limited indication of life cycle increases in voter turnout in the 1980s is partially the consequence of a unique syndrome of politico-economic polarization among the post-New Deal generation in the 1980s. That polarization results in offsetting trends in social-economic divisions within the generation.

The End of the Life Cycle

At the other end of the life cycle, the evidence of declining turnout is also very irregular. Once more, it is most clear-cut for the least well educated. Four of the oldest cohorts in this group, reliably represented in our sample data for at least three elections, showed a decline in turnout in the last two or three of those elections. In the other two education groups, the record of decline is often limited to the last or, at most, the last two elections.

Given the beginning of our data set in 1952 and the termination in

Figure 3.1 Temporal matrix for three political generations (26 cohorts × 40 elections).

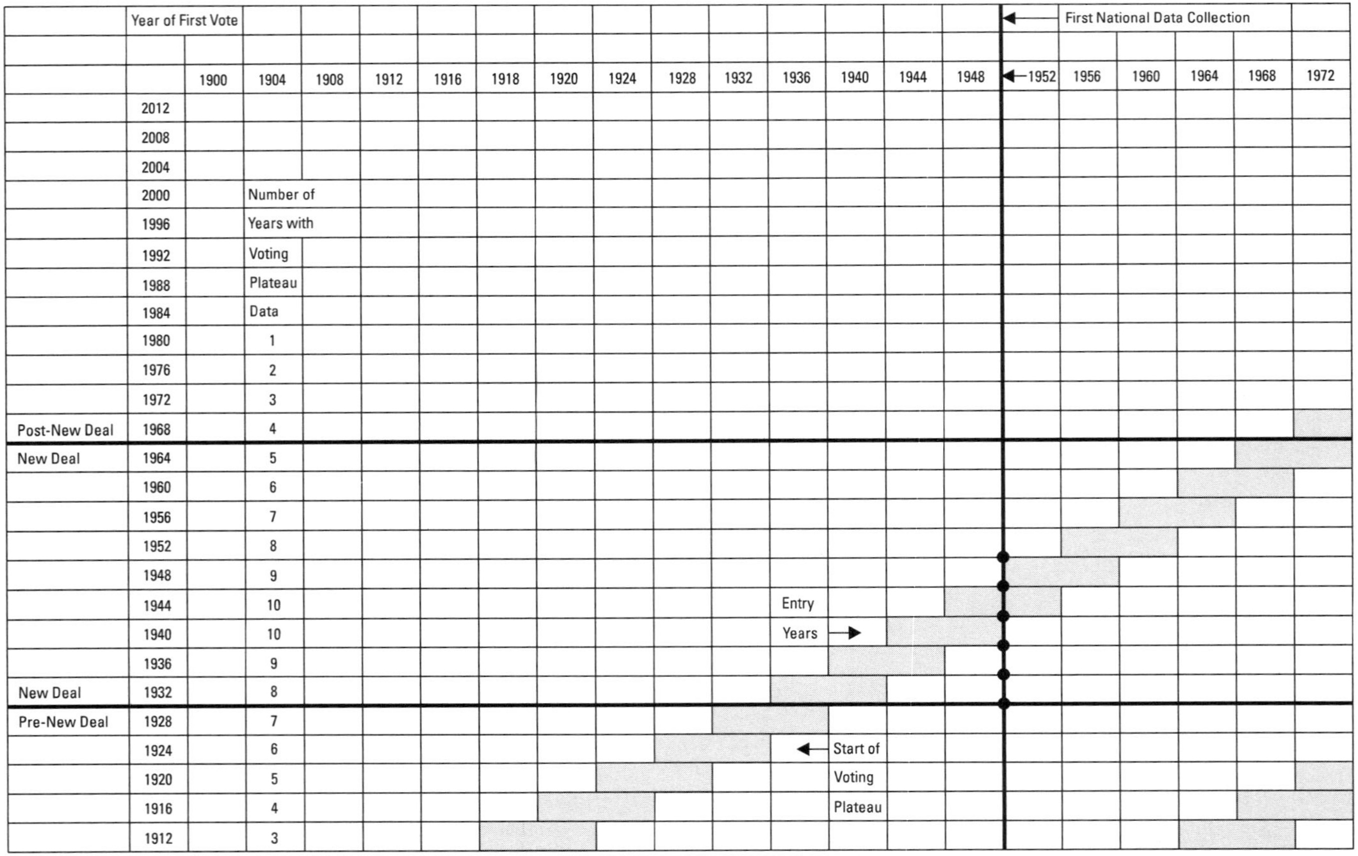

Year of First Vote

1992 Data

	1976	1980	1984	1988	←1992	1996	2000	2004	2008	2012	2016	2020	2024	2028	2032	2036	2040	2044	2048

2012								Entry											
2008								Years											
2004																			
2000																			
1996																			
1992																			
1988														End of					
1984														Voting					
1980			Start of											Plateau					
1976			Voting																
1972			Plateau																
1968														Terminal					
Post-New Deal														Years					
1964																			
1960																			
1956																			
1952																			
1948																			
1944			End of				Terminal												
1940			Voting				Years												
1936			Plateau																
1932																			
New Deal																			
1928																			
Pre-New Deal																			
1924																			
1920																			
1916																			
1912																			

1992, seven of the nine cohorts old enough to reflect a decline in voting in their last elections are members of the pre-New Deal generation. It will be 2024 before we have full data for the New Deal generation, and 2052 before the last of the post-New Deal (as defined in 1992) will have been counted. We will return to life cycle effects when we consider the analysis of each generation in the next chapter.

Life Cycle and the Turnout Plateau

In the meantime, we are left with the major consequence of shifting attention away from cross-sectional data on age to cohort-based evidence of aging. For 17 cohorts (from those entering in 1912 to those who came of voting age in 1976) we have turnout records that suggest a turnout "plateau" beginning with the second or third election beyond that in which they are first eligible to vote and ending before terminal decline sets in one or at most two elections before the last election in which the cohort is represented in our samples.[17]

These cohort records have been evaluated by estimating the slope of the regression line formed by regressing election-year turnout for each cohort. This was done within each of our three education categories both across the *entire time period,* 1952–1988, and before and after the major generational boundary year of 1968. The estimates of slopes of the entire period for each cohort, within categories of education, are presented in the last three tables in Appendix A. The evidence provides strong support for the conclusion that there is no systematic variation in within-cohort aggregate rates of turnout over time *beyond* the second or third election after the first election of eligibility and prior to the next to last election before death. In other words, setting aside life cycle effects, very early and very late, there is no net increase or decrease in turnout after the age of 26 (±4) and before the age of 70 (±4). A lifelong propensity to go to the polls is established when the citizen is still fairly young and persists until the infirmity of old age forty or fifty years later.

Within those boundaries the electors of any given cohort maintain a turnout rate that does not reveal any trend above or below their forty-year average. The only partial exception is for college-educated members of the post-New Deal cohorts. For them the pattern varies from cohort to cohort, but, particularly for the two oldest cohorts, the trend after the second or third election continues upward. No other generation or education subset reveals any significant departure from a flat regression line. Beyond limited life cycle effects for cohorts in their introductory or declining years, the evidence for most of the people (for most of the time) is that neither short-term nor long-term influences have much of an impact on turnout. In general, turnout levels are set early in life and persist well into later years. In the face of close and exhaustive inspection, it is now apparent why the New Deal generation did not contribute to the declining turnout of the 1970s and 1980s.

An important theoretical point that emerges from our historical perspective argues that much of the evidence for "conventional wisdom" interpretations of the correlation of age and life cycle differences with voter turnout is actually the result of generational differences. This seems particularly true during that portion of the modern period where turnout dropped with the entry of each successive cohort. Cross-sectional data suggesting that turnout rates peak at ages 65 to 70 are now seen to be a product of higher turnout rates of older (earlier) cohorts. The age of 70 is not a peak so much as the end of an enduring plateau prior to an inevitable (but very irregular) life cycle decline. More generally, life cycle effects that have been so prominent in explaining voting among young adults have, in point of fact, a much more limited role to play. We will return to the question of whether generational differentiation has been accentuated in the Reagan/Bush era, but at first blush it would appear that for the past 40 years, the real effects of generation and the period in which the post-New Deal generation entered the electorate have been mistaken for the apparent effects of aging.

Turnout in Entry Years

The conclusion that our three generations are separated by much more than life cycle effects is supported by more than the aggregate generational differences in turnout presented in Table 3.4 or Appendix Tables A4, A5, and A6. At least two additional sets of evidence are contained within the many possible cohort comparisons in the full array of data suggested by Figure 3.1. The first of these is very direct. If cohorts can be assigned to different generations because of different formative experiences shared by cohort members when coming of age, then relevant cohort differences should be apparent as the cohorts enter the electorate. Comparing turnout rates of cohorts on entry is, of course, open to

Table 3.6 Average Turnout Rates for Cohorts As They Enter the Electorate

Political Generation	Education		
	0–11	12	13+
New Deal	26 (27/103)	70 (99/141)	82 (65/79)
Post-New Deal	29 (44/154)	52 (204/391)	71 (234/331)

NOTE: Entry shows the percentage voting followed by the number reporting voting/total number of cases.

uncertainties of interpretation insofar as short-term influences intrude on one or another cohort in one or another election. In our case, however, comparing entry levels of the 1950s and 1960s with those of the 1970s and 1980s seems to be a proper comparison of the consequences of postulated "pre-turmoil" circumstances with those of the "post-turmoil" period. In other words, the comparison of New Deal cohorts with post-New Deal cohorts on entry seems particularly appropriate, given the radical differences in the political environment at the time of their entry. The turnout rates for New Deal and post-New Deal cohorts on entry are shown in Table 3.6. The generational differences that we have observed in the aggregate comparisons did, indeed, apparently originate when the various cohorts each entered the electorate. Furthermore, it is (again) the high school graduates who contribute most dramatically to aggregate generational differences.

A second test for generational differences involves a familiar approach to "controlling" or taking account of possible life cycle differences between generations. In our previous comparisons with the New Deal cohorts (as in Table 3.5), we have compared different generations at the same point in time, with possible age or life cycle differences confounding the meaning of observed "generational" differences. True, to some extent we have taken differences in life experiences into account by matching cohorts with years of education; nevertheless, we have not accounted for other age-related attributes that may have led to generational differences in turnout.

We can, however, come close to precision matching both on education and political age. For the latter, we start with the six cohorts of the post-New Deal generation in 1984 and 1988. Strictly speaking, within our data set there is only one possible set of comparisons between these post-New Deal cohorts and those from the New Deal generation if we want to hold constant age or non-education life cycle effects. Only the 1952 data for the oldest six cohorts of the New Deal generation have *exactly* the same life cycle status as the six 1988 cohorts of the post-New Deal generation. The 1956 or 1960 data for the New Deal cohorts would capture them four or eight years further along in their life cycle—but then we would have no comparable data for the post-New Deal electors. It is not possible to compare earlier New Deal cohorts with the post-New Deal cohorts of 1980 or 1984 because there are no 1944 or 1948 New Deal data. Only the single set of comparisons, 1952 with 1988, permits precision matching of the two generations on life cycle effects (see Figure 3.1).

In Table 3.7 we have in fact slightly compromised the goal of precision matching by combining 1956 election data with those from 1952, and 1984 data with those from 1988, in order to increase sample size and the reliability of our estimates. Despite this *a fortiori* blurring of generational effects, the post-New Deal turnout rate is 25 points lower than that of the New Deal, both among electors with no more than grade school and those with completed high school educations. The ameliorating influence associated with college attendance produces differences that average only five points. (In the pure contrast of 1952 New Deal cohorts with 1988 post-New Deal cohorts, the same comparisons produced differences of 32, 36, and 7 points.)

These observed generational differences in turnout, under rather stringent controls for age and education, are the more important because they are of the same magnitude as comparable differences that can be noted in Table 3.5. In that table, among the high school graduates, generational differences between New Deal and post-New Deal were 28, 30, 25, 31, and 33 points. It would now seem that such generational differences, observed at a given point in time, should not be attributed to *age* or *life cycle* differences between the generations, but rather should be interpreted primarily as true generational differences, the result of period effects that are radically different between these two generations.

Finally, any direct comparison of pre-New Deal and post-New Deal cohorts is, of course, impossible. Matching pre-New Deal life cycle stages

Table 3.7 Turnout Rates and Generational Differences, for New Deal and Post-New Deal Cohorts, Matched on Age and Education

	Education										
	0–11 Years			High School Graduate			One Year or More of College				
Cohort Ages	1952–56 New Deal	1984–88 Post-New Deal	Difference	1952–56 New Deal	1984–88 Post-New Deal	Difference	Cohort Ages	1952–56 New Deal	1984–88 Post-New Deal	Difference
21–24	33 (20/60)	19 (5/26)	−14	67 (52/78)	41 (40/97)	−26	21–24	78 (32/41)	69 (74/108)	−9
25–28	56 (51/91)	16 (4/25)	−40	76 (91/120)	44 (52/117)	−32	25–28	89 (46/52)	79 (111/140)	−10
29–32	62 (63/101)	43 (12/28)	−19	74 (90/121)	55 (69/126)	−19	29–32	89 (58/65)	85 (137/162)	−4
33–36	61 (89/147)	30 (9/30)	−31	87 (106/122)	65 (75/115)	−22	33–36	89 (69/78)	87 (183/210)	−2
37–40	63 (92/145)	50 (14/28)	−13	88 (87/99)	61 (60/98)	−27	37–40	91 (39/43)	91 (167/185)	0
41–44	71 (106/149)	** (6/15)	−31	90 (71/79)	69 (24/35)	−21	41–44	95 (57/60)	92 (65/71)	−3
Average:			−25			−25	Average:			−5

NOTE: Entry shows the percentage voting followed by the number reporting voting/total number of cases.

** Too few cases for estimation.

with the six post-New Deal cohorts would require data from 1928 (24 years before the first Michigan data collection) for the pre-New Deal cohorts.

However, we can match selected cohorts on life cycle and education as we observe the *closing* years of the life cycle for pre-New Deal and New Deal cohorts. A comparison of turnout rates of pre-New Deal and New Deal cohorts—controlling on life cycle—is possible with the 1952 and 1956 data for the pre-New Deal cohorts (13 and 14 elections beyond their coming of age) and the 1984 and 1988 data for the New Deal cohorts (also 13 or 14 elections beyond the beginning of their generation in 1932).

With striking uniformity within all three education levels, Table 3.8 shows that pre-New Deal electors have a higher voting rate than do New Deal electors. As with the New Deal/post-New Deal comparisons, the sharpest generational differences in period effects occur at the lower education levels.

▪ Summary

Given the temporal boundary definitions of the generations, and the relatively limited time span of our data base, there are severe limits to our ability to compare period, life cycle, and generation effects among and within our cohorts. Modeling all of these effects in a single equation, or set of equations, can produce coefficients that give statistically significant evidence of the independent effects for period, life cycle, and age or generation, but we have not found such analyses to be particularly fruitful. Instead of such equations, we submit the direct estimates given above of all three effects.

The most telling general conclusion to emerge from the disaggregated analysis of cohort histories of voting turnout is that from the third election in which citizens are eligible to vote to the fourteenth (from the ages of 26–29 to 69–72) there is no apparent net change in the turnout for non-Black citizens. Life cycle effects lead to increased rates in the second and third elections of eligibility, and to diminished rates in the fifteenth or later elections, but there is a 40-year-wide level plateau of turnout for most cohorts. A second generalization is that the turnout rates which characterize each cohort differ by political generation, particularly among citizens with no more than a high school diploma;

Table 3.8 Turnout Rates and Generational Differences, for Pre-New Deal and New Deal Cohorts, Matched on Age and Education

	Education										
	0–11 Years			High School Graduate			One Year or More of College			
Cohort Ages	1952–56 Pre-New Deal	1984–88 New Deal	Difference	1952–56 Pre-New Deal	1984–88 New Deal	Difference	Cohort Ages	1952–56 Pre-New Deal	1984–88 New Deal	Difference
45–48	71 (52/73)	** (7/17)	−30	** (21/22)	82 (32/39)	−14	45–48	** (19/21)	88 (49/56)	−3
49–52	78 (107/138)	** (11/18)	−17	89 (41/46)	78 (55/71)	−11	49–52	90 (35/39)	86 (76/88)	−4
53–56	82 (103/126)	66 (25/38)	−16	93 (39/42)	86 (57/66)	−7	53–56	96 (27/28)	89 (62/70)	−5
57–60	83 (92/111)	57 (27/47)	−26	88 (30/34)	89 (54/61)	+1	57–60	80 (20/25)	93 (50/54)	+13
61–64	80 (76/96)	57 (34/60)	−23	** (15/16)	93 (39/42)	−1	61–64	** (22/23)	95 (69/73)	−1
65–68	79 (76/96)	68 (30/44)	−11	** (17/17)	88 (63/72)	−12	65–68	** (10/10)	96 (51/53)	−4
69–72	74 (63/85)	78 (42/54)	+4	** (14/16)	83 (44/53)	−5	69–72	** (10/10)	93 (51/55)	−7
Average:			−17			−7	Average:			−2

NOTE: Entry shows the percentage voting followed by the number reporting voting/total number of cases.
** Too few cases for estimation.

pre-New Deal turnout is higher than that for the New Deal generation and post-New Deal turnout is well below that of the New Deal.

There are two important consequences of these generalizations. Because of the large numbers in the post-New Deal generation, their replacement of the habitual voters in the pre-New Deal cohorts inevitably resulted in a net decrease in national turnout rates. Even though the turnout rates of the young post-New Deal cohorts increased steadily, in accord with traditional theories of life cycle effects and the sheer passage of time, the starting point for post-New Deal turnout was so low that throughout the 1970s and 1980s their addition to the eligible electorate continuously depressed net national turnout rates.

Quite apart from the mechanics of population turnover and generational replacement, the discovery of the turnout plateau forces a sharp revision in our view of the impact of life cycle effects on turnout. The picture of a decelerating but continuing increase in turnout rates through citizens aged 50, 60, and 70 is now properly seen as the result of misinterpreting cross-section data that really reflect generational differences—not the consequence of aging. The cohort data explore changes associated with the aging of the cohort, and those data show an early end to life cycle effects of aging, a long mid-life interlude, and a resumption of aging effects as citizens enter their seventies and eighties. The immediate implications for our generational persistence model of societal change are both obvious and profound. They are modified by the possibility that the low starting point for the turnout of the post-New Deal cohorts is, in some sense, as unique as other generational attributes that we shall examine in the next chapters. Extrapolation from the turnout plateau thesis, dominated by the New Deal cohorts, may not be appropriate for the younger post-New Deal population. And if not, the generational differences originating in the post-New Deal period may fade quite rapidly.

It seems reasonable to expect life cycle influences to produce an increase in the turnout of the post-New Deal cohorts at some future point in time. Such influences may soften the differences between them and the remaining members of the New Deal generation. But as of 1988, the low point in turnout since 1960, generational differences in voting rates had translated into a continual national decline in turnout because of the demographic machinery of generational replacement.

4
★ ★ ★ | The Three Stages in the
Political Life of the Citizen

The existence of inter-generational differences in voter turnout has redirected our efforts to understand the origins or causes of voting. If the rates of turnout vary by generation, do the social and psychological antecedents to turnout also vary? Do the standard explanations or descriptions of the differences between voters and non-voters apply to any, or to all, generations? Or, as with age, is the conventional interpretation of the correlates also subject to change when the analysis is structured by a generational perspective? Inquiry into the established correlates of turnout, generation-by-generation, opens up the possibility of addressing still further questions. Can we better explain why the generational differences exist? If the correlates of turnout change over time within generations, can we learn more about their meaning through an inspection of change?

As a first step in answering such questions, we will begin with a generation-by-generation inspection of all the correlates of turnout contained in the NES studies from 1952 to 1988. We will retain our scheme of comparing three generations within three levels of education across four subsets of adjoining elections. Given the fact that the NES studies included more than a score of predictors associated with turnout in all ten elections, we are confronted with a substantial challenge to simplify and reduce both the sheer magnitude and the potential complexity of our investigation. We continue our inquiry by considering each of the three generations separately.

Among the three generations of electors in our study, only the pre-

New Dealers can provide evidence helpful in understanding the origins of declining rates of turnout. Our interest in them is clearly not confined to concern with turnout in the particular election of 1992. The pre-New Deal generation's youngest members were 81 years old in 1992, and they constituted only a very small part of the 1992 electorate. Rather, we expect that analysis of this group of voters can lead to a better general understanding of voter turnout, and of declining turnout among the elderly in particular. This phenomenon, also present among the aging cohorts of the New Deal generation, is likely to be of increasing concern in the years immediately ahead.

The New Deal generation provides an opportunity for describing differences between voters and non-voters over an uninterrupted 40-year span. A host of national social and political changes were experienced by this continuing component of the electorate, as well as by the post-New Deal generation. However, these changes did not appear to affect rates of voter turnout within the New Deal generation. This prompts us to ask whether the correlates of turnout among the New Dealers re-mained the same in the 1990s as in the 1950s. Analysis of the New Deal generation opens up other areas of inquiry as well: (1) How was the 1950s level of turnout within that generation sustained in the face of the changing political context described in Chapter 2, to say nothing of the social and economic life-cycle changes experienced by the generation as their mean age rose from 35 (in 1952–1960) to 59 (in 1984–1988)? (2) How does the explanation of their turnout in the 1980s compare with conventional explanations of electoral participation? (3) How does the explanation for the New Deal generation's turnout in the 1950s and the 1980s compare with the explanation for turnout in the two other generations? Our theoretical interest turns on the New Deal generation because it can possibly provide a baseline from which we can learn more about the nature of the generational differences that have led to a compositional, structural reduction in overall voter turnout between 1952 and 1988.

Finally, the exploration of the post-New Deal generation can be help-ful in completing the analysis of turnout in the Republican era of the 1980s. It may also provide some insight into the evolution of individual electors' early participation after coming of voting age. Because we can follow the oldest members of this youngest generation for 24 years, from the time they were first old enough to vote in 1968, we should also be able to learn something from them about the processes of political maturation. However, it should be noted that there will be an inevitable element of indeterminacy about the generalizability of our conclusions concerning the youngest generation. After all, the entire generational inquiry is germane, and was initiated, because the post-New Deal generation seems to be atypical, so very different from preceding generations. Whether those differences become apparent in the general process of political maturation may not be evident in our subsequent analysis.

▪ Pre-Election Participation in Partisan Politics

Let us begin by considering briefly the place of voting in the fuller panoply of political activities. To be more specific about the scope of our problem, we have explored the possibility that declining turnout was only one aspect of a broader disengagement from partisan political activity. On this point, evidence that spans our full 40-year period is not all that we might wish. Some indicators of important forms of campaign participation other than voting (such as joining local citizens' groups, writing letters to public officials, or engaging in political protests) appear in the NES data only intermittently. The few comparisons over time that can be made with such indicators have led to speculation that political activity other than voting increased rather than decreased during that period, corresponding to the increase in citizen resources such as education (Miller, 1980).

Because of the episodic nature of survey questions on the topic, we cannot make a comprehensive test of all such generalizations. However, while continuing to note period differences in generational turnout rates, we can employ a limited battery of NES measures of non-electoral participation for the full period from 1952 to 1988. This battery includes five items: attending political rallies or meetings, working for a party or candidate, wearing a campaign button or displaying a campaign sign, giving money to a party or candidate, or—most basic of all—trying informally to influence someone's vote.[1] To facilitate the inquiry, we combined the five available items to form a summary measure of pre-election participation ranging from none to participation in all five activities.

The results of an election-year-by-election-year inspection of campaign activities among our three political generations, holding educational attainment constant, are quite straightforward. First, as detailed in Table 4.1, within *each* generation and within *each* education level there is an apparent small period effect separating the elections of the Reagan-Bush era (1984–1988) from the previous elections of 1972–1976–1980. Overall, pre-election participation *dropped* ten points in the Reagan-Bush era across the nine comparisons that can be made, including small declines among those with twelve or more years of education in both the New Deal and post-New Deal generations. There was no similar pattern of decline in *voting* turnout within the same cohorts.[2]

Second, in comparisons of the generations, the New Deal generation exhibited substantially *more* pre-election participation than did the pre-New Deal generation. (The two exceptions, high school graduates in 1952–1960 and 1964–1968, involve one somewhat unreliable estimate for the pre-New Deal cohorts in 1964–1968.) The pattern of sustained levels of political participation other than voting, particularly in the ranks of the college-educated, is consistent with the legitimacy accorded to extra-electoral activity, particularly by the young, during the late 1960s and early 1970s (Barnes and Kaase, 1979). Moreover, the pattern differs sharply from the generational differences in election day turnout where the older pre-New Deal generation had recorded greater turnout (see Table 4.1).

There was evidence of only limited change in pre-election participation rates pertaining either to intra-generational change or to inter-generational replacement among the high school graduates and college groups. Because of the tremendous growth in the *numbers* of the college-educated, and the relative constancy of their individual *rates* of pre-election participation, the overall aggregate level of pre-election participation across the country had actually *risen* over the decades as voting turnout was falling. Except for the high school graduates of the New Deal generation, the 40-year records suggest little change within or among the generations.

Decline in voter turnout does not seem to be a manifestation of a broader withdrawal from partisan political activity. In essence, the threshold separating voters above the line from non-voters below the line *rose* between the 1950s and the 1980s: the threshold separating those engaging in pre-election activity from the remainder of the electorate actually dropped, increasing the proportion of activists. This creates at least a minor puzzle. Both the proportion of non-voters and of activists increased, the former *despite* increasing levels of educa-

Table 4.1 Pre-Election Participation in Partisan Electoral Politics: Proportions of Non-Black Citizens of Voting Age Engaging in One or More Voluntary Electoral Activities Other Than Voting

Years of Education	Generation	1952–60	1964–68	1972–80	1984–88	1992
0–11	Pre-New Deal	32 (395/1243)	26 (106/407)	24 (103/426)	16 (12/73)	** (2/5)
	New Deal	31 (363/1162)	33 (192/585)	33 (301/926)	23 (89/380)	24 (49/205)
	Post-New Deal	—	** (2/17)	33 (77/233)	17 (31/179)	36 (42/117)
12	Pre-New Deal	47 (132/284)	51 (50/99)	35 (49/140)	21 (7/34)	** (2/8)
	New Deal	42 (459/1082)	42 (289/686)	44 (460/1044)	40 (194/482)	41 (148/359)
	Post-New Deal	—	57 (17/30)	36 (248/689)	32 (207/643)	48 (295/613)
13+	Pre-New Deal	55 (152/279)	54 (58/108)	48 (51/105)	39 (10/26)	—
	New Deal	57 (367/644)	62 (322/518)	60 (575/965)	56 (292/518)	59 (93/157)
	Post-New Deal	—	47 (24/51)	61 (498/816)	52 (464/896)	57 (243/423)

NOTE: Entry shows the percentage participating followed by the number participating/total number of cases.

** Too few cases for estimation.

— No cases in sample.

tional attainment, the latter perhaps because of this upgrading of their resources.

▪ The Analysis of Changing Correlates of Turnout

In considering a portfolio of 22 variables to account for differences between voters and non-voters, multivariate analyses will serve to summarize the main results. The list of variables includes all of the variables relevant to turnout that are available from the Michigan studies in the period 1952 through 1992. Prior to organizing the variables for a sequence of analytic considerations, we have examined each variable, one at a time, in their bivariate relationships to voter turnout within each of our 36 categories (where each category is defined by three generations and three levels of education in each of four election periods).

Bivariate (cross-tabular) analyses remind us that there are at least two key types of information involved in each correlation: one is the distribution of the independent variable—what proportion of the population is found in categories associated with higher turnout, what proportion in categories with lower turnout? The second piece of information concerns the magnitude of the differences in turnout between categories facilitating turnout and those inhibiting turnout. Let us use a simple correlate, church attendance, to illustrate what may be learned about turnout as each generation passes through our four election periods. The leading hypothesis is that church attendance captures one facet of social connectedness, and we can learn about voter turnout as we examine different conditions under which frequent church attenders vote more often than do non-attenders.

As Table 4.2 illustrates, even a simple idea—relating frequency of church attendance to voting turnout—can produce a complicated maze when placed in the context of a basic analysis design which has 36 possible categories (of generation, epoch, and education) within which to observe the relationship between two variables. Across the four columns in the top portion of Table 4.2 we see evidence within the *pre-New Deal* generation of a small decline in regular church attendance from 1952–1960 to 1984–1988. Among the *New Dealers* there was a steady *drop* in regular church attendance across the four election periods; 8 percentage points or a 27 percent decline (8 out of 30) among the non-graduates, 14 points or a 30 percent drop among high school

Table 4.2 Inter-Period Changes in Church Attendance and Frequency of Voting

Years of Education	Proportion Attending Weekly or More Often				
	1952–60	1964–68	1972–80	1984–88	1992
0–11					
Pre-New Deal	38	44	33	30	**
New Deal	35	30	27	27	35
Post-New Deal	—	**	13	17	12
12					
Pre-New Deal	41	43	38	**	**
New Deal	47	44	31	33	36
Post-New Deal	—	**	22	23	17
13+					
Pre-New Deal	45	49	40	**	—
New Deal	49	47	31	34	38
Post-New Deal	—	35	23	24	24
Years of Education	Turnout of Regular Attenders				
	1952–60	1964–68	1972–80	1984–88	1992
0–11					
Pre-New Deal	84	77	78	70	**
New Deal	72	79	73	84	80
Post-New Deal	—	**	33	44	—
12					
Pre-New Deal	91	88	88	**	**
New Deal	82	88	89	91	91
Post-New Deal	—	**	57	65	58
13+					
Pre-New Deal	95	89	86	**	—
New Deal	92	88	92	96	94
Post-New Deal	—	81	80	91	92

** Too few cases for estimation.
— No cases in sample.

graduates (14/47) and 15 points or a 31 percent drop among those who had attended college. For the *post-New Deal* cohorts the distribution of regular church attendance did not change appreciably between the two sets of elections for which we have reliable data.

Next, looking at the turnout data for our two categories of church

Table 4.2 (continued)

Years of Education	Turnout of Less Than Regular Attenders				
	1952–60	1964–68	1972–80	1984–88	1992
0–11					
Pre-New Deal	73	69	55	52	**
New Deal	60	64	59	58	57
Post-New Deal	—	**	34	30	26
12					
Pre-New Deal	94	84	83	67	**
New Deal	81	78	77	80	80
Post-New Deal	—	**	51	50	66
13+					
Pre-New Deal	89	88	80	84	—
New Deal	86	87	88	90	94
Post-New Deal	—	60	74	77	84

** Too few cases for estimation.

— No cases in sample.

attenders (regular + less than regular = 100%): among those with the least education in the *pre-New Deal* cohorts there was a small decline in turnout between 1952 and 1988 for the regular church attenders (from 84 percent reporting having voted to 70 percent); for the less than regular attenders the decline in voting was a bit sharper, 21 points or a 29 percent drop from the base of 73. The same pattern is repeated for those pre-New Deal cohorts in the high school graduate category, but among those with some college, both the regular attenders and the less regular dropped their *rates* of voting by about the same magnitude. Overall, the data support or are consistent with the inference that the decline in voting turnout within the pre-New Deal generation was both a consequence of a small decline in the "social connectedness" provided by regular church attendance *and* a disproportionately larger decline in voting turnout among the increasing numbers of irregular attenders.[3]

Within the *New Deal* generation, turnout among regular church attenders was up among high school graduates; among those who were less regular church attenders, there was no significant change in turnout between the 1950s and the 1980s. The increase in the voting *rates* of regular church attenders was almost exactly offset by the decline in their *numbers*; there was no overall net change in turnout among New Dealers.

Among the *post-New Deal* cohorts, church attendance was essentially unchanged between the 1970s and 1980s, but turnout of both regular and less than regular attenders was up substantially in the upper two education group levels.

There are, therefore, three different patterns connecting church attendance and voting turnout within our three generations. The *decline* in turnout within the pre-New Deal cohorts came predominantly from a disproportionate decline among those less bound to the church through attendance; the increase in turnout among post-New Deal cohorts apparently came from those more connected to the church through regular church attendance. Turnout rates held steady within the New Deal generation as the effects of a reduction in regular attendance were overcome by increased voting by the smaller and smaller groups of regular attenders.

This is only the starting point for a comprehensive analysis of church attendance. Subsequent inquiry will take account of the possibly confounding effects of other social and economic attributes, and should ultimately consider possible differences among religious traditions and denominations. Prior to such multivariate complications, the illustrative exercise we have reviewed leads to the following observations: If, over time, the proportion of non-attenders within a group (the pre-New Deal generation) increases, the overall turnout of the group may go down. By the same token, if (say, among the young post-New Deal cohorts) more and more people attend church, turnout will go up. A change in the *distribution* of values of the independent or presumed "causal" variable ($+1$ for attending, 0 for non-attendance) will result in a change in the values ($+1$ for voting, 0 for non-voting) of the dependent variable.

Second, if the turnout *rate* for the non-attenders goes down, or if the rate for regular attenders goes up (relative to the rate for non-attenders), the correlation between church attendance and voting turnout will also go up. If the turnout rate for church attenders goes down (or the rate for non-attenders goes up) the correlation will decrease. In these situations, it is *relative differences in the rate of turnout* between church attenders and among non-attenders that affects the correlation.

The simple point is that changes in the distribution of the independent variable *or* changes in the dependent variable *within* categories of the independent variable can each be responsible for overall changes in turnout and in the correlation between church attendance (the independent variable) and voting turnout (the dependent variable). The much more difficult point is to understand *why* each different change occurs. Both the decline in attendance and the turnout among irregular attenders in the pre-New Deal cohorts seem "reasonable," but do they have the same explanation? Within the New Deal, if church attendance is going down, why doesn't turnout go down among the increasing number of former regular attenders? Does the increased turnout among the regular church attenders in the post-New Deal generation (where attendance is not changing) have the same explanation as the increased turnout among regular attending New Dealers?

Although there is only limited research literature on points such as this, it would seem that life cycle effects early in life are reflected primarily in changes in the distribution of social or sociological variables such as education, church attendance, income, residential mobility, or marital status: more and more people over the age of 18 acquire attributes (scores) associated with voting turnout, fewer and fewer do not have those characteristics. And of those possessing attributes that promote voting, more and more actually vote. At the other age extreme, it seems possible that declining turnout among the elderly is more often tied to psychological variables such as withdrawal and loss of interest or loss of social support networks; turnout goes down as fewer people pay attention to political campaigns, and as those who don't pay attention vote even less often than they had.

Doubtless both sociological and psychological factors come into play at both ends of the life cycle. However, we often note patterns of change which seem reasonable, or at least not unreasonable, but for which it is very difficult to specify precisely why the change occurs. For example, why should a decline in turnout be the result of a decline only among those less interested in politics (with no increase in their numbers), with no change in turnout among the comparably unchanging numbers of the more interested? Or, in another case, why does an increase in turnout occur *both* because the number of people with higher incomes increases *and* their turnout rate increases while the turnout rate among the decreasing number of low-income citizens does not change? The general idea that correlations with turnout reflect the relevance or a changing relevance of one explanation or another is useful. However, that idea is seldom translated into the details about distributions and rates of turnout that can provide much more specific and elaborate ideas about the causes of turnout, ideas that, in turn, can prompt further empirical examination and testing.

Multivariate Analysis

Our analytic approach, both here in the study of voting turnout and later in our more extensive treatment of voters' preferences between candidates, is a multivariate attempt to cope with a very large number of alternative explanations displayed in the literature. We will rely on regression coefficients when we move to the multivariate mode of analysis. Nevertheless, prior knowledge of the distributional and relational attributes derived from preliminary bivariate cross-tabulation will prove useful in the multivariate interpretation of regression coefficients.

In order to connect our examination of bivariate cross-tabulations with the results of multivariate analysis, we shall first and most directly address changes over time in those variables for which there is statistically significant evidence of an ultimate "apparent total effect" derived from a general multi-stage, multi-variable, causal structure for variables associated with voting turnout.

The "apparent total effect" coefficient (which we feature in the second of each pair of columns in Tables 4.3–4.5) represents the unstandardized regression coefficient for the given independent variable with the dependent variable *after* we have statistically taken account of, or controlled, all other independent variables that might be joint causes of both, antecedents both to the given independent variable and turnout.[4] By restricting our attention to relationships involving "significant" total apparent effects, we guard against giving attention to possibly spurious or confounded evidence that a presumably causal relationship exists between the two variables in question. (Such a situation prevails when a simple bivariate "zero order" coefficient, in the first of each pair of columns, drops to statistical insignificance when possibly confounding variables are all "controlled" in the second column.)

The multivariate structure of our analysis sequence has four blocs or stages: (1) twelve social-economic characteristics; (2) party identification (as a separate bloc); (3) seven medium-term attributes reflecting interest, efficacy, and citizen duty; and (4) two short-term reflections of attitudinal involvement in elections.[5] An "apparent total effect" for any given variable in the *first* bloc will exist if there is a statistically sig-

Table 4.3 Bivariate Regression Coefficients and Apparent Total Effects on Non-Black Voter Turnout: Pre-New Deal Generation

	1952–60 N = 554		1964–68 N = 312		1972–80 N = 357		1984–88 N = 112	
	Bivariate b	Total Effect	Bivariate b	Total Effect	Bivariate b	Total Effect	Bivariate b	Total Effect
Age	−.07	*	−.10	*	−.14	−.13	*	*
Education	.16	.11	.16	.12	.20	.14	.22	.22
Gender	−.14	−.13	−.13	−.15	−.21	−.21	*	*
Residence/House	*	*	*	*	*	*	−.12	*
Marital Status	.14	.06	*	*	.19	*	*	*
Home Ownership	.10	*	.10	*	.13	*	*	*
Church Attendance	.12	.12	.08	*	.18	.17	.12	*
Union Family	.03	*	.08	*	.05	*	*	*
Urbanism	.07	*	.10	*	*	*	*	*
Income	.19	*	.14	*	.21	*	.13	*
Social Class 2	.14	.08	.15	.12	.14	.10	*	*
Residence/Locale	—	—	.14	.15	*	*	*	*
PID 2	−.06	*	.07	*	*	.08	−.16	*
Gov't. Pays Attention	—	—	.09	*	*	*	*	*
Elections Help	—	—	.21	.12	.13	*	*	*
Interest in Public Affairs	.27	.18	.24	.12	.35	.22	.39	.35
Gov't. Too Complicated	.17	*	.09	*	.10	*	.16	*
No Say	.22	.11	.20	*	.21	*	.18	*
Officials Care	.22	*	.24	.14	.16	*	*	*
Don't Care Don't Vote	.19	.11	—	—	.17	.10	.17	*
Interest in Campaign	.28	.09	.28	.19	.38	.23	.24	*
Care	.19	*	.18	*	.21	*	.20	*

* Coefficients not significant at .10.
— Missing data for years specified.

nificant correlation between it and voter turnout, *with all other variables* in that bloc *held constant*. Party identification, in the second bloc for the analysis of voting turnout, will, in turn, have an apparent total effect on turnout if there is a significant coefficient, with the effects of all variables in the preceding bloc held constant. Similarly, in the third bloc of attitudes, each of the seven variables will be tested for the existence of an apparent total effect with all of the other variables in that bloc—*as*

Table 4.4 Bivariate Regression Coefficients and Apparent Total Effects on Voter Turnout: New Deal Generation

	1952–60 N = 766		1964–68 N = 863		1972–80 N = 1788		1984–88 N = 1255		1992 N = 616	
	Bivariate b	Total Effect	Bivariate b	Total Effect	Bivariate b	Total Effect	Bivariate b	Total Effect	Bivariate b	Total Effect
Age	.16	.11	.15	.10	.04	.09	*a	.07	-.07	*
Education	.26	.20	.20	.18	.27	.24	.28	.23	.31	.24
Gender	-.10	-.10	*	*	-.06	*	*	*	*	*
Residence/House	14	.13	.17	*	.15	.05	.09	*	.14	.11
Marital Status	*	*	.06	*	.13	.05	.08	*	.17	.07
Home Ownership	.10	*	.21	.11	.17	.08	.12	.05	.16	*
Church Attendance	.12	.09	.12	*	.15	.11	.20	.16	.20	.15
Union Family	-.03	*	*	*	.05	.05	*	*	.05	*
Urbanism	.07	*	*	*	.02	*	.10	.07	.11	.07
Income	.20	.10	.22	.13	.23	.11	.18	.06	.23	*
Social Class 2	.18	*	.14	*	.15	*	.16	*	.15	*
Residence/Locale	—b	—	.15	.14	.11	.09	*	.06	.09	*
PID 2	-.11	-.09	-.11	-.10	-.09	-.09	-.05	*	-.07	-.08
Gov't. Pays Attention	—	—	.09	*	.13	*	.14	*	.10	*
Elections Help	—	—	.08	*	.13	*	.12	*	.07	*
Interest in Public Affairs	.31	.19	.23	.15	.28	.16	.23	.13	.24	.14
Gov't. Too Complicated	.19	*	.11	*	.16	*	.12	*	.14	*
No Say	.17	*	.12	*	.21	*	.23	.10	.18	*
Officials Care	.19	.07	.18	.08	.22	.08	.21	.06	.14	*
Don't Care Don't Vote	.16	.10	—	—	.19	.11	.13	.07	.18	.12
Interest in Campaign	.27	.06	.26	.11	.25	.07	.29	.15	.40	.28
Care	.22	.08	.18	.09	.21	.10	.18	.07	.22	*

a. * Coefficients not significant at .10.

b. — Missing data.

Table 4.3 Bivariate Regression Coefficients and Apparent Total Effects on Non-Black Voter Turnout: Post-New Deal Generation

	1952–60	1964–68 N = 94		1972–80 N = 1233		1984–88 N = 1233		1992 N = 1088	
		Bivariate b	Total Effect	Bivariate b	Total Effect	Bivariate b	Total Effect	Bivariate b	Total Effect
Age	—[a]	*[b]	*	.11	.07	.23	.12	.18	.07
Education	—	.31	.23	.34	.33	.39	.28	.39	.35
Gender	—	*	*	*	*	*	*	*	.04
Residence/House	—	—	—	*	*	.12	.09	.08	*
Marital Status	—	*	*	.04	.05	.12	*	.12	*
Home Ownership	—	.14	*	.05	*	.23	.09	.18	.07
Church Attendance	—	.14	*	.11	.07	.18	.11	.07	*
Union Family	—	*	*	*	*	.08	*	.11	.07
Urbanism	—	*	*	*	*	.07	.05	.08	*
Income	—	.17	*	.13	*	.31	.11	.28	.11
Social Class 2	—	.32	.22	.13	*	.23	.08	.16	*
Residence/Locale	—	*	*	.03	.07	*	-.04	.04	*
PID 2	—	*	*	-.16	-.13	-.21	-.14	-.16	-.10
Gov't Pays Attention	—	.14	*	.10	*	.13	*	.07	*
Elections Help	—	*	*	.12	.05	.14	*	.12	*
Interest in Public Affairs	—	.31	.20	.31	.20	.33	.17	-.29	-.18
Gov't Too Complicated	—	*	-.25	.16	*	.18	*	.17	*
No Say	—	.33	.30	.21	.08	.25	.11	.20	.07
Officials Care	—	.31	*	.17	*	.19	*	.17	*
Don't Care Don't Vote	—	—	—	.16	.10	.24	.11	.20	.09
Interest in Campaign	—	.41	.26	.34	.14	.38	.15	.36	.18
Care	—	.27	.27	.21	.06	.27	.08	-.23	*

a. — Missing data.
b. * Coefficients not significant at .10.

well as in the first and second blocs—taken into account and held constant. The statistical threshold we have used for "significance" is not severe; for an effect coefficient to be shown in a table, instead of being replaced with an asterisk, the estimated probability of getting a coefficient that large (or larger) due to chance alone must be no greater than .10. (Bivariate regressions are also included in the tables if they are significant at the .1 level, even though the variable does not survive our multivariate test.)[6]

The Pre-New Deal Generation

Of the 22 variables used in our multivariate analysis of turnout, seven can confidently be said to have an independent, "apparent total effect" on turnout among the *pre-New Deal* cohorts in at least two of the first three election periods in Table 4.3 for which we can produce reliable estimates. In the fourth set of elections, 1984–1988, the pre-New Deal generation is represented in our study by only 112 electors. Despite the small sample size for these elections, it seems significant that only two variables appeared to make independent, total effect contributions to explaining the level of turnout among the oldest cohorts in their last years. One was education, the sole item from the 12 social attributes of the first bloc; the second variable was "general level of interest in public affairs," the sole "political" item from the third bloc.

Both of these variables represent long-term influences. Education, completed a half-century earlier, apparently subsumes all other social differentials as an influence promoting voter turnout (or representing other factors that promote turnout) within this group of elders. Earlier statistically significant total effects for gender, church attendance, and social class disappear as the octogenarians move into their last elections. Education continues to carry a significant total effect and is interestingly more potent in the 1984–1988 period than in any prior election set. However, the influence of education pales in the presence of an attitude closely connected to voting, namely, the virtually lifelong interest in public affairs held by the voters in the pre-New Deal cohorts. Moreover, during the 1950s and 1960s in particular, pre-New Deal electors within each education level reported higher levels of voting turnout associated with greater interest in public affairs than did members of the New Deal generation (Jennings and Markus, 1988).

In the 1984–1988 elections, our measure of one's sense of political efficacy, the one item representing sense of civic duty, and the two short-term measures of interest in the campaign and the election outcome each showed quite visible bivariate relationships with voter turnout. However, none of these zero-order coefficients persisted in the face of statistical controls placed on the full set of items. General interest in public affairs is the only *political* variable that makes an independent contribution to the electors' decisions whether to vote in 1984 and 1988.

On the other hand, in the first three time periods, 1952–1980, the total effect explanations involve an extended list of variables as independent predictors of voter turnout. Education and interest in public affairs lead the list; they are joined, from among the social variables, by gender, church attendance, and social class. On the political side, sense of civic duty and short-term interest in following the campaign both show significant apparent total effects for those time periods.

The usefulness of our multi-stage analytic model is apparent as we examine in bivariate tabular detail the decline in turnout over time between 1952 and 1980 among members of the pre-New Deal generation. An overall deterioration in turnout rates across the 30 years is unmistakable. Between the 1950s and the 1980s, there was a 15-point drop in the turnout percentage within the generation. The decline was an inverse function of education (which, of course, did not itself change in a generation in which the youngest member was 45 in 1952). There was a drop of more than 25 percent (from 77 percent voting in the 1950s to 56 percent turning out in 1984–1988) among those who did not graduate from high school, a 17 percent drop for high school graduates (from 93 percent to 77 percent), and only an 11-point drop for those with some college education (from 91 to 81). The overall decline was thus accentuated by limitations in prior education, and was not a consequence of changes in the citizens' education (we detected no educational differences in mortality rates).

Throughout the four decades and across all generations, education was an unmistakable correlate of turnout, particularly in the elections of the past 20 years—from 1972 through 1992. However, the *change* in turnout among the pre-New Deal generation was also a function of differences in education, as the decline was caused primarily by a sharp decline in the voting rate of the *least well educated*.

More generally, within the pre-New Deal generation, declining turnout was consistently associated with disproportionate decreases (over time) in voting among citizens least inclined to vote in the first place. Of the six variables most clearly associated with declining turnout (education, gender, church attendance, civic duty, interest in public affairs, and interest in campaigns), distributional changes minimizing support for voting exacerbated the ubiquitous drop in turnout among those less disposed to vote. (In the instance of gender, with the passage of the years there were relative increases in the proportion of women who, in turn, were increasingly inclined not to vote.) Among the older citizens, representation of the nominally "least often represented at the polls" was, across time, often further depressed for reasons we do not yet understand.

▪ Turnout in the New Deal Generation

If the declining years of the pre-New Deal generation (1984–1988) saw a withering away of independent roles for traditional antecedents of the decision to vote, the mid-years of the New Deal generation produced a sustained display of familiar causal relationships. All ten of the attitudinal variables associated with voter turnout had a significant role at the zero-order bivariate level in all four sets of elections. Among twelve social and economic characteristics, only gender and union family membership were insignificant in more than one of the election periods, and all of the relationships were remarkably consistent across all four election periods. There are occasional reminders that although the oldest of the New Deal cohorts were in their late thirties or early forties in 1952, the youngest did not enter the electorate until 1964, in our second set of elections. Thus, residential mobility differentiated between voters and non-voters in the early elections, but mobility had largely disappeared as an independent factor by the 1980s. Conversely, home ownership differentiated New Deal voters from non-voters only *after* the 1960s saw home ownership leveling off with a norm established for the generation.

The relative constancy of the turnout rates for the New Deal generation provides an exceptional commentary on the stability of voting behavior within established elements of the electorate. It is relatively easy to account for this stability in terms of both the distributional and relational features of our predictor variables related to New Deal turnout. This is not to say that the New Deal generation was impervious to all of the political winds of change, nor was it devoid of experiences with social and economic change. However, when one or another potential source of change did threaten to change turnout, compensating changes forestalled any net shift up or down.

In general, the variable-by-variable analyses show that among the New Deal generation cohorts both the distributions of the dominant predictors of turnout and the turnout differences between categories of explanatory variables were themselves virtually constant across all four time periods. For example, the proportions expressing interest in the campaign, within the education controls, did not vary by more than one or two percentage points between the 1950s and the 1980s. Among the top two education groups, one relationship with turnout decreased slightly as the *disinterested* among the college-educated increased their voting rate from 74 percent to 85 percent. On the other hand, although interest did not decline among those who had not graduated from high school, the turnout rate of the less interested among them did *drop* markedly, from 52 percent in the 1950s to 41 percent in 1984–1988. Again, however, this did not produce a significant overall change across the New Deal generation.

Education, the strongest predictor, did not change perceptibly in this generation whose mean age was 35 in 1952–1960. From the beginning of the period to the end, both distributional and relational properties sustained a constant rate of turnout. Caring about the election outcome also emerged as a strong correlate of voter turnout in the New Deal generation. The proportions who cared were almost without change in election after election, just as the differences in voting rates between those who cared more and those who cared less were also large but unchanging through time.

Finally, at least among the attitudinal variables, the presence or absence of party identification did make a significant difference to voting rates in the New Deal generation, at least during the years preceding 1984–1988, whereas party identification had been largely absent from the considerations of the older pre-New Deal group. However, the propensity to profess or reject identity as a Republican or Democrat did not change overall within the New Deal generation (Miller, 1991, 1992). There was a dip in the 1970s, particularly among high school graduates and those with some college education, but the latter led the rebound in 1984 and 1988. Throughout the 30 years, the voter turnout difference between the identified and the non-identified varied slightly from period to period, but the net result was to sustain turnout at a relatively constant rate.

If our intent were to attain a fine-grained description of the many nuances in the structures and processes that lead to voter turnout, we might be less than satisfied with some of the generalizations we have just offered. It might be, for example, that interest in election campaigns or caring who wins the election might actually have been responsible for the minuscule upturn in voting we noted in the last chapter. Our present purpose is served by the generalization that apparent stability in the rates of reported voting in the New Deal generation is thoroughly supported by the distributional and relational attributes of all of the predictors that multiple regression analyses document as having important independent relationships with voter turnout.

Nevertheless, our interest in New Deal generation turnout is still piqued by the knowledge that other variables in their portfolio, also related to voting rates, have changed markedly over time. For example, home ownership had risen over the 30-year history that we can observe, and church attendance was down; but voting among non-owners was also down and voting among regular attenders was up. The popular sense of the responsiveness of government was lower, and we know that the entire generation had aged. However, an extension of our variable-by-variable inquiry supports the conclusion that theoretically meaningful but consistently offsetting changes prevented either an increase or a decrease in overall rates of turnout.[7]

Finally, income was not a significant factor in the turnout of the pre-New Deal generation, but it was a consistent contributor to voter and non-voter differences in the New Deal cohorts. Nevertheless, its contribution was, again, to help stabilize turnout levels. Except for the fragment of the generation who had not completed high school (where relative income dropped over the years and where the correlations with turnout disappeared in the 1980s), income levels and the contribution to voter and non-voter differences did not change over time within the New Deal generation.

Returning to a general consideration of the effects of variables conventionally thought to determine voter turnout, there is little evidence of the unexpected where the New Deal generation is concerned. Neither of the two items assessing "institutional responsiveness" made an independent contribution to distinguishing voters from non-voters in any of the four sets of elections. Except for 1984–1988, the same was true of the two items assessing one's personal sense of political efficacy. In the 1980s, however, the assertion that "people like me don't have any say about what the government does" joined the statement "I don't think public officials care what people like me think" (measuring "external efficacy") with an independent effect on turnout. The first item had no independent effect in the other three sets of elections, as was true for the efficacy item in which government is considered "too complicated."

All the remaining political attitudes (including involvement in the election outcome) made their expected independent contribution to voter turnout. Finally, in accord with the earlier observations of Wolfinger and Rosenstone (1980), Republicans outvoted Democrats by a small margin in all four of our election periods. Along with education, these attitudes were among the stable predictors of turnout in each of the election periods. They are joined—as was not the case for the pre-New Deal generation—by almost the full set of social and economic attributes generally associated with voter turnout. Some factors were relevant only in one or two sets of elections (union membership in 1972–1980, social class and urbanism in 1984–1988). In general, the accepted wisdom on most questions about the relevance of social and economic experience to voter turnout applies to the behavior of the New Deal generation across the full span of ten presidential elections.

The Disappearance of Gender Differences in Turnout

One final comment is needed to highlight the social transformation of the active electorate. In the last chapter we noted that the mobilization of African-American citizens into relatively full participation as voters requires separate treatment from our concern with generational transformation. We also noted earlier in this chapter the persistent gender gap that was present within the pre-New Deal generation, at least up to 1984 and 1988. However, the pattern of higher rates of male voting was just as common within the New Deal generation during the elections of the Eisenhower period (1952–1960) as it was for the pre-New Deal generation. In both generations, the gender difference was most pronounced among citizens who had not attended college. However, by the time of the 1964 and 1968 elections, this earlier version of a gender gap had disappeared among high school graduates in the New Deal cohorts, and by 1984–1988 it no longer appeared at any education level within the New Deal generation. The mobilization of women thus joined the mobilization of Black voters to mark major socio-political changes in the composition of the active voting electorate during the period of our inquiry.

▪ The Post-New Deal Generation

There was a forewarning in the previous chapter that the cohorts of the post-New Deal generation might prove distinctive in terms other than their rate of voting turnout. This turned out to be at least partially true concerning the impact of life cycle effects on their rate of voting. On the one hand, their experience with changes in social and economic circumstances in early adulthood seems normal enough. Between the elections of the 1970s and those of the 1980s, residential mobility declined: the proportion reporting living in the same house for five or more years went up 50 percent for high school graduates (from 28 percent to 43 percent), almost a third among non-graduates (26 percent to 34 percent), and 20 percent for the college group (from 64 percent to 76 percent). In a similar vein, home ownership increased, incomes were up, and larger and larger proportions identified with a party (from 48 percent to 55 percent among high school graduates and from 54 percent to 63 percent among the college group).

Moreover, for virtually all of the social correlates of turnout, regardless of whether there was a change in the distribution or the mean of the predictor variable, there was an increase in the correlations describing differences in vote turnout. In a mirror image of the pre-New Deal generation, the turnout rate of those with attributes positively associated with voting (middle class instead of working class, home owners rather than non-owners, those who cared compared to those who did not care) *increased* as the proportions in the social category also increased. (Among the elderly, the turnout rates of those with attributes negatively associated with voting, for example, women, those with low income, or those who were disinterested, decreased as the proportions in the category increased.) The social effects of life cycle changes among these young adults were accompanied by predictable political effects. The trends in both social and political effects brought the post-New Deal cohorts closer to the norms already in place for the established New Deal generation. Between the 1970s and the 1980s the two generations converged, both in the incidence of attributes associated with higher turnout and in the turnout rates of persons with such attributes. All of this seems understandable not only as the consequences of but actually as the very definition of life cycle effects.

Alienation in the 1980s

At the same time, however, and against this early life cycle trend of increasing engagement, the voting rates of those in the post-New Deal generation with relatively "negative" social or economic attributes (low income, short-term residents, non-identifiers) often declined, accounting for at least a part of the limitations on life cycle effects noted earlier. This phenomenon may well be the generational consequence of coming of political age in a period of increasing social and political polarization. The decline in turnout among the less advantaged was often not large, but it was always juxtaposed with an increase among the more advantaged. For the two sets of party *non*-identifiers with less than college education the drop between the 1970s and the 1980s was only two points, while turnout among the party identifiers in the same cohorts was up as much as 20 points. Among young citizens who were not high school graduates, income made little difference and turnout was down 6–7 points across the board. However, both for high school graduates and those with some college (see Table 4.6), if their family incomes were in the top 20 percent, turnout was up seven and five points, respectively;

Table 4.6 Change in Turnout Among Post-New Deal Cohorts: Income

Years of Education	1972–80		1984–88		Change in Turnout	
	High Income	Low Income	High Income	Low Income	High Income	Low Income
0–11	47 (19/41)	30 (27/90)	41 (7/17)	23 (20/88)	**	−7
12	58 (98/170)	50 (69/136)	65 (99/152)	39 (66/170)	+7	−11
13+	83 (249/300)	70 (127/181)	89 (380/426)	61 (76/125)	+6	−9

NOTE: The income variable is constructed from the NES Cumulative file income variable. The low income category is composed of the first two categories in the NES variable and the high income category is composed of the last two categories.

Entry shows the percentage voting followed by the number reporting voting/total number of cases.

** Too few cases for estimation.

Table 4.7 Change in Turnout Among Post-New Deal Cohorts: Home Ownership

Years of Education	1972–80		1984–88		Change in Turnout	
	Homeowner	Non-Owner	Homeowner	Non-Owner	Homeowner	Non-Owner
0–11	36 (45/124)	29 (32/111)	45 (37/83)	21 (21/98)	+9	−8
12	58 (239/413)	50 (139/275)	62 (237/385)	41 (106/259)	+4	−9
13+	82 (332/407)	76 (317/414)	90 (512/573)	72 (238/330)	+8	−4

NOTE: Entry shows the percentage voting followed by the number reporting voting/total number of cases.

but for those in the bottom 20 percent, turnout was *down* by eleven and nine percentage points. Among non-home owners, there was a drop in turnout from the 1970s to the 1980s of eight, nine, and four points, respectively, across the education groups (see Table 4.7); at the same time, turnout was actually going up by nine, four, and eight points among the increasing numbers of homeowners.

This particular pattern of declining turnout among the materially or socially less advantaged was not present either in the New Deal or the pre-New Deal generations. Despite the fact that we cannot look for analogous patterns in the comparably early years of the other generations, we are inclined to interpret this accentuation of turnout differences within the ranks of the post-New Deal cohorts as further evidence of generational differences between them and the older generations.

In the New Deal generation, the patterns of the *correlates* of turnout across time reflected great stability and persistence. Within the *pre*-New Deal cohorts, the rather widespread pattern of change was one of a limited decline in turnout among persons generally predisposed to vote, with a large decline—accounting for most of the net decline—among those normally less likely to vote. The disproportionate drop in turnout among those less likely to vote produced an increase in the magnitude of the vote turnout correlations in the last voting years of the pre-New Deal cohorts. Among the *post*-New Deal cohorts there was also an increase in correlations over time, but it was largely the result of the growing numbers of electors predisposed to vote who were voting at ever higher rates. However, the increase of the correlations with turnout was accentuated by the drop in turnout among those less predisposed to vote. That decline, in turn, slowed the overall rate of increase in turnout in the early years of the post-New Deal generation.

We do not mean to overdramatize the theme of increased disaffection or alienation among the disadvantaged post-New Deal cohorts. The pattern of an actual decrease in voting from the 1970s to the 1980s is not repeated at the bivariate level for any of the dozen *attitudinal* correlates of voter turnout that we have examined. It is present, and only mildly so, where the social or economic correlates of turnout are concerned.

Nevertheless, the more important explanation for the failure of early life cycle experiences to increase post-New Deal turnout apparently lies in the depressed turnout rates of the Reagan/Bush cohorts as they entered the eligible electorate in 1980, 1984, and 1988. Their numbers are large—they make up one in five of all eligible voters in 1988 (see Table 3.1 in the previous chapter)—and they constitute half of the entire post-New Deal generation in 1992. Their addition to the generation that began a full decade earlier, and their maintenance of that generation's record for low turnout, extends the span of years that produced a continued depressing effect on turnout.

▪ Summary: Lessons Learned

The experiences of early adulthood may, in time, raise the post-New Deal generation's rate of voting. For the moment, though, it is important to note that the social dynamics that produce life cycle effects on turnout always seem to be tied to the level of engagement that marks a cohort's entry into the electorate. Beyond this, it must also be noted that the inquiry into life cycle effects, for both the New Deal and post-New Deal generations, has exposed some of the pitfalls inherent in assuming a one-to-one correspondence between changes in different aspects of the life cycle and changes in voting turnout. Distributions of social circumstances may change, but the effects may be offset by changes in the relationship of those circumstances to turnout—or they may be accentuated (as in the case of gender differences with the pre-New Deal cohorts). Conventional wisdom has often compounded the error of mistaking cross-section estimates of turnout differences associated with age for turnout differences caused by aging. The mistake is to assume that changes in social circumstances that extend into middle age must produce continuous changes in net turnout. The two dimensions of causal relationship are at least somewhat independent; and there is no need to presume that life cycle changes in social circumstances will inevitably produce net life cycle effects in politics.

We can now appreciate that the continued low turnout rates among the post-New Deal generation were at least partially the consequence of the increase in the turnout gap between the more advantaged and the less advantaged citizens, despite the continued progression of life cycle changes that otherwise might have been expected to produce an increase in turnout for the entire generation as it aged. At least a partial explanation for the persistently low turnout levels may be found in the reasons for polarization of the haves and have-nots, as well as in the pervasiveness of the influence of the "times of troubles" that introduced the post-New Deal generation to the electorate.

A review of the evidence of the full cohort-by-election-year displays modifies previous analytic constructions that saw life cycle influences extending over most of the course of an elector's lifetime. In our view, the data as we have organized them do not so much argue against the thesis that adults are characterized by lifelong openness to change; rather, the data argue that such change will be an overlay on behavioral norms acquired during early times of susceptibility to change in response to temporally bounded period effects.

And after all is said and done, we are more than ever aware of the limited base provided by four decades of data. We know a bit about the entry of one generation into the electorate, the exit of a second, and the mid-life of a third. We know enough to think that we are dealing with three distinctive generations; we do not know enough to be certain which of them support the most enduring generalizations and which are the result of unique events and processes that are not likely to be seen again soon. We are, nevertheless, in a position to be better informed about some of the reasons for the sharp differences in turnout rates among the three generations.

5

★ ★ ★ | Explanations of Generational Differences in Turnout

Beyond the turnout gap between the economic haves and have-nots among the young, two phenomena shed further light on the depressed voting rates of the post-New Deal generation. First, we will examine generational differences in the role that party identification plays in voter turnout. Second, following the lead of Teixeira (1987) and Knack (1992), we will explore "social connectedness" as a precursor to turnout. In the latter case we will combine into a single index of social connectedness a selection of the predictors of turnout we reviewed in the last chapter. In both cases we will compare the post-New Deal generation with the base line established by the New Deal cohorts. We will observe conditions that accentuate generational differences and those that limit or inhibit those differences. Throughout we will note that the changing distributions of antecedent variables have compounded the effects of changing relationships with voter turnout.

Generational Changes and Party Identification

If the national upgrading of education over recent decades forestalled sharper declines and blurred the gross evidence of generational differences in turnout, other societal changes contributed to the decline in voting turnout of the post-New Deal generation and accentuated the difference from the generations of the New Deal. One such change occurred in the incidence of party identification. Different versions of party identification have been specified in many models developed to

Table 5.1 Incidence of Independents[a] Among Non-Blacks, by Year, Within Generations Within Education

Years of Education	Political Generation	1952	1956	1960	1964	1968	1972	1976	1980	1984	1988	Period Averages 1952–60	Period Averages 1980–88	Proportion of Independents
0–11	Pre-New Deal	23	25	19	(15)	(16)	22	(25)	*	*	*a	22	(26)b	
	New Deal	26	27	30	26	30	32	29	27	30	28	28	28	
	Post-New Deal	—c	—	—	—	*	59	50	(59)	(58)	(55)	—	57	
	Intra-Generational Change													0
	Pre-New Deal/ Post-New Deal Replacement													+35
12	Pre-New Deal	(24)	*	*	*	*	*	*	*	*	*	19	*	
	New Deal	25	32	27	26	31	36	37	35	32	36	28	34	
	Post-New Deal	—	—	—	—	*	56	52	51	48	46	—	48	
	Intra-Generational Change													+6
	Pre-New Deal/ Post-New Deal Replacement													+29
13+	Pre-New Deal	*	*	*	*	*	*	*	*	*	*	19	*	
	New Deal	33	29	22	32	40	38	39	36	29	27	28	31	
	Post-New Deal	—	—	—	—	(60)	49	49	40	37	39	—	39	
	Intra-Generational Change													+3
	Pre-New Deal/ Post-New Deal Replacement													+20

NOTE: Proportions of "Independents" include all those who do not identify with either the Republican or the Democratic party in response to the single question, "Generally speaking, do you usually think of yourself as a Republican, a Democrat, an Independent, or what?"

a. *, N < 25.

b. (N), 50 > N > 25.

c. — No cases in sample.

explain the decline in turnout in general, as well as the decline in a single election (Abramson and Aldrich, 1982; Kleppner, 1982; Shaffer, 1981). Party identification is also well known as a phenomenon that has changed over recent years in a manner to encourage decreased turnout.

In keeping with our focus on long-term differences in generational attributes, we again consider the long-term component of party identification—the distinction between having a sense of self-identification ("Generally speaking, I usually think of myself as a Democrat/Republican") and not having such an identification ("I usually think of myself as an Independent/as having no preference/as something else").[1] The introduction of party identification to our study of generational differences in turnout has a number of consequences. First, as Abramson forcefully demonstrated, the generational exchange producing a change in the composition of the electorate (see Table 5.1) is largely responsible for the dramatic increase in the national proportion of non-identified citizens between the 1950s and the 1980s. Change in the generational composition of the electorate produced changes in the period averages of proportions of non-identifiers that paralleled changes in the proportions of non-voters. The pre-New Deal cohorts have somewhat fewer non-identifiers than do the New Deal cohorts (22 to 28 among the least well educated, 19 to 28 among the remainder); the post-New Deal cohorts that replaced the pre-New Deal generation have a much higher number of non-identifiers than do the New Deal electors (57 to 28, 48 to 34, and 39 to 31 among the three educational comparisons).

The story of the impact of these generational exchanges on voting turnout is slightly more complex. Table 5.2 simplifies the period and generation comparisons by separating party identifiers from non-identifiers. Among party identifiers, turnout rates within the *continuing* New Deal cohorts show the familiar evidence of stability over time (for example, 68 percent in the 1960s, 67 percent in the 1980s). With regard to the two generations participating in the compositional change of the electorate, however, there was visibly higher turnout during the 1950s by the party identifiers among the high school graduates within the older cohorts, and there was markedly *lower turnout* in the 1980s among the party identifiers in the youngest, post-New Deal replacement generation. Generational transformation between the 1950s and the 1980s was clearly responsible for reduced turnout even *among the party identified.*

At the same time, the generational differences among the party iden-

Table 5.2 Voting, Among Non-Black Party Identifiers and Non-Identifiers, by Time Period and Political Generation Within Education

Years of Education	Political Generation	Identified with Party			Not Identified		
		Period Averages			Period Averages		
		1952–60	1980–88	Differences in Voting	1952–60	1980–88	Differences in Voting
0–11	Pre-New Deal	78	62		75	*ᵃ	
	New Deal	68	67	Intra-Generational Change −1	53	51	Intra-Generational Change −2
	Post-New Deal	—ᵃ	*ᶜ	Pre-New Deal/Post-New Deal Replacement *	—	(23)ᶜ	Pre-New Deal/Post-New Deal Replacement (−52)
12	Pre-New Deal	94	(79)ᵇ		87	*	
	New Deal	87	86	Intra-Generational Change −1	73	84	Intra-Generational Change +11
	Post-New Deal	—	64	Pre-New Deal/Post-New Deal Replacement −30	—	43	Pre-New Deal/Post-New Deal Replacement −44
13+	Pre-New Deal	92	(89)		(85)	*	
	New Deal	89	92	Intra-Generational Change +3	93	89	Intra-Generational Change −4
	Post-New Deal	—	85	Pre-New Deal/Post-New Deal Replacement −7	—	75	Pre-New Deal/Post-New Deal Replacement −10

NOTE: Entries are average proportions reporting turning out to vote.

a. — Missing data.

b. (N), 50 > N > 25.

c. *, N < 25.

tified were somewhat less than those within education sub-groups for the full electorate. For example, within the middle education group (12 years of education), the generational difference in turnout between all of the pre-New Deal and all of the post-New Deal citizens was 35 percentage points; among *party identifiers* in Table 5.2, the comparable difference was only 30 points. Party identification apparently inhibited the decline in turnout. It then follows that the decline in turnout must have been more pronounced in the ranks of the non-identified. Indeed, among non-identified "independents," generational turnover differences in turnout between our two generations were truly impressive. The 30-point difference between generations just noted among the party identified became a 44-point difference among the non-identified.

Such differences take on massive dimensions when they are based on groups (non-identifiers) that have more than doubled in size in the replacement generations over the 30-year period as shown in Table 5.1: from 19 percent of the high school graduates in 1952–1960 to 48 percent in 1980–1988. These dual effects—the increase in the relative number of the non-identifiers, and the doubling and tripling of their rates of non-voting—are an important part of the story of the decline in turnout.[2]

At this point, it is useful to remember that the many trends and counter-trends among the various themes of our analysis seem complex and confusing only if one is trying to figure out separate, incremental contributions of each theme to the overall national decline in turnout. Our goal is simply to identify the origins of generational differences in non-voting. We now have evidence from Tables 5.1 and 5.2 that more education, along with party identification, limits the generational differences in voting rates. In order to assess the consequences of generational replacement in the electorate on overall turnout, we would have to take systematic account of the many ways in which the young post-New Deal generation has had an impact on national turnout figures: (1) they have added disproportionately to the fraction of citizens with relatively high educational attainments; (2) they have added disproportionately to the fraction of the electorate with no party identification; (3) the non-identified among them contain an increasingly high proportion of non-voters (when non-identified and identified are compared); and, finally, (4) the sheer size of the youngest generations compounds the impact of all sources of change.

However, without attempting to apportion these contributions to net change in turnout, it is clear that the generational differences between the swiftly departing pre-New Deal cohorts and the rapidly growing post-New Deal cohorts are the source of reduced turnout among *both* party identifiers and the better educated, as well as among the non-identified and less well educated. The increase in the numbers of non-identified among the new generations has simply highlighted the location of the differences between generations, just as the increase in the numbers of citizens who have gone to college has restricted generational differences in turnout.

The fact that citizens who identify themselves with a particular political party are more likely to participate than those without such ties makes intuitive sense. However, why this is even more true among the new generations than it is among the old is not at all obvious, even with recourse to notions of political socialization inherent in our emphasis on political generations. More generally, the uniqueness of the new generations when compared with their elders—both with regard to the number who are party identified and with regard to turnout, *whether identified or not*—calls for the exploration of other ways in which political generations differ from each other.

Social Connectedness and the Decline in Turnout

A second promising line of inquiry concerns the topic of social structure. A growing body of literature and thought has built on earlier analyses of social structure and political involvement and has explored hypotheses suggesting that voting turnout rests, in part, on socially induced incentives (Morton, 1991; Peterson, 1992; Uhlaner, 1989).[3] Teixeira explored this possibility in his treatment of declining turnout (Teixeira, 1987); Pomper and Sernekos had taken up the same theme in their 1984 analysis (Pomper and Sernekos, 1989). One of the most recent discussions is presented by Knack (1992). Each of these treatments has its own theoretical twist. Knack emphasizes "social cooperation," Teixeira uses "social connectedness" as the organizing concept, Pomper and Sernekos talk about "community integration," and Rosenstone and Hansen present evidence of "social involvement." Each discussion also employs slightly idiosyncratic operational measures of the phenomena in question. In addition, some analyses are more explicit than others in the presumption of probable generational differences in the nature and consequences of social structure and context (Knack, 1991).

Our analysis of the impact of social context on generational differences in turnout is hampered both by the limited time span of our inquiry and by the paucity of comparable indicators covering even that limited period. The NES data collections in the 1980s contain only five clearly relevant indicators of social connectedness or community integration: home ownership, number of years in the home, number of years in the community, marital status, and church attendance.[4] Combining them in a simple additive index and then dividing the electorate into those scoring high and those scoring low produces the picture of social committedness presented in Table 5.3.

The political consequences of social connectedness appear to parallel those related to party identification. Citizens who are better tied into social structures of family and community consistently turn out to vote with greater frequency. There is variation by year and by generation, but the voting rates of the more integrated are always higher than those who are rated low on social connectedness, and sometimes by margins of as much as 15 to 20 points.

As with party identification, some of the post-New Deal generation's

Table 5.3 The Social Connectedness of Generations, 1964–1992

Political Generations	1964	1968	1972	1976	1980	1984	1988	1992
Pre-New Deal								
1. Pre-1920	48	(40)[a]	(36)	(71)	*[b]	*	*	*
2. Republican Normalcy, 1920–1928	50	27	53	69	58	79	76	*
New Deal								
3. Roosevelt Era, 1932–1944	52	65	67	75	74	76	77	75
4. New Deal Consolidated, 1948–1964	29	47	56	66	66	67	74	76
Post-New Deal								
5. Years of Turmoil, 1968–1976		(19)	25	33	38	44	49	57
6. Reagan Era, 1980–1988					22	31	27	33

NOTE: Entry is proportion scored high on social connectedness; see Table 3.1 for approximate number of cases.

a. 50 > N > 25.

b. * N < 25.

lack of social connectedness may be the consequence of their just being young—they are still early in the life cycle. Here, more than any other place in our analysis, we are handicapped by the absence of full life cycle information from earlier generations with which to guide contemporary assessments. Consequently, we cannot specify how much of the apparent generational distinctiveness concerning social connectedness stems from period effects that will become true generational effects for the older three-quarters of the generation, and how much is from life cycle effects among the younger cohorts that will disappear with time. Certainly social maturation of the youngest will soften some of the differences apparent in the 1980s.

However, as with lack of party identification, the effects on turnout of the increased *numbers* of the less well integrated or less connected were compounded by their extraordinary failure to vote on election day. Table 5.4 shows that, as with party identification (see Table 5.2), the impact of generational replacement on voter turnout, particularly for those within the high school group, was somewhat greater for those with fewer social connections than for those presumptively better integrated into the community. The difference was exemplified in the post-New Deal generation, where overall only 44 percent of the less well integrated turned out to vote, in contrast to the 66 percent turnout rate among those who scored high on social connectedness. (In the continuing New Deal generations, the differences in turnout associated with high and low connectedness, within each of three levels of education, were 15, 12, and 13 percentage points in the 1952–1960 period and 23, 9, and 19 points in the 1980–1988 period—against differences of 17, 22, and 15 points in 1980–1988 among the post-New Deal generations and 11, (−2), and 7 in 1950–1960 with the pre-New Deal group.)

The parallelism in the roles of partisan independence and lack of social connectedness in limiting voter turnout among the post-New Deal generation is the more striking given the almost complete statistical independence of the incidence of the two sets of phenomena. Neither within the education/generation subsets during the 1960s nor within the education subsets of the three generations during the 1980s did the bivariate distribution of the two factors exhibit correlations above .08. Thus, both at the heart of partisan political involvement (party identification) and at the core of social integration, generational differences resulted in diminished political involvement *and* reduced voting turnout.

Table 5.4 Voter Turnout and Social Connectedness, by Time Period and Political Generation Within Education

Years of Education	Political Generation	High on Social Connectedness			Low on Social Connectedness		
		Period Averages			Period Averages		
		1952–60	1980–88	Differences in Voting	1952–60	1980–88	Differences in Voting
0–11	Pre-New Deal	88	61		77	47	
	New Deal	77	69	Intra-Generational Change −8	62	46	Intra-Generational Change −16
	Post-New Deal	—a	42	Pre-New Deal/Post-New Deal Replacement −46	—	25	Pre-New Deal/Post-New Deal Replacement −52
12	Pre-New Deal	(91)b	(79)		93	*c	
	New Deal	94	88	Intra-Generational Change −6	82	79	Intra-Generational Change −3
	Post-New Deal	—	66	Pre-New Deal/Post-New Deal Replacement −25	—	44	Pre-New Deal/Post-New Deal Replacement −49
13+	Pre-New Deal	97	(86)		90	*	
	New Deal	96	95	Intra-Generational Change −1	83	76	Intra-Generational Change −7
	Post-New Deal	—	91	Pre-New Deal/Post-New Deal Replacement −6	—	76	Pre-New Deal/Post-New Deal Replacement −14

a. — Missing data.
b. (N) 50 > N > 25.
c. *N < 25.

The interaction among party identification, social connectedness, and voting turnout—along with a suggestion of the magnitude of the combined effects of the absence of identification and the lack of connectedness—is illustrated in the changes over time in the joint distributions among identification and connectedness. First of all, there were intergenerational differences in the joint distributions of identification and connectedness among the pre-New Deal and post-New Deal generations. The principal result of exchanging post-New Deal cohorts for members of the pre-New Deal generation was to replace electors who were heavily involved, both socially and politically, with electors who were often neither identified with a party nor connected to their social environment. This replacement, depicted in Table 5.5, should by itself have reduced turnout, even if turnout rates "within cells" did not change at all.

In fact, the effects leading to a net reduction in support for voter turnout were compounded by changes in voting rates, as illustrated in Table 5.6. Disaggregating both by identification and connectedness reveals that the reduction in turnout was limited to 3 percentage points among electors who were socially connected party identifiers. However, among those who were independents (including "leaners") or who had limited social ties, there were reductions in turnout of 11, 12, and 16 percentage points.

The theme of generational contrasts is even more vivid as we note the

Table 5.5 Compositional Change in Replacement of the Pre-New Deal with the Post-New Deal Generations: Joint Distribution of Party Identification and Social Connectedness

Social Connectedness	Pre-New Deal 1964–1968 Party Identification			Post-New Deal 1980–1988 Party Identification			Difference between the Replacement Generations	
	ID	Non-ID		ID	Non-ID		ID	Non-ID
High	69	13	82	41	24	65	−28	+11
Low	15	3	18	19	16	35	+4	+13
	84	16	100	60	40	100		
			N = 579			N = 1904		

NOTE: Entries for each generation add to 100%.

Table 5.6 Generational Differences in the Turnout Rates

Social Connectedness	Pre-New Deal 1964–1968 Party Identification		Post-New Deal 1980–1988 Party Identification		Difference between the Replacement Generations Party Identification	
	ID	Non-ID	ID	Non-ID	ID	Non-ID
High	81	80	78	64	−3	−16
Low	75	(59)	64	47	−11	−12

NOTE: Entry is the average proportion turning out to vote.
( ) N < 50.

Table 5.7 Joint Distributions of Party Identification and Social Connectedness for New Deal Generation, 1964–1968 and 1980–1988

Social Connectedness	New Deal 1964–1968 Party Identification			New Deal 1980–1988 Party Identification			Difference between Time Periods	
	ID	Non-ID		ID	Non-ID		ID	Non-Id
High	59	24	64	60	27	70	+1	+3
Low	12	5	36	9	4	30	−3	−1
	71	29	100	69	31	100		
			N = 2238			N = 2596		

NOTE: Entries for each generation add to 100%.

contrast with analogous differences in Table 5.7 within the continuing cohorts of the *New Deal* generation. We have already observed their stability over time with regard to party identification and social connectedness. The difference in the joint distribution of the two variables in the 1950s and the 1980s is consistent with such stability with only a small net shift from less well connected party identifiers to well connected independents. The differences in turnout rates presented in Table 5.8 were of similarly limited magnitude, and they were consistent with the net evidence of a small net increase in turnout for the New Deal cohorts.

Table 5.8 Turnout Rates Within the Joint Distributions of Party Identification and Social Connectedness for New Deal Generation, 1964–1968 and 1980–1988

Social Connectedness	New Deal 1964–1968 Party Identification		New Deal 1980–1988 Party Identification		Difference Between Time Periods	
	ID	Non-ID	ID	Non-ID	ID	Non-ID
High	86	79	85	83	−1	+4
Low	69	57	69	83	0	+26

NOTE: Entry is the average proportion of self-reported voters.

The evidence of the conserving influence of party identification and social connectedness supports our general theoretical notions about the role such factors play in the dynamics of change at the individual level. Nevertheless, our analysis has raised new interpretive questions. First, we need to know why the post-New Deal generation was less likely than the older generation to be identified with a party or blessed with primary social contacts. We have made the rhetorical argument that the reason lies in the different socializing events experienced by each generation. However, it remains a rhetorical argument buttressed by inference rather than by empirical measures of the impact of those events. More analysis is necessary to determine the impact of external, exogenous events on social connectedness.

Second, we need to know why the non-identified *and* the less connected of the post-New Deal generation were even less likely to vote than were the non-identified and less connected of the New Deal generation. Did the quality and meaning of political independence change in the 1960s and 1970s? Did social connectedness and solidarity incentives become more important for voter turnout in the 1980s? The third question, derivative of our first one but perhaps even more challenging, is why were there also intergenerational differences in turnout among the party identified and the socially connected? More generally, whatever the citizens' educational background, race, region of residence, social connectedness, or state of party identification, why do we observe generational differences in voter turnout?

▪ The Search for an Explanation

In his 1978 article, Brody employed an extended battery of attitudinal indicators to explore declining turnout. He examined (1) citizens' interest in the campaign and (2) their interest in the election outcome, and so have we. He also examined (3) four indicators of citizens' sense of civic obligation to vote; (4) two items reflecting citizens' sense of governmental responsiveness; and (5) four measures of citizens' feelings of political efficaciousness. Only six of these twelve items have survived for our use.

Psychological Involvement in Political Participation

As a sequel to the inquiry into the inter-generational decline of party identification and the intra-generational growth in the numbers of the socially connected, we reviewed the possible role which each of these other dimensions of psychological political engagement (including interest and care) played in the creation of generational differences in turnout. Our discussion first addresses the elementary questions of whether there were generational differences in the sheer incidence of these potential explanations, and then whether or not there were generational differences in the level of turnout associated with each value of each explanatory variable.[5]

The NES data across all the years of our analysis include three indicators of a citizen's sense of political efficacy. The assessment of citizens' belief that "public officials don't care very much what people like me think" is among the most revealing for our purposes of exploring generational differences in turnout. Along with the other two indicators of political efficacy, increased agreement with this statement marked a sharp national decrease in sense of political efficacy across the 30-year span. But, in contrast to changes in national parameters of turnout, education, or party identification, *none* of the changes in the indicators of efficacy reflect *generational* differences.

In the 1950s there was no substantial difference between the New Deal and pre-New Deal generations' responses to "the officials don't care" question. Table 5.9 shows that thirty years later there were still no systematic differences unique to the generations. The decrease in citi-

Table 5.9 Incidence of Beliefs That "Public Officials Don't Care Very Much What People Like Me Think," Within Political Generations by Year, Controlling on Education

Years of Education	Political Generation	1952	1956	1960	1980ᵃ	1984	1988	1992	Period Averages 1952–1960	Period Averages 1980–1988	Differences in Non-Efficacious Responses	
0–11	Pre-New Deal	46	42	34	(76)ᵇ	72	*ᶜ	*	41	*	Intra-Generational Change	+36
	New Deal	37	33	31	73	63	74	76	34	70		
	Post-New Deal	—ᵈ		—	73	59	78	71	—	80	Pre-New Deal/ Post-New Deal Replacement	+39
12	Pre-New Deal	22	20	27	*	*	*	*	23	*	Intra-Generational Change	+29
	New Deal	27	16	17	50	43	57	62	21	50		
	Post-New Deal	—		—	57	42	63	63	—	54	Pre-New Deal/ Post-New Deal Replacement	+31
13+	Pre-New Deal	9	13	13	*	*	*	*	12	*	Intra-Generational Change	+27
	New Deal	17	8	13	41	33	44	48	12	39		
	Post-New Deal	—		—	45	29	44	48	—	39	Pre-New Deal/ Post-New Deal	+27

NOTE: Entry is the proportion who agree with statement.

a. The relative sensitivity to election specific circumstances is reflected in the entries for 1980.

b. (N), 50 > N > 25.

c. *, N < 25.

d. — Missing data.

zens' sense of political efficacy was an across-the-board change among all generations and within all levels of education.

When beliefs about public officials are juxtaposed with non-voting *within* any of our time periods, all of the cross-sectional relationships, as seen in Table 5.10, seem quite normal. Both during the 1950s and the 1980s, among all three generations, and within all education groups, the more efficacious had higher rates of voter turnout. During both periods, but particularly the earlier period, differences in turnout associated with appropriate differences in efficacy were greater for those with limited education and less for those with some college experience.

However, despite these familiar contours, neither efficacious nor in-efficacious sentiments appeared to have had any impact whatsoever on the pattern of *generational differences* established when we first examined turnout within educational levels. In fact, Table 5.10 suggests that within both the efficacious and inefficacious groups, the contrast is sharpened between *decreased* turnout attributable to "generational replacement" and *increased* turnout within the continuing New Deal generation. In any event, changes in this measure of political efficacy provide no explanation for the effect of generational replacement on the national decline in turnout.

The same conclusion follows from analyses of the other two indicators of political efficacy, "people like me don't have any say about what government does" and "sometimes politics and government seem so complicated that a person like me can't really understand what's going on." In neither case were there first-order effects from generational differences or generational replacement that accounted for the thirty-year overall decline in efficacy. The decline in efficacy was again across the board, affecting all generations equally. Generational differences in turnout were not accounted for by taking into account variations in feelings of efficacy.

"Citizen interest in following campaigns" and citizens "caring about who wins the election" were also scrutinized for their possible contri-bution to generational differences in turnout. In contrast to the three measures of political efficacy, both a long-term decline in interest (or increase in lack of interest) and a smaller long-term decline in involve-ment in election outcomes *could* be traced to the extraordinary disin-terest and lack of political or social involvement on the part of the post-New Deal generation—quite in keeping with their propensity to

Table 5.10 Voting Turnout and Beliefs About Public Officials

Years of Education	Political Generation	Public Officials Do Care			Public Officials Don't Care		
		1952–60	1980–88		1952–60	1980–88	
0–11	Pre-New Deal	85	(60)[b]		68	55	
	New Deal	70	74	Intra-Generational Change +3	51	59	Intra-Generational Change +8
	Post-New Deal	—[a]	*[c]	Pre-New Deal/Post-New Deal Replacement *	—	30	Pre-New Deal/Post-New Deal Replacement −38
12	Pre-New Deal	95	(78)		85	(77)	
	New Deal	85	91	Intra-Generational Change +8	79	79	Intra-Generational Change 0
	Post-New Deal	—	63	Pre-New Deal/Post-New Deal Replacement −32	—	47	Pre-New Deal/Post-New Deal Replacement −38
13+	Pre-New Deal	92	(93)		(94)	*	
	New Deal	92	94	Intra-Generational Change +2	78	86	Intra-Generational Change +8
	Post-New Deal	—	85	Pre-New Deal/Post-New Deal Replacement −7	—	76	Pre-New Deal/Post-New Deal Replacement −18

NOTE: The entry is the proportion of self-reported voting.

a. — Missing data.

b. (N), 50 > N > 25.

c. *, N < 25.

forgo identification with a political party. In neither case, however, did "controlling" these first-order effects on the distribution of the political engagement variable eliminate the evidence of generational differences in turnout.[6]

Finally, we examined the single NES indicator pertaining to the citizen's sense of civic duty that bridges our full time span. Among all but the college-educated, the generational exchange of the new post-New Deal for the old pre-New Deal induced a modest increase in acceptance of the statement that "if people don't care how an election comes out they shouldn't vote in it." Again, however, taking into account variations in this sentiment did not diminish the generational differences in turnout.

The overall conclusion at this stage of our inquiry is that persons who exhibit above-average social connectedness, hold a sense of party identification, show an interest in elections, and have more formal education were visibly less likely to contribute to declining turnout over time as a consequence of generational differences. Those who are non-identified, disinterested, less integrated socially, and less well educated exhibited a larger consequence for turnout resulting from generational turnover. However, in contrast, none of the six *attitudinal* predispositions seemed to have any impact on changes in turnout due to generational replacement even though they provide a partial explanation for the turnout of citizens in all three generations. Indeed, neither set of explanations (social connectedness, party identification, and so on, nor the attitudinal predispositions) accounts for inter-generational differences in turnout.

▪ The Puzzle Transformed

The successor to Brody's puzzle—why have there been successive generational decreases in voting turnout—should promote a new temporal perspective on contemporary electoral analysis—new at least for most political scientists.[7] Recent history—too recent to be called history by traditional historians—has clearly played a largely unrecognized but crucial role in shaping the contours of the current American electorate, and perhaps equally in providing an essential context for individual level, micro-explanations of contemporary American mass politics.

Conventional scholarly wisdom about mass electoral behavior has been fundamentally ahistorical in its approaches to explaining the persistent downward trend of electoral participation in the United States between 1960 and 1988. The disaggregation of the electorate into the historically based generational components of the non-Black portion of the citizenry radically redefines the phenomena in need of explanation. The historical record of the New Deal generation can now be viewed as producing stable, if not increasing, turnout over thirty years. The across-time record of sustained turnout within the New Deal generation pretty much rules out potential sources of reduced turnout that would have been expected to impinge on the older generations as well as on the new additions to the electorate. On the face of it, this denies explanations of declining turnout that posit a *pervasive* national decrease in citizens' sense of political efficacy or a declining sense of obligation to the civic duty of voting, or those explanations that posit a decline in mobilization efforts as the use of the mass media replaces the traditional local campaign organization.

As a complement to our description of the three stages of political development in the last chapter, all of this points to possible causes of change that are related to *age* in cross-sectional analyses, but *not to aging* in longitudinal analyses. The explanatory problem is that we have not, in the present analysis and discussion, been able to identify or account for the essential causal elements. The search for correlates of the observable generational differences in turnout has been wide, if not yet exhaustive. We have noted phenomena that do account for a portion of the turnout differences among our three political generations, such as party identification, community integration or social connectedness, interest in election campaigns, and caring about election outcomes. These phenomena meet the double test of being in accord with *stability* within the New Deal generation while accounting for *change* between pre-New Deal and post-New Deal generations that is consonant with the inter-generational differences in turnout. However, these phenomena do not explain enough. At best they identify considerations that minimize (or maximize) generational differences.

Beyond our surmise that four decades of discouraging news about our political system had depressed the willingness of post-New Deal electors to participate on election day, we have no direct evidence to account for the inter-generational differences in turnout. Our correlates of turnout do not explain the very large differences in turnout that persist between comparably engaged, or disengaged, members of the contrasting generations. Moreover, the generations themselves now need explaining as a part of the infinite chain in which each endogenous explanation, in turn, needs explaining.

Our difficulties in attempting to account for differences in generational turnout rates, both in the 1950s and in the 1980s, clearly define a new set of problems. Table 5.11 illustrates that (1) both in the 1950s and in the 1980s, the "younger" generations voted less than the "older" generations; (2) the psychologically less involved participated less than did the more involved; and (3) both findings were generally more true for the less well educated than for the better educated. However, for the continuing New Deal generation (the younger of the generations during the 1950s, the older generation during the 1980s), the voting participation levels, within education and within motivation, either remain con-

Table 5.11 Average Rates of Voting, by Generation Within Education, for Citizens More Involved and Less Involved in Various Predispositions Relevant to Voting Turnout

Involvement	Years of Education	Pre-New Deal 1952–60	New Deal 1952–60	New Deal 1980–88	Post-New Deal 1980–88
Involved: High on	0–11	91	82	78	41
Efficacy, Citizen Duty,	12	96	90	95	77
Care, Interest	13+	93	92	94	90
Less Involved: Low	0–11	69	54	60	30
on Each Indicator	12	85	76	80	48
	13+	87	83	87	74
SUMMARY:					
Differences Related to	0–11	+22	+28	+18	+11
Involvement	12	+11	+14	+15	+29
within Levels of Education	13+	+6	+9	+7	+16
SUMMARY:					
Generational Differences	0–11		−9	−4	−37
in Turnout among	12		−6	+5	−18
More Involved	13+		−1	+2	−4
SUMMARY:					
Generational Differences	0–11		−15	+6	−30
in Turnout among	12		−9	+4	−32
Less Involved	13+		−4	+4	−13

stant or appear to increase, at least marginally, across the thirty-year time span. Beyond suggesting the generality of the relationships involving the six indicators of psychological involvement in politics, Table 5.11 is presented to emphasize the distinctiveness of all *three* of our broad generational groupings. Although the contrasts are greatest between the less well educated members of the New Deal and post-New Deal generations, the generational differences for both the more and the less involved members of the pre-New Deal and New Deal generations call for explanation.

At this point there seem to be few lines of inquiry with which to address the differences between the pre-New Deal and New Deal generations. There may be untapped resources in studies from the 1950s and 1960s, but the most obvious leads have been introduced in this analysis. They have helped define the problem, but they have not suggested a solution. There must have been attributes of pre-New Deal politics that were influential in socializing pre-New Deal cohorts to a high level of political participation. And yet, as a historian reading this manuscript observed, "One has to wonder: your pre-1920 and Republican normalcy generations represent the wildest imaginable mixes of peoples: the native born of the native born, immigrants, second-generation ethnics, Blacks still in the South, Blacks who had moved into cities and into the North, even women! These people had quite an array of experiences in childhood, and adulthood, which even if we confine them to the explicitly political, must have been fantastically different. What is the experience common to all that provoked them to drop the ballot in the box?"[8]

PART III

★ ★ ★

PARTISAN IDENTIFICATION

6

Conceptualization and Measurement of Party Identification

The concept of party identification, and its measurement, have been central to the evolution of the study of electoral behavior. They play crucial roles in our own multiple-stage, multiple-variable explanation of the vote. Party identification is also one of the most controversial concepts in all of electoral research. One end of the controversy is anchored in European national election studies, which have concluded that party identification does not exist, at least not in the political cultures of Europe (Thomassen, 1976). A milder statement argues that party identification exists, but only as a political attitude that is the product of contemporary short-term factors with no more durability or centrality than other political attitudes such as preferences on questions of public policy. Our own view, as alluded to in Chapter 1, is that party identification is the most enduring of political attitudes, responsible for shaping a wide variety of values and perceptions, and, therefore, an appropriate starting point for any analysis of a partisan political preference, such as a choice between presidential candidates.

Our discussion of party identification is divided into five parts. We begin with the nature of party identification. As background for reviewing party identification in the voting literature, we will discuss its abstract or theoretical nature and its functional role in the formation of voting decisions. That discussion reviews some of the major issues in the definition of party identification and its measurement through survey-based procedures. Next, we will consider some of the possible origins of citizens' sense of identification, as well as some of the sub-

117

sequent sources of change in that identification. We conclude by noting that contemporary changes in the alignment of the two parties differ by region and, outside the South, by political generation and religion.

The second part of our discussion illustrates the evolution of our contemporary view of party identification as a dominant influence on voting behavior. We arrived at our current understanding of party identification after a long journey through time and circumstance. There were occasions when progress in validating and extending our ideas seemed swift and certain. One of the first of these occasions took place with the completion of the first Michigan panel study, 1956–1958–1960. Prior to that, much of our sense of the stability and long-term persistence of citizens' party identifications was supplied by arguments, either by analogy or by evidence based on citizens' recall of past attitudes and behavior. Such evidence was entirely based on temporal snapshots provided by surveys of cross sections of the electorate, each taken at a single point in time.

The panel data in 1960 provided the first direct evidence of the extent to which individuals reported the same party identifications at three successive points in time—during a presidential election, an off-year election, and a second presidential contest. A Republican presidential landslide had been followed by a large Democratic congressional sweep, followed in turn by a narrow Democratic presidential victory. Throughout this period of massive electoral change, party identification remained relatively stable, both at the individual and the aggregate national levels. In accordance with our theoretical expectations, party identification was viewed as the most stable of all political attitudes.

The nature of party identification as a stable, persistent attribute was reaffirmed with data from a second Michigan panel study carried out in 1972–1974–1976. Both panel studies demonstrated that the strength of party identification was susceptible to the influence of short-term, election-specific forces; however, both studies also revealed that it is rare for citizens to cross the boundary between identification and non-identification. It is exceedingly rare for anyone actually to switch parties, from Democrat to Republican or vice versa, even though one might switch one's votes from Eisenhower to Kennedy, from Nixon to Carter, or from Bush to Clinton. This conclusion was in accord with the larger presumption that adults do not often change their personal identities, their ongoing sense of social location in relation to other people and to the values and institutions of their society (Converse and Markus, 1979).

Of equal theoretical importance, the two panel studies revealed that voters' departure from the party with which they are identified—such as when Republicans voted for Stevenson or for Kennedy or when Democrats voted for Nixon or for Ford—were explicable in terms of different short-term, election-specific forces that countered long-term identification. Both panel studies illustrated how unique sets of "defectors" can respond to the idiosyncratic forces of one election and yet revert to traditional or established party loyalties once those short-term, election-specific forces change. Republican Catholics could easily vote for Eisenhower in 1956 but then switch to Kennedy, a Democratic Catholic, four years later; conservative Democrats who could not support a radical George McGovern in 1972 would gladly return to the fold and support a Democratic centrist, Jimmy Carter, in 1976 (Converse et al., 1961 and 1979). Thus, in general, year after year most elections and most election studies provide new opportunities to test evolving notions, hunches, or hypotheses about one or another aspect of party identification.

In the next chapter, we initiate a third theme in our discussion of party identification and offer some generalizations from the accumulated time series amassed by the National Election Studies. Here our avowed and explicit purpose is to challenge some of the more hyperbolic treatments of realignment and dealignment that dominated the journal literature of the 1970s and 1980s (Burnham, 1970). With the advantage of historical hindsight, we will also counter some of the revisionist generalizations concerning the decline in the role of party identification as a determinant of national vote decisions (Fiorina, 1981). In both instances, we will emphasize our view of party identification as a remarkably stable predisposition that is crucial to the evaluation of that which is unique to a particular election and that which is generic to a series of elections. Our arguments are presented in the context of ubiquitous historical period effects on party identification after 1968, accompanied by selective generational effects responsive to the national political events of the past four decades.

The fourth theme concerns the immediate context of the Reagan/Bush/Clinton elections. Here we review the evidence of a national change in party balance that occurred between 1980 and 1988, only to be reversed in 1992. As with the preceding section, we shall try to establish the persistence of party identification's role in shaping both individual and collective vote decisions.

The conclusion in the next chapter summarizes our reasons for treating party identification as a point of departure for analyses that distinguish between the long-term forces that provide continuity in American presidential politics and the short-term forces that make each election unique and that often determine the election outcome.

▪ The Concept of Party Identification[1]

Party identification is a concept derived from reference and small group theory positing that one's sense of self may include a feeling of personal identity with a secondary group such as a political party. In the United States, the feeling is usually expressed as "I am a Democrat" or "I am a Republican." This sense of individual attachment to party need not reflect a formal membership in or active connection with a party organization. Moreover, one's sense of party identification does not necessarily connote a particular voting record, although the influence of party allegiance on electoral behavior is strong, and there is evidence of a reciprocal relationship in which voting behavior helps establish, and solidify or strengthen, one's sense of party allegiance. The tie between individual and party is psychological—an extension of one's ego to include feeling a part of a group. Party identification can persist without legal recognition or formal evidence of its existence; it can even persist without resting on or producing a consistent record of party support either in one's attitudes or one's actions.

In seeking to describe the nature of party identification without direct reference to politics, it is sometimes helpful to turn to the example of religion as a comparison that is much more than an analogy. Party affiliation, like religious affiliation, often originates within the family, where it is established as a matter of early socialization into the family norms. In addition to the primary group experience, however, the maturing child has a clear sense of belonging to a larger body of adherents or co-religionists. The sense of self in the religious context is clearly established by the sense of "We are Roman Catholic," "I am a Jew"; in politics, "We are Democrats" or "I am a Republican."

There is an affirmative exclusivity to group identification. Neither religious identification nor party identification necessarily speaks to one's regard, positive or negative, for other persuasions. Insofar as group identifications involve cultural, ethnic, religious, or social entities that are antagonistic or in conflict, the sense of identifying as a protagonist may lead to negative attitudes toward the "other" or outgroups. This is not a necessary condition, however; identification may simply denote a sense of oneness with the identified group that sets it off from other groups.

To push the direct religious comparison another step or two: in matters of religion, very few ordinary citizens are creative theologians, just as very few party identifiers are creative political ideologues. One of the roles of the church, or the party, is to provide structure to the ordinary person's understanding of the external world, specifying which of the phenomena of the secular world are relevant to one's religion, or to one's politics. The function of ideology, as with theology, is often to provide structure, organization, and coherence to one's thinking with regard to matters that the ideology (or theology) defines as relevant to politics (or religion). We use the term "ideology" as a symbol for the systems of political belief—however enriched or impoverished—that ordinary citizens espouse. We intend to include cognitive matters—beliefs and patterns of attitudes—as well as affective matters—values and preferences. Party ideology, or sectarian theology, thus plays a central role in facilitating understanding of the nature of one's world.

Beyond such contributions to cognitive structure, the role of faithful parishioner, or party follower, also provides many cues for normative assessments of the outside world: What is good, what is bad? What is acceptable, what is unacceptable? As a consequence of the many psychological functions performed by one's identification with the group, the citizen is given answers to a multitude of questions: What should I believe? What is the nature of reality? What should be done, what should not be done?

The Role of Party Leaders

Beliefs relevant to the group, whether theological or ideological, are usually conveyed through group leaders, who may specify the attitudes that are appropriate to one's affiliation as well as highlight the values that are central to that component of one's life. Thus, political leaders, presidential candidates or presidents, and others perceived to be legitimate party spokespersons articulate party ideology, or the party line, just as ministers or rabbis, bishops or the Pope, articulate religious dogma. Almost by definition, leaders articulate the creed of the faithful, and they stand as symbols representing any and all of the meanings attached to group affiliations. Followers who have a strict definition of orthodoxy may have been influenced by homogeneity in their leaders' views; followers who hold a pluralism of heterogeneous beliefs and perspectives may have been influenced by ideological factionalism among their leaders.

However, at the same time that the generic function of leadership is to articulate group values and beliefs, many individual leaders are perceived, at least in their early days of prominence, to possess the attributes associated with their party, unless, or until, they establish a more or less unique personal identity. Party identifiers initially ascribe to emerging leaders the characteristics that they have previously associated with the party. The group leadership may be a highly personal leadership, as in that of many contemporary religions—Mary Baker Eddy, Joseph Smith, the Reverend Billy Graham—or in the field of politics, as in the personages of Franklin Roosevelt, Norman Thomas, and Barry Goldwater, or, at the intersection of politics and religion, with the Reverends Falwell, Robertson, and Jesse Jackson. Although some leaders ultimately put their own stamp on the party and contribute to reshaping the party image, they are initially perceived as having the attributes of their predecessors.

Thus, for each individual, party identification can be understood to serve a function similar to that served by religious identification. The identifications are ultimately voluntary choices of allegiance; at their root meaning, they are extensions of self. They provide partial answers to such social reference questions as: "Who am I? Who are you? Who is he? What do they believe?" Such partisanship may be acquired in the first instance through family membership, but, as with religion, it may subsequently be influenced and affected by other social relationships and life experiences.

As new issues arise, and as new social problems develop, leaders must determine, help define, and then prescribe the appropriate beliefs and behaviors for the party or for the church. This is not to say that there is no creative thinking within the party rank and file about the issues of the day. Although no mass electorate meets the idealized standards for being sufficiently well informed to engage in mass decision-making through direct democracy, large numbers of attentive citizens do formulate opinions and policy preferences on their own. But transforming the welter of individual opinions into a party consensus is the challenge of democratic politics, and the task for party leaders.

If, as in the American context of two-party politics, a party must aggregate interests in order to command a base sufficiently broad to achieve a viable competitive position in electoral politics, the articulation of a party's program becomes a complex rhetorical exercise. The process directs, or redirects, the beliefs of the party followers, or it establishes an appeal that attracts or mobilizes new adherents. In the former case, party identification leads to, or "causes," policy-related preferences; in the latter case, there are instances in which policy-related preferences lead to, or influence, party identification.

Measuring the Concept

The importance of stable party loyalties has been widely recognized in electoral studies. Much disagreement, however, has been expressed concerning the way in which such loyalties should be defined and measured. In keeping with the concept of party identification as a psychological bond between the individual and the group, the National Election Studies have measured party identification by asking individuals to describe their own *sense of being* a Democrat or Republican. In contrast, however, other studies have chosen to measure stable partisan orientations by using individuals' past voting records, or their attitudes on a set of enduring partisan issues. Thus, Republican and Democratic identifiers are sometimes defined as those who consistently vote for the same party, while Independents are those who do not.

Such definitions should be characterized as definitions of *partisanship,* not of *party identification.* As definitions of partisanship, they serve many practical and scholarly purposes; however, as operational definitions of party identification, they blur the distinction between the psychological state of one's identification with party and its consequences. Party identification cannot be measured by one's vote or one's evaluation of partisan issues if, at the same time, there is an interest in exploring the influence of party identification on voting behavior or its consequences for policy-related preferences.

The extent to which behavioral measures confound the definition of party identification becomes particularly apparent when one focuses on the study of *change* in party identification. The familiar phenomenon of ticket splitting, for example, is clearly related to party identification; indeed, it is taken by some scholars to be a measure of party identification. The stronger one's identification, the less frequently one "splits" the ticket and votes for candidates from another party. The stronger one's identification as an Independent, the more often or the more completely one splits the ticket. However, in studying changes in ticket splitting, one realizes that it may be just as much the attractiveness of the opportunity to split one's ticket as it is a change in the propensity to demonstrate one's party loyalty that influences voting for all or only some of the candidates of one's party.

In an early exchange in the journal literature, Rusk made a closely related point in an argument with Burnham (Norpoth and Rusk, 1982). In that case Rusk argued for the recognition of two different meanings of ticket splitting—one that involved ticket splitting on a Massachusetts-type ballot, organized by elective office; and the other, ticket splitting with a party column-type ballot, organized by political party. Applied to the contemporary context, the implication is that if a voter is repeatedly confronted with a ballot in which candidates are arranged in party columns to facilitate the casting of a straight party vote, a number of visits to the polls may create or strengthen a sense of party identification. However, the contrasting experience, in which one must select from among all candidates, office-by-office—as found in a so-called Massachusetts-type ballot—may encourage ticket splitting and thereby forestall the development of a sense of party loyalty in party identification. The central point is that whatever the cause-and-effect relationship, an act of voting for a particular party and a sense of party identification are not the same and should not be confused as such.

More generally, given a multivariate view of the origin of personal opinions or individual behaviors, it must be recognized that an opinion, or behavior, may change as the result of any one of a number of origins or causes. The implications that flow from this perspective are central to all interpretations of the meaning of party identification based on changes in its correlation with a dependent variable such as vote choice. Party identification is properly recognized, year in and year out, as the most important contributor to one's voting behavior, but it is, nevertheless, only one contributor. Consequently, changes in voting behavior may occur without affecting one's sense of party identification; the changes may stem from one or more of the other influences that contribute to the vote decision. Year-to-year variations in the correlation between party identification and vote preference may occur without any change in the importance, or meaning, of party identification, but rather solely as a result of changes in vote preference stemming from other sources. This of course illustrates a ubiquitous problem of causal inference in any multivariate structure; but awareness of it forestalls simplistic reliance on the correlational approach for the validation of a measure. It also becomes even more evident that we can never establish the conditions under which party identification is a "cause" if party identification is measured in terms of the behavioral consequences it is thought to influence.

The most appropriate, and most widely accepted, measures of party identification rest fundamentally on self-classification. Since 1952, the National Election Studies have repeatedly asked cross-sections of the national electorate a sequence of questions inviting each individual to state the direction and strength of his or her partisan orientation. The dimension presupposed by these questions appears to have psychological reality for virtually the entire electorate.

The manifestation of party identification is provided by answers to the question: "Generally speaking, do you usually think of yourself as a Republican, a Democrat, an Independent, or what?" Those who classify themselves as Republicans or Democrats are then asked: "Would you call yourself a strong Republican (or Democrat) or a not very strong Republican (or Democrat)?" This sequence permits researchers to array the entire population on a continuum, running from strong Republican to weak Republican to Independent to weak Democrat to strong Democrat. It is important to note that the effort to measure enduring group identification rather than transitory feelings of partisan preference is reflected in the phrase, *"Generally speaking, do you usually think of yourself . . .?"* The result of this choice of language is often visibly different from that produced by measures such as the Gallup Poll measure, which begins: *"In politics as of today,* do you think of yourself . . .?"

The significance of attending to "details" of measurement when analyzing party identification has been forcefully argued by Converse and Pierce (1987). They emphasize that there are "two elements which have been absolutely central to the whole notion of party identification: an *extended time horizon* and some engagement of partisan feelings with *self-identity* . . . These two elements . . . imply . . . that numerous forms of partisan feelings may be experienced by an individual, and reported upon to investigators, which *do not* constitute the possession of a party identification as such" (p. 143; emphasis added).

For purposes *other than that* of measuring one's party identification, the National Election Studies' question sequence contains further probes for those individuals who do not think of themselves as Democrats or Republicans. Independent "leaners" are sorted from those who classify themselves as Independent (or, more often, who volunteer the fact that they have no party preference); they are asked the follow-up question: "Do you think of yourself as closer to the Republican or Democratic party?" This question permits a subdivision of the non-identifiers into three categories: (1) those professing a sense of feeling closer to the Republican party; (2) those professing a sense of feeling closer to the Democratic party; and (3) those who twice resist any suggestion that they have a partisan predisposition or inclination.

Independent Leaners

In our subsequent discussion we ignore the differentiation of independent leaners. We have done so in part because in the original interview sequence, the Independent leaners clearly deny a "temporally extended self-identity" as Democrat or Republican. It is also true that the follow-up question, "Do you think of yourself as closer to the Republican or Democratic party?" does not attempt to elicit even a qualified or limited sense of an "enduring engagement of partisan feelings with self-identity"; the question is asked only in the present tense, and it calls only for a cognitive assessment of current circumstance.[2] The answers may indicate partisanship, but they do not necessarily reflect a sense of party identification. We agree with Converse and Pierce when they note that there may be no "right" way to measure *partisanship,* but "it is of great importance not to treat diverse measures of partisanship as functional equivalents of one another. Partisanship has multiple facets, and keeping clear which facet is being measured, is a basic investigator responsibility" (Converse and Pierce, 1985).[3]

The subdivision of the non-identifiers proves very useful for a number of purposes, including that of using the entire question sequence as a maximally powerful, seven-category predictor of the actual individual vote. The same sequence—subdividing "Independents" into those with some partisan coloration and those who are staunchly non-partisan—is, however, responsible for a good bit of confusion in the electoral behavior literature. The people who reject a sense of party identification but do confess to a closer proximity to a particular party are presumptively devoid of any psychological sense of belongingness or allegiance to a party; nevertheless, they may behave very much like partisans. For example, their partisanship may be manifest in their positions on questions of public policy that are the object of partisan dispute, and at times it may be more thoroughgoing than the partisanship of those who actually are party identifiers (Keith et al., 1986, 1992; Zaller and Feldman, 1992). In such circumstances, this partisanship is not born of a sense of group identity or belonging, but of the quite different consequence of a particular leader's attractiveness or the coincidence of one's policy preferences matching one party's position on issues. *Independent* "leaners," or non-identifiers with party preferences, should *not* be confused with party identifiers, despite occasional treatment as such by other scholars.

At the same time as we strive for clarity and precision in our operational definition of "party identification," we must acknowledge the problems inherent in assigning meaning to the responses to questions in the survey interview (Feldman and Zaller, 1992). Given the inevitable slippage between the intent and the results of our measurement efforts, it is also appropriate to note that the reasons for our attempt at a strict interpretation of the meaning of party identification are more firmly grounded in theory than in data. There is little question that variations in the "strength of party identification" have reflected variations in the short-term fortunes of the respective parties, and have led to changes in the sheer intensity of partisan enthusiasms. It has also been well documented that the same short-term forces have both attracted and repelled many citizens who, while *not* major party identifiers, have on different occasions considered themselves closer to one of the two major parties. However, neither of these considerations speaks directly to the question of individuals responding to the same short-term influences by self-consciously moving *across the boundary* separating identifiers from non-identifiers. The question is not whether "independent leaners" may, from time to time, be more partisan in their voting behavior or issue preferences than are weak identifiers. The question is not whether independent leaners are covert partisans; they are often demonstrably and overtly partisan. The question is the stability (and the meaningfulness) of one's self-identification as a Democrat or a Republican (Keith, 1992).

One result of the common practice of attending to variations in strength of party identification (strong or not so strong) and variations in the partisan sympathies of non-identifiers (the so-called independent leaners) has been to obscure the relative stability of the basic sense of the political self, elemental party identification. Short-term enthusiasms for a Lyndon Johnson, Democratic dismay with a George McGovern, and Republican distress with Watergate are clearly reflected in abrupt changes in the widely used *seven point* measure of partisanship; however, we shall document the very limited impact of such phenomena on answers to the basic identification question, "Generally speaking, do you usually think of yourself as a Republican or a Democrat?" (Brody, 1988; Shively, 1979; Claggett, 1981).[4]

The relative stability of party identification, both at the level of national aggregate distributions and at the level of individual measurement through time, is impressive as well as necessary if it is to be a point of departure for the analysis of mass electoral behavior. As should be true of a standing decision, or continuity in one's sense of political self, measures of the stability and durability of various political attitudes consistently place party identification in the top rank, virtually unchallenged by the stability of feelings toward national political leaders or by commitments on matters of public policy as indicators of enduring political predispositions (Converse and Markus, 1979). Party identification is by no means an immutable commitment; but, given accumulated evidence of its relatively greater stability, it is often properly used as the beginning point for studies of change in the more transitory perceptions, attitudes, and beliefs that may be involved in election day decisions.

▪ The Origins of Party Identification

Despite the profound importance of party identification as a conditioner of individual behavior and as a shaper of the politics of the society, the precise origins of individual party loyalties are not well understood (Niemi and Jennings, 1991). At one point in the development of the study of party identification, the family was deemed to be all-important. The presumed centrality of the family's role in creating a sense of party was, in part, a direct consequence of early measurement practices among professional students of electoral behavior. In many early studies of political socialization, great attention was paid to individuals' *recall* of parental partisanship. These reports were used in lieu of data that might result from a direct examination of the shared sense of party within the context of the family, when both parent and child could be studied at the same time. In the virtual absence of the more appropriate evidence in national election studies, heavy reliance was placed on the recollections of children—often "children" in their adulthood—regarding their parents' partisanship, a partisanship that might well have existed decades earlier and whose memory might have been blurred by the passage of time. Such parental characteristics were too often remembered as identical to the current partisanship of the "child." The thesis that the family is the primary source of partisanship, and that the continuity of party identifications in the United States is therefore a reflection of the presumed conserving influence of familial party loyalty, has been substantially modified by research that details evidence of great slippage between the partisanship of the childhood family and that exhibited in later life.[5]

A major contribution to rethinking the origins and evolution of party identification was made by Jennings and his coauthors, beginning in the 1970s. Their work is based on a unique three-wave panel study of parents and their offspring conducted by the Center for Political Studies in 1965, 1973, and 1982. In the first major volume drawn from Jennings's study, where much attention was given to the origins of young adults' party identifications, a full 40 percent of the child-parent pairs showed the offspring departing from a perfect match with their parents across the three categories—Democrat, Independent, and Republican (Jennings and Niemi, 1974; Niemi, Katz, and Newman, 1980).

Verification that familial socialization cannot be responsible for a large fraction of those citizens who are party identifiers opened the search for alternative explanations of the origins of party identification. Throughout the 1980s, a voluminous literature explored the question. One of the most influential contributions came from Fiorina's reconceptualization of the role of party identification in the shaping of the voter's choice between candidates. Fiorina's study, *Retrospective Voting in American National Elections,* followed important contributions to the journal literature by Jackson, among others (Jackson, 1975; Fiorina, 1980).

Jackson's work argued that, contrary to any assumption of recursive models in which causal influence flows from party identification to other variables that intervene prior to voting, there was evidence of statistically significant feedback. In particular, policy preferences were held to shape party identification, even in the short-run period of a given election.

Party identification was thus viewed as the result of, as well as the cause of, voters' preferences on policy issues. More extreme revisionist arguments have attributed absolutist positions to the traditional view, as though party identification had once been thought to be an immutable first cause, exogenous to theories elaborating the origins of voters' decisions. The extreme revisionist view argues that, in contrast, party identification is simply another political attitude, susceptible to influence and change by short-term phenomena, thoroughly endogenous to explanations of electoral behavior. In particular, it is sometimes argued that party identification is primarily the consequence of the assemblage of issue or policy preferences held by the voter prior to voting.

Our own view rejects both extremes in favor of a position that is closer to the revisionists' caricature of orthodoxy. We believe that party identification is much more than just another expression of a short-run preference for one candidate over the other, or a cumulative summary of policy preferences, or a performance evaluation that rewards or punishes an incumbent administration. At the same time, we also believe that questions about the origins and the causal status of party identification and its impact on the vote are an essential part of the process of theory building in which we are all still engaged. In the first instance, for example, the Jennings studies provide evidence, seldom cited, of students' acquisition of party loyalties through their association with their secondary school peers, and, to a very limited extent, through association with their teachers (1974). From early in the 1970s, the thesis has been argued that the evolution of party identification is a matter of social learning that apparently begins in young adulthood and may extend well into one's adult life.[6]

As with initial childhood socialization, however, the *process* by which the high school senior's disdain for party is replaced twenty years later by a strong sense of party loyalty has not been fully documented. The most persuasive studies of the evolution of party identification within maturing individuals have been based on the Jennings study. As a result, the beginning and some intermediate stages of political socialization have been well studied, even though we still do not understand the micro-mechanics of that process. We do not know whether the process is one in which the citizen is mobilized largely by the successes of party leadership, or whether questions of urgent public policy do more to facilitate the growth of, and changes in, party loyalties. Do people begin by feeling a sense of remoteness from both parties, move to a modest preference for one party or its leaders, reflect that preference in their behavior, and ultimately develop a sense of self that is consonant with an established behavioral pattern? Or is the process much more cognitive—does one rationally choose between the parties on the basis of one's maturing values, social perspectives, and preferences on policy matters?[7]

Whatever the psychological mechanisms are that lead adult citizens to identify with a political party, recent decades have greatly increased our understanding of the external conditions that lead to new identifications or reinforce old ones. Some are conditions that are apolitical in origin, such as change in individual social locations. Going away to school, marrying, acquiring a job, and moving to a new home all intrude on familial origins and the political context of childhood. Thus, sequentially experienced life-cycle changes may produce changes in the social environment that, in turn, may produce changes in individual political identities.

Jennings and his coauthors have juxtaposed their data from parents and offspring, which cover a 17-year time span, to estimate the age when the party identifications of young adults settle down and become more stable, or, in their terms, join in a general crystallization of political attitudes. They are properly wary of being too specific in pinpointing ages, given the limitations of temporal coverage in their data, but they settle on the age span from 25 to 35 (Beck and Jennings, 1991; Jennings and Markus, 1984). This accords nicely with subsequent estimates based on our own analyses. Both the timing of the acquisition of some party identity other than "Independent," and the leveling off of voting turnout noted in Chapter 4, fit the notion that for most young adults (ages 26–29), there is much less malleability after the third election experience.

This is not to deny some degree of lifelong openness to influences and political change, but it does suggest that social "life cycle" effects on political involvement and experience are of limited duration. This is particularly true if life cycle effects are defined in traditional terms of phases of social experience, such as going away to school, getting married, getting a job, buying a home, and the like. There is, however, a more extended period of "political" life cycle effects that can be measured in terms of the duration of political experience. If we note the number of years—or number of elections—that have passed after a person reaches voting age, political life cycle effects may continue to contribute to the political maturation of the individual beyond the time span marking "social" life cycle experiences. Nevertheless, barring idiosyncratic intrusion from some social or economic discontinuity, party identification is an enduring long-term attribute for most people, from early adulthood until the last years.

▪ Social Change and Change in Party Identification

In some periods, however, large-scale societal changes may shift the geographic balance in partisan alignments, as with outward migrations from central city to suburbs, or with the great mid-century migrations from the rural South to the West Coast and the urban North.[8] Moreover, the political changes induced by pervasive social change may be of substantial consequence, as in the erosion of the Democratic dominance of the one-party South. At times the effects of social change may be overshadowed by changes induced by more directly political causes, as in the apparent impact of the Reagan presidency on party realignment following 1980, or the shifting of party loyalties in 1964.

Large, cataclysmic events of national scope and extended temporal duration may entirely reshape the national parameters of party identification. Two of the major epochs of American politics were formed by the Civil War of the 1860s and the Great Depression of the 1930s. Our earlier analysis of the thirty-year decline in turnout between the 1950s and the 1980s led us to the conclusion that a third sequence of national political events has produced an as yet little studied watershed in American political life, beginning in the last forty years of the twentieth century. This third epoch in American political history has not acquired a name or a unifying label. However, as our discussion in the earlier chapters suggested, this period is marked by the unprecedented succession of failed presidencies, beginning with Lyndon Johnson's abdication in 1968.[9]

Although much of the evidence is indirect, and the strongest arguments are inferential, it would seem that all three historic periods put a unique stamp on citizens' party loyalties. During the first two periods, the perspectives of each age, once established, shaped the partisanship of families and communities for generations to come. But, as with the generic problem of understanding the establishment of an individual's party identification following an adolescence of political independence, the precise mechanisms of the major historical transformations have not been established. For the post-Depression period in the twentieth century, it is not clear how much credit should be given to the Democratic mobilization of previous non-voters, and how much should go to the conversion of Republican sympathies into Democratic loyalties. And, whatever the balance between mobilization and conversion, what proportion of those who changed did so because of the appeal of the New Deal policies? Or did the Democrats benefit from the bitter disappointment over the performance of Herbert Hoover and the Republican party, or from the charismatic appeal of the nation's only four-term president, Franklin Delano Roosevelt, or from the Al Smith candidacy of 1928, which began the mobilization of an urban, ethnic, Catholic constituency? Similar questions must be addressed concerning the upsurge in Republican numbers that eliminated the Democrats' decades-old advantage in party identification among voters prior to 1988. There is much yet to be learned from the reconstruction of such periods of national upheaval. Given the development of survey research in the middle of this century, scholars now have an unparalleled opportunity to study the origins, consequences, and future of long-term changes that have shaped the post-New Deal generation.

▪ Learning about Party Identification

With the proliferation of research on party identification, recent decades have produced major additions to our knowledge about its nature. Where the importance of party identification was once assessed largely in terms of its simple correlation with vote choice, well-specified credit is now given for its many indirect contributions as well. These occur as party identifications shape perceptions and transmit values to the attitudes and beliefs that, in turn, lead to the individual's vote choice.

The earliest theorizing about party identification presumed that one of its major functions was to shape citizens' views of politics. Early evidence was found in the pervasive differences characterizing Democratic and Republican views on a variety of themes, from policy preferences to the choice of candidates. However, it was not until the study of the 1980 election that we had data which clarified the way in which party identification shaped other political attitudes, thereby exerting an indirect influence on citizens' vote decisions.

Democrats and Republicans began that election year with established long-term differences in their issue preferences, as well as in their perceptions of the candidates' relative proximities to those policy preferences. These differences were maintained or only mildly accentuated throughout the nominating period. However, during the general election campaign period the perceptions of the candidates' positions changed significantly, increasing to a point of ultimate partisan polarization. Among ideologically defined subsets of the electorate, the patterns of the candidates' perceived issue positions also shifted with a timing that coincided with the three stages of the campaign: the early primary period, the primary election campaign, and, ultimately, the general election campaign.

The net result of the year's changes was increased polarization between Democrats *and* Republicans as well as between liberals *and* conservatives. Both sets of partisans and both sets of ideologues changed their perceptions of the two candidates in ways that brought liberals and Democrats into rapport with the Democratic, more liberal candidate, while conservatives and Republicans increased their relative affinity for the more conservative Republican. There is, then, a central role for both partisan and ideological predispositions in the process of the voters' arriving at a choice between candidates.

These conclusions are theoretically gratifying. Our subsequent conclusions about the determinants of the vote choice in 1980, however, also rely heavily on the facts that (1) while polarization of *perceptions* of the relative proximities of the candidates changed throughout the year in intuitively satisfying patterns and in very substantial magnitudes, (2) perceived discrepancies between *citizens' policy preferences* and their *perceptions of current federal-government policies* were highly stable—and at election time reflected the *same* degree of partisan and ideological polarization that had existed even before the first presidential and primary elections. This configuration of research findings establishes the importance of separating the direction and magnitude of citizens' implicit preferences for government policy changes from citizens' perceptions of the relative proximities of the candidates' positions on these same policy issues. In conjunction with the observed stability of partisan and ideological predispositions throughout the year, patterns of stability and change in perceptions of the candidates are important; they strongly support the particular sequential ordering of causal factors we follow in our analyses of the elections of the Reagan-Bush era (Miller and Shanks, 1982).

In particular, we interpret this configuration of results as positive evidence that, for most people, the formation of policy preferences and perceptions of government policies preceded, rather than followed from, their perceptions of candidates' policy positions. Were policy preferences and perceptions of government policy to have covaried across time, along with the changes in perceived candidate positions, it would have been difficult to establish any causal ordering; perceptions of governmental policies could just as well have been imagined to flow from extensions or projections of the positions espoused by one's preferred candidate. In the case in point, however, it seems reasonable to presume that causal influences flowed from stable, long-standing predispositions to intermediate policy preferences and evaluations of perceived government policy that did not change appreciably during the election year. Subsequently, preferences for policy and policy changes were even more tightly connected to the vote choice by the changes in voters' relative perceptions and evaluations of the candidates.

Clearly, neither stable predispositions nor relatively fixed preferences for policy and policy changes were the causes of *change* in the perceptions of the candidates' policy positions. But those factors did apparently interact with the *events* of the campaign. Unfolding campaign events eventually influenced voters to make changes in their perceptions of candidates' positions as they went through the resolution of conflict en route to an ultimately clarified or reinforced preference for one candidate over the other.

Further Lessons from Earlier Elections

Following *The American Voter,* which was based on the studies of the elections of 1952 and 1956, virtually every study in the Michigan time series has cast new light on our understanding of party identification. We already noted that 1960 produced invaluable evidence of the stability of party identification at the individual as well as at the aggregate level. Panel analyses also demonstrated that party identification was not simply an error-filled synonym for the intended presidential vote, as some early critics had claimed.

Moreover, the intrusion of religion into the presidential politics of 1960 provided a first occasion for demonstrating the usefulness of party identification as a foil for the interpretation of the explanatory roles played by other factors relevant to vote choice. There were those who had noted the 1960 victory of the Catholic Kennedy, and the vote among Catholics that favored him overwhelmingly, and had concluded, therefore, that Kennedy had won the election because of the support of co-religionists.

The introduction of party identification into the analysis of that election conveyed a radically different story. True, Kennedy received a larger Catholic vote than had Adlai Stevenson, the Democratic candidate in 1956; it was larger both among Catholics who were Republican party identifiers and among those who were Democratic party identifiers. Among Protestants, however, Nixon received the traditional heavy vote from Republican identifiers and an unusually heavy vote from Democratic Protestants. Moreover, the "defection" rates of Democratic Protestants who voted Republican (after having voted their party line against the Eisenhower landslide of 1956) were strongly correlated with their frequency of church attendance. Almost four out of ten regular church attendants among Protestant Democrats voted for Nixon. Because of sheer numbers, Protestant Democrats for Nixon more than offset the number of Catholic Republicans who voted for Kennedy. We estimated that Kennedy's Catholicism cost him a net loss of some 2 percent of all the votes cast; far from assuring his victory, his religion cost him millions of votes (Converse et al., 1961).[10] Had it not been for the overall preponderance of Democrats among the voters of 1960, Nixon would certainly have won the election. Such a conclusion, however, rests on the assumption that the aggregate effects of short-term factors *other than* religion pretty much balanced out and left party identification (and religion) as explanations of the aggregate result of the election.

Four years later, in 1964, the combination of a great disparity in the appeal of the presidential candidates, coupled with Senator Goldwater's misreading of the ideological temper of the times, again demonstrated that party identification was not at all impervious to the short-term forces of politics. This episode has not been fully exploited for the information it provides regarding the operation of party identification in extreme circumstances. Nevertheless, there are many suggestive leads in the basic descriptive data. There was a surge in Democratic identifications between 1960 and 1964, but it was concentrated among non-Southern non-voters. In the South, the erosion of Democratic strength in party identification continued unabated among voters. The differences associated with political involvement (voting and non-voting) and region will resurface later in this discussion as we argue for specifying the conditions under which generalizations about party identification can be expected to be sustained. But in 1964, outside the South, the disparity in the popularity of presidential candidates led to an electoral landslide as well as to a perturbation in the trend of stable party identification, at least among politically peripheral non-voters.

The chaotic election of 1968 provided another natural experiment in probing the nature of party identification. In that instance, the crucial factors in understanding responsiveness to short-term forces were the age of the voter and the importance of party. We have already mentioned in Chapter 2 the significance of 1968 as a watershed year in American politics; in the present discussion, however, 1968 provides a different insight into how longstanding party identifications may influence voters' decisions. Before the election it was evident that the third-party appeal of the Wallace-Lemay American Independent party extended across the entire age spectrum. Nevertheless, the anti-Black, militaristic platform of their third party apparently appealed more to older voters than to the young. After the election there was still a clear relationship between voters' ages and their support for Wallace and Lemay; however, that relationship had reversed—the support was greatest among the young, and least among the old. Once again, party identification explained the difference. Among Democrats, the Wallace vote was heaviest among young identifiers; defection rates were much lower among older voters, for whom party identification was strong enough to withstand the appeal of the Wallace-Lemay ticket (Converse et al., 1969). This evidence, of course, provided additional support for the larger theory which predicts that the strength of one's partisanship increases with the passage of time. A more complete statement of that argument was presented by Converse in his article entitled "Of Time and Partisan Stability," which incorporated the age of the party system into the theory and drew further lessons about party identification from cross-national comparisons (Converse, 1969).

Incremental progress in the study of party identification can also be noted in connection with the election of 1972. In that election the failure of Democratic leadership to present a viable argument for new policies produced disarray among Democratic party identifiers, which resulted in a pointed demonstration that party loyalty is anything but impervious to short-term forces when confronted with unpopular policies and ineffectual leadership (Miller and Levitin, 1976). The election of 1972 constituted another example where the real world provides the analyst with a natural experiment providing theoretical insights along with practical consequences. Since the real world of politics is shaped by actors who must cope with external events as they strive to influence the authoritative allocation of values, the theoretician or analyst must be patient. Crucial tests of theories seldom occur in the sequence that would be optimal for theory building. When such tests do occur, however, their results can have a verisimilitude that is missing in the most elaborate of contrived laboratory experiments.

There is a sense in which the challenge confronting the political analyst is much like that facing the astronomer. The research plan must prepare the way for observation and measurement, but that which is to be observed and measured is clearly beyond the control of the researcher. When the researcher's plans and expectations are confounded, the only course is to wait for "nature" to create further experimental situations that may test hypotheses about the reasons for the confound. But in the study of elections, as in the study of the stars, programmatic research can also rest on the re-examination of recorded observations from prior inquiries. Indeed, much that we have learned about party identification has become evident only as we assemble the full portfolio of data from previous studies.

Clarifying the Role of Party Identification

Contemporary discussion of the nature of party identification—its origins and its consequences—has been informed by an assortment of contributions. Some have been predominantly conceptual or theoretical (Beck, 1974, 1976; Converse and Pierce, 1987); most have combined analytic modeling with reconceptualization or conceptual elaboration (Converse, 1976; Page and Jones, 1979; Converse and Markus, 1979; Weisberg, 1980; Fiorina, 1981; Franklin and Jackson, 1983; Miller, 1992); still other contributions have relied heavily on innovations in measurement (Carmines, McIver, and Stimson, 1987; Green and Palmquist, 1990; Mattei and Niemi, 1991; Abramson and Ostrom, 1991) or on the exploration of unique data sources (Jennings and Niemi, 1968, 1981; Jennings and Markus, 1984; Beck and Jennings, 1991; Teixeira, 1992; Abramson and Claggett, 1989).

Here we shall try to identify the conditions under which our operational definition produces evidence that accords with our notions of the nature of party identification. A basic difference from virtually all of the work cited previously has to do with the various populations of citizens that we select for special attention. For example, when considering the relative stability of party identification, we will take account of the changes in the aggregate national distributions of party identification during the massive realignment that swept the Southern states between 1960 and 1990. Taking account of this evidence of change in the South, as well as the contrast provided by the absence of similar change elsewhere, will give us a more complex sense of the conditions under which party identification is, or is not, to be treated as a relatively stable, enduring predisposition.

Another such specification is that provided by what we know about differences between voters and non-voters. We know that there are year-by-year variations in the similarity of the party identifications among voters and non-voters, with no obvious generic reason for the variations. For example, it is not clear whether non-voters simply manifest a greater volatility among politically less involved citizens, or whether they are prone to more measurement error in their responses to survey questions, or whether some more substantive difference separates them from voters. Nevertheless, the evidence is clear (as in 1964) that patterns for voters and non-voters differ. This must certainly mean that interpretations of the role of party identification in shaping national election outcomes will miss the mark if attributes of non-voters are not separated out and thus prevented from coloring the interpretation of partisan divisions among voters.

Following the lead of Abramson, we will also separately analyze Black and non-Black voters (Abramson and Claggett, 1991; Converse, 1979). Just as we have recognized different temporal patterns in the mobilization of Black, White, and Hispanic turnout, so we must recognize the unique political circumstances that have created ethnic differences in party identification. Given the dramatic changes that followed from federal legislation in the mid-1960s, changes in Black party identification may add to our general understanding of the functional relationship between mobilization of turnout and the acquisition of political orientations. But unless given separate (and equal) treatment, racial differences and changing patterns among Black citizens will only confound national analyses that do not differentiate the party identification of Blacks from non-Blacks. In sum, in order to avoid or minimize confounding conditions, simultaneous and coordinate consideration must be given (1) to all Black voters, (2) to Southern non-Black voters, and (3) to non-Southern non-Black voters. (Because of the limited sample size, Black voters will not be subdivided by region.) Inasmuch as our interest is confined to the ultimate explication of the *voters'* choices in recent presidential elections, we will center our inquiry on these three categories of voters.

The evolving treatment of party identification, its measurement and meaning, can be seen as an extended case study in the problem of providing an operational definition that then permits the delineation of circumstances to test the meaningfulness of the concept as measured. The present discussion adds to our understanding of party identification by identifying circumstances under which the basic measure of party identification, applied to a significant body of voters, has produced results fully in line with the original concept that it is an enduring predisposition, relatively impervious to changing or election-specific events.[11]

▪ The Distribution of Party Identification

We first draw attention to evidence related to party realignment and the regional contrast, South and North, depicted among White voters in Table 6.1. Between the elections of 1952 and 1980, outside the South, neither men nor women voters revealed any significant change in the net balance of their partisan sentiments across the 30-year interval. This is a remarkable demonstration of stability. For Northern Whites, the "steady state" period of relatively unchanging party identification apparently lasted not 12 years—1952 to 1964—but a full 30 years and was finally interrupted only *after* the first Reagan election.[12]

This extraordinary display of persistence in the net party balance among the Northern White voters, who made up between 75 and 80 percent of all White voters over the past four decades, provides a striking implicit commentary on the literature of the stability of party identification and party alignment. It does not, of course, necessarily negate analyses of short-term fluctuations between the quadrennial readings, although both Green and Palmquist (1990) and Abramson and Ostrom

Table 6.1 Partisan Balance of Party Identification Within Selected Subsets, Groups of Voters and Non-voters,[a] 1952–1992

Election Year	Non-South		South		Nation	
	Men	Women	Men	Women	Blacks	Total
VOTERS						
1952	4	3	58	54	55	14
1956	3	−2	58	38	36	12
1960	3	−2	47	34	32	13
1964	13	11	43	48	73	25
1968	4	4	29	39	89	18
1972	2	1	21	23	68	12
1976	3	−1	23	15	78	12
1980	2	5	6	15	82	14
1984	−8	−2	8	22	72	8
1988	−10	−9	−8	22	75	3
1992	−9	7	−1	11	69	9
% Distribution						
1952	39%	40	8	8	4	100%
1992	31%	34	12	12	12	100%
NON-VOTERS						
1952	25	25	53	51	32	35
1956	13	−4	48	38	29	21
1960	19	14	23	51	17	27
1964	31	38	51	37	57	41
1968	11	19	17	28	72	26
1972	15	15	19	29	53	34
1976	−4	14	17	40	57	21
1980	1	19	30	25	49	22
1984	1	5	17	12	34	11
1988	7	7	20	28	32	18
1992	−5	7	−31	15	42	9
% Distribution						
1952	17%	27	9	23	25	100%
1992	23%	25	18	19	16	100%

a. Each entry is the proportion of Democratic identifiers (strong plus weak) minus (−) the proportion of Republicans identified (strong plus weak). A negative sign indicates a Republican plurality.

(1991) have recently spoken to this point. However, the evidence of pervasive, long-term, aggregate stability outside the South is so dramatic that it would seem to call for a reexamination of many revisionist conclusions about the origins of change in party identification. It calls into question analyses that have, for example, used changes in *national* economic indicators to explain *national* changes in party identification, when electorally relevant change in party identification apparently did not take place outside the South.

Long-term, aggregate stability of party identification outside the South raises more direct questions about the implications of the thesis that party identification changes incrementally as the consequence of prior voting behavior. From 1952 to 1980, according to National Election Studies data, the Northern vote division among White voters averaged 57 percent *Republican*. Despite very large Republican pluralities in virtually every year except 1964, the Republican share of party identifiers did not increase as a simple extrapolation of the work of Markus and Converse (1979) might have suggested.

The same evidence of stability in the partisan balance of party identification calls attention to the absence of any cumulative impact of a series of "running tallies" that should have produced a Republican increment between 1952 and 1980 (Fiorina, 1981). The aggregate stabilities may, of course, conceal compensatory changes that have offset a drift away from the Democrats and into the Republicans' camp. No reasons for, or evidence of, such compensatory, pro-Democratic changes come immediately to mind. Consequently, it seems fair to conclude that the evidence of aggregate stability among non-Black voters outside the South should prompt further study of the dynamics of micro-level change in party identification.[13]

▪ Realignment in the South

Equally clear evidence of the mutability of partisan loyalties is provided by Table 6.1 and its depiction of change among Southern White voters in general, and White Southern males in particular, across the same time span. Apparently the beginning of the end of single-party dominance among Southern White male voters started shortly after the Kennedy election of 1960. By the time of the first Reagan presidency, 20 years later, an 80–20 division favoring the Democratic party had been replaced by near parity for the Republican party. This would seem to be evidence of a classic version of the realignment of partisanship. It was a realignment of massive proportions, involving a Democratic-to-Republican switch of at least 3 out of every 10 Southern non-Black male voters. It was apparently a secular realignment as defined by V. O. Key, Jr. (1959) and introduced in the current discussion by Converse (1976).

Further analysis is needed to determine the relative importance of contributions from conversion, mobilization, and cohort replacement among Southern White voters over the 36 years included in Table 6.1, but the net effect is unmistakable. While conditions outside the South did not provoke any net change in the party alignment of non-Black voters between 1952 and 1980, changes within the South produced a virtual revolution. A closer examination of both sets of circumstances should tell us more about party identifications. Earl Black and Merle Black (1987) have suggested major themes to be explored in the analysis of the South. Outside the South, the suggestion of cohort replacement in the changing composition of the electorate offers a promising first line of inquiry.

▪ The Gender Gap

The possible unitary nature of regional factors capable of producing such party realignment among Southern White male voters is initially reflected in the parallel shift among non-Black Southern female voters across the seven elections between 1952 and 1976. A complicating anomaly then appears. Changes in party identification among Southern female voters after 1976 do not match the pattern of any other set of non-Black voters. This is striking because the other three groupings all reveal a shift to small Republican pluralities at the conclusion of the Reagan era in 1988, while White Southern women continuously exhibited a set of clearly pro-Democratic preferences throughout the 1980s. Their Democratic plurality in 1992 matches the figures from 1980, and, in the meantime, non-Southern women voters have joined in contributing to the gender gap. Why this should be so is not obvious.

The importance of explaining the male-female differences among non-Black Southern voters is accentuated by the realization that those differences in the 1980s are primarily responsible for the much discussed "gender gap" for those years (Frankovic, 1982). Even without fully understanding these gender differences, it seems possible to conclude that the appearance of the gender gap in the Reagan years was not as much a function of a liberal, pro-Democratic growth in the partisan sentiments of women as a function of the sharply conservative pro-Republican move among men (Wirls, 1986). At least until 1992 the Republicans did not have a new problem with women so much as the Democrats have had a continuing problem among men. And once regional data are sorted out, the specification of the gender problem of the 1980s is largely confined to the South.

▪ African-American Voters

Turning away from region and gender differences within White voters to consider the partisan sympathies of the African-American citizenry, the separation of Black voters and Black non-voters from the remainder of the electorate highlights the recent contributions of African-American voters to partisan national elections. The apparent impact of the Kennedy-Johnson era was more dramatic among Black voters than non-voters. And, given their mobilization beginning in the mid-1960s, Black voters across the nation were ultimately only slightly fewer in number than were Southern, White male voters. As a consequence, the fact that Black voters across the nation more than doubled their margin of support for the Democratic party between 1960 and 1968 by itself more than offset, in sheer numbers, the 50 percent decline in the Democratic plurality among Southern White males.

The countervailing moves within these two politically significant segments of the electorate underline the hazards of drawing conclusions based on national aggregations. National totals did not suggest any net change in the national balance of party identifications between 1956 and 1980. This is true, in general, because the precipitous pro-Republican shift in the White (male) South was counterbalanced by the large growth in Democratic pluralities among newly mobilized Black citizens.[14]

A suggestion that variations in the nature and meaning of party identification may be associated with variations in political awareness and involvement is provided by the comparison of voters with non-voters among Blacks. Although changes within each group were similar between 1960 and 1964, sharp differences appear after 1968. Those differences are accentuated by the contrary movements between 1984 and 1988. It was Black *non-voters,* but not Black voters, who contributed to the aggregate evidence suggestive of party realignment during the Reagan years.[15]

▪ Voters and Non-Voters

More generally, the analytic separation of voters from non-voters exposes relatively well-ordered evidence of stability among Northern White voters, stability that contrasts with greater volatility among Northern non-voters. Both in the unevenness of patterns of change across time and in the variability of gender differences, party identification among non-voters seems less a matter of stable, long-term predispositions and more a matter of responsiveness to short-term, election-by-election fluctuation of circumstances than is true for voters. A similar contrast appears both among Black citizens and among Southern Whites, although it is less striking on first inspection because of the pervasive patterns of change within these groups. In investigating the reason for these differences between voters and non-voters, it should also be recognized that the differences may contain the basis for reconciling other scholars' conclusions about the apparent general responsiveness of party identification to short-term influences with the new evidence of interelection stability among Northern White voters.

▪ The Reagan Realignment

As a final comment on Table 6.1, it may be noted that the particular disaggregations that are so revealing of different patterns of stability and change between 1952 and 1980 do not serve particularly well to cast new light on the more recent changes in the distribution of party identifications that reflect a limited national realignment during the Reagan era. The 1980–84 and 1984–88 changes in party balance were primarily a Northern, White phenomenon and were not apparent at all among Black voters or Southern White women voters. A detailed analysis of the realignment of the Reagan years, to be developed in the next chapter, indicates two quite distinct stages of change in which Reagan's personal leadership and then his partisan ideology first moved the younger, less politicized voters and then the older, more politicized ones into the Republican party. In neither stage of the realignment after 1980 were race, region, or gender as relevant as age, ideology, and political involvement (Miller, 1992). The narrowest point to be drawn from this introductory analysis is, quite simply, that systematic inspection of disaggregated time series data may have been a good starting point for questioning much conventional wisdom about party realignment and the stability of party identification, but it does not provide answers to many of the questions that it raises or that we have posed. The broader points of theoretical interest in the analysis are the many implications for shaping future inquiry into the nature of party identification and into the conditions that facilitate its stability, or provoke change.

▪ Party Identification and the Vote

Just as conventional wisdom about the stability of Democratic and Republican party identifications encouraged faulty interpretations of changing *distributions* in party identification, questions have also been raised concerning the meaningfulness of party identification as a *determinant* of the vote during the 1970s and 1980s. It seems reasonable to presume that two notable deviations in the correlation of party identification with preferences for presidential candidates, first in 1964 and then again in 1972, have been the remembered evidence for presuming a generally diminished importance for party following the elections of the 1950s (Miller et al., 1976). A systematic examination of the simple national bivariate relationships between party identification and vote choice over time, presented in Table 6.2, documents both episodes of declining correlation; it also documents the atypicality of the 1964 and 1972 elections.

The left-hand column of Table 6.2 reveals only two elections in which the bivariate correlation falls well below the 10-election average of .67. They were the Johnson-Goldwater contest, in which Republicans voted against their conservative senator from Arizona, and the Democrats' disastrous experiment with the radical-liberal McGovern challenge to an immensely popular Republican incumbent, Richard Nixon. After having risen steadily from the 1972 low, the party identification/vote choice correlation was up to postwar highs by 1984 and 1988. There is no indication from any recent election that party identification is less relevant to the vote decision in the 1980s than it was three decades earlier.

Table 6.2 Correlations of Party Identification with
the Presidential Vote Choice, 1952–1988

Election Year	Bivariate	Partial[a]
1952	.69	.64
1956	.67	.65
1960	.68	.60
1964	.57	.48
1968	.69	.55
1972	.52	.43
1976	.69	.64
1980	.73	.63
1984	.74	.65
1988	.75	.68
Mean	.67	.60

a. Partial correlation with controls on race, education,
gender, religion, income, and union membership.

As a further test of the constancy of correlations with the vote, the second column of Table 6.2 presents the *partial* correlations of party identifications and vote choice after the simultaneous imposition of controls on race, gender, religion, education, income, and union membership. The dual message of the partial correlations is clear: (1) year after year very little of the party-vote correlation can be considered the spurious consequence of their sharing these common antecedents; and (2) the passage of time has seen no diminution in the total effect of party identification on vote choice.

The causal role of party identification in the shaping of the attitudes and perceptions that are the immediate or proximate causes of a voter's preference for one candidate over the other has been a continuous topic of inquiry among students of electoral behavior. Evidence that the causal role of party identification as an antecedent to the vote is largely indirect through its influence on policy preferences and appraisals of presidential performance and candidate traits is provided by Shanks and Miller (1990) in their analyses of the Reagan elections. Over time, the *correlational* evidence is stronger, not weaker, for assigning a major explanatory/causal role for party identification in the context of presidential elections (Beck, 1976, 1982; Fiorina, 1977, 1981; Markus and Converse,

1979; Page and Jones, 1979; Petrocik, 1981; Wattenberg, 1984; Whiteley, 1988; Jacoby, 1988).

▪ Party Voting

The more general conclusion that there has been no across-time decrease in the extent to which the national presidential vote is a party vote is neither challenged nor further illuminated by our disaggregation of voters by gender, region, or race. Year in and year out, women have been no more likely than men to cast a party vote *nor* to defect and cross party lines to vote for a president. After 1960, the Black vote was as unwaveringly Democratic as were Black voters' partisan loyalties. And within regional comparisons, as with the others, party voting in the 1980s was every bit as common—or as uncommon—as it had been in the 1950s. Voting in line with one's party in 1984 and 1988 was as common as it had been in 1952 and 1956.

This conclusion holds for partisans on both sides. Republicans in the South have an almost perfect record; they have reported voting for Republican candidates an average of at least 95 percent of the time from the days of Eisenhower and Nixon to the era of Reagan and Bush. Outside the South the Republican vote has been slightly more variable, but Northern Republicans have reported more than 90 percent support for their party's presidential candidates. The most noticeable, if still minor, occasions for defections came in 1964 and 1976, but the Republican figures for 1984 and 1988, for both South and non-South, and among both men and women, were fully equal to their reported party votes in 1952 and 1956.[16]

The record of Democratic identifiers at the polls is a persistent record of substantially *less* party support than given by Republicans, and it is somewhat more varied than the record of Republicans. Nevertheless, the Democratic patterns of regional party voting do not appear to have changed at all over three decades. Democrats, regardless of either region or sex, were just as faithful—or unfaithful—to party in their 1984 and 1988 votes as in earlier decades. There is no evidence pertaining to either party in either region of any difference in the level of party voting among party identifiers that would distinguish the 1980s from the 1950s.

There are real-world consequences of this observation that extend well beyond what it says to political scientists about the more or less enduring nature and role of party identification. The data presented in Table 6.1, as well as the earlier discussion, indicate that Democrats quite apparently declined in numerical strength in the South between 1960 and 1980, and across the entire nation during the Reagan era, 1980–1988. This happened without the emergence of greater loyalty or more faithful voting performance from those who *remained* as Democrats. At the same time, Republicans increased their numbers among party identifiers without suffering any dilution of party loyalty at the polls. Even in the changing South, the party identification/vote choice relationship has been stable for more than three decades for *both* Democratic and Republican identifiers. Thus it would appear that there as elsewhere, typically less-than-faithful Democrats have converted to become typically faithful Republicans. Because Republican identifiers are substantially more faithful party voters than are Democratic identifiers, both elements in the exchange argue a greater increase in the election-day strength of Republicans than is implied by the simple distributional shifts in party identifications. Even though a massive regional realignment, followed by a limited national realignment, has cost the Democrats much of their one-time advantage in the distribution of party identification, the implications of party identification for the presidential vote have not changed materially with the passage of time and the change of political circumstance. And in 1984 and 1988, the Republican ticket benefited doubly from the leveling of the partisan playing field.

▪ Summary

Persuasive evidence that party identification is a long-term predisposition, largely exogenous to the vote decisions within a given election campaign, is provided by the overwhelming stability of identifications among non-Southern, non-Black voters from 1952 through 1980. Evidence that party identification is not impervious to changing political contexts is provided by changes in Black identification following the Civil Rights and Voting Acts of 1964–1965, and by a politically very significant realignment in the South throughout the decades of the 1960s, 1970s, and 1980s. One by-product of Southern realignments was the emergence of a gender gap as men became more Republican and less Democratic than women. A limited national realignment occurred between 1980 and 1988, a result of Ronald Reagan's appeal as a clearly conservative Republican President. Neither the national realignment of the 1980s nor the Southern realignment across three decades resulted in any change in the association between party identification and partisan choices at the polls. Voting Republicans are massively loyal partisans, seldom crossing party lines; voting Democrats are less constant in their party voting, by a substantial margin in the North and by a very large margin in the South.

7

★ ★ ★

Realignment and Generational Change in Party Identification

In 1952, when the University of Michigan's Survey Research Center was conducting its first major study of electoral behavior in an American presidential election, V. O. Key, Jr. released the third edition of his classic text, *Politics, Parties, and Pressure Groups* (Key, 1952). In the opening paragraphs of the chapter entitled "Electoral Behavior: Inertia and Reaction," Key offered two broad conclusions characterizing the American electorate: "In substantial degree the electorate remains persistent in its partisan attachments. The time of casting a ballot is not a time of decision for many voters; it is merely an occasion for the reaffirmation of a partisan faith of long standing. . . . A second main characteristic evident in electoral behavior is that under some conditions voters do alter their habitual partisan affiliations." Key then asked: "To what conditions is their shift in attitude a response?" Latter-day political scientists have spent the better part of four decades testing these two conclusions and trying to answer Key's single question. Under the impetus of the Michigan restatement, "party identification" replaced "habitual partisan affiliation," but the basic terms of the query into the nature of the citizens' enduring partisan attachments have remained very much as Key identified them.

Results of the first three major Michigan studies of the national electorate were entirely in line with Key's first assertion and his preoccupation with persistence and inertia as attributes of mass electoral behavior. Bolstered by a panel study that plotted individual change over time, national survey data from 1952 to 1960 documented a great persistence in citizens' identifications with the Democratic and Republican parties. As we have noted, there was a brief upturn in Democratic support in 1964, but it disappeared four years later, drawing perhaps too little attention to a condition under which partisan attitudes shifted. Other than that temporary perturbation, Democrats enjoyed a consistent 15- to 20-point edge over Republicans for some thirty years, from 1952 to 1980. Throughout much of the same period, the measures of the strength or intensity of partisan attachments seemed to confirm the thesis of partisan stability; in election after election until 1968, strong identifiers outnumbered non-partisans by virtually identical margins of about 25 percentage points.

Without destroying the suspense or giving away our story line—since the latter is not without its complexities—it is fair to note that the first period in our study—1952 through 1960—is now often referred to as the "steady state" era (Converse, 1976). During this era, a series of inquiries established party identification as distinctly different from the partisan character of the single vote, both in concept and in operational measure. The role of party identification was anticipated as a predisposition that powerfully influences citizens' perceptions and judgments (Campbell, Converse, Miller, and Stokes, 1960). In some subsequent reifications (or glorifications of more sober analysis), party identification was sometimes referred to as the "Unmoved Mover," or the "First Cause" of electoral behavior. Certainly, the evidence appeared to be all that Key could have hoped for as confirmation of his hypothesis that partisan attachments had great stability at both the individual as well as the aggregate level.

During that same time period, the theme of party realignment attracted the attention of many political analysts. This was particularly so among Republican enthusiasts who saw in the Eisenhower victories (and in the initial Republican congressional successes that accompanied them) the possibility of a resurgence of the Republican party. The narrow Kennedy victory in 1960, in the face of a presumably daunting Democratic plurality in the eligible electorate, added fuel to the Republican fire. This led, at least in part, to the Republican nomination of Goldwater in 1964 on the premise that he would mobilize latent conservative Republican sympathies and bring an end to the Democratic hegemony (Converse, Clausen, and Miller, 1965).

Although the Goldwater candidacy was something less than a triumph of Republican expectations, his Southern strategy did foreshadow the growth of Republicanism in the changing South. Another four years later the Republican Nixon *was* elected, and, for the first time since systematic, modern measurement had dominated social scientific analysis of electoral behavior, the bedrock of party identification cracked. Because the mobilization of Black voters concealed the realignment under way in the South, the national partisan balance was not disturbed in national aggregate estimates. But the *strength* or the intensity, of partisanship declined nationally. First in 1968, again in 1972, and finally again in 1976, each successive reading taken at election time revealed fewer strong partisans and more citizens devoid of any partisan preference.[1]

▪ Realignment, Dealignment, and Non-alignment

For two decades the literature on party identification was dominated by various interpretations of this sequence of apparent decay in partisan preferences. The signs of weakened party identification in the early 1970s spawned a sometimes frenetic discussion of partisan dealignment and realignment. As with alternatives to the alarmist interpretations of declining voter turnout during the same period, we believe that the aggregate contours of national change in the strength of party identification can be satisfactorily described by the parsimonious theory of generational replacement, while bolstering the belief in the persistence of party identification as an enduring long-term predisposition characteristic of most voters. The first *national* decline in the aggregate strength of party identification after 1952 occurred in 1968, coincident with the retreat among White citizens (largely non-voters) outside the South from the partisan Democratic high of 1964. The drop in aggregate measures of the strength of party identification was apparent in national estimates and was widely interpreted as an indication that partisans were rejecting old loyalties and taking on the role of non-partisans.[2]

A relatively simple cohort analysis of changes in the relationship between a citizen's age and party identification might have forestalled— or at least modified—such interpretations. It is true that a decline in the aggregate strength of "partisanship" was reflected across the board in 1968 in a *temporary* diminution of partisan intensity among *older* citizens as well as younger. But the portent for the future, and the reason for the apparent decline in party fortunes, were contained largely in the contrast between the party identifications of the youngest and the old-est cohorts. In keeping with established regularities, which had found strength or intensity of party identification to be a function of increasing age, the oldest cohorts in 1968 had the strongest partisan attachments. Their "replacements," the young cohorts newly eligible to vote, not only followed the pattern of having the weakest partisan attachments, but in 1968 and again in 1972 and 1976, they far exceeded their counterparts from previous years in the extent to which they were *non-partisans*—they neither identified with nor had any preference for one party over the other.

Throughout the 1950s and early 1960s, the youngest members of the eligible electorate had been less partisan than their elders, but they nevertheless had always counted many more strong partisans than non-partisans among their ranks, usually by a margin of 10 to 20 percentage points (compared to margins of 40–55 percentage points among the oldest cohorts). In 1968, however, for the first time (at least since 1952), the cohort of those newly eligible to vote for President actually contained more non-partisans (with no preferences) than strong party identifiers. Four years later, the recently eligible cohorts—this leading edge of the post-New Deal generation of voters—counted among its members even fewer party identifiers.

To the extent that 1968 ushered in an anti-party era with weak party control in government and weak party loyalties in the electorate, the origin of the latter was immediately and massively evident among the young. According to the Jennings data, the cohort of high school seniors from 1965 reflected an even lower incidence of party identification in 1972 than they had seven years earlier (Jennings and Markus, 1984). However, the impact of the political turmoil of the times was much less dramatic in the partisanship of the middle-aged and older cadres. Indeed, by 1976, the strength of party sentiments among citizens over age 50 had returned pretty much to the levels of 1960–1964. However, among the very large number of citizens under 40, non-partisans continued to outnumber strong partisans. In 1976, these younger cohorts made up approximately half of the total electorate. The contribution of these younger electors to national estimates of the strength of partisan senti-ments was the primary source of the nationwide aggregate decline in strength of party identification that continued until sometime after the election of 1976 (Miller and Shanks, 1982).

Examining the full set of four-year cohort data (Table 7.1) permits one to follow the entry of each new cohort into presidential politics across the 40 years and 11 presidential elections covered by the Michigan data. It seems reasonable to conclude that the traumas of the late 1960s and early 1970s—failed presidencies, international frustrations, domestic turmoil, and the disruptive effects of civil rights protests, anti-Vietnam demonstrations, and countercultural happenings—did initiate a *period* effect felt throughout the electorate. So, for a pointed bit of evidence, even though in 1972 and 1976 the strength of partisan sentiments among the older cohorts rebounded, during the 1980s those sentiments still did not reach levels comparable to those set by the oldest cohorts of the same age 30 years earlier.

At the same time, the impact of the "anti-politics" decades seems to have produced an enduring generational effect as well: the young reacted to the events of the period much more sharply than did the older cohorts. In summary, it was the reluctance of the young to accept partisan ties—not the lasting rejection of loyalties once held by their elders—that produced the indicators of apparent dealignment in the mid-1970s.

This is clearly of a piece with the generational discontinuity in voter turnout of the same period and among the same cohorts. The timing of the changes in the national parameters of turnout and partisanship was slightly different. The high water mark for turnout was 1960; the peak in the national mean of the strength of partisanship came in 1964. Turnout rates declined slowly in 1964 and 1968. Coincident with the lowering of the voting age to 18 years in 1972, turnout rates then dropped more than five points and continued to drop every year until 1984, resuming the decline and hitting bottom in 1988. Strength of partisanship, on the other hand, as Table 7.1 shows, plunged in 1968 from the plateau established in the 1950s. Strength of partisanship dropped again in 1972 and bottomed out in 1976. From 1976 to 1988, as turnout continued to *drop*, partisanship was *on the rise*, although it recovered only 12 points out of the 21-point drop between 1964 and 1976.

Nevertheless, throughout the twenty years from 1972 to 1992, the discontinuity between the New Deal and post-New Deal generations was evident both for party identification and for voter turnout. Inter-generational differences in turnout were greatest among citizens not identified

Table 7.1 Strength of Partisanship, by Four-Year Age Cohorts, 1952–1992

Age in 1952	Year of First Vote for President	1952	1956	1960	1964	1968	1972	1976	1980	1984	1988	1992	Age in 1992
	1992											−1	18–21
	1988										5	1	22–25
	1984									0	6	4	26–29
	1980								−5	6	10*	11*	30–32
	1976							−9	−8	10	14	18	33–36
	1972						−10	−3	0	11	14	22	37–40
	1972						−1	−8	2	9	17	21*	41–44
	1968					−4	−4	−1	10	10	16	20	45–48
	1964				16	−3	1	0	4	10	18*	18	49–52
	1960			14	20	17	1	3	18	23	25*	27	53–56
	1956		15	23	23	19	3	6	23	25	31	34	57–60
21–24	1952	23	13	17	25	15*	12	11	23	36	35	28*	61–64
25–28	1948	24	23	28	29	11	20	25	18	23	28	27	65–68
29–32	1944	23	23	24*	24	12	20	21	20	31	31	38	69–72
33–36	1940	16	22	27	30	13	19	25	27	35	34	33	73–76
37–40	1936	30	24	29	27	27	28	20	25	31	41	37	77–80
41–44	1932	26	31	32*	37	30	23	23*	42	40	26	43	81+
45–48	1928	25	32	24	36*	32	24	40	33	34	38		
49–52	1924	36	36*	38	37	36	34	35*	40	40			
53–56	1920	38	35	40	30	34	37	36	30				
57–60	1916	44	40*	32	53	43	31	32					
61–64	1912	37	40*	23	50	43	37						
65–68	1908	36	38	53	42	35							
69–72	1904	45	51	54									
73–76	1900	33	47										
77–80	1896	38											
National Totals		29	27	26	30	19	12	9	13	18	21	17	

*Entries are differences between the proportion of strong party identifiers and the proportion of Independent-Independents. The entries of 16 cells (out of 178), marked by *, have been "smoothed" by replacing those entries with the average of those in adjoining years and cohorts, when that single entry was markedly inconsistent with the entries for adjoining years and cohorts. The assigned values for these cells, reading by column, are: 36 was 24, 40 was 29, 40 was 52, 24 was 11, 32 was 19, 24 was 11, 32 was 19, 36 was 52, 15 was 27, 38 was 34, 23 was 11, 35 was 25, 10 was 17, 18 was 32, 25 was 18, 11 was 3, 21 was 11, and 28 was 21. This smoothing attempts to remove the most obvious instances of sampling error by substituting innocuous entries for those that are otherwise anomalous. The data are all based on the Michigan SRC/CPS/NES data collections.

with either party, and the impact of the presence or absence of party identification on turnout, within generations, was greater in the post-New Deal generation than with the New Deal cohorts. Conversely, the relation between voting or non-voting and having or not having a partisan identification was much stronger in the post-New Deal generation.

Noting the small disjunctures in timing of changes in identification and turnout indicates that we have more to learn about rates of change, and conditions for change, in these two phenomena that are so basic to individual electoral behavior. We know little about what determines the rate at which adults with no partisan preference acquire a party identification, or what determines change in the rate at which eligible citizens turn out to vote.

The confusion engendered by early misinterpretations of "dealignment" was compounded by unrecognized differences in partisanship between voters and non-voters. In the steady-state elections of 1952–1964, strong partisans among voters outnumbered those with no partisan preference by a ratio of 39 percent to 7 percent; among non-voters, on average, across the four elections, 26 percent declared themselves strong partisans and 8 percent had no partisan preference. At the height of the excitement about dealignment, from 1968 to 1976, the ratio of strong partisans to non-partisans among voters was still a robust 30 percent to 10 percent; however, that ratio among non-voters had actually reversed to 16 percent strong partisans and 19 percent with no partisan preference. The high point of contrast occurred in 1976, when strong partisans among *voters* still outnumbered non-partisans by a ratio of 28 to 11, but that ratio was reversed, 12 strong party identifiers to every 22 non-partisans, among *non-voters*. The contrast in 1976 was, of course, occasioned in part by the disproportionate incidence of the young among the non-voters. In the elections of the 1980s, the ratio among voters was still 35 percent with strong preference to 8 percent with no preference; and for non-voters, it was 18 percent with strong preference to 17 percent with no preference. There thus *was* some modest temporary ebb and flow in the aggregate indicators of the strength of partisanship among voters; among non-voters, however, the years of disturbance seem to have had a more lasting effect, a "period effect" on the strength of their partisanship.

The dramatic decline in the intensity of partisan sentiments that began in 1968 and persisted through the 1980s occurred primarily among non-voters, who did not participate in the presidential elections of the period. The point is that the cry of alarm that "the partisan sky was falling," with all of its strong implications for the future of the electoral process, was occasioned by indicators emanating primarily from non-participants in presidential politics. A "dealignment" of these inert non-participants might also have deserved comment and even some analytic thought, but unfortunately most analysts and commentators shared the mistaken belief that future elections would no longer be shaped by a continuation of the party identifications of the past. As a result, the diagnosis—alienation of the voters—and the prognosis—realignment of partisanship at the polls—were both flawed because the *non-voters* were largely the source of the alarming (or promising) indicators of impending change.

Moreover, those arguing the rejection and disintegration of two-party politics did not anticipate the resurgence, from 1976 through 1988, of the strength of partisanship. That pervasive upturn since the 1970s has been led by the same young cohorts who were so heavily non-partisan at their original entry into the electorate. As the political climate normalized, the younger cohorts who contributed so much to the apparent national dealignment experienced a dramatic increase in both the incidence and intensity of partisan sentiments in the elections of the 1980s. Their level of party affiliation by 1988 remained much below the norm we now associate with their generational counterparts from the 1950s, but this is because they started from such an abnormally low level when they first entered the electorate. These cohorts have in fact made a large contribution to the national indications of renewed partisanship.

In a striking reversal from 1976, strong partisans in 1988 outnumbered non-partisans among all but the youngest cohorts by larger margins (14 or 15 percentage points) than non-partisans had outnumbered strong partisans (9 or 10 percentage points) among the same cohorts just 12 years earlier (see Table 7.1). This change had a major impact on national parameters, because by 1988 the post-1976 cohorts constituted more than 40 percent of the total electorate. From another perspective provided by Table 7.1, between 1976 and 1992 the eight youngest cohorts *from the 1976 electorate* increased their strength of partisanship by an average of 21 percentage points; among the remaining six oldest cohorts, strength of partisanship went up only 7 percentage points. During the same time, the composition of the electorate continued to change because the oldest cohorts, whose feelings of party loyalty also continued to strengthen as they aged, were leaving the electorate. The departure of these strong identifiers slowed the overall rate of recovery in national estimates of the strength of partisanship, which otherwise would have reflected more clearly the increase in partisanship of the younger cohorts since 1976.

In sum, many analysts mistakenly interpreted the aggregate indications of declining national strength of party identification in 1972 and 1976 as indicators of impending widespread party realignment. An actual *reduction* of intensity of *individual* partisan commitments between 1964 and 1976 was real within the four youngest cohorts, but that reduction was demonstrably limited in magnitude and constituted a very brief episode for the older members of the electorate. The turmoil of the late 1960s and the political failures of the 1970s and 1980s delayed the development of party loyalties among the younger members of the electorate. The magnitude of that delay was extensive among cohorts that had been a large and rapidly growing part of the electorate. As a consequence, their contribution to changes in aggregate national partisanship has been largely unrecognized and unappreciated.

▪ Party Alignment, 1952–1980[3]

Fortunately for the stability of the country, it was largely political scientists and not national political leaders who reacted to the apparent decline in the fortunes of partisanship among the electorate. Political scientists, however, made the most of it, and some made far too much of it (Burnham, 1975). Even though persuasive evidence of a national party realignment was not to appear for another 20 years, the literature devoted to parties, elections, and electoral behavior, from 1968 on, was replete with analysis and discourse on party dealignment and realignment. When such analysis rested on a proper disaggregation of national totals and the examination of subsets of citizens experiencing real change under local political conditions, the facts are not in dispute. Change *was* occurring in the South (Beck, 1976). Hindsight makes it particularly clear that change in party identification had begun among White southerners as early as 1960 and was simply accentuated and accelerated in the late 1960s under the combined impetus of the Goldwater candidacy and the Johnson promotion of civil rights. Legislation such as the Voting Rights Acts of 1964 and 1965 was, of course, only a part of Johnson's vision of the Great Society. However, that legislation, along with the economic and foreign policies of the Democratic party leaders in the 1970s and 1980s, discouraged Democratic loyalties in the conservative South (Black and Black, 1987).

The most vivid contrast between the changes occurring in the South and the virtual total absence of change outside the South is provided in the regional comparison of White male voters, shown in Table 6.1 in the previous chapter. During the 1950s, the one-party nature of the post–Civil War South was reflected in the numbers of self-declared Democrats, who outnumbered Republicans among Southern White male voters by almost 7 to 1.[4] Twenty years later, the McGovern candidacy of 1972 saw that margin reduced from 42 points to 21 points; and, after another 20 years, 1992 found a virtual dead heat. The multifaceted realignment described by Black and Black continued relentlessly through Reagan's second candidacy (Black and Black, 1987, chap. 11). The Democratic candidacies of Johnson and Carter apparently slowed the tides of change without stemming them.

Outside the South, there is no evidence among men or women voters of a trend either away from the Democrats or toward the Republicans until 1984. Johnson's election in 1964 precipitated a brief surge of Democratic sympathies that was immediately followed by a decline or a return to "normalcy" among White voters. Even so, the two regional patterns stand in stark contrast to each other.

The changing distributions of the party identifications of Black citizens is, of course, a story unto itself. The figures in Table 6.1 in the previous chapter understate the spectacular changes in the contributions made by Blacks to recent political history, because they do not reflect the changes in the politicization and mobilization of Blacks as voters during the 1960s. Even without assessing their enlarged contribution to the active electorate, the dramatic shift in partisan balance among Blacks illustrates the real as well as symbolic contribution of the Johnson civil rights policies.

Despite occasional election day evidence of some resurgence of Republican affinities, and despite reports of increased Republican organizational strength in the South (Huckshorn and Bibby, 1983), the dominance of Democrats over Republicans in the eligible electorate across the remainder of the nation scarcely wavered throughout the 1960s or

1970s. The election and re-election of Richard Nixon in 1968 and 1972 meant that the Republicans had won four of the last six presidential elections; yet the data on the underlying partisan balance of party identifications did not change. Not even in 1980, with Ronald Reagan making it five out of eight wins for Republican presidential candidates, and with another Republican landslide making history with the defeat of an incumbent (Democratic) President, was there a suggestion of basic changes in partisan sentiments outside the South.

In order to reconcile all of the evidence of stability and change in party identification and in the vote from 1952 through 1980, it is necessary to conduct separate analyses. First, we need to ascertain the *directional balance* of party identification between Democrats and Republicans; and second, we need to study changes in the *strength* of party identification, the ratio of strong partisans to non-partisans.

▪ Generational Replacement and Changes in National Estimates of the Balance of Party Identification

In the elections of 1952, 1956, and 1960—aptly named by Converse the "steady state" period in contemporary politics—the then-established differences between the highly competitive two-party politics of the North and the one-party Democratic politics of the South were dramatically apparent. As Table 6.1 revealed, Democrats outside the South outnumbered Republicans among non-Black voters by a persistent but only wafer-thin margin that endured for three decades, embracing every election from 1952 through 1980. This fact went virtually unnoticed and therefore has received scant attention in most analyses of party identification as an element in voting behavior.

By the election of 1988, the partisan division among Southern male voters had come to be indistinguishable from that of Northern male voters. The erosion of the Democratic margin among Southern women at first equaled that among Southern men during the six elections from 1952 to 1972, but then the erosion of Democratic sympathies stopped. Since 1972, the standing division of party identification among Southern women has varied somewhat but has consistently given the Democrats a 15- to 20-point edge. Nevertheless, the aggregate division in the South, including both men and women, found the Democratic lead in sympathies cut from an average of some 55 points in 1952 to no more than

10 points in 1980 (Black and Black, 1960). These patterns and their effects on national parameters had gone unrecognized and therefore unappreciated for their contribution to erroneous depictions of the nature of party identification as an element of American electoral behavior.

Before considering further the realignment of national partisan sympathies, it is useful to reflect on the implications of the period effects and generational differences that have been suggested. The very idea of cohort analysis emphasizes the possible consequences of compositional change in the electorate during a period of political turbulence that is exacerbated by rapid growth of the electorate. However, except for noting the rapid if ultimately incomplete rejuvenation of partisanship among older voters between 1972 and 1976, a focus on the changing composition of the electorate begs the direct question of our basic interest in individual-level stability and change in partisanship.

In approaching the question of stability and change in partisanship, we should first note that the generational differences that appeared rather suddenly in 1968 suggest that we should modify some of the traditional as well as the revisionist notions of the origins of party identification. Historically, party identification was thought to have been altered by national traumas—watershed events such as the Civil War or the Great Depression. The lasting effects of such realigning epochs were thought to be carried by the parents' influence on the social and political attitudes of the successor generations.

The evidence of cohort differences in partisanship would, of course, be consonant with the thesis that new disruptions of the party system simply accelerated the decay of family traditions and familial transmission of party loyalties. But there was more to it than that. The very abruptness of the cohort differences that appeared in 1968 (documented in Table 7.1) suggests a very active intrusion of new events on the process of the acquisition of partisanship among the young. The sharp decline in transmission of partisanship that began in 1968 and lasted through 1976 stands in sharp contrast to the "steady state" maintenance of identification among the older cohorts. This disruption in familial transmission may or may not have lasting effects leading to real generational discontinuities in the partisanship of the electorate. It certainly produced short-term change not anticipated in the early theories of political socialization. In addition, the rapid recovery of partisanship among the older cohorts, with a much slower rate of development and growth in the younger (filial) generations, has created a generational gap that belies a pervasive influence of the older on the younger (Jennings and Niemi, 1981). In short, whatever the role of the family in shaping and preserving party traditions, the events of the late 1960s and early 1970s had an impact of their own on the partisan predispositions of the younger cohorts then entering the electorate. Those most affected were not *re*aligned, not even *de*aligned; they simply entered the electorate more often *un*aligned, with no partisan preference.

Moreover, the immediacy of that impact of events on the young did not allow for habituation to behavioral patterns, which has become a choice explanation of the origins of party identification. The thesis that defections from partisanship—Democrats voting for Eisenhower in 1952 and 1956, for Nixon in 1968 and 1972, or for Reagan and Bush in 1980, 1984, and 1988—have an impact on one's sense of party identification is not at issue. Rather, as with generational differences and family traditions, the sharp break with partisanship that entering cohorts exhibited prior to 1968 makes the absence of partisanship among the new cohorts from 1968 and after more of a comment on the immediate impact of historical context than on an extension of either family influence or habituation theories.

The amassing of new data that captures variations in historical context enriches our understanding of the origins of party identification and partisanship. As an aside, we should note that the growing evidence of a multiplicity of origins may upset some old orthodoxies; however, this does not necessarily address whether the significance, the meaning, or the consequences of party identification are similarly enriched or altered. The meaning of "I generally think of myself as a strong Democrat/Republican" *may* vary with the origin of the sentiment. In the meantime, we may note the proliferation of evidence that, in its origins, party identification is a fascinatingly complex thing. At the same time, we should emphasize the fidelity with which party identification, once established, is translated into presidential vote choice and the persistence of its contribution to voters' partisan perspective on the world of national politics.

▪ Political Involvement and Party Voting

Just as the disaggregation of the eligible electorate into voters and non-voters casts a very different light on the historical ebb and flow of partisan sentiments, so too does deeper probing into differences in the

Table 7.2 Party Voting, 1952–1988, by Party, Region, and Ideological Involvement

	High on Ideological Involvement				Low on Ideological Involvement			
	Non-South		South		Non-South		South	
	Dem.	Rep.	Dem.	Rep.	Dem.	Rep.	Dem.	Rep.
1956	81 (273)	94 (169)	77 (109)	100 (16)	64 (77)	98 (176)	53 (57)	96 (27)
1960	89 (184)	94 (99)	70 (79)	100 (15)	74 (65)	92 (132)	60 (63)	96 (23)
1964	93 (214)	75 (141)	77 (86)	91 (21)	90 (123)	67 (104)	79 (68)	85 (20)
1968	82 (151)	90 (115)	73 (44)	100 (18)	67 (86)	96 (103)	69 (32)	93 (14)
1972	63 (113)	98 (90)	37 (35)	93 (28)	61 (64)	95 (76)	65 (53)	100 (21)
1976	85 (186)	85 (160)	70 (71)	94 (33)	77 (95)	86 (124)	75 (71)	92 (49)
1980	78 (96)	95 (86)	63 (51)	97 (36)	65 (62)	94 (65)	63 (32)	100 (27)
1984	89 (188)	96 (157)	83 (59)	96 (46)	58 (73)	97 (161)	59 (57)	97 (33)
1988	90 (167)	91 (180)	81 (73)	96 (48)	73 (60)	91 (134)	53 (34)	97 (39)
Mean	83	91	70	96	70	91	60	95

NOTE: Entries are proportions voting for their own party's presidential candidate. Numbers in parentheses are the number of non-Black respondents on whom the proportions are based.

level of political engagement *among voters* amplify our understanding of those sentiments. In general, there is clear if not dramatic evidence that those voters who are the least engaged by, or sophisticated about, politics are the most volatile in their political attitudes, including their political identities. In order to explore this possibility, a simplified version of the measure of "levels of conceptualization" introduced in *The American Voter* can be used to sort voters into two groups: the more politicized (the higher two levels in Chapter 10 of *The American Voter*) and the less politicized (lower two levels). Using this measure is a step toward further refining our sense of the conditions under which the consequences of party identification are persistent and stable, and the circumstances under which voters do alter their adherence to a habitual party affiliation (Campbell et al., 1960).

Table 7.2 presents the simple time series data on party voting (proportion of votes cast for the identifiers' party). Voters are categorized by party, region, and level of ideological involvement or political sophistication. The first and in some ways most notable discovery is the persistence of the degree of party voting through time within each category. Within each of the eight categories, election-specific variability is provided almost exclusively by only two of the nine presidential elections. For both Democrats and Republicans outside the South, 1964 was an exceptional year. The Johnson landslide was provided by the extraordinarily high rate of party voting among Democrats and the uniquely high rate of defections on the part of Republicans. However, the Democratic party's disarray in 1972 was marked by even more striking defections, with Democrats outdoing the Republicans of 1964 in the frequency with which they crossed party lines to vote for President. The aftermath of Watergate produced the second low point for Republicans. But these exceptions aside, one must mark the lack of election-specific variability in party voting. Even though the realignment in the South continually added newcomers to the ranks of the Republicans, there was no dilution of the proportions voting the party line at the polls. And, however much the Democratic ranks were "purified" by their loss of identifiers to the Republicans, those who remained voted their party's choice at the same rate in election after election.

Other regularities apparent in the data pertain to party differences. Republicans are absolutely as well as relatively notable for their demonstrated loyalty at the polls. Whatever their region of residence or their level of political sophistication, year after year (with the exceptions noted) 90 to 95 out of every 100 self-professed Republicans support their party's candidate for President. The Democrats, on the other hand, exhibit both absolutely and relatively higher rates of defection, by both region and level of involvement. Why this should be is unclear. But one fact is clear: most of the behavioral variability associated with party identification occurs on the Democratic side of the fence. Southern Republicans, whether as a beleaguered minority or as numerically co-equal to the Democrats, have been more faithful party voters than have their Northern peers. In addition, if this support for party standard bearers has not been affected by Republican voters' level of ideological involvement, the less involved among Democrats have been markedly less faithful on election day than have their more involved counterparts, both North and South. The explanation for Democratic variability and Republican constancy should rank high on electoral researchers' agenda for future research.

▪ Presidential Leadership and the Realignments of the 1980s

Between 1980 and 1988, at least a limited version of the long-heralded partisan realignment took place. After nine post-war elections, bracketing a span of 32 years, in which Democrats outnumbered Republicans by almost identical national margins among those voting for President, the Democratic edge virtually disappeared in the elections of 1984 and 1988. In Table 6.1 we saw the Democratic national plurality among voters drop from a "normal" 14 points in 1980 to no more than 3 points in 1988. The 1980–1988 realignment among voters apparently took place in two phases, each phase affecting one of two clearly different groups of voters. Between 1980 and 1984, changes in party loyalties took place pretty much across the board, but the shifting loyalties were disproportionately concentrated in two sectors. First, the young shifted more to the Republican side than did the old, suggesting greater malleability or susceptibility to the winds of change among the less experienced voters. At the same time, among young and old alike, the voters with limited formal education swung more heavily to the Republicans. Consequently, it was the less well educated young who changed the most: a Democratic margin of 23 points dwindled to 9 points, a 14-point shift between 1980 and 1984. Among the better-educated older voters, a small 3-point plurality of Republicans grew to an 8-point margin, a shift of only 5 points.

In the second phase of the realignment, there was a further shift to the Republicans but in only one sector of the voting population. Apparently, all of the Republican gain between 1984 and 1988 was concentrated in the ranks of the older, better educated voters. This group had been most resistant to the national move into the Republican camp between 1980 and 1984; it was precisely this group that went from a modest 40 to 32, 8-point Republican margin in 1984 to a solid 46 to 28, 18-point plurality in 1988, even though the vote margin favoring Republicans declined in the same period. If the first phase of the realignment was a tribute to the charismatic attraction that Ronald Reagan held for the less involved, less politicized voters, then the second phase seems to have engaged the more ideologically predisposed voters who had come to appreciate that Reagan really was a *conservative* Republican president (Miller, 1986).[5]

It is possible, of course, that the realignments of the Reagan years may vanish as swiftly as did the increment given to the Democrats in 1964 with Lyndon Johnson's election. Indeed, in 1992 the Democrats recovered a good portion of their 1980–1988 losses. Certainly every national leader is well aware of the speed with which short-run disaster can overtake long-term expectations. Prior to the election of 1992, however, the forecast was that the realignment of the late 1980s would be a relatively durable part of the Reagan legacy to American politics. The rationale for such a forecast derives from a basic perspective on the nature of democratic political processes. That perspective, in turn, brings the argument of this chapter full circle with another insight expressed by V. O. Key, Jr., in the metaphor of the electoral process as an echo chamber in which voters echo the message of political leaders. The more elaborate version of Key's perspective is presented as the conclusion to *Public Opinion and American Democracy* (Key, 1961). Key's basic argument posits political leadership as the wellspring of mass politics; thus it is the political elites, the subculture of activists, who articulate the alternatives that shape public opinion.

Political elites, including political leaders such as presidents, give definition to the political party. There are many reasons for the half-century Democratic party dominance of American politics, but not the least of these may include the sense of habitual party affiliation that became ingrained in many citizens who voted four times for Franklin Delano Roosevelt as the leader of the Democratic party, and three times to reaffirm a preference that he continue as President. At this remove it is difficult to reconstruct public opinion of fifty years ago; however, the incomparable longevity of Roosevelt's presidential leadership, followed by the contrast with a Thomas Dewey or a Harry Truman, must have contributed much to the contemporary meaning of being a "New Deal Democrat."

As we search for the roots of party identification, it is easy to forget that, following Truman, Eisenhower's hallmark was his emphasis on bipartisanship. Although Eisenhower's signal contribution to post-war domestic politics may well have been his conversion of the Republican party from the party of isolationism and "America First" to the party of internationalism and the United Nations, his legacy was not the redress of the partisan balance in the electorate (Campbell et al., 1954). Whatever the hopes of Republican partisans may have been during his first term of office, only the rare commentator foresaw a party realignment at the end of Eisenhower's second term.

We have already commented on the Kennedy-Johnson era, but it is worth noting again that the aftermath of the euphoria from the New Frontier, Camelot, and the Great Society was filled with the hot summers and burning, riot-torn cities of the late 1960s; Woodstock and the counterculture; and protests against Vietnam and for civil rights. As an antidote to the chill experienced during the 1950s, including limited dissent on American foreign policy and the heritage of racial discrimination, the decade of protest was undoubtedly overdue. However, the rejection of politics as usual was not calculated to endear the Democratic party to Main Street America, any more than to the hearts of the protesters. In hindsight it is remarkable that the Democratic party did not suffer more as a consequence of the widespread rejection of its leadership in 1968 and 1972, but there was in fact little subsequent evidence of realignment outside the South.

The Nixon era, as with the Eisenhower years, constituted another forgone opportunity across eight years of presidential leadership for the Republican party. Nixon's personal triumph was almost unequaled in his re-election in 1972—but that re-election, Watergate, and the Committee to Re-Elect the President were all well separated from the Republican party. This separation may have prevented another "failed president" from actually placing his party at a disadvantage.

Carter presided over yet another "failed presidency" in large part because he was not the party's leader. He campaigned as an outsider from Plains, Georgia, and he presided as an outsider. He, along with Johnson, benefited from his regional identification, and he momentarily slowed the Southern "white flight" from his party with his 1976 campaign when he ran against the Washington establishment. As with presidents before him, Carter did not appear to hurt his party—at least not at the grassroots level where party identification flourishes—but he scarcely took honors as a revitalizing leader of the party among the electorate.

Ronald Reagan was the only president of the post-war era who took office as an avowed partisan and unvarnished ideologue, held office for eight years, championing his conservatism *and* his Republicanism, and retired at the end of two full terms with a legacy of goodwill sufficient to elect his successor. The textbooks say that the President is the titular head and leader of the party. Reagan may not have satisfied all the factions within the Republican party, but that wasn't because he was not an articulate Republican spokesman or an active, openly partisan campaigner, both on the election trail and in Washington. Indeed, despite trials and tribulations that would have ended some careers, Reagan remained relatively popular to the end, when he retired from office with the country relatively at peace with itself and others. It seems likely, however, that the economic and social legacies of the Reagan administration contributed heavily to the political disenchantment of many young citizens in 1988 if not 1992.

A more detailed account of the changes in party identification between 1980 and 1984 attributes much of the 1980–1984 change to Reagan's personal popularity with the less experienced and less sophisticated sectors of the electorate (Miller, 1986). That analysis explicitly examined and rejected the hypothesis that it was the Reagan administration's conservatism rather than its Republicanism that provided the foundation for that change of partisanship. Four years later it would appear that Reagan's sustained personal popularity as President prevented any visible backsliding on the part of the recent converts to Republicanism.

An analysis of the 1988 election provides two sets of evidence that conform to our interpretation of the two-stage sequence of realignment. In the first place, there is pervasive and powerful evidence of Reagan's contribution to the Bush victory. The election was in some ways a Reagan retrospective triumph—a triumph of popular satisfaction with his policies, with the general state of the world and of the nation as he left office, and with his overall performance (Shanks and Miller, 1991). In the absence of evidence to the contrary, there seems no reason not to attribute the carryover of 1984 increases in Republican party identification to Reagan's popularity.

The second pertinent finding from our previous election analyses is of a different order. Across the three elections preceding 1988, the distribution of ideological predispositions among voters had not changed from a display of a 13-point margin of self-designated conservatives over self-designated liberals. In 1988 that margin *increased* overall by 8 points. Disaggregating voters by age and education, as we have done to locate those who changed their party identification, it becomes apparent that it was the older, better-educated voters—those who had experienced a 15-point increase in the Republican margin between 1980 and 1988 (from a slim 34 to 31 in 1980 to a solid 46 to 28 in 1988)—who also experienced a very substantial and disproportionate *17-point* increase in their self-declared conservatism during the same interval. Among the better-educated young voters, the increase in conservatism was associated with a 7-point increase in Republicanism. On the other hand, among the less well educated, whose pro-Republican shift occurred entirely between 1980 and 1984 (in response to the Reagan popularity), there was no 1980–1988 increase in conservative predispositions at all. In 1988 the less well educated were more Republican than they had been in 1980, but they were not more conservative; the better-educated, both young and old, were both more Republican *and* more conservative.

The above analysis of the 1988 elections thus supports the thesis that ideology and personality, both articulated and presented by the same presidential party leader, may each have reshaped the sense of party loyalty among different sections of the voting public. We are persuaded by this two-pronged explanation of the 1980–1988 realignment because it seems to fit a relatively broad view of the origins of party identification while it makes explicit the importance of presidential leadership for party as well as for country.[6]

Our rendering of the persistence of partisan attachments and our examination of the conditions under which voters alter their habitual partisan affiliations are obviously incomplete. Except for our limited speculation about recent presidencies, we have virtually ignored party in other aspects of politics as a partner in the shaping of mass political attitudes. Moreover, our disaggregations of the mass did not reach up to the political activists or the non-governmental elites who are so important in political processes. Nonetheless, our accumulated resources have permitted explorations and reconstructions not available to earlier generations of scholars. The old question, "What is a political party?" is answered as before—it is people, the people's leaders, and the symbols they present for public approval. The old question, "What causes stability and change in people's attachment to party?" is now more important than ever, with a very complex set of answers.

▪ Generational Differences in the Balance of Party Identification

In extending our inquiry into the origins of voters' choices, it is useful to return to the analysis of the changing incidence of party identifiers and to conduct a parallel examination of generation replacement among Southern and non-Southern non-Black *voters*. A regional comparison of changes over the past thirty years helps to explain some otherwise conflicting evidence of the nature of aggregate changes in party identification.

First, when we look at White citizens living outside the eleven states of the Old South, we find substantial confirmation of an earlier generalization holding that party identification was relatively stable across much of the time period preceding the election of 1984.

As Table 7.3 reveals in greater detail, there are striking *generational* differences within the *first three* time periods of our analytic scheme applied to the non-Black North. However, there seem to be no significant *period* or *life cycle* effects altering the party balance in the transition from the 1950s to subsequent elections prior to 1984. The cohorts politicized under Democratic New Deal leadership included many more Democratic identifiers—or fewer Republican identifiers—than did the cohorts of the *pre-New Deal* era, and at times by large margins of 25 or more points. There are also occasional suggestions of election-specific effects that vary by generation or education level (as with non-graduate New Dealers in the 1964–1968 elections). Thus, disaggregation exposes more variability among voters in the North than appeared in Table 6.1. Nevertheless, despite these perturbations, there is little evidence of either persistent period effects or pervasive life cycle effects.

However, generational replacement contributed by the post-New Deal cohorts has produced two contrary streams of influence on partisan balance in the Northern non-Black body of voters. First, Table 7.3 illustrates that in the third time period covering the three elections leading up to the Reagan era (1972–1976–1980), post-New Deal cohorts identified substantially less often as Republicans than did the other cohorts (those in the pre-New Deal and New Deal generations). By much smaller margins, those cohorts were also more Democratic, among high school graduates and those with at least some college.

Therefore, it seems that the initial entry of the post-New Deal generation into the electorate benefited the Democratic party at the beginning of the 1970s. For example, in the period from 1972 to 1980, among the large group of voters with at least some college education, the *Democratic* plurality of 4 points (29 Dem.–25 Rep.) within the post-New Deal generation contrasted with a 12-point *Republican* plurality (24 Dem.–36 Rep.) among the older New Deal generation.

However, the future balance of party alignments is difficult to predict;

Table 7.3 Party Identification of Non-Black Voters, Non-South

Years of Education	Generation	Democratic				Independent				Republican			
		52–60	64–68	72–80	84–88	52–60	64–68	72–80	84–88	52–60	64–68	72–80	84–88
0–11	Pre-New Deal	38	51	43	*	25	14	24	*	37	35	33	*
	New Deal	52	59	50	43	25	22	24	24	23	19	25	34
	Post-New Deal	—	*	31	38	—	*	52	38	—	*	17	25
12	Pre-New Deal	32	22	32	*	18	22	23	*	50	56	46	*
	New Deal	43	45	33	36	28	36	33	33	29	29	34	31
	Post-New Deal	—	*	35	27	—	*	50	39	—	*	14	33
13+	Pre-New Deal	17	20	19	*	14	14	9	*	69	67	72	*
	New Deal	22	26	24	26	32	33	40	26	47	41	36	49
	Post-New Deal	—	26	29	29	—	56	46	35	—	19	25	37

NOTE: In each row the combined entries for Democratic, Independent, and Republican total 100 percent for each time period.

*N < 20.

— No cases in sample.

we note that the same post-New Deal generation that favored the Democrats as they entered the electorate from 1972 through 1980 also led the absolute growth of *Republican* strength between the Nixon/Carter years and the following Reagan/Bush era. Republican party identifications increased in 1984 and again in 1988, but most sharply in those cohorts of the post-New Deal generation. The initial advantage to the Democrats of the changing composition of the active electorate was thus short-lived.

Somewhat less evident, but of perhaps greater theoretical significance, are the origins of the post-1980 shift in partisan balance in the North. Table 7.3 shows that the numbers of Democratic identifiers *did not decline* appreciably. Second, the proportions of Republicans increased by substantial margins—by 12 percentage points and 13 percentage points among the college-educated, and by 8 and 9 percentage points among the non-graduates. All of this could happen, of course, because Republican growth came at the expense of a commensurate decline in the numbers of non-identifiers. The large supply of non-identifiers, in turn, had been produced by the post-New Deal cohorts as they were first mobilized to vote in the elections of 1972, 1976, and 1980. All told, little more than one in two of all post-New Deal generation voters went to the polls *as party identifiers* in those elections (in contrast to 60 to 75 percent identifiers among older voters). However, in the next electoral period, the Reagan/Bush electoral epoch, the large asymmetrical movement of Independents into the partisan Republican ranks meant that the remaining proportions of Independents had dropped to normal magnitudes, similar to those of the New Deal generation in earlier time periods.

In the South, the story was dramatically different. As has been noted elsewhere, the realignment of Southern voters had begun with the Kennedy election in 1960. The realignment was not marked among the least well educated (those with fewer than 12 years of formal education); the erosion of Democratic strength and the growth in Republican numbers in the South was most pronounced among the better-educated. Thus the rate of change was apparently a direct function of education.

The most dramatic example is illustrated in Table 7.4 in a juxtaposition of the oldest and youngest generations at two points in time. Starting with the pre-New Deal generation in the 1950s, traditional Democratic pluralities ranged from 33 percentage points among the less well educated up to 54 percentage points among the college-educated. This was, of course, an inversion of the Northern pattern of relatively

Table 7.4 Party Identification of Non-Black Voters, South

Years of Education	Generation	Democratic				Independent				Republican			
		52–60	64–68	72–80	84–88	52–60	64–68	72–80	84–88	52–60	64–68	72–80	84–88
0–11	Pre-New Deal	62	76	50	*	9	8	16	*	29	16	35	*
	New Deal	70	64	64	54	17	22	20	26	13	14	17	20
	Post-New Deal	—	*	(54)	(48)	—	*	(36)	(44)	—	*	(10)	(8)
12	Pre-New Deal	(52)	*	(39)	*	(21)	*	18	*	(27)	*	44	*
	New Deal	75	50	47	46	12	27	32	35	13	24	21	19
	Post-New Deal	—	*	39	42	—	*	27	28	—	*	30	29
13+	Pre-New Deal	65	(52)	(32)	*	25	(20)	(20)	*	11	(28)	(43)	*
	New Deal	61	54	35	36	17	30	33	36	23	16	33	29
	Post-New Deal	—	*	34	31	—	*	37	34	—	*	29	36

NOTE: In each row the combined entries for Democratic, Independent, and Republican total 100 percent for each time period.

( ) 50 > N > 20.

* N < 20.

better educated Republicans contesting with less well educated Democrats. Thirty years later, in the 1980s, the analogous figures for the New Deal generation in the South were as follows: there was still a 34-point margin for the Democrats among non-graduates, a 27-point margin for graduates, and only a 6-point margin among the college-educated. Among post-New Deal voters, margins of +40 among non-graduates and +13 for high school graduates contrasted with a 5-point *Republican* margin among those with some college.[7] In thirty years the socioeconomic alignment had been sharply reversed.

The realignment begun in the 1960s continued in the Reagan/Bush years, but the largest shift came with the political trauma of the late 1960s and early 1970s, with most change occurring among the best-educated Southern voters. The picture across our four time periods is one of continuing realignment which by 1988 had produced both a massive erosion of the one-time Democratic dominance in the South and an inversion of the relationship between partisanship and education levels.

A close inspection of Tables 7.3 and 7.4 makes evident the extent to which the mobilization of the post-New Deal generation was responsible for much of the excitement about party alignment, dealignment, and realignment in the political science literature of the 1980s. Without sorting through voter turnout across time, region, race, and generation, it is impossible to know that the appearance of dealignment in the national electorate was, in fact, the result of the mobilization of a new generation of voters from the North who had limited party identification. There is virtually no evidence, in either the North or the South, of an increase of non-identified non-party voters in either the pre-New Deal or New Deal generations.

In both regions, the shifts in party numbers between 1952 and 1988 were accompanied by, if not caused by, a realignment of social groups. We have already noted that in the South, the educational correlates of party identification were inverted. There the college-educated voters underwent a massive realignment as Democratic pluralities of 50 percent (70 Democrats to every 10 Independents and 20 Republicans) were replaced in the post-New Deal generation by parity or even a small Republican advantage. Among the least well educated Southerners, however, there was simply no discernible decrease in the preponderance of Democrats. The net result was to reverse historic relationships and to associate Democratic preferences with the least well educated voters and

Table 7.5 Correlation of Partisan Direction of Party Identification (D-I-R) with Years of Education

	1952–60	1964–68	1972–80	1984–88
	Northern, Non-Black Voters			
Pre-New Deal	.21	.28	.26	.18
New Deal	.23	.24	.16	.16
Post-New Deal	—	(.06)	.08	.03
	Southern, Non-Black Voters			
Pre-New Deal	−.10	.20	.11	.15
New Deal	.09	.07	.23	.15
Post-New Deal	—	.18	.11	.16

NOTE: Entries are T_b correlations.
( ) N < 20.

Republican preferences with those with some college education in the South as well as in the North.

In the North, the social composition of partisan groupings also changed, but in a somewhat different manner. Our understanding of the North is complicated by the generational differences in the social correlates of partisan preferences. As Table 7.5 suggests, however, in both the early and middle election periods, members of the pre-New Deal generation exhibited a strong traditional correlation of better-educated Republicans and less well educated Democrats. In all four time periods, the education/party preference correlation within the New Deal generation was still substantial, although apparently in decline during the 1980s. Within the post-New Deal groups, however, there is little question that by the 1980s, party identification had only a limited tie to formal education and all the social and economic attributes that education represents. While the social composition of party groups in the South underwent a revolutionary inversion, the partisan relevance of educational attainment among voters in the North simply disappeared.

If the correlates of party identification such as education and election-day turnout were dramatically different in the 1980s, some of the other political correlates of party identification in the post-New Deal generations were perhaps surprisingly familiar. For example, although a very large proportion of the Republicans in the youngest generation were

Table 7.6 National Party Vote Frequency of Non-Black Party Identifiers

Years of Education	Political Generation	1952–1960	1964–1968	1972–1980	1984–1988	1992
		DEMOCRATS				
0–11	Pre-New Deal	77 (311/405)	85 (131/155)	66 (75/113)	** (19/19)	—
	New Deal	79 (322/410)	86 (183/214)	62 (193/313)	82 (89/108)	89 (55/62)
	Post-New Deal	—	—	87 (27/31)	** (20/23)	—
12	Pre-New Deal	76 (50/66)	** (16/16)	79 (22/28)	—	—
	New Deal	78 (221/285)	85 (147/174)	60 (112/187)	80 (84/105)	89 (75/84)
	Post-New Deal	—	—	73 (50/69)	73 (57/21)	84 (52/63)
13+	Pre-New Deal	71 (80/113)	71 (30/42)	63 (21/34)	—	—
	New Deal	69 (227/331)	81 (171/212)	64 (212/330)	74 (126/44)	89 (42/47)
	Post-New Deal	—	** (10/14)	75 (183/244)	77 (179/233)	91 (126/138)
		REPUBLICANS				
0–11	Pre-New Deal	97 (319/330)	85 (73/86)	89 (78/88)	** (12/14)	—
	New Deal	91 (139/153)	72 (47/65)	83 (111/133)	94 (63/67)	** (18/21)
	Post-New Deal	—	—	** (9/11)	** (7/10)	** (10/10)
12	Pre-New Deal	92 (69/75)	81 (21/26)	95 (28/29)	** (7/10)	—
	New Deal	96 (140/146)	82 (83/101)	93 (142/153)	93 (69/74)	88 (45/51)
	Post-New Deal	—	—	91 (38/42)	92 (76/83)	86 (38/44)
13+	Pre-New Deal	98 (161/164)	86 (57/66)	95 (70/74)	** (15/15)	—
	New Deal	97 (305/316)	86 (184/215)	93 (378/405)	95 (229/241)	88 (70/80)
	Post-New Deal	—	—	93 (185/198)	96 (287/299)	94 (133/142)

NOTE: Entries are average proportions of party identifiers reporting voting for their party's candidate, followed by the number voting/total number of cases.

** Too few cases for estimation.

— No cases in sample.

newcomers to the party, their votes in the elections of the 1980s matched the partisanship of Republicans in the older generations. As Table 7.6 indicates, party voting by the post-New Deal generation was sustained on both sides.[8]

▪ Party and Policy

In fact, on a number of questions of public policy preference, the party differences within the young post-New Deal cohorts were, if anything, somewhat sharper than within the older cohorts. This was particularly true of attitudes toward such "contemporary" issues as defense spending, government aid for minorities, popular support for civil rights leaders, and attitudes toward abortion. On each of these topics the addition of the young post-New Deal cohorts sustained or heightened the issue polarization among partisan voters. In every instance, as Table 7.7 illustrates concerning aid to minorities, younger Democratic party identifiers were at least marginally more liberal than were older Democrats of the New Deal generation, and younger Republicans more conservative than were older ones.

A slightly different pattern of generational differences characterized another set of "traditional" issues that included such diverse and long-standing topics as détente, the expansion of government service and domestic spending, an active role for the federal government in maintaining jobs and a high standard of living, and gender equality. On each of these topics, represented in Table 7.8 by responses to the issue of government spending and government service, party differences within the post-New Deal generation were not consistently different from those within the older New Deal cohorts. The striking contribution of the post-New Deal voters to these policy conflicts lay in the clear fact that in virtually every instance the attitudes of the younger voters—Republicans, Independents, and Democrats alike—were distinctly to the left of those of the New Deal generation. In general, younger Republican party identifiers were every bit as much to the left of their elders as the younger Democrats were to the left of their older cohorts. This was true both for the domestic issues on which the parties are traditionally and sharply divided (domestic service and spending; jobs and standard of living) as well as for more recent questions such as support for increased de-

Table 7.7 Net Policy Preference, 1980–1988: Governmental Aid to Minorities[a]

Education	Political Generation	Party Identification			Party Polarization	
		Democrat	Independent	Republican	Difference of Party Means	Tau Gamma Correlation[b]
Grade School	New Deal	−7[c]	−20[c]	−32[c]	25	.09
	Post-New Deal	*	*	*	*	*
High School	New Deal	−7	−35	−41	34	.16
	Post-New Deal	+2	−31	−49	51	.22
	Generational Differences	+9	+4	−8	+17	+.06
College	New Deal	+4	−18	−33	37	.16
	Post-New Deal	+15	−1	−42	57	.24
	Generational Differences	+11	+17	−9	+20	+.08

a. Entries based on pooled data from 1980, 1984, and 1988 NES.

b. Entry is Tau Gamma correlation Party Identification (three categories) and uncollapsed issue preferences (seven categories).

c. Entries are means based on proportions Favoring Aid MINUS proportions Opposed to Aid. See Chapter 12.

* Too few cases for estimation.

Table 7.8 Net Policy Preference, 1980–1988: Increase Government Services and Domestic Spending[a]

Education	Political Generation	Party Identification			Party Polarization	
		Democrat	Independent	Republican	Difference of Party Means	Rank Order Correlation[b]
Grade School	New Deal	+46[c]	0	-26	72	.29
	Post-New Deal	*	*	*	*	*
High School	New Deal	+29	-20	-41	70	.32
	Post-New Deal	+34	+10	-16	50	.21
	Generational Differences	+ 5	+30	+25	-20	-.11
College	New Deal	+18	-20	-44	62	.28
	Post-New Deal	+44	+ 4	-38	82	.33
	Generational Differences	+26	+24	+ 6	+20	+.05

a. Entries based on pooled data from 1980, 1984, and 1988 NES.

b. Entry is Tau Gamma correlation of Party Identification (three categories) and uncollapsed issue preferences (seven categories).

c. Entries are proportions Yes MINUS proportions No. See Chapter 12.

* Too few cases for estimation.

Table 7.9 Net Policy Preference, 1980–1988: Decrease in Defense Spending[a]

Education	Political Generation	Party Identification			Party Polarization	
		Democrat	Independent	Republican	Difference of Party Means	Tau Gamma Correlation[b]
0–11	New Deal	+37[c]	−3	−4	40	.19
	Post-New Deal	+45	+20	+36	9	.08
	Generational Differences	+8	+23	+40	−31	−11
12	New Deal	+19	−8	−43	62	.32
	Post-New Deal	+35	+15	−13	48	.20
	Generational Differences	+16	+23	+30	−14	−12
13+	New Deal	+25	−17	−43	68	.34
	Post-New Deal	+37	+7	−39	76	.34
	Generational Differences	+12	+24	+4	+8	0

a. Entries based on pooled data from 1980, 1984, and 1988 NES.

b. Entry is Tau Gamma correlation of Party Identification (three categories) and uncollapsed issue preferences (seven categories).

c. Entries are proportions Yes MINUS proportions No. See Chapter 12.

fense spending. This pattern of generational differences is illustrated in Table 7.9.

▪ Summary: Party Identification at the End of the Twentieth Century

At the aggregate level where national parameters are found, generational analysis has been an indispensable diagnostic tool. We have learned that the post-New Deal generation not only contributed massively to diminished partisanship in the electorate, but was responsible for much of the thirty-year national decline in turnout. In the South, the post-New Deal generation is making a continuing disproportionate contribution to a regional realignment of the social foundations of Democratic and Republican politics.

The analyses underlying these conclusions carry implications for a number of theories about the nature of party identification. First, we now have two large regional sets of evidence pertaining to stability and change. In recent years the literature on party identification has been characterized by numerous inquiries emphasizing short-term changes in party identification (measured as partisanship with a seven-point distribution rather than the three nominal categories of Democrat-Independent-Republican), with most analyses based on the total eligible electorate, South as well as North, Black as well as non-Black, and non-voters as well as voters. In fact, the historical record for non-Black Northern voters is one of remarkable resistance to change over a thirty-year period, 1952 to 1980. If the test of the stability of party identification is confined to non-Black voters outside the South, it is appropriate to conclude that party identification was remarkably resistant to short-term, election-specific change from 1952 to 1980. Moreover, with the notable exceptions of 1964 and 1972, the direct linkages between party identification and the vote for presidential candidates were comparably constant. When changes ultimately occurred in the social/economic correlates of party identification and in the policies associated with partisanship, or in the distribution of party identification itself, the young, post-New Deal generation led the change.

At the same time, for an almost equally long interval between 1960 and 1988, the changing conditions confronting voters in the South have been associated with a continuing realignment of regional support for the Democratic and Republican parties. Both the erosion of Democratic dominance and the shift in the social cleavages differentiating the parties are most evident in the younger, post-New Deal generation in the South. More generally, the Southern model for describing change seems to have involved a relatively direct exchange of partisan loyalties—Republican numbers increasing as the number of Democrats decreased. It is, of course, possible that the pattern of unidirectional aggregate net change could rest on a transformation matrix populated by Democrats first becoming non-partisans and then evolving into Republicans. This would be consistent with Beck's thesis that dealignment, as the result of a relaxation of the bonds of intra-familial transmission, would precede realignment (Beck, 1974, 1976).

The treatment of this realignment by Earl Black and Merle Black is seen as a regional version of policy-driven conversion in party identifications (Black and Black, 1987, chap. 11). To the extent that this is true, systematic inquiry should find party identification changing coincident with, and perhaps in response to, large contextual changes in policy preferences. This leads to one important qualification to generalizations based on the stability of party identification in the White North: participants in pervasive social change may well change partisan commitments at roughly the same time. The sharp differences in the regional patterns of stability and change favor an interpretation in which change in party identification in the South occurred in response to change in relevant policy preferences. The ultimate consequence of the changes still under way in the South would appear to be a highly rational simplification of the two-party system of American politics. The liberal Democratic North, conservative Republican North, and conservative Democratic South are being transformed into a national system without the regional ideological aberration in the South. Although this change is partially being brought about by an extension of the Goldwater-Nixon Republican strategy for building mass support for the Republican cause in the South, it is doubly significant to note the numbers of conservative Democratic politicians who have been converting to Republicanism and removing the conservative Democratic anomaly at the elite level as well.

Consistent with this attribution of change in party identification, the latter-day *national* realignment from 1980 to 1988 suggests yet other conditions under which change in party identification takes place, in this instance when non-partisans move into allegiance to a party. Two phases, 1980–1984 and 1984–1988, captured the transformation of the

Reagan years. Non-identified voters certainly fueled the first phase of realignment in the North. The second phase, however, not only was *not* concentrated in the post-New Deal generation, but was limited largely to older voters who were also in the process of shifting their ideological identities into the conservative camp. In the face of thirty years of national stability in party identification outside the South, the period of 1980–1988 produced a double conversion of both ideology and partisanship at the national level. This supports our second generalization: under conditions of pervasive change in the social or political context, party identification may change in tandem with and in response to the contextual changes.

Beyond these large generalizations, we have noted several other aspects of conditions under which party identification is more, or less, stable. Both strength and stability of identification at the individual level are a function of the passage of time, usually reflected in the age of the identifier. Changes in social conditions and political context are more likely to produce changes in party identification among the young—or the newly identified—than among the old. In a related vein, susceptibility to change seems to be a function of the intensity of political involvement—greater among the less involved (non-voters), and less among the more psychologically involved (voters).

Finally, the stability of party identification is clearly a function of the larger political environment: subject to great and pervasive change under the upheavals of a Civil War or a national depression, stolid and phlegmatic under conditions of normalcy. But the Civil War aside, the catalyzing events of the American setting have needed a political translation by political leaders in order to produce pervasive change in the party loyalties of the mass electorate. Roosevelt and the spokesmen for the Democratic New Deal provided the leadership that enrolled and converted new Democratic followers in the 1930s. Lyndon Johnson and Hubert Humphrey did the same for Black citizens in the mid-1960s, as did Ronald Reagan for conservatives in the 1980s. We have noted earlier the failure of Eisenhower, and Nixon after him, to convert personal popularity to partisan advantage. The rise and fall of Republican fortunes in the late 1980s provided yet another lesson in the importance of sustained leadership, as the Bush failure prior to the election of 1992 joined the earlier failure of Johnson on the Democratic side to deny a possibly enduring party realignment.

As the last decade of the twentieth century draws to a close, it should be noted that in both parties the lineage of leadership is changing. The change is most evident on the Democratic side. President Clinton ran and was elected as a "New Democrat." His Vice President preserved the prominence of a nationally known political family name, but stood almost alone as age, disenchantment, ill health, or tarnished personal reputations thinned the ranks of familiar Democratic leaders. Among Republicans, Dole of Kansas stood out as an established partisan symbol of conservatism, but he was at least temporarily outshone by the likes of Gingrich and Buchanan. And none of these new leaders presented themselves to the electorate as the heirs to a decisive ideological tradition from previous decades. Insofar as party identification is influenced by a cadre of known leaders associated with shared positions on a broad range of public policies, party identification in the middle of the last decade of the century may not be reinforced by the leadership of either party.

PART IV

EXPLANATION OF VOTE CHOICE

8

★ ★ ★ | Multiple-Stage Explanation of Political
Preferences: Explanatory Themes, Temporal
Sequence, and Survey Methods

In Parts II and III we discussed both individual and aggregate change concerning electoral participation (or turnout) and long-term partisan identification. At this point, we shift our attention to the explanation of individual differences in vote choice for President among those citizens who cast their ballots for one of the two major candidates.

We defer consideration of the Perot candidacy to Chapter 16 for two closely connected reasons. First, Perot's support was drawn equally from the potential supporters of the two major candidates. Allocating Perot voters to Bush or Clinton, depending on which was their second choice, would not have made a significant difference to the outcome of the election. Second, as we shall illustrate in Chapter 16, our decision to set aside the Perot voters preserves our ability to pursue our basic interest in the competition between the candidates of the two major parties and still permits a full-blown discussion of the Perot vote.

As outlined in Chapter 1, our strategy for explaining individual differences in vote choice involves a comprehensive set of explanatory ideas or hypotheses that have been suggested by a wide variety of theories and approaches. Our approach to this theoretical and conceptual diversity has been to classify all potential explanations into a small number of general "themes," each of which may include several specific factors that share the same kind of content and may influence the vote through similar processes or mechanisms. Our strategy has been inclusive in two senses. Most of our explanatory themes incorporate a variety of potential explanatory variables of the same general type (for example, current preferences concerning policy direction in many different substantive areas), and our definitions of the various alternative themes are designed to cover the range of explanatory hypotheses that have been suggested by the scholarly literature on electoral behavior. Our conclusions concerning the role of particular explanatory factors or variables in a given election may diverge from those advanced by other analysts because we have used different measurement or statistical procedures, or because of the other explanatory variables involved in our analyses. Our collection of general explanatory themes, however, should incorporate most, if not all, of the suggestions that have been discussed by other scholars concerning the explanation of individual electoral decisions.

▪ Explanatory Themes and Causal Stages

We have classified potential explanations of the vote (and their associated survey-based variables) into one of eight general themes, depending on whether the voter attributes involved are primarily defined in terms of: (1) stable social and economic characteristics, (2) long-term partisan identifications, (3) policy-related predispositions, (4) preferences concerning current policy issues, (5) perceptions of current conditions, national or personal, (6) retrospective evaluations of the current President concerning governmental "results," (7) evaluations of the personal qualities of the candidates, or (8) prospective evaluations of the potential future effectiveness of the two parties and their candidates. As emphasized below, two of these explanatory themes are defined in terms of policy-related conflicts within the society (including general policy-related predispositions and current policy preferences), and two themes are defined in terms of consensual criteria for political evaluations (concerning current conditions and personal qualities of the candidates). Within each of these pairs of general explanatory themes, all specific variables share the same kind of analytic content and are assumed to influence vote choice through the same types of causal processes. Because of those similarities, we will eventually be able to assess the combined relevance of all the variables within each explanatory theme as well as the role of each variable. For example, we will be particularly interested in the combined explanatory power of all policy-related preferences, including both predispositions and policy preferences. That combination or aggregation will be mentioned briefly in discussions of specific policy-related variables. We will defer explicit assessments of the overall power or "importance" of each of our eight explanatory themes until Part V—after we have examined the apparent effects of individual variables in each of those themes.

In addition to the substantive distinctions among different explanatory themes, our analytic conclusions also rest on crucial assumptions concerning temporal sequence, based on a causal order of six stages in which we believe voters acquire their positions on different types of variables. Within this structure, all of the variables in a given *stage* may have been influenced by variables in earlier stages (as well as by other variables within the given stage), and may have had some influence on one or more variables in later stages, as well as having some direct or unmediated impact on the vote. All of the variables in each explanatory theme have been assigned to the same causal position (or stage), on the basis of our assumptions about the similar kinds of processes involved in their development. It should be noted that we have assigned some explanatory themes to the same causal stage (for example, partisan identification and policy-related predispositions to one stage—the second—and current policy preferences and perceptions of current conditions to another stage—the third). We have made these assignments because of the similarity of the themes in each pair with regard to temporal sequence and because of our conviction that questions about causal relationships between them cannot be resolved. These assumptions about temporal sequence, including the assignment of each explanatory theme to one of six causal stages before the vote, can be seen in Figure 8.1. This aspect of our approach to electoral explanation deserves special emphasis, for these assumptions represent the foundation for our interpretation of all the statistical results to follow.

We have assumed that a variety of stable social and economic characteristics (which constitute the first stage of our model) have played some role in shaping voters' continuing predispositions toward many policy-related conflicts within the society, as well as in shaping their long-term partisan identifications—both of which have been assigned to the second major stage in our model. On the basis of a variety of evidence, we have concluded that all of the other attitudes that had some impact on voters' choices for President should be assigned to later or subsequent stages in our model. All of those other attitudes may have been influenced by policy-related predispositions or partisan identifica-

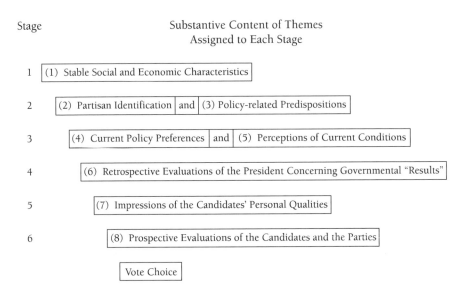

Figure 8.1 Explanatory themes and causal stages.

tions, or by social or economic characteristics—and they may sub-sequently mediate the relationships between variables in our first two stages and the vote. Such attitudes, however, are not likely to have "caused" the characteristics grouped together in the first two stages. In effect, both types of predispositions, as well as social and economic characteristics, are treated as "givens" for the current election—on the assumption that they were already "in place" before the current campaign began and were generally not changed by short-term forces based on campaign issues or candidate personality (which are the basis for our other explanatory variables).[1]

The third major stage in our model (following partisan and policy-re-lated predispositions) also includes two distinct explanatory themes, neither of which involves any explicit connection with the candidates or parties that are competing in the campaign being analyzed. These two themes are defined in terms of voters' opinions concerning the two different types of "issues" that were emphasized during the current campaign. These two types of opinions are defined in terms of voters' own preferences concerning current conflicts over policy direction and their perceptions of current conditions concerning consensual objectives. None of these opinions and perceptions are expressed in terms of evaluations of the parties or the candidates. As with the partisan and policy-related predispositions in our second stage, the explanatory variables in the third stage (concerning current policy conflicts and conditions) may have had some influence on each other. As in our second stage, we have deliberately not attempted to unravel such relationships and have simply included both types of variables in the same causal stage.

Following voters' preferences concerning current policy issues and their perceptions of current conditions, all of the remaining explanatory themes (and all of the remaining stages in our model) are expressly defined in terms of explicitly partisan *evaluations*. Specifically, the variables in our fourth stage involve retrospective evaluations of the current President concerning the "results" of his administration. Unlike subsequent stages, these evaluations are asymmetric in their focus on only one side of the partisan contest in the current election, on the grounds that most evaluations of the President have been established before the other candidate becomes well known; and, in any event, a challenger has no record for which he can be held accountable in a manner comparable to the incumbent.

Our fifth stage, then, introduces comparative evaluations of the two major candidates with respect to exclusively personal qualities of the leaders, qualities that are not defined in terms of partisanship, policy, conditions, or governmental results. Finally, the variables in our sixth stage, which we assume to be the most proximate to the vote, represent prospective evaluations concerning potential governmental "results," based on hypothetical questions that ask which candidate or party would do "a better job" in handling specific problem areas.

In our model, each successive stage is thus temporally located closer and closer to the vote decision. For that reason, the values of each (successive) set of variables are more and more vulnerable to influence from early choices by the voter. Despite that possibility, however, we shall argue with some care that it nevertheless makes sense to do the best one can with available evidence to consider an independent role for the factors in stages 5 and 6 rather than conclude that "feedback" from an early preference for one candidate overwhelms any attempt to separate cause and effect concerning our most proximate variables and the vote.

▪ Analytic Strategy and Procedures

The succeeding chapters in Part IV explore the apparent electoral "effects" for specific survey-based variables within each of our general explanatory themes. In the sequence dictated by our multiple-stage model, and illustrated in Figure 8.1, most chapters are devoted to a single explanatory theme. Each chapter reviews the rationale and evidence for suggesting that specific attributes of voters within that general theme played some role in shaping their choices between Bill Clinton and George Bush in 1992. In preparation for each chapter, *all* potential explanatory variables with the same type of content (or within the same general theme) from the 1992 NES survey have been subjected to the same statistical procedures in order to identify specific variables that appear to have had a significant impact on the vote—even after we take into account other significant variables located in the same or earlier themes.

For each potential explanatory variable that is identified (or selected) by those procedures, we present a series of descriptive statistics concerning its relationship to the vote. Each such series begins with summaries of the simple bivariate relationship between the given variable and the vote. Each series then shifts to coefficients from a sequence of multivariate analyses which allow the analyst to consider statistical controls for different combinations of the other explanatory variables in our model. The more important of these analyses are designed to remove the confounding effects of other explanatory variables that we have assigned to a prior stage, or to the same stage, in our model. These analyses take into account or control for variables whose apparent influence on the vote might otherwise be confused with that of the explanatory variable being examined. From those analyses, we have designated one coefficient for each explanatory variable as our preferred estimate of its "apparent total effect" on the vote.

In general, we believe that the designated total effect coefficient represents the most appropriate descriptive statistic, sometimes among several potential alternatives, to suggest the overall or average impact of that characteristic on voters' choices for President in 1992. Coefficients from analyses which precede the equation that produced this apparent total effect are still potentially biased by confounding variables, and coefficients based on subsequent analyses reflect the mediating influence of variables that presumably intervene between it and the vote. After identifying the apparent total effect of a given explanatory variable, we present several additional coefficients to suggest the ways in which that total effect may have been mediated by variables which we have assigned to causal stages lying between it and the vote. In general, each of the total effects for an explanatory variable in "earlier" stages in our model may include a variety of indirect effects, based on that variable's influence on other explanatory variables that are more proximate to the vote.

The statistical procedures we have used to assess the electoral impact of specific variables are the same within each of our explanatory themes, based on our assumptions about the general causal structure (and sequence) which has "produced" all of the relationships among our survey-based variables. Our rationale in using these multivariate procedures is based on the "logic of elaboration" developed by Paul Lazarsfeld and his associates and subsequently codified as the "logic of causal order" by James Davis (1990). Three examples from the 1992 election may clarify the analytic objectives for these procedures:

- One of the simplest social or economic characteristics discussed in Chapters 9 and 10 is defined in terms of the voter's ownership of his or her home. As with other indicators of social or economic status, voters who rented their homes in 1992 were substantially more likely than non-renters to vote for Bill Clinton rather than George Bush. The magnitude of this difference in the division of the vote between renters and other respondents is somewhat smaller after we adjust or control for other social or economic characteristics, in order to remove any portions of that difference between renters and non-renters which could be attributed to other, related characteristics in the initial stage of our model—rather than to the apparent total effects of home ownership per se. Almost all of the remaining total effects of home ownership subsequently disappear when we also account for, or control for, voters' partisan identifications. This result clearly suggests that the apparent impact of home ownership on the vote should be attributed to the "long-term" tendency for renters to be more likely to consider themselves as Democrats (and for homeowners to consider themselves as Republicans)—rather than to any "short-term" relevance of home ownership in the 1992 campaign.

- Voters' attitudes toward traditional morality and moral tolerance, as documented in Chapter 11, appeared to play a substantial role in shaping voters' decisions in 1992. The apparent impact of general attitudes in this area is quite visible even after we take into account or control for voters' partisan identifications and other policy-related predispositions, as well as social and economic characteristics. Further analyses then suggest that some of that total effect appears to have been mediated by voters' preferences on specific policy issues, including gays in the military, but a substantial coefficient remains as a direct or unmediated effect on the vote after we control for all of the other (intervening) variables in our model.

- Finally, the results discussed in Chapter 13 suggest that voters' perceptions of the "state of the economy" in 1992 also played a major role in their choices between Bill Clinton and George Bush, even after we control for all of the earlier stages in our explanatory model. As might be expected, however, *all* of that apparent effect disappears when we then take account of voters' explicit evaluations of George Bush's performance as President. As a consequence, we conclude that the electoral effects of economic conditions appear to have been entirely mediated by voters' evaluations of the President. (This same connection must be considered in assessing the electoral impact of direct evaluations of the President, based on a similar sequence of descriptive statistics for those variables.)

Each of our "apparent effects" represents a descriptive statistic for which we have deliberately accepted a somewhat conservative interpretation. For each coefficient, our interpretation represents a clear suggestion—without decisive "proof"—that it should be regarded as an approximation of the overall extent to which differences between voters on that variable were in fact responsible for "producing" differences between them in their vote for President in 1992. As discussed in the last section of this chapter, these approximations should not be regarded as formal "estimates" because of the assumptions we are, and are not, prepared to make about the underlying causal structure. At this point, we simply emphasize the explanatory motivations for the analyses to be presented in the following chapters.

▪ Sources of Evaluations Based on Conflict or Consensus

At several stages in the evolution of electoral preferences, political evaluations of candidates and parties may be influenced by three fundamentally different external sources of positive or negative impressions. The first of these three sources is found in the partisan competition between the Republican and Democratic candidates for President and voters' general partisan identifications, which are activated during the campaign. Those identifications reflect the cumulative impact of previous (positive or negative) impressions of the parties and have a pervasive impact on all evaluations of the current President and candidates. As we emphasized in Part III, the concept of "long-term" partisanship and the NES measure of party identification have been central to the evolution of the electoral field and play a crucial role in our own multiple-stage explanation of the vote. The impact of all *other* sources of electoral evaluations or preferences, in addition to partisan identification, can be attributed to contrasting attitudes or opinions based on the extent of conflict or consensus within the electorate concerning the desirability of the phenomena being evaluated.

With a second conflict-based criterion for evaluation, individual voters acquire positive impressions of leaders (both incumbents and challengers) who emphasize policy positions that "sound right" to them—in areas where both citizens and candidates disagree about government policies, priorities, or benefits. Similarly, voters acquire negative impressions of candidates whose positions "are not on the right track" given their own views in those areas.

The third or consensual criterion for evaluation comes into play if voters obtain positive impressions of incumbent leaders when current circumstances are "good" or favorable with respect to universally desirable objectives—such as "prosperity" or "peace"—and voters acquire negative impressions of those leaders when such conditions are "bad" or subject to negative criticism.

In the first of the latter two contrasting criteria for evaluation, the external *sources* for voters' positive or negative impressions of the can-

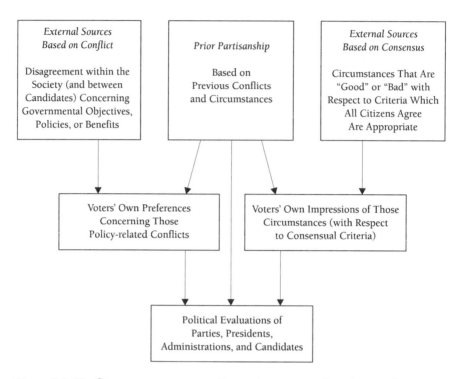

Figure 8.2 Conflict versus consensus: Alternative sources of partisan evaluations.

didates are the public positions taken by the candidates or the parties, as emphasized and interpreted in the campaign by those candidates and the media. For the latter criterion for evaluation, the external sources for positive or negative impressions of the candidates are current conditions or circumstances with respect to consensual governmental objectives—as emphasized either in the campaign or through regular coverage of "the news."

These general distinctions among three sources of partisan impressions and two contrasting criteria for evaluation are depicted in Figure 8.2. In our multiple-stage model, these three sources for partisan impressions are responsible for *activating* prior partisan identifications, conflict- (or policy-) related preferences, and values concerning current circumstances with respect to consensual objectives—thereby "producing" partisan evaluations at several stages in the evolution of electoral preferences.

Before saying more about the distinction between conflictual and consensual bases for evaluation, we should make two general observations. Well before any current election, prior conflicts within the society and between parties, *and* prior episodes of successful and unsuccessful governmental administrations of both parties, will have had a cumulative impact on voters' long-term partisan identifications—thereby modifying or reinforcing any partisanship they may have acquired from their parents or other interpersonal interactions. Second, explicit evaluations of the "job done by" the current President will usually be shaped by all three sources of partisan impressions before any campaign begins. They will be the result of (1) the activation of voters' own preferences or party sympathies concerning policy-related conflicts (where the President has taken a visible position), and (2) voters' sometimes partisan perceptions of the current administration's success or failure in reaching consensual objectives, as well as (3) following directly from their partisan identifications. Similarly, conflict-related preferences and expectations concerning future "results" (with respect to consensual objectives) are presumably important, along with partisan identification, in shaping prospective evaluations of the candidates and parties.

Types of Policy-related Conflicts

Most electoral analysts believe that partisan evaluations and preferences are at least partially shaped by current conflicts within the society concerning governmental objectives or priorities. Analysts often disagree about the electoral impact of specific conflicts, but all observers of recent elections would agree that voters and leaders have disagreed with each other concerning many policy-related topics, including:

- support for the poor or disadvantaged, including food and shelter,
- assistance to racial minorities and women, including affirmative action,
- the size and use of U.S. military forces,
- assistance to anti-communist groups in other countries,
- union organization (and strikes) in both the public and the private sectors,
- regulation of business and consumers to protect the environment,
- alternative approaches to preventing crime,
- governmental regulation of and subsidies for health care,

- prohibition of abortion (under various circumstances),
- restrictions on rights of homosexuals,
- the role of religion in the public schools, and
- the reduction of the national budget deficit.

This list of topics could easily be expanded to several dozen policy-related conflicts that have been suggested as partially responsible for electoral decisions since 1980. Most of these and other explanatory possibilities are discussed in Chapters 11 and 12. At this point, we simply note the existence of a wide variety of policy-related areas in which voters and politicians have taken opposing positions during the 1980s and 1990s. In each of these areas, some voters have presumably reacted to one candidate's position as sensible or "right" or to another candidate's as inappropriate or "wrong." Such reactions may have influenced voters' evaluations of those candidates—whether or not they retained any conscious association of either leader with that topic.

Several different types of policy-related conflicts may become relevant in a given election, depending on the kind of governmental objectives or activities that are emphasized in the campaign. (1) In some areas, conflicting views may be expressed in fairly general terms, based on broad topics like equality or morality, or on differential benefits (or costs) for particular groups or "interests." (2) In other areas, such as controversies concerning abortion and religion, policy-related conflicts may involve "absolute" preferences concerning alternative objectives or policies. (3) In still other areas, however, such as defense spending and assistance to the poor, nearly all voters (and politicians) agree on the government's general responsibilities, but conflicts may still arise concerning the relative priority to be given to governmental objectives in that area—given the inevitable tradeoffs in allocating scarce resources.

In these types of current issues (assigned to the third stage in our model), voters prefer different policies or priorities in areas where the major parties and their candidates have advocated visibly different positions. As emphasized in Chapter 12, the apparent electoral effects of voters' preferences concerning current policy-related issues may be "produced" by a variety of social or psychological processes. For some voters, the electoral impact of policy preferences may reflect a classical kind of issue voting or "rational choice." As discussed repeatedly below, however, statistical relationships of this sort (between policy preferences and the vote) may also arise through a variety of other less conscious or deliberate processes. For all such issues the defining element is some kind of *conflict* or disagreement within the electorate—and between the two major candidates—concerning the most appropriate *direction* for federal policy.

Types of Consensus-related Conditions

In areas where voters agree on the general appropriateness of governmental objectives and priorities, evaluations of incumbent leaders' performance may also be shaped by positive or negative perceptions of current conditions that might be attributable to governmental policies or actions. Several kinds of external conditions may become relevant for political evaluations of this second type, precisely because of widespread agreement concerning the government's responsibilities in those substantive domains. In particular, most voters would presumably agree that the federal government is at least partially responsible for:

- national economic conditions, including opportunities for employment;
- national social or environmental conditions, such as safety from crime or pollution;
- the way such conditions affect their own lives; and
- the international status of the United States.

Any of these external conditions may have some impact on evaluations of the current administration's performance, based on positive or negative impressions of current circumstances *provided* they are emphasized in the current campaign by the candidates or the media. Most electoral analysts believe that perceptions of the national economy can have a powerful influence on the voters' evaluations of the President, but no agreement has emerged concerning the impact of voters' own financial circumstances or other (non-economic) conditions (Kinder and Kiewiet, 1979).

Unlike policy-related conflicts, however, *all* of the electoral effects of voters' perceptions of current conditions should be mediated by their evaluations of the candidates' past or future performance. In practice, perceptions of current conditions may also be influenced by voters' policy-related preferences as well as their partisan identifications. For that reason, we have included (or controlled for) such variables in assessing the electoral impact of current conditions.

Distinguishing "Issues" from Personal Qualities of the Candidates

In this introduction to explanatory themes and causal stages, we have distinguished between two general types of "issues" that may be emphasized in any campaign. In this formulation, issues may be based on policy-related conflicts or they may rest on perceptions of current national or personal conditions. In every election, however, there are some controversies that are informally referred to as "issues" that cannot be described in terms of policy-related conflicts, current conditions, or governmental priorities. In particular, both media interpretation and scholarly research often refer to "issues" that are really controversies about the personal characteristics of the candidates. Such controversies may involve candidates' private lives as well as general characteristics like honesty, intelligence, or morality that are relevant to performance in the public sector. Despite this conventional terminology, we have reserved the term "issue" for campaign controversies about governmental activities or outcomes—that is, about policy-related conflicts or about perceptions of current conditions. Evaluations of the President may be shaped by either type of issue. Controversies about the candidates' personal qualities, however, such as Clinton's morality in 1992, will not be described as an "issue." We believe this definition is helpful in clarifying our results concerning specific explanatory variables, and it preserves a traditional distinction within the electoral field.

To be sure, most survey-based evaluations concerning purely personal (or non-governmental) aspects of the candidates are primarily defined in terms of characteristics that are consensually seen as desirable. In that sense, such evaluations may be provisionally located on the "consensus side" of our distinction between two contrasting criteria of partisan evaluations. However, evaluations of personal qualities may also be powerfully influenced by conflict- or policy-related preferences. In any event, our list of potentially important campaign "issues" does not include any personal qualities of the candidates. Such qualities are assessed in a separate analytic stage, after we have controlled for policy preferences and perceived conditions.

Redefining Political "Performance" in Terms of Conflict and Consensus

Several electoral analyses have featured a distinction between explanations of the vote that are based on voters' preferences concerning policy *direction* versus explanations based on evaluations of presidential *performance*.[2] Such analyses try to compare explanations that are defined (and aggregated) in terms of "policy" versus "performance," as if evaluations of "performance" are entirely based on the sources *other* than conflicts concerning policy direction. In preparing this book, however, we have concluded that all evaluations of the President or presidential candidates (including their "performances") should be seen as based on the above alternative sources for partisan impressions: partisanship, conflict, and consensus. Rather than explain political preferences in terms of "policy versus performance," we prefer to reduce ambiguity and distinguish between external sources of political evaluations that define conflict over governmental objectives or priorities and external sources that assume or emphasize a broad consensus concerning the government's responsibility for particular conditions or "results." In this reformulation, evaluations concerning any leader's "performance" should be seen as influenced by both types of external sources—and both criteria for evaluations as well as partisan identification. Thus, voters may see a particular leader as doing a good (or bad) job for two very different kinds of reasons—because they support (or oppose) what that leader is trying to accomplish *or* because they see that leader as successful (or unsuccessful) in "pursuing" acceptable governmental objectives.

▪ Alternative Approaches to Survey-Based Explanation

In many electoral analyses based on survey data, analysts have attempted to explain an individual voter's choices between the major candidates by reconstructing the psychological "forces" (at the small end of the funnel of causality) that apparently influenced that voter's choices. In some analyses, including those in *The American Voter*, the authors have summarized specific impressions, or psychological "forces," that were apparently responsible for each voter's final decision by classifying responses to open-ended questions about those aspects of the candidates (and parties) that each voter "liked" and "disliked." In that approach, the apparent importance of any substantive topic or area is usually based on the number of respondents who mentioned that topic as a "reason" for liking or disliking one of the candidates—as well as the relationships between such responses and the vote. In the years after *The American Voter,* however, many scholars concluded that the impact of some types of attitudes on the vote could not be reliably assessed on the basis of volunteered, self-reported "reasons," but could be better approximated through multivariate analyses of evaluations based on structured questions.[3] On the basis of that rationale, comparative evaluations of the candidates have been developed for a wide variety of criteria, including explicit measures of the candidates' relative proximities to the respondents' own policy preferences, as well as assessments of the candidates' personal qualities and leadership abilities.

We are convinced, however, that all candidate-related evaluations, however elicited, represent a kind of partisan "conclusion" that will have been heavily influenced by positive or negative impressions of the candidates based on a variety of *other* considerations—in addition to the topic identified in the survey questions eliciting the evaluations. For example, many factors may lead survey respondents to report that one candidate seems closer than the other to their own policy preferences in a given area. To counter such potentially confounding effects, we have concentrated on explanatory variables that acquired their current values well before the current campaign—that is, that are located "further back" than explicit evaluations near the small end of the funnel of causality. We are impressed with the inherent difficulty in any attempt to reconstruct causal connections among the specific psychological factors, or proximate forces, that immediately precede each voter's decision. In trying to "solve" that problem, we have emphasized voters' own attitudes toward topics which may have been emphasized (and activated) in the campaign and which thereby may have generated the proximate impressions (or psychological forces) that are responsible for all partisan evaluations—as well as the vote.

Regardless of the type of evaluations involved, however, the *external* sources of voters' positive or negative impressions of political leaders (or parties) should not be confused with the resulting *internal* impressions. Specific impressions expressed by a given voter (concerning a particular candidate or party) are generated by the interaction of that voter's exposure to some external "source" or circumstance with prior attitudes of the voter. Ultimately, both contributions to such interactions should be measured separately.

Generalized descriptions of the logic of elaboration, such as that presented by James Davis, rely on terms such as "independent," "intervening," or "dependent" to clarify the explanatory role of different types of variables (Davis, 1990). Although we rely heavily on the image of a succession of explanatory stages, it is clear that the relationship of various stages to each other could be presented in terms of independent (social and economic characteristics), intervening (predispositions), and dependent (candidate evaluations or, more clearly, vote choice). Elsewhere in this book we comment on the utility of describing stable variables in terms of long-term influences that are more or less "independent," and malleable or volatile attitudes or opinions as short-term, more or less dependent.

At this point we simply want to emphasize the perspective that sees all attitudes, perceptions, or opinions as the consequence of people's interactions with stimuli external to themselves as provided by the world of politics. In a very real sense, most of our survey-based variables are more or less "dependent" because the real independent variables are the external stimuli (partisan, conflictual, or consensual) that provoke or evoke the responses to the questions put to NES respondents. However we classify or categorize those responses, they represent the consequences of interactions among prior attitudes and voters' exposure to events in the world of politics.

Methodological Issues Concerning "Apparent Effects"

In discussing the electoral impact of specific explanatory variables, we will periodically emphasize the statistical procedures involved and our reasons for relying on a bloc recursive model and ordinary least squares (OLS). Some comparisons between our results and results based on alternative statistical procedures are presented in a Methodological Appendix to this book (Appendix D), along with a discussion of the issues involved in using one procedure instead of another.

In addition to that technical discussion, however, we offer the following observations on the estimates we have presented concerning the apparent "effects" of specific variables—and the consequences of the statistical procedures we have used. First, we must emphasize our view that estimates of the "apparent effect" for each individual variable in our model conceal significant variation among voters in the degree to which that characteristic was activated by the campaign, and in the degree to which, when activated, that characteristic exerted some influence on vote choice. The true influence of a given attitude on the vote is almost certainly higher for some voters than for others, and thus all of our estimates represent a kind of average over the entire sample of voters—or an "apparent average effect." Unfortunately, the additional assumptions required for our coefficients to be unbiased estimates of the (true) average of individual level effects are not easily testable. In the absence of such tests, we have repeatedly described the resulting coefficients as "approximate" or "apparent."[4]

Ideally, we would incorporate this kind of variability in the "true" impact of individual explanatory variables by including a direct measure of the salience or importance of each topic in our explanatory model for each voter. With such a measure, each explanatory variable in our multivariate analyses would be replaced by the product of the voter's position on that variable and its causal "weight" *for that individual.* The 1992 NES survey does not include any measures that can be used as approximations for such weights, and we note that several previous attempts to develop and validate such measures have not been successful.[5] In any event, we would be reluctant to use as causal "weights" any survey-based variables that were based on respondents' own reports concerning the importance of specific factors in explaining their choice. The electoral field has not yet resolved this issue, and we are reluctant to trust voters' self-reports concerning the impact of specific factors on their own choice—whether those reports are based on structured questions about the relative importance of specific topics or open-ended questions about the positive and negative aspects of the candidates.

Since *The American Voter* appeared, many analysts have been concerned that effect estimates for any attitude-based explanatory variables (especially issue proximities and other explicitly comparative evaluations of the candidates) will be biased if they rely on conventional multivariate procedures. As indicated briefly in Chapter 1, such concerns are frequently discussed in terms of "simultaneity," whether they involve reciprocal causal relationships between explanatory variables and the vote or relationships between such variables and omitted causes of the vote. The same kinds of problems may also arise because of (non-trivial) measurement error in the explanatory variables. On the basis of assumptions concerning reciprocal causation, correlated disturbances, or measurement error, several analysts have suggested that effect estimates for "endogenous" explanatory variables (which are themselves caused by contemporary or "short-term" forces) will be seriously biased if they are based on a single equation model.[6]

In these formulations, "simultaneity" effects concerning issue proximities can occur through two types of substantive processes, as well as from unspecified correlations between the disturbances and independent variables in the model. In the first of these processes, usually called "projection," respondents who do not know the position of a given candidate simply attribute their own preferences to that candidate, thereby maximizing their *apparent* proximity to that candidate. In the other confounding process, usually called "persuasion," respondents shift (or create) their own policy preferences to match the position of the candidate they have already chosen because of other factors. Of course, in neither case is the apparent preference a basis for a choice between candidates (Page and Brody, 1972).

Analysts who are critical of the single equation model have typically noted that believable estimates of causal effects may still be possible in models that involve reciprocal causation, measurement error, or unavoidable relationships between measured and omitted causes of the vote—provided the analyst is willing to endorse a different set of assumptions. To produce such estimates, analysts must adopt a simultaneous equation model which includes assumptions (usually called "exclusion restrictions") that assign some potential effects to a nonexistent status (that is, zero).

The history of simultaneous equation models of the voter has been as controversial as the two single-equation traditions they were designed to replace (based on open-ended questions and issue proximities). Disagreement about such models has primarily focused on the validity of the exclusion restrictions which are required for any simultaneous equation model to be "identified"—so that its coefficient can be estimated. Each exclusion restriction stipulates that the impact of one explanatory variable on the vote (or some other dependent variable) is entirely mediated by other endogenous variables in the model—that is, does not have any direct effect that does not go "through" the endogenous explanatory variables that appear in the equation.[7] The most frequently cited simultaneous equation models of the vote can be found in Franklin and Jackson (1983), Page and Jones (1979), and Fiorina (1981). Simultaneous equation models may also be used to correct for bias in effect estimates caused by measurement error in the explanatory variables. Examples of this kind of rationale and analysis can be found in Green and Palmquist (1990) and Rosenstone et al. (1988).

The basic rationale for the multi-stage model we have employed provides at least one contrast to the logic of two-stage least squares procedures based on simultaneous equations. In the latter, the presumed endogeneity of an explanatory variable is countered by replacing that variable with an alternative that cannot have been influenced by the short-term factors that may have confounded the single-equation estimates for the explanatory variable in question. This substitute or alternative explanatory version is typically constructed in the first stage of the two-stage procedure by using clearly exogenous variables (such as education, race, gender, income, or age). The resulting predicted score is then inserted in the second stage of the analysis with the assurance that its values cannot be the consequence of (or correlated with) any omitted endogenous influences on the vote.

The logic of elaboration that underlies our model also treats the same kind of "instrumental" variables in the first stage of the two-stage process as exogenous, in that we do not attempt to explain them or account for their origins. All of those variables, however, are considered as possible antecedents of *both* the other explanatory variables and one or more dependent variables. They are included in our analysis because of their own independent effects *and* because of the possibility that they represent shared antecedents that may "confound" any relationship observed between other explanatory variables and the vote. We "control" them statistically, thereby removing their confounding influence on the apparent impact of these variables.

Instead of replacing a given explanatory variable with its predicted score (based on the influence of exogenous variables), thereby "throwing away" the rest of that variable's variation as "confounded," our bloc recursive model explicitly retains all of our exogenous factors as explanatory variables at each stage of the analysis. By controlling for exogenous variables at each stage, we remove their possibly spurious contribution to each relationship between independent and dependent variables. This perspective, based on the logic of elaboration and our bloc recursive model, also highlights a frequent lack of attention to temporal sequence in causal analysis. This tradition emphasizes such a focus with its distinctive terminology for characterizing the explanatory role of specific *variables*—antecedent, independent, intervening, and dependent— as well as for presumed causal *processes*—defined in terms of the origin and transmittal of direct, indirect, and total apparent effects.

As mentioned above, our previous analyses of recent elections gradually moved away from explanatory models that relied on explicit evaluations of the candidates in favor of concentrating on the apparent total effects of variables that are presumably located farther back in the funnel of causality. In particular, we have shifted our policy-related analyses from issue proximities to measures of voters' general predispositions and current preferences concerning policy direction—all of which are defined without any reference to the (perceived) positions of the candidates or current federal policy. One of our major objectives in that shift away from explicitly evaluative explanatory variables has been to reduce the amount of "simultaneity" or "feedback" from other causes of the vote.

Moreover, as noted, we have adopted a bloc recursive model to estimate the total effects of specific variables in each of our stages because of the consequences of false exclusion restrictions in any of the simultaneous equation models we have considered. Our continuing use of a multiple-stage and bloc recursive model is based on our general belief that respondents' own policy preferences and perceptions of current conditions are only moderately affected by "persuasion" (based on influence from the campaign of the candidate that voters prefer because of other factors), and that all candidate evaluations are subject to substantial "projection" effects—in which evaluations in one area are affected by candidate preferences (which were caused by other considerations). In general, we agree that effect estimates based on our bloc recursive model may be slightly biased because of uncontrolled "feedback" (from the vote) due to factors that we have omitted from our analyses. Those biases, however, should be much smaller than those caused by false exclusion restrictions in the simultaneous equation models we have considered.[8] In the meantime, we have presented our results in ways that make evident their dependence on the (approximate) validity of our assumptions.

Comparisons with "The American Voter"

As outlined in Chapter 1, our explanations of individual choice involve many of the same substantive ideas that were used in *The American Voter*. The variables we have used to explain vote choice during the 1980s and 1990s are defined substantively in terms of the same kinds of psychological "forces" that were used to explain voters' decisions in 1952 and 1956. These include policy-related or ideological differences between the candidates, perceptions of current national conditions, and the personal qualities of the candidates, as well as the performance of the parties as "managers of government" and voters' long-term identifications with one of the two major parties. Furthermore, both formulations assume that voters acquire a wide variety of positive and negative impressions about the major candidates and parties in their reactions to specific events or experiences over a substantial period of time—both before and during a current campaign.

Nevertheless, the two approaches to multivariate analysis are different in several important respects. In our multi-stage analysis, each explanatory variable has been constructed from one or more *structured* questions concerning voters' opinions about a specific explanatory topic, whereas the explanatory variables used in *The American Voter* were based on voters' responses to evaluative questions about their reasons for "liking" or "disliking" the candidates or parties. Furthermore, although our overall approach is consistent with *The American Voter's* metaphor of a funnel of causality, our multi-stage model is based on a more differentiated set of assumptions concerning the sequence in which voters acquired their "positions" on different types of explanatory variables.

These differences between our current approach and the procedures used in *The American Voter* might be responsible for differences in some detailed conclusions about a given election. Unfortunately, however, methodological differences of this sort *can* also lead to more substantial differences in substantive interpretation; indeed, major controversies about individual elections may be attributable to such fundamental differences in measurement and analytic procedures. Because of these possibilities, and because of the continuing influence of *The American Voter* as well as other analyses based on the same kind of methods, we have concluded several chapters with comparisons of the apparent roles played by specific aspects of the 1992 campaign as assessed by these two quite different approaches to electoral explanation.[9]

Several explanatory factors appear to have had the same kind of impact on electoral decisions in 1992, whether the evidence of that influence is based on structured questions about voters' attitudes or on open-ended questions about their "reasons" for liking or disliking the candidates. However, these contrasting methods also lead to *quite* different conclusions concerning the role played by some other factors. We will use such comparisons in several chapters to suggest that measures based on structured questions concerning voters' opinions usually provide a more appropriate assessment of the electoral "relevance" of specific aspects of a given campaign than do voters' own explanations for their vote preferences. The same comparisons, however, will also suggest the possible advantages of a mixed strategy for electoral explanation, since both kinds of data are available in the traditional NES design for presidential elections.

9

★ ★ ★ The Political Importance of "Non-Political" Variables: Stable Social and Economic Characteristics

If modern studies of electoral behavior began in 1923 with the innovative work of Gosnell and Merriam, the intervening seven decades have demonstrated that virtually every socioeconomic attribute of citizens in the United States is relevant to one or another of the voting decisions (Gosnell and Merriam, 1924). Both the decisions whether to vote and whom to vote for are statistically related to social characteristics that have become politically relevant at some point in the nation's recent history. The connections between social characteristics and political behavior are so ubiquitous that they led the founder of survey-based political analysis, Paul Lazarsfeld, to suggest that one's social being defined one's political preferences.[1] Subsequently, Lazarsfeld modified his language to say that he had intended only to claim that social pressures reinforced behavioral intentions. Nonetheless, such works as *The People's Choice* (Lazarsfeld et al., 1948), *Voting* (Berelson et al., 1954), *The People Elect a President* (Campbell and Kahn, 1952), and many other successor studies of voting behavior treat social characteristics such as age, education, gender, and religion as major "causes" of political differentiation.

Electoral scholars have often noted what they see as a continuing tension, if not a major conflict, between such sociological "explanations" of voting behavior and the more psychological explanations based on attitudes, perceptions, values, and beliefs. Some interpretations have even drawn a contrast between a neo-Marxist emphasis on social structure (at private universities such as Chicago and Columbia) and a liberal capitalist preoccupation with context-free individualism (at a public

212

university like the University of Michigan) (see Natchez, 1970). Such interpretations are a more extreme version of a commonly held view that there are important differences between the sociological tradition in electoral analysis, which began at the Columbia Bureau of Applied Social Research, and the social psychological approach, which was introduced by the Michigan Survey Research Center (and continued by the Center for Political Studies).[2]

In our view, longstanding controversies of that sort are less important than our understanding of the intimate and complementary relationships among the social, psychological, and political dimensions of civic life and electoral behavior. People in different social (or economic) categories hold different political views as a result of their social experiences and the ways in which the political relevance of those experiences is defined by the contemporary political context. We have argued, quite vociferously, that generational differences exist—in political attitudes, values, and behavior—because of differences in political experiences during the stages in individuals' lives when each generation's definitions of self and political values were shaped by events that are more or less unique to that generation. In like manner, more recent differences in political identification and preferences reflect very different personal histories and social circumstances for the Southern Black, the urban Cuban Hispanic, or the devout Evangelical churchgoer.

Some political differences among social categories have endured so long that they literally constitute "long-term" influences on political behavior. For example, some of the political differences between households with one or more labor union members and those with no union members trace back fifty years or more to the political mobilization of workers during the Depression of the 1930s. Although organizational efforts to change or enhance the partisan relevance of union membership may vary from election to election (as when the union leadership broke with tradition to endorse Mondale early in the 1984 contest), the substantial difference in vote choice between union and non-union households seems virtually frozen in time.[3] Because of such "social" continuities in electoral behavior, we might well expect such differentiation to be reflected in the enduring political attribute of party identification—an attribute that has had a relatively unchanging relevance for the quadrennial presidential contests between the two major parties.

On the other hand, as we shall note in some detail, changes in the topics or issues emphasized by political elites may bring new political meaning to very traditional social differences. In the domain of religion, for example, some religious categories have acquired new political relevance within the twelve years that separate the Carter-Reagan contest in 1980 from the Clinton-Bush election in 1992. It will take more intensive and extended analysis than we can pursue in this book to clarify the precise nature of the newly emerging symbiotic relationship between religion and politics. At this point, however, and within the general framework of this book, it is possible to trace changes in some of the statistical relationships as they involve issue-related predispositions, voting preferences, and enduring changes in partisan identification.

Our general outlook on the causal processes that we are exploring does not suggest conflict or tension between sociological and psychological approaches to electoral explanation. Both approaches view voting behavior as a continuation of relationships over time as well as evidence of substantial change. This view is based on the notion that it is really the external events of politics, and changes in the nature of the political context, that "cause" short-term change in voters' behavior by interacting with their prior beliefs and preferences. Stable differences in citizens' social "locations" provide different expectations confronting political change (when it occurs); and changes in social characteristics often accelerate or highlight the meaning of significant change in the external world of real politics.

Social and economic attributes remain the most "independent" variables with regard to voters' preferences; such attributes are (usually) the cause rather than the consequence of individuals' political activities or commitments. In most relationships, therefore, social and economic attributes are the fixed or unchanging "first causes." Such characteristics only acquire political "effects," however, when specific categories become politically relevant as the result of political interaction with the external world. We shall note that, where religion is concerned, political changes within "social" categories may be the consequence as well as the source of political values and perspectives.

▪ The Impact of Stable Social Characteristics

The field of electoral studies began by emphasizing relationships between the vote and a variety of social or "background" characteristics, including socioeconomic status, urbanism, age, religious affiliation, and gender. More recently, political scientists have been increasingly interested in explicitly political—and more proximate—determinants of the vote, including policy preferences, performance evaluations, and perceptions of the candidates' personal qualities. This preoccupation with explicitly political attitudes is both understandable and appropriate, for the reasons that are emphasized throughout this book, but any comprehensive explanation of the vote must also include social and economic characteristics—for two quite different reasons.

First, many differences in political attitudes have their origins in differences in the objective well-being or other life experiences among social groups. Our analysis would be concerned with voters' social and economic circumstances even if we were certain that their impact on the vote was ultimately interpreted or entirely mediated by the explicitly political (and attitudinal) variables in our model. In general, we learn more about the meaning of each explanatory political variable if we understand how or why different kinds of voters have arrived at different attitudes in that area. For that reason, our subsequent chapters include analyses that treat each of the political variables that we use to understand the vote as dependent variables whose origins—particularly those shared with vote preference—must be explained. In most of what follows, however, we have concentrated on how the impact of each explanatory variable (including social characteristics) can be interpreted as mediated by some or all of the factors that we assume intervene between it and the vote, with particular attention to some of the specific attitudes that appear to be responsible for that mediation.

The second reason for including social and economic characteristics in our analysis is intimately related to the logic of our multiple-stage model of the vote. In general, we do not assume that *all* of the impact of each social characteristic is going to be mediated by the intervening variables in our model. In other words, we assume that the effects of some social characteristics will be only partially mediated by the intervening variables that have been included in any given stage. It follows, then, that any effect estimate for a *political* variable, at any given stage, which is based on an analysis that does not include social and economic characteristics, may be at least partially spurious (or biased) because of its "origin" in the confounding impact of prior variables.[4]

The field of survey-based electoral analysis began with a strong theoretical interest in the potential connections between vote choice and social or economic characteristics; *The American Voter* included an extended discussion of the conditions under which many such characteristics are linked to the vote. Explanatory interpretations of this type of relationship have been fairly diverse, including the attribution of causal force to economic interests shared by members of the same group, to social influence based on group membership or association, and to common political experiences shared by group members (in the current campaign, earlier elections, or childhood socialization). Many interpretations embrace the possibility that specific issues in a given election may be defined in terms of particular groups or social characteristics (for example, women, minorities, labor unions, corporations). Despite the historical emphasis on the "social basis" of electoral choice, however, relatively few contemporary explanations of vote choice have considered a comprehensive set of potential connections between social or economic characteristics and the vote. We attempt to do so in the next two chapters.

In addition to a substantive interest in the impact of social and economic characteristics, variables based on such characteristics are often included in multivariate models precisely because they are exogenous to most ongoing electoral processes. Therefore, as discussed in the last chapter, they may be useful as instruments in estimating coefficients in models that would otherwise be troubled by "simultaneity bias"—because the other explanatory variables are thought to be as endogenous as vote choice itself. Our purpose, however, is to summarize the evidence concerning a variety of possible connections in the 1992 election between vote choice and social or economic characteristics, and then to suggest the kinds of social or psychological processes that appear to have been involved in generating such relationships. Put somewhat differently, our motivation in examining these social and economic characteristics is primarily substantive, instead of procedural or methodological. We will, however, try to be clear about the assumptions that we have made in attempting to take account of social and economic variables in assessing the role played by other types of explanatory variables.

As in our previous reports on the Reagan, Bush, and Clinton elections, our multivariate analysis of the contest between Bill Clinton and George Bush begins by identifying those social or economic characteristics that appear to have had some effect on voters' eventual choices between those candidates. After identifying such characteristics, we introduce (or control for) a variety of other variables that are defined in terms of attitudes or opinions, in order to clarify the many ways in which social or economic differences between citizens may have influenced their choice on election day. In particular, we will emphasize the extent to which visible "connections" between the vote and social and economic characteristics appear to have been produced by the prior influence of those characteristics on several continuing or long-term predispositions, instead of by a direct role in generating the "short-term forces" associated with the 1992 campaign.

▪ Social Attributes and Voter Turnout

Earlier chapters on voting turnout and party identification provided many illustrations of the political relevance of social and economic determinants on voting behavior. Those determinants were discussed in fairly general terms, based on broad periods defined by adjoining elections and generationally defined subsets of the potential electorate. At this point we turn to a more detailed election-by-election inspection, from 1980 to 1992, of regularities and changes in the relationship between vote decisions and various social and economic factors. We give particular attention to voting behavior in the most recent of those contests.

With regard to voter *turnout,* we find little evidence of change in relationships between 1980 and 1992 that was not suggested in the earlier chapters. At the level of simple bivariate relationships, the most noteworthy results concern the consistency or stability of most relationships with turnout. As we have observed, voting turnout varies by generation (or age) and education, and it does so in all four elections of the Reagan/Bush/Clinton era. There are also persistent differences in turnout between groups of people—differences that are defined by gender, union membership, marital status, income, region, home ownership, ethnicity, and religion (for details see Tables B1.1 to B11.2 in Appendix B). National turnout may decline, as from 1984 to 1988, or rise, as from 1988 to 1992, but the magnitudes of inter-group differences (or their relative deviations from national totals) are nearly constant during the entire 12-year period. Some of these persistent inter-group differences in turnout, as with age, education, and income, seem particularly important. Other social differences are equally persistent but less pronounced, including those between groups defined in terms of religion, ethnicity, region, and marital status.

In 1992 all of the standard social and economic attributes were at least moderately correlated with voter turnout. For all of those attributes, with one exception, the size of inter-group differences (in turnout) was stable across the Reagan/Bush/Clinton elections, with only occasional single-year aberrations. Only religious categories exhibit any interesting shifts in voting rates between 1980 and 1992, and even these examples are few in number and limited in scope, but interesting because of related changes in vote divisions. The turnout of Jews increased steadily throughout the period, rising from 81 percent voting in 1980 (only 10 percentage points above the self-reported national figures) to a reported 97 percent turnout in 1992 (more than 20 percentage points higher than the self-reported national rate). On the other hand, the turnout of Mainline Protestants who felt religion to be a very important part of their lives dropped from a rate some 13 percentage points above the national average in 1980 to only 4 percentage points above the national average in 1992.

In general, turnout differences between social categories simply persisted throughout the Reagan/Bush/Clinton elections; and they endured in much the same patterns as had emerged in earlier elections of the mid- and late twentieth century. Thus, as suggested by our earlier comments on social connectedness, marital status seems to have a persistent influence on civic participation (see Tables B6.1–B6.3 in Appendix B). Married citizens voted from 9 to 14 percentage points above the national average, and those who had never been married or were currently divorced voted at rates 10 to 14 percentage points below the national norms (20 to 27 percentage points below the rate of the married citizens). In the South, turnout rates continued to lag behind those of the other regions, running from 11 to 13 percentage points behind the Midwest after 1980 (see Tables B8.1–B8.3). These (selected) categorical differences in turnout are typical of a large number of subgroup differences that remained virtually unchanged from 1980, or earlier, to 1992.

▪ Social Differences and Partisan Preferences: The Case of Religion

As with voter turnout, subgroup differences concerning partisan preferences are also quite constant between 1980 and 1992, with relatively few instances of systematic change over time. There is, however, one type of "social" characteristic for which that pattern is emphatically not true, and from which we may learn about the circumstances under which strong connections may be created between social and political attributes. The circumstances that have created these changes concern religion, and they have produced dramatic shifts in partisan identification as well as voting behavior across the relatively brief period of our analysis.

Religion and Presidential Politics

In the broadest of terms, religion has long been recognized as an important part of the political mosaic of the United States. Professional students of religion, however, have argued for some time that political scientists (among others) have generally erred in emphasizing differences among the three main religious traditions of the United States (that is, differences defined in terms of Catholics, Protestants, and Jews) without differentiating among strikingly different subsets of Protestants. Thirty years ago, Glock and Stark declared: "When we speak of 'Protestants,' as we so often do in the social sciences, we spin statistical fiction . . . Protestantism [in contrast to Catholicism] includes many separately constituted groups and the only possible ground for treating them collectively would be if they shared in a common religious vision. Since this is clearly not the case, we shall have to change our ways" (p. 65). Despite such admonitions, the role of religion in the social science discussions of twentieth-century American politics has been largely confined to the religious differences that emerged during the elections of 1928 and 1960. The "connection" between religion and politics was presumably documented by Al Smith's defeat in 1928, which demonstrated a barrier to the election of a Catholic president that persisted until Kennedy's victory in 1960. More recently, the collection of essays assembled by David Leege and Lyman Kellstedt responds to the Glock/Stark criticism with well-reasoned hypotheses and empirical tests concerning politically relevant distinctions among the major Protestant religious traditions. In their book, the gross contrast between Protestant and Catholic is replaced by careful presentations of several politically relevant dimensions that divide churches, sects, and denominations within the overall ranks of "Protestants."

Fortunately for the simplicity and coherence of electoral analysis, Kellstedt notes that "grouping of Protestant denominations into religious traditions serves as an aggregating mechanism, allowing the great number of [Protestant] denominational groups to come together to provide support for issue positions, political parties, and candidates for public office. These religious traditions, and particularly in the institutions that have developed to serve them, become the focal point of campaign efforts on the part of candidates and parties" (Leege and Kellstedt, 1993, p. 275). Throughout much of the Leege/Kellstedt volume, the editors and their collaborators refer to five major religious traditions—Evangelical Protestants, Mainline Protestants, Catholics, Jews, and the Non-religious—which capture most of the relevant political differences among denominations.

In a highly provocative chapter, Kellstedt and coauthor Corwin E. Smidt utilize NES data to document (and clarify) the dramatic shift in voting between the 1960s and the late 1980s for subgroups within the three largest religious traditions (Evangelical Protestants, Mainline Protestants, and Catholics) that emphasize some special character of the Bible. The progression of religious politics from 1980 through recent time becomes even more striking if we employ a concept introduced by James L. Guth and John C. Green in another chapter of the Leege/Kellstedt volume entitled "Salience: The Core Concept?" (Leege and Kellstedt, 1993, chap. 8). In an effort to identify those citizens for whom religion is most relevant to politics, Green and Guth constructed an indicator of religious involvement based on two NES questions that were introduced in 1980. The first of these questions asks: "Do you consider religion to be an important part of your life or not?" Those who answered "yes" to that question were then asked: "Would you say your religion provides some guidance in your day-to-day living, quite a bit of guidance, or a great deal of guidance in your day-to-day life?" Guth and Green combined answers to the "importance of guidance" questions with measures of church attendance and devotional behavior to form a highly reliable measure of religious involvement, or religiosity.

Our search for a summary indicator of the potential political relevance of voters' religions is well served by the NES questions concerning religious "importance" and "guidance." Both questions help isolate striking patterns of change in the sheer size of religious sub-groups between 1980 and 1992. In addition, they help clarify even more striking patterns of change in the partisanship of different religious groups. For our purposes, we have also included church attendance in our analysis to identify sources of change that may be tied to political communications within the local congregation. Following Leege's lead, however, we will not incorporate attendance in an overall measure of religiosity (Leege, 1993). Instead, we will treat attendance as an indicator of probable exposure to political communications within the church, whether directly from the pulpit, from politically active fellow parishioners, or from casual conversation among like-minded co-religionists. With these measures of religious salience and frequency of church attendance, we can describe some of the short-term changes in religio-political relationships (among the major religious traditions) that have taken place during the Reagan-Bush-Clinton years.

The Changing Fortunes of Different Religious Traditions

Before considering political matters, we must make clear that the religious profile of the electorate in the United States has been undergoing large and portentous changes. In studying these structural changes, we have set aside the smaller ethno-religious groupings because of their heterogeneity and size. For the major groupings, however, we can document striking volatility, both among the seculars (with no religious affiliation) and among the followers of the three most prominent traditions. In the twelve years from 1980 to 1992, as shown in Table 9.1, Mainline Protestants declined in numbers from more than one out of three in the electorate (36 percent) to a little less than one out of four (24 percent). In the same brief interval, Evangelical Protestant numbers grew from 26 percent to 32 percent. And, more dramatically, the number of citizens with no religious preference apparently almost doubled (from 7 percent in 1980 to 13 percent in 1992).[5] Furthermore, the proportion of Mainliners who regularly attend church and consider religion a very important guide in daily living dropped from one in four to one in six *within* that tradition (from 24 percent to 17 percent). On the other hand, among Evangelicals during that time period, the same definition of commitment produced a slight increase in the rate of committed religionists (from 38 percent to 40 percent of all Evangelicals). Nationally, among Protestants the ratio of committed Evangelicals to committed Mainline adherents went from near parity in 1980 (10 to 9) to an overwhelming Evangelical dominance (14 to 4) in 1992. Mainliners declined in both numbers and commitment, while Evangelicals flourished.

Table 9.1 Religious Attachments Among Non-Blacks: Major "Traditions," 1980 and 1992[a]

Tradition	Importance of Religion	1980		1992		Change[b] 1980 to 1992	
		Regular Attend.	Less Regular	Regular Attend.	Less Regular	Reg.	Irreg.
Mainline	Most Important	9	5	4	2	−5	−3
Protestant	Less Important	4	18	4	14	0	−4
Evangelical	Most Important	10	3	14	4	+4	+1
Protestant	Less Important	3	10	4	10	+1	0
Catholic	Most Important	5	2	6	2	+1	0
	Less Important	7	10	6	10	−1	0
Other		15		21		+6	

a. Entries for each year total 100%, including Jews and "Other" minor religions who totaled 8% in both 1980 and 1992, and Non-religious who totaled 7% and 13%, respectively, in 1980 and 1992.

b. Some of the drop in members of Mainline Protestants is a consequence of improved measurement in 1992.

Despite all the well-publicized ferment within the Catholic church, the numbers within comparable categories of Catholic followers changed very little in size and virtually not at all either in church attendance or the importance of religion in daily life.

Within the Black community, changes in religious affiliations have been even more dramatic. Because of limited sample sizes in NES surveys, it is not possible to assess differential changes for Blacks within the Mainline Protestant or Catholic traditions.[6] We can, however, note that Black Mainline Protestants apparently lost a third of their number, dropping from 15 percent to 10 percent of all Blacks. As with non-Black citizens, Black Catholics held steady (at 10 or 11 percent of the total). In contrast to the non-Black citizens, however, there may have been some *decrease* in the secular ranks among Blacks: the non-religious represented 7 percent of Blacks in 1980 and only 5 percent in 1992. Among Black Evangelicals (up from a little less than 70 percent of the Black total in 1980 to almost 75 percent in 1992), both the importance of religion and the frequency of church attendance were even higher than among non-Blacks, and both appeared to increase between 1980 and 1992.

The complex pattern of movement among denominations and between traditions is discussed in the Leege/Kellstedt volume in the chapter by Green and Guth entitled "From Lambs to Sheep: Denominational Change and Political Behavior." Their analysis of recall data inhibits any facile generalization about patterns of micro-change over time.

Apart from changes in the size of religious groupings, a few other indicators of change in participation are worth noting from the more detailed Table B9.1 in Appendix B. Inter-group differences in voting turnout over time were generally constant during the 1980–1992 period, with all groups moving down or up together. Thus, turnout rates for nominal Evangelicals and the non-religious have been consistently below the rest of the nation. Similarly, Jews consistently had the highest turnout of all religious sub-groups after 1980, especially in 1992 when their self-reported rate reached the extraordinary level of 97 percent. Those least involved with religion among both Catholics and Mainline Protestants exhibited a mild increase in turnout, moving from a level near that of the rest of the country in 1980 to 6 points above the rest of the nation in 1992. Nominal Mainline Protestant contribution to national vote totals was minimized by the apparent decline in the size of the group—from 27 percent of the electorate in 1980 to 20 percent in 1992. During that period, the political role of the more religious Mainline Protestants was doubly constricted as a decline in sheer size was accompanied by a relative decline in their turnout.

Religious Commitment and Voter Turnout

The patterns of political change that accompanied shifts in religious traditions and salience have nuances that go beyond the trends reported in this volume. The most important features of those changes, however, can be captured with the one simplification that we have implicitly used in the foregoing discussion. To be explicit: In subsequent analyses we shall distinguish between the subset of regular church attenders for whom religion is highly salient (called the committed) and the subset including all other members of that tradition (called the nominal adherents, for whom religion is apparently less central, either in terms of its importance in daily life or frequency of church attendance). Even with this simplification, comparisons of religious groups in terms of voting turnout provide ample grist for interpretations of political change. From Table 9.2, it is immediately evident that committed Protestants (both Mainline and Evangelical) did not reflect national changes in turnout

Table 9.2 Changes in Voter Turnout, 1980–1992

	Committed Supporters		Nominal Supporters
Mainline Protestant	−1 (4%)		+8 (20%)
Evangelical Protestant	−1 (14%)		+7 (18%)
Catholic	+7 (6%)		+11 (18%)
Jew		+16 (3%)	
Non-Religious		+4 (13%)	
Other		+10 (5%)	

NOTE: Each entry is the change in the proportion of the group reporting having voted in 1980 and 1992. Entries in parentheses are proportions of non-Black two-party voters (excluding Perot supporters). The data on which these measures of change are based are presented in Tables B9.1 and B9.2.

between 1980 and 1992. In most cases, as with the nominal supporters of the major traditions, voter turnout in 1992 exceeded that of 1980 by somewhat more than the margin observed for the rest of the electorate (up 6 points from 70 percent self-reported voting in 1980, to 76 percent in 1992).

Among committed followers, however, changes in turnout varied significantly across traditions. For traditional Mainline Protestants, the earlier suggestions of decline carried over into the political arena. Indeed, in an era in which core followers among the Catholics seemed politically energized and mobilized, committed Evangelicals as well as committed Mainline Protestants turned out at no greater rate at the end of the Reagan-Bush era than they had at the beginning. If there were short-term forces that made for a higher turnout in the Christian Coalition in 1992, they were clearly offset by other forces among the two Protestant core groups.

Among Catholics, voter turnout increased in line with national totals, with the largest increase occurring between 1980 and 1984. Equally notable is the increase in turnout among followers of other (smaller) religious categories. These increases in turnout take on added significance when we explore simultaneous changes in the partisan division of the vote. First, however, we should note a racial discontinuity in the turnout figures for Black citizens. Among nominal Black Evangelicals, the picture was much like that among non-Blacks; between 1980 and

1992, turnout rose about 5 points. Among committed Black Evangelicals, however, turnout dropped from a strong 84 percent in 1980 to 76 percent in 1992. This apparent change accounts for most of the overall decline in turnout among all Evangelicals (regardless of race). These estimates are based on fairly small numbers of cases, but they suggest that Black Evangelicals did not follow other committed Evangelicals in maintaining or increasing their political engagement on election day.

Religious Traditions and Vote Choice

The relevance of religion to the national shift in political fortunes that replaced the clear-cut Reagan-Bush victories with Bill Clinton's narrow win is documented in Table 9.3.[7] Voting changes within five of the nine categories of voters as defined in Table 9.2 were more or less in line with the national swing from Reagan's defeat of Carter in 1980 to Clinton's victory over Bush in 1992. All three of the "nominal follower" groups for the three major religious traditions shared in the pro-Democratic

Table 9.3 Partisan Pluralities in Vote Divisions, 1980 and 1992, by Religious Category

	Committed Supporters			Nominal Supporters		
	1980	1992	Change in Democratic Plurality	1980	1992	Change in Democratic Plurality
Mainline Protestant	−28[a]	−10	+18	−29	+7	+36
Evangelical Protestant	+12	−13	−25	+2	+19	+17
Catholic	−23	0	+23	−5	+32	+37

	1980	1992	Change in Democratic Plurality
Jew	+15	+85	+70
Non-Religious	−13	+47	+60
Other	−30	+26	+56

a. Entry is Democratic percentage of two-party vote minus (−) Republican percentage among Non-Black two-party voters. Data for 1984 and 1988 are presented in Table B9.2.

shift. Nominal Mainline Protestants and Catholics, however, shifted more than twice as much (+36 and +38) as did nominal Evangelicals (+17). The shift to the Democratic column was almost twice as large among nominal followers as among committed supporters within both Catholics and Mainline Protestants. Voters in the three categories outside the major religious traditions (No religion, Jewish, and "Others") clearly exceeded the rest of the nation in rather massive pro-Democratic movements from 1980 to 1982.

The ninth group in our analysis of the new religious theme in presidential politics, the committed Evangelicals, defied the national swing. They moved from a clear vote favoring Democrat Carter over Republican Reagan in 1980 (+12) to a 1992 vote giving Republican Bush a plurality (−13) comparable to their 1980 vote for Carter. As in the case of voter turnout, the distinctiveness of changes in the vote division for the religious core of each tradition suggests the kinds of dynamics that may be involved. In particular, while some religious groupings within the active electorate were moving as much as 40, 60, or 70 percentage points away from Reagan and his successor, George Bush, nominal Evangelicals shifted less than 20 percentage points in the same pro-Democratic direction. Committed Evangelicals actually moved in the opposite direction, giving as much support to the Republican candidate in 1992 as they had given to the Democrat in 1980. This political switch is the more remarkable in that in 1980 they favored an Evangelical Democrat while in 1992 they voted Republican *against* another Evangelical, Bill Clinton.

It should be noted (see Appendix B, Table B9.2) that changes in the voting behavior of committed Evangelicals are even more striking than suggested by overall differences between them and their committed counterparts in the other religious traditions. By 1992, committed Evangelicals were also quite different from fellow Evangelicals for whom religion was of great importance in their daily lives but who did *not* attend church frequently. Nominal Evangelicals for whom religion was important but who did not attend church frequently shifted their votes toward the Democrats along with the rest of the nation.

It should be noted, however, that committed adherents in all three major traditions were clearly more pro-Republican (both in their 1992 votes and in their shift from 1980) than were their nominal fellow co-religionists, and that committed Mainliners were virtually as heavily pro-Republican in 1992 as committed Evangelicals. The latter stood out primarily in their *change* of vote choice against the national grain.

It seems apparent that the active growth in support for Republicans (and in opposition to Democrats) that emerged after the election of Ronald Reagan in 1980 was centered in the ranks of churchgoing Evangelicals for whom religion provides a great deal of guidance in their daily lives. There were, however, three other instances of partisan change in voting that were at least a match for the magnitude of the pro-Republican shift among committed Evangelicals; and they may be equally important for our understanding of the growing relevance of religion to politics in 1992.

First, the increase in the size of the secular, non-religious contingent in the electorate was as great as that of core Evangelicals—from 7 to 13 percent of the two-party voters between 1980 and 1992. In 1980, such voters were less numerous than the Mainline or Evangelical core groups, and only slightly larger than the committed Catholics; by 1992, those voters were the second largest of all religious categories, and almost as numerous within the electorate as the committed Evangelicals. The turnout rate for the non-religious has run well below that of the core groups in all three traditions, and by factors of 10 to 20 percentage points (65 percent voting to 77, 84, and 87 percent among the three groups of committed religious followers in 1992). Without much public attention, however, voters with no religious affiliation had moved further in partisan terms since 1980 than any of our religious groups. Voters with no religious preference supported Reagan over Carter in 1980 with a 56 percent to 44 percent plurality (much like the vote of committed Evangelicals); in 1984, they voted 55 percent to 45 percent for Mondale; and in 1992, they supported Clinton over Bush with a 74 percent to 26 percent vote—a 12-year swing in partisan pluralities of 60 points (−12 to +48) toward the Democrats, in contrast to the core Evangelical swing of 25 points toward the Republicans (see Table B9.2 in Appendix B).

Second, the proportion of Jews who voted for Clinton in 1992 was equally remarkable, for it represented a comparable swing of more than 70 points from their lukewarm support of Carter in 1980. In 1992, as in 1980, Jews constituted no more than 3 percent of the active electorate. Nevertheless, both among the Jews and among the growing number of non-religious, the ultimately large Democratic pluralities of 1992 had begun to emerge in 1984 at the very time of Reagan's overwhelming defeat of Mondale, and they continued to increase through the Dukakis loss in 1988 and on through the Clinton victory in 1992.

The third exceptional location for religion-oriented electoral change was the residual group remaining after most voters are classified into one of the major religious traditions. Such individuals represent a heterogeneous collection of minor religions—too varied to suggest any conclusions about the consequences of church attendance or the salience of religion in daily life. At this juncture, however, we can note that the overall voting behavior of this group suggests some awareness of political changes on the religious right. In particular, these adherents of minor religious traditions shared with Jews and the non-religious a very large shift to the Democrats. In 1980, followers of the minor religions matched the rest of the nation in a vote division clearly favoring Reagan over Carter. By 1992, however, they had reversed themselves with a 63 percent to 37 percent vote for Clinton over Bush. Although the minor or "other" religions made up only 5 percent of the electorate, the combined numbers for all three groups (who moved to the Democratic side much more sharply than did the remainder of the nation) reached 21 percent—at least one in five—substantially larger than the group of committed Evangelicals who shifted less sharply in the Republican direction.

▪ Other Social Groups

Within religious groups, the variability in the size and magnitude of changes in voting between 1980 and 1992 is the more striking in the face of comparisons with other social dimensions. No other social differentiation exhibited such significant changes in partisan voting over the same four elections. Other differences in social location or experience were sometimes marked by a sharp difference in the partisanship of votes in a given year, but there was no systematic change in political differentiation over the period of the Reagan-Bush-Clinton elections. Without exception, the secular components of Lazarsfeld's Index of Political Predispositions were as highly related to partisanship in voting in each and every election as the traditional literature would lead us to expect. As recorded in Appendix B, education, income, union membership, and similar indicators of socioeconomic status were all strongly and consistently correlated with the partisan direction of the vote. Despite indications of increased Republican strength in the South, the Democratic distinctiveness in the presidential vote in the South was evident in all but the election of 1992. Vote choices of Black voters were as decisively more Democratic than the votes of non-Blacks as the general literature on electoral behavior would lead us to expect. The gender gap, which emerged during the 1980s, persisted through 1992, with the female vote favoring Democratic candidates by a repeated 10 to 15 percent. Similarly, married voters remained as distinctively pro-Republican in 1992 as they had been throughout the 1980s.

Only one set of socio-political relationships appeared to change between 1980 and 1992. But as a result, interdenominational differentiation among the major religious traditions and differences between the more religious and the less religious appear to be key aspects of a new social base for political conflict during the 1990s. Whether these changes are primarily due to the Moral Majority, the Christian Coalition, or the Republican party, the new religious right has become a likely source of broad-based, enduring change in partisan national politics. The evidence suggesting such enduring changes is strengthened as our analysis shifts from changes in voting behavior to changes in partisan identification.

▪ Religion and Party Identification

Although there are mild patterns of change in the balance of party identifications within religious groups that seem to conform to the larger year-by-year changes in the division of the vote, very little net change can be seen in the partisan balance of those groups between 1980 and 1992—with two striking exceptions. One exception is within the Evangelical tradition. The entire set of Evangelicals for whom religion is of great daily importance moved sharply *away* from an earlier affinity for the Democratic party. In 1980, they were outdone only by Jews in their identification with the Democrats; twelve years later, the Democratic advantage among the more religious Evangelicals had almost completely disappeared (see Appendix B, Table B9.2). The second exception to the general pattern of minimal national change in party identification is provided by those members of "Other" religions, who moved even more sharply toward self-identification with the Democrats.

In contrast to the opposing shifts in party identification among the Evangelicals and the "Others," the secular non-religious were virtually

Table 9.4 Changes in the Partisan Balance of Party Identification, 1980–1992

	Committed Supporters		Nominal Supporters
Mainline Protestant	−3		−6
Evangelical Protestant	−34		−15
Catholic	+10		+1
Jew		−5	
Non-Religious		+3	
Other		+50	

NOTE: Each entry is the percentage point change in the Democratic Plurality (%Democrat-%Republican) of party identifications. Data on which measures of change are based are presented in Table B9.2.

unmoved in their net partisanship between 1980 and 1992, while their absolute numbers were growing substantially. The division of the vote for the non-religious was more volatile than for other religious groups, but their responses to new forces in national politics did not lead to any visible changes in their party loyalties. *Relative* to the rest of the country, however, because of the widespread shift to Republican identification between 1980 and 1988, the non-religious went from being among the less Democratic of religious groups in their partisan identifications in 1980 (see Table B9.3 in Appendix B) to being slightly more Democratic than the overall national margin in 1992. Nevertheless, the pro-Democratic shift in voting had not yet led to a complementary change in their party identification. It seems persuasively possible that the intense partisan emphasis on moral values that appealed to committed Evangelicals may have accounted both for the increase in the number of voters who had no religious preference and for the shared resistance among the non-religious, the Catholics, and the other non-Protestants to joining the Evangelical move toward Republican identification. A continuation of the Evangelical religious emphasis in partisan politics might, therefore, lead to further changes in party identification, as well as to a further accentuation of religious differences in voting behavior.

In Table 9.4, the elements of our puzzle are assembled in a summary of recent religion-related changes in partisan identification. We again note the dramatic differences between committed Evangelicals and the other major religious categories. Although followers of both Protestant traditions reflect a move from Democratic to Republican ranks, only core Evangelicals display a movement of historic significance. After a 65 percent to 36 percent split in identifications favoring the Democrats in 1980, committed Evangelicals in 1992 favored the Republican party in their partisan identifications, albeit by a very slender margin. Among nominal Evangelicals, party identification also shifted away from the Democrats, despite a voting shift toward the pro-Democratic direction. Elsewhere, the more familiar picture of stable party loyalties is maintained, except for those among "Other" religions and the non-religious. Catholics show little net change in partisan identification, and Jews appear to have become somewhat more Republican in their party identifications (despite a large pro-Democratic shift in their voting behavior).

Our evidence of stability and change in both partisan identifications and voting suggests some of the strengths and weaknesses inherent in political appeals delivered from the pulpit. Such appeals have increasingly been credited with shaping the votes of parishioners. The absence of any substantial increase in turnout among the more religious suggests that it has been the Republican emphasis on "family values" (that is, opposition to abortion, support for prayer in the public schools, opposition to changed roles for women, and hostility to pornography and homosexuality) rather than traditional party-organization mobilization that has attracted the more religious, just as it has perhaps alarmed the more secular. (A somewhat different perspective is offered in *Rediscovering the Religious Factor in American Politics* in Chapter 12: "Are the Sheep Shearing the Shepherds?")

The Christian Coalition of the 1990s did not evolve as the result of conservative politicians suddenly persuading Evangelical parishioners to adopt new values and seek new standards for evaluating political adversaries. Rather, political change was apparently induced in the early 1980s by religious leaders, such as Pat Robertson, matching one set of partisan alternatives with the existing values of rank-and-file parishioners in Evangelical congregations. Despite much public fanfare to the contrary, political leaders in the religious ranks were not necessarily successful in persuading their followers that political action is the road to a better life, if not to salvation. Voting turnout did not go up at all among committed members of either Protestant tradition; in fact, compared with the rest of the country, turnout declined among the strongly Republican committed Protestants. But for those who were already socially engaged and relatively active as social and political participants, a selective church-based linkage may have made one set of partisan alternatives more attractive than the other.

Whether unintended beneficiaries or active partners, Republican candidates Reagan, Bush, Buchanan, Quayle, and Robertson appeared to emphasize the values held by the more intensely religious Protestants, and they argued successfully that those values were more attuned to the goals of the Republican party than to the Democrats. Their campaigns reflected the message that family values, orthodox heterosexuality, and traditional morality are associated with the Republican party. The high point for this strategic perspective may have been reached in 1988, although its public culmination was clearly reached in Houston at the Republican convention of 1992.

This strategy does have some risks. No one knows at this point (1996) how far the Republicans will go in this direction, or which party will benefit. Measured by the highly publicized and visible fund-raising accomplishments of the "Moral Majority," the numbers favored the Republicans in the early stages of this strategy. More recently, leaders of the Christian Coalition have taken the initiative in their selective support of particular candidates and viewpoints. At this point, however, it would seem that the partisan tradeoffs associated with further emphasis on this strategy may have become more balanced. Despite journalistic emphasis on the growing role of the religious right in domestic politics, the "bad news" for this group is that its population base may not have grown, in part because of a decrease in the sheer numbers of highly religious Mainline Protestants, and turnout rates may have dropped. Of at least equal significance, the growth of Democratic support outside the religious right has been notable, even in the period of national Republican dominance prior to 1992.

10

★ ★ ★

Explanations of Group Differences in the Vote

To extend our discussion of changes in the religious base of presidential politics, we now introduce the general approach to multivariate explanation, discussed in Chapter 8, which we will follow throughout the remainder of this section. We begin by clarifying the impact of religious denominational preferences on voters' choices for President in 1992. We then apply the same analytic approach to assessing and interpreting the influence of other social and economic characteristics on the 1992 vote.

Our analytic procedure reviews the electoral correlates of a wide variety of non-political variables that are defined in terms of social or economic characteristics. Each such variable is selected for further analysis if it exhibits some relationship with the vote, after we control for all other social and economic variables but do not control for party identification. For each social or economic variable which passes that test, we then examine a variety of political factors that might mediate *between* that social or economic variable and the vote, thereby providing a political "translation" for characteristics that are defined in non-political terms. Several different types of variables may play such a mediating role, based on the different explanatory themes in our multiple-stage explanation of voters' decisions.

▪ The Elaboration of Electoral Explanations Based on Religious Differences

In general, we begin our discussion of each selected explanatory variable by documenting its bivariate relationship with individual vote choice.

We therefore begin our explanation of religious differences in the 1992 vote by first noting the vote division or the average vote (for example, an average of .04 for a group that voted 52–48, or 52 percent Democratic) within each category that involves a particular type of religious observance. We then compare that average with the vote division in a "base" group specially designated for this purpose: in this instance, the average vote among the Non-religious. These average scores and differences in averages appear in Rows 1 through 3 in Table 10.1. Each simple difference in average vote between a religious group and the Non-religious is necessarily the same as the bivariate regression coefficient for the relationship between the vote (scored $+1$ or -1) and a dummy variable (scored $+1$ for voters with that attribute), which appears in the fourth row of Table 10.1.

Given the heavily Democratic vote among the Non-religious (see Appendix Table B9.2), it is not surprising that the average vote in each of the six non-Jewish religious categories is much more Republican, or less Democratic, than the vote division in our Non-religious group. All of the coefficients in Row 4 for these six (non-Jewish) categories have negative signs. Each is the same as the corresponding differences (in average vote) in Row 3. The next observation is also reassuring; within each of the three major religious traditions, the difference between their vote division and that for the Non-religious base group is visibly larger among the Committed than among the Nominal adherents of that tradition.

Confounding and Suppressing Effects

Our analysis provides another insight into the role of religious differences as we reexamine the apparent effects for each category (in Row 5) based on multivariate analyses which hold constant all other social and economic characteristics that differentiate between the voters in each category and those in the base (Non-religious) category. To the extent that controls for the other social and economic differences *reduce* the magnitude of an original (bivariate) coefficient, we may conclude that the difference between groups was probably "spurious" in the sense that it was "produced" by differences between the two religion-based categories with regard to other social or economic characteristics. These revised estimates (in Row 5) have eliminated or removed the confounding role of other social and economic characteristics. The coefficient in Row 5 for each religious attribute, therefore, represents its "apparent total effect" on the vote, expressed as the difference between vote divisions (between the designated category and the Non-religious) that remains after we hold constant all other social and economic characteristics.[1]

Across the six categories of non-Jewish religious adherents, at least one conclusion seems clear: "controlling" for the various social and economic attributes that might distinguish members of a given religious category from those with no religious preference produces no substantial change from the simple coefficient based on the original bivariate relationships, *except* within the Evangelical tradition. Thus, the 39-point difference in Row 4 (−.39) between the two-party vote division of the Nominal Mainliners and the Non-religious remains a 38-point difference (−.38), after all of the other social and economic attributes of the two groups (other than religion) are taken into account in Row 5.[2] Similar changes in the effect coefficients among Committed Mainliners and for both groups of Catholics are also of minor significance. This simple pattern, however, does not apply for Evangelicals.

In both Evangelical groups, taking account of, or controlling for, other social and economic differences between each group and the Non-religious base *accentuates* the differences in vote divisions between the Evangelicals and the Non-religious. This result suggests that members of both groups of Evangelicals have one or more other social characteristics that would predispose them to vote more Democratic than they actually did. Such a hypothesis, suggesting that other relatively static social characteristics would predispose Evangelicals to a more Democratic vote than they actually cast in 1992, seems quite reasonable when we recall the behavior (and partisanship) of both Evangelical groups in 1980, just three elections earlier. At that time, Evangelical groups reflected their historically lower socioeconomic status as they favored the Democrat Carter over the Republican Reagan (see Appendix B, Table B9.3). Once such influences are taken into account, the uniqueness of both Evangelical groups' vote divisions in 1992 (when compared to socioeconomically similar voters among the Non-religious) is re-estimated as substantially larger, and therefore even more Republican, than we had originally thought (by .21 among Nominal Evangelicals and by .25 among the Committed).

At each stage in our hierarchically structured analysis, we look for

Table 10.1 Elaboration of the Two-Party 1992 Vote Differences Between Seven Religious Categories and the Non-Religious

	Nominal Mainline Protestants	Committed Mainline Protestants	Nominal Evangelical Protestants	Committed Evangelicals	Nominal Catholics	Committed Catholics	Jewish
1. Average Vote (−1 or +1) in Designated Category	+.09	−.13	+.21	−.12	+.29	+.03	+.83
2. Average Vote in Base Category (Non-religious)	+.48	+.48	+.48	+.48	+.48	+.48	+.48
3. Difference: Average Vote (Designated Category minus Base)	−.39	−.61	−.27	−.60	−.19	−.44	+.35
4. Bivariate Unstandardized Regression Coefficient (Religion Scored 1 for Designated Category, 0 for Base)	−.39	−.61	−.27	−.60	−.19	−.44	+.35
#5. Coefficient from Multiple Regression with Other Social/Economic Characteristics Held Constant	−.38	−.61	−.48	−.85	−.15	−.45	+.44
6. With Party Identification (Party ID) Also Held Constant	−.18	−.36	−.36	−.53	−.20	−.52	(+.13)
7. With Specific Policy-related Predispositions (But NOT Party ID) Also Held Constant	(−.06)	(−.11)	(−.07)	−.17	(−.00)	(−.13)	+.31

	Nominal Mainline Protestants	Committed Mainline Protestants	Nominal Evangelical Protestants	Committed Evangelicals	Nominal Catholics	Committed Catholics	Jewish
8. With Liberal vs. Conservative Self-designation Also Held Constant	(.00)	(−.09)	(−.01)	(−.09)	(+.07)	(−.06)	+.28
9. With Party ID and all Policy-related Predispositions Also Held Constant	(+.01)	(−.08)	(−.07)	(−.10)	(−.03)	−.23	(+.11)
10. With Preferences on All Current Policy Issues Also Held Constant	(+.02)	(−.05)	(−.05)	(−.10)	(−.02)	(−.16)	(+.14)
11. With Perceptions of Current Personal and National Conditions Also Held Constant	(+.02)	(−.08)	(−.05)	(−.11)	(−.02)	(−.16)	(+.14)
12. With Retrospective Evaluations of Current President's Performance in Office Also Held Constant	(+.00)	(−.09)	(−.05)	−.14	(−.02)	−.16	(+.12)
13. With Evaluations of the Candidates' Personal Qualities Also Held Constant	(−.01)	(−.09)	(−.06)	−.14	(−.01)	(−.13)	(+.13)
14. With Prospective Evaluations of the Candidates' and Parties' Future Performance Also Held Constant	(−.01)	(−.11)	(−.06)	(−.11)	(−.02)	(−.12)	(+.08)

NOTE: Parentheses indicate that the coefficient is not reliably different from .00 at the .1 level.
#The entries in Row 5 are designated as the "apparent total effect" of that variable.

such indications that the introduction of additional considerations (by adding other explanatory variables or themes) changes our estimate of how similar—or different—each group vote division is when compared with the base group for that characteristic. In presenting our results, we will frequently reiterate this question: How different is the vote division within Group A from the division within the designated base group (for that characteristic), both before and after we have taken account of an additional variable that may be confounding or suppressing the characteristic's apparent impact on the vote? If it can be demonstrated that a set of possibly antecedent circumstances—for the moment collectively called Variable X, which has been suggested as partially responsible for some portion of an initial difference—actually does account for some of that difference (as seen in the reduction of the regression coefficient for Group A *after* taking these circumstances into account), then we have improved or "elaborated" our understanding of the initial difference—by concluding that "it was partially due to X." The magnitude of that reduction is a measure of the contribution of Variable X to the difference we had observed *before* taking X into account. If "taking account" of Variable X does not change the magnitude of the initial difference or coefficient, we conclude that X is not "responsible" for that prior result. On the other hand, if taking account of X appears to *increase* the group differences, we conclude that X appears to have obscured the "true" difference in the vote divisions between the two groups (such as the Evangelical and Non-religious groups) by "suppressing" some portion of that difference.

The question of whether a given variable or theme (called "X") confounds our understanding of a relationship by obscuring evidence of differences among members of two groups can be answered empirically. If, as in the present case, it seems true that "other social characteristics" mask the actual vote differences between each group of Evangelicals and a truly comparable base group of the Non-religious, we may be content to conclude that we now know more about *how unique* the vote division (of the Evangelicals) really is (when compared to the comparable vote division of the Non-religious). We may then simply move on and try to account analytically for the newly specified difference by introducing controls for other *subsequent* factors that serve as intervening or mediating variables.

Alternatively, we might choose to stop and try to understand the nature of the suppression of the group "effect" before examining the role of any intervening variables. In the present case, the suppressing influences lie somewhere within the entire "X" collection of eleven social attributes, other than religion, that we have taken into account in this first stage of our elaboration. Given the difficulties that would confront any attempt to explain the causal interrelationships that connect the several disparate social attributes to the political preference of a particular religious commitment, we have left that problem as unresolved in order to concentrate on the *consequences* of that commitment.

Mediating Effects

In the initial phases of our inquiry, our interest is usually directed toward understanding the electoral consequences of given characteristics (such as religious commitments) rather than identifying or assessing the possible sources of the differences among them. Because our goal in the present instance is to understand the *consequences* of apparent differences among religious traditions by introducing factors that lie between them and the vote, rather than to first identify the particular factors which may be responsible for those religious differences, we move on to the next explanatory stage. It is of course true that the meaning or significance of what we subsequently discover may rest on the reasons for, or the sources of, the initial (religious) differences that have been exposed. We could then be driven back to search for the origins of those (religious) differences, in turn, for a more satisfactory explanation of their political consequences. Elsewhere in this volume we make just such a choice for other types of explanatory variables, by trying to understand the origins of those factors before we elaborate their consequences.

▪ Consequences of Religious Group Differences

As we discussed in Chapter 8, our assumptions about the hierarchical structure of interrelationships among the many antecedents of the vote specify a causal order for several distinct stages in the evolution of electoral preferences. For the average voter, party identification "follows" social and economic factors in the next stage within a sequence of possible influences on vote choice. In causal terms, we believe that the different political experiences reflected in various social categorizations (such as those reflecting religious traditions and commitments) may have led to the formation of persistent (long-term) differences in individuals' party identifications. We locate party identification as a second explanatory theme (following social and economic characteristics) situated in the second causal stage (along with a third general theme based on policy-related predispositions).

Party Identification and Religious Group Differences

Party identification is thus treated as a potential mediating connection between any established social attribute, such as religion, and the vote. In no sense is party identification taken into account because we are trying to "explain away" or minimize religious differences in vote division. On the contrary: we are trying to elaborate our understanding of those differences, and, to the extent that party identification is relevant to them, we postulate that past political experience—whether as a child or as an adult—appears to have left group members with different predispositions to favor one partisan choice over the other.

In Table 10.1, we introduce party identification into our analysis in Row 6 as we "hold its effect constant"; that is, we take account of the effect of differences in party identification between those with one set of religious characteristics and those with no religious preference. We then can observe what portion of the differences in vote preferences between the religious and the Non-religious can be attributed to long-standing differences between those groups in their partisan identifications. As we thus accommodate the effects of differences in party identification, we may alter our view of the meaning of observed differences in voting behavior between each of the religious groups and the Non-religious. (See Appendix D, Methodological Commentary, for a clarifying discussion of the meanings that might be attached to the ideas of "holding other variables constant" or "controlling" them to clarify relationships.)

When we compare the coefficients in Row 5 with those in Row 6 of Table 10.1, it is evident that the apparent role of party identification in explaining religious differences varies substantially across our different religious groups. In religious groups where voters had earlier acquired distinctive partisan identifications that were consistent with their preferences in the 1992 election, "controlling for party" accounts for some visible portion of the relationship between religion and their vote. In effect, the remaining coefficient represents the difference between the votes of the religious and the Non-religious who share the same party identifications. Where party identification is less related to the other contemporary short-term forces influencing vote choices, it may be less robust as a link between a pre-existing religious attribute and a subsequent vote preference. In such cases, removing (or controlling for) the effect of partisan identification makes less difference to the electoral difference between the two groups, so that we infer that the observed differences in voting behavior have less often occurred as a simple result of differences in longstanding party identification.

In the case of Mainline Protestants in Table 10.1, after taking account of the possible confounding effects of other social and economic characteristics, there are substantial differences in the vote divisions between the Committed (those regular church attenders for whom religion is a very important guide in daily life) and the Nominal Mainliners, for whom religion is less important. The "Committed" voted .61 more Republican than did the Non-religious base group. The Nominal Mainliners were only .38 more Republican than the same base group of the Non-religious; both of these are differences that exist (in Row 5) after eliminating possibly confounding differences that may be attributed to other social and economic attributes. However, among *both* Protestant groups, party identification accounts for about half of the *remaining* difference between their vote and that of the Non-religious (comparing Rows 5 and 6, the coefficient of .38 is reduced to .18, and .61 becomes .36). These two groups are thus roughly similar in the extent to which the differences between their vote choices and those of the Non-religious can be attributed to longstanding differences in party identification.

Against this similarity in the role of party identifications among Mainline Protestants, the comparison of the Nominal Evangelicals and the Nominal Mainliners reveals a substantial difference in the role played by party identification in explaining the electoral difference between those two groups. After taking into account possible differences in social and economic attributes, both groups voted much more Republican than did the Non-religious in 1992—the Mainliners by .38 (as noted above), and the Nominal Evangelicals by .48. By taking into account differences in party identifications between the Mainliners and the Non-religious, however, we can account for about half of that apparent effect (.20 of the .38). Among Evangelicals, in contrast, our control for party identification accounts for only one-fourth of the apparent effect (.12 of the .48 which separates them from the Non-religious). Nominal Mainliners differed less from the Non-religious than did Nominal Evangelicals, but a larger proportion of that apparent effect could be attributed to party identification. Whatever the intergroup similarities and differences, party identification played a relatively larger role in explaining—if not producing— the electoral distinctiveness of Nominal Mainline Protestants than of Nominal Evangelicals.

For both sets of Catholics, party identification plays yet a different role—that of a countervailing influence analogous to the suppressing influence of other social factors on the vote divisions, as noted above in the case of the Evangelical groups. Contrary to the situation with the subsets of Protestants, or any of our other religious groupings, our control for differences in party identification between voters in either group of Catholics and voters in the Non-religious group exposes slightly *larger* differences between their vote divisions than are apparent without such a control. Once we take account of the fact that Catholic party identifications are more pro-Democratic than are the identifications of the Non-religious, the difference in vote choices between Catholics and the Non-religious is increased over that which appeared without taking their prior partisan differences into consideration. Far from explaining why Committed Catholics voted more Republican than did the Non-religious, taking into account their differences in party identification *increases* the apparent difference in vote divisions between the two groups from .45 more Republican (or less Democratic) than the Non-religious in Row 5 to .52 in Row 6. For Nominal Catholics, establishing the same equivalencies for party identification also increases the apparent pro-Republican effect of being a Nominal Catholic (instead of Non-religious). Thus when we take into account the extent to which Catholic party identifications were more heavily Democratic than the identifications of the Non-religious, the electoral preferences of both Catholic groups are slightly more pro-Republican (compared to the Non-religious) than was apparent before we controlled for party identification.

More generally, Table 10.1 shows the varied role of party identification in interpreting the electoral effects associated with our religious categories. These variations suggest that there are substantial differences in the degree to which the electoral distinctiveness of different groups of voters can be attributed to long-term partisan identifications: sometimes such identifications explain major portions of vote differences with the Non-religious; at other times such identifications appear to play only a minor role.

▪ Policy-related Predispositions and Religion

In every election, voters' preferences for President are influenced by their attitudes concerning a variety of conflicts within the society—particularly when those conflicts are emphasized and relevant attitudes are activated by the election campaign. For conflicts that are longstanding, as in the competition between Democrats and Republicans, or recurring, as in persistent liberal/conservative disagreements over policy, many citizens become predisposed to take one side or the other whenever those conflicts become salient. This chapter introduces several such predispositions and their apparent influence on the vote. Policy-related predispositions constitute a third theme in our model, separate from party identification but also located in our second causal stage.

In earlier chapters, we discussed partisan predispositions in terms of voters' long-term identifications with one of the major parties which influence many other political attitudes as well as exerting a direct influence on the vote. In the next chapter we discuss in some detail the policy-related predispositions that are introduced in this chapter, each of which is linked to policy-related conflicts although not defined in terms of specific policy alternatives. These predispositions are relevant to both partisan and policy-related conflicts that are more or less persistent and therefore largely "in place" before any given election campaign begins.

Some of these policy-related predispositions have been considered at length by other scholars under different labels. Given the relatively recent emergence of "predispositions" as a widely used analytic category, there is still considerable ambiguity attached to the meaning of specific measures in this area. Sometimes such variables are interpreted in terms of social values or goals. At other times, the central meaning is less affective or evaluative and more cognitive, emphasizing perceptions or beliefs. Some predispositions represent very general or generic concerns, while others are no more than slightly generalized versions of contemporary policy choices. Other than voters' self-designation as "liberal" or "conservative," policy-related predispositions were not introduced into NES data collections until 1984. For that reason, it is not clear as this book is being written that they are all as "long-term" and generic as, say, party identification. Given the relatively short history of research in this area, the resulting measures also doubtless vary in the extent to which they are measured with comparable validity and reliability.[3]

Each of these predispositions, however, is conceptually as well as empirically tied to ongoing conflicts within the society. None of them is articulated or defined in terms of current policy alternatives—choices presented to the electorate in the election campaign by the competing parties or candidates—but each defines two conflicting positions that have been associated with opposing political leaders. As we shall note in a moment, many of the predispositions that we have examined appeared to play some role in shaping voters' choices between Clinton and Bush.

We have assigned all such conflict-related predispositions to a fairly early causal position in our multiple-stage model of the vote. Along with partisan identification, we have assumed that, in our model of sequential stages leading ultimately to the vote decision, all such predispositions come *after* voters' stable social and economic characteristics, and *before* all of the other explanatory variables in our model.

In some areas (and for some voters), attitudes toward continuing conflict within the society have almost certainly played some role in the evolution of their partisan identifications long before any given campaign begins. In other areas (and for other voters), longstanding partisan identifications have surely influenced voters' attitudes toward policy-related conflicts—through the cumulative impact of the "positions" advocated by party leaders. As a consequence, as we noted in detail in Chapter 8, policy-related predispositions have an ambiguous causal relationship with voters' long-term partisan identifications that we cannot resolve with any combination of available data and theory; therefore we have assigned predispositions from both themes to the same causal bloc in our multiple-stage model.

This kind of causal ambiguity is emphasized in Figure 10.1, which suggests the overlapping sources of partisan identifications and policy-related predispositions. In that diagram, events or circumstances that took place in previous elections appear at the top, while current voter characteristics appear at the bottom. As suggested by the arrows in the

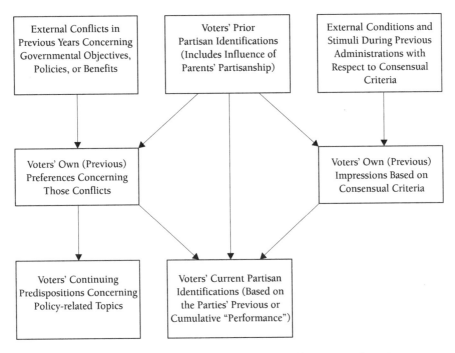

Figure 10.1 Sources of policy-related and partisan predispositions based on conflict versus consensus.

figure, partisan *and* policy-related predispositions may have been shaped by prior conflicts in areas where leaders of the two major parties have taken opposite "sides," while partisan identifications are also shaped by the parties' prior success or failure in areas where a consensus (instead of conflict) exists concerning the criteria for such evaluations.

In order to examine the unique role of the specific policy-related predispositions, we next examine the coefficients for each social or economic category (religious categories, at this point) while holding constant the full set of other social and economic characteristics *and* the full set of seven policy-related predispositions—but *not* party identification nor liberal/conservative ideology. The resulting coefficients are entered in Row 7 of Table 10.1. One can now compare coefficients in Rows 5 and 6, which reflect the apparent effect of holding party identification constant, with the differences between the coefficients in Rows 5 and 7, which reflect the combined impact of controls for all seven specific policy-related predispositions.

Row 8 coefficients then follow Row 7 and reflect the result of simply adding controls on ideology (self-classification as liberal or conservative) to the controls on social and economic characteristics *and* specific policy-related predispositions. Row 9 then reintroduces a control for party identification, *in addition* to those variables already controlled in Row 8. On the basis of these results, we can compare coefficients which reflect the impact of party identification, with or without the other predispositions (in Rows 6 and 9), as well as the effects of policy-related predispositions, with or without party identification (in Rows 7 and 9).

This sequence may initially seem a bit cumbersome, but it should be kept in mind that the goal is to permit us, as analysts, to view the results of specifying *alternate* causal formulations. If one is willing to assume that party identification is a probable source for the other predispositions, one can examine the consequences of adding controls for policy-related predispositions (in Row 9) *after* noting the role of party identification in Row 6. If one is not inclined to give precedence to party identification—and we believe there is no definitive evidence on the point—one can go from Row 5 directly to Row 9 and note the result of adding controls for *all* of our second-stage predispositions (party identification, ideology, and seven specific policy-related predispositions) to those for our first-stage variables. Or one can emphasize the sequence of Row 7 (the apparent effect after we control for seven specific policy-related predispositions), followed by Row 8 (adding liberal/conservative ideology) and finally, Row 9 (adding party identification).

In any event, after comparing Rows 5 and 9 of Table 10.1, we conclude that our complete battery of nine predispositions (seven specific policy-related predispositions, party identification, and ideology) provides an important set of connections between the members of the religious categories and their votes (after we have accounted for their differences in other social/economic characteristics with the Non-religious). The pattern holds for all seven religious groupings. Indeed, for six of the seven groups, the differences between their vote choices and those of the Non-religious are so diminished after taking into account all nine predispositions that the remaining coefficients fall below our standard threshold for statistical significance.[4] In those instances, the remaining differences between the vote divisions of each of these groups and the Non-religious cannot be reliably distinguished from zero. At the very least, as mediating agents, both in relative and absolute terms, the full set of predispositions accounts for virtually all of the apparent effects (on the vote) associated with membership in each of the six religious groups instead of the Non-religious group.

Perhaps the next most instructive general conclusion is derived from comparing the alternatives offered by Rows 6 and 7 of Table 10.1: predispositions reflecting social values seem more relevant than party identification in differentiating the votes among citizens with different religious affiliations. The absolute magnitudes of the differences between Rows 5 and 7, reflecting the impact of policy-related predispositions *other* than party, are much larger for the non-Jewish groups than those between Rows 5 and 6, which reflect differences associated with party identification alone. The apparently greater relevance of policy-related predispositions is also particularly evident in Rows 8 and 9, where we observe the relatively small incremental reduction in coefficients that results when party identification is added to the controls for the other eight predispositions (except, of course, in the case of Catholics). Whether examined separately or in combination, party appears to be the lesser contributor to the vote differences between our religious groups and the Non-religious. The other eight policy-related predispositions are both relatively and absolutely of greater importance in connecting religious perspectives to electoral decisions.

Our explanatory objective must be kept firmly in mind at this stage of our exploration of apparent effects associated with different religious groups. We do not conclude from the foregoing inspection of Rows 6, 7, 8, and 9 that party identification is less important than other predispositions in separating Republican voters from Democratic voters within each of the religious groups. We conclude only that party identification is less important than policy-related predispositions in generating the electoral differences between each religious group and the Non-religious group. Our first-level question is: Why do groups that differ in religion differ in their votes? Our first answer is: more because of policy-related predispositions than because of party identification.

The Indirect Effect of Religion on the Vote Through Policy-related Predispositions

Up to this point in our analysis of religious differences in vote choice, specific policy-related predispositions (not party identification nor ideology) have always been considered together (in Row 7 of Table 10.1) as a single component in our multi-stage explanatory model. In the absence of the appropriate long-term, longitudinal data that might permit us to disentangle causal relationships among various policy-related predispositions, we cannot specify with any precision the roles played by different predispositions in generating the (observed) electoral differences between specific religious groups.

We can, however, take one further step in extending our understanding of the electoral consequences of predispositional differences among the major religious groupings. We do so by introducing each individual predisposition both as a dependent variable explained by social and economic characteristics and as an intervening variable, connecting those characteristics with vote choice. This intervening role for specific predispositions is based on a vote prediction equation which controls for the other seven predispositions as well as the social and economic characteristics. With this information, predisposition by predisposition, we have noted the extent to which each religious category appears to have had an independent effect on the vote "through" that specific policy-related predisposition. (Party identification has been deliberately excluded from those controls in order to accentuate the role played by policy-related predispositions, despite our uncertainty about the causal relationships between those policy-related variables and long-term partisanship.)

The algorithm we use in this step not only estimates each predisposition's capacity to distinguish each religious group from the Non-religious, but it also suggests how the relationships between social attributes and predispositions may be used to disaggregate the impact of a given social attribute on the vote. As we shall see, the results of the procedure provide a telling illustration of how misleading the use of even complex bivariate description of public opinion can be, and how important it is to spell out the multi-stage nature of the processes that link social attributes to electoral decisions.

The first part of our algorithm examines the bivariate relationship between each social attribute and each policy-related predisposition. Table 10.2 presents the results of regressing each predisposition on each religious characteristic. It depicts the extent to which the predisposition (as a "dependent variable") distinguishes between Non-religious voters and those who possess a given set of religious attributes. For example, we note in column 4 of Table 10.2 that one's position on morality,

Table 10.2 Regressions of Eight Policy-Related Predispositions on Differences in Vote Division Between Religious Groups and the Non-Religious

Policy-Related Predispositions	Nominal Mainline Protestants	Committed Mainline Protestants	Nominal Evangelicals	Committed Evangelicals	Nominal Catholics	Committed Catholics
Limited Government	−.26	−.40	−.14	−.33	(−.05)	(−.06)
Egalitarianism	−.14	−.18	−.20	−.23	−.08	(−.08)
Morality	−.18	−.43	−.32	−.58	−.12	−.34
Gays-Fundamentalists	−.14	−.29	−.30	−.53	−.08	−.19
Ideology (Lib./Cons.)	−.35	−.37	−.43	−.66	−.26	−.36
Isolationism	(−.06)	−.30	(.10)	−.18	(+.04)	(−.04)
Union/Business	−.24	(+.02)	−.15	−.24	(−.06)	(−.07)
Vietnam Service	−.23	−.44	−.34	−.41	−.20	−.45

liberal/conservative ideology, and comparative evaluations of homosexuals versus Christian fundamentalists (with coefficients of $-.58$, $-.66$, and $-.53$) are all highly related to the difference between *Committed* Evangelicals and the Non-religious; but, in the third column, they are substantially less related (coefficients of $-.32$, $-.43$, and $-.30$) to the distinction between *Nominal* Evangelical voters and those in the Non-religious base group. This pattern of differences between Nominal and Committed religionists on the three predispositions is repeated across both of the other two major religious traditions.

Each of the eight predispositions is clearly relevant to the distinction between the Non-religious and at least one religious group. Some, such as the predisposition toward isolationism, and the conflict between labor and business, are not very relevant to most religious groupings. Others, such as moral tolerance, liberal/conservative ideology, and comparative evaluations of homosexuals and fundamentalists, are broadly involved in distinguishing between all of the religious groupings and the Non-religious.

Assessing the indirect effect of social (religious) differences on the vote next rests on the significance of the relationships connecting each religious category, each policy-related predisposition, and the vote choice, Democratic or Republican. It was at this stage that four predispositions, those pertaining to civil religion, authoritarianism, patriotism, and attitudes toward Blacks, were dropped from further analysis.[5] When we held constant the effects of the other predispositions, the relationship between each of the four and differences in vote choice compared to the Non-religious dropped below the threshold of statistical significance. This was true even when we searched for interactions that might relate to vote choice *within* a religious group (rather than in comparison with the Non-religious) for which the predisposition is salient. Very strict attitudes toward child rearing, for example, distinguished sharply between each religious group and the Non-religious base group, and also between the Committed and the Nominal groups among both Evangelicals and Catholics (although not within Mainline Protestants). Nevertheless, once the other predispositions were taken into account, the same attitudes toward child rearing were unrelated to vote choice *within* the groups, including the Non-religious. Similarly, although a predisposition concerning civil religion (the relevance of a belief in God to being characterized as a true American) distinguished Committed Mainliners and Catholics from the Non-religious, it did not reliably distinguish between the Democratic and Republican voters within either group.

The general lesson is that even when public opinion appears to be associated with different locations in the social structure, such opinions may have only limited political consequences. The same opinions that distinguish one group from another may be of limited relevance to differences in subsequent vote decisions, between or within them. On the other hand, predispositions that are relevant for vote choice *and* are associated with particular social attributes may indeed provide a linkage between those social attributes and vote choice.

Table 10.3 contains all of the statistically significant indirect effect coefficients in the full matrix of eight policy-related predispositions among six religious categories. One of the predispositions, isolationism, appears to play no role in distinguishing the vote decisions of any of the various religious sub-groups from the Non-religious. Three predispositions, moral tolerance, evaluations of homosexuals versus fundamentalists, and traditional liberal/conservative ideology, show particular prominence in their influences on religious voting. The first two are no surprise, and the marked similarity of their coefficients in Tables 10.2 and 10.3 suggests the correlation between them; however, it should be noted that both are retained in subsequent analyses because each has a statistically significant relationship to vote choice *after* the effect of the other has been controlled. The strong showing of the liberal/conservative predisposition across all six groups is somewhat unexpected, at least in terms of magnitude, in that it is nearly identical to moral tolerance in Table 10.2. This might have been anticipated, however, from work by Guth and Green reported in Leege and Kellstedt.[6]

Religious Political Conservatism

While we are illustrating the conservative inclinations of religious groups—particularly among the Committed of each major tradition—it is important to review evidence regarding some of the other predispositions that one might stereotypically expect to be involved in the politicization of religious conservatives. As we have just noted, many predispositions were demonstrably not closely tied to the religious/Non-religious differentiation in the 1992 presidential vote. The measures of authoritarianism (in child rearing), patriotism, support for civil religion,

Table 10.3 Indirect Effects of Religious Differences (from the Non-Religious) Through Predispositions

Predisposition	Nominal Mainline Protestants	Committed Mainline Protestants	Nominal Evangelicals	Committed Evangelicals	Nominal Catholics	Committed Catholics
Limited Government	-.02*	-.03	-.01	-.03	.00	.00
Egalitarianism	-.03	-.04	-.04	-.05	-.02	-.02
Moral Tolerance	-.04	-.10	-.07	-.13	-.03	-.08
Gays-Fundamentalists	-.02	-.04	-.04	-.08	-.01	-.03
Ideology (Lib./Cons.)	-.09	-.10	-.11	-.18	-.07	-.10
Isolationism	.00	-.02	-.01	-.01	.00	.00
Union/Business	-.02	.00	-.02	-.02	-.01	-.01
Vietnam Service	-.02	-.04	-.03	-.03	-.02	-.04

NOTE: Entries of .03 or .04 are significant at .01 < p < .05; entries of .05 or larger are significant at p < .01. Positive signs indicate pro-Democratic effect; negative signs indicate pro-Republican effect.

Table 10.4 Mean Values of the Three Policy-Related Predispositions for Six Religious Groups Composed of Main Christian Traditions Subdivided by the Centrality of Religion

	Mainline Protestants		Evangelicals		Catholics	
	Nominal	Committed	Nominal	Committed	Nominal	Committed
Moral Traditionalism (L = +1, C = −1)	−.17	−.46	−.25	−.53	−.08	−.37
Gays-Fundamentalists (L = +1, C = −1)	−.08	−.23	−.24	−.47	−.01	−.14
Ideology (L = +1, C = −1)	−.12	−.17	−.12	−.35	−.02	−.14

NOTE: Entry is the mean score for the group; positive sign indicates a plurality of liberal sentiments, negative sign signifies a plurality of conservative sentiments.

a limited role for government, and isolationism (in international affairs) seemed singularly devoid of relevance for any religious/Non-religious differentiation among voters in 1992. The measure of predispositions toward Blacks and racial discrimination showed only a marginally significant relevance for distinguishing between Nominal (White) Evangelicals and the Non-religious; it was not distinctive for the other five groups, and it was devoid of independent implications for vote choice between Democrats and Republicans among all groups. All of this suggests that among religious groups, ideological concepts may be correlates of partisan votes, but they may have application to only a limited range of political choices outside social issues involving "family values" and sexuality. This, in turn, should suggest potential limits on the influence of the increasingly activist new religious right.

Nevertheless, the relative positions of the six religious groups regarding the policy-related predispositions most relevant to vote decisions suggest that characterizing Committed Evangelicals as the core of a politically right-of-center religious vote is not far off the mark. Table 10.4 presents mean scores for the three predispositions that were most distinctive in terms of differences between religious groups and the Non-religious. Within all three major Christian traditions, Committed adherents were more conservative on each of these predispositions than were nominal co-religionists—and markedly so among Evangelicals. It is also true that Committed Evangelicals were much more conservative in these three predispositions than either Mainliners or Catholics, as was anticipated by their precipitous swings away from the Democrats and toward the Republicans (see Tables 9.3 and 9.4 in Chapter 9) or their truly remarkable reversal of partisanship between 1980 and 1992 that produced a 56 to 44 percent vote in 1992 favoring Bush over fellow-Evangelical Clinton.

As a group, partisan and policy-related predispositions apparently played a substantial role in accounting for the distinctiveness of the 1992 vote decisions of our religious sub-groups. Four of the predispositions among those we examined—party identification, moral traditionalism, homosexuality, and liberal-conservative ideological identifications—were important as influences on individual vote decisions. All four revealed substantial differences among the values held within the different Christian traditions; and all continue to be relevant in the contemporary partisan political debate over social issues and family values.

The absence of any extraordinary increase in voter turnout among religious groups, and the presence of recent religion-related shifts of party identifications as well as vote preferences (both noted in the last chapter), are consistent with the hypothesis that church-based cues, perceived by regular church attenders, played a significant role in shaping political preferences among the Committed members of each tradition. At the same time, a strong counter-movement in the preferences of voters outside the religious "mainstream" also suggests a political reaction to the rise of a new religious right. We reviewed no direct evidence, however, to indicate whether such changes, as in the vote preferences among those preferring a minor religion or no religion at all, were predominantly a response to church-initiated or party-instigated partisan arguments, or have some other explanation.

▪ Race, Ethnicity, and Voting

If partisan strategies in the Reagan-Bush-Clinton elections suggest that religion is contributing a new cultural dimension to American politics, then race and ethnicity have been central dimensions for many decades. It has often been observed that the magnitude of the Black-White cleavage in the politics of the United States is unequaled by any socio-political cleavage in any other contemporary industrialized Western democracy. For thirty years, since and slightly before the civil rights voting legislation of 1964 and 1965, the Black vote has been monolithically Democratic. With the enforcement of civil rights legislation, that vote has grown stronger at the polls. NES data (see Table B7.1 in Appendix B) suggest a relatively constant racial differential in voter turnout, with Blacks voting about 10 percent less often than non-Blacks in the Reagan-Bush-Clinton elections.

This marks a substantial lessening of the massive gap in turnout that existed before the 1965 Voting Rights Act. The remaining difference, however, also reflects racial differences in education, income, and other factors that work against voting turnout. Rosenstone and Hansen estimate that when such social and economic differences are taken into account, the racial gap in voter turnout averaged only about 4 percent between Blacks and Whites in the nine presidential elections from 1956 through 1988 (Rosenstone and Hansen, 1993, Table 5.1, p. 131). This certainly means that during the limited later time period covered in our present analysis—the four elections of 1980 through 1992—the purely racial gap was smaller yet. Rosenstone and Hansen also note a slightly larger margin for citizens of Hispanic descent, and they estimate larger differences in off-year elections than in presidential years for both Blacks and Hispanics.

With many of the social and legal barriers to non-White voting participation removed, the full electoral impact of minority groups has been brought to bear on voters' choices. In all four elections, Blacks cast approximately 90 percent of their two-party ballots for the Democratic candidates. An inevitable consequence of such a one-sided distribution is that when we turn to relationships between race and partisanship, virtually all of the year-to-year variation is supplied by non-Black voters. For example, the difference between Black and non-Black voters in the average vote (or vote division) in 1992, .82, was considerably smaller than the corresponding difference in the preceding three elections, but almost all of that reduction can be attributed to the fact that the non-Black voters (in 1992) were so much less pro-Republican and therefore less different from Black voters.

Heterogeneity among Hispanics

As the proportion of citizens of Cuban, Mexican, and Puerto Rican origins has grown in recent decades, the so-called Hispanic vote has drawn increased attention. That attention has included distinguishing

Table 10.5 Party Identification, 1988 and 1992, for Hispanic Two-Party Voters[a]

	Democratic	Independent	Republican	Total	D-R	N
Non-Mexican Origin	46	27	17	100%	+29	108
Mexican Origin	59	30	11	100%	+48	76

a. Based on combined 1988 and 1992 NES samples of voters.

Table 10.6 Vote Division, 1988 and 1992, for Hispanic Two-Party Voters[a]

	Democratic	Republican	Total	D-R	N
Non-Mexican Origin	55	45	100%	+10	108
Mexican Origin	81	19	100%	+62	77

a. Based on combined 1988 and 1992 NES samples of voters.

between Cubans and Puerto Ricans, as well as between former Mexicans and others from Central and South America. We are restricted in what we can say about Hispanic voting both because of their limited numbers in our national samples, and because the distinction between non-Mexican and Mexican Hispanics has been well drawn in NES data only since 1988. Nevertheless, data from 1988 and 1992 suggest that there has been striking heterogeneity in the Hispanic vote. Separate estimates for each year suggest little change between years. Turnout for all Hispanics is estimated at 66 percent in 1988 and 65 percent in 1992. Hispanics of non-Mexican origins reported little more than 70 percent turning out to vote in both years. Among those of Mexican origin, just under 60 percent reported voting. The vote division and party identifications of two-party voters are, of course, based on even smaller numbers, but as Tables 10.5 and 10.6 show, the partisan preferences of the two subsets are also quite different, with Hispanics of Mexican origin providing stronger support for the Democratic party.

Black Voting

There are too few Hispanic respondents in each group to provide stable estimates for our sequential elaboration of explanations for vote choice. Taken together as a single group, the vote division among Hispanics in 1992 was not reliably different from that of non-Hispanics once other

Table 10.7 Elaboration of Two-Party 1992 Vote Difference Between Blacks and Non-Blacks

	Coefficients
1. Average Vote (-1 or $+1$) in Designated Category — Black	+.89
2. Average Vote in Base Category (Non-Black)	+.06
3. Difference: Average Vote (Designated Category minus Base)	+.82
4. Bivariate Unstandardized Regression Coefficient (Race Scored 1 for Black, 0 for Others)	+.82
#5. Coefficient[a] from Multiple Regression with Other Social/Economic Characteristics Held Constant	+.91
6. With Party Identification (Party ID) Also Held Constant	+.43
7. With Specific Policy-related Predispositions (but NOT Party ID) Also Held Constant	+.46
8. With Liberal vs. Conservative Self-designation Also Held Constant	+.46
9. With Party ID and all Policy-related Predispositions Also Held Constant	+.28
10. With Preferences on All Current Policy Issues Also Held Constant	+.27
11. With Perceptions of Current Personal and National Conditions Also Held Constant	+.25
12. With Retrospective Evaluations of Current President's Performance in Office Also Held Constant	+.13
13. With Evaluations of the Candidates' Personal Qualities Also Held Constant	+.10
14. With Prospective Evaluations of the Candidates' and Parties' Future Performance Also Held Constant	+.12

#The coefficient in Row 5 is the "apparent total effect" of the designated category on the vote.

social and economic attributes were taken into account. However, we do have reliable estimates that Blacks have differed sharply from non-Blacks in their vote preferences. Table 10.7 shows that the vote difference in 1992 between Blacks and non-Blacks is even greater (Rows 4 and 5) after we take other social and economic differences between the two groups into account.

The enduring nature of the political schism between these two major racial groups becomes evident when we note in Table 10.7 that the long-term factor of party identification reduces the apparent effect of race on vote choice by more than half. By holding party identification constant, we reduce the effect coefficient for race from .91 to .43 (as shown in Rows 5 and 6). The entire collection of policy-related predispositions makes almost the same independent contribution to racial differences; controlling for racial differences in those predispositions (instead of party identification) reduces the apparent effect of race from

.91 to .46 (in Row 7). The relative independence of these two components of racial differences is suggested by Row 9 of Table 10.7; taken
together, party identification and our set of policy-related predispositions
account for .63 of the initial .91 apparent total effect. The combined
reductions in the coefficient for race produced by controls for all of our
predispositions suggest that much of the race-related differences in
voting in 1992 were based on long-term differences, although a significant remainder (.28) suggests that some of those differences should
be attributed to the short-term circumstances in that election. The latter
conclusion stands in clear contrast to the Bush-Dukakis contest in 1988.
In that election an initial coefficient of 1.07 (after taking other social
and economic characteristics into account) was reduced to .24 by a
similar package of predispositions. The residue of .24 is not unimpor-
tant, but it does suggest that the race-related effects of the 1988 campaign and the circumstances surrounding it were based on pre-existing
predispositions that were activated during that campaign rather than
issues that were unique to 1988.

Both the famous "Willie Horton" television ad and the focus on
Dukakis's opposition to the death penalty (in one of the debates with
Bush) may have constituted effective short-term forces in 1988. The
effects of such events, however, can be primarily interpreted as activating
pre-existing predispositions concerning race, without requiring the formation of any new attitudes that were unique to 1988. To test such an
interpretation, we would have to evaluate responses to the ad or the
debate as independent explanatory variables. Unfortunately, however,
those two events occurred virtually simultaneously, and the 1992 NES
data collection does not include the questions or time sequence that
would permit a direct test of either hypothesis. This kind of analytic
problem illustrates a general point we will emphasize in subsequent
chapters concerning the nature of long-term and short-term factors in
the shaping of electoral decisions.

The indirect effects of predispositions that link racial differences to
the 1992 vote seem to make sense intuitively. Five predispositions appear
to have made a statistically significant contribution to the vote differences between Black and non-Black citizens. Neither of the two predispositions relevant to foreign policy discriminated between the votes of
the racial groups; nor did attitudes toward homosexuals. Of the remaining five policy-related predispositions, the most striking differentiation
was produced by predispositions pertaining to egalitarianism. The indi-

rect effect on the vote that appeared to operate "through" that predisposition was a substantial .08, which is comparable to the role of morality for our religious groupings, as shown in Table 10.3. Another indirect effect of race appears to have been contributed by liberal/conservative self-designations (.08). Not only was egalitarianism clearly associated with racial voting differences, but race was the only variable among our social and economic characteristics for which the apparent indirect effect "through" egalitarianism exceeded .05.

The short-term components of our explanatory scheme add to the general picture of Black/non-Black differences in the 1992 vote. Preferences on current policy issues and appraisals of national and world conditions played only small incremental roles in explaining racial differences (see Rows 10 and 11 of Table 10.7), but a much larger effect can be attributed to retrospective evaluations of the performance of George Bush and the Bush administration. Taking such performance evaluations into account reduces the remaining effect coefficient from .25 to .13. After that stage, no further changes or reductions occur in the apparent impact of race when we control for comparative evaluations of the two variables concerning personal qualities or future performance.

Whatever the respective contributions of long- and short-term factors, it is true that a visible electoral difference remains between the two racial groups after we have considered all of the explanatory variables in our several explanatory stages. As with the Committed Catholics (for which we have no complete explanation), some portion (.12) of the tendency for the Black vote to be more Democratic than the non-Black vote remains as "unexplained." This may be the result of influences that were never translated into attitudes, values, or beliefs, or were not captured in the various measures we extracted from the NES interviews; some direct effects may have been produced by social group pressure or direct messages from the pulpit. Or we may have incomplete or inaccurate measures of the variables that we included, and there may be errors of omission or commission that have been obscured by our rhetoric. In any event, we have accounted for most, but not all, of the apparent total effect of race on voter choice (.79 out of .91).

▪ The Gender Gap

Gender-related conflicts have been a prominent feature of contemporary presidential politics in the United States at least since 1972, when formal efforts were made to increase the role of women in national presidential selection. Male/female differences in voting behavior were evident in all four Reagan-Bush-Clinton elections, and they were of a fairly constant magnitude, both in the proportions turning out at the polls and in the partisan division of their votes (see Tables B2.1 and B2.2 in Appendix B). The turnout differences are minor; what has drawn attention is the greater proclivity of women to support the Democratic party and its candidates—or of men to support Republicans. In an earlier chapter on party identification, we suggested that the gender gap originated when Southern women failed to duplicate the trajectory of changes made by male Southerners in the post-1972 realignment of party identifications. While this explanation for the existence of the gender gap is not entirely satisfactory, it does appear to rule out some alternative theories; in particular, it reduces the likelihood that the explanation lies in a simple, pro-Democratic swing unique to the female vote.

In our explanation of gender differences in voting in 1992, we next document a somewhat more satisfactory accounting of the gender gap, yet one that poses its own unresolved questions. In adding gender to the consideration of the cultural themes of race, ethnicity, and religion, we do not observe the same magnitude of initial group differences that we have noted in the other domains. Instead of initial apparent effects of .90, .60, or even .18 (the smallest of the coefficients for a religious group), we start with an apparent effect of being female (instead of male) of .13, which is, nevertheless, consistent with very stable gender differences in the votes for 1980, 1984, 1988, and 1992 (see Appendix Table B2.2). In our hierarchical causal structure, that coefficient is not affected by taking into account other social and economic characteristics of voters (.13 becomes .12 in Table 10.8). Party identification does have an effect, however, and reduces the size of the gender coefficient in Table 10.8 from .12 (Row 5) to a statistical insignificance (.01, Row 6). Superficially, this might end the story, for the overall gender gap (whatever its source) appears to be the simple consequence of a long-term imbalance in party identification that gives the Democrats an advantage among women relative to the even division of party loyalties among men.

It would appear from Table 10.8, however, that the impact of gender in the 1992 vote is more complicated than a single long-term difference based on partisan identification. If, *instead* of party identification, we first

Table 10.8 Elaboration of Two-Party 1992 Vote Difference Between Men and Women

	Coefficients
1. Average Vote (−1 or +1) in Designated Category (Female)	+.23
2. Average Vote in Base Category (Male)	+.10
3. Difference: Average Vote (in Designated Category minus Base)	+.13
4. Bivariate Unstandardized Regression Coefficient (Race Scored 1 for Female, 0 for Male)	+.13
#5. Coefficient[a] from Multiple Regression with Other Social/Economic Characteristics Held Constant	+.12
6. With Party Identification (Party ID) Also Held Constant	(+.01)
7. With Specific Policy-related Predispositions (but NOT Party ID) Also Held Constant	(−.06)
8. With Liberal vs. Conservative Self-designation Also Held Constant	(−.06)
9. With Party ID and all Policy-related Predispositions Also Held Constant	−.07
10. With Preferences on All Current Policy Issues Also Held Constant	−.12
11. With Perceptions of Current Personal and National Conditions Also Held Constant	−.14
12. With Retrospective Evaluations of Current President's Performance in Office Also Held Constant	−.07
13. With Evaluations of the Candidates' Personal Qualities Also Held Constant	−.06
14. With Prospective Evaluations of the Candidates' and Parties' Future Performance Also Held Constant	(−.05)

#The coefficient in Row 5 is the "apparent total effect" of the designated category on the vote.

take account of the other predispositions, the sign of the effect coefficient for gender actually changes (from +.12 to −.06). After we control for specific policy-related predispositions we see a tendency for women to vote more Republican—or for men to vote more Democratic (although the coefficient is not reliably different from zero). Women were apparently more likely than men to cast a Democratic vote (or men more likely to vote Republican) because of their predispositions *other* than party identification. As a consequence, when those differences (between men and women) are removed or controlled, the resulting coefficient suggests an effect of the opposite sign (−.06), which is the consequence of the combined indirect effects through policy-related predispositions. By holding constant both party identification (which favors the Democrats) and policy-related predispositions (which also favor the Democrats), we detect gender differences in which women reacted more favorably than men to George Bush—or men more positively to Bill Clinton—as shown by a statistically significant −.07.

Policy preferences and perceptions of politically relevant external conditions also appear to have encouraged women to a Democratic vote and men to Republicanism such that adding them to the list of variables "taken into account" produces a pro-Republican effect of being female (or a pro-Democratic effect of being male) instead of the opposite-signed difference of +.13 in the actual votes cast by these two groups.

It would appear that among short-term influences in 1992, only retrospective performance evaluations favored Bush's cause among women (or Clinton's among men), thereby offsetting some of the traditional gender effects based on partisanship and policy-related preferences. The addition of explicit comparative evaluations (of Bush versus Clinton) based on personal qualities and future performance accentuate that trend so that our final effect coefficient is reduced to an insignificant (−.05).

At this point we have accounted for an initial pro-Democratic total effect (of being female instead of male) as well as for a set of opposite-signed influences associated with the two candidates in 1992. As is often true in the search for plausible explanations for behavior, new analyses may raise as many questions as they answer. This is true in the present case: Why should women more often exhibit liberal/Democratic predispositions than men? Why should the two genders hold different policy preferences and perceptions of current conditions? And why should women have responded more positively than men to George Bush as President? The difficulty of such questions was recognized in *The American Voter*, but they were largely neglected in favor of an emphasis on the apparently most proximate influences on the vote.

▪ Marital Status

Our review of the roles of social and economic characteristics in shaping the votes of the Reagan-Bush-Clinton years has dealt with four themes—religion, ethnicity, race, and gender—that are new to presidential politics, at least in their late twentieth century incarnations. A fifth element in the continuing American social revolution concerning social relations or "cultural" orientations pertains to marital status. Although some aspects of marital status are related to differences in social class, the popular emphasis on its relevance to politics seems to lie more in attention to the growth of sexual activity outside marriage and the phenomenon of single-parent homes than in attention to changes in the partisan division of the votes.

The distribution of the electorate across the major categories of married, never married, divorced, and widowed changed in the 1960s and 1970s, but did not change dramatically during the 1980s; for the most part, the political relevance of those categories did not change either. As of 1980, the married were already distinctive in the rates with which they went to the polls (see Appendix Table B6.1) and in their pro-Republican choices. By a margin of 20 percentage points, married voters favored Reagan over Carter, while each of the other marriage-related groupings favored Carter over Reagan by razor-thin margins. In their large numbers, married people dominated national politics until 1992. In that year, married citizens divided their votes very evenly between the major parties but gave the Democrat, Clinton, a thin 3-point edge (much like the others had in 1980). The other 40 percent of the voting electorate favored Clinton by margins ranging from 23 percent among the widowed to 55 percent among the never married. Where the married moved from the Republican column in 1988 to the Democratic column in 1992 with a swing of 16 percentage points, the swing in the same direction among the divorced and never married was 39 and 40 points.

As a result, the vote division of married men and women was much more Republican in 1992 than was the division in any other marital category (see Appendix Table B6.3). Given the partisan contest over the sponsorship of "family values," these data invite inquiries as to whether the differences in partisan voting behavior reflected a Republican advantage among the married or an anti-Republican backlash (among the divorced and never married) against the new religious right, as suggested earlier. Students of the 1992 election should note that the contrasting voting behavior between the married and the never married was apparent even in 1980. The 1992 vote differences, however, were roughly twice as large; the 77 percent Democratic vote among the unmarried contrasted with a nearly even division (51 percent Democratic) among the married (see Appendix Table B6.2). In 1992, these differences were of the same magnitude as the differences in the votes between the highest and lowest income quintiles or those between voters with no more than grade school educations and those with some exposure to college. Only race clearly exceeded marital status as a social-political cleavage.

Table 10.9 Elaboration of the 1992 Two-Party Vote Difference Between Never Married Citizens and Others

	Coefficients
1. Average Vote (−1 or +1) in Designated Category (Never Married)	+.52
2. Average Vote in Base Category (All Others)	+.11
3. Difference: Designated Category minus Base	+.41
4. Bivariate Unstandardized Regression Coefficient (Gender Based 1 for Female, 0 for Male)	+.41
#5. Coefficient[a] from Multiple Regression with Other Social/Economic Characteristics Held Constant	+.23
6. With Party Identification (Party ID) Also Held Constant	+.22
7. With Specific Policy-related Predispositions (but NOT Party ID) Also Held Constant	(+.02)
8. With Liberal vs. Conservative Self-designation Also Held Constant	(−.02)
9. With Party ID and all Policy-related Predispositions Also Held Constant	(+.06)
10. With Preferences on All Current Policy Issues Also Held Constant	(+.08)
11. With Perceptions of Current Personal and National Conditions Also Held Constant	(+.08)
12. With Retrospective Evaluations of Current President's Performance in Office Also Held Constant	(+.03)
13. With Evaluations of the Candidates' Personal Qualities Also Held Constant	(+.03)
14. With Prospective Evaluations of the Candidates' and Parties' Future Performance Also Held Constant	(+.00)

#The coefficient in Row 5 is the "apparent total effect" of the designated category on the vote.

Although marital status is usually used to contrast the "married" and the "never married," it should be noted that the divorced members of the electorate divided their votes just halfway between the other two groups—the never married voted 28 points more Democratic than the married (after taking account of other social and economic differences), while the divorced vote average was 14 points more Democratic. The widowed voted 3 points more Republican, a difference not statistically distinguishable from the married.[7]

Table 10.9 presents some suggestive evidence concerning the possible origins of these differences, based on comparisons of the never married (plus those currently living with a partner) with all of the other marriage-related categories. First, of course, is the discovery that much of the .41 difference between the average votes of these two groups in 1992 is a consequence of the other social and economic differences between those groups. When these correlates are taken into account, the apparent impact of being "never married" is reduced to .23. As we might expect from the nature of party identification, party plays virtually no part in this distinctiveness of the vote division for the unmarried. And, as with religion, value-laden policy-related predispositions other than party account for virtually all of the remaining differences pertaining to marital status and vote choice. With other social and economic attributes held constant, and with predispositions *other* than party taken into account, there is no statistically significant difference (+.02) between the vote choices of the never married and those of the married (which are the polar political groups where marital status is concerned).

Among our policy-related predispositions, all but those concerning foreign involvements and the conflict between labor unions and business play some visible role in distinguishing the political behavior of the unmarried. Among the other six, moral tolerance and liberal/conservative ideological preferences are most relevant to the vote choice and provide a clear difference between the unmarried and those in other marital groups. In both cases, more liberal predispositions among the never married promoted support for Clinton and prompted a distinctly larger Democratic vote than among the married (see Table 10.10). The pro-Democratic influences associated with the never married also included liberal preferences concerning the role of government, egalitarianism, Vietnam, and evaluations of homosexuals versus fundamentalists. Not only are the unmarried predisposed toward the liberal side in all of these eight predispositional domains, but the overall difference between them and other voters is *greater* than that between all other pairs of politically polarized sets—Black and non-Black, the lowest and highest income groups, or Evangelical Protestants and the Non-religious. The two groups based on marital status were the most polarized groups in three of the six specific domains of policy-related predispositions; they were bested by only one polar pair in two domains, concerning the role of government and egalitarianism (on which Blacks and non-Blacks differed more sharply) and by one other pair, based on income, that was more polarized on limited government.

Much like the Non-religious, individuals who have never been married are a minority in a society in which veneration of the traditional family is not only the national norm but holds a monopoly on media

Table 10.10 Differences in Mean Scores on Selected Policy-Related Predispositions, for Voters with Selected Social and Economic Characteristics

	Gender	Race	Post-ND	College Graduate	Union	South	Low Income	High Income	Unmarried
Limited Government	+.28	+.45	+.09	-.26	+.22	.00	+.20	-.29	+.34
Egalitarianism	+.04	+.37	+.13	+.08	+.02	-.05	+.02	-.10	+.21
Moral Tolerance	-.01	+.10	+.20	+.10	-.03	-.05	+.11	-.01	+.39
Gays-Fundamentalists	+.08	-.07	+.10	+.18	+.01	-.17	-.06	+.09	+.19
Ideology (Liberal/Conservative)	+.11	+.22	+.10	+.07	+.04	-.06	+.27	-.16	+.38
Isolationism	+.14	+.18	-.08	-.27	-.07	+.03	+.27	-.16	+.04
Union/Business	+.07	+.22	-.02	-.23	+.28	-.05	+.08	-.25	+.01
Vietnam	+.21	+.11	+.21	+.21	+.15	-.18	-.05	+.13	+.26

NOTE: Positive scores are Liberal, negative scores are Conservative on indices ranging from +1 to -1.

attention concerning politics. It may well be that "spinsters" and "bache-lors" are no longer held in low regard. Nevertheless, social issues are defined in terms of the dominant groups in the social structure; coun-tervailing forces among the rest of society are given voice only when they can be organized—as has been at least somewhat true for women, Blacks, and Hispanics. Members of unorganized social categories remain invisible to all but the social analyst. It is therefore particularly impor-tant—for reasons of social theory as well as political analysis—to capture noteworthy features of unorganized political behavior. In 1992, the Non-religious and the fragments of minor religions were joined with the never married to make up two large sets of unorganized voters who were predisposed toward countervailing social and political perspectives. As we suggested in our brief commentary on variations in political change across religious groups, the behavior of the unorganized may be an important consequence of the behavior of the highly organized. Where the never married are concerned, the concentration of their numbers among the younger post-New Deal cohorts has added to their suscepti-bility to appeals that run counter to the traditional values of established society.

▪ Income and the Vote

We next consider several traditional or standard measures of socioeco-nomic status, using the NES data on three "factual" characteristics: income, education, and home ownership. In the original Lazarsfeld formulation of the Index of Political Predispositions, such variables were joined with others, such as religion and rural or urban residence, in a simple additive manner, presumably grouping together the like-minded among voters. In that formulation, pressure for social conformity accen-tuated the Democratic voting propensities of the disadvantaged, the Republican inclinations of those with high socioeconomic status, and the vulnerabilities of the cross-pressured in categories of mixed status. Beyond a general assumption of a commonality of political meanings cutting across high and low status on each variable, little attention was given to possible differences in political meaning associated with the different components of the Index of Political Predispositions. There have been many refinements and conceptual reformulations of the social structural perspectives on the analysis of electoral behavior, including

Table 10.11 Alternative Perspectives on the Electoral Relevance of Social or Economic Position

	Income (1st Quint.)	Income (Top Quint.)	Education (Coll. Grad.)	Homeowner (Renter)	Union Household
1. Average Vote (−1 or +1) in Designated Category	+.59	−.03	+.06	+.47	+.34
2. Average Vote in Base (Middle-income, Non-union, Non-college, Homeowner, Other)	+.18	+.18	+.22	+.08	+.13
3. Difference: Average (Designated Category minus Base)	+.41	−.21	−.16	+.39	+.21
4. Regression Coefficient from Bivariate Analysis	+.41	−.21	−.16	+.39	+.21
#5. Other Social and Economic Characteristics Held Constant[a]	+.22	−.13	−.08	+.12	+.24
6. Party Identification (Party ID) Also Held Constant	+.13	(+.02)	(−.03)	+.11	(+.08)
7. With Specific Policy-related Predispositions (but NOT Party ID) Also Held Constant	+.17	(−.01)	−.11	(+.03)	+.11
8. With Liberal vs. Conservative Self-designation Also Held Constant	+.16	(+.00)	−.13	(+.02)	+.12

	Income (1st Quint.)	Income (Top Quint.)	Education (Coll. Grad.)	Homeowner (Renter)	Union Household
9. With Party ID and all Policy-related Predispositions Also Held Constant	+.12	(+.05)	−.09	(+.05)	(+.05)
10. With Preferences on All Current Policy Issues Also Held Constant	(+.10)	(+.04)	−.10	(+.06)	(+.05)
11. With Perceptions of Current Personal and National Conditions Also Held Constant	+.10	(+.04)	−.09	(+.06)	(+.02)
12. With Retrospective Evaluations of Current President's Performance in Office Also Held Constant	(+.08)	(+.06)	−.10	(+.05)	(+.02)
13. With Evaluations of the Candidates' Personal Qualities Also Held Constant	(−.06)	(+.04)	−.09	(+.06)	(+.03)
14. With Prospective Evaluations of the Candidates' and Parties' Future Performance Also Held Constant	+.11	(+.05)	(−.05)	(+.06)	(+.04)

NOTE: Parentheses indicate that the coefficient is not reliably different from .00 at the .1 level.

#The entries in Row 5 are designated as the "apparent total effect" of that variable.

some direct contributions from *The American Voter.* We, in turn, join that line of commentary, albeit briefly, to note ways in which our approach adds to our understanding of some of the complexities involved in the social classification of voters in terms of their social "status" or position.

The data pertaining to family income epitomize our earlier assertions about the general stability over time of vote differences related to social and economic characteristics. In Appendix B, Tables B5.1–B5.3, we see rocklike stability in the voting patterns arranged by relative quintile assessments of family income. Both vote turnout and vote divisions consistently conform to well-established stereotypes; the poor vote less often and more Democratic, the well-to-do vote more often and heavily Republican. Virtually the only item of interest concerning changes in vote division is the distinct progression of the middle-income voters from a Republican vote in 1980 to a Democratic plurality in 1992.

Because of the frequent deviations from monotonicity in the income-vote relationship, we have chosen to elaborate explanations of the vote for only the top and bottom quintiles and to use the middle three quintiles (in combination) as the base group for our analysis of income-related differences. Consonant with this decision, we discover differences as well as similarities in our elaborations of apparent effects for the two extreme income quintiles. As seen in Table 10.11, it appears that our initial differences based on income are modified substantially when other interrelated social and economic attributes are also included in the analysis. For the highest quintile group, the apparent effect drops from −.21 to −.13 when we control for other social characteristics. For the lowest quintile the reduction in apparent effect is even greater—from .41 to .22. Thus, almost half of the initial .62 difference in vote division between top and bottom quintiles disappears once we take other social attributes into account.

By re-estimating the apparent effects associated with our lowest and highest quintiles at each stage in our model, we can identify some of the factors that are presumably involved in "producing" the impact of income on vote choice. At the second stage in our model, after taking account of other social and economic characteristics, party identification predictably "explains" some of the pro-Democratic tendencies of low-income voters and even more of the pro-Republican tendencies among voters in the top income quintile. In particular, the historical association of low income with the Democratic party accounts for .09 of the .22 apparent effect in the lowest quintile based on controls in our other social characteristics. The association of high incomes with the Republican party accounts for *all* of the .13 apparent pro-Republican effect of being in the highest quintiles, and more. After taking account of party, the combined effect of moving between the lowest and highest quintiles is reduced to .11 from the original .62 (based on coefficients of $+.13$ and $(+.02)$ in line 6 of Table 10.10).

When measured against the baseline coefficients established by estimating the apparent effects for low- and high-income groups (compared to middle-income voters) with all other social and economic characteristics held constant, predispositions concerning party and ideology, as well as the newer policy-related predispositional domains, are minor but congruent influences in explaining the tendency of high-income voters to support the Republican candidate. Short-term influences, including current issues and retrospective evaluations of Bush and the Bush administration in 1992, appear to add nothing of consequence to the interpretation of income differences provided by the long-term predispositions in our model.

As a supplement to conventional wisdom, we note that we are unable to reduce further the pro-Republican impact of being in the high-income group after we have accounted for the traditional ties of the upper-income group to the Republican party and to conservative ideology. The effect estimate in that group which remains after we control for long-term factors is insignificant, and does not change appreciably when we also take account of current policy preferences, national conditions, and candidates' personal qualities or expectations concerning future performance. In roughly parallel fashion, once we take into account reactions to President Bush's performance, the apparent impact of being in the low-income group cannot be reliably distinguished from that of the middle-income base. By attending largely, if not exclusively, to long-term factors, we have accounted for almost all of the initial gap (.62) that separated the lowest and highest quintiles. Short-term issues relevant to family income may play a large role in presidential campaigns, but in the 1992 vote they were overshadowed by the impact of longstanding predispositions that have long separated the well-to-do from the poor.

▪ Education and the Vote

Against the backdrop of the social correlates for voting during the New Deal era, a comparison of our conclusions concerning the electoral impact of high income with parallel estimates for college graduates clarifies the changes that have taken place in the role of social status on the national electoral scene. Traditional approaches to the analysis of electoral behavior have treated education as a significant indication or component of socioeconomic status. Measurement of education seems quite straightforward, based on the number of years spent in formal education institutions. We have continued to use this approach, although we acknowledge that the content of education may have changed over time and that therefore there may be changes in meaning for specific "levels" that cannot be captured by continued reliance on the number of years spent in school.[8] Education is, of course, much more than a measure of status alone; as an enabling experience and a screening procedure, education has profound implications for the citizen's inclination and capacity to learn about politics. These implications are immediately evident in the relationship of education to voter turnout.

When the data were collected for the writing of *The American Voter*, half of the electorate had no more than an elementary school education, and college graduates were rare indeed. Forty years later, with the post–World War II G.I. Bill and a continuing surge of enrollment in higher education, having at least some college experience has become the modal category within the electorate. Although dropout rates are high among central city youth, in 1992 more than four out of five of all citizens of voting age reported completing 12 years in school, and one of every two reported having attended college. This record is unique in the modern world of industrialized nations, and the trend continues. Even in the brief period of 12 years that is the focus of this book, there has been a visible shift in the educational composition of the electorate: there has been a 25 percent increase in the proportion attending college, up 10 points from 39 percent in 1980 to 49 percent in 1992, and there has been a 30 percent decline in the numbers who have not completed high school, a seven-point drop from 24 percent to 17 percent (see Appendix Table B1.1).

In the face of rapid turnover, as better educated young voters replace less well educated senior citizens, one can speculate about the extent to which educational quality may have declined. From our perspective as political analysts, it is difficult to discern what is really happening in the classroom, and thus we have spent much time in earlier chapters examining rates of political participation within education levels as well as across political generations. Tables B1.1–B1.3 in Appendix B provides some useful additional information within our four-election span. As educational levels have increased, the participation gap between the top and bottom of the inverted education pyramid has also increased, at least in recent years. In absolute terms, the less well educated are voting less, and the better educated are voting more. This observation does not accord with the thesis that higher education has less effect on political involvement than it did when it was limited to fewer people.

The complexities of the relationship between educational experience and electoral behavior are even more apparent in the domain of partisanship. The status relationship—that equating higher education with Republican predispositions—has weakened across our twelve-year time span. Appendix Table B1.2 portrays the steady decline in the differences in partisan voting between the top and the bottom: a 56-percentage-point difference in the proportions of high and low education groups voting Democratic in 1980 had dwindled to a 28-point difference—a 50 percent drop—by 1992. This was, of course, foreshadowed by our earlier regional analysis in which we concluded that a dramatic reversal of the socioeconomic correlates of vote choice in the South has been accompanied by a fading away of some traditional relationships in the rest of the nation.

As with income, the relationship between years of education and the partisan division of the vote has also varied somewhat each year. Table B1.2 in Appendix B shows that, in 1980 and 1984, there was little difference between the high school graduates and those with some college education. On the other hand, in 1992 there was less difference between the bottom and the middle than between the middle and the top. In general, our criterion for choosing a particular social characteristic for multivariate "elaboration" was based on the apparent significance of its total effect on the voter after we had taken other social and economic characteristics into account. It should be noted that this selection criterion is not necessarily infallible in the search for insights into the political meaning of a complex variable, such as education. An analysis of the difference between elementary school attendees and high school graduates might prove illuminating. In 1992, however, only college graduates exhibited apparent electoral effects (when compared to other education categories), so our elaboration of education-related effects is based on the contrast between that group and all the others.

The alternative estimates for the impact of college graduation in the third column of Table 10.11 provide a number of interesting comparisons. First, a modest preponderance of Republican party identifications explains a visible portion of the pro-Republican departure of college graduates from all those with less formal education. However, where the other predispositions complemented party identification in explaining the electoral differences associated with race and gender, both policy-related predispositions *and* policy preferences among college graduates encouraged Democratic, rather than Republican, voting. By removing the effect of policy-related predispositions, or taking them into account, the pro-Republican coefficient for college graduates, −.08, becomes even more pro-Republican, −.13, although adding party identification brings it back to −.09. Similarly, when we also control for current policy preferences, the pro-Republican coefficient of −.09 is enlarged to −.10. The remaining potential explanations of vote choice have no consistent impact on the remaining coefficients for college graduates.

The impact of controlling for some predispositions on the apparent effects of college graduation and high income suggests countervailing changes that may be occurring in American society. First, as we have noted, the policy-related predispositions of college graduates are predominantly liberal when contrasted with the strongly conservative predispositions of the wealthy. This pattern includes general liberal/conservative self-description (see Table 10.10). Income and education also produce different coefficients in Table 10.10, with college graduates more liberal on our measures of morality, attitudes toward homosexuality, and egalitarianism. These differences lead us to two concluding comments: first, our explanatory scheme does not account for the pro-Republican plurality in the votes of the college graduates, −.09, compared to high school graduates; second, while a college degree may be necessary (in most cases) for the voter to become prosperous, financial prosperity and educational success are not the same, at least not in politics.

▪ Renters versus Homeowners

Home ownership represents a third traditional indicator of socioeconomic status in the United States. As is true of most social and economic attributes of American citizens, the political correlates of owning or renting one's dwelling place have not changed significantly in recent years. Homeowners are more regular visitors to the polls than are renters, and they persistently vote more heavily Republican. Until 1992, when even homeowners gave an edge to Clinton over Bush, the elections of the 1980s consistently found renters supporting the Democratic candidate with pluralities somewhat smaller than those enjoyed by the Republican candidates among homeowners. Although renters led the surge away from Bush, or toward Clinton, in 1992, there is little suggestion of a more enduring trend; the differential in party identification in 1992 was almost identical to those of the 1980s.

The difference in the vote divisions between homeowners and renters is largely attributable to differences between these two groups on other social and economic characteristics. When we control or account for such differences, the apparent impact of renting (instead of owning) declines from .39 to .12. In a pattern similar to that of the "never married," party identification among renters makes little contribution to the remaining differences, while controlling for policy-related predispositions reduces the difference in their voting divisions to statistical insignificance. Three of these predispositions were not relevant to the group differences in vote preference, but each of the other five clearly was at least marginally relevant. In particular, statistically significant indirect effects (at the .01 or .05 level) appear to exist for ideology, egalitarianism, moral tolerance, support for governmental activism, and attitudes toward homosexuals versus religious fundamentalists. Compared with the indirect effects of the different religious categories, however, none of their indirect effects are very strong. The social orientations associated with the differences between renters and homeowners were not as relevant to their vote choices as those orientations were for the vote decisions of the more Committed among the various religious categories, but they do combine to illuminate or interpret most of the differences between these groups. Beyond these policy-related predispositions, however, none of the other sources of electoral influence, either long-term or short-term, appeared to contribute substantially to the differences in the vote decisions of homeowners and renters.

▪ The Union Family Vote

Traditional Democratic coalitions—from the New Deal to the Great Society—included not only Catholics, Blacks, and the economically disadvantaged, but union families (with one or more family members belonging to a labor union) as well. This affinity was signaled by the creation of one of the earliest political action committees, the CIO/PAC. The political distinctiveness associated with union membership in 1992 differed from that of the Reagan-Bush years only in slight degree. While the ebbing of labor union membership has produced a gradual decline in the number of union-affiliated electors, their propensity to vote at a higher rate than those with no union affiliation has increased (see Appendix Table B11.1). Although it is misleading to talk of a trend in voting partisanship, 1992 did see a reduction in the gap between preferences of union and non-union voters. Although the union vote had been increasingly Democratic, the sharp increase in the Democratic share of the non-union vote in 1992 (paralleling the Democratic increase in the non-Black vote) reduced the difference with the union vote from approximately 15 points in 1980 to 10 points in 1992.

The long history of the unions' pro-Democratic bias is nicely captured by the consequences of controlling for party identification in Table 10.11. A total effect of union membership of .24 in 1992 (after controlling for the effect of other social and economic characteristics) is reduced to a statistically non-significant coefficient of (.08). Controls for policy-related predispositions, instead of party identification, also reduced the apparent pro-Democratic effect of union membership from .24 to .11, but *adding* those controls to that for party identification did not produce a substantial further reduction. Furthermore, no significant changes were produced by adding controls for any subsequent stage in our model. The "union vote" in 1992 seems to have been singularly based on union members' historical differences from non-union voters, and may have been based on party identifications alone.

▪ Age

Contrary to political tradition and recent conventional wisdom, neither voters' ages nor residence in the South exhibited a large impact on the 1992 vote. As could be forecast from our discussion of generational differences in earlier chapters, fewer younger than older cohorts participated on election day, as was true in the other three presidential elections we have reviewed. But in 1992—or 1988 or 1984, for that matter—no significant age-related differences emerged in the two-party vote for President.

The absence of any simple age-related difference in the division of the voters between Bush and Clinton can be seen as the result of several offsetting differences. In the earlier analysis of turnout and party realignment, the bottom line seemed straightforward: generational differences separated the aging New Deal generation from the burgeoning post-New Deal successor cohorts. Our multiple-stage elaboration of generational differences in the 1992 vote discloses some complementary explanations for long-term influences, supplemented by short-term consequences of the political context of the election period.

First, long-term influences apparently have countervailing effects on vote choice: once the effects of other social and economic attributes are taken into account, a small (statistically insignificant) pro-Republican tendency ($-.05$) among members of the post-New Deal generation is replaced by a much more substantial apparent effect of $-.16$ in Table 10.12. At the next analytic stage, after we take account of the full roster of partisan and policy-related predispositions, the remaining difference between the New Deal and the post-New Deal cohorts is essentially unchanged, at $-.16$ in Row 10, Table 10.12. This result, however, is the apparent consequence of contradictory, or offsetting, effects. Party identification favors the Republicans; thus, removing its effect *reduces* the pro-Republican tendency of the post-New Deal group (from $-.16$ in Row 5 to $-.09$ in Row 6; or from $-.23$ in Row 8 to $-.16$ in Row 9). Specific policy-related predispositions, on the other hand, are clearly more liberal among the young, so controls for those variables accentuate the pro-Republican tendencies of the post-New Deal generation (from $-.16$ in Row 5 to $-.26$ in Row 7). The liberal, or pro-Democratic, predispositions with the greatest pro-Democratic consequences for this group concerned egalitarianism and morality. Although tolerance for opposition to participation in the Vietnam War had no statistically significant independent effect on the vote difference between younger and older voters, the direction of that difference is consonant with the general expectation of generational differences caused by anti-Vietnam sentiments among the young.

Further controls for short-term influences produce a modest reduction in the remaining pro-Republican effects of being in the post-New Deal generation, leaving our analysis with a final unexplained pro-Republican effect of $-.10$. In short, policy-related predispositions were virtually the only factors that were responsible for any pro-Democratic influence on

Table 10.12 Alternate Perspectives on the Electoral Relevance of Generation

	Post-New Deal Generation
1. Average Vote (−1 or +1) in Designated Category (Post-New Deal)	+.15
2. Average Vote in Base Category (All Others)	+.20
3. Difference: Average Vote (Designated minus Base)	−.05
4. Bivariate Unstandardized Regression Coefficient	(−.05)
#5. Coefficient[a] from Multiple Regression with Other Social/Economic Characteristics Held Constant	−.16
6. With Party Identification (Party ID) Also Held Constant	−.09
7. With Specific Policy-related Predispositions (but NOT Party ID or Liberal/Conservative) Also Held Constant	−.26
8. With Liberal vs. Conservative Self-designation Also Held Constant	−.23
9. With Party ID and All Policy-related Predispositions Also Held Constant	−.16
10. With Preferences on All Current Policy Issues Also Held Constant	−.15
11. With Perceptions of Current Personal and National Conditions Also Held Constant	−.12
12. With Retrospective Evaluations of the Current President's Performance in Office Also Held Constant	−.10
13. With Evaluations of the Candidates' Personal Qualities Also Held Constant	−.10
14. With Prospective Evaluations of the Candidates' and Parties' Future Performance Also Held Constant	−.10

NOTE: Parentheses indicate that the coefficient is not reliably different from .00 at the .1 level.
#The coefficient in Row 5 is designated as the "apparent total effect" of that variable.

younger voters. Those influences offset most of the countervailing pro-Republican forces for the post-New Deal group, but they did not erase an unexplained pro-Republican tendency that is statistically significant.

None of this denies the importance of generational differences and age-related responses to the politics of the 1970s and 1980s, but the cumulative consequences of the more recent passage of time cannot be overlooked. The decisiveness of our explanation of declining voter turnout between 1960 and 1988 rested in part on the contrast between the turnout rates of the oldest and youngest cohorts. As the composition of the electorate changed as a result of the young replacing the old, so the survival of secular realignment of party strength in the South following 1960 (and nationwide in the 1980s) depended on the relatively greater malleability of the partisanship of the young. The sharpest contrast between the generations, however, both in voting turnout and in partisan realignment, has slowly disappeared through the sheer passage of time and the disappearance of the pre-New Deal generation.

The data recording the partisanship of the different cohorts from 1980 to 1992 are too uneven to sustain generalizations about any "convergence" of different cohorts during that time. Nevertheless, Part B of Appendix Table B3.3 indicates the virtual absence of significant cohort differences in the vote within New Deal and post-New Deal generations after 1980. Pinpointing an earlier depiction of a pro-Republican shift in party identification in the 1980s, there is a potentially optimistic note for Republicans concerning the vote in Part B of Table B3.3. There it appears that the youngest cohorts have been on the move—relative to the rest of the electorate—in shifting their long-term party loyalties from a Democratic plurality in 1980 (+18) to an even split between the parties from 1981 to 1992. The detailed results in the appendix tables also depict *intra*-generational differences between cohorts in 1980; however, averages for the New Deal and post-New Deal generations after 1980 leave only mild inter-generational differences.

▪ The South

The political nature of the last component of the old Democratic coalition, the South, is somewhat similar to that of age. No significant electoral distinctiveness between Southerners and other voters appears (see Table 10.13) *unless* one takes account of policy-related predispositions as well as other social characteristics but *not* partisan identification. From that analysis (in Row 7) we see a significant pro-Democratic Southern tendency (+.16), but that apparent effect becomes inconsequential when we also control for party identification, as shown in Row 9. In effect, the pro-Democratic consequence of partisan identification in the South is offset by the very conservative policy-related predispositions of that region.

At the same time, it appears that electoral behavior in the East and the Midwest in 1992 (see Appendix Table B8.3) differed from that in other parts of the country as well as from each other. In Table B8.3 we can see indications that the South is still in flux. Party identification no longer favors the Democrats in absolute terms, and our long-term pre-

Table 10.13 Alternate Perspectives on the Electoral Relevance of Southern Residence

	South
1. Average Vote (-1 or $+1$) in Designated Category (South)	$+.19$
2. Average Vote in Base Category (Midwest)	$+.05$
3. Difference: Average Vote (Designation minus Base)	$+.14$
4. Bivariate Unstandardized Regression Coefficient	$+.14$
#5. Coefficient[a] from Multiple Regression with Other Social/Economic Characteristics Held Constant	$(.11)$
6. With Party Identification (Party ID) Also Held Constant	$(.00)$
7. With Specific Policy-related Predispositions (but NOT Party ID or Liberal/Conservative) Also Held Constant	$+.16$
8. With Liberal vs. Conservative Self-designation Also Held Constant	$+.14$
9. With Party ID and All Policy-related Predispositions Also Held Constant	$(.05)$
10. With Preferences on All Current Policy Issues Also Held Constant	$(.07)$
11. With Perceptions of Current Personal and National Conditions Also Held Constant	$(.06)$
12. With Retrospective Evaluations of the Current President's Performance in Office Also Held Constant	$+.09$
13. With Evaluations of the Candidates' Personal Qualities Also Held Constant	$+.08$
14. With Prospective Evaluations of the Candidates' and Parties' Future Performance Also Held Constant	$(.06)$

NOTE: Parentheses indicate that the coefficient is not reliably different from .00 at the .1 level.
#The coefficient in Row 5 is designated as the "apparent total effect" of that variable.

dispositions reflect the evolution of the South as a home for conservative Republicans. The likelihood of a new role for the region may be reflected in the fact that the ultimate analytic "bottom line" from our analysis suggests only an insignificant Democratic advantage in the South in the 1992 election, even with both Democratic candidates coming from that region.

▪ Summary

Our search for substantive interpretations of the apparent effects of social and economic characteristics on vote choice affirms most of our general conclusions concerning stable patterns of voting across the four elections from 1980 to 1992. Despite great volatility in the vote itself, ranging from Reagan's landslide in 1984 to Clinton's narrow victory in 1992, differences across social and economic characteristics seemed almost impervious to change. Only in the case of religion—and then only within categories of Evangelical Protestants—were there indications that encourage speculation about important changes within linkages between social relations and politics.

Moreover, although there is a general presumption that most social and economic characteristics are interrelated to form what is appropriately described as social structure, there is a substantial degree of uniqueness in the relationship of political attributes to each social dimension. In general, our efforts to control for variations in other social and economic characteristics do little to explain or diminish associations between political preferences and any particular characteristic. Taking account of other social characteristics does not greatly change our estimates for the apparent electoral effects of vote choice with race (Table 10.7), education, high income, or union membership (Table 10.11). There are some predictable exceptions when the social or economic variable involved is associated with life cycle differences. Consequently, the political choice correlates of marital status or home ownership change markedly when other social attributes are taken into account.

In keeping with the presumption of stable, long-term associations between social attributes and partisan preferences, our explanations are largely based on second-stage variables, long-term predispositions concerning party and ideology, and major dimensions of policy-related conflict. Elements found in the third or later stages of our hierarchical causal structure, such as current policy issues or various evaluations of the candidates, appear to explain only minor components of social or economic differences in vote choice in any given election year.

We have documented the fact that most social and economic attributes that were used to explain electoral choice fifty years ago are still relevant today. We have noted many instances in which continuity within political traditions has provided explanations of voting choices almost solely in the language of long-term predispositions: union membership, race, socioeconomic status, and some aspects of religion fit the definition of socio-political cleavages that continue to shape contemporary voter decisions without much responsiveness to new problems or short-term issues. We have noted several circumstances in which policy-related predispositions (as well as party identification) are crucial elements in explaining electoral differences between social or economic groups. In every instance, we have accounted for most of a given inter-group difference with some combination of our explanatory stages. In some cases, however—as with gender, race, and age—our search for explanations of group differences comes up somewhat short, so that we must reconsider a new set of alternative explanatory hypotheses. And in others, as with Protestant Evangelicals, we see evidence that enduring social values may have been engaged by new political circumstances in a manner that promises a new cultural dimension for the politics of the next century.

Continuing Conflicts within the Society: Policy-related and Partisan Predispositions

In the previous chapter, we introduced several general predispositions toward continuing ideological or policy-related conflicts in the society, because of the role they appear to play in mediating the influence of social or economic characteristics on vote choice. We began that consideration of policy-related predispositions with voters' general self-identification as liberal, moderate, or conservative, for that is the only measure (besides party identification) of a "long-term" factor that has exhibited a continuing relationship with many different policy domains as well as vote choice. We then considered three specific predispositions based on general beliefs in quite different policy domains. These three measures summarize voters' beliefs concerning equality, morality, and the role of government, based on sets of items that were developed and tested for NES surveys of the 1984, 1988, and 1992 elections. The conceptual status of these and other measures concerning general policy-related topics has not been fully resolved in the literature. Like other analysts, however, we have used several of these measures in our earlier work on the 1988 election (Shanks and Miller, 1991), and we continue to expand that emphasis in our present work, as illustrated by their role as mediating variables in the previous chapter.

In the present chapter, we consider the electoral impact of each of our partisan and policy-related predispositions in their own right. We begin by clarifying several of the additional ways in which voters' choices for President appear to be influenced by their long-term partisan identifications. That review includes the significance of relationships between party identification and prior social and economic characteristics, the ambiguous causal relationships between partisan and policy-related predispositions, the indirect impact of long-term partisan identifications through other intervening variables that influence the vote, and, finally, the "direct" effect of party identification that remains when we control for *all* of the other explanatory variables in our model. We then explore, one by one, the other predispositions (introduced in the last chapter) that are defined in terms of continuing policy-related conflicts within the society that may be activated in shaping voters' choices on election day.

Our analysis of specific predispositional measures also includes four variables concerning group-related conflict and foreign affairs. Each of these adds to our explanation of voting behavior in 1992, although their theoretical status is more ambiguous than the other four policy-related predispositions concerning ideological self-designation and general beliefs about equality, morality, and the role of government. This chapter concludes with a review of several methodological issues concerning the validity and interpretation of our effect estimates for individual policy-related predispositions, including a comparison of results from our current analysis with those based on the very different analytic procedures used in *The American Voter.*

Party Identification: Long-Term versus Short-Term Forces

In previous chapters, we discussed voters' continuing identifications with one of the two major parties and referred to the pervasive influence of those identifications on other political variables. As emphasized in *The American Voter* and many other studies of the American electorate, we believe that long-term partisanship exerts an indirect influence on vote choice by shaping voters' attitudes toward many of the short-term forces in a given campaign, as well as by exerting some direct or unmediated influence of its own on the vote decision.

At this point, however, we should restate our conviction that, given the available data and our repertoire of analytic procedures, the causal relationships between partisan identification and policy-related predispositions must remain both conceptually and statistically indeterminate. Most voters in 1992 had acquired their current partisan identifications *and* their own predispositions toward continuing policy-related conflicts well before that campaign had begun. We assume that the statistical relationships between party identification and our policy-related predispositions are based on a complex and thus far unknown combination of processes that include childhood socialization, exposure to prior events with substantial political consequences, and the persuasive efforts of party leaders—as well as the cumulative influence of policy-related preferences on partisan identifications. Causal interpretation of those statistical relationships lies outside the scope of this volume, and our recognition of the complexities involved represents a notable departure from our previous work.[1]

Instead of presenting a single set of estimates which would imply a resolution of this causal ambiguity, Table 11.1 documents the strength of the statistical connections between party identification and the vote, both before and after we take account of different combinations of other explanatory predispositions. Our discussion is based on the same analytic procedures that were used in the preceding chapter's discussion of social and economic characteristics. Thus, Rows 1 and 2 of Table 11.1 present the vote divisions or average votes (scored +1 for Clinton and −1 for Bush) among voters who described themselves as Democrats (rounded to +.81) and Republicans, −.77, and Row 3 presents the simple difference (1.58) between those averages. Row 4 then presents the bivariate (unstandardized) regression coefficient, .78, from an analysis that includes only the trichotomous measure of party identification (based on the initial NES question on that topic). The scoring for party identification includes only two "units" (from −1 for Republicans to 0 for Independents, and from 0 to +1 for Democrats), so that the bivariate regression coefficient for party identification, .78, is very close to half of the simple difference between Democrats and Republicans in their average score on the vote (1.58). Rows 5, 7, and 8 present the corresponding regression coefficients for party identification from multivariate analyses which include progressively more explanatory variables, beginning with the social and economic characteristics discussed in the previous chapter, .70, followed by the specific policy-related predispositions discussed in this chapter, .53, and finally general liberal versus conservative self-designation, .48.[2]

From the modest reduction in coefficients between Rows 4 and 5 (from .78 to .70) it would appear that the electoral effects of partisan identifications are only slightly biased or confounded by the impact of

Table 11.1 Alternative Perspectives on the Impact of Party Identification

1. Average Vote (−1 or +1) Among Those Who Generally* Think of Themselves as a Democrat (N = 489)	.81
2. Average Vote (−1 or +1) Among Those Who Generally* Think of Themselves as Republican (N = 323)	−.77
3. Difference in Average Vote: Democrats Minus Republicans	1.58
4. Bivariate Unstandardized Regression Coefficient (Party Identification Scored −1, 0, or +1)	.78
5. Coefficient from Multiple Regression with Social and Economic Characteristics Held Constant	.70
6. (Not Relevant for This Table Concerning Party Identification)	—
7. With All Specific Policy-related Predispositions Also Held Constant	.53
#8. With Liberal vs. Conservative Self-designation Also Held Constant	.48
9. (Not Relevant for This Table Concerning Party Identification)	—
10. With Preferences on All Current Policy Issues Also Held Constant	.46
11. With Perceptions of Current Personal and National Conditions Also Held Constant	.44
12. With Retrospective Evaluations of the Current President's Performance Also Held Constant	.25
13. With Evaluations of the Candidates' Personal Qualities Also Held Constant	.22
14. With Prospective Evaluations of Candidates' and Parties' Future Performance Also Held Constant	.16

*The number of cases associated with extreme positions on these and similar measures simply indicate the base on which extreme scores were calculated. Note that the number of cases is unweighted; all other results are weighted.

(Coefficients Appear in Parentheses if the Estimated p Value is > .1).

#Indicates estimate of the "apparent total effect" discussed in the text.

(usually prior) social or economic characteristics on both party identification and the vote. In contrast, the substantial reduction between Rows 5 and 8 (from .70 to .48) suggests that the impact of long-term partisanship may indeed be confounded with that of ideological and other policy-related predispositions—that is, with variables in the other explanatory themes that we have assigned to the same causal stage in our model.

Unfortunately, because all of our predispositions have been assigned to the same causal stage, we are unable to assess the indirect effects of party identification *or* policy-related predispositions on the vote that operate "through" their impact on the other type of predisposition. Such indirect effects seem particularly likely, given the cumulative influence of party leaders on voters' policy-related predispositions and the impact of basic values on adult partisan orientations. Because of this ambiguity, we have selected a "preferred" estimate for the apparent total effect of each predisposition from explanations of equations that include both types of predispositions, as well as social and economic characteristics. Given these uncertainties, the coefficient in Row 8 of Table 11.1 (.48) must be interpreted as a conservative estimate of the "apparent total effect" of party identification on the vote, because it neglects any indirect effects of partisanship through our other (policy-related) predispositions.

The progressive reduction in the remaining coefficients (following the apparent total effect) in Table 11.1 suggests the extent to which the total impact of long-term partisanship on the vote is mediated, or transmitted, by the other intervening variables in our model. In particular, the potential indirect effects of partisanship can be seen in the degree to which the remaining apparent effect of party identification is reduced when we also account for retrospective evaluations of presidential performance (Row 12), comparative evaluations of the two candidates' personal qualities (Row 13), and evaluations of the future performance of the parties and candidates (Row 14). In this sequence of coefficients, the largest single decline in the remaining (or unmediated) impact of party identification can be seen in the difference between .44 (in Row 11, from an analysis which includes current policy preferences and perceptions of current conditions as well as all prior variables) and .25 (in Row 12, from the analysis which also includes explicit evaluations of the current President's performance in office).

Party identification also represents the only type of general attitude or predisposition that is nearly guaranteed to have a continuing "long-term" influence on national elections, for it is always activated (albeit in slightly varying degrees) in elections that call for voters to choose between the two major parties. Finally, it should be noted that party identification retains some apparent "direct effect" on the vote, .16, after we have controlled for *all* of the other explanatory variables in our model. This remaining or uninterpreted effect estimate represents an unknown combination of intervening variables that have been omitted or badly measured in our multivariate analysis. It also includes any direct impact of partisan identification per se—especially when it acts as a "tie breaker" because the effects of other political attitudes are balanced, or as the only influence for individuals who do not have any other basis for choice.

Before turning to the examination of policy-related predispositions, we should note an alternative way of describing the role of intervening or mediating variables. When we describe specific intervening variables as "transmitting" some portion of the total effect of party identification, the same variables must be directly influenced by party identification. This aspect of partisanship is seen most clearly in our discussions of explanatory variables located in stages subsequent to our first and second "long-term" stages. For example, we have just noted that retrospective evaluations of Bush's performance appeared to play a major role in mediating the influence of party identification in vote choice, thereby transmitting some of the total impact of identification on the vote. In Chapter 14 we will examine the influence of these same retrospective evaluations on the vote. In that analysis, we shall note that party identification represents an important confounding variable because it presumably has an impact on both retrospective evaluations and the vote. When we control for party identification, we eliminate some of the spurious components of the relationship between evaluations and the vote and sharply reduce the apparent effect of the former on the latter. Evidence that any variable mediates or transmits some of the influences of party identification rests on our conviction that the mediating or intervening variable has been influenced or caused, in this case, by party identification.

Policy-related Predispositions

Policy-related predispositions represent "long-term" influences on the vote in the sense that they are acquired well before the current campaign. For that reason, we have assigned all of them to the same early stage in our model where we have located partisan identification. It is useful, however, to distinguish between the long-term *existence* of a predisposition and the degree of continuity in its *activation*. The electoral effects of some policy-related predispositions are often interpreted as "long term." However, differences between one election and another in the extent to which specific predispositions are activated surely represent variations in short-term forces.

One of the major limitations in our analysis (as well as most other electoral research) is that we have no direct measure of short-term forces that are external to the voter. That is, we have no systematic measures of the voter's exposure to campaign events, candidate behavior, or other phenomena that provide the stimuli for that voter's decisions. Consequently our designation of long-term and short-term applies only to the attitudes or predispositions of the voters; the less malleable and more persistent predispositions are called "long-term," the more volatile and changeable attitudes are "short-term." This is not a serious problem where attitudes toward a new candidate are concerned—they are short-term by almost any definition. However, the conceptual status of long-term forces becomes less clear where the "activation" of stable predispositions is concerned. For example, the waxing and waning of the party identification/vote relationship may be described as changes in a long-term influence when this is really a reflection of changes in the (unmeasured) influence of short-term external factors that differ in the extent to which they elicit the voters' sense of party identification.

Ideological Self-Designation

The concept of a liberal/conservative ideological identification as a counterpart to Democratic/Republican party identification has emerged with increasing clarity—and popularity—over recent years. This was particularly true after methodological studies produced an alternative measure based on a two-question sequence. That "branching" format, parallel to that used to measure party identification, probes respondents' self-designation on a liberal-moderate-conservative continuum. The branching technique has become a standard component of the NES studies. This is not to say, however, that there is no longer any controversy over the meaning of this measure of ideological position. In some uses it has been interpreted as a summary of citizens' policy preferences; in other discussions it has been seen more as a symbolic identification whose meaning is derived from partisan candidates; and still others have found it to be the most comprehensive base for political belief systems in the mass public (Levitin and Miller, 1979). In any event, no electoral analysis based on policy-related predispositions would be complete without considering voters' general (if not ideological) orientations based on the terms "liberal" and "conservative."

Since the 1970s, NES surveys have included a variety of questions about voters' opinions concerning these terms or symbols and the way they are used to describe politicians and other citizens. Many of our measures concerning policy-related predispositions and current policy preferences can be interpreted in terms of disagreement between "liberal" and "conservative" positions in specific areas. The combined effects of those topic-specific "issue" variables should capture most of the electoral consequences of the ongoing conflict between people whose general orientations can be described as "liberal" or "conservative." In each of those areas, however, we need to assess the extent to which the apparent effect of a specific attitude or preference may in fact be misleading, or spurious, precisely because it is based on the more general, prior underlying difference between people who think of themselves as "liberals" or "conservatives."

To address that problem, we have constructed a measure of voters' ideological self-description in terms of the familiar distinction between "liberal," "moderate," and "conservative." This measure (also scored from -1 to $+1$) combines voters' answers to the NES root question about ideological self-designation with questions eliciting their sense of "closeness" to the groups "liberals" and "conservatives."[3] A second purpose of this measure is to capture any electoral consequences of conflicts between liberals and conservatives in specific policy areas that are not covered by explicit NES questions, as well as to assess the impact of "liberal" or "conservative" self-identification per se. Table 11.2 presents our standard series of descriptive statistics concerning the relationship between this measure and the vote.

As in our subsequent summaries of general beliefs about equality and morality, voters with the most liberal self-descriptions were nearly unanimous in their support for Bill Clinton (instead of George Bush), and those with the most conservative self-descriptions were almost as united in their support of Bush over Clinton. As shown in Rows 1 and 2 of Table 11.2, voters who considered themselves to be liberals and designated "liberals" as a group they felt "close to" exhibited an average score (on the vote) of $+.93$, and comparably conservative voters exhibited an average vote of $-.78$. As before, the bivariate regression coefficient in Row 4, .90, presents an exaggerated impression of the electoral impact of a one-"unit" difference in ideological self-designation—that is, of the electoral consequences of shifting from a self-description as a "conservative" and feeling "close to conservatives" to a moderate or neutral

Table 11.2 The Electoral Relevance of Ideological Self-Designation

1. Average Vote Among Liberals Who Also Feel* "Close to" Liberals (N = 147)	.93
2. Average Vote Among Conservatives Who Also Feel* "Close to" Conservatives (N = 203)	−.78
3. Difference in Average Vote: Most Liberal Minus Most Conservative	1.71
4. Bivariate Unstandardized Regression Coefficient (Self-designation Scored from −1 to +1)	.90
5. Coefficient from Multiple Regression with Social and Economic Characteristics Held Constant	.78
6. With Party Identification (Party ID) Also Held Constant	.47
7. (Not Relevant for This Table Concerning Ideological Self-designation)	—
8. With All Other Predispositions Also Held Constant	.44
#9. With Party ID AND All Policy-related Predispositions Also Held Constant	.27
10. With Preferences on All Current Policy Issues Also Held Constant	.22
11. With Perceptions of Current Personal and National Conditions Also Held Constant	.21
12. With Retrospective Evaluations of the Current President's Performance Also Held Constant	.13
13. With Evaluations of the Candidates' Personal Qualities Also Held Constant	.13
14. With Prospective Evaluations of Candidates' and Parties' Future Performance Also Held Constant	.08

*The number of cases associated with extreme positions on these and similar measures simply indicate the base on which extreme scores were calculated. Note that the number of cases is unweighted; all other results are weighted.

(Coefficients Appear in Parentheses if the Estimated p Value is > .1).

#Indicates estimate of the "apparent total effect" discussed in the text.

position, or from a neutral position to a self-description as a "liberal" and feeling "close to liberals." However large the "true" electoral consequences may be for one-unit differences on this measure, it seems unlikely that the underlying attitudes involved completely dominated voters' decisions in 1992—as would be implied by an effect estimate of .90. At the very least, any estimate of the "true" total effect of this characteristic must take account of the confounding influence of factors (such as race or income) that may be antecedent to both one's ideology and one's vote. Row 5 presents such a coefficient (.78), based on controls for all of our social and economic characteristics.

Because of the ambiguities concerning the causal relationship among the various partisan and policy-related predispositions, we have not come to a definitive conclusion about the most appropriate estimate for the total effect of voters' ideological self-designation. For that reason, as described in Chapter 10, the coefficients in Rows 5 through 9 again present the results of five alternative approaches to removing the confounding influence of other causes of the vote.

The impact of ideological self-designation is very sharply reduced to .27 (in Row 9) when we control for party identification *and* specific policy-related predispositions, as well as social and economic characteristics. Given the general nature of ideological self-designation and its relationship to our other predispositions, however, it seems likely that the "true" total effect of this general orientation is larger than this "preferred" estimate in Row 9, .27, because of its indirect influence on the vote through partisan identification and the other (specific) predispositions which we were able to measure. On the other hand, the "true" total effect of ideological self-designation per se may also be smaller than the coefficient in Row 6, .47, which controls for party identification but does not reflect any controls for policy-related predispositions in specific areas. Ultimately, the overall influence of liberal versus conservative sentiments on the vote should be examined by *combining* the apparent effects of specific policy-related attitudes *and* ideological self-designation. The results of such analyses, however, have been deferred until Chapters 12 and 17.

Pending a definitive resolution of the interplay between party and ideology in the voters' decision-making process, we note that the apparent total effects of the two self-designation variables in the second stage in our causal sequence—Rows 8 and 9 in Tables 11.1 and 11.2—are quite different, .48 for party identification and .26 for liberal-conservative position. Although we believe both coefficients to be underestimates for both variables, we cannot, at this point, determine the extent to which either should be adjusted, nor can we disentangle the causal relationships that connect the variables to each other or to the several other predispositions we placed in the same stage.

The small difference between Row 9, .26, and the coefficients found in Rows 10 and 11 (.22 and .21), suggests that relatively little of the apparent total effect of ideological self-designation is mediated by the campaign-related issues in our model, based on voters' perceptions of conditions as well as preferences concerning specific policies. Apparently, most of the overlap between the electoral effects of specific conflicts between liberals and conservatives and those stemming from general ideological orientations has already been captured by our controls for other policy-related predispositions.

This assessment of limited mediation or transmittal of general ideological predispositions through specific policy preferences or conditions has at least two possible additional explanations—beyond the power of our measures of specific predispositions. In the first place, it is not evident how often specific policy conflicts should be subsumed under the conservative/liberal labels; those labels may not be appropriate for summarizing some conflicts. The literature on the nature or meaning of being a conservative or a liberal is not at all clear about the extent to which ideological identifications should be thought of as summarizing all of one's specific policy preferences. In the second place, whatever the generic relationship between the generality of the labels and the specifics of the policy conflicts, the extent to which specific policy preferences mediate the influence of general ideological orientations must certainly depend on the completeness with which such policies were covered by the NES survey. If more policy questions had been posed to NES respondents, in ways that accentuated their relevance to liberal or conservative identifications, the inclusion of such policy preferences in the explanation of liberal/conservative differences in vote choice might have produced larger, more striking results.

At the same time, the apparent effect in Row 11 of Table 11.2 (.21), based on additional controls for current policy issues and conditions, is visibly reduced (to .13, in Row 12) when we also control for voters' evaluations of George Bush's performance as President. This suggests some ideological aspects of evaluating presidential performance that were not reflected in the NES questions about current policies and conditions but that were activated by the pre-election campaign.

Finally, Row 14, .08, suggests that ideological self-designation had a "direct" (or unmediated) impact on voters' choice for President which is still visible after we control for all of the other explanatory variables in our model—including comparative evaluations concerning personal qualities and future performance. As indicated earlier, we believe that this remaining or uninterpreted effect represents an unknown combination of campaign issues that have been omitted (or badly represented) in our analysis and the influence of "symbolic" attitudes toward the "ideological" terms used by political leaders to summarize their positions. In the latter context, given the prevalence of popular use of the terms, it seems reasonable for personal identifications as liberals and conservatives to have a direct unmediated effect on the vote just as it is for Democrats and Republicans to make choices that are partially influenced by their party loyalties without mediation by other attitudes.

▪ Measuring Beliefs Concerning Specific Political Conflicts

When attitudes toward any particular conflict within society are "activated" by the candidates (or the media), they may influence vote choice through a variety of mechanisms. These may include voters' conscious comparisons of the candidates' positions in that area as well as the acquisition of positive or negative impressions of the candidates through more indirect or less conscious processes (Rahn et al., 1993). The substantive content of predispositions that are activated in this way may be defined in terms of very broad orientations, as in general attitudes toward "liberals" versus "conservatives," or in terms of a specific area of conflict, such as the scope of the role of government in the allocation of goods and services.

Because of the conviction that stable policy-related predispositions play a significant role in shaping voters' choices, a succession of NES pilot studies and election studies have produced at least four established multiple-item measures of policy-related predispositions in specific areas—in addition to party identification and ideological self-designation. The challenge of refining appropriate concepts and creating new operational indicators is daunting, and only the six measures just referred to were explicitly included in the 1992 NES data collection.

In preparing this volume, however, we explored the full range of NES questions in an effort to construct additional predisposition-like measures that might cast additional light on our understanding of voters' choices in 1992. Each of the many candidates for inclusion was held to a minimal standard concerning the evidence for their distinct (or independent) explanatory power. Surviving measures of policy-related predispositions exhibited a statistical relationship to vote choice that appeared to be significantly different from zero, based on a *p* value of less than .1, in an analysis which included all prior social and economic characteristics, party identification, *and* all other policy-related predispositions.

This analytic strategy (with its not very demanding threshold for statistical significance) was intended to ensure that no general explanation of attitudes toward current controversies over policy would be overlooked, in part because such an omission might thereby also bias conclusions concerning the importance of other specific issues. Our search for potential predisposition-related measures resulted in three groups of variables: (1) multi-item measures which exhibit an independent relationship to the vote as well as appropriate measurement quality; (2) measures based on one or two items that passed our standard statistical threshold for inclusion ($p < .1$) but may not satisfy conceptual or measurement requirements as generic predispositions; and (3) measures which did not meet our threshold for an independent relationship with the vote (including one of the four multi-item measures referred to above). We now present alternative effect estimates for the first of these three groups of variables. Because of their previous history in NES surveys, our analyses of these measures (concerning equality, limitations on governmental responsibilities, and morality) are presented in some detail. Successful, but less well established, measures (in the second category) are given somewhat shorter treatment. Unsuccessful or "rejected" measures are discussed in a subsequent section.[4]

General Beliefs about Equality

In recent discussions of American national politics, few policy-related disagreements have received more attention than conflicts posed by alternative goals or objectives that are defined in terms of "equality." Starting from the "self-evident" statement that "all men are created equal" in the Declaration of Independence, observers from several ideological perspectives have seen equality-related issues as extremely important in political conflicts *within* the national government. No parallel treatment exists, however, concerning the relevance of voters' attitudes toward equality for their voting behavior in recent presidential elections. Public opinion research has often focused on alternative policy objectives concerning equality (McClosky and Zaller, 1984), as have analyses of the structures and processes of democratic governmental institutions. Surprisingly, however, very few studies of American electoral behavior have focused on the role of controversies concerning equality in shaping voters' decisions at the polls.

The issues of equality among individuals and between social groups, in addition to conflicts among the major economic sectors of the nation concerning policy relating to banking, transportation, and industrial production, have been persistent sources of partisan conflict. The economic disaster of the Great Depression, which left a third of the nation ill-fed, ill-clothed, and ill-housed, provided a rallying point for a New Deal that had as part of its mission the goal of equalizing the political and economic strengths of labor and management. As the century ends, conflicts centered on economic inequality and political power still have their counterpart in arguments over the adequacy of the "social net" that provides assistance to the disadvantaged. Gender, religion, and ethnicity, in various guises, have defined the struggle for equality through much of the nation's existence. And, of course, the struggle for racial equality has been one of the major defining conflicts in the elections of the current period.

Since the 1984 election, NES surveys have enabled analysts to examine the relationship between voters' choices for President and their general beliefs about equality. Survey-based measures of those beliefs rely on a series of questions which ask respondents if they "agree" or "disagree" with statements about various equality-related ideals, including "equal chances," "equal rights," "equal treatment," or simply "equality." These general statements do not include any reference to specific groups, beneficiaries, or policy alternatives, nor do they address any distinctions between alternative goals within the area—like the familiar contrast between "equality of opportunity" and equality in "results."[5]

As in 1984 and 1988, voters in the 1992 election whose answers to these questions suggested a strong commitment to equality were much more likely than those who had obvious reservations about such objectives to vote for the Democratic (instead of the Republican) candidate. In 1992, this bivariate tendency was evident for each of the six NES questions in which respondents were asked to agree or disagree with a general statement about the importance of equality or the government's responsibility in that area. For example, only 44 percent of those who agreed that "we have gone too far pushing equal rights in this country"

Table 11.3 The Electoral Relevance of Beliefs Concerning Equality

1. Average Vote Among Most Liberal* (None of the 6 Responses Anti-Equality, N = 356)	.66
2. Average Vote Among Most Conservative* (None of the 6 Responses Pro-Equality, N = 40)	−.72
3. Difference in Average Vote: Most Liberal Minus Conservative	1.38
4. Bivariate Unstandardized Regression Coefficient (Equality Index Scored from −1 to +1)	1.05
5. Coefficient from Multiple Regression with Social and Economic Characteristics Held Constant	.84
6. With Party Identification (Party ID) Also Held Constant	.50
7. With Specific Policy-related Predispositions (But NOT Party ID) Also Held Constant	.43
8. With Liberal vs. Conservative Self-designation Also Held Constant	.29
#9. With Party ID AND All Policy-related Predispositions Also Held Constant	.22
10. With Preferences on All Other Policy Issues Also Held Constant	.12
11. With Perceptions of Current Personal and National Conditions Also Held Constant	.11
12. With Retrospective Evaluations of the Current President's Performance Also Held Constant	(.07)
13. With Evaluations of the Candidates' Personal Qualities Also Held Constant	(.05)
14. With Prospective Evaluations of Candidates' and Parties' Future Performance Also Held Constant	(−.00)

*The number of cases associated with extreme positions on these and similar measures simply indicate the base on which extreme scores were calculated. Note that the number of cases is unweighted; all other results are weighted.

(Coefficients Appear in Parentheses if the Estimated p Value is > .1).

#Indicates estimate of the "apparent total effect" discussed in the text.

voted for Clinton (instead of Bush), compared with 76 percent among those who disagreed with that statement. For the rest of this analysis, responses to these six questions have been combined into a single additive index of support for (or opposition to) the general concept of equality in the United States.

Table 11.3 presents our standard sequence of descriptive statistics concerning the relationship between vote choice in 1992 and this summary of respondents' general beliefs concerning equality. As with voters' ideological self-designation, individuals with polar opposite beliefs concerning equality voted overwhelmingly for the candidate that was conventionally associated with their views. The bivariate regression coefficient for this measure, in Row 4, is slightly over 1.0, and is reduced to only .84 (in Row 5) when we control for our social and economic characteristics. Approximately half of that coefficient disappears when we control for voters' long-term partisan identification (which yields a coefficient of .50 in Row 6) *or* for all of our policy-related predispositions but not party (which produces a coefficient of .29, in Row 8). The coefficient in Row 9, .22, is our preferred estimate of the "apparent total effect" of general atitudes concerning equality on the vote in 1992 after we have taken account of relationships with their likely antecedents and other predispositions in the same stage in our model.

As emphasized before, we believe that the electoral impact of policy-related beliefs or preferences may be based on several different causal processes, including voters' selection of the candidate whose "position" minimizes the distance from their own, as well as more diffuse impressions that are influenced by voters' predispositions in that area without any (conscious) comparison of candidates' positions.

It appears that voters' opinions on current issues (based on both conflict-related and consensual objectives) are responsible for (or mediate) half of the total influence of general beliefs about equality on the vote. The remaining effects of those beliefs, however, appear to have been entirely mediated by voters' evaluations of George Bush's performance as President and their evaluations concerning personal qualities and future performance.

Limited Governmental Responsibility

If the concept of equality is given historical precedence as a founding principle of the American version of democratic government, so should the idea of "limited government." In its commitment to checks and balances and the comprehensive delegation of power to the states (in areas not explicitly reserved for the federal government), the U.S. Constitution anticipated the long and continuing history of conflicts over the size of the federal government and the scope of its responsibilities. In many ways, American politics in the late twentieth century has featured Democratic advocacy of an active, expansive national government against Republican defense of a much more limited (if not passive) role for the same government. The labels historically used by partisans, particularly Democrats, to portray the spirit of presidential eras are revealing in this respect—the New Deal, the New Frontier, the Great Society—for they suggest governmental action on behalf of new causes. With the rhetoric of the congressional elections of 1994 still fresh in mind—recalling Reaganesque promises to "get government off the backs of the people"—it is evident that concerns over the size of government and the scope of its responsibilities lie at the heart of much of the partisan politics in the 1990s. Whether the specific issues are defined in terms of governmental protection of the environment, industrial regulation in the name of industrial safety, welfare for those whose economic circumstances force them below a minimum (poverty) level, a lessening of the tax burden, or freedom from governmental regulation (to promote economic growth), the major issues of the day are often framed in terms of "more" government versus "less."

Because of the visibility of such issues, many observers have suggested that recent voters' decisions have been at least partially shaped by their preferences concerning the degree to which economic decisions should be made by the government rather than left to the private sector and individual responsibility. According to that formulation, voters who are generally supportive of governmental intervention and are skeptical about leaving many decisions to "market forces" or the "profit system" have responded more positively to Democratic candidates, while voters who are generally opposed to governmental intervention have responded more positively to Republican candidates.

National partisan politics following the Clinton election were predictably more complex than this emphasis on conflict over economic policy suggests. For example, throughout the 1980s the Republican leadership, in particular, had paid increasing attention to the "social issues" and often supported governmental *intervention* on behalf of the preservation or restoration of traditional concepts of morality. In this arena, preference for limited government was often articulated by liberals and Democrats who wanted to "keep government out of the bedroom," and more than one commentator noted that support for limited government did seem to vary with the values presumably at issue.

To assess the general hypothesis related to economic policy, we combined responses to three questions in the 1992 NES survey concerning governmental responsibility which have been shown to exhibit consistent relationships with partisan evaluations (Markus, 1992). Each of these questions involved a choice between two statements, one of which expressed an anti-government (or pro–private sector) opinion, and the other a pro-government (or anti-market) opinion.[6] Our summary measure of attitudes toward limited government was constructed by scoring each "pro-government" response as +1 (since such views presumably encouraged support for the Democratic victor in 1992), each "pro-market" response as a −1 (since such views presumably encouraged support for the losing Republican candidate), and all other responses as 0, and then calculating the average of those three values. Based on this summary measure, Table 11.4 presents our standard sequence of descriptive statistics concerning the relationship between voters' general views on limited government and the vote.

As with equality, voters with opposing views in this domain cast their ballots for the two major party candidates in very different ways. As shown in Rows 1 and 2, voters with the most pro-government views divided their votes in a sharply pro-Democratic fashion, .54, and voters with consistently anti-government views were just as consistent in voting Republican, −.59.[7]

Row 5 documents the considerable extent to which the apparent impact of predispositions toward limited government is reduced when we control for social and economic characteristics (from .55 to .41), and Rows 6 through 9 suggest the varying degrees to which that effect may be confounded with those of other partisan or policy-related predispositions.

Row 9 presents the coefficient which we have designated as the apparent total effect of attitudes toward limited government, .08, for it represents the relatively modest extent to which vote choice in 1992 appears to have been influenced by attitudes in this specific area—after we have controlled for all other partisan or policy-related predispositions.

As with our total effect estimate for equality, we believe that this coefficient, .08, represents an underestimate of the electoral role played by attitudes in this area, for it ignores any indirect effects of such attitudes (on the vote) that might be traced to their impact on the other predispositions in our model. Nevertheless, the theme of limited government, which loomed so large in partisan rhetoric following the congressional elections of 1994, does not, at this stage in our analysis, seem

Table 11.4 The Electoral Relevance of Attitudes Toward Limited Government

1. Average Vote Among Most Liberal* (All Pro-Government Responses, N = 469)	.54
2. Average Vote Among Most Conservative* (All Anti-Government Responses, N = 189)	−.59
3. Difference in Average Vote: Most Liberal Minus Most Conservative	1.13
4. Bivariate Unstandardized Regression Coefficient (pro- vs. anti-Individualism Scored −1 to +1)	.55
5. Coefficient from Multiple Regression with Social and Economic Characteristics Held Constant	.41
6. With Party Identification (Party ID) Also Held Constant	.21
7. With Other Specific Policy-related Predispositions (But NOT Party ID) Also Held Constant	.23
8. With Liberal vs. Conservative Self-designation Also Held Constant	.15
#9. With Party ID AND All Policy-related Predispositions Also Held Constant	.08
10. With Preferences on All Current Policy Issues Also Held Constant	.07
11. With Perceptions of Current Personal and National Conditions Also Held Constant	.05
12. With Retrospective Evaluations of the Current President's Performance Also Held Constant	(.03)
13. With Evaluations of the Candidates' Personal Qualities Also Held Constant	(.03)
14. With Prospective Evaluations of Candidates' and Parties' Future Performance Also Held Constant	(.01)

*The number of cases associated with extreme positions on these and similar measures simply indicate the base on which extreme scores were calculated. Note that the number of cases is unweighted; all other results are weighted.

(Coefficients Appear in Parentheses if the Estimated p Value is > .1).

#Indicates estimate of the "apparent total effect" discussed in the text.

to have been a major factor two years earlier. It is well to keep in mind, however, that we are now focusing, variable by variable, on contributions to explaining individual vote choices. If preferences for limiting governmental responsibility in 1992 overwhelmed support for extended government, it would still be possible for the issue to have played a significant role in that election by limiting the size of the Clinton margin. As with many other questions of comparative importance, however, we will reserve our analytic resolution of this possibility until Chapter 17. In the meantime, the possible importance of taking into account the confounding effects of common antecedents is apparent as we watch evidence of a central role for attitudes toward limited government dwindle from a coefficient of .41 in Row 5 to .05 when we control for both types of current issues. Finally, all of the remaining influence of beliefs in this area appears to have been mediated by voters' evaluations of George Bush's performance as President and their evaluations of the candidates' personal qualities and prospective (or future) performance.

Traditional Morality and Moral Tolerance

If it was the confluence of popular concerns over civil rights, Vietnam, and the counterculture that transformed politics in the United States in the 1960s and 1970s, those three themes have played quite different roles in the partisan politics of the 1980s and 1990s. The Republican successes of the early 1970s, the end of the Cold War with the Soviet Union, and lesser military initiatives under Reagan and Bush apparently blunted the lingering conflicts associated with the Vietnam War, at least as a direct influence on presidential politics. Racial tensions may have relaxed by 1992 and have become less central to partisan conflict, but they remained a potential source of electoral support—as seen in the 1988 campaign of Jesse Jackson and the "Willie Horton" controversy in that year. When race, war, and anti-communism receded as the focuses for partisan conflict, however, a very different set of domestic concerns was articulated by the religious right. As of the mid-1990s, the various issues had not coalesced into an integrated set of controversies, but many growing conflicts over social values and norms shared an emphasis on different aspects of traditional morality.

By the 1992 election, concern over divorce rates had been joined by increasing attention to the proportion of single-parent families; increased acceptance of homosexuality was accompanied by increasingly vocal opposition by some to the "homosexual life-style" or single-sex marriages; the separation of church and state was challenged by advocates of prayer in the public school and support for "voucher" programs to provide governmental support to private education (as well as more choice between public schools); and the moral, and therefore the legal, status of abortion surpassed all other topics as a focus for single-issue

politics and a symbol for a wider range of issues concerning the "traditional family." Whether these concerns represent a logical or inevitable
consequence of the promotion of alternative (if not countercultural)
life-styles twenty years earlier may be debatable. There seems little
question, however, that this set of political issues was introduced by the
"Moral Majority" of the 1970s and sustained by the Christian Coalition
of the 1990s.

Since the late 1960s, electoral campaigns in the United States have
involved increasing attention to areas that had previously been regarded
as "private" instead of "public." Over time, lines have been drawn
between citizens who are angered by a national decline in "traditional
morality" and those advocating greater tolerance for "alternative life-
styles." These abstract formulations have clearly been based on intense
disagreement about several specific topics, including sexual behavior
outside marriage, homosexuality, and abortion. During the 1980s, opposing positions in this area became increasingly associated with specific
leaders and parties. In 1980 the Republicans opposed the Equal Rights
Amendment, which Democrats supported. By the late 1980s Republican
leaders were emphasizing the importance of the "traditional" family
(with a mother and a father) and "traditional morality," while Democratic leaders were associated with tolerance and equal rights for homosexuals and increased governmental assistance to single parents and
families with dependent children. In the 1992 campaign, this focus was
epitomized by Vice President Quayle's criticism of a popular television
series whose female character (Murphy Brown) had a child outside of
marriage. The Republican Convention called for an end to legalized
abortion and support for "traditional values." The campaign was also
marked by Bill Clinton's visible support for abortion rights and for
military service by homosexuals.

Our assessment of the electoral relevance of predispositions concerning morality is based on a summary of general beliefs in this area and
attitudes toward groups that are often defined in terms of morality-re-
lated issues. (Preferences concerning current policy issues in this area
are discussed in Chapter 12.) Our measure of general beliefs is based on
agree/disagree questions concerning "traditional family ties," "newer
life-styles," and "moral standards," rather than any specific controversies
or policies (see Conover and Feldman, 1986). Our summary measure
concerning morality is the simple average of responses to four such

Table 11.5 The Electoral Relevance of Beliefs Concerning Traditional Morality

1. Average Vote Among Most Liberal* (All Responses Anti-Traditional, N = 48)	.84
2. Average Vote Among Most Conservative* (All Responses Pro-Traditional, N = 257)	−.38
3. Difference in Average Vote: Most Liberal Minus Most Conservative	1.22
4. Bivariate Unstandardized Regression Coefficient (Morality Index Scored from −1 to +1)	.91
5. Coefficient from Multiple Regression with Social and Economic Characteristics Held Constant	.78
6. With Party Identification (Party ID) Also Held Constant	.47
7. With Other Specific Policy-related Predispositions (But NOT Party ID) Also Held Constant	.40
8. With Liberal vs. Conservative Self-designation Also Held Constant	.29
#9. With Party ID AND All Policy-related Predispositions Also Held Constant	.22
10. With Preferences on All Current Policy Issues Also Held Constant	.15
11. With Perceptions of Current Personal and National Conditions Also Held Constant	.16
12. With Retrospective Evaluations of the Current President's Performance Also Held Constant	.12
13. With Evaluations of the Candidates' Personal Qualities Also Held Constant	.09
14. With Prospective Evaluations of Candidates' and Parties' Future Performance Also Held Constant	.11

*The number of cases associated with extreme positions on these and similar measures simply indicate the base on which extreme scores were calculated. Note that the number of cases is unweighted; all other results are weighted.

(Coefficients Appear in Parentheses if the Estimated *p* Value is > .1).

#Indicates estimate of the "apparent total effect" discussed in the text.

items, each of which has been scored from −1 (for the most conservative response concerning traditional morality) to +1 (for the most liberal or tolerant response).[8] Table 11.5 presents our standard sequence of descriptive statistics concerning the relationship between this summary measure and the vote.

As with equality and the other predispositions, Rows 1 and 2 document a dramatic difference in the division of the vote between individuals at the opposite ends of the measure of attitudes toward morality. As shown in Rows 5 through 9, however, most of the apparent impact of morality on vote choice is confounded with other policy-related and partisan predispositions—in much the same fashion as was true for equality and governmental responsibility.

Specifically, our estimate for the apparent impact of morality declines from .78 to .47 (in Row 6) when we control for party identification as well as social and economic characteristics, suggesting that the influence of beliefs in this area may be partially incorporated in voters' long-term partisan identifications. At the same time, however, the apparent effect of morality drops even more (to .40, in Row 7) when we control for other specific predispositions *without* party identification, and that co-efficient is further reduced to .29 (in Row 8) when we also control for liberal versus conservative self-designation. These results suggest that the most important "confound" concerning the electoral relevance of morality may involve our other policy-related predispositions, instead of long-term partisan identifications. In any event, the apparent effect for morality is reduced to .22 when we (again) control for party identification as well as *all* of our other policy-related predispositions and so-cial/economic characteristics. As with equality and limited government, this estimate for the apparent impact of morality is almost certainly lower than its "true" total effect, for it unavoidably neglects any indirect impact of beliefs in this area that operate through other policy-related and partisan predispositions.

Our effect estimate for the electoral relevance of morality declines from .22 to .15 when we take account of voters' preferences on current policy issues, suggesting that some of the overall impact of morality-re-lated predispositions may be mediated by current policy conflicts in that area (including homosexuals in the military). Our estimate of the re-maining (or unmediated) impact of beliefs in this area is reduced only slightly by additional controls for evaluations of the candidates' personal qualities and the future (or prospective) performance of the parties and candidates—most of which are devoted to economic (as opposed to "social") topics.

This result suggests that voters' positions concerning traditional mo-rality had a substantial impact on vote choice in 1992 that must be distinguished from liberal or conservative positions in other areas—most of which (unlike morality) are largely mediated by voters' evaluations of the candidates' prospective performance. In contrast to the not unreasonable conclusion that it makes sense for both party identification and ideology to have some direct unmediated influence on vote choice, the very generality of our items assessing attitudes toward morality cannot sustain the same argument for our summary measure in that area. The very visible coefficient in Row 14 suggests that we are still missing something—or are poorly measuring some of the intervening variables—in our accounting for the total effect of general beliefs about morality.

Group-related Conflicts

In addition to general beliefs concerning policy-related controversies, as described by established NES multi-item measures, we have also examined voters' attitudes toward "groups" in the society that are involved in contemporary conflicts about specific policy areas. It is clear that attitudes toward several group-related conflicts were related to vote choice in the 1992 campaign, but only two of the measures we constructed exhibited apparent effects which were large enough (after controlling for our other predispositions) to meet our threshold for statistical significance. The conflict between homosexuals and Christian fundamentalists, quite visible in the media, was reflected in a significant total effect estimate for the difference between the "thermometer" ratings given by NES respondents for those two groups.[9] This result held even while taking account of the role of "morality" in our analysis. The political relevance of conflicts between labor unions and corporations can also be seen in a significant total effect estimate for voters' identification with (and feelings of "closeness" toward) those (often) opposing groups. Table 11.6 presents the standard series of descriptive statistics concerning the relationships between these two variables and the vote.

As with the multiple-item measures concerning general policy-related beliefs, the bivariate relationships between both of these two group-related variables and the vote are dramatically reduced when we control for party identification and other policy-related predispositions, as well as social and economic characteristics. Furthermore, as shown in Row 9 of Table 11.6, the apparent total effect of attitudes toward homosexuals and fundamentalists, .15, is entirely eliminated (to −.00, in Row 10) when we control for preferences on current policy issues—without any controls for current conditions or evaluations concerning performance or personal qualities.

Table 11.6 The Electoral Relevance of Group-Related Feelings

	Homosexuals vs. Fundamentalists	Unions vs. Business
1. Average Vote Among Those with the Most Liberal Views* (N = 36) (N = 90)	.78	.88
2. Average Vote Among Those with the Most Conservative Views (N = 172) (N = 296)	−.23	−.17
3. Difference in Average Vote: Most Liberal Minus Most Conservative	1.00	1.05
4. Bivariate Unstandardized Regression Coefficient (Group-related Attitudes Scored from −1 to +1)	.81	.47
5. Coefficient from Multiple Regression with Social and Economic Characteristics Held Constant	.74	.32
6. With Party Identification (Party ID) Also Held Constant	.47	.16
7. With Other Specific Policy-related Predispositions (But NOT Party ID) Also Held Constant	.27	.20
8. With Liberal vs. Conservative Self-designation Also Held Constant	.16	.15
#9. With Party ID AND All Policy-related Predispositions Also Held Constant	.15	.09
10. With Preferences on All Current Policy Issues Also Held Constant	(−.00)	.09
11. With Perceptions of Current Personal and National Conditions Also Held Constant	(−.01)	.08
12. With Retrospective Evaluations of the Current President's Performance Also Held Constant	(−.05)	(.05)
13. With Evaluations of the Candidates' Personal Qualities Also Held Constant	(−.06)	(.05)
14. With Prospective Evaluations of Candidates' and Parties' Future Performance Also Held Constant	(−.06)	(.04)

*The number of cases associated with extreme positions on these and similar measures simply indicate the base on which extreme scores were calculated. Note that the number of cases is unweighted; all other results are weighted.

(Coefficients Appear in Parentheses if the Estimated p Value is > .1).

#Indicates estimate of the "apparent total effect" discussed in the text.

In contrast, the apparent total effect of general orientations toward unions and corporations (.09) is relatively unaffected by controls for current policy issues and conditions. It is reduced to an insignificant level, however, when we control for evaluations of George Bush's performance as President. This apparent difference between our two group-related measures (in the role of alternative intervening variables) may be explained by noting that our analyses include a policy-based variable that is very relevant for the first of these group-related conflicts (concerning gays in the military) but does not include any policy issues concerning the ongoing conflict between business and unions.

Foreign Affairs

In all three presidential elections in the 1980s, the role of voters' policy-related attitudes concerning foreign policy and defense was dominated by conflicts involving communism and the Soviet Union. Because of the salience of those topics, our final explanatory model for the 1988 election included general attitudes toward communism and patriotism as well as preferences concerning current defense-related issues (Shanks and Miller, 1991). By 1992, many observers assumed that the end of communist regimes in Eastern Europe and the Soviet Union would lead to a substantial reduction in the electoral relevance of public attitudes toward foreign affairs. Despite those developments, however, underlying disagreements within the electorate concerning the U.S. role in the world still influenced voters' choices in the 1992 election, given the many current international conflicts where the United States had played some role, as well as the U.S. victory in the 1991 Persian Gulf War.

We have classified our most important explanatory variable concerning foreign affairs as dealing with "current policy preferences," and thus our discussion of its electoral role in 1992 has been deferred until the next chapter. However, to suggest that there were general effects in the domain of foreign policy which were still at work after the demise of the Soviet Union, we examined the electoral relevance of general attitudes toward U.S. involvement in (or isolation from) conflicts involving other countries, and voters' attitudes toward military service in the Vietnam War. The latter was appropriate, in part, because of Bill Clinton's apparent efforts to avoid the draft during that conflict.[10]

As shown in Row 9 of Table 11.7, general attitudes toward interna-

Table 11.7 The Electoral Relevance of Foreign Affairs

	Isolationism	Vietnam Service
1. Average Vote Among Those with Isolation or Anti-Vietnam Draft Responses (N = 258) (N = 607)*	.47	.45
2. Average Vote Among Those with Interventionist or Pro-Vietnam Draft Responses (N = 906) (N = 524)	.08	−.13
3. Difference in Average Vote	.40	.58
4. Bivariate Unstandardized Regression Coefficient (Foreign Affairs Measures Scored from −1 to +1)	.20	.29
5. Coefficient from Multiple Regression with Social and Economic Characteristics Held Constant	.14	.24
6. With Party Identification (Party ID) Also Held Constant	.06	.15
7. With Other Specific Policy-related Predispositions (But NOT Party ID) Also Held Constant	.13	.14
8. With Liberal vs. Conservative Self-designation Also Held Constant	.11	.10
#9. With Party ID AND All Policy-related Predispositions Also Held Constant	.07	.08
10. With Preferences on Current Policy Issues Also Held Constant	.05	.06
11. With Perceptions of Current Personal and National Conditions Also Held Constant	.04	.05
12. With Retrospective Evaluations of the Current President's Performance Also Held Constant	(.01)	.04
13. With Evaluations of the Candidates' Personal Qualities Also Held Constant	(.01)	(.03)
14. With Prospective Evaluations of Candidates' and Parties' Future Performance Also Held Constant	(.01)	(.02)

*The number of cases associated with extreme positions on these and similar measures simply indicate the base on which extreme scores were calculated. Note that the number of cases is unweighted; all other results are weighted.

(Coefficients Appear in Parentheses if the Estimated p Value is > .1).

#Indicates estimate of the "apparent total effect" discussed in the text.

tional involvement and Vietnam service appear to have exerted some influence on vote choice (.07 and .08) after we control for party identification and other policy-related predispositions as well as social and economic characteristics. The impact of isolationist sentiment appears to be primarily mediated by voters' evaluations of George Bush's performance as President. It is reduced to an insignificant (.01) in Row 12 after we control for those evaluations. Attitudes toward Vietnam service, however, appear to retain some impact on the vote after we control for evaluations of Bush as President as well as current policy and conditions. Given Bill Clinton's attempts to avoid the draft during that war, the survival of this apparent effect is at least consistent with some analysts' expectations, as is the fact (not shown in this table) that the apparent effect of this variable is substantially larger among voters in the post-New Deal generation—who were young enough to have been directly affected by the draft in that war.

▪ Other Potentially Relevant Predispositions

The policy-related variables discussed in the preceding section were selected because their relationship to vote choice in the 1992 NES Survey was still visible (or significant) after we introduced statistical controls for other predispositions as well as for voters' social and economic characteristics. As noted in Chapters 1 and 12, several other policy-related conflicts were also mentioned during the 1992 campaign, and thus predispositions in those areas might have played some role in shaping voters' choice between Bill Clinton and George Bush. Because of those possibilities, we carried out similar analyses for a variety of other policy-related controversies, including general attitudes concerning poor people, feminists, social class, patriotism, child rearing, civic religion, immigration, racial minorities, and environmentalists. For most of these conflict-related topics, our estimates for the apparent electoral effects of general attitudes (or predispositions) on the 1992 vote were very small, so we have omitted reporting any results for those conflicts on the grounds that they were both substantively and statistically insignificant. In one of those areas, however, our analyses produced a series of negative or at least ambiguous results which deserve a separate discussion.

Negative Results Concerning Race-related Attitudes

Since 1984, NES surveys have included a substantial number of questions devoted to race-related attitudes because of widespread academic and public interest in the impact of such attitudes on electoral decisions and (through elections) public policy. Recent descriptions of the electoral relevance of racial attitudes range from suggestions that they are the dominant factor in presidential politics (Kinder et al., 1989) to the limited thesis that they represent a continuing social conflict with intermittent impact at the national level (Shanks and Miller, 1991). To assess the impact of race-related attitudes on the 1992 election, the NES questionnaire included the following variety of measures:

- the traditional seven-point scale concerning the appropriateness of government aid to improve the social and economic position of Blacks;
- a single question in a battery of items concerning federal spending for "programs that assist Blacks";
- three questions based on alternative definitions and goals for equal treatment or affirmative action for Blacks in employment and education;
- the traditional NES question concerning the speed of the Civil Rights movement—that is, whether it has gone "too fast," "too slowly," or "about the right speed";
- thermometer ratings for groups defined as "Blacks" or "Whites" and options to declare an "identification" with those groups;
- ratings of Whites, Blacks, and other minorities concerning three traditional stereotypes, namely, the extent to which persons in those groups are hardworking, violent, and intelligent; and
- four agree/disagree questions about Blacks and racial discrimination, based on general statements about the extent and consequence of past discrimination and the degree to which Blacks need special assistance or should "get ahead on their own."

We have examined relationships between the vote and measures of race-related attitudes in each of these areas. This collection of measures includes general attitudes or predispositions toward race-related topics as well as preferences concerning current policy issues (which are discussed in the following chapter). For the present chapter, most of our analyses focused on a summary measure of voters' beliefs about "Blacks and racial discrimination," based on their responses to the agree/disagree statements at the end of the above list.[11] Measures based on the same agree/disagree questions have been used in several other reports, and the underlying attitudes have been given several different names, including "racial prejudice" and "racism" as well as more neutral expressions such as "beliefs about Blacks and racial discrimination"—which we prefer.

At the outset, we expected to find that voters' choices for President in 1992 would appear to be influenced by their general beliefs about Blacks and discrimination because of the association of the Democratic party with the Civil Rights movement and various Republican leaders' explicit and implicit statements on several race-related topics (such as their opposition to affirmative action or racial "quotas"). We also expected, however, that the apparent total impact of voters' general beliefs concerning race would be primarily mediated or interpreted by their preferences concerning a variety of current policy issues (including those concerning race). As shown in Table 11.8, our summary measure of beliefs in this area does fit those general expectations, but in a fashion which we find surprising.

There *is* a strong bivariate relationship (.61, in Row 4) between our summary measure of beliefs concerning Blacks or racial discrimination and the vote. That relationship is substantially reduced (to .43, in Row 5) when we take account of prior social and economic characteristics, and it completely disappears when we control for other policy-related predispositions (in Row 7).

Given our analytic strategy, this abrupt result precludes any conclusions that involve a significant (independent) electoral effect of general beliefs about Blacks or racial discrimination per se. In short, we have *no* evidence for electoral effects of beliefs in this area in 1992 that remain after we control for our *other* policy-related predispositions. Indeed, as shown in Row 8, the apparent impact of general beliefs about Blacks is both insignificant and slightly *negative* ($-.07$) after we control for all of our other policy-related predispositions, and that coefficient is still insignificant and negative ($-.03$) (see Row 9) when we also control for party identification. On the basis of those results, it would appear that any electoral effects for general attitudes in this area that may have occurred in 1992 should be attributed to their (indirect) impact through other partisan or policy-related predispositions. For that reason, we have not included any race-related predispositions in our final model.[12]

We do not necessarily regard the larger question of race-related electoral effects as "resolved." General race-related attitudes *may*, of course, have played an indirect role in the 1992 election, despite the negative results reviewed in Table 11.8. Such a conclusion would be particularly appropriate for analysts who assume that racial attitudes are acquired before (or at least have a substantial influence on) other policy-related predispositions. For example, it is possible that general beliefs about

Table 11.8 The Electoral Relevance of Beliefs About Racial Discrimination

1. Average Vote Among Most Liberal* All Responses Liberal, N = 141	+.78
2. Average Vote Among Most Conservative* All Responses Conservative, N = 252	−.17
3. Difference in Average Vote: Most Liberal Minus Conservative	.95
4. Bivariate Unstandardized Regression Coefficient (Index Scored from −1 to +1)	.61
5. Coefficient from Multiple Regression with Social and Economic Characteristics Held Constant	.43
6. With Party Identification (Party ID) Also Held Constant	.28
7. With Other Specific Policy-related Predispositions (But NOT Party ID) Also Held Constant	(−.04)
8. With Liberal vs. Conservative Self-designation Also Held Constant	(−.07)
#9. With Party ID AND All Policy-related Predispositions Also Held Constant	(−.03)
10. With Preferences on All Current Policy Issues Also Held Constant	(−.07)
11. With Perceptions of Current Personal and National Conditions Also Held Constant	(−.06)
12. With Retrospective Evaluations of the Current President's Performance Also Held Constant	(−.06)
13. With Evaluations of the Candidates' Personal Qualities Also Held Constant	−.08
14. With Prospective Evaluations of Candidates' and Parties' Future Performance Also Held Constant	(−.05)

*The number of cases associated with extreme positions on these and similar measures simply indicate the base on which extreme scores were calculated. Note that the number of cases is unweighted; all other results are weighted.

(Coefficients Appear in Parentheses if the Estimated p Value is > .1).

#Indicates estimate of the "apparent total effect" discussed in the text.

Blacks and racial discrimination may have influenced voters' basic predispositions toward equality, and, therefore, controlling for equality (as one of the other predispositions in a multivariate model) eliminates any apparent impact of direct attitudes toward racial discrimination on the vote. Given our sense of the larger role that the concept of equality has played in American political thought, as discussed earlier in this chapter, we are reluctant to assume that racial equality has become the dominant theme in contemporary understanding of the meaning of "equality."

As previously emphasized, we are unable to clarify the causal relationships among the various explanatory variables that we have designated as "predispositions." Because of that uncertainty, we are reluctant to assume that the statistical relationships among those variables should be interpreted in terms of causal priority (or precedence) for *any* specific predispositions—including race-related beliefs. We should note, moreover, that we have been unable to find any evidence for independent (or distinguishable) effects of other race-related attitudes on presidential voting (in 1992) that remain after we control for voters' beliefs and preferences in other policy-related areas—and the same result is almost as clear for 1988. This kind of negative result concerning distinct electoral effects for racial attitudes is consistent across a variety of alternative analyses, based on alternative measures and statistical procedures.[13] Because of the consistency of those negative results, we have not included any race-related predispositions or policy preferences in our final model. We anticipate some controversy about the validity of our negative conclusions in this area, however, because of the continuing political visibility of race-related issues.

▪ Alternative Approaches to Assessing the Role of Predispositions: The Relevance of Methodological Concerns

To this point, we have relied on a single set of survey-based measures and statistical procedures to assess the electoral relevance of partisan and policy-related predispositions. On the basis of these procedures, we have identified eight policy-related predispositional variables that appear to have made some independent contributions to the vote (as well as several whose effect estimates fell below our threshold for statistical significance). We have also suggested several ways in which such predispositions appear to have had an indirect influence on the vote— through intervening or mediating variables that we have assigned to later causal stages in our overall explanatory model. All of our results so far, however, have been based on only one general approach that could be used to assess the impact of continuing predispositions on the vote. As in any survey-based explanation, our conclusions could be misleading insofar as they are vulnerable to one or more methodological criticisms—particularly if some other survey-based procedures would produce different (and more accurate) results.

For example, consider the policy-related predispositions discussed earlier that have not been included in our final model (for example, general attitudes toward "Blacks" or "poor people") because their total effect estimates were very small. Judging from the measures and analytic procedures discussed above, the electoral impact of general attitudes in those areas appears to have been insignificant, in both substantive and statistical terms. In general, effect estimates from multivariate analyses of this sort may be wrong, spurious, biased, or otherwise misleading for several different reasons. For each specific predisposition with an "insignificant" apparent effect, analysts should consider the following alternative interpretations:

- The specific predisposition involved may, of course, have had no real impact on vote choice. If so, the selection process described above has led to the correct conclusion about that policy-related topic.
- Another possibility, although unlikely, is that the specific predisposition had a substantial impact on the vote in the population as a whole, but we obtained a very small effect estimate for the NES sample, due to chance.
- The given predisposition may also have had a substantial (true) impact on the vote which has been suppressed or hidden by the omission of explanatory variables that measure related (and offsetting) causes of the vote. If so, a substantial coefficient for the given predisposition might still emerge from a somewhat different analysis (based on the same sample) which would include additional "controls" for potentially confounding factors.
- Alternatively, the impact of a given predisposition-related variable may have been incorrectly designated as "insignificant" because of excessive overlap with another predisposition; because of a serious misspecification of the nature or shape of that predisposition's relationship with the vote; because that overall estimate conceals major differences between subpopulations; or because of errors in the survey-based measure for that predisposition.

These general concerns are, of course, also relevant for variables that *do* appear to have a significant impact on the vote. Thus, the apparent effects of predispositions that have been included in our model may also be misleading in the sense that they are higher or lower than the "true" effects of those variables—due to chance, omitted confounding variables, incorrect specifications concerning functional form, subpopulation differences in effects, or measurement error. For variables that do appear to have some impact on the vote, we should add the possibility of incorrect conclusions based on a misspecification concerning causal *direction*, if that variable is at least partially influenced by "feedback" from the vote.

For most of the explanatory variables in our analysis, we have considered a variety of alternative specifications concerning survey measurement and the shape (or form) of relationships with the vote, and we have included selected results from those alternative analyses in our discussion of specific explanatory themes. (We have deferred the general possibility of "simultaneity" or reciprocal causation until Appendix D.) At this point, we merely note that the above potential threats to the validity of explanatory conclusions are relevant for every stage and variable in our model. For our policy-related predispositions, we believe that these potential problems are not serious enough to discourage our interpretation of the resulting estimates in terms of the overall (or average) impact of those variables on voters' choices between Clinton and Bush in 1992. Beyond these standard threats to the validity of survey-based explanations, however, we have also considered the possibility of major differences in results between the methods described above and the fundamentally different approach to electoral explanation that was used in *The American Voter*—and is frequently used in contemporary public opinion research.

▪ Differences in Conclusions Based on "Reasons" versus "Variables"

After fifty years of election surveys, social scientists have been unable to agree concerning the comparative advantages (or disadvantages) of two fundamentally different approaches to electoral explanation, based on contrasting assumptions about measurement and causation. As in *The American Voter,* contemporary explanations of vote choice are often based on answers to questions which, in essence, ask respondents to identify those aspects of the candidates that they "like or dislike" or the "reasons" they prefer one candidate over the other. For example, the popular media often report the reasons voters give for their choices when interviewed in exit polls. In contrast, as we suggested in Chapter 8, other analysts (including ourselves) prefer to rely on explanatory variables that have been constructed from quite different kinds of responses. We prefer to rely on questions asked about respondents' views concerning each topic that might have played some direct or indirect role in shaping their choice without invoking any implicit or explicit connection with any political party or candidate.

In surveys conducted by the National Election Studies, this distinction between measures based on respondents' views about a specified topic (for example, the state of the national economy, attitudes on abortion, views on equality) and measures based on respondents' volunteering a topic as one reason for their own partisan preference or vote choice (their "likes" and "dislikes") is confounded by the methodological difference arising from the type or format of the survey questions involved. In particular, the questions concerning those aspects of the candidates and parties that voters "like" or "dislike" are unstructured or open-ended, while the measures of voters' attitudes that we employ in our analysis are based on structured questions about specific topics, with answer alternatives that are offered to each survey respondent. Our general preference for electoral explanations that are based on such structured questions about respondents' views instead of open-ended questions about their rationale for candidate or party evaluations is based on several arguments, including the following:

- *Indirect Effects.* Some types of explanatory variables have an impact on vote choice that is primarily (if not entirely) indirect, in the sense that their influence is mediated by more proximate intervening variables—especially those variables that are defined in terms of explicit partisan evaluations. We should expect that voters' responses to open-ended "like" and "dislike" questions about the candidates would underrepresent explanatory themes that lie behind their proferred responses and that their responses would be dominated by explanatory themes that we have placed fairly "close" to the vote as mediating explanations in our multiple-stage model. In particular, as we have seen, general predispositions exert most of their influence on the vote through a variety of intervening variables that are defined in terms of specific preferences, perceptions, and evaluations that become salient during the campaign. It therefore seems reasonable to expect that measures of policy-related *predispositions* that are constructed from voters' own explanations of their candidate evaluations will not be as strongly linked to the vote as parallel measures (for the same predispositions) that are based on specific issues stressed in the campaign. In other words, the *consequences* of general policy-related predispositions in specific campaign-related areas are more likely to surface in respondents' "reasons" concerning policy preferences than are the predispositions themselves.

• *Misleading Self-Reports Concerning the Basis for Choice.* Voters may not provide very accurate accounts of the causes of their own evaluations of the candidates, because they do not remember or choose not to report factors or considerations that had some impact on those evaluations at some earlier point in time. This kind of criticism of explanations based on "reasons" is usually based on social psychological research (see Nisbett and Wilson, 1977), as well as the general likelihood of "reverse causation"—in which such responses are influenced by the campaign of the candidate they have chosen to support for other reasons. In recent criticisms of this kind,[14] some voters' responses to the NES "likes and dislikes" questions have been described as *rationalizations* concerning the causes of their own preferences, rather than the true sources or origins of those preferences.

• *Differential Underreporting.* Furthermore, survey respondents are not equally motivated and skilled in the kind of verbal behavior required by open-ended questions. As a consequence, even respondents who can recall the factors or considerations that influenced their candidate evaluations may differ in the accuracy of their responses to such questions, as a result of differences in verbal ability and involvement in the interview.

For these reasons, many analysts and nearly all of the measurement development activities associated with the National Election Studies since the 1960s have moved toward multiple-item measures of voters' attitudes as a replacement for the "reasons" or "likes and dislikes" that are produced by open-ended questions. To this point, our own analyses of the elections since 1980 have been powerfully shaped by these arguments, and our previous essays made very little use of the traditional NES open-ended questions about the parties and candidates. After more than two decades of measurement and analytic development based on structured instead of open-ended questions, however, electoral scholars still disagree about the relative merit of electoral explanations that are based on these two very different methods.

Despite serious reservations about such explanations, we are persuaded that the NES open-ended questions about the candidates and parties should be maintained, for a variety of reasons. On the basis of recent publications and informal communications, it seems clear that each of the following positions concerning the NES open-ended questions about the candidates and parties is defended by research colleagues: (1) The traditional NES "likes and dislikes" questions may be useful in suggesting the range of considerations that may have played some role in structuring voters' choices. It is difficult to cover every relevant topic when designing an NES survey instrument; some important topics may not be covered by structured questions in any given survey. Colleagues with this view, however, tend to argue that NES open-ended questions should not be used in quantitative or statistical explanations of vote choice, because they are often rationalizations for decisions that were really made on other grounds, as well as being unreliable sources for the "true" causes of choice.

(2) Even though explanations based on open-ended questions will be generally inferior to those based on structured questions, they may still be used to summarize voters' positive and negative impressions of the major parties and candidates. This would be true without differentiating between specific issues or criteria for evaluation, but they may be helpful in clarifying the apparent impact of variables based on structured questions.

(3) Despite their potential shortcomings, explanations of the vote based on the NES open-ended questions still provide the best way of characterizing the overall role played by different types of explanations, like the major "components" of electoral decisions reported in *The American Voter* (concerning attitudes toward domestic issues, foreign issues, group-related benefits, the parties as managers of government, and the candidates). Advocates of this view may also believe that the NES open-ended questions provide a useful way to assess the role played by specific campaign issues, since the electoral relevance of those topics

is self-evident in responses that are volunteered by the voter—instead of inferred from statistical relationships between the vote and variables based on structured questions about that topic.

"Likes" and "Dislikes" as Reasons for Vote Choice

To assess these conflicting perspectives on the validity of these two types of explanations, we constructed a second set of measures (in parallel to those based on structured questions). We attempted to create a second measure for all of the explanatory variables in our model from the answers to NES "likes and dislikes" questions. Each of these measures is the simple sum of individual (signed) responses to the four open-ended questions about the candidates that dealt with criteria for evaluation. Each such response was scored −1 (for pro-Bush or anti-Clinton responses) or +1 (for pro-Clinton or anti-Bush responses). For our policy-related predispositions, this procedure produced seven variables which summarized all of the positive or negative responses concerning Clinton and Bush that involved some explicit reference to predispositions concerning equality, scope of governmental responsibility, morality, unions (or workers) versus business (or the wealthy), isolationism, Vietnam, and general views that were described as liberal versus conservative.

Table 11.9 shows the results of multiple regression analyses which permit us to compare statistical relationships between our two types of predisposition-related measures and vote choice for Clinton versus Bush. The first four columns present standardized regression coefficients for our predisposition-related measures, comparing responses to structured questions with those from open-ended questions, from two different analyses, one with and one without variables that capture the effects of all other (measured) influences on the vote. Both of these analyses include controls for our standard social and economic characteristics and party identification, as well as the other measures of policy-related predispositions based on the same method.

Table 11.9 makes it clear that alternative methods based on structured questions (eliciting voters' attitudes on each topic) or open-ended questions (which simply ask for respondents' reasons for liking or disliking the candidates) sometimes lead to similar conclusions concerning the electoral relevance of given policy-related predispositions *for those voters*

Table 11.9 The Impact of Predispositions Based on Structured vs. Open-Ended Questions: Comparing Explanations Based on Voters' Own Positions vs. Their "Reasons" for Choice

	Standardized Regression Coefficients for Measures Based on Structured Questions, Respondents' Own Views		Standardized Regression Coefficients for Measures Based on Open-ended Questions about the Candidates		Percentage of Clinton/Bush Voters Who Provided One or More Responses within the Designated Category
	Total Effect* (with Other Predispositions Held Constant)	Direct Effect (with All Other Variables Held Constant)	With Summaries of Likes/Dislikes for Other Predispositions Also Held Constant	With Summary Measures for All Other Likes/Dislikes Also Held Constant	
Unions vs. Business (includes workers vs. wealthy for likes/dislikes)	.05	(.02)	.06	.03	15.9
Limited Government	.06	(.01)	.06	.04	4.8
Isolationism	.06	(.01)	(.03)	(.00)	5.2
Homosexuals vs. Fundamentalists (no mentions for likes/dislikes)	.06	(−.02)	—	—	0.0
Vietnam	.08	(.02)	(.02)	(.01)	0.2
Equality	.09	(−.00)	.05	.05	1.6
Morality	.10	.05	.10	.06	7.8
Liberal vs. Conservative	.16	.05	.08	.05	6.4
Party Identification (Same for both Methods)	.40	.14	.52	.26	—

*All analyses also include controls for the standard set of social and economic characteristics used in this chapter. The number of cases (N) for all of these comparisons is 1193.

(Coefficients for Which the Estimated Value of p is > .1 Appear in Parentheses).

who were scored something other than zero on the pertinent measure. This caveat is important because our two methods are very different in the sheer number of voters who have non-zero values on the relevant explanatory variables. Typically, the unstructured questions yield only a handful of voters who give a response in the content domain involved.

For the 1992 election, both approaches suggest that general attitudes concerning morality and liberal or conservative self-designation played a larger role (as measured by effect coefficients) in shaping the vote choice (between Clinton and Bush) than did other predisposition-related variables. That partial convergence in results, however, does not extend to the other topics discussed in this chapter. Both methods suggest that voters' general attitudes toward equality, scope of governmental responsibility, and identification with business (or the wealthy) versus unions (or workers) had *some* impact on vote choice for President in 1992, but the two methods do not suggest the same rank order in terms of their relative importance in explaining individual choice. Furthermore, the two methods suggest quite different conclusions concerning the impact or relevance of attitudes toward international involvement (or isolation), service in Vietnam, and the ongoing conflict between homosexuals and fundamentalists. That final theme was not mentioned by *any* respondents in the 1992 NES open-ended questions concerning Clinton and Bush, although our analysis of voters' feelings about those groups based on structured questions suggests that attitudes in that area did have some indirect impact on the vote.

In each of these comparisons, the substantial difference between variables in their cross-sectional variability is a major source of the difference between the standardized regression coefficients for the two alternative explanatory variables. As shown in the final column of Table 11.9, very few Bush or Clinton voters gave responses to the NES open-ended question about the candidates that can be assigned to any of our policy-related predispositions. The largest percentage (of Clinton/Bush voters) who volunteered responses pertaining to one of our predispositions is 15.9 percent (which included a somewhat broader range of answers than the responses used in our measure for "business versus unions" based on structured questions). The proportions who provided responses in each of our other predisposition-related topics are well below 10 percent.

In addition to the small percentage of voters who mentioned these predisposition-related topics in answering the NES open-ended question,

Table 11.10 Differences in the Apparent Total Effects of Specific Predispositions (Based on "Mentioning" the Topic as a Reason for Choice)

Topic of Policy-related Predisposition	Percentage Mentioning Topic	Unstandardized Effect for all Clinton/Bush Voters	Unstandardized Effect for Base: No Mention	Difference in "b" for those Who Mention
Equality	1.6	.22	.21	(.30)
Limited Government	4.8	.08	.08	(.03)
Morality	7.8	.22	.21	(.13)
Business vs. Unions	15.9	.09	.10	(−.02)
Isolationism	5.2	.07	.08	−.20
Vietnam	0.2	.08	.08	(.11)
Liberal vs. Conservative	6.4	.26	.27	(.00)

we should draw attention to the impact of policy-related predispositions, elicited by structured questions, on the vote among those respondents who did *not even mention* the topics in giving their reasons for "liking" or "disliking" either of the candidates. As shown in Table 11.10, the total (unstandardized) effect estimates based on structured questions were only slightly modified when the estimates were limited to those who did *not volunteer any* "reasons" for choice in that area. Analyses of the role of policy-related predispositions based on open-ended questions appear to have "missed" the impact of those predispositions for substantial numbers of voters—individuals who may have been influenced by their views but did not happen to mention that topic in response to the NES open-ended question.

On the other hand, responses to open-ended questions that can be assigned to the same general topics as our measures of policy-related predispositions may be helpful in identifying voters whose predispositions in that area were strongly activated by the campaign—and played a different role in shaping their choice. The final two columns in Table 11.10 present separate estimates for the apparent effects of specific predispositions, as measured with structural questions, for respondents who did not—and who did—mention a "reason" for choice in that area. None of the differences between the apparent effects for those two groups were statistically significant, but the three on equality, morality,

and Vietnam suggest that the NES open-ended questions may have identified individuals for whom those topics were somewhat more salient or
important.

Because of the many differences produced by these two approaches to
measurement, we will repeat this kind of analysis in subsequent chapters. By emphasizing these comparisons, we hope to focus attention on
the differences (and similarities) between electoral explanations based
on "reasons" given in response to open-ended questions and explanations that are based on structured questions about the respondents' views
in each area. Both of these approaches to electoral explanation continue
to be used in scholarly research as well as in media coverage of national
elections. As a consequence, political observers and scholars should be
aware of the possibility that conflicts between different electoral explanations may be attributable to the fundamental differences between these
two methods. At the same time, as the fourth column of Table 11.10
illustrates, respondent-supplied "reasons" for choice may be useful in
clarifying the apparent "effects" of specific topics, when they are combined with structured measures of voters' opinions in those areas.

▪ Summary

This chapter's detailed review of partisan, ideological, and policy-related
predispositions is important in its own right because it clarifies the way
in which such predispositions may influence electoral decisions. Our
analyses concerning these predispositions, however, are also useful as a
means of underscoring their relevance for understanding the political
consequences of the social and economic characteristics discussed in the
previous chapter. Indeed, the interplay between the two chapters often
clarifies what might otherwise remain ambiguous. For example, it is
clear from Table 11.5 that moral traditionalism is closely related to our
other predispositions, including party identification. Our conclusions
concerning unique effects based on morality, however, are strengthened
by the evidence in Chapter 10 that such beliefs are disproportionately
relevant to the vote decisions of the committed among Mainline Protestants, Evangelicals, and Catholics, in contrast to a limited role among
their nominal co-religionists. In Table 10.3, no other predisposition
displays a comparable pattern.

The impact of general beliefs in our three conflict-related areas is substantially mediated both by voters' positions on current policy conflicts and by their assessments of current conditions. We note that the 1992 NES instrument did not include all of the policy questions that could have mediated the relationship of moral traditionalism with vote choice. The effects of all three belief-related measures might have been completely mediated by a more comprehensive set of measures concerning current issues. In that connection, however, we also note that party identification and ideology both exhibit direct effect coefficients which are conceptually or theoretically appropriate in that both types of characteristics can have a direct (unmediated) influence on voters' preferences for President.

12

★ ★ ★

Voting and Current Policy Preferences

In the previous chapter we reviewed the apparent electoral impact of voters' general predispositions toward policy-related topics. We now turn to evidence which indicates that voters' policy preferences concerning some of the specific conflicts highlighted in the 1992 campaign also had an independent impact on their decisions to vote for Clinton or Bush. By shifting our attention to these contemporary policy conflicts, still without any explicit references to the candidates or their parties, we advance to the next or third stage in our overall explanatory model—following social and economic characteristics and partisan and policy-related predispositions. In focusing on specific policy conflicts that were emphasized during the campaign, however, this chapter considers only one of several approaches to topics that are defined in terms of contemporaneous or "short-term" forces.

In particular, voters' perceptions of current conditions concerning consensual governmental goals, such as having a "strong economy," are also included in the third stage of our model, but are not explicitly discussed until Chapter 13. All of the other short-term forces we will examine are defined in terms of explicit partisan evaluations and have been assigned to still later stages in our model—as well as to subsequent chapters. Voters' retrospective evaluations of the President's success in office and prospective evaluations of both candidates and their parties are discussed in Chapter 14. Finally, voters' impressions of the candidates' personal (or non-governmental) qualities are covered in Chapter 15. Because of this analytic strategy, some of the "issues" or "problems" that were emphasized in the 1992 campaign will be discussed in several different chapters, since their topics may involve evaluations of past or future performance—by the President, the candidates, or the parties— and perceptions of current conditions, as well as conflicts over policy preferences and policy-related predispositions.

This point deserves special emphasis, for our treatment of policy-related conflicts represents only one of several ways in which frequently mentioned "problems" or "issues" may have played some role in shaping voters' choices for President. In 1992, at least 5 percent of the Bush/Clinton voters mentioned each of the following topics as the "most important problem" facing the country: unemployment (40 percent), the economy (32 percent), the deficit (30 percent), health care (20 percent), assistance to the disadvantaged, including welfare (16 percent), crime and drugs (13 percent), education (11 percent), pollution or the environment (8 percent), morality (6 percent), and race (6 percent). Still other areas were mentioned, but by less than 5 percent of the sample. Each of those general areas involves some conflict over policy direction, but several can also be seen in terms of general concerns about the current state of affairs in the nation without any explicit connection to controversies about federal policy.

For example, as discussed below, we believe that much of the argument about health care (or the high cost of health insurance) in the 1992 campaign was defined in terms of a general "problem" without a clear linkage to opposing possibilities for federal policies. As a consequence, the topic surfaces in prospective evaluations of the candidates' future effectiveness without activating conflicts concerning the degree to which, or way in which, the government should be involved.

An even clearer case of "problem" instead of "policy-" related voting has to do with the national economy. As Ross Perot often repeated, the public wanted the President to "get under the hood and fix the problem" posed by continuing high levels of unemployment. Many voters were apparently influenced by their disapproval of President Bush's "handling" of the economy, and their favorable impression of Bill Clinton's likely success, without taking sides as to precisely what should be done. In contrast, policy conflicts were more clearly linked to the vote in domains where the definition of current "problems" was less consensual, such as assistance to the disadvantaged or aid to private schools.

Published accounts of the 1992 election identify an impressive list of policy conflicts which included the following: the preferred level for national defense, economic assistance to the poor, action to reduce unemployment, reduced social security, federal aid to public education, public policies concerning homosexuality, commitment of national resources to government-supported "infrastructure" (such as highways and communications), level of personal income taxes, capital gains taxes, governmental regulation of business and industry, the death penalty, affirmative action, prayers in public schools, environmental protection, reduction of pollution, the federal deficit, and consumer protection—in addition to the overall level of government spending and abortion.[1]

As in our treatment of other explanatory themes, we will discuss statistical evidence regarding a somewhat smaller list of variables concerning policy preferences that were related to the vote. It should be noted that the NES coverage of possible policy-related topics was very comprehensive and permitted some examination of virtually every area mentioned in the 1992 electoral analysis literature. Our analysis of the NES 1992 survey indicated, however, that several policy-related conflicts covered in the NES interviews did not appear to be sufficiently visible or "important" to produce a significant connection between voters' preferences in that area and their choice for President. This negative result was occasionally true for the simple bivariate relationship with the vote, but it usually appeared after we introduced statistical controls for other significant policy-related preferences, partisan identification, policy-related predispositions, and our full set of social and economic characteristics.

Consequently, it bears reemphasizing that our assessment of topics conventionally defined as substantive issues related to governmental action extends over at least five chapters. The components will not be drawn together until the final section of the book. At this point, however, we should like to note one very interesting and perhaps controversial result of our analysis. It concerns the frequency with which we find limited evidence of any role in influencing voters' decisions attributable to topics that received widespread publicity during the campaign. In the second half of the chapter we will comment at length on issues that we think should not be counted among the short-term forces that played a significant role in shaping the ultimate presidential vote in 1992, despite their prominence in media presentations of the campaign.

Nevertheless, as noted in the previous chapter, voters' preferences concerning a number of current policy issues appear to have mediated or accounted for some of the total effects of policy-related predispositions. This suggests that those specific issues were the mechanisms that "activated" our more general predispositions in the 1992 campaign. At the same time, some of our measures of current policy preferences also add to our overall explanation by tapping policy-related disagreements relevant to the vote that were not captured by any of our predispositions.

As in the previous chapters, all of our analyses of the effects of current policy conflicts are based on the standard sequence of descriptive statistics concerning the empirical relationships between independent and intervening variables and vote choice. For each policy issue, that sequence of results begins with the simple (bivariate) relationship between policy preferences and the vote, and then documents the changes in the strength of that relationship as we control for a growing set of other explanatory variables. Each of the additional explanatory variables is introduced for one of two reasons—in the first instance because they are causally prior, or coterminous, with the policy-related measure and may therefore confound its apparent impact on the vote; subsequently, additional variables are examined because they may be intervening or mediating variables that help explain the impact of the policy preference on the vote.

We should note again that the distinction between those explanatory variables that are "policy-related predispositions" and those that are "current policy preferences" is clearly one of degree rather than kind. Both types of measure are designed to capture differences between voters in their own positions concerning policy-related conflicts or disagreements within the society. In general, the variables we have designated as "predispositions" are based on questions about broad conflict-related topics, but they do not refer to specific policy alternatives that were currently being considered or proposed for the federal government in 1992. In contrast, the variables we have designated as "current policy preferences" *are* based on questions about policy alternatives that were emphasized by one of the candidates, or the media, during the campaign. Some policy-related variables, however, could be classified as somewhere in between a general predisposition and a current policy preference. For example, our measure of policy preferences concerning the military is fairly general, but we have considered it along with other current issues because of defense-related priorities that were emphasized during the 1992 campaign.

Most of this chapter is devoted to examining the electoral relevance of specific policy conflicts in order to identify each of those areas where voters appear to have made voting decisions that were at least partially shaped by their preferences concerning policy direction. For some purposes, however, electoral analysts are also interested in the extent to which *all* of the policy-related conflicts have influenced vote choice—in combination, without reference to the specific conflicts involved. That question is discussed at some length in the last section of this book, but in this chapter we present a preliminary discussion of the combined relevance of *all* policy-related preferences in order to suggest their aggregate explanatory power. We then close the chapter by examining the degree to which electoral analysts may obtain a different impression of the relevance of current policy issues if they rely on voters' own accounts of their issue-based "reasons" for their positive or negative evaluations of the candidates.

▪ Electoral Effects of Specific Policy Issues

This first section of the chapter describes the electoral relevance of voters' own preferences in five policy domains that appeared to play some role in the 1992 campaign. The specific policies involved concern governmental assistance to the disadvantaged, the strength and use of military force, allowing homosexuals in the military, the overall level of income taxes, and allocation of public funds to private schools. Similar analyses were carried out for NES questions concerning policy issues in many other areas, but none of the others exhibited effects on the vote that were large enough to be statistically or substantively significant— once we controlled for preferences in other policy areas as well as prior predispositions and social characteristics. We will comment on some of these "surprises" in passing, but will reserve most such commentary for the latter part of the chapter.

Governmental Assistance to the Disadvantaged

Since 1980, NES surveys have included a battery of questions concerning voters' preferences for the level of federal spending in a wide variety of areas. Each of those questions asks the respondent whether spending should be increased, kept the same, or reduced for specific governmental programs or objectives, several of which are defined in terms of assistance to persons with some kind of economic disadvantage. In the Clinton-Bush contest, as in each of the presidential elections in the 1980s, this topic was very visible in the campaign, and answers to questions about "spending" in particular problem areas were all strongly related to the vote. Respondents who preferred an increase in federal spending to assist poor or disadvantaged citizens were *much* more likely to vote for Bill Clinton—or against George Bush—than were those who preferred a reduction in those areas. This bivariate tendency was evident for all of the eight relevant NES questions in which respondents were asked if they would prefer more, the same, or less federal spending on programs that were at least implicitly defined in terms of assistance to persons with some kind of economic disadvantage.[2]

In 1992, on the basis of multivariate analyses that also included economic conditions, respondents' preferences concerning other current issues, general policy-related predispositions, partisan identification, and social or economic characteristics, the two NES questions which asked about spending on "food stamps" and "the poor" captured most of the statistical connection between spending preferences and the vote. No other question about governmental assistance that could be interpreted in terms of economic disadvantage exhibited a similarly significant relationship with the vote (for Clinton or Bush) when our policy-related variables in other areas, as well as the above two items concerning the disadvantaged, were held constant.

Furthermore, as will be discussed in the following section, that negative result, in which questions about government spending were *not* independently related to the vote choice, includes *all* of eight additional questions about the preferred level of federal spending, as well as the three traditional NES issue questions concerning (1) the government's responsibility for health insurance, (2) the current level of "services and spending," and (3) the familiar question on maintaining a "good job and standard of living." There is, therefore, a surprisingly long list of conflicts related to social welfare policies that, when considered one by one, did not pass even our relatively lenient standard of probable statistical significance (requiring $p < .1$ for distinguishing between Bush and Clinton voters). The list not only includes many topics that had been part of past NES surveys, but also some that NES has considered part of the "core" questions in that series.

For these many reasons, our 1992 analysis of social welfare issues, long a staple of liberal Democratic/conservative Republican disagreements, is based on the simple average of two trichotomous variables concerning government expenditures for food stamps and aid to the poor, labeled as a summary index of policy preferences concerning federal assistance to the disadvantaged.

Table 12.1 presents our standard sequence of descriptive statistics for the relationship between this summary measure and vote choice. In light of the 1994 Republican "contract with America" it is interesting to note that among voters with the clearest sentiments for and against aid to the disadvantaged, those favoring aid outnumbered those opposing aid by a margin of 3 to 1. As with the other explanatory variables discussed in previous chapters, Row 4 of Table 12.1, with an effect coefficient of .72, provides a convenient way of summarizing the overall strength of this variable's bivariate relationship with the vote. Analysts may disagree, however, concerning the most appropriate set of variables to include or control for in assessing the impact of policy preferences.

At the outset, the original bivariate coefficient linking attitudes toward aid to the disadvantaged and the vote is reduced to .53 (from .72 in Row 4 of Table 12.1) by the inclusion of controls for social or economic characteristics (in Row 5). That coefficient, in turn, is reduced even more, to .31 (in Row 6), when we take account of party identification. The strength of the effect coefficient is further reduced to only .14 after the introduction of additional controls for all of our policy-related predispositions (in Row 9), and to .12 with controls on other policy preferences and conditions (Row 11). Thus, most of the original bivariate coefficient, .60/.72, appears to be confounded in the sense that the policy preferences we are analyzing share a variety of common social, partisan, and policy-related predispositional antecedents with the vote.

The sharp reduction in the apparent effect of policy preferences on aid to the disadvantaged when we control for these three sets of long-term variables is more generally noteworthy. The size of that reduction is similar to the results for other explanatory variables defined by policy conflicts. The explanatory variables which represent long-term influences predating the election campaign consistently account for a very large portion of the simple bivariate relationship between each set of current policy preferences and the vote.

Table 12.1 Policy Preferences Concerning the Disadvantaged

1. Average Vote for Most Liberal Preference (More Spending on Both Questions, N = 176)*	.74
2. Average Vote for Most Conservative Preferences (Less Spending on Both Questions, N = 57)	−.50
3. Difference in Average Vote: Most Liberal minus Most Conservative	1.24
4. Bivariate Unstandardized Regression Coefficient (Policy Preference Index Scored from −1 to +1)	.72
5. Coefficient from Multiple Regression with Social and Economic Characteristics Held Constant	.53
6. With Party Identification (Party ID) Also Held Constant	.31
7. With Specific Policy-Related Predispositions (But NOT Party ID) Also Held Constant	.22
8. With Liberal vs. Conservative Self-Designation Also Held Constant	.19
9. With Party ID AND All Policy-Related Predispositions Also Held Constant	.14
10. With Preferences on All Other Policy Issues Also Held Constant	.13
#11. With Perceptions of Current Personal and National Conditions Also Held Constant	.12
12. With Retrospective Evaluations of the Current President Also Held Constant	(.05)
13. With Evaluations of the Candidates' Personal Qualities Also Held Constant	(.06)
14. With Prospective Evaluations of the Candidates and Parties Also Held Constant	(.04)

*The number of cases associated with extreme positions on these and similar measures simply indicate the base on which extreme scores were calculated. Note that the number of cases is unweighted; all other results are weighted.

(Coefficients Appear in Parentheses if the Estimated p Value is $> .1$).

#Indicates estimate of the "apparent total effect" discussed in the text.

Next we should note that it is also generally true that adding the control for preferences pertaining to *other* policy conflicts has little impact on the apparent effect estimates for any of the policy areas that have a significant apparent total effect, that is, for the five topics named earlier. This is not the case for many of the policies that do not meet our threshold of a statistically significant independent effect on the vote. Many of the campaign topics that fall below our rather low threshold for inclusion in our topic-by-topic analysis fail to reflect statistically significant independent effects with the vote because they are placed in competition with other variables that are defined in terms of current policy conflicts. Such variables may in some sense be important when considered apart from other policies in that their relationship to the vote cannot be accounted for by long-term factors. However, it turns out that they are so interrelated with each other, as well as with other policy questions, that controlling for the others eliminates the coefficient that would represent statistical independence for the "failed" items. This pattern not only limits the size of the apparent effect on the vote for specific policy variables, but it compounds the problem of anticipating the extent to which an entire set of policy-related variables may influence the vote—a subject to which we will turn in a later section of this chapter.

A final note before proceeding with our analyses of other specific policy conflicts in 1992: in the early stages of the analysis we had come to believe that the causal relationships between current policy preferences and perceptions of "current conditions" were ambiguous or indeterminate. Prior to completing our analysis we had no way of knowing how much current policy preferences were shaped by perceptions of current conditions—or vice versa. For that reason, the perceptions of current conditions are included in the same causal stage in our model as current policy preferences. Row 11 of Table 12.1 presents the apparent impact of policy preferences concerning the disadvantaged, .12, after we control for those conditions, as well as other policy preferences and all prior variables. This is the coefficient that we have designated as the "apparent total effect" of policy preferences in this area. A by-product of our alternative routes to explaining or understanding is the discovery that "perceptions of conditions" and "policy preferences" do not appear to be strongly intercorrelated and, therefore, the question of their causal location relative to each other is not one with major empirical consequences.

Furthermore, most of the apparent effect of policy preferences concerning the disadvantaged noted in Table 12.1 appears to have been mediated by evaluations of George Bush as President, rather than by any impressions of Bill Clinton. The apparent effect of this policy conflict over government aid to the disadvantaged is reduced to an insignificant value (.05) in Row 12 of the table when we also control for evaluations of the President—and it remains insignificant when we also control for other evaluations of the candidates and parties. It would appear that the primary mechanism by which policy preferences in this area influenced the 1992 vote involved their impact on voters' overall assessments of President Bush, rather than their comparison of alternatives offered by Clinton and Bush.

Defense Policy and the Use of Military Force

In the last chapter we noted that the disappearance of communist governments throughout Eastern Europe and the collapse of the former Soviet Union had led some observers to expect that disagreements concerning the size and use of U.S. military forces would lose most of their relevance for voting behavior in presidential elections. Furthermore, after the Persian Gulf War began in 1991, the Bush administration's policies were supported by a large majority of the electorate, including the Democratic candidate for President. Specific conflicts over "defense" or the use of military force might therefore have been expected to have a much smaller impact than in other recent elections.

It is not possible to offer a precise estimate of how much that influence was reduced. The dramatic changes in the international situation did however have a sharp impact on the content of NES interviews. Previous "baseline" questions about communism, the Soviet Union, "Star Wars," and the Nicaragua Contras were deleted from the 1992 interview schedule. On the other hand, several questions were added about the Persian Gulf War. All told, general expectations concerning the declining relevance of this area are at least partially supported by other estimates of the apparent impact of preferences related to military affairs on voters' choices between Clinton and Bush.

A good example is provided by the NES 7-point question about the level of federal spending on "defense." This question played a visible role in many analyses of previous elections that focused on policy-related preferences. In 1992, however, preferences concerning federal expenditures for national defense were not significantly linked to vote choices, at least not independent of related predispositions toward foreign policy. The only two defense- or military-related questions that did exhibit a relationship to the 1992 vote, after we control for prior variables and other policy-related preferences and conditions, were very general in nature. They concerned the importance of "maintaining a strong defense" and the appropriateness of using military force to "solve international problems," without any explicit reference to the Gulf War.[3] For these reasons, our 1992 version of defense and foreign policy analysis is based on a summary of responses to two questions, rather than on opinions about current defense expenditures, the Gulf War, or any other specific policy alternatives concerning defense or the military covered in the NES survey.

Because of the general nature of these two questions, concerning a strong defense and the use of military force, our summary measure could easily be reclassified as a policy-related predisposition, joining the two-item measure of predispositions toward foreign policy introduced in the last chapter. Such a change would have no appreciable impact on our overall conclusions other than a modest shift in explanatory credit from disagreements over current policy to more general beliefs or predispositions. Despite that ambiguity, however, we have interpreted the apparent electoral effects of this variable in terms of "current policy issues" because of the proximity of the Gulf War to the 1992 election—and because events in Somalia, Haiti, and Bosnia had transformed the context of policy debates in this area for future elections.

Table 12.2 presents our standard series of descriptive statistics for the relationship between our two-item summary of military policy preferences and the vote. As with policy preferences concerning the disadvantaged, the statistical relationship between military-related preferences and the vote is moderately reduced when we control for social and economic characteristics (from .78 to .65, in Row 5). That coefficient, in turn, is sharply reduced when we also control for partisan identification (to .42 in Row 6), for all policy-related predispositions without party identification (to .23 in Row 8), or for all partisan and policy-related predispositions (to .20 in Row 9). The apparent electoral effects of defense-related preferences might therefore be easily confused with those of more general political orientations. Moreover, we note that the strength of this connection goes down only slightly (to .19 in Row 10) when we also control for voters' preferences in other policy areas— which suggests that the confounding influences of other policy-related conflicts have been removed by our controls for more general predispositions.

As with policy preferences concerning the disadvantaged, the remain-

Table 12.2 Policy Preferences Concerning the Military

1. Average Voter for Most Liberal (Against Staying Strongest and Use of Force, N = 50)*	.85
2. Average Voter for Most Conservative Preferences (Agree Strongly and Extremely Willing, N = 117)	−.34
3. Difference in Average Vote: Most Liberal minus Most Conservative	1.19
4. Bivariate Unstandardized Regression Coefficient (Policy Preference Index Scored from −1 to +1)	.78
5. Coefficient from Multiple Regression with Social and Economic Characteristics Held Constant	.65
6. With Party Identification (Party ID) Also Held Constant	.42
7. With Specific Policy-Related Predispositions (But NOT Party ID) Also Held Constant	.30
8. With Liberal vs. Conservative Self-Designation Also Held Constant	.23
9. With Party ID AND All Policy-Related Predispositions Also Held Constant	.20
10. With Preferences on All Other Policy Issues Also Held Constant	.19
#11. With Perceptions of Current Personal and National Conditions Also Held Constant	.16
12. With Retrospective Evaluations of the Current President Also Held Constant	(.03)
13. With Evaluations of the Candidates' Personal Qualities Also Held Constant	(.01)
14. With Prospective Evaluations of the Candidates and Parties Also Held Constant	(.02)

*The number of cases associated with extreme positions on these and similar measures simply indicate the base on which extreme scores were calculated. Note that the number of cases is unweighted; all other results are weighted.

(Coefficients Appear in Parentheses if the Estimated p Value is $> .1$).

#Indicates estimate of the "apparent total effect" discussed in the text.

ing coefficients in Table 12.2 suggest that all of the apparent impact of defense or military-related preferences was mediated by voters' retrospective evaluations of George Bush as President. The introduction of such evaluations reduces the remaining effect estimate to an insignificant value—even without considering variables based on the candidates' personal qualities or any prospective evaluations. In our view, the electoral relevance of military-related preferences in 1992 was almost entirely based on the influence of those preferences on voters' evaluations of President Bush. Bill Clinton tried to adopt a low profile on the strength and use of U.S. military forces, and appears to have succeeded.

Homosexuals in the Military

During the 1992 campaign, Bill Clinton and the Republican party adopted visible and contrasting positions concerning the role of homosexuals in American society. The Republican convention and platform emphasized the importance of the "traditional" family in a fashion which suggested clear opposition to homosexual life-styles as well as heterosexual promiscuity. In contrast, the Democratic ticket was visibly supported by organizations that advocated gay and lesbian rights, and candidate Clinton took a clear position against the continuing ban on military service by homosexuals.

Issues related to sexual orientation had clearly been developing for several years; NES Pilot Surveys have explored a variety of alternative policy-related questions concerning homosexuals.[4] The 1992 NES interview schedule included three policy-related questions concerning laws against anti-gay discrimination, military service by homosexuals, and adoption of children by homosexual couples. Responses to each of these questions exhibited some relationship to voters' choices between Clinton and Bush.[5]

As in the preceding analyses of policy-related preferences concerning the disadvantaged and the military, we examined the relationships between each of these questions about homosexuals and the vote in order to identify specific policy conflicts which exhibited an independent relevance for the vote after we controlled for other policy preferences and all of the variables from earlier stages in our model. Of those three items, *only* the question about support of or opposition to military service by homosexuals exhibited a clear and significant independent relationship to the vote, as shown in Table 12.3. Neither of the other two questions provided any significant explanatory power once other variables in the same causal stage or preceding stages were taken into account.

We should add, however, that our sequence of analyses suggests that the electoral relevance of potential policies toward homosexuals in 1992

Table 12.3 Policy Preferences Concerning Homosexuals in the Military

1. Average Vote for Strongly in Favor (N = 387)*	.61
2. Average Vote for Strongly Opposed (N = 366)	−.28
3. Difference in Average Vote: Liberal minus Conservative	.89
4. Bivariate Unstandardized Regression Coefficient (Policy Preference Index Scored from −1 to + 1)	.42
5. Coefficient from Multiple Regression with Social and Economic Characteristics Held Constant	.36
6. With Party Identification (Party ID) Also Held Constant	.25
7. With Specific Policy-Related Predispositions (But NOT Party ID) Also Held Constant	.15
8. With Liberal vs. Conservative Self-Designation Also Held Constant	.15
9. With Party ID AND All Policy-Related Predispositions Also Held Constant	.13
10. With Preferences on All Other Policy Issues Also Held Constant	.12
#11. With Perceptions of Current Personal and National Conditions Also Held Constant	.12
12. With Retrospective Evaluations of the Current President Also Held Constant	.08
13. With Evaluations of the Candidates' Personal Qualities Also Held Constant	.08
14. With Prospective Evaluations of the Candidates and Parties Also Held Constant	.05

*The number of cases associated with extreme positions on these and similar measures simply indicate the base on which extreme scores were calculated. Note that the number of cases is unweighted; all other results are weighted.

(Coefficients Appear in Parentheses if the Estimated *p* Value is > .1).

#Indicates estimate of the "apparent total effect" discussed in the text.

may have been based on the repeated (and more general) Republican emphasis on the "traditional family" rather than Bill Clinton's specific advocacy of "gays in the military."

Taxation

In recent national elections, no topic has been more frequently mentioned than the possibility of increases or reductions in the taxes paid by ordinary citizens. Republican charges that the Democrats will continue to "tax and spend" have become a traditional component in contemporary presidential campaigns, although Bill Clinton complicated that picture in 1992 with his pledge to reduce taxes for the "middle class." For some years candidates from the two major parties have advocated different policies in several tax-related areas, including the extent to which marginal tax rates should be different for different income levels (that is, should be "progressive"), the degree to which rates should be different for businesses and for individuals, the degree to which lower-income families should be given tax relief, the degree to which wealth should be taxed at death (that is, inheritance taxes), and the degree to which rates should be lower for profits on investments and the sale of property (that is, taxes on capital gains). These topics are often regarded as too complex for public opinion surveys, and the 1992 NES interview schedule included only one question about voters' own preferences concerning federal taxes of any kind. That question simply asked: "Would you personally be willing to pay more in taxes so that the government could spend more on the services you favor, or would you rather keep your taxes the same even if this meant the government couldn't increase its spending as you would like?" Note that this question emphasizes the respondent's *own* willingness to "pay more in taxes" instead of a general preference concerning the overall level of taxes paid by other individuals. Table 12.4 presents our standard sequence of descriptive statistics concerning the relationship between those preferences and the vote, both before and after the introduction of controls for the other variables in our model.

Only a minority of voters appeared to be "willing" to pay more in taxes, but those individuals provided very strong support for Bill Clinton with an average vote of +.63. Among the larger group of voters who were "unwilling" to pay more in taxes, however, George Bush received only a slight majority, with a vote division of −.05. The strength of the relationship between attitudes toward taxes and the vote declines from a modest bivariate coefficient of .34 to .14 after we control for both social and economic characteristics and party identification. Much of that relationship, moreover, appears to be confounded with more general policy-related predispositions, for it is further reduced to .05 when we also control for all of those variables (in Row 9). That coefficient declines only slightly when we control for preferences concerning other policy issues and perceptions of current conditions, to .04 in Row 11—the

Table 12.4 Policy Preferences Concerning Taxes

1. Average Vote for Those Willing to Pay More (N = 388)*	.63
2. Average Vote for Those Not Willing to Pay More (N = 773)	−.05
3. Difference in Average Vote: Willing minus Not Willing	.68
4. Bivariate Unstandardized Regression Coefficient (Policy Preference Scored from −1 to + 1)	.34
5. Coefficient from Multiple Regression with Social and Economic Characteristics Held Constant	.28
6. With Party Identification (Party ID) Also Held Constant	.14
7. With Specific Policy-Related Predispositions (But NOT Party ID) Also Held Constant	.12
8. With Liberal vs. Conservative Self-Designation Also Held Constant	.10
9. With Party ID AND All Policy-Related Predispositions Also Held Constant	.05
10. With Preferences on all Other Policy Also Held Constant	.04
#11. With Perceptions of Current Personal and National Conditions Also Held Constant	.04
12. With Retrospective Evaluations of the Current President Also Held Constant	.04
13. With Evaluations of the Candidates' Personal Qualities Also Held Constant	.04
14. With Prospective Evaluations of the Candidates and Parties Also Held Constant	(.03)

*The number of cases associated with extreme positions on these and similar measures simply indicate the base on which extreme scores were calculated. Note that the number of cases is unweighted; all other results are weighted.

(Coefficients Appear in Parentheses if the Estimated p Value is > .1).

#Indicates estimate of the "apparent total effect" discussed in the text.

coefficient that we have designated as the "apparent total effect" of voters' preferences in this area.

This coefficient is fairly modest, but its size may conceal a larger underlying role for tax-related preferences—because of limitations in the NES questions devoted to this topic. It is suggestive that the modest impact of this variable is not reduced by controls for evaluations of George Bush as President (in Row 12), and is only slightly reduced by controlling for the personal qualities of the candidates (to .04 in Row 13). The modest coefficient for this variable is not reduced to a non-significant value until we control for prospective evaluations of both the candidates and the parties. However understated it may be in our analysis, it seems likely that the apparent impact of tax-related preferences in 1992 reflected real differences in voters' tolerance for additional taxes— and some response to repeated Republican claims that Bill Clinton and the Democrats would continue to "tax and spend." This latter, stronger conclusion is supported by evidence from the NES "like and dislike" questions which we will review later in this chapter.

Public Funding for Private Schools

The final domain where we identified some independent impact of specific policy preferences on the vote concerns evolving proposals that public funding for education should be made available directly to parents—instead of public schools—so they can assign that support to the public or private school they choose for their child to attend. Proposals of this sort are strongly opposed by most organizations associated with public education, but have gained significant political support by critics of the public schools and prominent Republican leaders, including George Bush in the 1992 campaign. The 1992 NES question in this area was: "Some people think that we should use government funds only to support children who go to public schools, others feel that we should use government funds to support children's schooling regardless of whether their parents choose to send them to public, private, or parochial school. How do you feel, or haven't you thought much about this?"

In contrast to the preceding question concerning taxation, a substantial minority of NES respondents indicated that they didn't have an opinion about this topic, but those who did exhibited quite different choices between George Bush and Bill Clinton. As shown in Rows 1 and 2 of Table 12.5, voters who favored some choice in the type of school to be supported by government funds divided their votes equally between Bush and Clinton (with an average of −.01), but the roughly comparable number of those who opposed any support for non-public schools provided fairly strong support for Bill Clinton (with an average vote of +.34). The bivariate relationship between this variable and the vote is largely unchanged when we control for social and economic characteristics. This result suggests relatively little confounding net impact associated with religious affiliation (that is, of Catholic, Lutheran,

Table 12.5 Policy Preferences Concerning Aid to Private Schools

1. Average Vote for Those Opposed (N = 565)*	.34
2. Average Vote for Those in Favor (N = 404)	−.01
3. Difference in Average Vote: Opposed minus In Favor	.34
4. Bivariate Unstandardized Regression Coefficient (Policy Preference Scored from −1 to + 1)	.17
5. Coefficient from Multiple Regression with Social and Economic Characteristics Held Constant	.16
6. With Party Identification (Party ID) Also Held Constant	.11
7. With Specific Policy-Related Predispositions (But NOT Party ID) Also Held Constant	.08
8. With Liberal vs. Conservative Self-Designation Also Held Constant	.05
9. With Party ID AND All Policy-Related Predispositions Also Held Constant	.05
10. With Preferences on all Other Policy Also Held Constant	.05
#11. With Perceptions of Current Personal and National Conditions Also Held Constant	.06
12. With Retrospective Evaluations of the Current President Also Held Constant	(.02)
13. With Evaluations of the Candidates' Personal Qualities Also Held Constant	(.02)
14. With Prospective Evaluations of the Candidates and Parties Also Held Constant	(.02)

*The number of cases associated with extreme positions on these and similar measures simply indicate the base on which extreme scores were calculated. Note that the number of cases is unweighted; all other results are weighted.

(Coefficients Appear in Parentheses if the Estimated p Value is $> .1$).

#Indicates estimate of the "apparent total effect" discussed in the text.

or Christian schools) or the possibly offsetting economic circumstances that have traditionally been associated with private schools. The remaining coefficient is reduced to .05 when we control for partisan and policy-related predispositions (in Row 9). That coefficient is unaffected by additional controls for other policy issues or current conditions, but the apparent total effect is reduced to a non-significant value when we also control for evaluations of President Bush. This suggests that the electoral relevance of this topic, however limited, was linked to voters' reactions to the President's proposal rather than Bill Clinton's campaign.

■ Policy Issues with Non-Significant Apparent Effects

Several conflicts that played a visible rhetorical role in the pre-election campaign are not included in the above set of policy preferences that appear to have influenced voters' choices between Clinton and Bush in 1992. In particular, readers who are familiar with other accounts of the 1992 campaign, or with controversies associated with the subsequent Clinton administration, may be surprised at the omission of preferences concerning the overall level of federal spending, if not the "size" of the federal government, or the absence in 1992 of any vote-related policy issues concerning health insurance, unemployment, abortion, affirmative action, student loans, or the environment. On each of those topics, our failure to identify independent electoral effects of a specific policy conflict is due to some unknown combination of inadequate survey measurement or the true absence of any significant influence on the vote that could be traced to a specific conflict over proposed policies.

The Overall Level of Federal Spending

Following the 1992 election, a central arena for Republican criticisms of the Clinton administration was a recurring claim that the federal government is "too big" and "spends too much"—both of the taxpayers' money and borrowed funds, as evidenced by the large budget deficit and the growing national debt. This topic was clearly anticipated in the 1992 campaign in George Bush's repeated charge that Clinton would emphasize "liberal" policies of "tax and spend." However, Republican criticism of the federal budget of the *current* administration in 1992 as "too big" may have been muted by the fact that the incumbent President was the Republican candidate and Republicans had controlled the White House for twelve years. Nevertheless, because of Republican campaign emphasis on the deficit, it seemed possible that voters' general preferences concerning federal spending would have some influence on their choices between Bush and Clinton—in addition to or instead of the influence of their specific preferences concerning the resolution of various problems facing society.

To test that idea, we constructed a summary index of preferences concerning federal spending on all sixteen of the topics covered by the

NES "government spending" questions (including eight items with no obvious connection to aiding the disadvantaged). The resulting index is strongly related to the vote at the bivariate level, and that connection is not eliminated by controlling for social and economic characteristics, partisan identification, or policy-related predispositions (including the predisposition toward limited government). The connection between that index and the vote *is* eliminated, however, when we add controls for the five measures of current policy preferences that had an apparent total effect on the vote. More particularly, the statistical "connection" between our new summary of all preferences concerning federal spending and the vote disappears when we control for our summary of only two of those questions—concerning "food stamps" and "the poor."

Because of the part-whole relationship between our summary of all spending preferences and those concerning spending for the disadvantaged, we repeated the above analyses for an alternative summary of spending-related preferences which included all fourteen questions in that series, *except* those which had some clear (direct or indirect) relationship to economic disadvantage. The resulting measure has a substantial, although smaller, relationship to the vote, but its coefficient is *entirely* eliminated when we control for spending preferences concerning the disadvantaged. On the basis of that result, we have concluded that *all* of the connection between spending preferences and the 1992 vote should be attributed to voters' policy preferences concerning assistance to the disadvantaged—and not to their general views concerning "federal spending."

A similar result can be seen in coefficients associated with the traditional NES seven-point question concerning preferences for the current levels of "government services and spending." Voters who expressed a preference for increased federal "services and spending" were much more likely to vote for Bill Clinton than those who expressed a preference for a general reduction. The relationship between those preferences and the vote, however, is reduced to an insignificant value when we control for policy-related predispositions, partisan identification, and social or economic characteristics—even without any controls for other policy preferences, such as those included in our multi-item summary measure. This negative result could be at least partially caused by flaws in the somewhat double-barreled survey question involved, but it is consistent with the conclusion that voters' choices in 1992, as in 1988, did not seem to be influenced by their general attitudes toward the size or cost of government.

Race-related Policies

In the previous chapter, we discussed the failure of any measure based on race-related preferences to exhibit an independent apparent impact on voters' choices between George Bush and Bill Clinton, and this despite the presence of several different survey questions concerning ongoing conflicts in that area. Several race-related variables exhibited substantial bivariate relationships with the vote, but the coefficients for those variables declined to the point where they could not reliably be distinguished from zero after we controlled for our policy-related predispositions. That is, the apparent impact of preferences concerning race-related policies was usually reduced to a non-significant value by controls for general predispositions even without any controls for other current policy preferences or other variables from subsequent stages in our model.

As politicians prepare for the 1996 election, evidence is accumulating that longstanding disagreements concerning affirmative action may increase the electoral relevance of conflicts that are explicitly defined in terms of race as well as those that are indirectly related, such as "welfare." The omission of any race-related policies from our explanatory model for electoral decisions in 1992, however, represents a continuing source of uncertainty. Indeed, as we noted in an extended discussion in the last chapter, our attempt to use NES measures as predispositions to respond to race-related policy conflicts ended in failure. We could not construct a race-related predisposition that possessed a significant apparent total effect on the vote once other variables in the first two stages (including party identification and other policy-related predispositions) were taken into account.

Those who are prepared to stipulate or simply assume that voters' attitudes toward race-related topics are causally prior to all other policy-related predispositions, including attitudes toward "equality" and self-designation as a "liberal" or "conservative," can point to evidence for assigning a *substantial* amount of explanatory "credit" for vote choice to race-related conflicts. We, on the other hand, have taken the position that attitudes toward policy conflicts that are defined in terms of a specific topic should exhibit some independent connection with the vote choice—after we control for attitudes toward other policy-related conflicts—before they are included in our explanatory model. We have not found any evidence of such an independent link connecting race-related policy preferences to the vote in the NES surveys conducted during the 1992 *or* 1988 elections.

At this point, we should emphasize the general nature of the statistical "competition" between alternative explanatory variables in any attempt to identify specific policy conflicts that have an independent impact on electoral decisions. In all of the recent elections we have examined, *many* policy conflicts exhibit a substantial relationship with vote choice after we control for partisan identification as well as social and economic characteristics, but fail to maintain an independent "connection" with the vote after we introduce controls for policy-related preferences in other areas. As with other themes, the competition for "credit" among different theme-related variables should be seen as the result of a statistical procedure in which a substantial number of variables may be "called," but relatively few are likely to be "chosen." The competition is entered with rather lenient standards ($p < .10$) to assure a wide reach for correlates of the vote; the stringent competition is provided by the other candidates that also meet that requirement.

The Logic of Non-significant Policy-related Effects: The Case of Abortion

To illustrate the nature of that general competition, Table 12.6 presents our standard sequence of descriptive statistics for the relationship between voters' policy preferences concerning abortion and their choice between Bush and Clinton. Because of the considerable emphasis on that topic during the 1992 campaign, we present the entire sequence of estimates for abortion, even though the apparent total effect for that variable ultimately turns out to be non-significant. We do so because that sequence may clarify the more general statistical competition among other potential explanatory variables. The ongoing conflict over federal policy concerning abortion did not exert an independent impact on the

Table 12.6 Policy Preferences Concerning Abortion

1. Average Vote for Those Who Prefer "Always Permitted" (N = 558)*	.47
2. Average Vote for Those Who Prefer "Never Permitted" (N = 107)	−.15
3. Difference in Average Vote: Always minus Never	.62
4. Bivariate Unstandardized Regression Coefficient (Policy Preference Scored from −1 to + 1)	.40
5. Coefficient from Multiple Regression with Social and Economic Characteristics Held Constant	.34
6. With Party Identification (Party ID) Also Held Constant	.21
7. With Specific Policy-Related Predispositions (But NOT Party ID) Also Held Constant	.13
8. With Liberal vs. Conservative Self-Designation Also Held Constant	.08
9. With Party ID AND All Policy-Related Predispositions Also Held Constant	.07
10. With Preferences on all Other Policy Issues Also Held Constant	.06
#11. With Perceptions of Current Personal and National Conditions Also Held Constant	(.04)
12. With Retrospective Evaluations of the Current President Also Held Constant	(.01)
13. With Evaluations of the Candidates' Personal Qualities Also Held Constant	(.00)
14. With Prospective Evaluations of the Candidates and Parties Also Held Constant	(−.01)

*The number of cases associated with extreme positions on these and similar measures simply indicate the base on which extreme scores were calculated. Note that the number of cases is unweighted; all other results are weighted.

(Coefficients Appear in Parentheses if the Estimated p Value is $> .1$).

#Indicates estimate of the "apparent total effect" discussed in the text.

vote in the same sense that policy issues on the other five topics did, but it may be helpful to emphasize the *rationale* for its omission from the final set of issues with apparent significant effects on the vote.

Rows 1 and 2 of Table 12.6 document the extent to which voters who thought that abortion should "always" be permitted made quite different choices between Clinton and Bush than those who thought it should "never" be permitted. The much more numerous set of voters with the most liberal position concerning abortion were more loyal to Bill Clinton, with a vote division of +.47, than the much smaller group against abortion in all circumstances were in their support of George Bush, with a vote division of −.15. As indicated in Row 4, the bivariate regression coefficient is quite strong (.40) for the relationship between vote choice and a trichotomous measure of abortion-related preferences in which all "other" responses are grouped into the middle category. That coefficient is only moderately reduced by controlling for religion and all other social or economic characteristics (to .34 in Row 5). Most of the electoral "connection" is nevertheless removed when we control for voters' other policy-related preferences, including their general views concerning morality and homosexuality (down to .06 in Row 10).[6] Furthermore, given the statistical relationships among our full set of policy-related preferences, the coefficient is close to failing to meet our threshold for statistical significance at that point. As a consequence, the introduction of fairly innocuous additional controls for "current conditions" drops the coefficient to a non-significant value, (.04), in Row 11.

In this sense, policy preferences concerning abortion came quite close to being included in our final explanatory model for 1992 even though the independent influence of those preferences would have been fairly small. As in other domains or explanatory themes in our analysis, the electoral role of variables with fairly small effects may be particularly difficult to distinguish from those of closely related topics. In this case, it is difficult to ignore the strong connection between policy preferences concerning abortion per se and other attitudes toward sexuality and morality, but we do believe that the latter take causal precedence over the differences in policy preferences on abortion per se.

Policy-related Conflict Concerning Unemployment

The 1992 campaign involved a substantial emphasis on the continuing level of unemployment in a recession that had been under way since at least 1990. Furthermore, 19 percent of those who voted for Clinton or Bush mentioned unemployment as the "most important problem" facing the country, in addition to the 22 percent who mentioned the more general or undifferentiated problem of "the economy." Despite that fact, direct questions about voters' own policy preferences in that area did not exhibit a significant relationship to the vote after we controlled for other policy-related preferences. In particular, the specific item concerning federal spending on "unemployment" did not provide any significant additional explanatory power beyond that associated with "food stamps" and "the poor," and the same negative conclusion applies to the traditional NES question concerning the government's responsibility for everyone having a "good job and standard of living."

As with abortion, voters' policy preferences concerning unemployment appear to have had very little independent influence on their choices between Clinton and Bush. Many voters did see a major "problem" in the high level of unemployment, and (as discussed in Chapters 13 and 14) appear to have voted against President Bush because of his "performance" in that area, but there is no evidence to suggest that those effects were based on conflicts over the direction of federal policy in that area. At most, voters may have been influenced by differential priorities concerning the urgency of this problem for the federal government. Our measures of policy preference in this domain, however, are limited to the preferred level of governmental "spending" and views on the appropriateness of governmental responsibility for "jobs and standard of living"—neither of which exhibit an independent relationship to the vote.

Policy-related Disagreement Concerning Health Care

Finally, we should emphasize the fact that the standard NES question concerning governmental versus private health insurance also failed to exhibit a significant relationship to the vote after we controlled for partisan and policy-related predispositions. That is, as with preferences for governmental spending and services, we did not even need to introduce controls for current policy preferences in other areas (such as assistance to the disadvantaged) in order to reduce the coefficient associated with health care insurance to a non-significant level. The statistical connection between such preferences and the vote seems to be based on general attitudes toward equality and the role of the government, rather than disagreements over policy alternatives favoring either governmental or private-sector insurance. As in the area of unemployment, however, substantial numbers of voters identified "access to health care" as one of the nation's most important problems. Furthermore, whatever their policy preferences, voters' choices between Clinton and Bush may have been influenced by their prospective assessments of the two candidates concerning their ability to "make health care affordable."

As of the fall of 1992, however, voters' choices for President were not visibly linked to conflicts over articulated policy alternatives concerning health care and health care insurance. After the failure of the Clinton administration's 1994 initiatives in this area, future elections may be more visibly related to policy-related conflicts about health care, and such differences may be easier to detect. This will be true, in particular, if future NES surveys measure differences among voters in the *priorities* they assign to different problem areas—as well as the different policies they prefer. In 1992, however, the electoral relevance of popular concerns about "health care" seems to have been based on "results" rather than visible conflicts about "means."

▪ The Combined Relevance of Policy-related Preferences

So far, our analysis has been designed to clarify the electoral role of several different policy-related predispositions and specific current policy issues. The rationale for this topic-by-topic approach follows an established tradition in the electoral field. Both academic and media-based explanations of the vote are usually defined in terms of a specific set of alternative—or competing—ideas about policy conflicts that have played some role in shaping voters' decisions. As we noted at the beginning of this chapter, the list of potentially relevant policy-related conflicts in the 1992 election is fairly long, and we have devoted most of this chapter to identifying the specific policy-related controversies that might have been activated by the 1992 campaign.

In focusing on the electoral relevance of specific policy-related topics, however, we have not considered the degree to which voters' choices may have been shaped by those conflicts *in the aggregate.* By emphasizing the variety of specific policy preferences that could have played some role in shaping voters' decisions, we have assigned modest or minimal "effects" to each of several different explanatory variables—no one of which appears to have exerted a dominant influence on the vote. As a consequence, both analysts and general readers may underestimate the explanatory power of policy conflicts (as a general type of explanation for vote choice) because each of the specific explanatory variables in that category has been assigned a relatively modest amount of "credit" for influencing the vote. Consequently, in order to provide a more global assessment of the role of policy-related conflicts in elections, we have examined in detail an approach to summarizing the combined electoral role of all the variables that are defined in terms of ideological or policy-related preferences.

To this end we take advantage of the fact that at various points we have noted that voters' preferences in some policy-related areas seem visibly related to their views in other areas. Voters with "conservative" or "liberal" policy preferences in one area are likely to exhibit similarly designated views in other policy areas. It would be easy, however, to exaggerate the overall strength of these relationships. For example, the correlation between Clinton/Bush voters' attitudes toward equality and morality is .37, and the correlation between preferences concerning the military and assistance to the disadvantaged is similar in size. Because of the moderate nature of many such relationships between different policy-related preferences, many voters exhibit attitudes toward our full set of policy-related conflicts that are substantially "mixed," in that their views in some areas support what is generally recognized as a "liberal" and potentially pro-Democratic position while their opinions in other areas support the "conservative" and potentially pro-Republican position—in addition to those areas where they have no opinion or very weak preferences.

Nevertheless, while documenting the extent of "mixed" versus consistent policy-related preferences, we can illustrate the combined influence of those preferences on the vote. We have constructed a single index of liberal versus conservative views from all eight of our policy-related predispositions and the five measures of current policy preferences relevant to vote choice.[7] We must emphasize the fact that this index weighs each policy-related variable equally rather than by the strength of its apparent influence on the vote, and the resulting index should *not* be regarded as a "measure" of any underlying or theoretical variable. In the final section of this book, we discuss a variety of criteria for assessing the combined "importance" for all of our conflict-related variables—and for sets of variables that have been assigned to other explanatory themes in our model. The present thirteen-item index can, however, be used to suggest the combined power of all policy-related preferences in shaping vote choices for Clinton and Bush in 1992.

Table 12.7 presents the Clinton/Bush voters and their average votes for each of twenty-one categories that are defined in terms of seven categories of the summary index and the three categories of party iden-

Table 12.7 The Combined Relevance of Policy-Related Preferences Based on 7-Category Summary Index

Range of Scores on Summary Index (Average of All Policy-Related Opinions)	Republican Identifiers		Independents and Apolitical		Democratic Identifiers		All Clinton/ Bush Voters	
	%	Average	%	Average	%	Average	%	Average
Highly Consistent Conservative (−1.0 to −.5)	25.1%	−.97	8.3%	−.94	0.9%	−.32	9.8%	−.94
Moderately Conservative (from −.5 to −.3)	28.0	−.96	11.5	−.71	4.8	−.12	13.3	−.77
Slightly Conservative (−.3 to −.1)	24.7	−.78	21.5	−.29	16.8	+.64	20.5	−.14
Balanced or No Opinion (−.1 to +.1)	13.8	−.43	26.1	+.48	26.0	+.85	22.7	+.51
Slightly Liberal (+.1 to +.3)	7.8	−.14	14.4	+.74	27.0	+.91	17.8	+.74
Somewhat Liberal (+.3 to +.5)	.6	.56	12.2	+.82	15.8	+1.00	10.5	+.93
Highly Consistent Liberal (+.5 to +1.0)	0.0	....	5.9	+1.00	8.7	+.94	5.4	+.96
TOTAL*	100%	−.77 (328)	100%	+.17 (380)	100%	+.81 (492)	100%	+.17 (1201)

NOTE: Cell entries are average scores on the vote (Clinton = +1, Bush = −1).
*Based on weighted N.

tification. The same table also documents the overall extent to which liberal and conservative preferences are related to party identification. The distribution of the electorate across the five intermediate categories of this index suggests the extent to which voters held "mixed" opinions with an ideological or partisan "tilt" over the range of policy-related preferences that may have influenced voting for Clinton versus Bush.

In particular, Table 12.7 suggests that differences between voters in their conflict- or policy-related preferences may have been responsible for "moving" the average vote among Republicans and Democrats from near unanimity for their party's candidate to modest levels of support for the opposite party—and for moving voters who did not identify with either party all the way from virtual unanimity for Bush, among those who were consistently conservative, to actual unanimity for Clinton, among those who were consistently liberal. The strength of these overall differences has been suggested in several previous studies, including our own essays on the three elections in the 1980s (McClosky et al., 1960; Flanigan and Zingale, 1994; Miller and Shanks, 1981; Shanks and Miller, 1990, 1991). At this point, we simply note the *magnitude* of the overall differences in the vote between the policy-related categories in Table 12.7—both because of their potential relevance for any interpretation of the 1992 election, and because they underscore the rationale for "holding constant" all policy-related preferences when we assess the relevance of other explanatory themes.

The Prevalence of "Mixed" Preferences

Table 12.7 also suggests that more than half of the Bush/Clinton voters can be characterized as ideologically neutral or as only slightly conservative or liberal, based on the middle three categories of our summary index for all policy-related predispositions and current policy preferences. Only about 15 percent can be described as consistently conservative or liberal across all of these policy-related areas. Thus, although the combined set of explanatory variables that are defined in terms of liberal versus conservative opinions appears to have powerfully influenced voters' choices, a majority of voters have a mixture of liberal and conservative views (or "no opinion") which suggests an overall position that is fairly moderate.

Several comparisons of leaders and followers within the two major parties in the United States have emphasized the fact that most rank and file voters have "mixed" or moderate opinions concerning the full spectrum of policy-related issues that have been emphasized in recent presidential elections, while partisan leaders hold views that are much more consistent if not extreme.[8] In most recent elections the major parties have presented candidates and platforms that were designed to appeal to voters with conservative *or* liberal positions on most of the major issues in those campaigns.

The Explanatory Interpretation of Policy-related "Effects": A Cautionary Note

For our purposes, we can also turn to a three-category version of the summary index for policy-related preferences. It preserves the modest pro-conservative central tendency of both the seven-category version and the simple average of all our policy-related variables, and it uses similar "cut points" on both the ideological and the partisan dimensions. Table 12.8 presents the same kind of results as in Table 12.7 for this trichotomized version of our summary index.

From these results, it can more readily be seen that the differences in

Table 12.8 Partisan vs. Policy-Related Antecedents of the Vote Based on 3-Category Index

	Republicans	Independents	Democrats	Total
Conservative	−.93	−.70	+.21	−.69
(−1.0 to −.2)	(211)	(108)	(63)	(382)
Moderate	−.51	+.36	+.81	+.39
(−.2 to +.2)	(106)	(178)	(236)	(520)
Liberal	+.39	+.84	+.99	+.93
(+.2 to 1.0)	(6)	(95)	(190)	(291)
Total	−.77	+.17	+.81	+.17
	(323)	(381)	(489)	(1193)

Regression coefficients for both 3-category variables, from an analysis which holds social and economic characteristics and the "other" predisposition constant

	Unstandardized (b)	Standardized (B)
Party ID	.50	.41
Trichotomous Policy-Related Index	.51	.38

voting behavior that are associated with moving from a neutral or moderate position to a visibly liberal or conservative position for persons in the same category of party identification are apparently approximately as large as the corresponding differences in the vote associated with moving from an Independent to a Republican or Democratic identification for persons with the same approximate positions on our summary of policy-related preferences. As shown in the bottom part of Table 12.8, this general pattern can also be represented by the results of a multiple regression analysis based on these two explanatory "variables" (while also taking into account the voters' social and economic characteristics). As in the tabular format, both the standardized and unstandardized coefficients associated with those two variables are approximately the same when each is estimated with the other held constant. In the final section of this book we will note the consequences of taking account of the causal status of each component in this summary index of policy-related preferences.

Explanatory Interpretation of "Effects": The Relevance of Change over Time

In previous chapters, we have noted that estimates of electoral "effects" for specific political attitudes may be somewhat misleading or confounded if they are partially based on causal processes other than those producing the direct or indirect influences that we have considered. In particular, any analysis of the electoral consequences of voters' own policy-related predispositions or current policy preferences that relies on a single cross-section survey, such as our analysis which is based on the traditional NES design, must consider possible alternative interpretations of the statistical relationship between the preferences and the vote. The relationship may have been at least partially "produced" by a process in which the leader has *persuaded* at least some of his followers to adopt the policy positions he advocated during the campaign—rather than having had the voters select him because he advocated policies that his supporters already preferred. Either the persuasion of a leader or the *prior* policy preference of the voter may be the "cause" of the statistical relationship between policy preferences and votes.

    More generally, direct estimates of policy-related "effects" from single equation models and cross-section survey data may be challenged as troubled by simultaneity bias. The explanatory variables in question such as those based on policy-related preferences may themselves be endogenous to the campaign; they may have been influenced by the same factors (such as leadership and persuasion) that shaped vote choices, in addition to having had some separate influence on the vote. These general possibilities have been acknowledged in Chapters 8 and 11, and are discussed at greater length in our Methodological Appendix (Appendix D). At this point, however, we offer a relevant analysis of the subset of NES 1992 respondents who were also included in a 1990 NES survey (conducted before the 1992 campaign began). In general, these "panel" data permit analysts to re-examine the relevance of policy-related preferences for vote choice in 1992 on the basis of measures that were obtained well before they could have been influenced by the 1992 campaign.

Analysts who are concerned about such endogeneity of policy-related preferences may be suspicious of the size of the differences or coefficients we have reported as associated with our summary index and the 1992 vote. Indeed, several political scientists have expressed the same kind of misgivings about our effect estimates for party identification, because of their conviction that the NES measure of party identification is substantially influenced by short-term forces in any given campaign. Such analysts argue that effect estimates for party identification (from any single equation model) will be inflated because of the impact of other causes of the vote on the same current partisan identifications as well. Both of these potential criticisms, however, can be at least partially addressed by using the "panel" component of the NES 1992 study design.[9]

Specifically, that design makes it possible for us to answer the following question: What would happen to the regression coefficients associated with party identification *and* our summary (trichotomous) index for policy-related preferences if we were to replace both variables in our analysis of the *1992* vote with the same voter's scores on those same two variables measured in *1990*—nearly two years before the 1992 campaign began? If our 1992 indicators of partisan identification and overall policy-related preferences have themselves been influenced by aspects of the 1992 campaign, we should obtain very different results pertaining to the 1992 vote when both variables are replaced by identically constructed measures based on interviews with the same voters two years earlier in 1990.

Table 12.9 documents the changes in vote coefficients for party iden-

Table 12.9 Party ID and Policy-Related Preferences in Relation to the 1992 Vote (Based on Measures from 1990 and 1992*)

	Measures from 1992		Measures from 1990	
	b	beta	b	beta
Party Identification Republican (−1), Independent (0), Democrat (+1)	.57	.49	.58	.50
Trichotomous Policy-Related Summary Conservative (−1), Moderate (0), Liberal (+1)	.40	.31	.23	.16

Number of cases with data on both explanatory variables from both 1990 and 1992 and the 1992 vote (for Clinton vs. Bush) as well as standard social and economic characteristics (from the 1992 interview) = 342.

*(For the same respondents in both analyses.)

tification and our summary index for policy-related preferences when we replace the measures from the 1992 interviews with measures from interviews that were conducted right after the 1990 election. In replacing the two 1992 variables with their counterparts from 1990, *none* of the statistical relationships between those latter variables and the *1992* vote can be attributed to the influence of any aspects of the 1992 campaign— since the relevant data (apart from the 1992 vote) were all collected more than a year *before* Bill Clinton's campaign began and more than two years before the 1992 votes were cast.

In order to compare the coefficients of these two explanatory variables for 1990 and 1992, the number of voters involved must be substantially reduced from the 1992 totals to include only the respondents who were interviewed in both years. Furthermore, the summary index of policy-related preferences must be based on only the variables from 1992 that are also common to both years in order to ensure that identical questions are used for both 1990 and 1992 measures.

Because of these two "technical" changes, the size of the standardized and unstandardized coefficients in Table 12.9 for our summary of policy-related preferences in 1992 is somewhat smaller than the results presented in Table 12.8 for the set of explanatory variables that were used in our review of the full set of *all* policy-related preferences in the

1992 NES survey. In particular, some of the 1992 policy-related preferences that were not included in the 1990 survey had stronger relationships to the 1992 vote than did the remaining policy preferences that
were included in *both* NES surveys. For that reason, this analysis of the
1990–1992 panel begins with some reduction in the apparent explanatory process for policy-related preferences. The "b" for policy-related
preferences with the vote drops from .51 (in Table 12.8) to .40 in 1992
(Table 12.9). The "b" for party identification remains virtually unchanged for the reduced number of cases: in 1992, .50 (in Table 12.8)
becomes .57.

Table 12.9 suggests that *some* of the apparent impact of policy-related
preferences on the 1992 vote may have been based on *some* confounding
influences of the 1992 campaign on our measures of policy-related
preferences as well as the vote. We will turn to that possibility in a
moment, but this same analysis also suggests that *none* of the apparent
impact of party identification on the 1992 vote should be attributed to
its endogeneity in the 1992 campaign. The coefficient for party identification and the 1992 vote goes *up*, slightly, to .58, instead of down,
from .57, when the 1992 measure of party identification is replaced by
answers to the same question in the fall of 1990. As suggested in other
recent analyses (Green and Palmquist, 1990), political scientists who
believe there is a substantial amount of simultaneity bias in cross-section
estimates of the impact of party identification on presidential voting
must contend with fairly powerful evidence to the contrary.

As emphasized in several previous chapters, we believe that partisan
identifications change very slowly, and only rarely during the course of
a single election campaign. That conclusion is reinforced by the absence
of any reduction in the coefficient in party identification where we
replace the 1992 version of that variable with its counterpart from 1990.
This adds to our confidence in our decision to treat our measures of
party identification as a "given" for the analysis of vote choice in the
1992 election.

There are, however, ambiguities concerning the correct interpretation
of the two parallel coefficients for policy-related preferences in 1992 and
1990. On the one hand, it is clear that more than half of the 1992
coefficient (.23/.40) remains after we replace contemporary policy-related preferences from 1992 with answers to the same questions asked
nearly two years before. That much of the apparent electoral relevance

of those preferences in 1992 seems removed from criticism based on endogeneity stemming from the 1992 campaign. Next, it should be recognized that significant political developments took place between the two elections in several of the policy areas covered by our "summary index," including circumstances related to defense, employment, the standard of living, the size of the national debt, and the perceived cost of government welfare programs.

Because of such inter-election events and their influence on relevant policy preferences, those preferences two years later, as of 1992, should presumably be a *consequence* in part of those intervening events. Only *some* of the decline in the 1992 coefficient for policy-related preferences using the same variables from 1990 measures may, therefore, be attributed to "persuasion" or other troublesome forms of endogeneity based on the influence of the 1992 campaign. Given the available evidence, we can only suggest the outer limits to the upward bias described by those who are concerned about the confounding influences on policy-related preferences (from .40 to .23) from other causes of the vote. The nature of those biases and the challenges they pose for electoral analysts are discussed in our Methodological Commentary (Appendix D).

Caveats on Our Interpretation of Effects

It is appropriate here to emphasize again the complexities of the causal relationships that may be involved in shaping the vote according to our multiple-stage model. In addition to confronting problems of endogeneity and simultaneity, we have been led to a number of additional observations that bear emphasis. First, the analytic introduction of policy-related predispositions in the second stage of the model prior to assessing the impact of voters' policy preferences on their 1992 vote decisions has a massive impact on the policy preference/vote relationship. There is probably no single source of the differences between our analytic results and those of other analysts that is more significant than our employment of policy-related predispositions as *antecedents* to policy preferences. This should not be interpreted as suggesting a lesser role for "issue voting." Instead, it makes evident the extent to which specific policy preferences are particular instances of more generic, policy-related orientations. This observation is particularly relevant when reviewing the absence of several prominent topics from our roster of significant independent contributors to the 1992 vote.

A second observation pertains to another limitation imposed by what is essentially a single temporal cross-section view of the 1992 electorate. We have no basis for estimating the magnitude of the extent to which policy conflicts publicized by the campaign have activated relevant predispositions without necessarily changing or otherwise influencing them. In Chapter 8 we noted the ambiguities associated with designating causal elements in our model as "long-term" and "short-term." We see the current problem of interpretation rooted in the same domain of "that which is knowable but unknown" because of limits in the evidence we have. For example, the use of ideological terms may have become more frequent in recent campaigns, and more frequently associated with partisan choices as specific controversies or conflicts have been described as conflicts between liberal and conservative points of view. Therefore, the relationship of ideological terms to the vote may have increased, but not necessarily because the incidence of liberal and conservative sentiments has changed. The change may, instead, have been in the salience or the perceived relevance of the terms.

Data necessary to test such alternative propositions could have been collected with a study design different from that employed by NES in 1992. But in the absence of crucial evidence, we simply treat our predispositions as having developed *prior* to current policy preferences. General predispositions therefore get all of the analytic credit for influencing the vote decision when the credit may be due, as well, to the articulation of specific policy alternatives in the campaign. It is in part for these kinds of reasons that we have decided to reserve conclusions about the overall importance of policy preferences (or the variables in any other theme) until the last section of the book.

Yet another observation emerges from a review of the fate of various policy issues discussed in this chapter. We have often asserted that because of our inability to establish a temporal order for variables located *within* a given stage, we may seriously underestimate the apparent total effect of many specific variables. We are particularly concerned about policy variables that were eliminated in the analysis when placed "in competition" with other policy questions. Policy preferences, as well as other variables, were dropped from our analysis if they did not exhibit statistical independence from the contributions of other preferences in the same analytic state. Issues survived only if they were sufficiently unique or unrelated to other issues to avoid elimination for that reason. It is possible, therefore, that our decision rules inadvertently "dismissed" subsets of issue variables because they were all so highly interrelated with one another. The controls we imposed to minimize spurious relationships may have eliminated policy questions, one by one, that might have survived if they had been organized into multi-item sets of correlated issues, or had they not been placed in competition with items that met our criteria for inclusion in the ultimate set of questions.

At the same time, it should be noted that some of our surprises, such as the failures of the NES "spending and services" question or the question on health insurance, "failed" without reaching the competition with other policy questions. We are more impressed, however, with the fact that items such as those pertaining to government guarantees of full employment and a good standard of living or defense spending had become "core" items for quadrennial analysis *without* confronting the measure of more generic attitudes toward limited government or some of the other predispositions introduced in 1992.

To some extent, the presentation in Tables 12.8 and 12.9 is a reassuring indication that policy-related variables will not be seriously underrepresented when they are ultimately assembled in our assessment of importance in Chapter 17. However, this does not speak directly to the question of inadvertently excluding subsets of highly interrelated policy questions and thereby biasing our particular conclusions concerning the importance of specific issues that were present in the campaigns. Each of the foregoing observations emphasizes the importance of prior decisions on the design of data collections, and of assumptions about causality as important preconditions for multivariate analyses of complex problems.

▪ Explanations Based on Policy Preferences versus Policy-related Evaluations or "Reasons"

As in the preceding chapter on policy-related predispositions, we now turn to a comparison of the apparent role of current policy issues based on the two different approaches to survey measurement and analysis introduced earlier in Chapters 1 and 8. The first of these approaches, as used in this chapter, relies on structured questions concerning voters' own preferences on current policy issues; the second is based on the policy-related responses given by Bush and Clinton voters to the NES open-ended questions evaluating the candidates. We have constructed summary measures for the partisan direction of all responses to the NES open-ended questions on the candidates that deal with military force, assistance to the disadvantaged, homosexuals in the military, public funding to private schools, and taxes—and a similar measure concerning abortion, because of unique aspects of that issue discussed below.

As in Chapter 11, we have compared standardized regression coefficients for the relationships between the vote and two parallel sets of measures concerning the same policy areas, based on structured versus open-ended questions. For both of these methods, Table 12.10 presents coefficients for two different pairs of analyses. In each pair of analyses, one column includes only attitudes toward the five policy issues discussed in this chapter, as well as social and economic characteristics and party identification, while the other column is also based on measures for all of the other explanatory themes in our analysis—including those that presumably intervene between policy preferences and the vote.

For measures based on structured questions, the first of these analyses is similar to one that produced the total effects discussed earlier in this chapter and in Chapter 11. The resulting coefficients for each policy preference are slightly different, however, because they are based on analyses which do not control for perceptions of current conditions. The counterpart coefficients in Table 12.10 for responses to the open-ended questions are based on analyses which include *only* these (specific) policy-related measures, as well as social and economic characteristics and party identification, but which do not include either current conditions or policy-related predispositions.

An example may be helpful in clarifying the nature of these comparisons before we discuss any general conclusions from this table. The standardized regression coefficient for policy preferences concerning the military (based on the structured questions discussed above) is .07. That apparent effect is entirely mediated by the other more proximate variables in our multiple-stage model, so that the "direct effect" coefficient for that variable in our final equation is very small and insignificant, (.01). The standardized coefficient for our summary of all military-related responses to the NES open-ended questions is .05. That standardized coefficient for direct effects is slightly larger, .06, when we also control for the partisan direction of the other responses to open-ended questions about the candidates. It should be noted, however, that this variable based on military-related responses was scored zero for nineteen

Table 12.10 Impact of Current Policy Based on Structured vs. Open-Ended Questions Comparing Explanations Based on Voters' Own Positions vs. Their "Reasons" for Choice*

	Standardized Regression Coefficients for Measures Based on Structured Questions about Respondents' Own Views		Standardized Regression Coefficients for Measures Based on Responses to Open-Ended Question about Candidates		Percentage of Clinton, Bush Voters Who Provided One or More Responses within the Designated Category
	Total Effect (With Other Policies Held Constant)	Direct Effect (With all Other Variables Held Constant)	With Summaries of Likes/Dislikes for Other Policies Also Held Constant	With Summary Measures for All Other Likes/Dislikes Also Held Constant	
Party Identification (same for both methods)	.36	.13	.46	.26	—
U.S./Strength of Military	.07	(.01)	.05	.06	5.2
Aid to Disadvantaged	.07	(.02)	.06	(.02)	16.7
Homosexuals in Military	.10	.04	.04	(.03)	2.4
Public Aid to Private Schools	.05	(.01)	(.02)	(.02)	0.3
Tax Increase	.04	(−.02)	.08	.04	14.8

NOTE: The number of cases (N) used in all of these analyses is 1193.

*All analyses include controls for the standard set of social and economic characteristics, partisan identification, predispositions, and personal/national conditions used in this chapter.

(Coefficients for which the estimated value of p is $>.1$ appear in parentheses).

out of every twenty respondents in this analysis—because only 5 percent made explicit mentions of the topic in responding to the unstructured questions.

Similar results can be seen concerning assistance to the disadvantaged and military service by homosexuals. As with the issue of military strength, the standardized coefficients for both topics based on structured questions (.07 for aid to the disadvantaged, .10 for homosexuals in the military) are only slightly larger than the corresponding coefficients based on open-ended questions (.06 and .04, respectively). Nevertheless, they are larger even after having taken account of the policy-related predispositions that had substantial effects on the relationships in Tables 12.1 and 12.3. These two issue domains are quite different, however, in the frequency with which respondents mentioned these topics in response to the NES open-ended questions. Some 17 percent of all Bush and Clinton voters mentioned some aspect of assistance to the disadvantaged (including "welfare") as a reason for liking or disliking one of the candidates, but only 2 percent referred to military service by homosexuals.

Both methods suggest the distinctiveness of the ongoing issue concerning homosexuals in the military because neither method's standardized coefficient is reduced to insignificance when we control for all of the other explanatory themes in the analysis. However, neither method yields coefficients for attitudes toward assistance to the disadvantaged that are distinguishable from zero after we control for all the other variables in our model—suggesting that such preferences were entirely mediated by voters' more general evaluations of the candidates.

These two ways to assess the role of current policy issues lead to noticeably different conclusions for the remaining two issues in our analysis, concerning public funding for private schools and voters' "willingness" to pay more in taxes. The standardized coefficient for our single (structured) question concerning governmental support for private schools is .05, but the counterpart coefficient based on responses to open-ended questions about the candidates is not distinguishable from zero, in part because fewer than 1 percent of all voters mentioned that topic as a reason for liking or disliking one of the candidates. In contrast, many voters (15 percent) mentioned some aspect of "taxes" as an aspect of Bush or Clinton they liked or disliked, and the standardized coefficient for the variable based on those responses (to open-ended questions) is .08. This is somewhat larger than the marginally insignificant coefficient of .04 from our structured question in that area. We believe that this striking difference is primarily due to the unsatisfactory wording of the (single) NES question in 1992 that was devoted to policy direction concerning taxes. This difference does demonstrate, however, that open-ended questions can be helpful in identifying potentially relevant factors that are not captured by the structured questions in the NES interview schedule.

As with policy-related predispositions, we have also used responses to the NES open-ended questions to identify respondents for whom each issue may be more relevant or "important." Table 12.11 presents the *unstandardized* coefficients for our measures based on structured questions concerning policy direction in each of the above five areas, plus abortion. Each coefficient is presented for the entire sample (Column 2) and for the large subsample of voters who did *not* mention that topic in response to open-ended questions (Column 3). The fourth column assesses the degree to which that coefficient for the structured question is larger or smaller for the minority of voters who *did* mention that topic. In each of our five policy areas, the apparent effect of preferences for voters who did not mention that topic as a reason for choice is not appreciably lower than the estimated coefficient for all voters who did mention the topic. Thus, almost all of the "effects" we have reviewed in this chapter appear to be concentrated among voters who did not mention that topic as a "reason" for liking or disliking either of the candidates.

A notable exception to this general rule concerns the issue of abortion. As discussed earlier in this chapter, the apparent overall impact of policy preferences concerning abortion on the vote is not large enough to pass our standard threshold for statistical significance, and that result is confirmed (but not shown in Table 12.10) for the abortion-related measure based on responses to the NES open-ended questions. The insignificant coefficient for the NES structured question concerning abortion (.04 in Table 12.11) has been included along with evidence which suggests that the apparent impact of policy preferences on this topic is even smaller (.01) when the analysis is restricted to voters who did *not* mention that topic in response to the open-ended questions about the candidates. However, 19 percent of those who voted for Clinton or Bush *did* mention abortion as a reason for liking or disliking one of the

Table 12.11 Differences in Apparent Total Effects of Specific Policy Issues Based on "Mentioning" That Topic as a Reason for Choice

Topic of Current Policy Issue	Percentage Mentioning Topic	Unstandardized Coefficient (b) Based on ALL Voters*	Unstandardized "b" for Base: No Mention	Difference in "b" from Col. 2 Those Who Mention
Use/Strength of Military	5.2	.17	.15	.30
Disadvantaged	16.7	.12	.15	−.14
Homosexuals in Military	2.4	.11	.11	(.10)
Private Schools	0.3	.05	.05	(.16)
Tax Increase	14.8	.04	.05	(−.05)
Abortion	19.3	(.04)	(.01)	.22

*Bush-Clinton voters.

candidates, and the apparent impact of their preferences concerning abortion is a very substantial .22, from (.01) within that minority. In contrast to the results for taxes, we believe the standard NES structured question concerning abortion is a satisfactory measure of preferences, so we are not tempted to attribute the low overall coefficients for that policy issue to faulty measurement. For abortion, however, the NES open-ended question appears to be successful in identifying voters for whom this issue was particularly relevant.

▪ Summary

We have concluded that most electoral analysts would reach some-what similar conclusions about the relevance of some current conflicts concerning policy direction in 1992, regardless of whether they relied on "reasons" based on open-ended questions or structured questions about voters' own preferences on those specific topics. For other con-flicts, however, the results of these two methods diverge in several ways which illustrate the potential strengths and weaknesses of these two approaches.

In particular, the open-ended approach seems to have been successful in identifying individuals for whom the abortion issue was important in the 1992 election. Among voters who mentioned the topic as a reason for liking or disliking one of the major candidates, their preferences concerning abortion appear to have had a substantially greater than average impact on their choice for President. In general, however, the NES open-ended questions do not appear to have been very successful in identifying individuals for whom a specific policy played a larger role in shaping their vote.

Unless one presumes that attitudes toward equality are in some sub-stantial degree the result of attitudes toward race and racial discrimina-tion, we could not find evidence of a significant impact of racial attitudes on the 1992 vote. Neither the various measures of race-related predis-positions nor race-related policy preferences were independently related to the choice between Bush and Clinton—once the possibly confound-ing effects of other long-term factors in stages 1 or 2 were taken into account.

The topic of race was only one of several in which particular policy preferences did not exhibit the expected impact on the vote decision. In each instance, topics such as abortion, government spending, health insurance, or defense spending were strongly related to voters' choices at the bivariate level, but the relationships faded as the confounding influences of various predispositions or other policy preferences were considered and discounted. As a consequence, the inclusion of policy-related predispositions in an early stage of our analytic model must be seen as an important departure from traditional analyses of issue voting.

This component of our model leads to additional analytic considerations. Issues that are largely subsumed under one or another policy-related predisposition do not appear as independent contributors to the vote decision; issues that are not a particular instance of a predisposition, nor highly correlated with other issues, survive the competition for inclusion in our final equation. We may underestimate the importance of the former and be unduly impressed with the latter unless the constraints of our model are kept clearly in mind.

The demonstration, in passing, of the exogenous nature of party identification in 1992 does not resolve many uncertainties about the connections between campaign emphases, the relevance of specific policy-related predispositions, and the salience of pertinent policy preferences. Even with a different and more appropriate design for future data collection, disentangling the various long-term and short-term components of voters' decision-making will be a complex task. In the interim, we have anticipated the pervasive interest in assessing the relative importance of these components and will discuss this further in the final section of the book.

13

★　★　★ | Voters' Perceptions of Current Conditions: Electoral Reward and Punishment Relative to Consensual Governmental Objectives

In the previous two chapters, we concentrated on the apparent influence of a wide variety of policy-related preferences on voters' eventual choices for President. By definition, all of the explanatory variables discussed in those chapters reflected some kind of conflict or disagreement within the society. As anticipated in discussions in previous chapters, however, the electoral consequences of policy-related conflicts are often combined with those of a second—and fundamentally different—type of "issue" in a given campaign. This chapter deals with the electoral effects of this second type of issue, which is based on broad consensus (instead of conflict) within the electorate concerning those circumstances or conditions that are desirable (such as a strong economy) or undesirable (such as pollution). Issues based on consensually agreed upon objectives for government develop as incumbent politicians are evaluated positively when current conditions are seen as good and negatively when conditions are regarded as bad.

In theory, a "pure" issue in this second category would not involve any disagreement about governmental objectives, priorities, or benefits—for its electoral effects would be entirely based on the degree to which current conditions, usually attributed to the incumbent administration, satisfy some consensual desired objective. In practice, however, topics or "problems" that are emphasized in a campaign often involve a combination of *both* kinds of issues—with very different implicit criteria for political evaluations. For example, campaign issues that are defined in terms of the budget of the national government usually involve a combination of perceptions concerning the desirability of a balanced budget (a consensual objective) and disagreements (conflicts) concerning the relative priority of reducing taxes or cutting spending. For a variety of reasons, including this implicit combination of policy and conditions in the definition of current "problems," explicit political evaluations of the President or a candidate are likely to be influenced by both kinds of issues.[1]

Appraisals of conditions are conceptually quite different from appraisals of policies. Nevertheless, at times there is a temptation to think that voters judge conditions in the context of the policies that produced them, for instance, "the economy is in trouble because of Reaganomics." It is also true that perceptions of "conditions" may lead to preferences for ameliorating current policies, for example, "we should increase defense spending because our military establishment is out of date." Our uncertainty as to which is the chicken and which is the egg, or which has causal precedence, has led us to place both themes in the same (third) causal stage in our model. Both policy preferences and assessments of conditions are sources for political evaluations and both may have a major impact, even when the question involved appears to refer to an entirely consensual objective—such as approval or disapproval of the President's handling of the economy. These two types of sources for political evaluations are portrayed in Figure 13.1.

The final section of this book is devoted to comparisons of the aggregate role played by each of our eight explanatory themes when the effects of all variables that belong to each explanatory theme are combined—such as the combined effects of all "current conditions" or all "current policy issues." In the present chapter, we focus on the theme defined by the apparent impact of voters' perceptions of "current conditions" in several specific areas.

▪ Current Conditions and "Performance-Based" Voting

In some discussions of "performance-based" voting, the causal processes that link perceptions and evaluations of current conditions to the vote are described as simpler or "easier" for the voter than "rational choices" based on policy-related preferences. Voters who see current conditions, whether national or personal, as unsatisfactory or "bad" may well assign responsibility to the incumbent administration and therefore acquire a

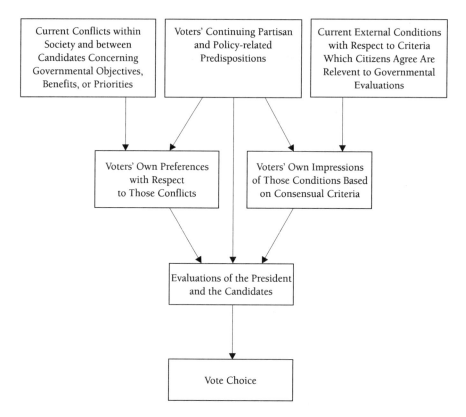

Figure 13.1 Sources of political evaluations based on conflict versus consensus.

negative impression of that administration. This will increase the likelihood they will vote *against* the President's party. In contrast, citizens who see current conditions as satisfactory, or "good," acquire positive impressions of the administration and this, in turn, increases the likelihood that they will vote *for* the President's party. Such processes are presumably likely to lead voters to punish (or reward) the incumbent party for the current "state of the nation" or other conditions where they see the President as at least partially responsible.

To clarify the role played by perceptions of current conditions per se, we explore in this chapter the impact of such perceptions on the 1992 vote. The analysis is based on survey questions that cannot be construed as "leading" questions because they make no reference to a current President or administration, nor to parties or policies that might be responsible for the perceived conditions.

At several points we have suggested that according to many analysts' evaluations, George Bush's performance as President made the largest single contribution to the aggregate result of the 1992 election—for example, substantially larger than the contribution of policy issues or the personal qualities of George Bush and Bill Clinton. Media presentations of the 1992 election were nearly unanimous in their conclusion that, in turn, the single most important factor in influencing voters' evaluations of President Bush's performance and, through those evaluations, their 1992 vote, was the voters' impressions of current economic conditions.

Current Conditions As the Most Important Problem Facing the Country

A context for our exploration of "conditions" surrounding the 1992 election is provided by responses to the perennial NES question concerning the most important problem facing the country. Voters' perceptions defining *the* most important problem have, over the years, captured highlights often provided by the campaign itself. In 1980, for example, the "Misery Index" that Jimmy Carter had invented in 1976 to encapsulate dissatisfaction with the combined levels of high unemployment, high interest rates, and high inflation preceding the election contest with President Ford was reemployed by President Carter's opponent, Ronald Reagan. It resonated with almost half of the Carter-Reagan voters, who named some aspect of the national economy as the nation's leading problem. At the same time, as shown in Table 13.1, one out of every seven major party voters reflected the attention that was focused on Iran and the hostage crisis of 1980 and named our relationship with Iran and the hostages as the nation's most pressing problem.

Four years later the Reagan re-election campaign benefited from the President's emphasis on national defense. But if one in six of the Reagan-Mondale voters in 1984 thought defense was the number-one national problem, an even larger group—21 percent of all voters—saw government spending as the major problem. In the Bush-Dukakis contest of 1988, government spending was again, by an even larger margin, the dominant preoccupation of the electorate. It had traded places with the inflation of eight years earlier and topped the array of national problems, while articulated concerns about inflation had virtually disappeared from the map. More generally, Table 13.1 illustrates the volatility with which the short-term conditions surrounding presidential

Table 13.1 The Single Most Important Problem Facing the Country as Described by Major Party Voters, 1980–1992[a]

	1980	1984	1988	1992
Social Welfare[b]	7%	12%	18%	16%
Health	—	—	2	6
Welfare	4	6	6	3
Law and Order	1	3	18	9
Drugs	—	*	11	2
Crime	1	1	3	2
Morality[c]	*	2	3	5
Racial Problems	*	*	1	2
Economic Problems	54	43	45	63
Inflation	33	4	1	*
Unemployment	7	10	4	19
Government Spending	2	21	33	16
"The Economy"[d]	3	2	1	22
Foreign Affairs	22	17	6	2
Iran	14	—	*	—
Latin America	*	2	*	—
Defense	9	15	3	1
Functioning of Government[e]	2	2	1	2
Natural Resources[f]	2	1	5	1
	97%[b]	93%	100%	101%

*Indicates less than one-half of one percent.

a. Entries are proportions of Two-Party Voters.

b. Columns do not total 100%: Unemployment is sometimes regarded as a component of "Social Welfare" but is listed under Economic Problems in this table; small categories such as Agriculture and Labor Management or idiosyncratic themes such as "Watergate" are not tallied.

c. In 1992 only one major party voter mentioned religion in government or politics as a problem.

d. "The Economy" refers to responses with no specific referent (such as inflation or unemployment).

e. "Government" includes all references to the functioning of government: Size, power, ethics, trust, efficiency or waste, states' rights, experience, etc., except for government spending.

f. "Natural resources" includes all references to pollution or the environment or resource development.

elections change. Although the arenas of foreign affairs, domestic social welfare, and the economy are omnipresent, the specific policy conflicts highlighted in election campaigns come and go with astounding speed and vigor.

The election of 1992 took place in a context literally defined by economic problems. It is true that popular concerns with public health and medical care were more visible than in recent years, but fewer than one in ten named health care as the nation's first concern. And the call for a resurrection of the nation's moral standards impressed even fewer voters: only 5 percent named some version of moral decay as their nominee for "most important problem." On the economic side, however, almost one in four of the Clinton-Bush voters simply said "the economy," with no further elaboration, when identifying the nation's most important problem; another one in five said "unemployment," and an additional one in six said "government spending." All told, 63 percent of the voters listed one or another economic problem as the most important of the problems facing the nation. Inflation was no longer the bugaboo concerning the future of personal finances, but the specter of unemployment and high government spending in the midst of a generally unpromising economic future provided a challenge for the incumbent Bush and an opportunity for the aspirant Clinton.

▪ Economic Conditions in 1992

In anticipation of economic rewards and punishment, the NES inquiry into the 1992 election devoted unprecedented attention to voters' perceptions of economic conditions—past, present, and future. Twelve separate questions dealt directly with the single topic; one was directed to perceptions of the American position as a competitor in international markets, four were centered on different features of the national economy, and seven were assessments of economic conditions focused on household and family finances. A thirteenth question somewhat more ambiguously assessed the United States' "position in the world" as having become stronger or weaker. A selective summary of our multi-stage analyses of the results of these inquiries is presented in Table 13.2.[2]

Perhaps the first thing to note, in the left-hand column of Table 13.2, is that the NES presumption of the electoral relevance of each condition was broadly supported in preliminary analysis. Ten of the twelve eco-

Table 13.2 Summary of Coefficients for Electoral Relevance of (Economic) Conditions for Two-Party Vote in 1992

	After Controlling Social and Economic Characteristics (Row 5)	After Adding Long-Term Elements to Controls (Row 9)	Total Effect After Adding Policy Preferences and Other Conditions (Row 11)
International			
U.S. Competitiveness Past Year	.44	.15	(.07)
U.S. Position in the World	.28	.09	.06
National			
Unemployment Past Year	.63	.21	(.08)
Inflation Past Year	.39	.12	(.02)
National Economy Next Year	.14	(.02)	(−.02)
Current State of the Economy	.63	.24	.19
Family			
Income Past Year	.22	(.05)	(−.02)
Economic Problems Past Year	.33	.09	(.04)
Future Family Finances	(.08)	(−.03)	(−.09)
Changes in Finances	.27	.12	(.04)
Fear of Future Unemployment in Family	.15	.08	(.05)
Experienced Layoff	(.35)	.44	.40

nomic items were clearly related to the two-party vote in bivariate analyses. Moreover, all items except for layoff experience and the query on family finances "next year" were significantly related to vote choice even after controlling for the possible confounding effects of voters' prior social and economic characteristics.

The apparent effect coefficients are reduced by almost two-thirds when the full set of long-term factors is taken into account. Particularly where perceptions of national and international conditions are concerned, long-term factors presumably in place well before the 1992 contest was joined were clearly very important antecedents. In two instances, taking account of the long-term factors reduced the coefficients reflecting apparent electoral relevance below the level of statistical significance (when $p > .1$).

The third column in Table 13.2 shows the consequences of next taking into account the factors in our third stage. Once policy preferences and the "other conditions" are taken into account, or controlled, only three out of the original twelve "conditions" continued to be significantly related to the vote. These three situations were based on NES respondents' perceptions of (1) changes in the national economy (since the previous year), (2) the U.S. "position" in the world, and (3) job layoff experienced by someone in the respondent's family.[3]

Table 13.3 presents our standard series of descriptive statistics concerning the relationships between perceived conditions in these three domains and the vote. As with the explanatory variables reviewed in other chapters, the three measures all exhibited strong bivariate relationships with the vote. Judging from the first four rows of Table 13.3, and without taking the possible effects of the various origins of voters' perceptions into account, it would appear that each of these three perceptions of conditions had a substantial impact on the voters' choice for President. In particular, it is clear that voters with different views of the national economy made quite different choices (on average) between Bill Clinton and George Bush.

The strength of the bivariate relationship between perceptions of the economy and the vote (.79 in Row 4) is only slightly reduced when we control for social and economic characteristics (to .63 in Row 5). Perceptions of the economy were, to a remarkable extent, shared by rich and poor, young and old, Black and White, men and women across all of the social and economic categories involved in our analysis. Views of

Table 13.3 The Electoral Relevance of Current Conditions

	State of the Economy	U.S. Position in the World	Layoffs in Household
1. Average Vote Among Those With Negative Conditions Much Worse, Worse, Some Layoff (N = 466) (N = 413) (N = 17)	.56	+.48	.58
2. Average Vote Among Those With Positive Conditions Much Better, Better, No Layoff (N = 55) (N = 327) (N = 1176)	−.69	−.28	.17
3. Difference in Average Vote: Most Negative minus Most Positive	+1.26	.76	.41
4. Bivariate Unstandardized Regression Coefficient (Economy/Position Scored −1 or +1, Layoffs 0 to 1)	.79	.38	.41
5. Coefficient from Multiple Regression with Social and Economic Characteristics Held Constant	.63	.28	(.35)
6. With Party Identification (Party ID) Also Held Constant	.36	.16	.40
7. With Other Specific Policy-related Predispositions (But NOT Party ID) Also Held Constant	.38	.15	.40
8. With Liberal vs. Conservative Self-designation Also Held Constant	.34	.13	.43
9. With Party ID AND All Policy-related Predispositions Also Held Constant	.24	.09	.44
10. With Preferences on All Current Policy Issues Also Held Constant	.22	.08	.45
#11. With Perceptions of Other Current Conditions Also Held Constant	+.19	+.06	+.40
12. With Retrospective Evaluations of the Current President's Performance Also Held Constant	(−.03)	(−.00)	+.24
13. With Evaluations of the Candidates' Personal Qualities Also Held Constant	(−.04)	(−.01)	+.30
14. With Prospective Evaluations of the Candidates' Future Performance Also Held Constant	(−.06)	(−.00)	+.25

*The number of cases associated with extreme positions on these and similar measures simply indicate the base on which extreme scores were calculated. Note that the number of cases is unweighted; all other results are weighted.
(Coefficients Appear in Parentheses if the Estimated p Value is > .1).
#Indicates estimate of the "apparent total effect" discussed in the text.

the nation's economy were only moderately influenced by past experiences captured in voters' social and economic attributes.

However, the value of the apparent effects coefficient for perceptions of the economy is reduced by more than half when we introduce the political considerations embedded in party identification (.36 in Row 6) or policy-related predispositions (.34 in Row 8). Although the long-term partisan predispositions and the policy-related predispositions are clearly interrelated, they are different enough to produce a still smaller coefficient, .24, when combined, as in Row 9. Perceptions of the national economy were defined by the relevant NES question as "short-term" influences, change within the past year, but a very large part of their connection with the vote (55/79ths) occurred through the activation of relatively longstanding predispositions. We noted the same pattern based on the influence of long-term factors on short-term evaluations in the preceding chapter in our analysis of policy preferences.

The coefficient for the state of the nation's economy is further reduced when we also take into account voters' current policy preferences and other current conditions (.19 in Row 11). Nevertheless, the apparent effect of economic perceptions on the vote still remains large enough to justify the widespread belief in the independent contributions of economic conditions to the 1992 election.

Furthermore, we should note that the NES question used to elicit voters' views of the state of the national economy could not produce a very precise assessment of the current state of economic affairs. Our measure of the total effect for perceptions of the national economy must underrepresent their real influence because the NES question was limited to perceptions of *change* in the past year. The substantial group of voters who saw the economy as "the same" as the year before must have included many individuals who thought the economy had been in trouble for some time, but had not actually gotten worse in the past year. In 1992 this was at least arguably the case because news headlines had dwelt on the prolonged high level of unemployment for well over a year. Moreover, as we continue our sequential analysis, the ultimate impact of voters' perceptions of the economy appears to have been entirely mediated by evaluations(s) of George Bush's performance as President. The effect estimate that remains after we control for those evaluations is small and insignificant ($-.03$ in Row 12).

The United States' Position in the World

Voters' impressions of the U.S. position in the world (as relatively strong or weak) were also related to vote choice at a level which, although somewhat weaker, is still quite visible (and statistically significant at .06 in Row 11) after we control for all other conditions and current policy preferences as well as all explanatory variables in previous stages in our model. As with perceptions of the national economy, the impact of voters' impressions in this arena appeared to have a significant effect that seemed to be entirely mediated by their evaluation of George Bush as President. Given the emphasis on foreign policy during the Bush administration and his campaign, it comes as something of a surprise to note the rather limited apparent total effect. On the other hand, it is not surprising that impressions of the U.S. position in the world had a relationship to the vote choice that was apparently completely accounted for in the explicit evaluations of President Bush.

Egocentric Voting

In addition to the apparent effects of various perceptions of national conditions, voters who reported that someone in their family had experienced a layoff from employment during the previous year were much more likely than other voters to choose Clinton instead of Bush. The explicitly short-term nature of the apparent effect of those layoffs is evident in that the effect remains approximately the same when we control for other conditions and all policy-related variables *and* party identification, as well as social and economic characteristics. However, that layoff-related effect is only moderately reduced when we control for voters' evaluations concerning presidential performance, the candidates' personal qualities, and future performance—suggesting a kind of electoral "effect" that was not mediated by any of the other political attitudes in our analysis.

These analytic results are thought-provoking on at least two dimensions. First of all, experience of layoff in the household would seem to be the essence of an egocentric "pocketbook issue." It stands in clear contrast to the socio-tropic focus of a concern with the national economy. And, at first glance, the relationships to the voters' choice seem a good fit with conventional wisdom: the bivariate relationship is much stronger for socio-tropic perceptions of the national economy, .79, than for the egocentric experience with layoff, .41. However, once the contributions of the long-term factors are taken into account, experience with unemployment in the household apparently played a more important role in voters' decisions than did perceptions of general economic conditions in the nation (.40 vs. .19 in Row 11). Put another way, emphasis on the national economy during the election campaign apparently activated a host of longstanding predispositions that were not similarly associated with personal experience with unemployment. This comparison is not a rigorous test of the relative political significance of egocentric and socio-tropic economic concerns, but it at least suggests a line for further inquiry.[4]

By the same token, the robust nature of the egocentric contribution as a *direct* effect on the vote calls for further examination in and of itself. The ultimate coefficient of .25 in Row 14 testifies to an apparent importance for family layoff experience as a direct antecedent to the vote. It is, therefore, also evidence of the failure of our assembly of explicitly political attitudes to account for the difference in vote choice between voters whose families had recently experienced a job layoff and those whose families had not. To the extent that our objective is to understand the explanatory role of each variable related to the vote, a large unexplained coefficient is a measure of failure and a challenge to pursue a more adequate solution.

The limits to our theoretical understanding of the political implications of voters' economic experiences are further suggested by juxtaposing yet a third result of our analytic procedures. In Table 13.2, an index of the voter's family's experience with "economic problems during the past year" has a bivariate relationship with the vote, .33, equivalent to that for layoff in the household, .35. And yet the relationship involving other economic problems of the voter's family, in contrast to that with layoff experience, is almost totally the result of common antecedents located in our first two stages of explanation. Once those confounds are removed, the relationship with vote choice completely disappears (.04) in the eleventh row of our model in Table 13.2. The same analytic procedures reveal an apparent *increase* in the effect coefficient, .40, associated with a job layoff in the family.

Economic Problems in the Household

A detailed scrutiny of the components of the index of family experience with economic problems does not resolve our quandary. As might be expected, those reporting problems reflected their relative socioeconomic marginality in their lower rates of voting turnout: the 11 percent of the total electorate who reported that they fell behind in rent or mortgage payments during the past year reported 28 percent less voting than did others; the 30 percent who said they had to put off medical or dental care because of family financial straits reported 17 percent lower turnout; and the turnout of the 52 percent who said they had to put off buying things they really needed was down 11 percent from that of those who did not have to report delaying needed purchases.

Bivariate relationships between experience with domestic household economic problems and vote choice were even stronger. Among those who had to postpone purchases, the Clinton share of the two-party vote was up over 50 percent (from 47 percent to 71 percent); problems with medical expenses were associated with a 35 percent larger vote for Clinton, as was true for those who fell behind in their housing payments. Despite such apparent evidence of the relevance of recent economic hardship, the removal of the (confounding) influence of such enduring or long-term antecedents as party identification and policy-related predispositions reduces the effect coefficient associated with the multi-item index of experience with economic problems by more than 70 percent (to .09, the middle column in Table 13.2). The removal of the possible confounding effects of intercorrelations with other "conditions" or with current policy preferences eliminates all remaining positive evidence of contributing to our explanation of the vote by considering family experience with financial problems during the previous year. This, of course, joins our other estimates as a conservative assessment of possible causal influence. This is so because the fact that the effect coefficient disappears when we estimate the total effect (an insignificant .04 in the right-hand column) does not include the possibility that "economic problems" had an indirect effect through the variables that we have added as controls. Nevertheless, with an estimated total effect of approximately zero, "family economic problems" joins a host of other indicators of egocentric self-interest reported in the literature as similarly not connected to the voters' choices.

Job Layoff and the Vote

The contrast with the impact of a job layoff in the family (with an apparent total effect coefficient of .40) is striking, and it may reflect the relatively greater severity of actual unemployment. It may also be that the difference lies in the persistent criticism of the Bush administration for denying that unemployment was really a serious problem during the year or more prior to the election. If so, much of this judgment was missed in voters' assessments of Bush's handling of the economy, and the direct effect of experience with employment layoffs remained a very substantial .25. The other side of the politicization coin is the conventional wisdom that holds that the heavily apolitical outlook of the less advantaged members of the electorate means they search for explanations of personal plight that are remote from national politics. In any event, it seems evident that both everyday experiences with economic hardship and the traumatic experience of being laid off can be given political interpretations. The different processes that connect the voters' economic and political worlds are not well understood, and the contrast between the political consequences of the two examples of presumed egocentric economic interest makes this point.

▪ Long-Term and Short-Term Elements of Policy-related Attitudes and Preferences

At the beginning of this chapter we observed the growth and decay of popular definitions of the most important problems facing the nation. The often dramatic shifts in the salience of different topics, as shown in Table 13.1, seemed to validate our treatment of policy preferences as medium-term if not short-term forces. References to drugs, inflation, defense, and unemployment come and go from one election to another as conditions change and produce changes in the definitions of the nation's most important problems. A review of the "elaboration" tables in this and the last two chapters provides at least two additional perspectives for viewing the role of long-term and short-term preferences in influencing voters' decisions.

The less surprising of two general conclusions supported by a review of the elaboration tables of the last two chapters is that "conditions" have a very limited impact on the apparent effect of policy preferences on the vote. The fact that controlling for conditions makes virtually no difference, issue after issue, to the policy preference/vote relationships suggests that policy preference influences on the vote are not highly correlated with voters' perceptions of conditions. "Conditions" were placed in the same causal stage as policy preferences simply because we did not, and do not, know which might be relevant to the other's relationship to the vote. We now know that the linkages between policy preferences and conditions, relevant to the vote, are not strong.

In the elaboration analysis of policy preferences in the last chapter, adding "conditions" (in Row 11 of the tables) to the controls for other policy issues made absolutely no contribution to our explication of issue voting. In this chapter we have seen in Table 13.3 that adding current policy preferences to the elaboration of the contributions of "conditions" (Row 10) adds nothing to our understanding of the role of conditions in shaping the vote decision. We still have little basis for placing preferences and conditions in separate stages following a presumption that one is more often contingent on the other, but at this point in our analysis the placement seems not to be a matter of great practical importance.

A much more significant by-product of our analyses is the discovery that very impressive bivariate relationships between conditions and the vote are as vulnerable to controls on long-term predispositions (the difference between coefficients in Row 5 and Row 9 in Table 13.2) as are the policy preference/vote relationships. The connections linking vote choice to perceptions of conditions as well as to "medium-term" policy preferences are often largely the result of the long-term factors located in the first and second stages of our model. Where policy preferences are concerned, taking account of social and economic characteristics as well as the second-stage partisan and policy-related predispositions reduces the regression coefficient for our measure of attitudes toward the disadvantaged from .92 to .14; for attitudes concerning the military, the reduction is from .79 to .20; and for taxes, .34 becomes .05. Where issues of more recent origin are concerned, the contrast is somewhat less sharp: the coefficient for attitudes toward homosexuals in the military goes from a bivariate .42 to .13, and aid to private schools from .17 to .05. Even then the coefficients that remain to be attributed to short-term influences after taking account of possible long-term origins are all very limited.

In the case of the three conditions analyzed in Table 13.3, the contrast is not quite as striking because the apparent total effects remain larger than was generally true for specific policy preferences. Nevertheless, the same generalization covers both policy preferences and perceptions of conditions: although there is enough volatility to warrant distinguishing preferences and conditions from *long-term* predispositions, much of their relationship to the vote is confounded by the same long-term predispositions. This provides strong evidence that what we observe in voters' attitudes and perceptions is the result of relatively stable, enduring political orientations being activated by the events surrounding the election and the election campaign itself. Campaigns come and go, but voters' partisan and policy-related predispositions change only slowly.

It is important to note that the same conclusion holds in every single case for the many instances of policy preference that did not have significant apparent total effects on the vote and, therefore, will not appear in our ultimate equation assessing the importance of different contributions to the vote. Several traditional NES seven-point scales had very substantial initial effect coefficients for their bivariate relationship to the vote, but they were coefficients that virtually disappeared when common antecedents defined by long-term variables were taken into account. Different preferences for public or private health insurance started with a bivariate coefficient of .57, which dropped to a non-significant (.05) once long-term antecedents were controlled; the choice between government services and reduced spending dropped to (.05) from an initial .76; attitudes toward the death penalty declined from a bivariate .30 to (−.02). Similar results held for attitudes toward abortion, government guarantees of jobs and a good standard of living, aid to Blacks, and affirmative action, among other contemporary policy topics. Long-term factors such as party identification, ideological self-placement, and policy-related predispositions are powerfully important in shaping voters' responses to the short-term elements of an election, including both the context provided by perceived conditions and that generated when candidates offer conflicting policy alternatives.

The contrast between the limited coefficients of apparent total effects and the unbridled partisan claims made in the midst of a campaign, or in the days after the election, is of profound importance to the interpretation or meaning accorded election results. Differences in policy preferences or assessments of conditions between—or among—different groups of voters suggest the starting point for the interpretation of election results. Taking possible confounding factors (variables) into account is essential and must usually go beyond the simple "control" for the voters' party identifications, age, or education.

The juxtaposition of the assemblage of thirteen policy-related attitudes with party identification, presented in the last tables in Chapter 12, was essential to make the point that policy-related attitudes and policy preferences *are* major, independent elements in electoral decision-making by the voter. The separation of long-term and short-term components is equally essential to placing the origins of issue voting in an appropriate temporal context.

Virtually every NES question on policy preferences revealed voter preferences highly related to their choice between candidates, but most of each such relationship can be accounted for in terms of established antecedents common to both policy preference and vote choice. And there are few policy preferences or perceptions of conditions identified with the 1992 election campaign that added to the influence of long-term factors on the vote in our issue-by-issue search for explanations of voters' choices. Of course, for such a conclusion to be valid, our descriptions of partisan and policy-related predispositions as relatively stable, enduring reflections of values more or less central to the voters' ways of perceiving and thinking about political matters must be accurate. On the face of the matter, the predispositions do not refer to the candidates, the parties, or current policy choices that could be made; and they are rather general in their referents. Furthermore, the more elaborate measures of morality, equality, and preferences for limited government activity have been rather stringently tested for statistical reliability and construct validity. But, as we noted early in Chapter 11, the difference between a predisposition and a policy preference sometimes seems no more than a matter of degree. The present level of uncertainty among researchers concerning policy-related predispositions is not unlike that which prevailed with the early interpretations of party identification. It took long-term panel studies in a variety of political contexts to provide independent evidence that confirmed the existence of presumptive qualities that earlier had been attributed to the concept.

If the presumed "long-termedness" of the policy-related predispositions can ultimately be verified, numerous intellectual challenges will follow. For example, since the days of Lazarsfeld and *The People's Choice* concepts of activation or mobilization have been set against conversion or persuasion. We mentioned earlier the possibility that campaign emphasis on a matter of public policy may "activate" relevant predispositions as well as add an independent influence on vote decisions. It is not clear that even with ideal designs for data collection we would have the analytic capacity to demonstrate that "activation" is not also persuasion. When activation occurs, can we give proper credit to the proximate cause—the stimulus of the campaign—or do our analytic procedures give unwanted precedence to the predispositions?

With appropriate allocation of variables to different causal stages, we can distinguish that which is more or less unique to the outcome of each election and that which successive elections have in common and which therefore reflects continuity in the mass politics of the nation. Inasmuch as a major objective for our present work is to advance our understanding of mass electoral behavior to permit the rigorous comparison of elections across time as well as across cultures, the distinction between longer term and shorter term lies at the heart of the enterprise.

▪ Summary

As in several previous elections, voters' perceptions of current conditions were clearly linked to their vote for President in 1992. Voters' perceptions of the national economy (largely negative) were strongly related to their choice between Clinton and Bush; and a visible portion of that relationship remained after we controlled for other current conditions and all policy-related variables as well as party identification and social or economic characteristics. The apparent effect disappeared, however, when we also controlled for voters' evaluations of George Bush's performance as President. That result reinforces the hypothesis that the effects of national conditions were entirely mediated by voters' evaluations of the "job" George Bush was doing as President. However, the much larger apparent effect associated with unemployment (a coefficient of .40 when someone in the family had been "laid off" within the past year) reveals a limitation of our explanatory scheme or the measures derived for it.

At the same time, the contrast between the socio-tropic view of the nation's economy and the egocentric response to unemployment in the household led us to elaborate our understanding of both. We observed that the greater strength of the socio-tropic relationship with the vote was eliminated when relevant predispositions were taken into consideration and their confounding of the relationship was removed. It is also important to note more generally that voters' contemporary views of "conditions" and their connection with the vote are subject to the same pervasive influence of partisan and policy-related predispositions as are policy preferences.

14

★ ★ ★ | Retrospective and Prospective Evaluations of Candidate and Party Performances

The transition from a focus on conditions—the voters' assessments of the state of the nation, or of self—to a concern with explicit evaluations of candidates and their parties is more than a simple move from one stage of our causal model to another. As we noted at some length in Chapter 8, the clarity and certainty with which causal relationships can be established, or at least presumed, diminish as we move analytically into realms based on voters' direct *evaluations* of candidates. This chapter proceeds by first examining explicit evaluations of the results of the current President's administration. After assessing the electoral effects of such evaluations, we will turn to the relationships between those evaluations and their antecedents. In particular, we will emphasize the degree to which presidential evaluations appear to be shaped by continuing conflicts within the society—in addition to perceptions of current conditions and long-term partisan identifications.

In this chapter, as we move closer and closer to the vote itself, we are more and more likely to encounter evaluations that have been shaped—or partially caused—by tentative vote choices. When such evaluations occur, that which we are attempting to explain, the voter's choice between candidates, becomes the cause. An "explanation," such as the voter's perception of the challenger's party as *more* likely to expand governmental activities, or the voter's conclusion that the incumbent did a good job in handling the nation's economy, often becomes a "rationalization" defending a vote choice that may, in fact, have been based on quite different "causes."[1]

389

The problem is ubiquitous. It need not concern only the vote. Retrospective evaluations of the accomplishments of the Bush administration (in the fourth stage of our model) might occasionally be the result of comparing the personal qualities of Bush and Clinton (in the subsequent fifth stage): "I think Clinton is much more competent than Bush—and I guess (therefore) Bush did not do as good a job as President as he could have." We believe, however, that it is much more likely, or more often the case, that the appraisal of Bush's personal qualities (for instance, competence) is based on his performance as President and head of the national government (for example, he did a good job and *thereby* demonstrated his competence) rather than the reverse. Nevertheless, once the analytic focus goes beyond the social and economic characteristics of the voter, the causal status of any set of variables is, in principle, open to question. In the later "short-term" stages, where simultaneity or feedback is more likely, establishing the direction of causality is most problematic.

We have assigned variables to one or another causal stage in our model because of theoretical notions—or because of relationships exhibited among sets of data other than those we are examining. In Chapters 6 and 7, for example, we reviewed the many collections of panel data that provided evidence for the location of party identification in the second stage of our model. In preparation for this book we tested these conclusions again, and we concluded that party identification in 1992 appeared to have much the same causal status as in 1956–58–60, 1972–74–76, January to November 1980, and so on. At the same time, we are very aware of the fact that party identification in 1992 may have been partially caused by voters' response to President Bush's performance as a Republican president—just as party identification in 1984 and 1988 was to some extent the result of President Reagan's emphasis on conservative Republicanism.[2]

The task of assigning probable temporal sequence and location in a causal order becomes much more difficult and the results less certain as we concentrate on causal stages that involve direct candidate evaluations. Because the candidate evaluations are more clearly influenced by short-term forces than are variables in earlier causal stages, it is more difficult to disentangle causal relationships (which always involve temporal sequence) among the evaluations.

Expectations for the Future

The last stage in our model—short of asking for the respondents' vote decision—is a comparison of expectations for the prospective performance of the parties and of the candidates competing for the presidency. These expectations should, we believe, have been preceded by all of the long-term, medium-term, and short-term considerations that were "in place" at the beginning of the election campaign or that emerged during the campaign. The effects of the campaign should have been to activate the long-term predispositions by altering the salience of the predispositions and the other medium-term policy-related considerations, *and* by bringing into view the incumbent's record and the short-term influences resulting from comparisons of the personal qualities of the two candidates—the latter being particularly important when the challenger (Bill Clinton in 1992) begins the campaign as an unfamiliar newcomer to national politics. All of this should add up to voters' expectations for the future—explicitly assessed in part through prospective party and candidate performance evaluations—as the considerations most proximate to the actual vote choice.

There are, however, at least two likely sources of error in any analysis of the voter's portrayal of expectations concerning candidates' future performance. First and most obvious, with a perspective we have already discussed, is the fact that the question "which candidate would do a better job at [solving the problem of poverty]?" is a close cousin to the question of which candidate you prefer as President. This is a particularly troublesome possibility the closer the NES respondent (as prospective voter) is to a choice between candidates. By the time of a late October NES interview, the answer to "how well the candidates would do at handling poverty" may be much more a rationalization for an emerging vote preference than a judgment that will *subsequently* influence a vote decision.

The second likely problem is that even when the question of future performance is posed in a very specific context—solving the problems of poverty, reducing the budget deficit, handling foreign affairs—questions about a candidate's future performance in complex policy domains must seem rather vague and ill-defined to many voters, and we should not assume a one-to-one correspondence between the content of the question and the answer. There may, consequently, be an element of residual *affect* in the judgment that is not precisely what the question calls for.

On the other hand, there are good reasons for asking such questions about the future. They refer implicitly—and sometimes very explicitly—to campaign promises with emphases that have varied from domain to domain as candidates try to match their own credibility against the opponent's weakness. Prospective evaluations will often be extensions of retrospective assessments, or judgments about the incumbent administration based on the voters' perceptions and evaluations of the "conditions" discussed in the last chapter. It is also the case that performance evaluations, both retrospective and prospective, involve the same kinds of judgments that are found in issue preferences and assessments of conditions. They differ in that they are expressly connected to one or both candidates, but as we noted in Chapter 8, the content of the conflict or consensus at issue in performance evaluations is manifestly quite different from the assessments of personal qualities also associated with the candidates. Selected personal traits of the challenger or the incumbent (to be discussed in the next chapter) may add a dimension that casts a different light on the future than the past. If the campaign has had an effect, prospective evaluations may also add a consideration that is missing from all of the other queries on which we base our reconstruction of the vote decision.

Because of the likely substantive as well as temporal links connecting retrospective and prospective evaluations to each other, this chapter will discuss evaluations of both party and candidate performance, retrospective and prospective, and the next chapter—the next to the last in this section of the book—will be concerned with the contribution of the personal qualities of the candidates to the voters' choices. It must be borne in mind, however, that the analysis actually proceeded in the sequence of stages as outlined earlier. The assessment of personal qualities followed retrospective evaluations (the evaluation of the record of the recent past) and *preceded* judgments about prospective performances. The evidence for prospective evaluation is considered after both retrospective evaluations of the incumbent administration and comparative evaluations of the candidates' personal qualities have been examined as prior stages in the model.

▪ Presidential Performance Evaluations

In the previous chapter, we examined the apparent initial impact of voters' perceptions of current conditions in the nation and their own lives on their vote for President. The NES questions which elicited such perceptions did not refer to any political governmental activities, and neither Governor Clinton nor President Bush was mentioned. The questions do contain implicit criteria for evaluating the effectiveness of the incumbent administration in specific substantive areas—areas where the electorate was doubtless in general agreement about the difference between "good" and "bad" conditions and the responsibility of the federal government for those conditions. Thus, almost all voters would have preferred that the "state of the economy" be better (or at least not worse) than it was a year ago, that the U.S. "position in the world" should be stronger (or at least not weaker) than a year ago, that the unemployment rate should go down (or at least stay the same), and that their own personal finances should be better than (or at least as good as) the previous year.[3]

In each of these areas, the potential impact of perceptions on vote choice is generally assumed to operate through a fairly simple model of electoral punishment or reward. The crucial difference between evaluations of conditions and retrospective evaluations of performance is the matter of attribution. Although hostile partisans may predictably link bad conditions to prior performance, more objective observers may see the same conditions as caused by factors out of an incumbent President's control—as in the case of the Iranian hostage crisis in 1980. Perceptions of "good" conditions *presumably* lead to positive impressions of the overall "performance" or the "job being done" by the incumbent President or administration, and "bad" conditions *presumably* lead to negative impressions—but it is precisely the necessity of a perceived causal link that turns our attention to retrospective performance evaluations.

At the outset of this section of the book we noted that evaluations of the results of governmental action (or inaction) may be influenced by policy-related conflict. Many potential governmental objectives are only partially consensual—such as "eliminating racial discrimination," or "strengthening the traditional family." In such cases, some voters do not agree that the stated objective is appropriate for the federal government, while others, if they do agree on the objective, may disagree about the priority given to it or about the policy that should be pursued to meet that objective. Because of such disagreements, evaluations of the current President's "performance" may be influenced by voters' own policy-related preferences through either of two mechanisms. First, voters who believe the government is responsible for a stated objective may reward or punish the incumbent administration for current conditions in that domain—even if the President has not taken a visible position in that area—while voters who do not support that objective (or give it a low priority) will not be influenced by their perceptions of current conditions in that area. Second, *if* the President has taken a visible position concerning controversial objectives, evaluations of the administration's performance may be directly influenced by voters' own policy-related preferences. Our interpretation of these empirical relationships is summarized in Figure 14.1.

The 1992 NES questionnaires include several types of questions that call for retrospective evaluations of George Bush's performance as President. In particular, respondents were asked each of the following questions:

- Do you approve or disapprove of the way George Bush is handling his job as President?
- Do you approve or disapprove of the way George Bush is handling our relations with foreign countries?
- Do you approve or disapprove of the way George Bush is handling the economy?
- Do you approve or disapprove of the way George Bush is handling the crisis in the Persian Gulf?

Table 14.1 presents our standard series of alternative estimates for the apparent impact on vote choice of the first of these, general approval or disapproval of President Bush's "performance" in office. The magnitude of the potential impact of voters' overall evaluations of the job President Bush has been doing is suggested by the enormous difference (1.71) between the average vote of the *minority* of the voters who strongly approved of Bush's performance as President (−.82) and the substantial *majority* who strongly disapproved (+.89); the bivariate regression coefficient is .90. The clear implication of the partisan imbalance of senti-

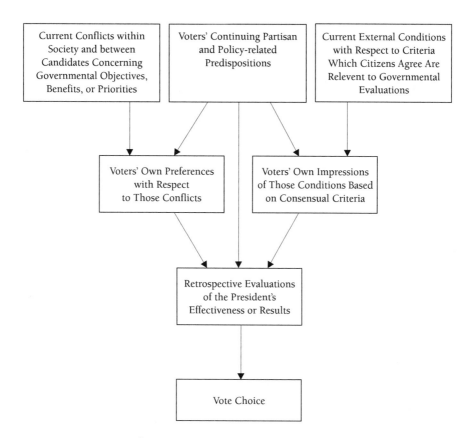

Figure 14.1 Sources of evaluations of the President's "results" based on conflict versus consensus.

ments (2.5 to 1.0 anti-Bush to pro-Bush) so strongly tied to individual vote choices is that Bush may have suffered on election day, 1992, because of these evaluations. This possibility will be examined more systematically in Chapter 17.

The bivariate coefficient is only modestly reduced to .80 when we remove the confounding effects of voters' social and economic characteristics; but it drops to .60 when we also hold party identification constant. The effect estimate is further reduced to .48 when we add controls for *all* conflicts or policy-related preferences, which may have influenced the vote through some other mechanism as well as influencing evaluations of the President.

Table 14.1 The Apparent Impact of General Presidential Evaluations

1. Average Vote for Those Most Disapproving (Strong Disapproval, N = 455)*	.89
2. Average Vote for Those Most Approving (Strong Approval, N = 193)	−.82
3. Difference in Average Vote: Most Disapproving minus Most Approving	1.71
4. Bivariate Unstandardized Regression Coefficient (Performance Evaluations Scored from −1 to +1)	.90
5. Coefficient from Multiple Regression with Social/Economic Characteristics Held Constant	.80
6. With Party Identification (Party ID) Also Held Constant	.60
7. With Other Specific Policy-related Predispositions (But NOT Party ID) Also Held Constant	.65
8. With Liberal vs. Conservative Self-designation Also Held Constant	.61
9. With Party ID AND All Policy-related Predispositions Also Held Constant	.50
10. With Preferences on All Current Policy Issues Also Held Constant	.48
11. With Perceptions of Current Personal and National Conditions Also Held Constant	.46
#12. With Other Retrospective Evaluations of the Current President Also Held Constant	.33
13. With Evaluations of the Candidates' Personal Qualities Also Held Constant	.25
14. With Prospective Evaluations of the Candidates' Future Performance Also Held Constant	.16

*The number of cases associated with extreme positions on these and similar measures simply indicate the base on which extreme scores were calculated. Note that the number of cases is unweighted; all other results are weighted.

(Coefficients Appear in Parentheses if the Estimated p Value is $> .1$).

#Indicates estimate of the "apparent total effect" discussed in the text.

There is no significant further decline in the remaining effect estimate for general presidential approval when we next control for perceptions of current conditions. The interpretation of this apparent lack of impact of "conditions" is consonant with the analysis of conditions in the last chapter. There we noted that the major reduction in the apparent total effect of conditions occurred as we introduced retrospective evaluations of the Bush administration into the analysis. Our conclusion was that those retrospective evaluations captured the impact of conditions on the vote. Now, the absence of any further decline in the apparent impact of the presidential evaluations when we control for current conditions is consistent with the deduction that the impact of such conditions has been largely captured (or mediated) by the explicit evaluations of the President's administration which we are examining. This conclusion from our analysis of retrospective evaluations of the President is not an additional test of our conclusions about the mediation of perceptions of conditions, but it is consistent with those conclusions and with the causal order we have postulated in the overall model. It suggests that not many voters somehow first evaluated the administration's performance and *from that* evaluation drew subsequent conclusions that conditions must be bad (or good).

Our estimate of the apparent total effect on the vote of the general appraisal of the "job" Bush was doing as President drops to .33 when the contributions of more specific evaluations are introduced and controlled. Finally, our effect estimate for this variable is still .16 after we also control for evaluations of the candidates' personal qualities and voters' future expectations. The size of that coefficient suggests the substantial extent to which the vote may have been based on explicit rewards or punishments for the results of the President's efforts—instead of any other factors in our model.

Retrospective Assessments of Foreign Affairs and the Nation's Economy

In addition to the impact of general approval (or disapproval) of President Bush, more specialized evaluations of the President's performance concerning the economy and foreign affairs also exhibited a significant relationship with the vote—even after we controlled for general presidential evaluations (or approval) as well as all prior variables. Based on Row 12 in Table 14.2, and discounting problems of measurement error in these single-item measures, it would appear that voters' assessments of the President's success in various domains of governmental activity or responsibility did indeed have visible consequences for vote choice that could be distinguished from more general evaluations of President Bush and his administration.

The modest coefficient for the apparent effect of Bush's handling of foreign affairs is one of the more dramatic illustrations of the hazards of

Table 14.2 The Apparent Impact of Presidential Evaluations in Specific Areas

	Handling Economy	Handling Foreign Affairs	Blame for Deficit
1. Average Vote for Those with Most Negative Perceptions (N)	.64 (719)	.81 (266)	.85 (455)
2. Average Vote for Those with Positive Perceptions (N)	−.78 (91)	−.45 (454)	−.60 (459)
3. Differences in Average Vote: Most Negative minus Most Positive	1.42	1.26	1.44
4. Bivariate Unstandardized Regression Coefficient (Performance Evaluations Scored −1, 0, or +1)	.85	.59	.72
5. Coefficient from Multiple Regression with Social/Economic Characteristics Held Constant	.73	.49	.63
6. With Party Identification (Party ID) Also Held Constant	.48	.30	.43
7. With Specific Policy-related Predispositions (But NOT Party ID) Also Held Constant	.53	.33	.48
8. With Liberal vs. Conservative Self-designation Also Held Constant	.49	.29	.44
9. With Party ID AND All Policy-related Also Held Constant	.36	.21	.34
10. With Preferences on All Current Policy Issues Also Held Constant	.34	.19	.33
11. With Perceptions of Current Personal and National Conditions Also Held Constant	.31	.17	.31
#12. With Other Retrospective Evaluations of the Current President Also Held Constant	.08	.05	.22
13. With Evaluations of the Candidates' Personal Qualities Also Held Constant	.07	(.02)	.18
14. With Prospective Evaluations of the Candidates' Future Performance Also Held Constant	−.02	(.03)	.13

#Indicates estimate of the "apparent total effect" discussed in the text.
(Coefficients Appear in Parentheses if the Estimated p Value is $>.1$).

projecting a relationship between public opinion and a future voting decision. Scarcely more than a year before the election of 1992, Bush reached a historic peak in approval by the nation, presumably because of his role as an international leader in the successful execution of the Persian Gulf War. It was widely noted that the failure of many national leaders of the Democratic party even to enter the contest for their party's nomination in early 1992 could be attributed to this unprecedented show of strength by the incumbent President.

The one-sided nature of public approval of Bush's handling of the nation's international affairs was not a mirage. It was real, and it was maintained all the way through the election of 1992 by a ratio of 454 to 266 (2 to 1 in Table 14.2) among NES respondents immediately before the fall election. The political miscalculation by Democratic hopefuls lay in the underestimation of the extent to which competing concerns, such as popular distress over the economy and dissatisfaction with the President's performance in that arena, might more than counter satisfaction with his conduct of the Gulf War. The "bottom line" of interest in Table 14.2, Row 12, shows the total apparent effect coefficient for voters' appraisal of Bush's handling of foreign affairs at .05—statistically significant and favorable to the President, but of limited substantive importance to voters' decisions at the polls.

The contrast with voters' assessment of Bush's handling of the national economy is largely found in the reversal of the imbalance between positive and negative opinions. Even larger numbers of voters held clear-cut positive or negative opinions on the economy than was the case for the President's handling of foreign affairs. But where sentiment on foreign affairs favored Bush by 2 to 1, negative appraisals outnumbered the positive when the handling of the economy was concerned, and by a staggering ratio of 8 to 1: 719 critical voters to 91 supportive voters in the NES sample for 1992. For well over a year, continual high unemployment, particularly in white-collar ranks plagued by the uncertainty over the ultimate impact of "downsizing," had received virtual daily lead-story treatment by the media. Increasingly, President Bush seemed frozen in a Hoover-like "recovery is just around the corner" pose. The burden of the resulting overwhelmingly negative appraisals is lightened only by the fact that the apparent total effect coefficient is only .08—larger than for foreign affairs, but not signifying overwhelming importance to individual vote choices.

The Deficit

The NES questions of 1992 included one item designed to elicit blame for the persistent annual national budget deficit. Voters were given a structured choice of attributing responsibility to the Republican President, Bush, or to the Democratic Congress.[4] The impact of this third very specific evaluation of the Bush administration was unmistakably greater than for either the economy or foreign affairs if measured by our apparent total effect coefficients. And yet the partisan balance of the evaluations in the third domain raises again the question of how we should assess the importance of an effect. The magnitude of the apparent total effect on the vote, .22, is clearly much larger than that of the President's handling of either the national economy or the nation's foreign affairs. However, the division of national sentiment on this question was precisely balanced: in the NES sample 459 voters blamed the Democratic Congress, while 455 blamed the Republican President.

In Chapter 1 we raised, as a hypothetical question, the problem of deciding the importance of a contribution to the election results. We pointed out that if the question is "What differentiates Democratic voters from Republican voters?" the answer might lie in the magnitude of the apparent total effects coefficient; however, if the question is "Why were there more Clinton voters than Bush voters?" the answer must take account of the partisan balance on relevant attitudes. In the arena of retrospective evaluations of the President and his administration, it now appears that honors are very mixed indeed. At first blush, it seems that blame for the budget deficit affected more voters' decisions than did either of the other two retrospective evaluations of the Bush administration, but the distribution of blame seemingly neither helped nor hurt the President's bid for re-election. Assessments of the President's handling of the national economy affected fewer people, but they must have produced more Democratic than Republican votes; and Bush's handling of foreign policy affected the smallest number of voters who, nevertheless, favored him over Clinton in this domain. The translation of these generalizations into specific conclusions about the importance of retrospective evaluations is a complex process, one that is not as straightforward as it might seem. We will present an explication of the process and a review of its results in Chapter 17.

▪ Evaluations of the President as Dependent and Intervening Variables

The preceding section presented the sequence of analyses which assess the apparent impact *on the vote* of evaluations concerning the "results" of the President's administration. As in other chapters, the initial analyses in that sequence were designed to assess the total effect of such retrospective evaluations by removing the confounding influence of prior factors that may have influenced those evaluations as well as the vote. By design, all of those analyses emphasized the *electoral consequence* of voters' evaluations of President Bush's performance in office. Because of that emphasis, however, our discussion of the causes or origins of such evaluations has been limited to the potentially confounding influences of such causal factors on our estimates of the electoral effects of the evaluations. Our understanding of the political role played by the evaluations of the President will not be complete until the explanatory variables in prior stages of our model are not simply "held constant" but are considered as potential sources or origins of those evaluations.

The Difference between Presidential Approval as a Separate and Independent Origin of Vote Choices and as a Consequence of Other Causes

A search for the "causes of one of the causes" is doubly useful where it is a search for the causes of current popular evaluations of the President. One of the oldest traditions in public opinion polling suggests that public opinion approval or disapproval of presidential performance can also be interpreted as a periodic "referendum" on the current administration between elections. From that perspective, survey questions about presidential approval can be used to assess the public's view of the current President's pre-election strength, or the probable current strength of his party. For that reason, political observers may be as interested in the sources or origins of such evaluations as they are in the next eventual vote. Just as previous discussions have dealt with vote choice, this section examines the apparent impact of antecedent causal stages, including policy- or conflict-related preferences *and* perceptions of current conditions, on the retrospective evaluations of President Bush and his administration.

As suggested in several accounts of the 1992 election, negative evaluations of the job George Bush was doing as President appear to have played an important role in his defeat. Furthermore, much of that negative sentiment seems to have been based on voters' perceptions of the state of the economy—without any visible connection to conflicts over policy direction. Not everyone, however, came to the same negative conclusion about the President's performance, and that variation among citizens in their evaluations of the President appears to have been powerfully shaped by voters' prior policy-related preferences and predispositions as well as their current perceptions of the economy and partisan identifications. This pattern can be seen in Table 14.3, which presents a familiar sequence of descriptive statistics, but this time concerning the relationships between policy-related preferences or perceived conditions and approval or disapproval of President Bush. As in our analysis of the vote, all of these analyses of presidential approval begin (in Column 1) with the simple bivariate relationships involved, with one row for each explanatory variable. The rows then present successive effect estimates for each variable from a sequence of multivariate analyses which progressively control for social and economic variables, party identification, other policy-related predispositions, other current policy preferences, and perceptions of current conditions. (In the tables in Chapters 11, 12, and 13, each column is the equivalent of a complete row in Table 14.3.)

Several aspects of Table 14.3 deserve emphasis and discussion. In the first place, most of the explanatory variables concerning policy-related predispositions or current policy issues that have been described as having influenced voters' choices between Bill Clinton and George Bush *also* appear to have influenced their disapproval or approval of the job George Bush was doing as President at the time of the 1992 NES pre-election interview. This is scarcely surprising to those who have, over the years, interpreted presidential approval ratings as between-election referenda. Nor should it surprise those who think retrospective performance evaluations are suspect as influences on the vote precisely because they are only rationalizations for votes about to be cast.

On the other hand, there are clear systematic differences in the explanatory elaborations that have presidential approval as the dependent variable and those that focus on the vote. These differences are informative in two general respects. First, comparing the rows in Table 14.3 with

Table 14.3 Apparent Effects of Policy-Related Variables on Presidential Approval

	Bivariate Regression Coefficient	With Social/ Economic Characteristics Held Constant	With Party Identification Also Held Constant	With (other) Predispositions Also Held Constant	With (other) Policy Preferences Also Held Constant	With Conditions Also Held Constant
Predispositions						
Party Identification	.54	.49	—	.34	.32	.29
Ideology (Lib./Con.)	.62	.55	.33	.18	.11	.09
Equality	.72	.56	.33	.11	(.03)	(.00)
Limited Government	.34	.25	.11	(.02)	(.01)	(−.01)
Morality	.60	.53	.31	.10	(.02)	(.04)
Unions vs. Business	.32	.24	.12	.07	.07	.06
Gays vs. Fundamentalists	.64	.63	.44	.24	(.10)	(.09)
Isolationism	.16	.12	.07	.08	.05	(.03)
Vietnam Service	.23	.21	.14	.09	.06	.05
Policy Preferences						
Military Strength	.70	.62	.46	.30	.30	.25
Aid to Disadvantaged	.52	.40	.25	.15	.15	.13
Gays in the Military	.30	.27	.19	.08	.06	.05
Tax Increase	.22	.17	.07	(.01)	(.00)	(.00)
Private Schools	.14	.13	.09	.05	.06	.06
Abortion	.32	.30	.21	.11	.11	.08
Conditions						
National Economy	.75	.67	.49	.41	.38	.34
U.S. Position	.36	.30	.22	.17	.15	.12
Layoff in Family	.39	.35	.39	.42	.42	.33

(Coefficients appear in parentheses if the estimated p value is $>.1$).

the elaboration tables in Chapters 11, 12, and 13 makes evident why retrospective assessments as inter-election "referenda" are *not* reliable surrogates for an election decision: the two are not the same, and presidential approval ratings should not be interpreted as a surrogate for voting
preferences without invoking many caveats. Second, the differences are
exactly as they should be: presidential approval ratings are relatively
more responsive to short-term forces—policy preferences and assessments of conditions—while vote choices are relatively more heavily
influenced by long-term factors—party identification and policy-related
predispositions in particular.

Retrospective evaluations of the President are neither totally contami-
nated by their proximity to the vote nor are they surrogates for the vote.
Retrospective performance evaluations, therefore, seem to be reasonable
candidates for inclusion in a separate stage in the vote analysis where
we emphasize their differences from the vote, and they should not be
casually taken as surrogates for inter-election referenda that mirror what
an actual election would produce. For our purpose, such evaluations
provide important intervening variables that help us to understand vote
choice.

Prospective Performance Evaluations

Continuity between the retrospective past and anticipation of the prospective future is captured in the 1992 NES data. Two of the three
retrospective assessments of President Bush were matched with questions
on comparative *prospective* expectations for both Bush and Clinton in
the same problem areas (the national economy and the budget deficit).
In addition, *prospective* performance evaluations for both candidates
were also measured concerning their ability to handle foreign affairs,
pollution and environmental protection, and the problem of poverty. In
this latter group, only "handling poverty" appeared to have an impact
on vote choice; of the three areas covered both by retrospective *and* prospective candidate orientations, only prospective candidate handling of
"the economy" displayed a significant effect in both temporal contexts.

The enduring institutions that are the political parties provide continuity from election to election and from decade to decade. In 1992 the
voters were also queried about their expectations for the prospective
performance of both *parties* in four domains. All four topics were cov-

Table 14.4 The Electoral Relevance of Prospective Candidate Performance

	Handling Nation's Economy	Solving the Problem of Poverty
1. Average Vote Among Those Saying Clinton Would Do a "Better Job" (N)	.92 (561)	.76 (667)
2. Average Vote Among Those Saying Bush Would Do a "Better Job" (N)	−.91 (302)	−.88 (207)
3. Difference in Average Vote: Clinton Better minus Bush Better	1.83	1.65
4. Bivariate Unstandardized Regression Coefficient (Prospective Performance Scored −1, 0, or +1)	.92	.88 (207)
5. Coefficient from Multiple Regression with Social/Economic Characteristics Held Constant	.85	.78 (207)
6. With Party Identification (Party ID) Also Held Constant	.68	.57 (207)
7. With Specific Policy-related Predispositions (But NOT Party ID) Also Held Constant	.73	.61 (207)
8. With Liberal vs. Conservative Self-designations Also Held Constant	.70	.57 (207)
9. With Party ID AND All Policy-related Predispositions Also Held Constant	.60	.47 (207)
10. With Preferences on all Current Policy Issues Also Held Constant	.57	.45 (207)
11. With Perceptions of Current Personal and National Conditions Also Held Constant	.56	.43 (207)
12. With Retrospective Evaluations of the President's Performance Also Held Constant	.41	.27 (207)
13. With Evaluations of the Candidates' Personal Qualities Also Held Constant	.38	.23 (207)
#14. With Other Prospective Evaluations of Candidates' and Parties' Performance Also Held Constant	.30	.10 (207)

#Indicates estimate of the "apparent total effect" discussed in the text.
(Coefficients Appear in Parentheses if the Estimated *p* Value is >.1).

ered by questions parallel to questions on the prospective performances of the candidates: health care, the national economy, poverty, and foreign affairs. Elaboration analyses produced statistically significant results for party evaluations in two domains, health insurance and the national economy. Neither domestic poverty nor foreign affairs evoked independent responses that enhance our understanding of individual voter choices by adding prospective evaluations of the parties.

It should be emphasized that the "findings" just reported were the apparent effects that remain *after* we control for *all* variables likely to have been confounding antecedents whose presence might have led to spurious conclusions. In other words, we have isolated two problem areas, each, for candidate and party expectations: the national economy and the problems of poverty for the candidates, the national economy and health insurance for the parties. In these domains the evidence, presented in Tables 14.4 and 14.5, suggests independent influences on the vote, although, as we have noted, we are not completely confident that the influences are as closely tied to the specified problem content as we might wish. Nonetheless, these evaluations of party and candidate do continue to show statistical independence after taking account of all other variables in all six stages.

Moreover, we read important implications into the variations of the empirical findings across different problem areas. Questions about the future handling of the economy, or poverty, or health insurance are not simply empty vessels into which emerging vote preferences are poured. If all queries about performance expectations were answered with the same implicit preference for candidate or party, the results of the inquiry into the several problem areas would be more or less uniform and the meaningfulness of each result would be open to question. But "foreign affairs"—surely the most ambiguous of terms describing a domain of popular concern for the recent decades—*did not* elicit optimistic forecasts for favored candidates or preferred parties. Such salient themes as protection of the environment or handling the national budget deficit did not evoke candidate evaluations of significant relevance to forthcoming vote choices. In other words, we believe that significant differences across content domains argue strongly against dismissing evidence of statistically independent influences on the vote when they do exist.

The conclusion that prospective evaluations of the anticipated performances of both candidates and parties make important contributions

Table 14.5 The Electoral Relevance of Prospective Party Performance

	Handling Nation's Economy	Making Health Care More Affordable
1. Average Vote Among Those Saying Democrats Would Do a "Better Job" (N)	.93 (481)	.70 (679)
2. Average Vote Among Those Saying Republicans Would Do a "Better Job" (N)	−.87 (278)	−.90 (159)
3. Difference in Average Vote: Democrats Better minus Republicans Better	1.79	1.60
4. Bivariate Unstandardized Regression Coefficient (Prospective Performance Scored −1, 0, or +1)	.90	.87
5. Coefficient from Multiple Regression with Social/Economic Characteristics Held Constant	.81	.75
6. With Party Identification (Party ID) Also Held Constant	.59	.51
7. With Specific Policy-related Predispositions (But NOT Party ID) Also Held Constant	.65	.57
8. With Liberal vs. Conservative Self-designations Also Held Constant	.61	.53
9. With Party ID AND All Policy-related Predispositions Also Held Constant	.48	.40
10. With Preferences on all Current Policy Issues Also Held Constant	.45	.38
11. With Perceptions of Current Personal and National Conditions Also Held Constant	.43	.36
12. With Retrospective Evaluations of the President's Performance Also Held Constant	.25	.22
13. With Evaluations of the Candidates' Personal Qualities Also Held Constant	.21	.19
#14. With Other Prospective Evaluations of Candidates' and Parties' Performance Also Held Constant	.07	.10

#Indicates estimate of the "apparent total effect" discussed in the text.
(Coefficients Appear in Parentheses if the Estimated p Value is $>.1$).

to our understanding of the antecedents of voter decisions is supported by yet another finding from our multi-stage multivariate model. The same finding, it is true, reveals the limitations of our understanding of these findings. Table 14.6 reproduces the last two rows of our standard elaboration tables for each of the six content domains in which future expectations for the performance of *either* parties or candidates seemed

Table 14.6 Apparent Effects Before and After Imposing Controls for All Other Variables in Sixth and Last Stage of the Model

	Handling National Economy	Handling Poverty	Handling Health Care Insurance	Handling Foreign Affairs	Handling Environment	Handling Budget Deficit
Prospective Evaluations of Parties, With Evaluations of Candidate Traits Held Constant (Row 13)	.21	.16	.19	.06	—	—
All Other Significant Prospective Evaluations Also Held Constant (Row 14)	.07	(−.01)	.07	(.03)	—	—
Prospective Evaluations of Candidates With Evaluations of Candidate Traits Also Held Constant (Row 13)	.38	.23	.19	(.04)	.11	.15
With All Other Significant Prospective Evaluations Also Held Constant (Row 14)	.30	.10	(.04)	(.00)	(.02)	(.02)

(Coefficients Appear in Parentheses if the Estimated p Value is >.1.)

important as explanations of the vote. The uppermost in each pair of rows (one pair for parties, the second for candidates) is generic "Row 13," presenting the apparent effect coefficients *after* taking account of (controlling for) the traits that measure personal qualities, but *before* also taking account of "other" expectations for prospective performances. The second row shows the effect coefficients *after* then taking account of (adding controls for) the impact of the other performance expectations.

In eight of the ten comparisons of an upper row with a lower row we see evidence that substantial coefficients of both substantive and statistical significance exist *before* the given variable is put into competition with all other variables in the same stage measuring prospective evaluations. The result of adding the controls for the other variables in the same stage is a dramatic reduction in the effect coefficient in every instance, with the exception of handling the national economy where the ultimate coefficient remains very large. The positive interpretation of this is that prospective evaluations of the performance of both the parties and the candidates make large contributions to the voters' ultimate choices between candidates. The contributions vary by substantive domain; they are larger for concerns with the national economy, national health insurance, and the problems resulting from poverty. And the effect coefficients fade *only* when all prospective evaluations except the one being examined are added to the list of controls.

The negative side of this argument lies in the fact that we are not equipped conceptually or theoretically to describe or explain the differences among domains. For example, controlling for the other expectations reduces the impact of candidates' handling of the economy only from .38 to .30 (a 21 percent reduction) or that of handling poverty from .23 to .10 (56 percent), but the impacts of candidates' handling the environment, the deficit, or health care all virtually vanish (11 to .02, .15 to .02 and .19 to (.04), respectively) when we apply the same rule of imposing controls on all variables in the same stage. With some variation in the content domains, the same perplexities arise with evaluations of prospective performances of the parties. In sum, we have even less guidance to an interpretation of the effects of performance evaluations on one another than we have for the interpretation of differences among the traits used to assess candidates' personal qualities that we will examine in the next chapter.

Nevertheless, prospective performance evaluations of parties and candidates, *taken together as a bloc,* appear to make the final stage in the explanatory model a highly important stage. At the variable-by-variable level of accounting for differences between Republican and Democratic voters, the end of the causal chain does not appear to be relegated to the insignificant but stands, instead, as a testament to the importance of expectations. The challenge for future research is to understand better the meaningfulness of differences in expectations across domains, and to understand better the contribution of the election campaign to the creation of expectations for the future.

▪ Assessing the Impact of "Presidential Performance" Based on Structured versus Open-Ended Questions

In Chapters 11 and 12, we compared the evidence provided by structured versus open-ended questions concerning the relevance of policy-related predispositions and current policy issues. In both chapters, direct comparisons between coefficients produced by these two alternative methods were sometimes problematic, but we were reasonably confident that the two sets of measures were based on voters' opinions about approximately the same topics. When we move from the "conflict" to the "consensus" side of our distinction between two different types of issues, however, comparisons of apparent effects for measures based on structured questions rather than the NES open-ended questions become more problematic—in two respects. First, the impact of voters' perceptions of current conditions that is captured by respondents' answers to open-ended questions must be classified in terms of the incumbent administration's "performance" in handling those conditions, because the interview schedule contains no open-ended questions about national or personal conditions per se. For that reason, we did not offer comparisons of this sort in the previous chapter on current conditions. Second, although the current administration's perceived "performance" in handling foreign versus domestic affairs can be assessed by counting responses that have been classified (or coded) in those two broad areas, we can see no meaningful distinction between responses that are based on retrospective versus prospective assessments of the (incumbent) administration.

For these reasons, we have limited our comparisons between the two

Table 14.7 The Impact of Presidential Performance Based on Structured vs. Open-Ended Questions

	Standardized Regression Coefficients for Measures Based on Structured Questions About Respondents' Own Views		Standardized Regression Coefficients for Measures Based on Responses to Open-ended Questions About the Candidates		Percentage of Clinton/Bush Voters Who Provided One or More Responses Within the Designated Categories
	Total Effect* (With Other Presidential Performance Held Constant)	Direct Effect (With ALL Other Variables Held Constant)	With Summaries of Likes/Dislikes for Other Presidential Performance Also Held Constant	With Summary Measures for ALL Other Likes/Dislikes Also Held Constant	
General Performance	.26	.12	.13	.10	33.3
Handling the Economy	.05	(−.01)	.06	.05	21.7
Foreign Affairs	.04	(.02)	.09	.06	14.0

*All analyses include controls for the standard set of social and economic characteristics, party identification, policy-related predispositions, general policy preferences, perceptions of current conditions, and other evaluations of presidential performance. The number of cases (N) for all of these analyses is 1193.

alternative methods for assessing the impact of presidential performance to three broad categories which correspond to measures discussed in the first part of this chapter—overall evaluations of presidential perform- ance, similar evaluations concerning the economy, and evaluations that deal with some aspect of foreign affairs. Table 14.7 presents the same type of comparisons between standardized regression coefficients that we discussed in Chapters 11 and 12. In this broad area of "performance," it is clear that our two methods (based on structured versus open-ended questions) lead to quite similar conclusions concerning the relevance of voters' assessments (when offered) of President Bush's performance in shaping their electoral decisions in 1992. The standardized coefficients associated with both types of total effects are fairly similar despite the radically different methods involved, although the magnitude of the total effect for general evaluations is substantially greater for our structured questions. Evaluations of George Bush's effectiveness as President or the performance of his administration appear to have played a major role in shaping voters' choices between Bush and Clinton in 1992, regardless of which method is employed. The relatively stronger showing for the responses to open questions as each stage comes closer to the vote was anticipated in our first discussion of open versus structured questions when we presumed that the more indirect causes would be less well represented in response to the open questions.

As in our previous analyses of this sort concerning policy-related conflict, however, it seems generally true that voters' opinions based on the structured questions had as big an influence on voters' choices among those who did *not* mention performance in response to the NES open-ended questions as they did among those who did mention per- formance as a "reason" for liking or disliking the President. As shown in Table 14.8, the apparent impact of voters' general evaluations of presidential popularity as measured by the structured questions does not rise appreciably when we shift our attention from voters who did not mention such topics to those who did. It does appear that the small apparent effect of voters' evaluations concerning foreign affairs is con- centrated among the minority (14 percent) who mentioned that area in response to the NES open-ended questions, but no such differences are evident for our other two types of presidential evaluations. As stated in previous chapters, we have concluded that responses to the NES open- ended questions may identify a minority of respondents for whom

Table 14.8 Differences in Apparent Total Effects of Presidential Performance Based on "Mentioning" a Reason for Choice

Type of Presidential Performance Evaluation	Percentage Mentioning That Type of Performance	Unstandardized Effect (b) for All Voters*	Unstandardized Effect (b) for Base Those Who Did Not Mention	Change in Effect for Those Who Did Mention
General/Overall	33.3	.33	.33	(−.00)
The Economy	21.7	.08	.08	(.02)
Foreign Affairs	14.0	.05	(.04)	.12

*Bush-Clinton voters.

particular considerations were more salient at the time of their pre-election interview, but such responses do not appear to represent an accurate indicator of the electoral "importance" of that topic to the individuals involved. Many voters whose choices appear to have been influenced by their assessments of presidential performance mentioned other topics in response to open-ended questions.

In general, we regard the responses to these open-ended questions as unreliable indicators of the centrality or relevance of particular bases for choice. We note that responses to open-ended questions lead to the same general conclusions as structured questions concerning the overall relevance of voters' evaluations of President Bush's performance. The apparent relevance of performance evaluations for the vast majority of respondents who did *not* mention any such topic, however, suggests that we should base any assessment of the overall importance of such evaluations on the structured questions that have been included for that purpose.

15

Evaluations of the Candidates' Personal Qualities

By many accounts, in recent decades American presidential politics has been transformed from an older, unique preoccupation with two-party politics to a newer, equally unique emphasis on candidate-centered politics. When the Michigan/NES studies began, the Democratic and Republican parties were two of the oldest political institutions in western democracy, tracing their uninterrupted lineage back for a century and a half. Party identification—so dependent on continuity within a political system—was important to the politics of the United States in a manner virtually unknown elsewhere in the world. As the century draws to a close, however, parties in the United States have lost much of their centralized control over the presidential nominating process, and, by some accounts, they have lost the loyalties of their constituents in the electorate.

For the purposes of understanding electoral behavior, the question of whether or not current presidential politics in the United States is best characterized as candidate-centered is less important than the fact that the role of voter evaluations of the candidates is receiving more systematic attention. The subject has become more salient as political commentators and the media have picked up the "candidate-centered" theme. This chapter reflects the fact that in recent years much effort has been extended by the research community to understand the place of the personal attributes of candidates in the electoral matrix. We now consider those personal attributes as the last component in our examination of candidate evaluations.

414

This component is important in completing our efforts to understand better the simple act of voting in presidential elections. It is given added pertinence by the rise of the industry supporting election campaigns and the associated testimonials about the importance of candidate-centered politics. With the evolution of polling, campaign consultants, media experts, and a host of specialists in the promotion of candidates for office have come to dominate the electoral field. The "party in the electorate" may be of undiminished importance to the voter, but the party is clearly playing a much lesser role in the recruitment and promotion of candidates for office.[1]

The development of a "campaign and election" industry independent of party organizations provides at least a part of the answer to questions about the origins of the increasingly candidate-centered nature of politics in the United States. Those who profit from the belief that presidential politics is candidate-centered have taken advantage of their visibility and have promoted the thesis (or the mystique) of candidate-centered politics into a self-fulfilling prophecy. At least from the days of Joe McGinniss's *The Selling of the President,* the practitioners have been the articulate champions of their own cause to the point where the cost of a viable presidential candidacy was widely quoted as at least $20 million in anticipation of the Republican primary in 1966. With media consultants, pollsters, and campaign managers for hire, all asserting the importance of their contribution—usually outside the machinery of the political parties—there is good practical reason, as well as academic curiosity, behind our own interest in a better assessment of the extent to which presidential elections are, indeed, actually candidate-centered in the minds of the voters.

Until the advent of the National Election Studies in 1977, survey researchers' analysis of voter evaluations of the personal attributes of candidates did not stray far from the path first marked by *The Voter Decides* in 1954. *The American Voter* in 1960 continued that measurement tradition, with little embellishment on the earlier concept of an "orientation" (read "predisposition") revealed in responses to the nonpartisan, non-issue facets of personality exhibited by the candidates. In 1980, however, a first NES venture to assess the personal traits of political leaders through the use of structured questions was launched. It followed intensive work by the NES principal investigators, in collaboration with psychologists such as Robert Abelson, Susan Fiske, and

Shelley Taylor, to identify personal qualities—or traits—that might be relevant to the voters' evaluations of presidential candidates (or other political leaders).

The succession of NES studies in 1984, 1988, and 1992 included various attempts to improve on the construction of a battery of measures of personal traits that would reflect a range of relevant personal "dimensions." Under the leadership of Donald Kinder, the psychologists' literature on perception of people was reviewed and attempts were made to formulate a construct of the ideal president against which actual candidates might be measured (Kinder, 1980).

Over the ensuing years there has been a virtually continuous effort to find reliable measures that capture the variety of voters' reactions to presidential candidates as potential political leaders. The notion that voters might measure candidates against some widely shared concept of the ideal president could not be supported with systematic empirical evidence from early NES efforts. Nevertheless, there has been no diminution of enthusiasm for developing assessments of candidates' personal qualities that can be applied to different candidates in different circumstances. Wendy Rahn and her coauthors have concluded that "forming assessments of the professional and personal qualities of candidates plays a central role in determining the final vote decision."[2]

The Measurement of Personal Traits

As reported by Carolyn Funk, who summarized a very long list of publications based on the NES data, by 1992 the ultimate result of many efforts had been the identification of nine "traits" of political leadership that presumably measured four "dimensions."[3] In each of nine instances an NES respondent is told, "I am going to read a word or phrase people may use to describe political figures. For each, tell me whether the word or phrase describes the candidate I name."[4] The responses are phrased in terms of "very well, quite well, not too well, not well at all." The (1) *competence* of each candidate is evaluated with the terms "knowledgeable" and "intelligent"; (2) *effectiveness* is represented by "provides strong leadership," "inspiring," and "gets things done"; (3) *integrity* is measured by responses to "moral" and "honest"; and (4) *empathy* is composed of "compassionate" and "cares about people like you."

Funk's review of the literature on leadership traits emphasizes that inter-item correlations among evaluations and reliance on factor analytic techniques are the primary measurement tools by which traits have been combined by researchers to measure more or less unique dimensions of the personal attractiveness of candidates. Voters' evaluations of personal characteristics of these sorts may play an important role in shaping their conclusions concerning candidates' likely success or failure as President, even though the stated criteria for those personal evaluations make no reference to governmental or, indeed, political activities, objectives, or responsibilities.

Evaluations of a candidate concerning a specific personal quality (for example, "inspiring") presumably represent the accumulation of many impressions, both positive and negative, of that candidate. The actual sources of these impressions are the many episodes, from previous years (for incumbents) as well as from the current campaign (for both challengers and incumbents), in which relevant aspects of the candidates become visible to the voters.

One may attribute the origin of voters' impressions of a particular characteristic of a given candidate (for example, "honesty") to the frequency with which that individual has actually *exhibited* that attribute— that is, the attribute literally has been visible to voters (for instance, a tendency of the candidate to "tell the truth"). Other scholars, however, are convinced that voters' impressions of any personal aspect of a given candidate are shaped by many factors other than the objective visibility of that characteristic (for example, "intelligent") in the candidate's public life. In many cases, the relevant personal aspects of a given candidate are not visible or well known, so that voters' evaluations of that candidate concerning those qualities are almost certainly influenced by positive or negative impressions of the candidate from other sources—including descriptions of the candidate from various influential sources as well as from general attributions derived from the voter's own partisan sympathies.

The Candidates of 1992

Observers' impressions concerning the impact of the candidates' personal qualities seemed particularly pronounced during the 1992 campaign. Essentially negative stories about Bill Clinton's private life, his possible marital infidelity, his early political ambitions, his privileged education, and his avoidance of the draft during the Vietnam War received intensive media coverage. Both before and after his nomination, his opponents emphasized the "character issue" in their television ads and campaign appearances. On the other hand, media presentations of the campaign also described Bill Clinton as an effective campaigner and a challenger who seemed more knowledgeable or inspiring than the incumbent President.

Interest in Clinton's personal qualities was accentuated by the fact that he came onto the national political scene as someone totally unknown to the vast majority of the electorate, the governor of a little-known state whose prior national distinction was being an extraordinarily long-winded speaker at the Democratic convention of 1988. Curiosity was enhanced by some aspects of Clinton's self-promotion. Behavior such as appearing on late night television, wearing "shades" and playing the saxophone, was not in the mode of the typical presidential aspirant. In keeping with the populist theme, Clinton and Gore made an early decision to campaign by bus, "pressing the flesh" in a manner reminiscent of Lyndon Johnson three decades earlier. And Clinton's humble origins as a self-made political leader in small circles fit his self-proclaimed role as a "New Democrat," not a part of the Democratic establishment but a member of an insurgent Democratic Leadership Council out of the centrist, if not conservative, Democratic South. Candidate Clinton did not fit easily into the well-worn shoes of a Dukakis or a Mondale, nor indeed those of another Southerner, another governor of a small Southern state, Jimmy Carter of Georgia. This New Generation leader of an old party came to his campaign with an image to shape and a persona to create.

President George Bush, on the other hand, was a well-known veteran of national politics. But as well known as he may have been to Washington familiars, there were ambiguities arising from his presidency—was he a real macho Texan, or an effete Easterner? Was he the internationally acclaimed leader of the multinational coalition that humiliated the Iraqi dictator Saddam Hussein, or was he the President who had been ridiculed in the national media as a "wimp"? The latter charge had provoked a curious reaction consisting in part of non-presidential masculine vulgarisms clearly articulated for quotation, apparently a desire by Bush to establish himself as a "regular fellow." What kind of person was George Bush, anyhow?[5]

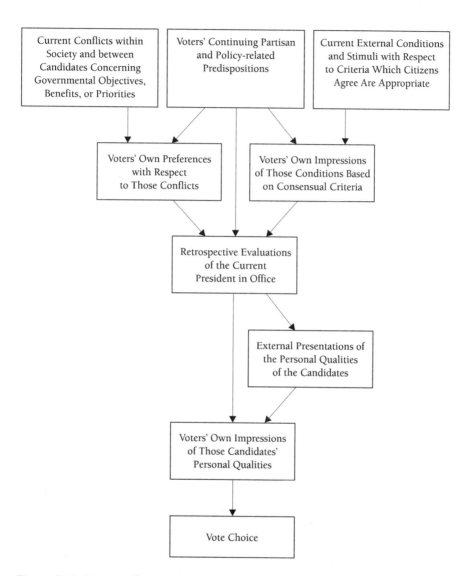

Figure 15.1 Sources of evaluations of the candidates' personal qualities based on conflict versus consensus.

Our analysis of personal qualities includes measures based on structured questions about each candidate with respect to the nine "general purpose" qualities or "traits," as well as the NES open-ended questions about both candidates. Without knowing how well the selection of traits fit either Bush or Clinton, voters and analysts would presumably agree in general about the desirability of the specific qualities included in the NES interviews—that is, we assume that relatively few voters prefer candidates who are dishonest instead of honest, or misinformed instead of knowledgeable.

Because of that agreement, survey respondents' evaluations of the candidates in response to these questions are analyzed in ways that assume they are based on consensual criteria rather than policy-related conflicts or other political attitudes. Put somewhat differently, as we noted in Chapter 8, the analytic purpose of evaluations of personal qualities is to assess sources of vote choice that are *not* influenced by major conflicts or group preferences within the society—precisely because they are defined in terms of "personal" characteristics that are seen as generally desirable. In this sense, personal trait assessments are more akin to evaluations of conditions than to policy preferences.

In practice, however, most analysts recognize the tendency for voters' assessments of the candidates' personal qualities to be influenced or "biased" by their partisan identifications and by tendencies to like or dislike the candidates for other reasons (non-personal, ideological, or party-related reasons). Thus, voters who identify with the Democratic party, or whose policy-related preferences are fairly liberal, or who disapprove of the job George Bush was doing as President, might describe Bill Clinton in a more positive fashion than George Bush on all of the NES questions concerning personal qualities or "traits." And the opposite tendency would exist for voters who were Republicans, or had conservative policy-related views, or approved of the job George Bush was doing as President. Figure 15.1 summarizes these general possibilities concerning the biasing effects of other political attitudes on evaluations of personal qualities.

▪ The Place of Candidates' Personal Qualities in the Analytic Model

Locating "personal qualities" in our multi-stage causal model is not intuitively easy. Particularly when an incumbent President is one of the candidates, impressions of personal qualities could have been formed over a considerable period of time. The final decision to locate "personal qualities of the candidates" where we did (in the fifth of six stages) was influenced by our generally conservative strategy of trying to minimize the likelihood that the apparent presence of a relationship between a given variable and the vote is in reality confounded by common antecedents that we have not taken account of, or controlled. One result, which we have often noted in earlier chapters, is that our estimates of apparent total effects are almost certainly minimal, conservative estimates. We offer little opportunity for a variable to be given undue credit for a causal role that might be spurious. By the same token, we are usually relatively confident that variables in a given causal stage have seldom been "the cause" of variables in a preceding stage. Such assumptions, of course, are intended to confront directly the incidence of "simultaneity" which gives some analysts pause when evaluating results produced by single equation analyses of cross-section data.

In the case of the personal qualities of the candidates, it seems unlikely to us that the voters' perceptions and evaluations of a given candidate's personal traits would be the basis on which the recent performance of the incumbent's administration (located in the previous stage) would be judged. It is always possible, of course, that some of the voters who, before the election, saw Clinton as an "inspiring" leader or one who "cared about people like themselves" concluded from those impressions that George Bush had not done a good job as President. It seems more likely that dissatisfaction (or satisfaction) with "conditions" or the performance of the President would lead to invidious (or flattering) personal comparisons with Bill Clinton. In most cases the causal arrow probably runs from conditions and performance to personal traits.

This illustrative line of argument is appropriate in part because the variables that were formed to measure each perceived trait were, in fact, *combinations* of the assessments of both candidates with regard to a given trait. If "honest" was a "very good" fit for Bush but did "not at all well" describe Clinton, the voter would be given an appropriately pro-Bush score on the trait "honesty." The fact that all nine trait variables are based on comparative evaluations of the two candidates does not foreclose the possibility that a given trait evaluation of the *two* candidates could have been partially responsible for a singular assessment of conditions or presidential performance that in fact resulted from the trait assessment—

particularly since one or both candidates may have proposed that linkage in the course of their campaigns. We believe, however, that assessments of past performance and conditions (from the fourth stage) are more likely to have caused evaluations of candidates phrased as personal traits than to have been caused by perceptions of the traits (measured in the fifth stage).

Personal Traits in 1992

The distributions of each of the nine constructed trait variables are presented in Tables 15.1 through 15.9. A systematic assessment of their contribution to the Clinton victory will be presented in Chapter 17. In the meantime, one can imagine scenarios that fit the broad contours of these "raw" data. The most obvious point is that differential public assessments of personal character were reflected in the relatively low ratings

Table 15.1 Personal Qualities: Candidate Traits as Seen by Voters.
            Trait: Cares about people like me

Trait is a better description of:	Bush Voters	Clinton Voters	Two-Party Voters
Bush	54%	4%	25%
Equal	37	14	24
Clinton	8	82	51
	100%*	100%	100%

*In this and the following tables, percentages may not add to 100 because of rounding. All results are weighted.

Table 15.2 Trait: Inspiring

Trait is a better description of:	Bush Voters	Clinton Voters	Two-Party Voters
Bush	54%	5%	25%
Equal	34	25	29
Clinton	12	69	46
	100%	100%	100%

Table 15.3 Trait: Compassionate

Trait is a better description of:	Bush Voters	Clinton Voters	Two-Party Voters
Bush	50%	8%	25%
Equal	40	28	33
Clinton	10	64	42
	100%	100%	100%

Table 15.4 Trait: Gets Things Done

Trait is a better description of:	Bush Voters	Clinton Voters	Two-Party Voters
Bush	56%	16%	32%
Equal	33	24	27
Clinton	11	61	40
	100%	100%	100%

Table 15.5 Trait: Intelligent

Trait is a better description of:	Bush Voters	Clinton Voters	Two-Party Voters
Bush	42%	10%	23%
Equal	54	51	52
Clinton	5	39	25
	100%	100%	100%

given Clinton by his own voters on matters of honesty and morals—Clinton voters even rated Bush above Clinton on matters of morality (see Tables 15.8, 15.9). The "character issue" had clearly reached many Clinton supporters, apparently providing evidence that voters reacted more or less discriminately to the various ways of describing positive features about the two candidates.

Emotional themes such as "caring," "inspiring," or "compassionate"

Table 15.6 Trait: A Leader

Trait is a better description of:	Bush Voters	Clinton Voters	Two-Party Voters
Bush	68%	12%	35%
Equal	27	30	29
Clinton	4	58	36
	100%	100%	100%

Table 15.7 Trait: Knowledgeable

Trait is a better description of:	Bush Voters	Clinton Voters	Two-Party Voters
Bush	51%	11%	27%
Equal	44	52	48
Clinton	5	37	24
	100%	100%	100%

Table 15.8 Trait: Honest

Trait is a better description of:	Bush Voters	Clinton Voters	Two-Party Voters
Bush	77%	18%	42%
Equal	21	37	31
Clinton	2	45	28
	100%	100%	100%

were, in turn, an advantage for Clinton—little more than a majority of Bush voters rated Bush above Clinton on these traits. However, in order to make a first assessment of the contributions of "traits" to individual vote decisions, we must turn to our multivariate model which removes the confounding effects of variables antecedent both to the voters' evaluations of traits and their vote choices.

Table 15.9 Trait: Moral

Trait is a better description of:	Bush Voters	Clinton Voters	Two-Party Voters
Bush	86%	34%	56%
Equal	12	42	30
Clinton	2	24	15
	100%	100%	100%

The Analytic Status of Personal Traits

In turning to the familiar sequence of descriptive statistics, we have a wide range of options for assessing the influence of the trait variables. In the first place, we continue the practice of item-by-item analysis first introduced in our scrutiny of the voters' social and economic characteristics, by examining the apparent impact of each trait on voters' choices of candidates. Following that inquiry, however, we shall also explore various generalizations offered by the research literature on which we are building. This will lead us to examine four dimensions of competence, integrity, leadership, and empathy created by the pairing of traits just described. Third, we can consider a further consolidation of measures, as discussed by Funk, and attempt to consolidate the four dimensions into two: competence (including leadership) and integrity (including empathy). Finally, we can forgo qualitative distinctions and look at a single composite or global assessment of the desirability of a candidate's personal traits.

Table 15.10 presents the results of our standard series of descriptive statistics for the relationships between the vote and comparative evaluations of single traits of the two major candidates, based on the extent to which they were described as "honest," "inspiring," and "cares about people like me." Those three qualities were the *only* traits for which the comparative evaluations of the two candidates (based on the difference between the ratings each voter assigned to Clinton and Bush) exhibited a significant relationship to the vote *after* we controlled for the other significant personal qualities (as well as all of the variables we have discussed in prior stages of our model).

As shown in Rows 1 through 4 of Table 15.10, the bivariate relation-

Table 15.10 Alternative Estimates for the Impact of Candidates' Personal Qualities

	Honest	Cares About People	Inspiring
1. Average Vote Among Most Pro-Clinton: Clinton "Very Much," and Bush "Not At All" (N)	.95 (84)	.94 (270)	.92 (138)
2. Average Vote Among Most Pro-Bush: Bush "Very Much," and Clinton "Not At All" (N)	-.92 (112)	-.97 (64)	-.85 (58)
3. Difference in Average Vote: Most Pro-Clinton minus Most Pro-Bush	1.86	1.91	1.77
4. Bivariate Unstandardized Regression Coefficient (Personal Qualities Scored −1 to +1)	1.41	1.45	1.43
5. Coefficient from Multiple Regression with Social and Economic Characteristics Held Constant	1.22	1.29	1.23
6. With Party Identification (Party ID) Also Held Constant	.81	.94	.82
7. With Specific Policy-Related Predispositions (But NOT Party ID) Also held Constant	.87	1.02	.90
8. With Liberal vs. Conservative Self-Designation Also Held Constant	.79	.95	.83
9. With Party ID AND All Policy-Related Predispositions Also Held Constant	.60	.75	.62
10. With Preferences on All Current Policy Issues Also Held Constant	.56	.70	.58
11. With Perceptions of Current Personal and National Conditions Also Held Constant	.52	.68	.55
12. With Retrospective Evaluations of the Current President in Office Also Held Constant	.23	.34	.27
#13. With Evaluations of the Candidates' Other Personal Qualities Also Held Constant	.10	.24	.14
14. With Prospective Evaluations of the Candidates and Parties Also Held Constant	(.04)	(.07)	(.05)

The entry marked with # is designated the "apparent total effect."

ship between each of these comparative evaluations and the vote is extremely strong. Almost all of the voters who described one candidate as *much* more honest, inspiring, or likely to "care about people like me" (in the NES pre-election interview) subsequently reported (in the post-election re-interview) that they voted for that candidate. The strength of these three relationships is summarized in the bivariate regression coefficients that appear in Row 4.

All three coefficients are still over 1.0 (in Row 5) after we remove the relatively modest confounding influence of social and economic characteristics. As emphasized in Chapter 10, voters with different social and economic backgrounds differed sharply from each other in their vote choices, but those differences were not much involved in the relationship between their perceptions of the candidates' personal qualities and the vote. All three coefficients are substantially diminished, however, when we control for either party identification *or* specific policy-related predispositions (in Rows 6 and 7). And, as shown in Row 9, all three coefficients are reduced by well over half (.60 from 1.22 for "honesty," .75 from 1.29 for "cares," and .62 from 1.23 for "inspiring,") when we control for party identification *as well as* all policy-related predispositions, including ideological self-designation. Although the traits were intended to isolate non-partisan non-ideologized assessments, they were quite clearly applied to the presidential candidates of 1992 with both partisan and ideological connotations.

The separation between short-term forces based on "issues, conditions, and candidates" is, however, suggested by the small difference between Rows 9, 10, and 11; the coefficients for personal qualities were much affected by the long-term variables, but they were only moderately reduced when we also controlled for current policy preferences and perceptions of current conditions. In other words, relatively little of the connection between these three personal qualities and the vote appears to have been misleading (or spurious) as a result of the influence of short-term issues in the campaign—beyond the impact of general predispositions, which have already been taken into account in our analysis.

Nevertheless, the somewhat unexpected magnitude of the connection between personal traits and long-term factors, including party identification and ideological preferences, suggests that some part of the association of traits with candidates is an association of traits with partisan and ideological preferences involved in societal conflict. To the extent that this is so, the political evolution of each of the nine "all-purpose" traits may be more clearly tied to group stereotypes and less uniquely matched to perceived personal uniqueness of the candidates than would be desirable.

However, in the next stage, as shown in Row 12, we encounter the apparent consequences of pertinent exposure to presidential behavior. *All* three coefficients are much diminished when our analysis also includes voters' retrospective evaluations of George Bush as President. The coefficients for comparative evaluations concerning "honest," "cares," and "inspiring" all drop by approximately one-half (from .52 to .23, from .68 to .34, and from .55 to .27) when we control for voters' evaluations of the current President's effectiveness (in office) preceding their comparative evaluations of both the candidates' personal qualities. Again, we have no way to be sure which kind of evaluation came first. Based on the assumptions of our model, however, these results suggest that much of the apparent connection between vote choice and evaluations of Bush and Clinton with respect to "honesty," "caring," and "inspiring" may be attributable to voters' assessments of Bush's success or failure as President, rather than to the candidates' personal qualities per se. This is not to argue that a candidate's personal attributes *should* or could be divorced from career experiences so much as it suggests origins for people's perceptions of personal attributes.

The remaining coefficients for each of the three personal traits are again reduced substantially (in Row 13) when we also control for our measures of the other two qualities. In our judgment, the resulting coefficients represent the most reliable estimates for the apparent total effects of voters' impressions of the candidates with respect to their honesty, .10, caring about "people like you," .24, and ability to inspire, .14. These coefficients describe the strength of the relationship between each specific evaluation and the vote that remains after we have controlled for all of our potentially confounding variables—including our measures for other personal qualities and the President's "performance" in office, as well as current issues and conditions, partisan and policy-related predispositions, and social and economic characteristics. As such, these results suggest a visible—but limited—extent to which voters' choices between Clinton and Bush may have been influenced by their comparative evaluations of Clinton and Bush concerning those specific personal qualities.

In part because we are taking advantage of very recent work done in defining several of our analytic dimensions, we are hard put to decide whether our analytic cup is half empty or half full. On the one hand, it seems remarkable that there is anything remaining to be explained at this late stage in our analytic game after having employed so many explanatory variables in the earlier stages. Nevertheless, the evidence is clear from the coefficients in Row 12 of Table 15.10, *before* we enter the traits in competition with each other, that comparative evaluations of candidates' personal traits exhibit some independent connection with voters' choices between Bush and Clinton.

Quite apart from the issue of assessing the electoral importance of these traits, which we will address in Chapter 17, the question remains: are these total effect coefficients of a magnitude we would expect from candidate-centered politics? This is a harsh test because it makes evident the limited rapport between the "large question" of the contours of candidate-centered politics and the finite answers our research has produced. In our judgment, however, the apparent total effect coefficients seem to be sufficient testimony to the absolute importance of non-party, non-issue, non-performance attributes of presidential candidates to merit continued work on the problem, whether or not this is an era of candidate-centered politics.

The last row of Table 15.10 also documents the extent to which these three personal qualities are correlated with prospective (and comparative) evaluations concerning the potential success or failure of the candidates and parties in future handling of major problem areas. As discussed in Chapter 14, we believe that these prospective evaluations capture a wide variety of residual influences on the vote, in addition to impressions of the candidates' prospective effectiveness in handling specific problem areas. As a consequence, the change in coefficients between Rows 13 and 14 (from .10 to (.04), from .24 to (.07), and from .14 to (.05)) is a combination of the true (indirect) impact of personal qualities on the vote which operates "through" those prospective evaluations and the influence of other confounding influences (based on governmental criteria) rather than a measure of the direct effects of the candidates' personal qualities on voter choices.

Other Qualities with No Apparent Effects: The Case of "Moral"

The 1992 NES interview schedule obviously contained questions about both Clinton and Bush concerning a larger set of personal qualities than the three discussed above. In particular, NES respondents were also asked questions about both candidates concerning the degree to which they were seen as "compassionate," "knowledgeable," "moral," "intelligent," "provides strong leadership," and "gets things done." In our judgment, one of these questions (concerning "strong leadership") presents a somewhat different criterion for evaluation than a "personal" or non-governmental quality, for it involves an implicit standard that is hard to distinguish from "would be a good President." It is also true that the inclusion of comparative evaluations based on that question substantially reduces the apparent impact of our three "personal" qualities. For both of those reasons, we have deferred consideration of comparative evaluations based on perceived "leadership" until Chapter 17, along with other prospective evaluations of the candidates' and parties' future success in specific problem areas.

The remaining five adjectives or expressions, however, do represent "personal" qualities of the candidate in the sense that they are not necessarily or explicitly defined in terms of that individual's potential effectiveness as President. For that reason, we have also examined the relationships between the vote and comparative evaluations of the two candidates concerning each of those adjectives or expressions. None of those measures exhibited any independent statistically significant relationship with the vote when we accounted for the above three qualities as well as all of our variables in prior stages. For that reason, it is tempting to conclude that those qualities played no visible role in shaping voters' decision-making in the 1992 election. Such a conclusion, however, is likely to be controversial.

In the first place, the absence of any apparent (or significant) impact for comparative evaluations based on the attribute "moral" will be surprising to many observers, given the substantial emphasis on charges concerning Bill Clinton's character and private life during the campaign. For that reason, we have also included in this chapter our standard sequence of descriptive statistics concerning the measures based on the question about "moral." These results appear in Table 15.11, which suggests that evaluations concerning "moral" were strongly related to

Table 15.11 Personal Qualities with Insignificant Effects: The Case of "Moral"

1. Average Vote Among Most Pro-Clinton:	1.00
Clinton "Very Much," and Bush "Not At All" (N = 28)	
2. Average Vote Among Most Pro-Bush:	−.74
Bush "Very Much," and Clinton "Not At All" (N = 147)	
3. Difference in Average Vote:	1.74
Most Pro-Clinton minus Most Pro-Bush	
4. Bivariate Unstandardized Regression Coefficient	1.35
(Personal Qualities Scored −1 to +1)	
5. Coefficient from Multiple Regression with Social and	1.11
Economic Characteristics Held Constant	
6. With Party Identification (Party ID) Also Held Constant	.72
7. With Specific Policy-Related Predispositions (But NOT Party	.72
ID) Also held Constant	
8. With Liberal vs. Conservative Self-Designation Also Held	.64
Constant	
9. With Party ID AND All Policy-Related Predispositions Also	.48
Held Constant	
10. With Preferences on All Current Policy Issues Also Held	.44
Constant	
11. With Perceptions of Current Personal and National	.41
Conditions Also Held Constant	
12. With Retrospective Evaluations of the Current President in	.18
Office Also Held Constant	
#13. With Evaluations of the Candidates' Other Personal Qualities	(.03)
Also Held Constant	
14. With Prospective Evaluations of the Candidates and Parties	(.00)
Also Held Constant	

(Coefficients appear in parentheses if the estimated p value is >.1).
The entry marked with # is designated the "apparent total effect."

the vote and were not reduced to an insignificant value until we controlled for other personal qualities. Nevertheless, given the impact of the three traits we have just discussed, the addition of a variable constructed from comparisons based on morality did not reveal any independent effect based on that criterion. However, as we shall note in more detail below, three of the five "failures" can be added to "honest," "cares," or "inspiring" to form three two-item dimensions for further consideration.

We now turn to the primary issue of the degree to which these specific items represent distinct personal qualities or, rather, more general criteria for evaluation. We do so, however, with little expectation that we will learn more about the characterization of Bush and Clinton in terms of morality.

General Dimensions of Trait Assessment

As we attempt to move from specific traits to more general "dimensions" and in the direction of a single global evaluation of the personal qualities of the candidates, it is important to keep in mind the extent to which our research strategy in this book is different from that of those who have contributed most to the study of political leaders' traits. Once we move beyond comparative evaluations concerning specific traits (where we do not sense any tension with the work of others), our criteria for statistical analysis differ markedly from those used by other scholars. In particular, other analysts may sometimes examine validating criteria looking for qualitative differences among traits while controlling against the intrusion of only selected other variables. We move the inquiry immediately into a larger multivariate context where the trait-based variables, or combinations of them, are placed relatively near the end of an extended sequence of possibly confounding antecedent variables. Where other scholars have been properly concerned with establishing content differences among traits, and discerning their ability to discriminate among different policy or performance domains, we have focused on a prior question: are we adding to our ability to distinguish between Democratic and Republican voters? It is not that we are uninterested in the degree to which alternative measures provide additional descriptive discrimination, but we give first priority to understanding and describing differences between voters who have chosen different candidates for President.

Our first effort to generalize by considering the four dimensions discussed earlier is modestly informative and, in one aspect, somewhat disruptive. Three of the four pairs of traits that have been used to define the two-variable dimensions contain one each of the three variables that achieve significant apparent effect "on their own." In each case, adding a second variable in combination with the first of the pair increases the magnitude of the apparent unstandardized effect of the dimension above that for either variable alone. The apparent total effect coefficient for effectiveness is .24 ("gets things done" plus .14 for "inspiring" alone); for integrity the coefficient is .14 ("moral" plus .10 for "honest" taken alone) and for empathy .25 ("compassion" plus .24 for "cares" by itself). Thus the dimensions based on pairs of variables seem substantively relevant as factors pertinent to voters' choices, and our analysis remains congruent with the work of scholars specializing in the study of the personal qualities of the candidates.

The one confusing result of our use of variable pairs to represent more general "dimensions" concerns the consequence of combining "knowledgeable" and "intelligent" to measure competence. When all four personal dimensions are included in our 1992 analysis, the coefficient for competence is visibly and significantly *negative*. We believe the unexpected value is an artifact of the extraordinary number of respondents who indicated "no difference" between Bush and Clinton—which sharply limited the amount of projection based on other sources of candidate evaluation. For that reason, and because neither variable alone produced a significant coefficient, we then deleted those traits from all subsequent analysis.

Because of this outcome of the attempt to assess competence as one of four dimensions, following the literature to a still higher level of generalization implied by the "two-factor" results of the work reviewed by Funk would result in a substantial problem of interpretation. At this level of generality, the two factors are again named competence (effectiveness plus competence) and integrity (trust plus empathy). According to Funk's analysis, confirmatory factor analysis of the eight variables shows a better fit to four factors than for two, but the two-factor results are still highly satisfactory by technical factor analytic standards.

The apparent total effect coefficients for the two-factor generalization of eight traits (as representing only two dimensions, competence and integrity) are in accord with the presumption that each of the four pairs involved does contribute a separate and more or less independent component to their respective dimensions. The coefficient for the four-variable measure of integrity does indeed look like the combination of its pair of two-variable components; .25 for empathy and .14 for integrity combine for an apparent total effect coefficient of .40 for integrity. Thus, although located very near the end of our long causal chain, voters' combined assessments of the candidate traits of "honest," "moral," "compassionate," and "cares about people like me" seem to be a major coherent influence on individual vote choice.

The second of the two dimensions also has an apparent total effect coefficient (+.10, which drops below our statistical threshold for significance) that looks almost exactly like a blend of the two-variable measures of competence ($-.16$) and effectiveness ($+.24$).[6] Although this is indirect evidence further confirming the uniqueness of each of the basic four dimensions, it also is evidence that the "mechanical" construction of a second, more general factor by simply following the factor analytic lead is not very sensible. The positive contribution of the four-variable two-component dimension is obscured by the artifactual, substantively meaningless negative contribution of the combination of "knowledgeable" and "intelligent," at least where assessments of Bush and Clinton in 1992 are concerned. Adding them to a measure based on the two-item measure of "effectiveness" will not enhance our understanding of voters' choices between Bush and Clinton. In like manner, the search for a single global assessment of all eight traits representing the theme of candidates' personal qualities is certainly doomed if one of the four constituent components is uninterpretable and serves to offset the explanatory contributions of the other three.

In short, our participation in the search for a global assessment of candidates' personal qualities comes up short of the impressive single-factor solution suggested by Funk. This may well be a matter of measurement operations and techniques rather than a problem of conceptualization. Nevertheless, we have no strong theory about the dimensionality of "presidential person perception" or about the psychological integration of traits measuring personal qualities of political leaders. Without a strong theory, and recognizing the heavily inductive, empirical base of at least the mechanics of all-purpose factor analysis, we have retreated from the search for a single, multiple-item global assessment to represent voter reactions to candidates' traits as one stage in our model. Instead, we will take advantage of the increase in analytic power produced by combining six of the traits into the three pairs reflecting empathy, integrity, and trust. As has been true for all other multi-variable themes in our model, we have deferred our summary assessment of the importance of the personal qualities of the candidates until Chapter 17.

■ Alternative Assessments of the Role of Personal Qualities Based on Structured versus Open-Ended Questions

As in our previous analyses of voters' policy-related attitudes and evaluations of presidential performance, we have compared two alternative approaches to assessing the role played by voters' impressions of the

Table 15.12 Impact of Personal Qualities Based on Structured vs. Open-Ended Questions: Explanations Based on Voters' Perceptions of the Candidates vs. Their "Reasons" for Choice

	Standardized Regression Coefficients for Measures Based on Structured Questions About Specific Qualities		Standardized Regression Coefficients for Measures Based on Responses to Open-Ended Questions About the Candidates		Percentage of Clinton/Bush Voters Who Gave One or More Open-ended Responses Within the Designated Category
	Total Effect:* With Other Personal Qualities Held Constant	Direct Effect: With ALL Other Variables Held Constant	With Summaries of Likes/Dislikes for Other Personal Qualities Also Held Constant	With Summary Measures for ALL Other Likes/Dislikes Also Held Constant	
Cares About People Like Me	.11	(.04)	(.02)	(.01)	1.3
Honest	.04	(.02)	.12	.08	24.2
Inspiring	.06	(.02)	.04	(.02)	3.7
Moral	(.01)	(.00)	(.01)	(.01)	5.6

*All analyses include controls for the standard set of social and economic characteristics, party identification, policy-related predispositions, current policy preferences, perceptions of current conditions, and retrospective evaluations of the current President in office. The number of cases (N) for all of these analyses is 1193.

(Coefficients for which the estimated value of p is >.1 appear in parentheses).

candidates' personal qualities. The first of these methods is based on the structured questions discussed earlier, and the second relies on those answers to the NES open-ended questions about the candidates that concern the same kinds of qualities.

From Table 15.12 we note that these two methods for assessing the electoral relevance of specific personal qualities lead to strikingly different conclusions. In particular, very few respondents volunteered candidates' concerns for "people like me," and the standardized coefficient for our summary of such responses was very small and insignificant (.02). In contrast, the standardized apparent total effect coefficient for comparative evaluations of the two candidates concerning the degree to which they "care about people like me" was very substantial (.11), and clearly larger than for the other personal qualities in this analysis. Both methods suggest that impressions of the two candidates' honesty and inspirational qualities also played some role in shaping voters' choices, although the impact of concerns about the candidates' honesty may have been more effectively captured by the NES open-ended questions. Neither method documented much popular reaction to the singular term "moral."

Furthermore, answers to open-ended questions that deal with the candidates' personal qualities were not very effective in identifying voters for whom those qualities were particularly important. As shown in Table 15.13, the apparent total effects for voters' evaluations of all three of these qualities (which had some significant impact on the vote) were no higher for voters who explicitly mentioned those topics than for voters

Table 15.13 Differences in the Apparent Effects of Personal Qualities Between Respondents Who Did and Did Not Mention That Topic as a Reason To "Like" or "Dislike" One of the Candidates

Name of Specific Personal Quality	Percentage Who Mentioned That Personal Quality	Unstandardized Coefficient (b) for All Voters	Unstandardized Coefficient (b) for Those Who Did Not Mention	Change in Coefficient for Those Who Did Mention
Cares About People	1.3	.24	.24	(.03)
Honest	24.2	.10	.10	(.03)
Inspiring	3.7	.14	.14	(−.01)

who did not—even in the case of concerns about the candidates' honesty, which were mentioned by about 25 percent of the respondents who voted for Clinton or Bush.

As in our previous comparisons of this sort, we conclude that structured questions concerning voters' evaluations of the candidates' personal qualities are, in general, better suited to describing the role of such evaluations in shaping vote choice than "mentions" of those qualities in response to open-ended questions about voters' reasons for liking or disliking the candidates.

16

★ ★ ★

Electoral Explanations for Third-Party Candidates: Understanding Support for Ross Perot

The primary purpose of this book is to clarify and evaluate alternative explanations of voters' choices between the Republican and Democratic candidates for President. Popular support for third-party candidates represents a significant—and recurring—aspect of the American electoral system, but a general explanation of such support would require an analysis that is well beyond the scope of this volume. Three elections in the post–World War II era have seen serious nationwide challenges to the Democratic/Republican hegemony over the U.S. electoral system. A fourth effort—or two fourth efforts—were launched in 1948 by Henry A. Wallace, a liberal Democrat, and his Progressive Party, and J. Strom Thurmond, leading a very conservative Democratic States' Rights Party. Only Wallace, Secretary of Agriculture under Franklin Roosevelt, was on the ballot in all of the then 48 states; the Progressive Party tallied 2.4 percent of the popular vote, doing best in New York with just over 8 percent of the vote. Thurmond, then a conservative Democratic governor of South Carolina, now a conservative Republican senator from the same state, also garnered 2.4 percent of the national vote, concentrated in the South where he won the electoral votes of four Southern states and came in second in Georgia.

Twenty years later, a half-century after the Bull Moose became the symbol of Theodore Roosevelt's third-party effort, another Wallace, the conservative Democratic governor of Alabama, George Wallace, led the American Independent Party to victory in five Southern states. In 1980, former congressman John Anderson won 10 percent of the national vote

438

as a moderate Republican alternative to Reagan; and in 1992 Ross Perot's national vote total reached 19 percent.

The one thing all four (or five) of these efforts had in common was that they had virtually nothing in common. They were all "minor party" efforts that were in fact not efforts of parties as much as personal efforts—although there was continuity in the Southern infrastructure connecting Thurmond and the various Wallace candidacies.[1] But the George Wallace/John Anderson/Ross Perot races had very little in common: one was a conservative bolt from the Democratic Party, one a liberal bolt from the Republican ranks, and one a centrist bolt from the blue. In our previous essays, we have paid only cursory attention to minor candidates and have left the explanation of popular support for such candidates to researchers who specialize in their campaigns. In 1992, however, Ross Perot's campaign was more successful than that of any third candidate since Roosevelt's "Bull Moose" campaign in 1912. At one point in the campaign Perot was actually ahead in the polls, and the magnitude of the success of his renewed campaign (after temporarily withdrawing from the race) could have had a major impact on the outcome of the close contest between Clinton and Bush.[2]

Because of the historic levels reached by the Perot vote, we reexamined all of the variables we considered to be explanations of voters' choices between Clinton and Bush to see if factors influencing the two-party vote also played a visible role in shaping voters' decisions concerning Perot. We were also persuaded that a direct examination of the Perot vote was important because some accounts of his campaign have led to what we think are unwarranted suggestions that the Perot candidacy was a forerunner to the emergence of a true third party in American politics. Other accounts, including our own, see the Perot vote as primarily understandable on the grounds that he tapped into a large pool of citizens who were very disenchanted with the continuing conflicts between Democratic and Republican leaders and their commitment to "politics as usual."

▪ The Perot Vote

Because of the uniqueness of third candidates in an electoral system historically dominated by a two-party hegemony, it is understandably tempting to focus on emergent third candidates and try to explain why they are preferred to *both* standard party alternatives. This definition of the analytic problem ignores the likelihood that for many normal two-party voters, the candidate of the "other" major party is anathema from the beginning and really not a viable alternative under any circumstance. For all such voters, an additional candidate is not a third alternative—other, perhaps, than as an alternative to abstention.

If the American electorate had no history of past party identification, it might be reasonable to begin an analysis of the Perot vote by treating all three candidates as real contenders for each voter's favor. In fact, as the thermometer scores suggested in 1992, for many Democratic partisans the pre-election sentiment was "anybody but George," and Republicans reciprocated with a foregone rejection of even a "New" Democrat. Among truly non-partisan voters it might be appropriate to consider a third candidate as the equivalent of a major party nominee. Even so, a modicum of familiarity with the handicap borne by "independent" candidates would raise the specter of a wasted vote. In an electorate in which fewer than ten percent of the voters are likely to be "pure independents," the number of nominal partisans who enter an election period with a strong predisposition to *avoid* voting for the "other" major party's nominee is certain to be large,[3] and for them the only contest is provided by the third candidate.

For this reason, any analysis which simply contrasts Perot voters with *all* others may be seriously misleading. In fact, many of the variables we have used to explain voters' choices between Clinton and Bush also appear to be quite relevant for explaining choices concerning Perot when that analysis is carried out in two parts—one for those voters who appeared to be choosing between Perot and Bush (who had in some sense rejected Clinton), and one for those who appeared to be choosing between Perot and Clinton (all of whom had in some sense rejected Bush).

The simplest approach to such an analysis simply deletes those who voted for Clinton from the analysis of voters who chose Perot or Bush and deletes Bush voters from the analysis of choices between Perot and Clinton. Because of its simplicity, we have primarily relied on that approach to distinguish between the two kinds of Perot-related decisions that voters may have made in 1992. We also carried out a more refined version of that strategy which was based on affective thermometer ratings of candidates in order to further restrict the analysis to the voters for whom one of the major candidates was demonstrably out of the running, and the results of those analyses largely confirm those based on the simpler analytic format.

On the basis of media reports and other scholars' analyses of the Perot campaign, we began our inquiry with several clear expectations concerning characteristics that might have distinguished the "Perot vote." In general, we expected that voters in the NES sample would be more likely to support Perot if they were: relatively young, male, not Black, not identified with either of the major parties, had a negative impression of both major candidates, or shared a distrust of an omnipresent federal government. Several of these predictions could have been based on prior research on other third-party candidates, and all are clearly suggested by Table 16.1, based on the NES 1992 survey.

We should note here that the frequently cited association between support for Perot and general cynicism or distrust concerning the federal government disappears if one takes into account negative attitudes toward both major party candidates in 1992. The bivariate relationship between distrust and voting for Perot can also be eliminated by replacing the 1992 answers to the trust-related questions with answers by the same respondents to the same questions from 1990 in the NES panel design spanning both years. This reveals that differences in "trust" in 1990 did not carry over to support for Perot two years later. Both of these results suggest that Perot's success was *not* based on exploiting accumulated long-term high levels of cynicism or distrust concerning government in general. In support of this contradiction of much conventional wisdom, an insightful analysis by John Zaller argues that Perot, in fact, was responsible for *creating* attitudes of distrust rather than benefiting from pre-existing cynicism.[4] Zaller's argument is impressive because of the rich array of data and the theoretical discussion he brings to bear on the topic. At the same time, it is clear that dissatisfaction with current political leaders played an important role in creating the base for Perot's support.

As in Chapters 10 through 15, we begin our analysis of the Perot vote by examining the degree to which familiar social and economic characteristics appear to have been activated in shaping voters' decisions to vote for Perot. We then consider the apparent influence of the variables we have assigned to the second stage in our model, partisan and policy-related predispositions. As before, the third bloc of variables to be

Table 16.1 Frequently Mentioned Correlates of Support for Perot

	Percent Vote for Perot	(Number of Cases)
Generation		
Post-New Deal	22%	(840)
New Deal or Prior	13%	(620)
Gender		
Male	24%	(686)
Female	14%	(774)
Race		
Non-Black	21%	(1297)
Black	3%	(163)
Partisan Identification		
No Identification	27%	(519)
Rep. or Dem. Identification	14%	(941)
Attitudes Toward Major Candidates		
Thermometers for Bush and Clinton below 50	59%	(63)
Both below 70 (but not both below 50)	29%	(411)
All other combinations	12%	(986)
Deficit as "Most Important Problem"		
Yes	23%	(461)
No	17%	(999)
Predispositions Concerning Limited Government		
Anti-government (−1 to −.1)	25%	(496)
Moderate (−.1 to .1)	17%	(57)
Pro-government (.1 to 1.0)	16%	(907)
Combined Policy-related Preferences		
Consistently conservative (−1 to −.2)	19%	(558)
Neutral or moderate (−.2 to +.2)	23%	(630)
Consistently liberal (.2 to +1)	10%	(272)

NOTE: Cell entries are percentages who voted for Perot.

considered involves voters' opinions about issues that were emphasized in the 1992 campaign, and includes their perceptions of current conditions as well as their preferences concerning various disagreements over federal policy. Our analysis concludes by assessing the combined effects of all policy-related conflicts and the impact of voters' evaluations of George Bush's performance as President.

For each of these explanatory variables and themes, our analysis stops short of the multiple-stage elaboration we used in Chapters 10 through 15. Moreover, the content of the first four stages does not include any measures of possibly unique relevance to a Perot voter. These limitations exist because the NES coverage of voter responses to Perot was limited due to his interruption of his own campaign. Consequently, we concentrate on the apparent total effects for each variable in the first four stages of our model.[5]

As discussed above, we present alternative estimates of those effects based on two quite different ways of thinking about the meaning of the Perot-related dependent variable involved. In the first and more conventional of these approaches, Perot voters are contrasted with all other voters—with the combined set of Bush and Clinton voters. Analysis using this approach suggests that the standard array of explanations for vote choice in two-party presidential elections is not highly relevant to understanding the Perot vote. In the alternative approach we take the voters' perspective. Utilizing candidate thermometer scores to measure evaluations of the three candidates, we estimate the effects of our standard roster of explanatory themes on two subsets of voters: the first subset presumably chose between Perot and Bush because both candidates, according to their thermometer scores, were clearly preferred to Clinton; the second subset appears to have chosen between Perot and Clinton because they were both clearly preferred to Bush. This procedure seems well suited to maintain the analytic language for talking about voters' apparent *choices* rather than simply describing *differences* among groups of voters.

There were, however, two serious drawbacks to this second approach. First, it left out voters for whom there was not a clear preference between Bush and Clinton as well as those for whom Perot was the clear third and least favored choice. Second, this procedure limited the analysis to relatively small groups of voters, so that our statistical estimates were more vulnerable to sampling variability.

As a compromise we also followed a third, slightly different approach that clearly separated three groups of voters: those who supported Bush, the Clinton voters, and the voters who supported Perot. Clinton voters were excluded from analyses in which the other voters appear to have chosen between Perot and Bush, and Bush voters were excluded from analyses in which the other voters appear to have chosen between Perot and Clinton. For each of our explanatory themes, this pair of analyses identifies factors which appear to have influenced voters' choices concerning Perot in ways that depended on which major party candidate was, *from the perspective of the voter,* the more plausible alternative. This procedure permits the coefficients for each variable to take on very different values for voters who may have made a conscious choice between Perot and Bush and for voters who chose between Perot and Clinton.

The results of this third procedure largely confirmed our conclusions from the second and somewhat more restrictive procedure discussed above. Furthermore, the third approach is based on a much larger number of voters, so that our statistical estimates are much more reliable. For that reason, we will primarily report on the results of the third (and simpler) procedure, but we will refer to the results of the second whenever they suggest a somewhat different conclusion.

▪ The Relevance of Social and Economic Characteristics

Some of the social and economic characteristics we have used to explain choices between Clinton and Bush have a clear and consistent connection with voters' decisions concerning Perot, no matter how we structure the analysis. Table 16.2 presents the apparent impact of each characteristic on voting for Perot, based on analyses that included all of these characteristics *and party identification,* in order to remove any influence that should be attributed to the relationships among these characteristics and long-term influences from other variables. Column 1, derived from our first approach, presents coefficients from an analysis which includes all voters, where voters who chose Clinton *or* Bush are scored 0 and Perot voters are scored 1. Column 2 presents coefficients for the same variables for an analysis which is restricted to voters who chose between Bush and Perot (thereby excluding all Clinton voters), and Column 3, also from our third approach, presents the results of an analysis that is restricted to voters who chose between Clinton and Perot (thereby excluding those who voted for Bush). Examining all three columns, it is clear that voters who were older (or were *not* in the post-New Deal generation), female, college graduates, and in the lowest quintile in family income (and not in the highest quintile) were visibly *less* likely to vote for Perot. These results are not modified in any consistent fashion when we restrict our analyses to voters whose

Table 16.2 Sources of Perot Support Based on Social and Economic Characteristics: Alternative Estimates Based on Different Definitions of "Choice"

Name of Explanatory Variables	Perot Vote for all Voters (P = 1, B + C = 0)	Perot vs. Bush (P = 1, B = 0, C = Excluded)	Perot vs. Clinton (P = 1, C = 0, B = Excluded)
Generation (Post-New Deal)	.10	.09	.18
Gender (Female)	−.10	−.10	−.17
College Graduate	−.11	−.13	−.12
Union Household	(−.01)	(.07)	(−.08)
Income: lowest 5th	−.08	(−.06)	−.15
Income: highest 5th	.05	(.02)	(.10)
Rent (vs. Own)	(.02)	.08	(−.01)
Never Married	(.03)	.12	(−.03)
Non-evangelical Protestants			
Uncommitted	(.02)	(−.06)	(.08)
Committed	(−.02)	−.17	(.09)
Evangelical Protestants			
Uncommitted	(−.04)	−.18	(.05)
Committed	−.14	(−.37)	(.10)
Catholics			
Uncommitted	(−.05)	(−.10)	(.04)
Committed	(.05)	(−.04)	.17
Jewish	(−.08)	(.23)	(−.14)
Other Religion/MD	(−.05)	(−.14)	(−.01)
	N = 1297	N = 745	N = 815

NOTE: All analyses restricted to non-Black respondents.
(Coefficients appear in parentheses if the estimated p value is > .1).

thermometer scores indicate that their first or second choices included Perot.

At this point, we should emphasize the fact that the results in Table 16.2 (and all subsequent results in this chapter) are based only on non-Black respondents, because of the nearly total absence of variability in voting support for Perot among Black respondents in the 1992 NES sample. For whatever reason, Perot was not at all successful in attracting Black voters. We have few insights into the sources of Perot's differential success among the various social and economic groups, although it is true that Perot's greater success among younger voters might have been predicted from similar tendencies where other third-party candidates were concerned, including George Wallace and John Anderson.

Some of the social and economic characteristics exhibit quite different relationships to support for Perot, depending on whether the choice was between Perot and Bush or Perot and Clinton. Thus, voters who rented (instead of owned) their home were more likely, +.08, to vote for Perot than Bush (when Clinton voters are excluded from the analysis), while the same coefficient is insignificant (and negative, −.01) for voters who chose between Perot and Clinton. Similarly, voters who had never been married were substantially more likely to vote for Perot than Bush, +.12, when Clinton voters were excluded, and the comparable coefficient was negative, but again insignificant (−.03), when the analysis was restricted to those who chose between Perot and Clinton. Furthermore, both of these contrasting effects are apparent when the two analyses are restricted to include only voters whose thermometer ratings placed Perot in first or second place.

The most suggestive examples of social contrasts between Bush and Clinton in competition with Perot, however, involve the religious groups discussed in Chapters 9 and 10. Perot's lack of support among Committed Evangelicals, −.37, is largely based on voters' choices between Bush and Perot; the corresponding coefficient is positive (+.10) but is not statistically significant in the analysis of Perot and Clinton voters. Similar, although weaker, patterns can be seen for other Committed Protestants and Catholics. Even Jewish voters exhibited opposite-signed coefficients concerning support for Perot when they were contrasted with voters with no religious affiliation, (+.23) for Perot versus Bush and (−.14) for Perot versus Clinton, although both coefficients are statistically insignificant because of the small sample size for that group. It seems clear that Bush won in the competition with Perot for votes of the committed in all major traditions. It is also true, although less unequivocally so, that Perot won in the competition for religious votes against Clinton. The rank ordering seems clear: Bush wins over Perot who wins over Clinton in the competition for support among the more religious. Clinton is the consistent choice among the non-religious. This simply extends our earlier hypothesis that religion is a growing foundation for contemporary political decisions. Most of these patterns are sustained or accentuated when our separate analyses are redirected to cases in which voters' thermometer ratings clearly put one of the two major party candidates in third place.

▪ Partisan and Policy-related Predispositions

In explanations of voting for third-party candidates, the role of partisan identification is often most properly expressed in terms of the existence of the *strength* of party identifications instead of their partisan *direction*. As shown in Table 16.1, the percentage of voters who cast their ballots for Ross Perot in the fall of 1992 was visibly higher (27 percent) among those with no partisan identification (including respondents with "no preference" or those who were classified as "apolitical" as well as Independents) than among those who described themselves as either Democrats *or* Republicans (14 percent). This apparent negative impact of identification with *either* major party is visible in all of our multivariate analyses of Perot support.

As in other areas, however, the impact of partisan identifications on vote choices concerning Perot is more substantial than the estimate suggested by this simple formulation. When we separate our Perot analysis into the two separate inquiries, each of which is based on the subsamples that chose Perot or one of the major party candidates, it appears that the impact of long-term partisanship involves the "direction" as well as the existence of such identifications. As shown in the first row and column of Table 16.3, the impact of our three-category directional measure of partisan identification on support for Perot appears to be nonexistent (−.01) when it is included along with other predispositions and social characteristics in explaining dichotomous choices between Perot and either of the other candidates. The second and third columns of that row, however, suggest that the same variable had a *positive* impact (Independents prefer Perot), +.14, on support for Perot among voters who chose between Perot and Bush, and a *negative* impact (Independents also prefer Perot), −.18, among those who chose between Perot and Clinton. These coefficients are only slightly reduced when the samples for our two (separate) analyses are further reduced by our second approach of excluding all voters who did not clearly prefer Perot to one of the two major candidates.

To be sure, voters with *no* partisan identification were (on average) more likely than Republicans to vote for Perot instead of Bush, and more

Table 16.3 Sources of Perot Support Based on Partisan and Policy-Related Predispositions: Alternative Estimates Based on Different Definitions of "Choice"

Name of Explanatory Variables	Perot Vote for all Voters (P = 1, B + C = 0)	Perot vs. Bush (P = 1, B = 0, C = Excluded)	Perot vs. Clinton (P = 1, C = 0, B = Excluded)
Party ID	(−.01)	.14	−.18
Lib./Con. Self-designation	(−.02)	.12	−.10
Equality	(.03)	.17	(−.05)
Limited Government	−.06	−.05	−.11
Morality	(.00)	.10	−.13
Unions vs. Business	(.00)	(.04)	(−.00)
Homosexuals vs. Evangelicals	(−.02)	(.04)	(−.05)
Isolationism	(.01)	.04	(−.02)
Service in Vietnam	.02	.06	(−.00)
	N = 1297	N = 745	N = 815

NOTE: All analyses restricted to non-Black respondents.
(Coefficients appear in parentheses if the estimated p value is > .1).

likely than Democrats to vote for Perot instead of Clinton. In addition, however, Republican identifiers were even more likely than Independents to vote for Perot instead of Clinton (after Bush voters are excluded), and Democratic identifiers were even more likely than Independents to vote for Perot instead of Bush (after Clinton voters are excluded). When the analysis is restricted to voters who appeared to be choosing between Perot and only one of the major candidates (most of whom had no intention of voting for the other one), partisan identification appears to have a strong monotonic influence on the likelihood of voting for Perot. The *sign* of that apparent effect, however, clearly depends on which major candidate has been set aside because he was presumably the clear third-place choice for those voters.

This same pattern can be seen in relationships between support for Perot and all but one of the policy-related predispositions. Thus, the apparent lack of visible connection between support for Perot and voters' self-designations as liberal or conservative is misleading when, as in column 1 of Table 16.3, the coefficient (−.02) is based on an analysis which compares Perot voters with the combined set of all voters who chose Clinton *or* Bush. When we restrict the analysis to voters who chose between Perot *or* Bush, that same variable appears to show a substantial positive impact on liberal support for Perot, +.12, and a similarly sized *negative* impact, −.10, with conservatives favoring Perot when our analysis is restricted to voters who chose between Perot or Clinton. This difference is *precisely* the pattern that would be expected if Perot's appeal is appropriately described in terms of moderate or "centrist" preferences. It should be noted, however, that these opposite-signed coefficients (for ideological self-designation) essentially disappear when we restrict both analyses to voters who clearly saw either Bush or Clinton as less attractive than both Perot and the other major candidate.

The apparent impact of predispositions concerning equality is not statistically distinguishable from zero when Perot voters are compared with all major candidate voters. That result conceals a clear positive impact, +.17, among those who chose between Perot and Bush (with egalitarians favoring Perot) and the suggestion of a negative impact (an insignificant −.05) with conservative sentiments favoring Perot among those who chose between Perot and Clinton. Furthermore, that difference (between opposite-signed coefficients for the two separate analyses) is *accentuated* when the two samples are further restricted to ensure that voters' thermometer ratings for one of the major candidates were in third place. This same pattern can be seen even more clearly in differential effect estimates for morality, with clearly significant coefficients of +.10 versus −.13.

The single deviation from the liberal/conservative reversal of signs— depending on who the major party alternative was—occurs in the domain of attitudes toward limited government. There the apolitical, non-partisan candidacy of Perot was highlighted—Perot received disproportionate support from voters favoring limited government, whoever his opposition was, −.05 and −.11.

In our view, the signed coefficients for all of our four established measures of policy-related predispositions are quite plausible in the context of these candidates' campaigns in 1992. Voters who were certain they were not going to vote for Bill Clinton (for whatever combination of reasons) were faced with a choice in which one of the remaining candidates, Perot, was less conservative, and the other, Bush, had exhibited a lesser commitment to equality and placed a greater emphasis on traditional morality. Both Bush and Perot emphasized the importance of the private sector and the need to limit government, albeit in different ways, so a smaller coefficient might be expected for that predisposition among voters who were in some sense choosing between these two similar candidates. Perot and Bush may also have been associated with somewhat different positions on foreign affairs, as suggested by the modest positive coefficient associated with isolationism and service in Vietnam. The absence of any significant difference between Bush and Perot seems plausible where the two group-related conflicts in our set of predispositions are concerned, and none have surfaced in our analysis of voters' choices between those candidates.

On the other hand, voters who were clearly opposed to Bush but were at least open to the possibility of voting for Perot found a choice in which Perot was clearly more committed than Clinton to "limited government"—and in which Clinton was presumably vulnerable among those who were strongly committed to traditional morality. Those two candidates did not present consistently different positions regarding our other predispositional variables (concerning group differences and foreign affairs), and we found no significant coefficients for those variables among voters who chose between Clinton *and* Perot.

▪ The Relevance of Current Issues

Ross Perot emphasized a somewhat distinctive set of policy issues and current conditions, including a strong commitment to deficit reduction and improving the economy in addition to his general criticism of "politicians in Washington." During the campaign, however, Perot took positions on several other policy issues that also appeared to influence voters' choices between Clinton and Bush.

Policy Preferences

Table 16.4 presents estimates for the apparent total effect of several current issues, based on the same alternative definitions of voters' decisions concerning Perot. As with our previous results, these analyses include controls for all of our partisan and policy-related predispositions and all but one of our standard set of social and economic characteristics—since we continue to exclude Black voters because of the lack of variability in support for Perot within that group.

It should be noted that in deference to Perot's campaign themes we

Table 16.4 Sources of Perot Support Based on Current Issues: Alternative Estimates Based on Different Definitions of "Choice"

Name of Explanatory Theme/Variable	Perot Vote for all Voters (P = 1, B + C = 0)	Perot vs. Bush (P = 1, B = 0, C = Excluded)	Perot vs. Clinton (P = 1, C = 0, B = Excluded)
Policy Preferences			
Aid to Disadvantaged	(−.03)	(.03)	−.08
Taxes	(.00)	.04	(−.01)
Private School Funding	(.00)	(.01)	(−.02)
Abortion	.06	.07	.07
Gays in Military	(−.02)	(.01)	−.06
Military Strength	.05	.13	(−.00)
Spending Cut	(.01)	(.05)	(.06)
Deficit MIP	(.03)	.08	(.02)
All Policy-related Conflicts			
Predispositions and Policy Index	(−.05)	.44	−.46
Perceptions of Conditions:			
State of Economy	(.03)	.13	−.08
U.S. Position in the World	.04	.05	(.01)
Recent Layoff in Household	(.10)	.22	(−.03)
	N = 1297	N = 745	N = 815

NOTE: All analyses restricted to non-Black respondents.
(Coefficients appear in parentheses if the estimated p value is $> .1$).

have added three policy topics that were not significantly related to vote choice in our earlier analysis of issue differences between Bush voters and Clinton voters: abortion, government spending cuts, and the budget deficit as the nation's "most important problem." As shown in column 1, only two of eight issues (concerning abortion and military strength) appear to have had any significant impact on support for Perot when the analysis includes all voters who chose either Bush or Clinton. As before, however, a somewhat different picture emerges when we conduct separate analyses for voters who chose between Perot and Bush and those who chose between Perot and Clinton.

In particular, the modest connection between military-related preferences and support for Perot (.05) appears to have been entirely concentrated among voters who chose between Perot and Bush, (.13); it is nonexistent (−.00) among those who chose between Perot and Clinton. Similarly, the initially insignificant negative coefficient concerning aid to the disadvantaged appears to conceal a substantial effect, −.08, for those who chose between Perot and Clinton. Both of these differences make sense in terms of the themes emphasized by the three candidates, and both are accentuated when we restrict both subsamples to voters who saw Perot as "better" than one of the major candidates.

Several policy issues were (at best) only weakly related to support for Perot, no matter which way we structure the analysis. Of particular interest is the fact that we found only the statistical suggestion of a relationship between support for Perot and voters' preferences for "less" spending on existing government programs—despite Perot's emphasis on expenditure control as a crucial component in reducing the federal deficit. There is, moreover, clear evidence that emphasis on the deficit (as one of the nation's most important problems) was relevant for choices between Perot and Bush, +.08, but not for those who voted for Perot or Clinton (.02). There is also evidence that attitudes toward homosexuals in the military had an impact on voting for Perot instead of Clinton, −.06, but that coefficient disappears when we further restrict the analysis to voters who gave Perot a higher thermometer rating than Bush— and may therefore have actually "chosen" between Perot and Clinton.

Perot's position in the middle between a more conservative Bush and a more liberal Clinton is dramatically portrayed when we turn to the summary measure for all policy-related predispositions and current policy preferences that we introduced late in Chapter 12. As shown in column 1 of Table 16.4, the apparent impact of those combined (or averaged) preferences on voting for Perot rather than *either* of the other candidates is insignificant (−.05). That small coefficient, however, conceals very large and opposite-signed coefficients for our two separate analyses. Thus, the apparent combined effect of policy-related attitudes on support for Perot was both positive and large, +.44, among those who voted for Perot or Bush. This result indicates a powerful tendency for more conservative voters to choose Bush and more liberal (or less conservative) voters to choose Perot—if they were *not* going to vote for Clinton. Similarly, the apparent impact of policy-related attitudes on support for Perot rather than Clinton is sharply negative, −.46. It is clear that more conservative voters voted for Perot and more liberal voters chose Clinton—if they were *not* going to vote for Bush. The overall size of these coefficients is similar to those from the Clinton-Bush analysis in preceding chapters.

When we approach the explanation of Perot support in this way, policy-related preferences appear to have played a very large role in the Perot vote. Given the demonstration in Chapter 12 that the Bush-Clinton choice was heavily influenced by conservative/liberal differences among their voters, and given that earlier in this chapter there seemed to be no ideological (or policy-related) relevance when Perot voters were compared to the combined Bush/Clinton electors, what we have just observed is a virtual logical necessity. Nevertheless, the centrism of the Perot candidacy can only be appreciated when contrasted with the more or less polarized constituencies on the right and on the left. Just as the Bush-Clinton contest was heavily influenced by liberal/conservative differences among their voters, those choosing between either of them and Perot were similarly impelled by ideological or policy-related comparisons.

Current Conditions

The rationale for separate analyses for those voters who chose between Perot and Bush compared with those who chose between Perot and Clinton is almost equally clear when we consider explanatory variables that are defined in terms of current conditions—concerning consensual objectives instead of policy-related conflict. All three of the condition-related variables that we have used to explain choices between Clinton and Bush were weakly linked to support for Perot when the voters who chose Clinton or Bush are combined into a single "anti-Perot" category. All three relationships, however, are substantially clarified when we conduct two separate analyses for choices between Perot and Bush or Perot and Clinton.

Specifically, perceptions of the national economy appear to have had a major positive impact on voters' choices for Perot instead of Bush, +.13. Our earlier suggestion that appraisals of "conditions" might include attitudes toward policy differences is made manifest in the visible negative impact of perceptions of economic conditions on voters' support for Perot instead of Clinton, −.08. Assessment of the size of this influence on support for Perot is unchanged when we further restrict those analyses to voters who gave Perot a higher thermometer rating than they did one of the other major candidates. In addition, the modest positive impact of voters' perception of the U.S. position in the world on support for Perot is shown to be entirely associated with choices between Perot and Bush, $+.05$, and is insignificant $(-.01)$ among voters who chose between Perot and Clinton. Finally, the initial suggestion of a positive consequence of any layoff in the household on support for Perot $(.10)$ is entirely based on voters who chose between Perot and Bush, $.22$, and that relationship becomes negative $(-.03)$ among voters who chose between Perot and Clinton. Both of these patterns are also sustained when our separate analyses are further restricted to voters who were clearly more positive about Perot than one of the major candidates.

▪ Alternative Interpretations of Perot-Related Effects

In reviewing these results based on restricted subsamples of voters, we have been sensitive to the possibility that our estimates of many coefficients are subject to selection bias, based on the statistical consequences of excluding those voters who did not appear to be "choosing between" the two candidates included in a given analysis. To be sure, it is possible that some factors which played a significant role in voters' rejection of one major candidate (so that they are *included* in our analysis of voters' choices between Perot and the other major candidate) and also played a role in shaping voters' choices concerning Perot may be omitted from our explanation of support for Perot for that group. To the extent that we have excluded such variables (and they are correlated with those we have included), they would introduce a misleading (or spurious) component in the statistical relationships between that Perot-related choice and the explanatory variables we have examined. We cannot rule out such a possibility, but we suspect that such biases are fairly small in this case.

▪ Summary

As others have emphasized, support for Ross Perot in 1992 was visibly greater among voters who did not identify with either party (than among those who did), among younger voters, among men, among Whites, and among voters with more "centrist" preferences concerning policy issues as well as ideological positions. All of these patterns persist in multivariate analyses, regardless of how we define the "choices" that voters have made concerning Perot.

Some analyses of support for Perot have reported only weak evidence to support the relevance of explanatory variables used to explain voters' choices between Clinton and Bush. We have noted that such results arise whenever the dependent variable combines all Bush and Clinton voters together as voting "against Perot." However, when potential sources of support for Perot are examined in properly segregated analyses, many of the variables we have used to explain voters' choices between Bush and Clinton appear to have played a substantial role in shaping voters' decisions concerning Perot, and the apparent effects of most variables are appropriately different between those two separate analyses. In particular:

- Partisan identifications influenced choices between both major candidates and Perot, in ways which involve the direction (as well as the existence) of such long-term identifications.
- Voters' choices between Perot and Clinton (among those who had clearly rejected Bush) were powerfully shaped by their policy-related predispositions, including ideological self-designation and attitudes toward limited government and equality. In those respects, Clinton clearly appeared as a more liberal (or less conservative) candidate than Perot, and voters who rejected Bush appeared to make their choice between the other two in ways that reflected those differences.
- Similarly, voters' choices between Perot and Bush (among those who had clearly rejected Clinton) were shaped by their policy-related preferences as well as liberal or conservative self-designation. In several areas Perot was visibly less conservative than Bush, and voters who made the choice between them appeared to act accordingly.
- The combined influence of all of the above policy-related attitudes in support for Perot was very large, according to an analysis which replaced all of our specific policy-related variables with the summary index of liberal and conservative views discussed in Chapter 12.
- Voters' perceptions of current conditions also had a substantial

positive impact on their choice for Perot rather than Bush, the incumbent President, but a more limited impact for voters who chose between Perot and the challenger Clinton.

We believe that these results should be helpful as a guide to analyses of voters' decisions concerning other third-party candidates, in addition to their relevance for understanding the "Perot phenomenon." When a significant portion of the electorate sees one of the major candidates as impossible to support, they must make a "hard choice" between the remaining major party candidate and a third candidate—even though that third candidate has only a small chance to win. When that occurs, such voters' choices might be shaped by considerations unique to the third candidate, but they should also be visibly shaped by their views concerning the topics that dominated the major party competition. Many such views were of demonstrable relevance to the Perot vote; other views, perhaps unique to the Perot candidacy, were not included in the NES survey because Perot's temporary absence from the campaign came just at the point when the survey instrument was completed. In particular, no appraisals of personal traits or prospective performance were obtained for Perot.

Analysis of the financial and media-related factors that shaped the viability of the Perot campaign lies beyond the scope of this book. Our results, however, clearly suggest that substantive concerns played an important role in shaping choices between Perot and each of the major candidates.

PART V

INTERPRETATION AND COMPARISON OF SPECIFIC ELECTIONS

17

★ ★ ★ The Importance of Specific Variables and General Themes in 1988 and 1992: Individual Differences and Aggregate Results

To this point, our statistical analyses of electoral decisions have focused on the estimation and interpretation of "apparent effects," based on the relationships between specific explanatory variables and vote choice. Our discussions of those results have occasionally referred to the relative "importance" of different types of explanations for the 1992 election, but all such statements have referred to the size of total effect coefficients for specific explanatory variables. We now shift both the rationale and the logic for evaluating and comparing the importance of different electoral explanations. As anticipated in previous chapters, we begin by distinguishing between two contrasting ways in which some of our individual variables may have played a more important role than others in a given election context. The first is based on their contribution to the *aggregate results* of that election; the second is based on their role in producing *individual differences* in voters' choices in the same election. After presenting both sets of results for specific explanatory variables, we will apply the same criteria to evaluate the importance of the eight general themes that we have used to classify all of the explanatory variables in our model.[1]

The apparent total effects derived in Chapters 10 through 15 identified those political attitudes which appear to have influenced voters' choices between Bill Clinton and George Bush. In addition to those effect estimates, we have occasionally referred to the distribution of opinions for specific variables within the electorate because of the implicit relevance of such distributions for their impact on the election outcome. In order

to use such information in assessing the importance of alternative explanations, however, we must decide which aspects of those distributions are relevant for the substantive questions we are trying to answer.

We begin by describing the rationale and logic involved in assessing
the role that each of our explanatory variables appears to have played
in determining the aggregate outcome of the 1992 election—or the
contribution that each factor appears to have made to Bill Clinton's
margin of victory. Conclusions of this sort, for a single explanatory
variable, rest on its apparent total effect on the vote *and* on the degree
to which the distribution of voters' opinions on that topic provided an
advantage to one of the candidates. In order to represent this contribution of each variable to the aggregate outcome, we will multiply the
overall apparent total effect of the variable by its mean value or average
score among those voters who chose either Bush or Clinton.

Within that general formulation, however, there are two different ways
of evaluating the central tendency or average score of each variable and
its potential (positive or negative) contribution to Bill Clinton's margin
of victory. The overall average or mean value for each explanatory
variable can either be defined in terms of the familiar simple mean score,
or it can be expressed as an "adjusted" mean. The adjusted mean would
reflect the degree to which voters had more positive (or negative) scores
on that variable than we would expect them to have—given their scores
on all of the other political variables that have been assigned to *earlier*
stages in our explanatory model. In other words, the adjusted mean is
that portion of the simple mean that cannot be attributed to sources
other than the variable under examination. When the apparent total
effect is multiplied by the adjusted mean, each of our explanatory
variables will be given a signed "contribution to the aggregate result"
that indicates the net advantage which that variable alone appears to
have provided to one candidate or the other. Each of those contributions
will be scored in terms of the net division of the votes cast for Clinton
or Bush as a component of the overall average score on the vote.
Differences between variables in the magnitudes of these contributions
are interpreted as differences in the importance of those variables in
shaping the aggregate results of the election. If there were no errors in
our statistical model, and if no variables were omitted or incorrectly
measured, the sum of this first type of contribution from all of our
political variables should add up to the overall average vote, or to
Clinton's margin of victory in 1992 (+.17).

We next shift our attention to the degree to which each explanatory variable appears to have been responsible for generating differences between voters in their choice for President. To address that question, we will combine the familiar "apparent total effect" of each variable with its standard deviation (or variability) among Bush or Clinton voters. As in our assessment of each variable's contribution to the aggregate result reflecting the winner's margin of victory, we can again contrast two different ways of defining the "importance" of a given variable in generating differences among voters, this time based on two different versions of the variable's empirical variability rather than its mean. In the first of these definitions, the variability of each variable is based on "all" of that variable, without any adjustments. In the second definition, however, we will only count that portion of each variable's standard deviation (or variability) that cannot be explained by the other political variables we have assigned to prior stages in our model. In assessing either type of importance, therefore, we will adjust our evaluation of each variable by removing the influence of prior variables in our model—thereby focusing on each variable's *unique* role in the 1992 election.

In the second section of this chapter, we move from emphasizing the roles played by individual variables to considering the combined importance of all of the attitudes that have been grouped within each of our general explanatory themes. Using an extension of the methods employed for individual variables, we offer contrasting estimates for the importance of each of our eight explanatory themes based on their apparent contributions to the aggregate result of the 1992 election *or* on their role in generating differences between voters in their choices for President.

The alternative assessments of our general explanatory themes will underscore the significance of our distinction between alternative types of importance. For example, we will emphasize the extent to which attitudes toward policy-related conflicts appear to have played a major if not dominant role in generating differences among individual voters in their choice for President, but the same attitudes appear to have made a very small net contribution to the aggregate results of the 1992 election.

With the results in hand for all eight themes in 1992, we then present the results of parallel analyses from the 1988 election. Many of the same variables are used in our explanations for both elections, but the two sets of measures are not identical. By comparing results for each of our general explanatory themes, however, we can highlight those areas where significant differences can be seen in the role played by the same factors in 1988 and 1992—either in shaping the size of the winner's plurality or in "producing" differences between individual voters in their choices for President. These comparisons between the 1988 and 1992 presidential elections suggest ways in which survey evidence might be used to compare any two electoral contests—including contests that are separated by political or national boundaries as well as time.

▪ The Apparent Importance of Specific Variables in 1992

Any explanatory variable that is based on a particular political attitude must have two empirical properties for us to suggest that it was "responsible" for some portion of the aggregate results of a given election—that attitudes on that topic made a visible contribution, either positive or negative, toward the winning candidate's margin of victory. Logically, such a contribution can only occur when voters' opinions on that variable have some apparent total effect on vote choice, *and* when the distribution of opinions in that area (or the adjusted mean value of that variable) favors one of the candidates instead of reflecting an even balance. In this section we will first assess the apparent contribution of each of our political variables to the aggregate outcome of the 1992 election by multiplying its apparent total effect by its average value or mean among Bush and Clinton voters. For each explanatory variable, the resulting product represents the extent and the direction of the hypothetical shift in the aggregate results of the election which would presumably have occurred if voters' opinions in that area had been balanced with an average score of zero, or if those opinions had not influenced voters' choices for President.

Assessing the Contributions of Specific Variables
to the Aggregate Results

Table 17.1 presents the apparent total effects for each variable along with the two different versions of the average score for all Bush/Clinton voters' opinions in that area. The first column in that table simply restates our estimates for the apparent total effects of each variable, based on the analyses discussed in Chapters 10 through 15. The second column represents our first description of the central tendencies (or average scores) for each explanatory variable that is defined in terms of a politically relevant attitude.

Because of the multiple-stage nature of the decision-making process implicit in our model, this simple average of voters' opinions in a given area is not the most appropriate indicator of the central tendency of those opinions when we wish to assess the *unique* contribution of opinions on that topic to the aggregate results of the election. For example, voters who consider themselves Republicans and have conservative preferences on several policy-related conflicts are very likely to have pro-Republican opinions on a variety of topics that are represented by explanatory variables in later stages of our model—such as evaluations of President Bush's performance in office or comparisons of the two candidates' personal qualities. Given this perspective, we must answer the following question about each explanatory variable that we have assigned to stages *after* partisan and policy-related predispositions: how much more (or less) pro-Republican (or pro-Democratic) were each voter's views than we would have expected them to be, *given* the voters' predispositions and their scores on other antecedent (political) variables? Or, more simply, how pro-Republican or pro-Democratic would the voter's views be if they were influenced only by sources that are *unique* to that variable—and not by opinions we have assigned to earlier stages?

Any answer to this question for an explanatory variable in our model located *after* partisan and policy-related predispositions must be based on a version of that variable from which we have "removed" all of the variation that can be attributed to the political variables in preceding stages. This alternative version of each variable represents that portion of the variation in that variable that can be attributed to its "unique" political content in that election (rather than to content derived from variables that preceded it in time). Such a variable is constructed as a "partial residual" from a multivariate analysis in which the given variable is treated as the dependent variable, to be explained by all of the other variables in the preceding causal stages.

Each voter's score on this unique component for a given variable is the difference between his or her actual, measured score on that variable and the score for that individual which is predicted by the apparent effects of that individual's positions on all prior partisan and policy-re-

Table 17.1 Total Effects and Average Values for Specific Political Variables in 1992: Components for Contributions to the Aggregate Result

Name of Explanatory Theme and Specific Variable	(Aggregate Result = Average Vote − +.17) Total Effect (unstandardized)	Average Score for Variable as a Whole	Average Score for Unique Component
Partisan Identification			
Party ID	.48	.14	.14
Policy-related Predispositions			
Lib./Con. Self-designation	.27	−.08	−.08
Equality	.22	.28	.28
Limited Government	.08	.28	.28
Morality	.22	−.21	−.22
Union vs. Business	.09	−.17	−.17
Homosexuals vs. Evangelicals	.15	−.14	−.14
Isolationism	.07	−.54	−.54
Service in Vietnam	.08	.07	.07
Current Policy Preferences			
Aid to the Disadvantaged	.12	.16	.09
Strength and Use of Military Force	.17	−.13	−.07
Homosexuals in the Military	.12	.09	.21
Willingness to Pay Increased Taxes	.04	−.34	−.49
Public Funds for Private Schools	.06	.12	.14

Perceptions of Current Conditions			
State of the Economy	.19	.53	.51
U.S. Position in the World	.06	.07	.08
Recent Layoff in the Family	.40	.01	.01
Retrospective Performance Evaluations			
General	.33	.18	.00
Economy	.08	.54	.30
Foreign Affairs	.05	-.13	-.26
Deficit Blame (vs. Congress)	.22	-.02	-.22
Evaluations of Personal Qualities			
Integrity	.11	-.15	-.14
Empathy	.24	.13	.08
Leadership	.19	.09	.02
Prospective Performance Evaluations			
of Candidates, re: the Economy	.30	.22	-.02
of Candidates, re: Poverty	.10	.38	.09
of Parties, re: the Economy	.07	.16	-.04
of Parties, re: Health Care Costs	.10	.43	.25

Table 17.2 Importance of Specific Political Variables Based on Contribution
to the 1992 Aggregate Result

Name of Explanatory Theme and Specific Variable	(Aggregate Result = Average Vote − +.174)	
	Transmission: Contribution of the Entire Variable	Source or Origin: Contribution of Unique Part of Variable
Partisan Identification		
Party ID	.07	.07
Policy-related Predispositions		
Lib./Con. Self-designation	−.02	−.02
Equality	.06	.06
Limited Government	.02	.02
Morality	−.05	−.05
Union vs. Business	−.02	−.02
Homosexuals vs. Evangelicals	−.02	−.02
Isolationism	−.04	−.04
Service in Vietnam	.01	.01
Current Policy Preferences		
Aid to the Disadvantaged	.02	.01
Strength and Use of Military Force	−.02	−.01
Homosexuals in the Military	.01	.02
Willingness to Pay Increased Taxes	−.01	−.02
Public Funds for Private Schools	.01	.01

lated predispositions and *any* other political or attitudinal variables that
have been assigned to prior stages in our model. The average values for
these partial residuals or unique components appear in the third column
of Table 17.1. These values represent the average value for that portion
of each political variable that cannot be attributed to prior political
variables—and may therefore be used to assess the unique contribution
of that variable to the aggregate result of the election.

Having obtained the effect estimates and averages in Table 17.1, we
now use the logic and computational procedures reviewed above to
examine the role that each of our explanatory variables appears to have
played in shaping the division of votes between Clinton and Bush in
1992—that is, the apparent contributions of each variable to Clinton's
aggregate plurality. Table 17.2 presents the results of those calculations
for each political variable in our analysis. The values in Column 1 are

Table 17.2 (continued)

Name of Explanatory Theme and Specific Variable	(Aggregate Result = Average Vote − +.174)	
	Transmission: Contribution of the Entire Variable	Source or Origin: Contribution of Unique Part of Variable
Perceptions of Current Conditions		
State of the Economy	.10	.10
U.S. Position in the World	.00	.01
Recent Layoff in the Family	.01	.00
Retrospective Performance Evaluations		
General	.06	.00
Economy	.04	.02
Foreign Affairs	−.01	−.01
Deficit Blame (vs. Congress)	−.00	−.05
Evaluations of Personal Qualities		
Integrity	−.02	−.02
Empathy	.03	.02
Leadership	.02	.00
Prospective Performance Evaluations		
of Candidates, re: the Economy	.07	.00
of Candidates, re: Poverty	.04	.01
of Parties, re: the Economy	.01	−.00
of Parties, re: Health Care Costs	.04	.02

the simple product of the apparent total effect on the vote of each variable (based on controls for the result of all prior variables) and its *unadjusted* average score for all Bush/Clinton voters, without any attempt to "remove" any of the average that might be attributable to political variables that we have assigned to earlier stages in our model. As such, the values in Column 1 represent that portion of the aggregate division of the vote that appears to have been produced by *transmitting* voters' positions on the given explanatory variable to the vote decision.

The entries in Column 2, on the other hand, represent the apparent contributions to the aggregate results of the unique portion of each explanatory variable—or the contribution that cannot be attributed to the average score of political variables we have assigned to prior stages in our model. For both columns, each entry represents an apparent contribution of voters' opinions in that area to the overall average vote, or to the division of the votes between Bill Clinton and George Bush within the NES sample (+.17). The only difference between the first and second columns concerns that portion of each variable's apparent contribution that can be attributed to the influence of variables we have assigned to earlier stages. Column 1 gives the variable credit for *all* of the contributions made by transmitting to the vote choice the influence of opinions in that area, regardless of their source or origin. Column 2 focuses on that portion of the given variable's contribution that appears to have "come from" the unique content of that variable in 1992—in the sense that it cannot be attributed to political variables that we have assigned to prior stages in our model.

As anticipated in several previous chapters, Table 17.2 suggests that voters' perceptions of the national economy in 1992 made the largest single contribution to Bill Clinton's victory over George Bush. That contribution remains essentially the same, .10 in both cases, regardless of whether we use the estimate in Column 1 or Column 2—that is, whether we give opinions in that area credit for *transmitting* the influence of perceptions that were shaped by prior partisan or policy-related predispositions, or restrict credit to voters' perceptions that were more or less critical of the economy than we would expect them to be because of the influence of those prior predispositions. In other words, none of the contributions of this variable to the election outcome can be attributed to the political variables that precede it in earlier stages of our model.

The apparent importance of several other variables, however, is substantially changed when we restrict their contribution to that portion of each variable that cannot be attributed to the opinions that we have assigned to prior stages in our model. The entries in Column 2 of Table 17.2 are necessarily identical to those in Column 1 for partisan and policy-related predispositions because they represent the first stage that is devoted to political variables. The contributions of current policy issues and conditions are only slightly modified when we adjust their average scores to remove the influences of the predispositions. As soon as we shift to explicit *evaluations*, however, the apparent contributions of many variables are substantially modified. For example, *all* of the apparent contribution of voters' general evaluations of President Bush's performance in office, .06, disappears when we remove the influence of voters' predispositions, policy preferences, and perceptions of current conditions—especially those concerning changes in the economy since the previous year.

That same procedure increases Bush's apparent benefit from voters' assignment of blame for the federal deficit to Congress rather than the President, from $-.00$ to $-.05$. On the other hand, only one of the variables in our final explanatory theme (concerning "prospective performance") retains a substantial contribution to the aggregate results of the election after we remove the influence of prior political attitudes. That variable is based on voters' assessments of the likely success of the two parties in "making health care more affordable."

Key Analytic Distinctions

Before turning to the importance of specific variables in producing individual differences in vote choice, it may be helpful to review the major conceptual and computational steps that lie between our initial description of each variable's bivariate relationship to the vote and our final assessment of its unique contribution to the aggregate election outcome. For selected variables, Table 17.3 presents a sequence of results from earlier chapters as well as from Tables 17.1 and 17.2. Each of these values has been selected to illustrate some of the possible ingredients in any conclusion about the importance of specific variables in determining the aggregate result of the 1992 election.

The first two columns of Table 17.3 are taken from the "elaboration" for the designated variable's relationship to voter choice in Chapter 12

Table 17.3 Analytic Steps Involved in Assessing the Importance of Specific Variables Concerning the Aggregate Election Outcome

Independent Variable	Bivariate Coefficient	Apparent Total Effect	Average Score	Unique Score	Unique Contribution
Homosexuals in Military	.42	.12	+.09	+.21	+.02
Economic Conditions	.63	.19	+.53	+.51	+.10
Bush: Economic Performance	.85	.08	+.54	+.30	+.02
Deficit Blame	.22	.22	−.02	−.22	−.05
Parties: Health Care	.87	.10	+.43	+.25	+.02

(for homosexuals in the military), Chapter 13 (for the state of the economy), or Chapter 14 (for Bush's handling of the economy, deficit blame, and for prospective performance evaluations of the parties on health care costs). The first column displays the simple bivariate regression coefficient for each variable, as an indication of its maximum potential influence on the vote. The second column contains the apparent total effect for each variable *after* we have removed the confounding influences of variables in prior (or the same) causal stages. The difference between these two columns is an essential result of the "logic of elaboration." It is not informative about *which* earlier stages or variables were responsible for the spurious component; such information must be obtained from the detailed elaboration tables for each variable. The coefficient of apparent total effects does, however, provide an essential starting point for subsequent analyses—either for assessing the variable's importance or for identifying the mediating variables that transmit its influence on the vote.

The third column in Table 17.3 presents the second ingredient needed to assess each variable's importance in shaping the aggregate result of the election—the average value, or the directional influence that follows from the central tendency of that variable's distribution among voters. That score could then be multiplied by the apparent total effect to indicate the aggregate contribution of that variable to the overall results of the election. That product, however, would include contributions based on the average scores of all prior variables, as well as any unique contributions from the (given) variable.

For that reason, the fourth column contains the "adjusted" mean for each variable, which is the "unique" portion of its current overall mean that cannot be attributed to potentially confounding variables. The product of that adjusted mean and the apparent total effect then appears in the fifth column—which represents that variable's contribution to the aggregate outcome of the election. This five-entry sequence is presented for five selected variables to illustrate the role of each step in assessing any variable's importance in determining the results of an election.

Chapters 10 through 15 were primarily devoted to identifying an apparent total effect coefficient for each variable by eliminating that portion of the original bivariate coefficient that should be attributed to preceding or confounding variables. The logic, indeed the necessity, of these controls for potentially confounding variables seems obvious to many social scientists. At several points, however, we have recognized the temptation to interpret the resulting apparent total effect coefficient as an indicator of a given variable's "importance." On those occasions, we have suggested that readers postpone such evaluations until the present chapter. For reasons that are highlighted in Table 17.3, the sequence of results for each variable in that table emphasizes the fact that *two* adjustments are needed to assess the unique contribution of a specific variable to the aggregate result—both of which involve the influence of political variables that have been assigned to prior stages in our model.

We note that the simple product of the apparent total effect for each variable and its unadjusted mean score would provide a useful description of that variable's impact on the aggregate result *provided* the analyst intends to give each variable credit for "transmitting" the overall impact of positive and negative average scores from prior variables which thereby influence the vote "through" the given variable. This distribution of importance is based on a total effect which reflects the "removal" of confounding influences from our estimates of that effect, but it does not similarly remove any of that variable's average score that may be attributable to variables in prior stages. Of course, any analyst or reader is free to emphasize this role of a given variable in *transmitting* the influence of prior variables as well as variation that is *unique* to that variable. Our own objective, however, is to emphasize the unique importance of each variable as the source of a positive or negative contribution to the aggregate election outcome. That contribution is limited to the product of the apparent total effect *and* the unique portion of its mean, and appears in the fifth column of Table 17.3.

That table highlights the limitations of the simple bivariate relationships (those usually expressed in bar graph comparisons for poll data in the popular press), which fail to consider either the statistical controls that are needed for a reasonable estimate of that variable's total effect or the unique contribution of that variable to the aggregate results. It is particularly important to note the differences between contributions to the aggregate results based on overall averages in contrast to contributions based on the unique component of those averages. For instance, the substantial *support* for George Bush that appears to have come "from" voters' perceptions of responsibility for the budget deficit was not visible until the unique component of that variable's mean was separated from the influence of prior variables.

It is also interesting to note that, because of the small total effect coefficient, Clinton received *less* net support from voters' retrospective assessments of Bush's handling of the economy and from expectations about the parties' future handling of health care guarantees than might have been suggested by the very large bivariate regression coefficients, .85 and .87, and by the unadjusted average scores for those variables, with pro-Democratic overall averages of +.54 and +.43. Similarly, the issue of homosexuals serving in the military provided even less support for Clinton than may be suggested by the bivariate relationship with the vote, .42, and his marginal advantage on the unadjusted average score for that variable, +.09.

Finally, the limited overview provided by this set of estimates suggests a provocative difference between the personal burden borne by George Bush, through retrospective evaluations of his handling of the economy, and the non-evaluative (where the candidates were concerned) appraisal of changes in the state of the economy. In 1992, the Republicans' problem was the economy much more than the President himself.

With Tables 17.1 and 17.2 and the elaboration tables from Chapters 11–15, the reader can construct rows like those in Table 17.3 for any of the political variables in our model that may be of particular interest. Such examples emphasize the point that neither bivariate relationships with the vote nor unadjusted mean scores provide appropriate indicators for the ultimate contribution of a variable to the outcome of the election.

The Role of Specific Variables in Producing Individual Differences

Our other major criterion for evaluating the importance of alternative explanations in a given election concerns the extent to which each explanation is responsible for generating the differences between individual voters in their choices for President. Specific variables may not make any net contribution to the aggregate result of the election because voters' opinions are evenly balanced between opposing points of view— but the same variables may have exerted a tremendous influence in leading voters with opposing views (in equally large numbers) to choose different candidates. In evaluating alternative explanatory variables with respect to this criterion for "importance," we are trying to compare the electoral relevance of different conflicts or disagreements within the society, or to assess the degree to which such disagreements were activated by the campaign.

Unlike apparent contributions to the aggregate results of the election, we cannot assess the importance of a given explanatory variable in generating individual differences in the vote by suggesting how the variability in the vote would have been different if we "removed" the influence of that one explanatory variable. The variability in our dichotomous variable (the vote) would be essentially the same in a hypothetical election in which every aspect of the current election remained the same *except* that the given variable did not exert any influence on individual decisions. In such an election, responsibility for that variability would simply be allocated to some other explanatory variable(s). To evaluate this kind of importance for a given variable, we will examine two different versions of a standardized regression coefficient, both of which give that variable "credit" for the size of its total effect on the vote *and* its variability.

As background for those coefficients, Table 17.4 again presents the apparent total effect for each political variable in our analysis, as in Table 17.1, along with two versions of its variability—its standard deviation—one for that variable as a whole and one for the residual component of that variable as discussed in the previous section. The latter residual component contains only that portion of the variable that cannot be attributed to the political variables we have assigned to previous stages in our model.

As with our average scores for these variables, the standard deviations for partisan and policy-related predispositions are necessarily the same for both columns in Table 17.4, and the values of our two types of standard deviations are only moderately different for current policy preferences and perceptions of current conditions. Beginning with retrospective presidential evaluations, however, substantial reductions are made in the variability of several variables when we remove that portion of those variables which can be attributed to political variables in prior stages.

Table 17.5 presents both versions of the standardized coefficient for the total effects of each political variable. Column 1 contains standardized coefficients based on all of the variability in each variable, and (analogous to our interpretation of Table 17.3) suggests the degree to which each variable was responsible for *transmitting* sources of differences between voters in their choices for President. Column 2, in contrast, presents standardized coefficients for that portion of each variable

Table 17.4 Total Effects and Standard Deviations for Specific Variables in 1992: Components for Importance in Explaining Individual Differences

Name of Explanatory Theme and Specific Variable	Total Effect (unstandardized)	Standard Deviation for Variable as a Whole	Standard Deviation for Unique Component
Partisan Identification			
Party ID	.48	.82	.82
Policy-related Predispositions			
Lib./Con. Self-designation	.27	.61	.61
Equality	.22	.41	.41
Limited Government	.08	.75	.75
Morality	.22	.46	.46
Union vs. Business	.09	.55	.55
Homosexuals vs. Evangelicals	.15	.40	.40
Isolationism	.07	.83	.83
Service in Vietnam	.08	.97	.97
Current Policy Preferences			
Aid to the Disadvantaged	.12	.54	.47
Strength and Use of Military Force	.17	.43	.38
Homosexuals in the Military	.12	.84	.67
Willingness to Pay Increased Taxes	.04	.93	.84
Public Funds for Private Schools	.06	.89	.87
Perceptions of Current Conditions			
State of the Economy	.19	.45	.42
U.S. Position in the World	.06	.78	.74
Recent Layoff in the Family	.40	.12	.12
Retrospective Performance Evaluations			
General	.33	.79	.55
Economy	.08	.68	.52
Foreign Affairs	.05	.80	.66
Deficit Blame (vs. Congress)	.22	.88	.69
Evaluations of Personal Qualities			
Integrity	.11	.39	.26
Empathy	.24	.40	.25
Leadership	.19	.36	.25
Prospective Performance Evaluations			
of Candidates, re: the Economy	.30	.83	.46
of Candidates, re: Poverty	.10	.77	.50
of Parties, re: the Economy	.07	.79	.48
of Parties, re: Health Care Costs	.10	.72	.52

Table 17.5 Importance of Specific Political Variables in 1992 in Explaining
Individual Differences in Vote Choice

(All Entries Are Standardized Regression Coefficients)		
Name of Explanatory Theme and Specific Variable	Transmission: Coefficient for Entire Variable	Source or Origin: Coefficient for Unique Part of Variable
Partisan Identification		
Party ID	.40	.40
Policy-related Predispositions		
Lib./Con. Self-designation	.16	.16
Equality	.09	.09
Limited Government	.06	.06
Morality	.10	.10
Union vs. Business	.05	.05
Homosexuals vs. Evangelicals	.06	.06
Isolationism	.06	.06
Service in Vietnam	.08	.08
Current Policy Preferences		
Aid to the Disadvantaged	.07	.06
Strength and Use of Military Force	.07	.06
Homosexuals in the Military	.10	.08
Willingness to Pay Increased Taxes	.04	.04
Public Funds for Private Schools	.05	.05
Perceptions of Current Conditions		
State of the Economy	.09	.08
U.S. Position in the World	.05	.05
Recent Layoff in the Family	.05	.05
Retrospective Performance Evaluations		
General	.26	.19
Economy	.05	.04
Foreign Affairs	.04	.04
Deficit Blame (vs. Congress)	.19	.15
Evaluations of Personal Qualities		
Integrity	.04	.03
Empathy	.10	.06
Leadership	.07	.05
Prospective Performance Evaluations		
of Candidates, re: the Economy	.25	.14
of Candidates, re: Poverty	.08	.05
of Parties, re: the Economy	.05	.03
of Parties, re: Health Care Costs	.07	.05

that cannot be attributed to the political variables in preceding stages—
or for the extent to which that variable represents the *unique source* or
origin of such influences. In contrast to our estimates for contributions
to the aggregate results, each variable in this analysis is assured of some
apparent "importance" because of the statistical threshold which each of
our variables had to pass in order to be included in the analysis (with
an apparent total effect coefficient such that $p \leq .10$). Some of our
variables, however, appear to have been responsible for a larger share
than others in producing the observed differences between voters in their
choices for President.

This sequel to our estimates of total effects and standard deviations is
the analogue to Table 17.2, a table showing the importance of each
variable's contribution to the difference between voters who chose between Bush and Clinton. The largest coefficients in Column 1 of Table
17.5, which presents the products derived from the first two columns of
Table 17.4, suggest that individual differences in vote choice were most
powerfully shaped by partisan identification, .40, liberal/conservative
self-designation, .16, general evaluations of President Bush's performance, .26, assessments of blame for the federal deficit, .19, and prospective evaluations of the candidates' future performance in handling the
economy, .25. Because of the reductions in the standard deviations for
the residual components of each variable discussed above, the standardized coefficients in Column 2 of Table 17.5 are substantially reduced
for explicit evaluations of the parties and candidates.

Party identification is clearly the most important unique source for
individual differences in the vote. Indeed, it towers over all other single
variables in our model. Relative to the other variables included in our
model, party identification was much more important in distinguishing
Democratic voters from Republican voters than it was in accounting for
Clinton's margin of victory (see Table 17.2). Overall, the national economy took top honors in terms of its contribution to the Clinton margin
in the popular two-party vote, but it was much less important in shaping
individual differences in vote choice. Second place in explaining individual differences was nearly shared by liberal/conservative self-designation, evaluations of President Bush's general performance and his struggle with Congress over the budget deficit, and prospective evaluations
of the candidates concerning the economy.

Restricting the importance of specific variables to the unique portion of that variable has only a modest impact on the apparent importance of voters' policy preferences and perceptions of current conditions in explaining individual decisions. Nevertheless, it is instructive to note that in the 1992 election, predispositions toward equality and morality (as well as liberal/conservative self-designations) played major roles in the explanation of individual differences.

In the last three stages of our model, the apparent importance of specific variables in explaining individual differences is substantially reduced by shifting the criterion for importance from the transmission of influence to the unique source or contemporary origin of that influence. This reduction is particularly evident for empathy as a personal quality and for prospective evaluations of the candidates. Nevertheless, several evaluations, including general approval of Bush's performance as President, the attribution of blame for the budget deficit, and prospective evaluations of the candidates' future ability to handle the economy, made substantial unique contributions to individual vote choices even after we had removed explanatory credit that should be allocated to prior variables.

■ The Apparent Importance of General Explanatory Themes in 1992

The results presented in Tables 17.2 and 17.5 describe the apparent roles played by voters' opinions about a wide variety of individual topics that were emphasized in the 1992 campaign. Such estimates, however, are only the starting point for evaluating the importance of different groups of attitudes which deal with the same kind of content—or for assessing the combined importance of all the variables which we have assigned to a given explanatory theme. Interest in such summaries is expressed in attempts to describe or interpret a given election as a whole. How relevant were voters' policy-related predispositions? How important were voters' impressions of the candidates' personal qualities?

Fortunately, the same methods used above to evaluate the importance of specific variables can be fairly easily extended to any set of variables. The following discussion presents results for the two contrasting types of importance discussed earlier for each of our general explanatory themes.

Table 17.6 Apparent Importance of General Explanatory Themes in 1992 Based on Contributions to the Aggregate Results

	(Aggregate Results = Average Vote = +.174)	
Name of Explanatory Theme	Transmission: Sum of Contributions Based on All of Each Variable	Source or Origin: Sum of Contributions Based on Unique Parts of Variables
Partisan Identification	.07	.07
Policy-related Predispositions	−.05	−.05
Current Policy Preferences	.00	.01
Perceptions of Current Conditions	.11	.10
Retrospective Performance Evaluations	.08	−.04
Evaluations of Personal Qualities	.03	.01
Prospective Performance Evaluations	.16	.03

The Importance of Explanatory Themes in Producing the Aggregate Results

Given the computational logic used in assigning credit for net aggregate results, we can produce combined estimates for the contributions by all the variables in the same explanatory theme by simply summing their signed individual contributions. Table 17.6 presents the simple sums of the apparent (positive or negative) contributions to Bill Clinton's plurality for all of the specific variables in each of our explanatory themes. Some conclusions from this table were already evident in our previous discussion of contributions for specific variables, but we offer the following highlights concerning the attitudinal sources or origins for Bill Clinton's victory in 1992.

As in all other presidential elections since World War II, more 1992 voters reported a continuing identification with the Democratic party than with the Republicans. That Democratic advantage made a substantial contribution, .07, to Bill Clinton's margin of victory, +.17, based on predispositions that were well in place before the 1992 campaign began. Given changes in the composition of the electorate, as well as occasional changes in party identification by individual voters, the size of that contribution can vary between elections. In 1964, for example, it was doubtless considerably larger than in 1992. This estimate for 1992, however, is similar to that for several recent elections.

Policy-related predispositions provided a substantial net advantage for George Bush, or a negative contribution to the Bill Clinton plurality, of −.05. This contribution offset much of Clinton's advantage in long-term partisan identification. That continued contribution represents a sum of offsetting positive and negative combinations for specific predispositions, seen in Table 17.2, each of which presumably was already in place before the election and, when activated by the 1992 campaign, appears to have produced little visible net advantage for one candidate or the other. In these respects, the pre-election playing field was close to level or even.

Similarly, voters' preferences on current policy issues appear to have provided no net advantage for either Clinton or Bush. The aggregate consequences for issues where liberal preferences outnumbered conservative views in Table 17.2 were almost exactly offset by the influences of preferences in policy areas where the distributions of those preferences provided some advantage for Bush. Some aspects of these results, of course, may be an accidental consequence of the NES selection of policy questions. In our view, however, no other issue or set of issues that might have decisively tipped the balance to favor one side or the other comes to mind. All of the most likely possibilities for such an influence have been examined and either failed to meet our modest threshold for statistical significance or have already been included in arriving at the above conclusion.

As emphasized in our discussion of specific variables, voters' perceptions of the economy appear to have made a decisive contribution, .10 in the second column of Table 17.2, to Bill Clinton's margin of victory in 1992. That contribution was supplemented by extremely small pro-Democratic contributions associated with other conditions, so that the combined (rounded) contribution of all the "current conditions" in the 1992 NES questionnaire was still .10. That substantial contribution, and the negligible contribution of preferences on current policy issues, were

not appreciably modified by removing those portions of policy preferences and perceptions of conditions that can be attributed to partisan
and policy-related predispositions.

As shown in the first column in Table 17.6, retrospective evaluations
of George Bush's performance as President also appear to have made a
substantial contribution to Bill Clinton's victory, +.08. As noted in our
discussion of specific variables, however, *all* of that pro-Democratic
contribution disappears when we remove the impact of prior variables
from the averages for these variables. Indeed, the net contribution of
voters' evaluations in this area, −.04, clearly suggests a Bush advantage
when we focus on the components of those evaluations that cannot be
attributed to the state of the economy and other variables that we have
assigned to prior stages in our model. In areas other than the economy,
such as foreign affairs and the deficit, voters' evaluations of George Bush
as President were more positive than we would have predicted given
their partisan identifications, policy-related preferences, and perceptions
of current conditions.

Evaluations of the personal qualities of the candidates appear to have
made only a modest net contribution to Clinton's plurality, +.03. This
result is based on pro-Clinton assessments concerning empathy and
effectiveness that were partially offset by negative contributions concerning his integrity. When we remove contributions that may have been
transmitted by these evaluations but have already been attributed to
prior variables, however, the remaining contribution that should apparently be attributed to the unique content of these personal qualities is
close to invisible, +.01. In our view, the personal qualities of the candidates did "make a difference" in the 1992 campaign, but their net
contributions were not large, and they involved offsetting evaluations.
When discussing the impact of candidates' personal qualities on the
outcome of the election, earlier cautionary notes should be kept in mind,
including the observation that personal appearances and other occasions
that may influence impressions of candidates' personal qualities are also
occasions for activating other sentiments concerning partisan and policy-related preferences.

Finally, voters' prospective evaluations of the candidates' and parties'
future performance appeared to *transmit* major contributions to Clinton's
victory, +.16. However, most of that apparent contribution is based on
the influence of prior variables whose impact on the vote was merely

transmitted through prospective evaluations of the candidates and parties. The only substantial contribution that remains after we remove the contributions we have already attributed to prior variables concerns health care. We are not surprised at this particular remaining contribution associated with prospective performance, for health care is not "covered" by any of our explanatory variables in earlier stages concerning policy-related preferences, current conditions, *or* presidential performance. We are not sure that this aggregate contribution of health care is correctly allotted to the parties instead of the candidates, or to prospective instead of retrospective evaluations, but we are confident that voters' opinions on that topic made some net contribution to Clinton's 1992 plurality.

The Importance of General Themes in Explaining Individual Differences

In mild contrast to the substantial differences among our explanatory themes in their contributions to the aggregate results, each of our general explanatory themes appears to have played a visible role in "producing" the differences between individual voters in their choice for President in 1992. Table 17.7 presents standardized regression coefficients for composite variables for each of our explanatory themes related to individual vote choice. Each of these variables was created as a partial predicted score from the same regression analyses reported in Table 17.5, so that each variable represents the combined effects of all of the variables in that explanatory theme. As before, Column 1 presents the standardized regression coefficient for the combined effects of all of those variables, while Column 2 presents the standardized coefficient for the combination of residual portions of those variables—after we have removed the influence of variables in prior stages.

As Table 17.7 illustrates, it appears that voters' policy-related predispositions, .41, were just as important as partisan identifications, .40, in producing individual differences in vote choice. We have anticipated this possibility in several previous chapters, and we believe it is an important characteristic of the 1992 election—as well as other recent elections. Voters' policy preferences on current issues provided some additional explanatory power, .20, as did perceptions of current conditions, .12, and those estimates are only moderately reduced to .14 and .11 when

Table 17.7 Apparent Importance of General Explanatory Themes in 1992 for the Explanation of Individual Differences in Vote Choice

Name of Explanatory Theme	Transmission: Standardized Coefficient for Composite Variable Based on All of Each Variable	Source or Origin: Standardized Coefficient for Composite Variable Based on Unique Parts of Each Variable
Partisan Identification	.40	.40
Policy-related Predispositions	.41	.41
Current Policy Preferences	.20	.14
Perceptions of Current Conditions	.12	.11
Retrospective Performance Evaluations	.47	.30
Evaluations of Personal Qualities	.19	.11
Prospective Performance Evaluations	.41	.20

we remove the variability in those variables that can be attributed to factors in prior stages.

Even though our model places perceptions of current conditions before presidential performance evaluations, thereby giving the former "credit" for what may be a joint influence on the vote, evaluations of Bush's performance as President loomed much larger than current conditions as a unique source of differences between voters in their choices for President. In terms of transmitting influence, evaluation of the President's performance, .47, clearly surpassed our other explanatory themes. As a *unique* source of individual decisions, such evaluations were still one of the most important themes. This seems appropriate to an election in which an incumbent President is running for re-election against an opponent who was previously largely an unknown quantity in national politics. Finally, the combined significance of prospective performance evaluations is, not surprisingly, cut in half once we remove the variability in those variables that can be attributed to prior stages.

The relatively limited apparent importance of the candidates' personal qualities calls for some additional comment. In an election in which the personal character of one candidate was given so much attention by the media, it seems surprising that the personal qualities of the candidates ranked at the bottom of our list of explanatory themes in terms of this criterion for electoral relevance. This result, of course, is partially due to our allocation of so much explanatory credit to variables that we have assigned to prior stages.

Furthermore, the focus on personal qualities in our analysis is more narrow than the range of content involved in Republican attacks on Clinton's personal characteristics. Nevertheless, despite NES efforts to provide a comprehensive assessment of the relevant personal traits of presidential candidates, differences between voters in their 1992 choices for President did not appear to be heavily based on personal qualities of the candidates.

In our view, the entries in the second column of Table 17.7 and the more detailed results in Table 17.5 describe the 1992 election in terms of what was really contested, or what was at stake in the minds of the voters. The explanatory variables or themes with the largest values identify those topics which provided the sources of *differences between voters* in their choices for President. These estimates for the relative importance of specific policy-related conflicts clarify the kinds of disagreements that appear to have been activated in shaping voters' choices. Similarly, our estimates concerning this kind of importance for current conditions and performance identify those areas where voters' choices appear to have been shaped by their differential perceptions of governmental results.

If our estimates concerning the importance of specific factors with respect to individual differences identify the political topics that constituted the *content* of a given election, our assessments concerning contributions to the winner's plurality clarify the factors that had the biggest impact on the aggregate *outcome* of the election. Social scientists are intensely interested in understanding the sources of inter-individual variability in electoral choice. Politicians, journalists, and historians, on the other hand, may be somewhat curious about the sources of that variability, but they are usually much more interested in identifying factors which helped or hurt the two candidates—and which "added up" to produce the winning candidate's margin of victory. Answers to the first of those two questions (concerning individual differences) must *not* be confused with answers to the second (concerning the aggregate result).

Alternative Conclusions Based on Conflict versus Consensus

At several points in this book, we have emphasized the substantive distinction between two different types of issues that play a visible role in every presidential campaign. Both types of issues are defined by opinions about governmental activities, but they involve quite different criteria for evaluating the candidates or the parties. The first criterion is based on *conflicts* or *disagreements* between the candidates and within the electorate concerning policy direction—or concerning the most appropriate objectives and priorities for the federal government. In the other type of issue, voters acquire positive impressions of an incumbent administration when current conditions (or results) are perceived in favorable terms, and they acquire negative impressions of the incumbent when those perceptions are unfavorable. Whether positive or negative, such evaluations are based on *consensual criteria*, generally agreed to by almost all voters. What can we learn about the combined importance of these contrasting types of issues?

From Table 17.6, we can simply *add* the apparent contribution to the aggregate results of voters' policy-related predispositions, $-.05$, and current policy preferences, $.01$, to produce an overall estimate of the negative contributions, $-.04$, which all policy-related or conflict-based preferences made to Bill Clinton's overall plurality, $+.17$. This Republican advantage was slightly more than offset by the Democratic advantage in conflicting partisan identifications, $+.07$, but it suggests a complex balance of preferences concerning the direction of federal policies in many different areas. More comprehensive or accurate measurement of policy-related preferences might yield a somewhat different impression of the net partisan consequences of all the areas in which the parties and candidates advocated opposing directions for federal policy. It is hard for us to imagine, however, that any alternative set of measures in this area, or any alternative analytic procedure, would yield an overall impression that is sharply different from this net Republican and conservative advantage with respect to the major conflicts between the candidates concerning the direction of federal policies.

In contrast, the positive contribution to Bill Clinton's victory—or George Bush's defeat—which can be attributed to voters' impressions of governmental "results" concerning consensual objectives was almost certainly *much* larger than the Republicans' apparent advantage concerning the (overall) balance of opinions about policy-related conflicts. The contributions of voters' perceptions of current conditions, $+.10$ in Table 17.6, and prospective performance evaluations, $+.03$, added up to a Democratic advantage for Bill Clinton that the favorable unique evaluations of George Bush as President, $-.04$, could not overcome.

Our summary of the relative importance of policy-related conflict versus performance, however, must be quite different when we assess the role played by the four most general explanatory themes in leading some voters to choose Bill Clinton but others to support George Bush. Unlike contributions to the aggregate results, the apparent combined importance of those themes in explaining individual decisions cannot be calculated by simply adding the coefficients in Table 17.7. Because of our emphasis on unique sources of influence in our bloc-recursive model, the standardized coefficients associated with each component can be calculated as the square root of the sum of the squared coefficients to be combined from Table 17.7—thereby summarizing the role of conflict and performance as general sources of electoral decisions. Using that procedure, we can see that the apparent importance of *all* policy-related variables in explaining individual differences is .43 (see Table 17.8). This value is the square root of the sum of the squared unique importance coefficients for policy-related predispositions, .41, and for current policy preferences, .14. Similarly, the combined importance of all impressions that were apparently based on consensual governmental objectives (rather than conflicts over policy direction) was .38, which is the square root of the sum of the squared coefficients for current conditions (.10), retrospective performance (.30), and prospective performance (.20).

These results show a strikingly different picture of the importance of our four most general explanatory themes in producing the variation in voters' choices for Clinton versus Bush than we saw in the contributions of those themes to the aggregate result of the election or to Bill Clinton's

Table 17.8 The Electoral Role of Conflict vs. Consensus Based on Contrasting Criteria for "Importance," for 1988 and 1992

	Sources of Contributions to the Aggregate Results Based on Unique Parts of Each Explanatory Variable		Sources of Individual Differences in Vote Choice Based on Unique Parts of Each Explanatory Variable	
	1988	1992	1988	1992
Partisan Identification	.01	.07	.43	.40
Combination of All Policy-related Conflicts (Predispositions and Current Issues)	−.02	−.04	.39	.43
Combination of All Consensus-based Evaluations (Conditions and Performance)	−.08	.10	.31	.38
Evaluations Concerning Personal Qualities	.03	.01	.20	.11

plurality. The stark difference between these two criteria for the importance of any explanation can be seen in the second and fourth columns of Table 17.8, which presents the same kinds of results for 1988 as well as 1992.

Long-term partisan loyalties and policy-related preferences appear to have made, respectively, visible but offsetting positive (.07) and negative (−.04) contributions to Bill Clinton's plurality over George Bush (+.17). In contrast, those two factors provided the two most important sources of individual differences in vote choice, .40 and .43.

After we remove the indirect influence of partisan identity and policy-related preferences, the remaining variation in voters' impressions of national and governmental performance may be seen as evaluations of governmental "results" based on consensual objectives rather than policy-related conflicts. Our combined estimate for the importance of such evaluations concerning consensual governmental criteria is .38—larger than that for the personal qualities of the candidates, .11, but not a singularly dominant source of differences between voters in their choice for President.

It is of equal interest to note that voters' preferences concerning policy-related conflicts appear to have been slightly more important than party identification. Party remains the most important single variable, but the general thesis that party "dominates" American presidential politics clearly needs substantial modification, at least for 1992. By the same token, however, "party in the electorate" remains a powerful influence on voters' decisions.

In our view, the above comparisons concerning relative importance provide approximate answers to general and persistent questions that arise after most partisan elections. How important *were* specific policy-related conflicts in generating differences between voters in their choice for President, and what can be said about the degree to which each of those conflicts provided an advantage for the winning—or losing—candidate? To what extent was the election candidate-centered, based on the personal qualities or the performances of the candidates? Or did the election provide persuasive evidence of one or another mandate for future governmental policies?

Because of the general interest in answers to those questions for any specific election, they may also be used to understand the differences between one election context and another. To illustrate that possibility, we next present similar results for the election in which George Bush handily defeated Michael Dukakis four years before the Bush-Clinton contest. Comparisons between parallel importance coefficients associated with the 1988 election and those from 1992 suggest the nature of the "most important" differences between those two partisan contests.

▪ Comparing Elections in Terms of Relative Importance

In 1988, George Bush overcame a substantial early lead by Michael Dukakis following the two party conventions to secure a clear-cut victory in November. Many of the themes that were emphasized in that campaign were similar to those in the 1992 election, but the two campaigns were different in several ways—differences which had a visible impact on the content of the NES instruments for those years as well as the sources of voters' choices between the Republican and Democratic candidates. Several of those differences were identified in our review of changing issues in the sequence of four elections covered by this book.

A few of those differences should be re-emphasized, however, before we discuss effect estimates and importance analyses that can be compared with those from 1992.

Unlike the situation in 1992, the incumbent President (Reagan) was not running for re-election, but his administration, including Vice President Bush, enjoyed a reservoir of good will or "approval." The country, in general, was seen as doing fairly well, and the national economy was viewed favorably from a Republican perspective—although not as positively as it had been preceding the Reagan landslide of 1984. The candidates emphasized policy-related differences from their opponents on somewhat different topics than in 1992, including communism, defense spending, the death penalty, and school prayer. Arguments over preferences on taxes, abortion, and private versus governmental responsibility, however, were similar to themes in the 1992 campaign. The Republican emphasis on "traditional values" and opposition to abortion were present in 1988 but not emphasized as much as in 1992, and the Democrats did not emphasize that theme as they had in 1992 but gave more attention to the performance of the national economy. The style of 1988 campaigning was similar to that of 1992; it involved "negative" campaigning with questions of patriotism and integrity high on the list of topics linked to the two opposing candidates. In summary, the two election contexts can be described in terms of overlapping but partially different combinations of policy-related issues, quite different economic conditions, and current records of incumbent Republican administrations that enjoyed very different levels of support or approval.

We have estimated the apparent total effects and average values for each of the explanatory variables that appear to have had some impact on voters' choices between George Bush and Michael Dukakis. The logic and structure of this analysis are exactly the same as for 1992, and many of the measures involved are constructed in exactly the same fashion, including party identification; policy-related predispositions concerning equality, morality, and identification with unions versus business; perceptions of the economy and the U.S. "position" in the world; general evaluations of presidential performance and specific presidential evaluations concerning the economy and foreign affairs; and comparative evaluations of the candidates with respect to integrity, empathy, and leadership. Several 1992 measures were not available in 1988, but other variables appeared to have some total effect on the vote within every explanatory theme. Specifically, somewhat different explanatory variables identified as having some impact on vote choice in 1988 concerned communism, feelings about Blacks and Whites, feminists versus pro-life activists, the death penalty, unemployment, the overall "condition" of the country, worry about layoffs, retrospective evaluations of President Reagan concerning the impact of his economic policies and honesty, and prospective evaluations concerning crime and the environment. Details of the statistical results can be found in Appendix C, which includes estimates for total effects with both types of means, both types of standard deviations and, consequently, both types of importance for each variable in the 1988 analysis.

The six tables in Appendix C provide some interesting commentary on voters' responses to media emphasis on particular campaign topics in 1988. Predictably, the mean scores in 1988 for voters' attitudes concerning anti-communism, race, patriotism, the death penalty, the economy, and crime clearly favored Bush and the Republican party. However, only voters' preferences concerning the death penalty and prospective evaluations of candidate performance concerning crime exhibited substantial apparent *total effects*. The same disparity between the partisan division among public opinions and their impact on the vote can be noted in 1992 where the topics of limited government and Bush's handling of foreign affairs were concerned. In both cases, one favoring Clinton and one favoring Bush, potential partisan advantages were not realized because conflicting opinions did not produce substantial apparent total effects.

We now turn to comparisons of the combined importance of our general explanatory themes in 1988 and 1992. As summarized in Table 17.9, the pro-Democratic contribution of party identification to the aggregate results was substantially larger in 1992 (+.07) than in 1988 (+.01) because of a combination of improved turnout among Democrats and a small aggregate shift in the partisan balance of identification in the latter year. The substantial Republican contribution associated with policy-related predispositions in 1988 also appeared to shift in a pro-Democratic direction four years later, with a decline from −.10 in 1988 to −.05 in 1992. This Democratic gain (or Republican loss) may reflect the "new Democrat" emphasis of the Clinton campaign, but in both years the Republicans benefited from long-term considerations as the influence of pro-Democratic average scores on equality was more than

Table 17.9 Comparing the 1988 and 1992 Elections in Terms of the Importance of General
        Explanatory Themes

	Importance Based on Source or Origin of Contribution to the Aggregate Results		Importance Based on Source or Origin of Differences Between Individual Voters	
	1988	1992	1988	1992
Partisan Identification	.01	.07	.43	.40
Policy-related Predispositions	−.10	−.05	.36	.41
Current Policy Preferences	.08	.01	.18	.14
Perceptions of Current Conditions	−.01	.10	.16	.11
Retrospective Performance Evaluations	−.05	−.04	.25	.30
Evaluations of Personal Qualities	.03	.01	.20	.11
Prospective Performance Evaluations	−.01	.03	.11	.20

offset by pro-Republican averages concerning morality and conservatism. Moreover, the Clinton candidacy as the choice of the centrist
Democratic Leadership Council did not appear to help the Democrats
with respect to voters' current policy preferences. In 1988 Dukakis
enjoyed a much more substantial advantage over Bush in that area (.08)
than did Clinton four years later (.01).

As emphasized earlier, voters' perceptions of the economy and other
current conditions were responsible for the greatest differences between
these two elections in the contribution of any of our explanatory themes
to the aggregate result. The small pro-Republican condition-related contribution in 1988, −.01, was replaced by a dominant pro-Democratic
contribution in 1992, +.10, thereby offsetting the continuing Republican advantage in policy-related predispositions and presidential performance in areas other than the economy. Bill Clinton might well have lost
the 1992 election if voters' perceptions of the economy had not been so
critical, or if the campaign had placed less emphasis on the recession.

We also note that voters' retrospective performance evaluations made
pro-Republican contributions to the aggregate result of both elections—

if we do not count the pro-Democratic contributions associated with perceptions of the economy in 1992. We note, however, that much of the pro-Republican contribution of retrospective evaluations in 1992 was based on the tendency for more voters to blame the Democratic Congress for the federal deficit than President Bush. In 1992, George Bush did not benefit from the same kind of generally positive evaluations that voters expressed concerning President Reagan in 1988.

Contrary to some popular interpretations, our results suggest that Michael Dukakis received a more positive evaluation than George Bush concerning the candidates' personal qualities. None of Bush's 1988 victory seems to have come from voters' evaluations of the non-political aspects of the candidates. In 1992, Bill Clinton may have benefited from a small advantage in this area—although that result represents offsetting positive contributions concerning empathy and negative contributions concerning integrity. Finally, we should note that our measures for prospective performances are quite different in NES surveys in 1988 and 1992, so that direct comparisons concerning that explanatory theme are difficult to interpret.

Nevertheless, with that caveat in mind, we return to Table 17.8 for a final comparison of these two elections. Although policy-related conflicts were approximately of equal importance in separating Democratic voters from Republican voters in the two years, there were modest changes in this type of importance for the consensual themes: "conditions and performance" went from .31 in 1988 to .38 in 1992, while the importance of personal qualities dropped from .20 to .11. The dual impact of these changes on the outcome of the election is fairly dramatic. As "conditions and performance" increased in importance, the partisan contribution of those opinions swung from the $-.02$ that had elected Bush as Reagan's successor to a pro-Clinton $+.10$ that produced the Clinton victory. The consequences of this shift in sentiments were enhanced by the declining relevance of personal qualities, minimizing the pro-Bush shift that had nearly eliminated the 1988 Democrat advantage in personal qualities of $+.04$.

▪ Summary

As we have emphasized, our results concerning both types of importance are subject to a variety of uncertainties concerning measurement and model specification—for specific variables as well as general explanatory themes. Alternative measures and analytic procedures *might* lead to somewhat different conclusions concerning the role played by different kinds of variables in "explaining" both individual and aggregate electoral decisions. At several points, we have noted that somewhat different results can be generated for 1992 with different analytic procedures and measures, and we have indicated where and why we think our own results could be improved as approximate answers to the descriptive questions we are trying to address. At this point, however, we offer the following general conclusions about the importance of different political attitudes in explaining voters' decisions in the 1992 election:

- Perceptions of economic conditions were clearly dominant in producing the aggregate result of the election, as hypothesized by most post-election analyses.
- A visible Republican advantage based on policy-related predispositions was largely offset by pro-Democratic contributions based on partisan identification and policy preferences.
- The major contribution of retrospective evaluations of President Bush appeared to be primarily based on perceptions of the economy, so that the unique contribution of retrospective evaluations actually helped the President, once we remove the influence of voters' perceptions of the economy.
- Evaluations of personal qualities made a small net positive contribution to Clinton's victory, because pro-Clinton evaluations concerning empathy offset modest negative contributions based on anti-Clinton impressions concerning integrity.
- Policy- or conflict-related preferences played a major role in producing individual differences in vote choice, even though the net contribution of consensus-based evaluations to the aggregate results more than offset Republican policy-related advantages to produce a Clinton victory.

Some of these conclusions also appear to be valid for the 1988 election in which George Bush defeated Michael Dukakis. Indeed, the general magnitude of our estimates (or approximations) for the importance of general explanatory themes in producing individual differences in vote choice is fairly similar between these two elections. Moreover, they resemble conclusions that we have offered elsewhere for the two elections won by Ronald Reagan in 1980 and 1984. In our view, differences between voters in most recent national elections have been shaped by similar combinations of policy-related predispositions, current policy issues, current conditions, presidential performance, and personal qualities of the candidates—in addition to longstanding partisan loyalties. Beyond these general similarities, however, our procedures have served to highlight the following differences between these two recent elections:

- The two elections appear to have been fairly different in the specific policy-related conflicts that were activated in generating voters' choices. Thus, voters' choices in the 1988 decision were visibly shaped by attitudes toward the death penalty and communism, which were invisible or irrelevant in 1992. Similarly, 1992 choices were apparently shaped by attitudes toward homosexuals, public funding for private schools, and Clinton-related attitudes toward Vietnam, most of which were irrelevant in 1988. Several other policy- or conflict-related attitudes, however, appear to have played a visible role in both elections, including ideological self-designations as liberals and conservatives, general attitudes toward equality and morality, and policy preferences concerning military strength.
- Our separate analyses for 1988 and 1992 suggest that the dominant explanatory theme in accounting for the large shift in aggregate results between those two elections was voters' perceptions of economic conditions. Such perceptions were on average moderately positive in the fall of Ronald Reagan's last year as President and made a modest contribution to George Bush's election. Comparable perceptions in 1992, however, were sharply critical and appeared to make the largest single contribution to George Bush's defeat and Bill Clinton's victory.

With the role of the national economy as a major influence on voters' decisions in 1992 emerging as one "bottom line" of our analysis, the results of using our complex model match the basic conclusion reached by many other analysts as well. However, we have also reached conclusions about the impact of other explanatory themes that have drawn much less consensus from other observers. Those conclusions are primarily based on results of the importance analyses of this chapter and would not otherwise be apparent.

18

★ ★ ★

General Conclusions and Future Directions

In our review of alternative explanations for vote choice, we have concentrated on the 1992 election because it is the most recent and therefore the most salient contest covered by the National Election Studies. The NES survey of that election also included the most comprehensive set of questions and, therefore, the most complete data on each of our explanatory themes. Several of the 1992 topics were not introduced until the 1988 or 1992 surveys; as a consequence, many of our analytic results cannot be strictly compared with similar kinds of results from earlier elections. However, on the basis of selected comparisons of our 1992 results with those from other years (Miller and Shanks, 1982; Shanks and Miller, 1990, 1991), we have come to a number of general conclusions about the way in which voting behavior is shaped in contemporary American presidential elections.

Education and Political Generation as Sources of Electoral Participation

While the last two sections of this book have been preoccupied with the state of presidential politics in the United States in 1992, the first three sections focused on the historical roots of current politics. These early chapters carried a dual message emphasizing inherent stability in contrast to occasional change, and localized change in the midst of national continuity. The analyses were motivated by a concern with the role of political leadership that was widely perceived to be in default during much of the past quarter-century, after a comparable time span in which triumph over dramatic kinds of adversity was demonstrably possible.

The generational transformation of the electorate over four decades places the momentary events of each presidential campaign and election in a perspective that discounts much of the hyperbole existing in popular accounts of presidential politics. Wars and depressions do make a difference, and bad judgments and presidential malfeasance in office do have an impact, but they do no more than modify political perspectives embedded in the social and economic context of the ongoing life of the electorate.

The Pervasive Influence of Partisan Identification

One of the major objectives of this book has been to restate the nature of voters' long-term identifications with one of the major political parties, and to emphasize the complementary nature of the explanatory role of party identification vis-à-vis the other political attitudes that must be included in any explanation of electoral choice. We conclude that this aspect of citizens' identity within the society is distinct from, even though shaped by, all of their previous impressions of the major parties. These, in turn, may have been based on the positions that those parties have taken on major policy-related conflicts in previous elections as well as their previous successes or failures in handling consensual governmental responsibilities while they were in power.

Partisan identifications are demonstrably not immune to change after their initial values have been shaped by childhood and early adult experiences. We have documented major changes in partisan identifications within the South. The changes accompanied a massive shift in social norms and policy preferences concerning race and society, and were, at least in part, popular reactions to the leadership of President Ronald Reagan. Nevertheless, partisan identifications respond *very* slowly to voters' impressions of current party leaders, their policies, and their success or failure in handling government. We have noted the resilience of partisan identification in several contexts, including that provided by the South, where the partisan realignment of the electorate has occurred over a span of more than three decades.

A recent illustration involves estimates of the impact of 1990 identifications on the 1992 vote. When answers to the root question on party identification *in 1992* are replaced by answers to the same question given by the same panel of individuals nearly two years before the 1992 campaign began, the relationship between party identification and the 1992 vote is virtually unchanged. Similar results are produced in analyses based on the NES panel design between 1972 and 1976 and in the year-long panel of 1980. The aggregate distribution of party identification may change (slowly) from time to time and election to election, but there has been a remarkable constancy in its impact on the vote.

In addition to its direct influence on vote choice—which remains visible after we control for all of the other variables in our model—long-term partisan identification clearly exerts a pervasive indirect influence by shaping many of the other mediating political attitudes that have an impact on the vote. Because both partisan and other policy-related predispositions were presumably all "in place" before the 1992 election began, we have not attempted to make any estimates concerning the size of any indirect effects of either type of predisposition which may operate through the other in the course of the election campaign. Most of our explanatory themes, however, exhibit relationships with the vote that appear to have been substantially confounded by the impact of predispositions on those relationships. As emphasized in many previous discussions, the short-term or election-specific impact of any explanatory variable on the vote should not be assessed without controlling at least for voters' partisan identifications and policy-related predispositions as well as the customary sets of social and economic characteristics.

Short- and Long-Term Effects of Social and Economic Characteristics

Throughout this book, another of our central objectives has been to clarify the ways in which voters' social and economic characteristics are relevant for the choices they eventually make for President. In general, the apparent total effects of a given social characteristic on the vote seem to be produced by the activation of a variety of predispositions, preferences, or perceptions that occur more frequently among voters possessing that characteristic. For example, active members of Evangelical Protestant denominations have distinctively conservative views on a wide range of topics, especially social or moral questions. As a consequence, they have voted increasingly for Republican candidates as relevant predispositions have been emphasized in Republican campaign challenges to the Democrats. This kind of activation is doubtless reinforced by informal communications among other, similarly inclined members of the same social category, as well as by more formal efforts to mobilize members of organized groups defined in terms of those categories. In our view, exploring relationships between social or economic variables and established cultural predispositions represents a necessary first step in any explanation of vote choice, especially if the relationships persist after taking long-term partisan identifications into account.

Social and economic characteristics of voters are sometimes used as exogenous "instruments" to remove biases in effect estimates for other (explicitly political) variables. The explanatory value of social and economic characteristics of voters is, however, considerably greater than such an instrumental or "technical" role may suggest. We view statistical relationships between social and economic characteristics and the vote as highly informative in their own right, in part because of the information they provide about the political alignments or coalitions in any given election (see Axelrod, 1972). In addition, however, such relationships provide important clues concerning the kinds of predispositions, political attitudes, or opinions that may be relevant as intervening variables in any comprehensive explanation of vote choice. Given the conflicts that have been emphasized in national debates over federal policy, and given the nature of likely candidates for both parties, including the current President, it seems probable that all of the social and economic characteristics we have included in our explanation of the vote choice in 1992 will be strong candidates for inclusion in policy-related explanations of turnout and choice in the next few elections.

Predispositions toward Policy-related Conflicts within the Society

Our emphasis on general policy-related attitudes should redress the tendency among many political scientists to underestimate the electoral consequences of continuing social and economic conflicts and disagreements within the United States. We are impressed with the electoral consequences of controversies where individual citizens hold quite different views concerning the most appropriate goals or priorities for the federal government, and where the two parties have been associated with opposing positions. Since *The American Voter* was published, presidential candidates have repeatedly (if not increasingly) taken opposing positions concerning several continuing conflicts. There has been partisan disagreement over the general role of government, the strength and role of the military (including unsuccessful and successful wars in Vietnam and Iraq, and military incursions in Central America, Africa, and Europe), efforts to eliminate discrimination based on race, gender, and age, efforts to reduce poverty or economic inequality, efforts to regulate business in the name of health, safety, and consumer interests, and conflicts over different social issues including various definitions or aspects of morality.

On several of these topics, policy-related predispositions represent "semi-exogenous" variables that have been largely in place before given election campaigns have begun. Some of them have been activated during ensuing campaigns by virtue of public positions taken by the candidates or emphasized in the media. The measures of policy-related predispositions developed by the NES enrich an earlier perspective that was largely confined to differences between self-defined "liberal" and "conservative" preferences. In 1992, voters' general attitudes toward traditional morality or moral tolerance were emphasized by a variety of interested parties during the campaign. Attitudes toward equality were the basis for other conflicts over policy, and still other topics evoked attitudes toward limiting the role of government in addressing various social and economic problems. As a consequence, voters' general attitudes on each of those particular topics appeared to play visible roles in shaping their choices for President in 1992. Continuing conflicts in these and other areas suggest that the same predispositions are likely to be engaged in 1996 and beyond.

Current Issues Based on Conflicts over Policy Direction

Throughout this book, we have emphasized a distinction between two quite different types of issues that may be prominent in election campaigns. The two types are differentiated by the degree of *conflict* or *consensus* that exists within the electorate concerning the appropriateness of governmental objectives. In the first type, voters and candidates have conflicting views about the *purposes* or *priorities* that the government should be pursuing. Candidates come to be evaluated in terms of their agreement (or disagreement) with a voter's own preferences in those areas. The relevance of such conflicts in a given campaign may be limited to general attitudes or predispositions, but the conflicts may also be defined in terms of current controversies about specific policies.

In practice, the distinction between general predispositions and current policy issues may be ambiguous, as in our view of policy preferences in 1992 concerning military strength. For that reason, we have emphasized the degree to which disagreements about current policy alternatives exhibit some distinctive connection to the vote after we have controlled for policy-related predispositions—and we have noted the ability of current issues to mediate the apparent impact of more general predispositions.

In the 1992 campaign, voters' choices between Clinton and Bush appear to have been influenced by their own specific policy preferences concerning the nation's military strength, aid to the disadvantaged, military service by homosexuals, taxes, and the possibility of government funding for private schools. Policy preferences in several other areas, including abortion, were related to vote choice, but exhibited only small and statistically insignificant coefficients after we had given consideration to preferences on other policy topics, and to general predispositions (as well as social and economic characteristics). We believe that many such topics played a role in shaping some individual choices for President, but their independent effects were apparently limited to groups of voters so small that they could not be detected in our overall analysis of the two-party voters.

We conclude that it is not wise to judge the impact of campaign themes when the evidence is limited to the images presented in the media or volunteered by voters. We expect the most salient issues involving societal conflict to shift considerably from one election to the next, as illustrated by the disappearance of issues concerning the choice between inflation or unemployment, the communist threat, or the enactment of the death penalty between 1988 and 1992. Noting the partisan trends associated with the political preferences of Evangelical Protestants, and observing efforts at political mobilization by the more conservative Republican leaders and members of the Christian Coalition, we anticipate that future conflicts will include cultural clashes over definitions of morality and the role of traditional family and personal values in national government and politics.

Issues Based on Current Conditions and Consensual Objectives

In contrast to preferences concerning current policy conflicts, our second type of current issue concerns topics where voters generally agree on the government's objectives but differ in appraisals of the results of governmental policy and action. Candidates who are associated with an incumbent administration can be evaluated in terms of the degree to which they have succeeded (or failed) in reaching such consensual objectives. As in several previous elections, much of the 1992 campaign focused on just such an issue: voters' perceptions of unemployment and the economy, which had been in recession since 1990. Conditions that have become important in this way in other elections include inflation, the likelihood of (or U.S. success in) military conflicts, the cost and supply of energy, the risk of violent crime, and the extent of environmental pollution. As with current issues that are defined in terms of conflicts over policy direction, we anticipate considerable fluctuation between elections in the particular conditions that may be important in shaping voters' choices for President. Our reading of the political history of recent decades, as well as that of the most recent elections, emphasizes the possibly overriding importance of "conditions" as the prime determinants of shifts in aggregate election outcomes. Policy conflicts may overshadow the evaluation of conditions in determining individual vote choices, but certainly in 1992 it was conditions that elected the President.

Retrospective Evaluations of the President: Success versus Failure in Office

Most explanations of presidential elections involve some component in which voters may cast their ballots against the incumbent party if they disapprove of the way the President is handling his job (either in general or in some aspect of those responsibilities, such as the domestic economy or foreign relations). Of course, they also may vote to keep the incumbent party in power if they approve of the current administration's performance. We have incorporated several explicit retrospective evaluations of this sort in our analysis. We have done so in a fashion which recognizes that such evaluations may have been shaped by voters' attitudes toward current policy conflicts and conditions as well as their prior partisan and policy-related predispositions. One consequence of that perspective has been to document the degree to which evaluations of presidential performance appear to share the same kinds of sources or origins as the vote.

This similarity between the sources of presidential evaluations and the determinants of vote choice provides a somewhat different perspective on the meaning of presidential performance, for it emphasizes the influence of voters' positions on policy-related conflicts as well as the President's perceived success or failure in handling the government's responsibilities in areas where little conflict exists. The ambiguities resulting from this overlap between "presidential approval" and the vote also call attention to the media's interest in survey-based measures of presidential "approval" throughout the periods between election campaigns.

By including or controlling for variables that we assume are causally prior to presidential evaluations, our analysis can suggest the extent to which the current President is seen as doing better (or worse) than we would expect, given voters' attitudes toward current issues and general predispositions. Thus, retrospective evaluations concerning George Bush's performance as President played an important role in the 1992 election, but the supportive nature of that contribution is obscured unless we consider the influence of other political attitudes on such evaluations. When such antecedents are taken into account, voters' evaluations of George Bush as President actually helped his re-election campaign, but this became apparent only after we "removed" the influence of voters' perceptions of the state of the economy. This suggests caution in regard to conflating characterizations of failed presidencies with judgments about the presidents themselves.

Personal or Non-Governmental Qualities of the Candidates

Most of the statistical relationships between vote choice and comparative evaluations of the candidates' personal qualities should be seen as misleading or spurious, in the classical sense of that term. That is, the very large bivariate relationships between personal evaluations and vote choice can be traced primarily to the impact on both variables of partisan identification and other predispositions and performances, rather than to the impact on the vote of the candidates' personal qualities per se.

In 1992, various explanatory variables appear to have played major roles in shaping voters' evaluations of the candidates with respect to several personal qualities (as well as shaping the vote through other causal processes). We expect such patterns to prevail in other presidential elections as well. Despite that qualification we are also persuaded that voters' choices between Bill Clinton and George Bush were influenced by their comparative evaluations of the two candidates concerning their honesty, their inspirational qualities, and the extent to which they appeared to care about "people like me." Each election, however, should exhibit a distinctive combination of this kind of "effect"—because of the unique characteristics of presidential candidates and the way in which they are portrayed during the campaign. Again, media emphasis on candidates' personal attributes and voters' volunteered appraisals of candidates' personalities should not be taken at face value in post-election analysis.

Electoral Explanations Based on Structured versus Open-Ended Questions

In several chapters we have emphasized the possibility of differing conclusions resulting from survey analyses that diverge because one set of conclusions is based on respondents' attitudes toward the content of the campaign while the other is based on the frequency with which the same attitudes toward campaign topics are volunteered as "reasons" for voting for, or against, one of the candidates.

In our analyses of the NES 1992 data, we have compared conclusions suggested by these two approaches for several explanatory themes. We carried out two parallel sets of analyses: the first was based on respondents' attitudes toward topics or issues or conditions as elicited by specific questions addressed to each theme (with no mention or evaluation of candidates or parties associated with the theme); the second set of analyses was based on volunteered responses in which voters mention the same topics or issues or conditions, but as answers to the NES open-ended questions about what the voters "like" or "dislike" about each candidate.

Information about respondents' own reasons for liking (or disliking) the candidate could, of course, be obtained through direct structured questions about a prespecified list of alternative potential "reasons," as is often done in media polls. Similarly, respondents' attitudes toward specific aspects of the campaign could in principle be measured through open-ended questions about goals or objectives that the respondent feels the government should be emphasizing—or that it should de-emphasize or discontinue.

The NES instrument, however, does not include either of these alternative methods of questioning respondents being interviewed. In our comparison of the two basic approaches to explanation, therefore, the distinction between "attitudes toward a given topic" and "reasons for choice based on that topic" is perfectly confounded with the distinction between structured and open-ended questions. In the interest of brevity, we often describe our comparisons of results based on these alternative approaches in terms of "structured versus open-ended questions." Nevertheless, any empirical differences between the results of those parallel analyses should be interpreted as an unknown combination of the different "logic" of explanation involved, the difference between structured and open-ended questions, *and* the detailed wording of all the questions involved.

We should note that we began this analysis with a clear expectation that results based on structured questions concerning the respondents' attitudes toward specified topics or issues would yield a clearer picture of the sources of voters' preferences than would their responses to the NES open-ended evaluative questions. In Chapter 8 we discussed the weaknesses inherent in respondents' explanations as the reasons or sources of their attitudes toward the candidates. We also noted the uneven or incomplete reports associated with open-ended questions.

In general, our expectations have been confirmed by the parallel analyses concerning policy-related predispositions, current policy issues, and the personal qualities of the candidate. In each of those domains, many campaign topics appeared to have stronger connections to the vote when explanatory variables were based on structured questions about respondents' attitudes toward those specified topics—rather than being based on "mentions" as reasons for liking or disliking one of the candidates (as elicited by the NES open-ended questions).

In some areas, however, we found clear suggestions that topics or aspects of the campaign mentioned in response to open-ended questions had played a visible role in voters' decisions, but had not been well covered or measured by structured questions. In 1992, large coefficients for measures concerning taxes and the candidates' honesty, based on the minority of voters who mentioned them in response to open-ended questions, are at least suggestive in this respect. In addition, we found evidence that open-ended questions may occasionally identify a minority of respondents for whom a particular topic covered by structured questions is particularly salient or "important"—as in the case of abortion in 1992.

Comparing the Importance of General Explanatory Themes

In the previous chapter, we emphasized the distinction between two quite different ways in which a given factor or variable may be described as playing an "important" role in a given election—depending on whether the analyst is trying to account for the aggregate outcome of that election or trying to explain differences in vote choice at the level of the individual voter. In each election we have examined since 1980, some political attitudes appear to have played a major role in leading some voters to choose the Republican candidate and others the Democratic candidate, while the same attitudes did not make any (net) contribution to the winner's margin of victory because the partisan distribution of voters' opinions was balanced or evenly divided. Similarly, some issues appear to have made a substantial contribution to the aggregate result of an election but played only a modest role in producing differences between individual voters because voters' opinions in that area were skewed to favor one candidate and exhibited only limited variability at the point of the vote choice.

The 1992 election presented clear illustrations of contrasting findings of that sort. Several policy-related predispositions and current policy preferences played a visible role in leading some voters to choose George Bush and others Bill Clinton, but the combined effects of those conflict-related preferences produced only a small net advantage for George Bush. Voters' perceptions of the economy, on the other hand, played only a modest role in explaining individual differences in vote choice (because of general agreement among both Clinton and Bush supporters that the recession posed serious problems), but made the largest single contribution to Bill Clinton's victory.

The procedures developed in Chapter 17 to clarify the importance of specific variables can also be used to summarize the role played by sets of variables which share the same type of content, or the same general explanatory "theme," such as policy-related predispositions or the personal qualities of the candidates. Such procedures are particularly helpful in comparing adjacent elections, where the same types of variables may have played some role in voters' decisions *and* were comparably measured in election surveys conducted during those campaigns. To illustrate those possibilities, we used "importance analysis" to clarify the extent to which the aggregate shift in votes between 1988 and 1992 should be attributed to changes in voters' perceptions of the national economy rather than to a reduction in the Republicans' advantage on conservative policy-related predispositions. The same importance analysis emphasized the considerable similarity between those elections in the importance attached to different explanatory themes in producing differences among individual voters in their choices for President.

▪ Some Lessons Learned

From the earliest plans to expand our analyses of individual elections and create a relatively comprehensive model for the analysis of elections in general, we expected that our analyses would provide a decisive integration and culmination of many individual arguments that had to be settled en route. We are not completely satisfied with the final results, but they have met our expectations in a number of respects. In the first place, the analytic comparison of voters' responses to structured questions with their volunteered reasons for liking the candidates produced anticipated results. We have noted the expected stronger performance of explanatory variables based on structured responses in estimating "apparent total effects" for individual variables or for themes. We have commented in passing on the evidence that reliance on "reasons" misses many voters for whom a particular variable—or theme—is of clear importance, according to the analyses of their responses to structured questions on the same topic.

A second reassurance concerning the validity of our multi-stage model was, perhaps paradoxically, provided by the limited importance assigned to the assessment of the personal qualities of the candidates. Widespread assumptions about the inevitability of the intrusion of simultaneity, or feedback from candidate preferences motivated by sources other than the actual personal attributes of the candidates themselves, led us to fear substantial overestimates of the impact of candidate personal attribute variables on the vote. However, the effect estimates from those measures most proximate to the choice between candidates by no means over-shadowed the apparent effects of variables less susceptible to feedback.

It may be that some part of the "importance estimate" for personal qualities is nevertheless inflated as a result of such feedback sources of error. If so, the resulting evidence is even less conducive to a belief that we are in the midst of an era of candidate-centered politics in which candidates are more important than party policy or national conditions. This is not to deny the probable impact of candidates and their cam-paigns on the activation of various predispositions, as well as on pol-icy preferences and assessments of candidate performance evaluations. It does, however, put the "character" issue and similar aspects of per-sonal campaigning—both positive and negative—in a quite different perspective.

A third generalization may be of even greater potential significance. Despite a newfound NES interest in the campaign, and in the volatility of campaign-induced preferences we have been surprised at the extent to which the apparent effects of current short-term responses of voters are in fact confounded by long-term factors—in particular by partisan and policy-related predispositions. We have seen repeatedly in the elabo-ration tables in Chapters 12, 13, 14, and 15 that impressive relationships of different variables with vote choice fade into substantive insignifi-cance as one takes various long-term factors into account.

This may not minimize the evidence of consequences of a campaign so much as it recasts the role of the campaign. The selling of a president may still be possible, but the creation of an appealing image would seem to be necessarily based on relatively enduring pre-existing predisposi-tions. At the same time, one should bear in mind that there is only limited evidence that all of the predispositions we have employed are long-term, stable elements well in place before campaigns begin. The results of the elaboration analyses in the 1988 and 1992 elections give added urgency to research that would verify, or challenge, the temporal durability of predispositions other than party identification and ideologi-cal self-designation.

If the data from 1988 and 1992 suggested an unanticipated importance for our policy-related predispositions, they also suggest unexpectedly "minimal effects" for selected other relationships. For example, in as-sembling the components of our six-stage, eight-theme model, much thought was given to unknown causal relationships between policy preferences and perceived conditions. It seemed plausible to assume that evaluations of current conditions, particularly concerning the economy, might influence attitudes toward government policy; it also seemed at least possible that strong opinions about policy might color perceptions of apparent results of the policy. Our decision was to include both themes in the same analytic stage. When we subsequently control, in alternating sequence, for all "other" variables in that stage to appraise the "independent" status of each single condition, or policy, it becomes apparent that neither conditions nor policies were substantially responsible for confounding the relationship of each other with the vote.

In like manner, despite strong preconceptions about the extent to which social and economic characteristics are interrelated, those interrelationships did not seem to intrude heavily on the relationships involving individual characteristics and vote choice. Nor, indeed, did controlling for social and economic characteristics reveal many confounds for other variables located in a stage more proximate to the vote. Controlling for fixed voter characteristics is always good policy before interpreting other relationships with the vote—as in the case of Protestant Evangelicals. Much more often, however, it is the predispositions— partisan and policy-related—rather than the social and economic attributes, that must be taken into account to avoid confounded explanations of electoral choice. Finally, the analysis in Part II of voter turnout of the pre-New Deal and post-New Deal generations suggests that there is much more yet to be learned about the structure of social and political attitudes as they are formed and then decay among the young and the old.

▪ A Broader View

In returning to many of the explanatory themes in *The American Voter,* we were motivated by a general belief that better answers could be obtained for evolving questions about the state of the national electorate than were being provided by prevailing academic and journalistic accounts. In particular, we were disturbed by the answers often given to questions about declining turnout on election day and the declining role of party in the electorate, questions concerning the basic foundations of partisan presidential politics. Whether or not these specific questions have been answered satisfactorily in this book, we think our inquiry has produced more than the specific answers we sought by presenting a comprehensive approach (and model) for the analysis of individual elections. This book, along with the complementary work of many colleagues, is intended to provide a continuing—and general—perspective on the foundations of individual electoral behavior in the contemporary United States.

We have, first of all, presented descriptions of behavior, and predispositions to behave, on the part of the national electorate that stand in sharp contrast to the hurly-burly of the short-term forces in the elections we have observed. The same descriptions run counter to much of the doomsaying that is characteristic of contemporary political commentary. It is relevant here to return to the three recurring questions that are posed after every election, the questions with which we opened this book: Why did some citizens participate while others did not? Of those who did go to the polls, why did some vote for one candidate and some for the other? Why did one candidate and not the other win; and why was the margin of victory so large (or small)?

In recent years, the answers to these questions given by politicians and commentators have often suggested something close to a consensus that things are sorely amiss with our system of selecting political leaders. Opinions about the public's responses to government seem to be divided between those who see only distrust and alienation and those who see rampant rejection. Fundamental distrust of government is represented by the call for term limits for elected officials (state legislators as well as U.S. senators and congressmen), the demand for reductions in taxes while simultaneously calling for a reduction in the federal budget deficit, and recommendations that the scope of federal governmental activities be sharply reduced, but with no reduction in governmental services— except perhaps assistance to the poor. According to public opinion polls, national political leaders in general—and Congress in particular—are held in contempt, and the major political parties are both condemned and rejected because they are seen as causes of the problem, rather than instruments for their solution. In this context, speculation continues about the likelihood of a third party or at least an "Independent" candidate.

"Proof" of public discontent has been seen in the increasing abstention from the polls on election day, or in the abrupt reversals of partisan political fortunes from election to election. Throughout most of the post–World War II period, the Democratic party has had control of both houses of Congress. However, given the dominant Republican control of the White House in 28 of the 40 years prior to 1992, the topic of "divided government" has emerged as a prominent theme for political commentary. Some observers, perhaps influenced by the popularity of "rational" choice theories, have conflated the existence of generalized political distrust with the fact of divided party control of Congress and the White House. Such observers occasionally suggest that divided government represents a deliberate choice by voters who are attempting to limit the scope of governmental actions through the constitutional provision for checks and balances. Such a scenario may seem fanciful to those knowledgeable about the severe limits that constrain "strategic voting" as an aspect of mass electoral behavior. Nevertheless, arguments of these sorts have underscored the extent to which all manner of evidence has been interpreted in terms of a presumed degeneration of the electoral links between a deserving but frustrated electorate and the corrupt and incompetent political leaders of the nation.

If one steps back from our attempts to understand declining turnout, dealignment in partisanship, and the reasons for the Bush and then the Clinton election victories, a quite different perspective comes into view. In the first instance, however responsive the electoral system may have been to the moods and electoral demands of the political moment, the regularities of the underlying correlates of voter participation seem to have been impervious to such surface changes. If we return to our analyses of voter turnout in the three stages of the political life of the citizen in Chapter 4 and look at Tables 4.3, 4.4, and 4.5 side by side, but in reverse order, we can see a remarkable sense of order and continuity. On the left side of those tables, we watch a new generation, the post-New Deal generation, appear on the political stage. With each passing set of elections, the normal consequences of life cycle changes and increased political involvement can be seen. More and more of the conventional correlates of voting turnout appear, with increased total effects, until, in the *last two* sets of elections, the maturing post-New Deal generation exhibits a pattern of relationships concerned with voting turnout that looks very much like the pattern in the next table for the *first set* of elections for the New Deal generation. The remarkable aspect of these comparisons is in the similarity between the post-New Deal generation in the 1980s and the older New Deal generation as of three or four decades earlier in the elections of the 1950s. Here we have two completely different generations and two completely different sets of elections with little suggestion of time-specific differences or changes in the foundations or sources of turnout.

The portrait of continuity across generations, and eventual stability within a generation, continues through the four successive sets of elections in which we can follow electors from the period of the New Deal as they age and vote. Their pattern in the elections of the 1980s is, in turn, very much like the pattern for the first elections in which we can observe their *pre-New Deal* elders four decades earlier. Ultimately, the relationships of other variables with turnout within the pre-New Deal cohorts progress through a veritable mirror image of the changing patterns for the very young post-New Deal cohorts, with appropriate allowances for the differences between emergent youth and declining old age.

Generational replacement has been a dominant source of change in participation in voting turnout for the electorate as a whole. The electors of each generation have had a characteristically different level of involvement and participation, based on their experiences at the time they entered the electorate. But the eventual social and psychological foundations of that participation appear to have been very much the same for each generation. Of course we cannot be sure that the emerging pattern of relationships with turnout for the post-New Deal generation would not have been different in different political times; or that the pattern for the New Deal generation when it emerged in the 1930s was truly like that for the emerging post-New Deal in the 1970s; or that the pattern in the years of decline of the New Deal cohorts will resemble that of the now-disappeared pre-New Deal cohort.

We do know that the correlates of turnout for the post-New Deal generation in the 1980s were like those for the New Deal cohort in the 1950s, and the pattern for the pre-New Deal generation in the 1950s was like that for the New Deal cohort in the 1980s. Although other patterns may have prevailed in earlier periods, or may prevail in subsequent (future) periods, all of our evidence emphasizes continuity. Furthermore, these results reject explanations of voter turnout based on withdrawal from participation by any but the very old—and then for reasons of physical infirmity, not political disenchantment. Despite wide partisan fluctuations in the division of the presidential vote, despite the transformation of election campaigns, despite a prolonged downward drift in aggregate turnout, and despite a wholesale turnover of personnel in the electorate, the social, economic, and social-psychological foundations of citizen participation at the polls have been remarkably constant and devoid of dramatic change.

In general, headlines and feature stories about election-day turnout have been more colorful than enlightening. And once voters have been separated from non-voters, the case for stability in the partisan underpinnings of the vote is only slightly more complex. The mobilization of African-American involvement in partisan politics is a straightforward exception. Changes in this area over the past half-century have been well documented by others. Our minor contribution has been to demonstrate the need to separate Blacks from non-Blacks in evaluating the nature of natural shifts in long-term partisan identifications.

A second complication has arisen from the very substantial and politically important changes in the South. Here, again, our contribution has been more in noting the change that has been documented by others. However, our generational descriptions of Southern realignment provide a starting point for further investigation; we believe there is more to be learned about adult acquisition and conversion of party identification by studying the Southern experience in greater detail.

A third complexity has been provided by the recent dramatic change of partisan loyalties among Protestants committed to the Evangelical religious traditions. If our suspicions concerning an opposite reaction among secular voters or among the young never-married are well founded, there will be more to learn about those changes in the next few elections.

Each of these three major venues for change in party identification—racial, regional, and religious—provides an opportunity to learn more about the various ways in which partisan identities are formed and change. In each case the impact of such changes on the vote has occurred over several elections and, including the dramatic shift of party loyalties among Evangelical Protestants, has come as a surprise only to the less observant. For two-thirds of the voters, changes in partisan identification have been of very limited scope for at least forty years. The noted exceptions aside, we have documented a continuity in the party identifications of the remainder of the electorate that is akin to the stability we have observed in the correlates of voter turnout.

As a long-term stable predisposition, party identification is not only a point of departure for electoral analysis; it is the most important of several predispositions that provide continuity across electoral epochs. We are very much in accord with the formulations of *The American Voter* which saw partisan loyalties limiting the frequency and magnitude of shifts in electoral preferences, an inertial force against change and a magnet drawing defectors back to a habitual partisan point of departure in time for the next election. Party identification is only one of a host of themes relevant to vote choice, but year after year it is the dominant predisposition in providing continuity in voters' perspectives and behaviors from one election to the next.

In a somewhat similar manner, we see policy-related predispositions as long-term factors with continuing implications for vote choice, but more subject to variability in their salience or relevance from one campaign to another. In our 1992 analysis, we noted the extent to which voters' preferences were tied to long-term factors through stable relationships with social and economic characteristics, party identification, and policy-related predispositions. Even the vote, which has fluctuated with 40-point shifts in the margins of partisan advantage in elections separated by only eight or twelve years, is more firmly anchored to a network of American social values than many post-election postmortems have suggested.

We began our inquiry by emphasizing the need to understand political change. We conclude, however, by emphasizing continuity and the importance of long-term predispositions that form early in political life and become a continuing aspect of national politics through the machinery of generational turnover and replacement. The partisan volatility of the presidential vote over short periods of time clearly merits the attention of politicians and political commentators alike. Changes in partisan control of government are newsworthy, and they do make a difference in the activities and priorities of government. Continuity in the values and identifications that shape the vote are not equally newsworthy, but they are certainly of equal importance to the continuing vitality of our electoral system.

Whatever the intent of the electorate has been in 1992 or 1994, the introduction of new political leaders to national politics is taking place in the midst of convulsive changes in social, technological, and economic conditions at the end of the twentieth century that will almost certainly produce another transformation in presidential electoral politics. The history recounted in this book will not be repeated, but we may be better prepared to understand the changes now under way as we clarify the sources of changes in the recent past.

From what we have learned in this book, it seems reasonable to expect voting turnout to continue to rise as the most recent additions to the post-New Deal generation look more like the new additions to the electorate of the 1950s and early 1960s. Turnout may be further enhanced as the influence of the generationally located period effect from the "time of turmoil" fades, and as older cohorts of the post-New Deal generations emulate the behavior of their predecessors—whom we have been able to observe before they faded from the stage of active participation.

Partisan loyalties may shift, and margins of advantage widen or narrow, but we should have a better sense of the likely pace of change in the years ahead because we have a better understanding of the years just behind us. We have not attempted to predict the future, but we do believe we have a better foundation on which to build an understanding of the fluctuating nature of racial politics, the political consequences of social and economic inequality, and the driving force of moral issues. In reconsidering the explanatory questions covered in *The American Voter,* nothing we have learned suggests that the basic institutions in our system of choosing a president are in need of repair, other than that which can be provided by wise and effective leaders.

Appendix A

★ ★ ★

Supplementary Data:
Cohort Analysis of Turnout

Table A1 Cohort Turnout Rates Within Three Categories of Education, Pertaining to Self-Reported Turnout Among Non-Black Members of the Electorate with 0–11 Years of Education

Age: 1952	Year of First Vote	Election Year											Age: 1992
		52	56	60	64	68	72	76	80	84	88	92	
	92											(18)	18–21
	88										(31)	(19)	22–25
	84									(22)	(20)	(33)	26–29
	80								(40)	(23)	(15)	19	30–33
	76							07	(0)	(31)	(27)	(11)	34–36
	72.1						37	(32)	(10)	(56)	(17)	(50)	37–40
	72.2		—	—	—	—	46	36	(40)	(43)	(57)	(45)	41–44
	68	—	—	—	—	(22)	40	46	(33)	(43)	(40)	(41)	45–48
9–12	64	—	—	—	28	(29)	43	52	(64)	(41)	(75)	(57)	49–52
13–16	60	—	—	(30)	44	71	48	55	(62)	(57)	(69)	(63)	53–56
17–20	56	—	33	54	67	(53)	61	38	(39)	64	(56)	(60)	57–60
21–24	52	31	51	63	73	64	65	79	(38)	(56)	52	(68)	61–64
25–28	48	60	57	72	71	53	63	61	(59)	65	53	72	65–68
29–32	44	67	57	63	76	82	66	63	(63)	60	59	69	69–72
33–36	40	63	55	62	73	66	57	72	68	77	75	61	73–76
37–40	36	76	71	86	69	83	75	71	64	79	(69)	(48)	77–80
41–44	32	71	77	83	84	63	62	68	79	58	67	79	
45–48	28	71	73	71	85	73	68	74	(77)	52			
49–52	24	83	81	82	73	73	71	69	53				
53–56	20	82	76	91	76	71	59	64	(44)				
57–60	16	86	78	94	76	66	58	49	(33)				
61–64	12	82	78	85	83	(35)	(36)	(18)					
65–68	08	80	74	72	(69)	(63)	(70)						
69–72	04	74	67	32	(90)								
73–76	1900	68	71	(77)									

( ) N < 25.

Table A2 Cohort Turnout Rates Within Three Categories of Education, Pertaining to Self-Reported Turnout Among Non-Black Members of the Electorate Who Are High School Graduates

Age: 1952	Year of First Vote	52	56	60	64	68	72	76	80	84	88	92	Age: 1992
												56	18–21
	92										39	47	22–25
	88									59	35	63	26–29
	84								51	47	38	72	30–33
	80							52	38	49	58	66	34–36
	76						40	45	50	57	56	73	37–40
	72.1						59	55	56	72	63	86	41–44
	72.2					58	68	56	72	59	69	78	45–48
	68				65	75	73	70	77	82	73	83	49–52
9–12	64			92	69	71	72	76	80	81	77	94	53–56
13–16	60		58	69	84	89	87	90	91	94	84	88	57–60
17–20	56	76	70	74	83	91	83	90	(84)	93	(88)	85	61–64
21–24	52	82	75	97	89	89	90	72	73	96	89	92	65–68
25–28	48	73	82	92	88	93	90	83	85	87	89	92	69–72
29–32	44	94	85	93	83	97	86	92	91	78	87	(82)	73–76
33–36	40	92	84	93	88	85	84	83	(100)	88	(92)	(68)	77–80
37–40	36	97	91	87	91	88	87	83	(77)	(93)	(88)	(88)	
41–44	32	96	93	100	(89)	(87)	88	95	(82)	(80)	(75)		
45–48	28	(83)	95	(92)	(75)	(100)	(73)	(70)	(80)				
49–52	24	91	(90)	(91)	(90)	(80)	(100)	(100)					
53–56	20	(87)	(91)	(100)	(100)	(75)	(88)	(31)					
57–60	16	(100)	(100)	(100)	(86)								
61–64	12	(100)	(100)	(100)									
65–68	08	(71)	(100)										
69–72	04	(50)											
73–76	1900												

(N), N < 25.

Table A3 Cohort Turnout Rates Within Three Categories of Education, Pertaining to Self-Reported Turnout Among Non-Black Members of the Electorate with At Least One Year of College

Age: 1952	Year of First Vote	52	56	60	64	68	72	76	80	84	88	92	Age: 1992
													(Election Year)
	92											73	18–21
	88									41	73	22–25
	84								57	75	85	26–29
	80							73	74	82	90	30–33
	76						67	67	81	81	89	34–36
	72.1						86	88	70	88	88	90	37–40
	72.2						79	77	86	87	86	83	41–44
9–12	68					68	84	81	84	94	92	92	45–48
13–16	64				82	77	88	82	83	88	82	94	49–52
17–20	60			(100)	72	76	85	96	86	91	97	94	53–56
21–24	56		70	91	89	79	91	98	(83)	80	92	98	57–60
25–28	52	86	92	89	72	91	88	84	93	93	91	100	61–64
29–32	48	85	88	87	97	94	96	98	96	98	97	95	65–68
33–36	44	92	92	95	96	97	88	85	(89)	95	90	94	69–72
37–40	40	89	92	92	96	92	91	91	(100)	96	(100)	94	73–76
41–44	36	(90)	97	90	96	100	86	97	100	(92)	85	(90)	77–80
45–48	32	91	91	97	(100)	(81)	95	95	(92)	(100)	(91)	(89)	
49–52	28	91	86	80	(88)	(91)	(81)	(74)	(89)	(91)			
53–56	24	(94)	(100)	(100)	(90)	(82)	(93)	(91)	(100)				
57–60	20	(90)	(77)	(100)	(73)	(100)	(89)	(79)					
61–64	16	(83)	(93)	85	(92)	(100)	(67)						
65–68	12	(100)	(100)	(100)	(83)								
69–72	08	(100)	(100)	(100)									
73–76	04	(100)	(100)										
	1900	(75)											

(N), N < 25.

Table A4 Voter Turnout Rates, by Cohort, with Time (Elections) Regressed on Turnout, for Non-Black Citizens, Less Than Completed High School, 1952–1988

Cohort	Mean Turnout, Percent Voting	Unstandardized Coefficients	Number of Elections (Observations)	Total Change in Percent Voting	T Value	P
Post-New Deal						
1976	27	.0216	4	06	0.8	.43
1972	45	.0053	5	03	0.6	.56
1968	40	.0014	5	01	0.2	.88
New Deal						
1964	48	.0137	6	08	1.6	.12
1960	58	.0043	7	03	0.8	.44
1956	56	−.0041	7	−03	0.8	.44
1952	64	−.0034	8	−03	1.0	.33
1948	63	−.0051	8	−04	1.5	.12
1944	66	.0004	10	00	0.0	.93
1940	63	.0030	8	02	1.8	.24
1936	75	−.0021	8	−02	0.9	.37
1932	73	−.0043	7	−03	1.6	.11
Pre-New Deal						
1928	73	.0000	7	00	0.0	.98
1924	79	−.0070	5	−03	1.6	.12
1920	83	.0015	4	01	0.2	.81
1916	84	−.0026	4	−01	0.5	.65
1912	82	.0043	3	01	0.4	.67

Table A5 Voter Turnout Rates, by Cohort, with Time (Elections) Regressed on Turnout, for Non-Black Citizens, Completed High School, 1952–1988

	Cohort	Mean Turnout, Percent Voting	Unstandardized Coefficients	Number of Elections (Observations)	Total Change in Percent Voting	T Value	P
Post-New Deal	1976	58	-.0037	3	-01	0.3	.08
	1972	61	.0084	5	04	1.7	.09
	1968	65	.0000	5	00	0.0	1.00
New Deal	1964	74	.0026	6	02	0.6	.55
	1960	75	.0052	7	04	1.6	.11
	1956	89	.0015	7	01	0.6	.55
	1952	87	.0026	8	02	1.1	.27
	1948	87	-.0048	8	-04	2.3	.02
	1944	86	.0017	10	02	1.2	.23
	1940	90	.0000	8	00	0.0	.93
	1936	88	.0000	8	00	0.2	.81
	1932	89	-.0045	7	-03	1.7	.08
Pre-New Deal	1928	93	-.0018	7	-01	0.7	.48
	1924	89	.0023	5	01	2.3	.73
	1920	90	-.0000	4	-00	0.0	.99
	1916	94	.0130	4	05	1.6	.11
	1912	100	—	3	—	—	—

Table A6 Voter Turnout Rates, by Cohort, with Time (Elections) Regressed on Turnout, for Non-Black Citizens, Completed Some College, 1952–1988

	Cohort	Mean Turnout, Percent Voting	Unstandardized Coefficients	Number of Elections (Observations)	Total Change in Percent Voting	T Value	P
Post-New Deal	1976	83	.0206	3	06	2.6	.01
	1972	83	.0062	5	03	2.0	.05
	1968	88	.0077	5	04	2.8	.01
New Deal	1964	84	.0020	6	01	0.6	.53
	1960	87	.0093	7	06	3.5	.00
	1956	89	.0000	7	00	0.1	.91
	1952	87	.0031	8	02	1.3	.20
	1948	95	.0031	8	02	2.3	.02
	1944	91	−.0000	10	−00	0.4	.70
	1940	92	.0014	8	01	0.7	.48
	1936	95	.0015	8	01	0.9	.39
	1932	93	.0000	7	00	0.3	.75
Pre-New Deal	1928	84	−.0040	7	−03	0.1	.34
	1924	94	−.0084	5	−04	1.8	.08
	1920	86	−.0050	4	−02	0.4	.63
	1916	88	.0023	4	01	0.3	.73
	1912	100	—	3	—	—	—

Voter Turnout and Partisanship of Selected Social and Economic Attributes, 1980–1992

Table B1.1 Voter Turnout by Years of Education

Turnout: Proportion Reporting Vote

Years of Education	A. Percent Voted				B. Deviations from Remainder of Electorate				C. Percent of Electorate			
	1980	1984	1988	1992	1980	1984	1988	1992	1980	1984	1988	1992
Less than High School Graduate (0–11)	55	55	51	49	−21	−23	−23	−33	24%	23%	20%	17%
High School Graduate (12)	69	70	61	73	−2	−5	−13	−5	37	35	35	34
At least some College (13+)	82	86	85	88	+18	+22	+28	+23	39	42	45	49
High-Low	27	31	34	39	+39	+45	+51	+56	+15	+19	+25	+32
National Self-Reported Turnout	70	73	69	76					100%	100%	100%	100%

Table B1.2 Political Partisanship and Years of Education

Party Identification and Presidential Vote
Among Major (2) Party Voters

Years of Education	A. %D_PI - %R_PI				B. %Dv - %Rv				Changes: 1980–1992		
	1980	1984	1988	1992	1980	1984	1988	1992	Turnout	P.I.	Vote
Less than High School Graduate (0–11)	+48	+30	+28	+39	+29	+12	+19	+37	−6	−9	+8
High School Graduate (12)	+12	+9	+8	+22	−21	−22	−1	+23	+4	+10	+44
At least some College (13+)	+1	−3	−8	−1	−27	−23	−15	+9	+6	−2	+36
High-Low	−47	−33	−36	−40	−56	−35	−34	−28	+12	−7	+28
National Mean	+15	+8	+3	+13	−12	−16	−6	+14	+6	−2	+26

Table B1.3 Political Partisanship and Years of Education with Group Means Expressed as Deviations from the Remainder of the Two-Party Electorate

Party Identification and Presidential Vote
Among Major (2) Party Voters

Years of Education	A. %D$_{PI}$ - %R$_{PI}$				B. %Dv - %Rv				Changes: 1980–1992	
	1980	1984	1988	1992	1980	1984	1988	1992	P.I.	Vote
Less than High School Graduate (0–11)	+42	+28	+30	+30	+53	+34	+29	+23	−12	−30
High School Graduate (12)	−3	+4	+9	+14	−13	−8	+7	+9	+17	+22
At least some College (13+)	−25	−19	−23	−25	−24	−13	−20	−18	0	+6
High-Low	−67	−47	−53	−55	−77	−47	−49	−41	−12	−36

Table B2.1 Turnout by Gender

Turnout: Proportion Reporting Vote

Gender	A. Percent Voted				B. Percent of Electorate				C. Change in Percent that Voted 1980–1992
	1980	1984	1988	1992	1980	1984	1988	1992	
Male	73	72	72	77	55%	56%	55%	53%	+4
Female	69	73	67	76	45	44	45	47	+7
Difference (Gender Gap)	4	1	5	1					−3
National Turnout	70	73	69	76	100%	100%	100%	100%	+6

Table B2.2 Political Partisanship and Gender

Party Identification and Presidential Vote
Among Major (2) Party Voters

Gender	A. %D$_{PI}$ - %R$_{PI}$				B. %Dv - %Rv				C. Change: 1980–1992	
	1980	1984	1988	1992	1980	1984	1988	1992	P.I.	Vote
Male	+9	+2	−4	+1	−19	−25	−13	+7	−8	+26
Female	+17	+12	+9	+16	−5	−10	0	+20	−1	+25
Gender Gap	8	10	13	15	14	15	13	13	+7	−1
National Mean	+15	+8	+3	+13	−12	−16	−6	+14	−2	+26

Table B3.1 Voter Turnout by Political Generation

Turnout: Proportion Reporting Vote

Generation	Year First Eligible to Vote	A. Percent Voted				B. Deviations from Remainder of Electorate				C. Percent of Electorate			
		1980	1984	1988	1992	1980	1984	1988	1992	1980	1984	1988	1992
Pre-New Deal	Pre-1920	*	*	—ᵃ	—					(*)			
	1920–1928	67	66	(61)	(62)	−4	−8	(−9)	—	7%	5%	3%	(*)
New Deal	1932–1944	83	80	79	82	+15	+9	+12	+6	21	18	15	11
	1948–1964	77	81	77	84	+9	+11	+11	+11	29	26	26	23
Post-New Deal	1968–1976	62	73	72	78	−14	0	+4	+2	35	35	35	32
	1980–1992	56	53	50	67	−15	−23	−25	−13	7	16	21	33
National Turnout		70	73	69	76					100%	100%	100%	100%

a. No citizens first eligible to vote before 1920 in NES sample.
*Less than one-half of one percent.
( ) N < 25.

Table B3.2 Political Partisanship and Political Generation

Party Identification and Presidential Vote
Among Major (2) Party Voters

Generation	A. %D$_{PI}$ - %R$_{PI}$				B. %D$_v$ - %R$_v$				Changes: 1980–1992		
	1980	1984	1988	1992	1980	1984	1988	1992	Turnout	P.I.	Vote
Pre-New Deal	—	—	—	—	—	—	—	—	—	—	—
	0	−9	(0)	(*)	0	−5	(16)	(*)	(−5)	(*)	(*)
New Deal	+29	+9	−1	+20	+2	−13	−8	+22	−1	−9	+20
	+11	+10	+3	+13	−22	−21	−5	+14	+7	+2	+36
Post-New Deal	+8	+5	+6	+16	−18	−16	−6	+18	+16	+8	+36
	+27	+3	−6	+4	+5	−17	−5	+16	+11	−23	+11
National Mean	+15	+8	+3	+13	−12	−16	−6	+14	+6	−2	+26

a. No citizens first eligible to vote before 1920 in NES sample.

* Less than one-half of one percent.

( ) N < 25.

Table B3.3 Political Partisanship by Political Generation with Group Means Expressed as Deviations from Remainder of the Two-Party Electorate

Party Identification and Presidential Vote
Among Major (2) Party Voters

Generation	A. $\%D_{PI} - \%R_{PI}$				B. $\%D_v - \%R_v$				Changes: 1980–1992	
	1980	1984	1988	1992	1980	1984	1988	1992	P.I.	Vote
Pre-New Deal	—	—	—	—	—	—	—	—	—	—
	-16	-16	(-2)	(*)	0	+12	(+23)	*	(*)	(*)
New Deal	+19	+3	-3	+10	+19	+4	-3	+6	-9	-13
	-5	+5	+1	0	-14	-6	0	-3	+5	+11
Post-New Deal	-10	-2	+6	+5	-8	+1	-1	+1	+15	+9
	+13	-4	-9	-12	+18	0	0	-1	-25	-19

a. No citizens first eligible to vote before 1920 in NES sample.
* Less than one-half of one percent.
( ) N < 25.

Table B4.1 Voter Turnout by Home Ownership

Turnout: Proportion Reporting Vote

Home Ownership	A. Percent Voted				B. Percent of Electorate				C. Change in Percent that Voted 1980–1992
	1980	1984	1988	1992	1980	1984	1988	1992	
Own	76	80	76	81	70%	68%	65%	66%	+5
Rent	58	58	56	64	28	30	33	32	+6
Difference	18	22	20	17					−1
National Turnout	70	73	69	76	100%	100%	100%	100%	+6

Table B4.2 Political Partisanship and Home Ownership

Party Identification and Presidential Vote
Among Major (2) Party Voters

Home Ownership	A. %D_PI − %R_PI				B. %Dv − %Rv				Changes: 1980–1992	
	1980	1984	1988	1992	1980	1984	1988	1992	P.I.	Vote
Own	+11	+4	−1	+8	−19	−25	−12	+8	−3	+27
Rent	+26	+18	+15	+28	+9	+9	+11	+46	+2	+37
Difference	15	14	16	20	28	33	23	38	+5	+10
National Mean	+15	+8	+3	+13	−12	−16	−6	+14	−2	+26

Table B5.1 Voter Turnout by Income Quintiles

Turnout: Proportion Reporting Vote

	A. Percent Voted				B. Deviations from Remainder of Electorate			
Income Quintiles	1980	1984	1988	1992	1980	1984	1988	1992
Lowest 1	58	51	47	56	-17	-27	-27	-24
2	68	68	64	66	-4	-7	-7	-12
3	67	73	69	77	-4	-1	-1	+1
4	77	82	78	86	+9	+11	+11	+11
Highest 5	81	87	86	88	+13	+18	+21	+16
High-Low	+23	+36	+39	+32	+30	+45	+48	+40
National Turnout	70	73	69	76				

Table B5.2 Political Partisanship by Income Quintiles

Party Identification and Presidential Vote
Among Major (2) Party Voters

	A. %D$_{PI}$ - %R$_{PI}$				B. %Dv - %Rv				Changes: 1980–1992		
Income Quintiles	1980	1984	1988	1992	1980	1984	1988	1992	Turnout	PI.	Vote
Lowest 1	+41	+32	+25	+37	+20	+20	+20	+52	-2	-4	+32
2	+35	+11	+13	+33	+9	-13	+8	+29	-2	-2	+20
3	+14	+5	+6	+23	-17	-11	+5	+26	+10	+9	+43
4	+4	+5	+6	+3	-28	-31	-7	+4	+9	-1	+32
Highest 5	-10	-3	-23	-9	-34	-35	-36	-3	+7	+1	+31
High-Low	-51	-35	-48	-46	-54	-55	-56	-55	+9	+5	-1
National Mean	+15	+18	+3	+13	-12	-16	-6	+14	+6	-2	+26

Table B5.3 Political Partisanship and Income Quintiles, with Group Means Expressed as Deviations from Remainder of the Two-Party Electorate

Party Identification and Presidential Vote
Among Major (2) Party Voters

Income Quintiles	A. %D_PI - %R_PI Deviations from Remainder of Electorate				B. %Dv-%Rv Deviations from Remainder of Electorate				C. Change 1980–1992	
	1980	1984	1988	1992	1980	1984	1988	1992	P.I.	Vote
Lowest 1	+31	+29	+26	+28	+39	+39	+29	+40	−3	+1
2	+25	+5	+13	+24	+27	+17	+18	+14	−1	−13
3	0	−3	+5	+13	−5	−7	+14	+12	+13	+17
4	−14	−2	+5	−12	−21	−18	−2	−16	+2	+5
Highest 5	−31	−14	−34	−31	−28	−25	−41	−28	0	0
High-Low	−62	−43	−60	−59	−67	−64	−70	−68	−3	+1

Table B6.1 Voter Turnout by Marital Status

Turnout: Proportion Reporting Vote

Marital Status	A. Percent Voted				B. Deviations from Remainder of Electorate				C. Percent of Electorate			
	1980	1984	1988	1992	1980	1984	1988	1992	1980	1984	1988	1992
Never Married	59	64	60	68	−14	−11	−11	−10	17%	18%	18%	20%
Married	76	77	75	81	+13	+9	+14	+13	60	58	56	62
Divorced	63	67	58	66	−9	−7	−14	−12	12	13	16	11
Widowed	70	74	69	71	−1	+1	0	−5	11	11	10	7
National Turnout	70	73	69	76					100%	100%	100%	100%

Table B6.2 Political Partisanship by Marital Status

Party Identification and Presidential Vote Among Major (2) Party Voters

Marital Status	A. %D_PI − %R_PI				B. %Dv − %Rv				Changes: 1980–1992		
	1980	1984	1988	1992	1980	1984	1988	1992	Turnout	P.I.	Vote
Never Married	+22	+16	+8	+24	+3	+10	+16	+55	+9	+2	+52
Married	+8	+2	−2	+3	−21	−26	−13	+3	+5	−5	+24
Divorced	+34	+11	+2	+34	+3	−7	+2	+42	+3	0	+39
Widowed	+31	+17	+15	+22	+1	0	−5	+23	+1	−9	+22
National Mean	+15	+8	+3	+13	−12	−16	−6	+14	+6	−2	+26

Table B6.3 Political Partisanship by Marital Status, with Group Means Expressed as Deviations from Remainder of the Two-Party Electorate

Party Identification and Presidential Vote
Among Major (2) Party Voters

Marital Status	A. %D$_{PI}$ - %R$_{PI}$				B. %Dv - %Rv				C. Change 1980–1992	
	1980	1984	1988	1992	1980	1984	1988	1992	P.I.	Vote
Never Married	+8	+10	+7	+14	+18	+31	+26	+45	+6	+27
Married	−21	−13	−9	−21	−23	−24	−19	−41	0	−18
Divorced	+21	+5	0	+24	+18	−1	+9	+28	+3	+10
Widowed	+19	+12	+14	+10	+15	+18	+1	+7	−9	−8

Table B7.1 Voter Turnout by Race

Turnout: Proportion Reporting Vote

	A. Percent Voted				B. Percent of Electorate				C. Change in Percent that Voted
Race	1980	1984	1988	1992	1980	1984	1988	1992	1980–1992
Black	65	65	59	70	11%	10%	11%	12%	+5
Non-Black	71	74	71	77	89	90	89	88	+6
Difference	−6	−12	−9	−7					
National Turnout	70	73	69	76	100%	100%	100%	100%	+6

Table B7.2 Political Partisanship and Race

Party Identification and Presidential Vote
Among Major (2) Party Voters

	A. %D_{PI} − %R_{PI}				B. %Dv − %Rv				C. Change: 1980–1992	
Race	1980	1984	1988	1992	1980	1984	1988	1992	P.I.	Vote
Black	+83	+59	+75	+60	+86	+81	+84	+87	−23	+1
Non-Black	+6	+2	−5	+1	−24	−26	−16	+4	−5	+28
Difference	77	57	80	59	110	107	100	83	−18	−27
National Mean	+15	+8	+3	+13	−12	−16	−6	+14	−2	+26

Table B8.1 Voter Turnout by Region

Turnout: Proportion Reporting Vote

Region	A. Percent Voted				B. Deviations from Remainder of Electorate				C. Percent of Electorate			
	1980	1984	1988	1992	1980	1984	1988	1992	1980	1984	1988	1992
South	69	66	57	67	+1	−7	−12	−9	35%	33%	36%	35%
West	77	76	79	81	+7	+4	+12	+7	18	20	19	20
Midwest	71	76	78	82	0	+5	+12	+8	26	29	27	25
Northeast	69	77	70	80	−3	+4	+1	+4	21	18	18	20
National Turnout	70	73	69	76					100%	100%	100%	100%

Table B8.2 Political Partisanship by Region

Party Identification and Presidential Vote Among Major (2) Party Voters

Region	A. %D$_{PI}$ - %R$_{PI}$				B. %Dv - %Rv				Changes: 1980–1992		
	1980	1984	1988	1992	1980	1984	1988	1992	Turnout	P.I.	Vote
South	+23	+27	+21	+20	−7	−9	−1	+18	−2	−3	+25
West	+8	+3	−10	+3	−22	−11	−4	+16	+4	−5	+38
Midwest	+14	−6	−3	0	−15	−25	−9	+4	+11	−14	+19
East	+6	+3	+1	+27	−13	−20	−9	+32	+11	+21	+45
National Mean	+15	+8	+3	+13	−12	−16	−6	+14	+6	+2	+26

Table B8.3 Political Partisanship by Region with Group Means Expressed as Deviations from Remainder of the Two-Party Electorate

Party Identification and Presidential Vote
Among Major (2) Party Voters

	A. %D$_{PI}$ - %R$_{PI}$				B. %D$_v$ - %R$_v$				Change: 1980–1992	
Region	1980	1984	1988	1992	1980	1984	1988	1992	P.I.	Vote
South	+8	+18	+17	+7	+6	+7	+5	−1	−1	−7
West	−8	−4	−1	−12	−11	−29	+3	−1	−4	+10
Midwest	−1	−19	−9	−17	−3	−13	−5	−17	−16	−14
East	−11	−5	+2	+18	−26	−5	−3	+19	+29	+41

Table B9.1 Voting Turnout and Religious Traditions

Turnout: Proportion Reporting Vote

Religions	Importance of Religion	A. Percent Voted				B. Deviations from Remainder				C. Percent of Electorate			
		1980	1984	1988	1992	1980	1984	1988	1992	1980	1984	1988	1992
Mainline Protestant	Committed	88	91	90	87	+20	+18	+22	+9	9%	9%	8%	4%
	Nominal	73	74	72	81	+4	+3	+4	+6	27	25	26	20
Evangelical	Committed	78	80	72	77	+8	+7	−3	+1	10	11	12	14
	Nominal	60	57	53	67	−14	−20	−20	−11	16	14	16	18
Catholic	Committed	77	89	85	84	+6	+17	+18	+9	5	6	5	6
	Nominal	70	77	73	81	−1	+4	+5	+6	17	21	20	18
Jew		81	86	82	97	+10	+15	(+13)	+22	3	3	2	3
Non-religious		61	67	60	65	−11	−8	−10	−13	7	8	8	13
Other		73	75	75	83	+3	+1	+6	+7	5	3	2	5
National		70	73	69	76					100%	100%	100%	100%

( ) N < 25.

Table B9.2 Political Partisanship and Religious Traditions

Party Identification and Presidential Vote
Among Major (2) Party Voters

Religion	Importance of Religion	A. %D_{PI} - %R_{PI}				B. %D_v - %R_v				Change: 1980–1992		
		1980	1984	1988	1992	1980	1984	1988	1992	Turnout	P.I.	Vote
Mainline Protestant	Committed	−14	−18	−13	−17	−28	−36	−25	−10	−1	−3	+18
	Nominal	−4	−13	−17	−10	−29	−36	−24	+7	+8	−6	+36
Evangelical	Committed	+31	+3	0	−3	+12	−26	−17	−13	−1	−34	−25
	Nominal	+35	+30	+26	+20	+2	−5	+3	+19	+7	−15	+17
Catholic	Committed	+21	+18	+23	+31	−23	−8	+10	0	+7	+10	+23
	Nominal	+27	+20	+11	+28	−5	−7	+5	+32	+11	+1	+37
Jew		+69	+42	(+30)	+64	+15	+39	(+45)	+85	+16	−5	+70
Non-religious		+15	+18	+16	+18	−13	+9	+26	+47	+4	+3	+60
Other		−20	+2	(−27)	+30	−30	−16	−25	+26	+10	+50	+56
National		+15	+8	+3	+13	−12	−16	−6	+14	+6	−2	+26

( ) N < 25.

Table B9.3 Political Partisanship and Religious Traditions, with Group Means Expressed as Deviations from Remainder of the Two-Party Voters

Party Identification and Presidential Vote
Among Major (2) Party Voters

Religion	Importance of Religion	A. %D_PI - %R_PI				B. %D_v - %R_v				Change: 1980-1992	
		1980	1984	1988	1992	1980	1984	1988	1992	P.I.	Vote
Mainline Protestant	Committed	−32	−28	−18	−31	−17	−21	−21	−28	+1	−11
	Nominal	−26	−28	−27	−28	−23	−29	−29	−13	−2	+10
Evangelical	Committed	+18	−5	−4	−19	+28	−11	−12	−36	−37	−64
	Nominal	+24	+26	+27	+9	+18	+13	+11	+2	−15	−16
Catholic	Committed	+7	+11	+21	+20	−11	+9	+17	−18	+13	−7
	Nominal	+16	+15	+10	+19	+9	+12	+14	+18	+3	+9
Jew		+56	+35	(+27)	+53	+28	+57	(+52)	+70	−3	+42
Non-religious		0	+11	+14	+6	0	+27	+35	+34	+6	+34
Other		−36	−6	(−31)	+18	−18	−1	−17	+9	+54	+27

( ) N < 25.

Table B10.1 Voter Turnout by Subjective Social Class

Turnout: Proportion Reporting Vote

Social Class	A. Percent Voted				B. Deviations from Remainder of Electorate				C. Percent of Electorate			
	1980	1984	1988	1992	1980	1984	1988	1992	1980	1984	1988	1992
Working	65	66	61	70	−12	−15	−18	−13	51%	51%	53%	51%
Middle	75	79	77	81	+6	+9	+11	+8	38	39	36	38
Upper Middle	85	90	87	89	+16	+19	+19	+14	11	10	11	11
UM-W	+20	+24	+26	+19	28	34	37	27	−40	−41	−42	−40
National	70	73	69	76					100%	100%	100%	100%

Table B10.2 Political Partisanship and Subjective Social Class

Party Identification and Presidential Vote
Among Major (2) Party Voters

Social Class	A. %D_PI - %R_PI				B. %D_v - %R_v				Changes: 1980–1992		
	1980	1984	1988	1992	1980	1984	1988	1992	Turnout	P.I.	Vote
Working	+30	+20	+22	+27	+3	−5	+12	−16	+5	−3	−19
Middle	+4	−3	−6	+7	−30	−24	−14	+16	+6	+3	+46
Upper Middle	−19	−12	−34	−20	−38	−41	−36	−11	+4	−1	+27
UM-W	−49	−32	−56	−47	−41	−36	−48	+5	−1	+2	+46
National	+15	+8	+3	+13	−12	−16	−6	+14	+6	−2	+26

Table B10.3 Political Partisanship by Subjective Social Class, with Group Means Expressed as Deviations from Remainder of the Two-Party Electorate

Party Identification and Presidential Vote
Among Major (2) Party Voters

Social Class	A. $\%D_{PI} - \%R_{PI}$				B. $\%D_v - \%R_v$				C. Change: 1980–1992	
	1980	1984	1988	1992	1980	1984	1988	1992	P.I.	Vote
Working	+32	+24	+35	+26	+34	+23	+32	+16	−6	−18
Middle	−17	−15	−15	−9	−24	−11	−16	−1	+8	+23
Upper Middle	−37	−21	−43	−37	−27	−26	−36	−32	0	−5

Table B11.1 Voter Turnout and Union Households

Turnout: Proportion Reporting Vote

Household	A. Percent Voted				B. Percent of Electorate				C. Change in Percent that Voted
	1980	1984	1988	1992	1980	1984	1988	1992	1980–1992
Union	73	78	74	85	26%	23%	21%	20%	+12
Non-Union	71	72	68	74	74	77	79	80	+3
Difference	+2	+6	+6	+11					
National	70	73	69	76	100%	100%	100%	100%	+6

Table B11.2 Political Partisanship and Union Households

Party Identification and Presidential Vote
Among Major (2) Party Voters

Household	A. $\%D_{PI} - \%R_{PI}$				B. $\%D_v - \%R_v$				C. Change: 1980–1992	
	1980	1984	1988	1992	1980	1984	1988	1992	PI.	Vote
Union	+29	+28	+22	+30	+10	+14	+18	+28	+1	+18
Non-Union	+8	+2	-2	+4	-19	-25	-12	+10	-1	+29
Difference	21	26	24	26	29	39	30	18	+5	-11
National	+15	+8	+3	+13	-12	-16	-6	+14	-2	+26

Appendix C

★ ★ ★

Supplementary Data: Importance Analysis for 1988

Table C1 Total Effects and Average Values for Special Political Variables in 1988: Components for Contributions to the Aggregate Result

Name of Explanatory Theme and Specific Variable	Total Effect (unstandardized)	Average Score for Variable as a Whole	Average Score for Unique Component
(Aggregate Result = Average Vote = .062)			
Partisan Identification			
Party ID	.51	.02	.02
Policy-related Predispositions			
Lib./Con. Self-designation	.50	−.09	−.09
Equality	.27	.20	.20
Anti-Communism	.08	−.43	−.43
Union vs. Business	.32	−.08	−.08
Blacks vs. Whites	.30	−.13	−.13
Feminists vs. Pro-life	.18	.00	.00
Patriotism	.07	−.11	−.11
Current Policy Preferences			
Military	.27	.12	.24
Aid to the Disadvantaged	.23	.16	.16
Abortion	.10	.19	.25
Death Penalty	.10	−.54	−.48
Perceptions of Current Conditions			
Country as a Whole	.16	−.18	−.18
Unemployment	.14	−.12	−.10
U.S. Position in the World	.06	.12	.17
Worry about Jobs in Household	.17	−.14	.13
Retrospective Performance Evaluations			
General	.26	−.18	−.14
Economy	.11	−.07	−.02
Economic Policies since 1980	.10	−.25	−.19
Foreign Affairs	.06	−.20	−.16
Personal Economic Help	.06	−.04	−.09
Honesty since 1980	.08	.21	.02
Personal Qualities of the Candidates			
Empathy (cares, compassionate)	.45	.06	.06
Integrity (honest and moral)	.14	−.01	−.02
Leadership (inspiring)	.31	.04	.03
Prospective Evaluations of Candidate Performance			
Concerning Crime	.23	−.14	−.10
Concerning Environment	.25	.03	.04

Table C2 Importance of Specific Political Variables Based on Contributions
to the 1988 Aggregate Result

	(Aggregate Result = Average Vote = +.062)	
Name of Explanatory Theme and Specific Variable	Importance in Transmission Coefficient for the Entire Variable	Importance as Source Coefficient for Unique Part of Variable
Partisan Identification		
Party ID	.01	.01
Policy-related Predispositions		
Lib./Con. Self-designation	−.05	−.05
Equality	.05	.05
Anti-Communism	−.03	−.03
Union vs. Business	−.02	−.02
Blacks vs. Whites	−.04	−.04
Feminists vs. Pro-life	.00	.00
Patriotism	−.01	−.01
Current Policy Preferences		
Military	.03	.06
Aid to the Disadvantaged	.04	.04
Abortion	.02	.02
Death Penalty	−.05	−.05
Perceptions of Current Conditions		
Country as a Whole	−.03	−.03
Unemployment	−.02	−.02
U.S. Position in the World	.01	.01
Worry about Jobs in Household	−.02	.02
Retrospective Performance Evaluations		
General	−.05	−.04
Economy	−.01	.00
Economic Policies since 1980	−.03	−.02
Foreign Affairs	−.01	−.01
Personal Economic Help	.00	.00
Honesty since 1980	.02	.02
Personal Qualities of the Candidates		
Empathy (cares, compassionate)	.03	.03
Integrity (honest and moral)	.00	.00
Leadership (inspiring)	.01	.01
Prospective Evaluations of Candidate Performance		
Concerning Crime	−.03	−.02
Concerning Environment	.01	.01

Table C3 Total Effects and Standard Deviations for Specific Variables in 1988: Components for Importance in Explaining Individual Differences

Name of Explanatory Theme and Specific Variable	Total Effect (unstandardized)	Standard Deviation for Variable as a Whole	Standard Deviation for Unique Component
Partisan Identification			
Party ID	.51	.84	.84
Policy-related Predispositions			
Lib./Con. Self-designation	.50	.33	.33
Equality	.27	.39	.39
Anti-Communism	.08	.52	.52
Union vs. Business	.32	.27	.27
Blacks vs. Whites	.30	.25	.25
Feminists vs. Pro-life	.18	.38	.38
Patriotism	.07	.75	.75
Current Policy Preferences			
Military	.27	.52	.43
Aid to the Disadvantaged	.23	.44	.37
Abortion	.10	.75	.67
Death Penalty	.10	.77	.72
Perceptions of Current Conditions			
Country as a Whole	.16	.58	.54
Unemployment	.14	.54	.49
U.S. Position in the World	.05	.78	.75
Worry about Jobs in Household	.17	.29	.29
Retrospective Evaluations of President Reagan			
General	.26	.81	.56
Economy	.11	.79	.55
Economic Policies since 1980	.10	.77	.61
Foreign Affairs	.06	.77	.59
Personal Economic Help	.06	.71	.61
Honesty since 1980	.08	.53	.49
Personal Qualities of the Candidates			
Empathy (cares, compassionate)	.45	.35	.26
Integrity (honest and moral)	.14	.31	.28
Leadership (inspiring)	.31	.38	.30
Prospective Evaluations of Candidate Performance			
Concerning Crime	.23	.40	.31
Concerning Environment	.25	.36	.28

Table C4 Importance of Specific Political Variables in 1988 in Explaining Individual Differences in Vote Choice

(All Entries are Standardized Regression Coefficients)

Name of Explanatory Theme and Specific Variable	Transmission: Coefficient for the Entire Variable	Source or Origin: Coefficient for Unique Part of the Variable
Partisan Identification		
Party ID	.43	.43
Policy-related Predispositions		
Lib./Con. Self-designation	.17	.17
Equality	.10	.10
Anti-Communism	.04	.04
Union vs. Business	.09	.09
Blacks vs. Whites	.07	.07
Feminists vs. Pro-life	.07	.07
Patriotism	.05	.05
Current Policy Preferences		
Military	.14	.12
Aid to the Disadvantaged	.10	.08
Abortion	.07	.07
Death Penalty	.08	.07
Perceptions of Current Conditions		
Country as a Whole	.09	.09
Unemployment	.08	.07
U.S. Position in the World	.04	.04
Worry about Jobs in Household	.05	.05
Retrospective Evaluations of President Reagan		
General	.21	.15
Economy	.09	.06
Economic Policies since 1980	.08	.06
Foreign Affairs	.05	.04
Personal Economic Help	.04	.03
Honesty since 1980	.04	.04
Personal Qualities of the Candidates		
Empathy (cares, compassionate)	.16	.12
Integrity (honest and moral)	.04	.04
Leadership (inspiring)	.12	.09
Prospective Evaluations of Candidate Performance		
Concerning Crime	.09	.07
Concerning Environment	.09	.07

Table C5 Apparent Importance of General Explanatory Themes in 1988 Based on Contributions to the Aggregate Results

	(Aggregate Result = Average Vote = −.062)	
Name of Explanatory Theme	Transmission: Sum of Contributions Based on All of Each Variable	Source or Origin: Sum of Contributions Based on Unique Parts of Variable
Partisan Identification	.01	.01
Policy-related Predispositions	−.10	−.10
Current Policy Preferences	.03	.08
Perceptions of Current Conditions	−.02	−.01
Retrospective Performance Evaluations	−.08	−.05
Evaluations of Personal Qualities	.03	.03
Prospective Performance Evaluations	−.03	−.01

Table C6 Apparent Importance of General Explanatory Themes in 1988: The Explanation of Individual Differences in Vote Choice

Name of Explanatory Theme	Transmission: Standardized Coefficient for Variable Based on All of Each Variable	Source or Origin: Standardized Coefficient for Variable Based on Only Unique Parts of Variable
Partisan Identification	.43	.43
Policy-related Predispositions	.36	.36
Current Policy Preferences	.25	.18
Perceptions of Current Conditions	.18	.16
Retrospective Performance Evaluations	.42	.25
Evaluations of Personal Qualities	.28	.20
Prospective Performance Evaluations	.16	.11

Appendix D

★ ★ ★

Methodological Commentary

▪ Potential Challenges to the Validity of Apparent Effects

In Chapter 8 we identified a variety of methodological perspectives concerning survey-based explanations of electoral decisions which recommend different analytic procedures from those we have employed in Chapters 10 through 17. Each of those perspectives reflects a different type of concern about the validity of our conclusions, based on the type of statistical procedures involved. One of those alternative approaches has been discussed in several chapters. That approach uses voters' own explanations for their candidate evaluations instead of apparent effects based on voter's opinions that are not themselves defined as "reasons" for candidate preferences. For the other methodological concerns identified in Chapter 8, however, we have only suggested the degree to which our conclusions may be vulnerable to such criticism and have cited other scholars' discussion of the issues involved.

In particular, we have so far only noted that some analysts have questioned (1) the validity of estimates for the electoral impact of political attitudes that have been estimated with a single cross-section survey and a bloc recursive (instead of a non-recursive) model; (2) the appropriateness of using ordinary least squares (OLS) for dependent variables (like ours) that have only two categories or values; and (3) the extent to which our overall estimates represent misleading summaries of "true" effects which actually vary significantly from one type of voter to another. Each of these methodological concerns is discussed in a separate section below, followed by a cautionary note concerning the meaning of statistical control. Each of these discussions includes a restatement of the potential problems involved and an introduction to alternative analytic procedures that have been proposed to address those possibilities. In each area, we have presented additional statistical results to clarify the tradeoffs associated with different approaches and the decisions we have made concerning causal structure and statistical procedures.

▪ Assessing the Plausibility of Electoral "Effects" Based on Bloc-Recursive versus Non-Recursive Models

Since the 1960s, several electoral analysts have expressed concern about the validity of effect estimates based on single-equation models for "endogenous" explanatory variables that are defined in terms of voters' political opinions. Such concerns are based on the possibility that opinion-based variables may themselves be influenced by the current campaign or other recent events that have had an impact on vote choice. Potential explanatory variables of that sort may be partial *consequences* (or at least correlates) of other causes of the vote that have been omitted from the equation which is used to estimate the relevant electoral "effects." Insofar as any explanatory variables are subject to campaign-based influences of this sort, the coefficients for all explanatory variables produced by ordinary least squares (or any other multivariate procedure based on a single equation) will be biased or distorted from the "true" effects involved. In principle, this kind of "endogeneity bias" can be present for explanatory variables in each stage in our model beyond the exogenous variables that we have assigned to our first stage. Some researchers believe that the magnitude of such biases is much greater for explanatory variables that are defined in terms of partisan *evaluations* because they are located fairly "close" to the vote. Most of the controversy in this area, however, has concerned the (approximate) magnitude of the bias in effect estimates from single-equation models for partisan identification and policy-related preferences.

At several points, we have noted others' preferences for analytic procedures based on simultaneous equation models, instead of a single OLS equation for each causal stage or bloc. Advocates of such procedures emphasize the fact that they were designed specifically to overcome the above kinds of problems, which have been variously described in terms of "endogeneity," "simultaneity," or "feedback" from other causes of the dependent variable. In Chapter 8 we discussed the general nature of our reservations concerning the use of simultaneous equation models to explain the vote, without any detailed arguments or evidence. In this section we present results from analyses that use both types of methods, both to clarify our reasons for using a bloc recursive (instead of a simultaneous equation) model in our own analyses, and to address more general issues associated with the use of simultaneous equation models in the electoral context.

In particular, we have compared the results of ordinary least squares with those from several alternative simultaneous equation models for an explanation of the vote that includes only two political variables, the traditional measure of partisan identification and our summary index of policy-related preferences,[1] in addition to exogenous variables based on social and economic characteristics. In our discussion of these two variables near the end of Chapter 12, a summary equation of this sort was introduced in order to provide an approximate comparison of the overall total impact of partisan identifications with the combined influence of all the policy-related preferences in our model—in a contest where the apparent effect for both variables is estimated with the other "held constant."

Alternative Models and Two-Stage Least Squares (2SLS). The general two-stage procedure for non-recursive models is usually referred to as two-stage least squares, or 2SLS. In that procedure, the combined set of exogenous variables is used to replace each endogenous variable by a predicted score which represents that portion of the endogenous variable that can be predicted from all of the exogenous variables in the model. In our case, the first stage of these procedures generates predicted scores for both party identification and our index of policy-related preferences. The second stage of this procedure then estimates the coefficients for partisan identification and policy-related preferences in the structural equation for the vote by using the predicted scores for those two explanatory variables instead of their original (potentially endogenous) versions. This second stage in the two-stage procedures presumably permits us to estimate the "true" effect of these two endogenous variables on the vote, because the "predicted" versions of those variables are now free of correlation with any influences that have been omitted from the structural equation for the vote—because they are constructed as a linear combination of all the exogenous variables on the vote. Those social and economic variables are assumed to be uncorrelated with all other causes of the vote, precisely because they are "exogenous" to the political process. As a consequence, any linear combination of these exogenous variables (like the predicted versions of our endogenous variables) must also be free of any correlation with the omitted causes of the vote (summarized in the disturbance term for that equation). The second stage of this analysis, however, will *only* yield reliable estimates of the "true" effects of our two endogenous variables on the vote *if* the other assumptions in our model are correct—and *if* we have excluded enough exogenous variables from the structural equation for the vote so that it is at least "just identified."

This final requirement concerning "identification" deserves special emphasis, for the exclusion restrictions that are built into any simultaneous equation model represent the heart of the issue concerning the application of this technique to electoral analyses based on cross-section survey designs. In our case, we are required to assume that *some* of our exogenous variables (for example, social or economic characteristics) do not have *any* impact on the vote beyond their indirect effects "through" our two intervening variables (that are defined in terms of partisan and policy-related orientations). Social or economic variables for which we are prepared to assume that *all* effects (on the vote) are *entirely* mediated by our two endogenous variables can therefore be excluded from the final structural equation for the vote, and (at least) one such exclusion is needed for each of the two endogenous explanatory variables in our structural equation for the vote. Ideally, we would prefer to include *all* (or exclude none) of our exogenous variables in the structural equation for the vote, thereby "permitting" them to have some impact on the vote through some other (presumably short-term) processes besides those that are defined in terms of partisan identification, policy-related predispositions, or current policy issues—such as through voters' perceptions of the economy or other causes of their evaluations of the President's performance in office. If we include all of our exogenous variables in the final equation, however, our analysis becomes statistically impossible—because both of our revised explanatory variables (that is, our predicted scores for partisan identification and policy-related preferences) represent perfect linear combinations of the exogenous variables that are included in the same equation. The role of these exclusion restrictions deserves special emphasis: the *only* way to use predicted scores for our two endogenous explanatory variables that are *not* perfect linear equations of the exogenous variables in our model is to delete (or exclude) some of those variables from the structural equation for the vote.

Comparison of 1992 Results Based on OLS and 2SLS. Table D1 presents the effect coefficients and standard errors for our two explanatory variables produced by two-stage least squares for six of seven (alternative) simultaneous equation models, each of which is based on a different set of exclusion restrictions, and OLS results for the single equation model (Model 8) which includes all of our social and economic variables as well as our two endogenous variables. As emphasized above, no estimates are possible for the first of these models, which is defined in terms of simultaneous equations (designated as Model 1 in Table D1). In that model, *every* exogenous variable may influence the vote through some other (omitted) intervening variables in addition to its indirect effects on the vote that operate "through" voters' partisan identifications and policy-related preferences. Models 2 through 6 are based on alternative sets of assumptions that exclude progressively more social and economic variables from the structural equation for the vote. This sequence culminates in Model 7, which assumes that *all* of the influences of all of our social and economic variables on the vote are entirely mediated by our two endogenous variables, so that it is "safe" to exclude all of our exogenous variables from that structural equation.

Before we discuss the substantial differences between the results for Models 2 through 8, we should emphasize our belief that the most appropriate explanatory model in this situation is the one we have designated as Model 1—for which we do not have enough information to estimate the coefficients. To some extent, we agree with the critics of single equation models of this sort, for we suspect that our measures of partisan identification and policy-related preferences are somewhat correlated with other (omitted) causes of the vote, so that there is *some* "simultaneity bias" or "feedback" from presidential preference to our two "endogenous" explanatory variables. Unfortunately, however, we have no way to estimate the "true" impact of these two variables on vote choice without *assuming* that one or more exogenous (social or economic) variables have no impact on the vote *except* their indirect influence through partisan identification and policy-related preferences. In our view, such assumptions may be very far from correct since the effects of our social characteristics are unlikely to be entirely mediated by our

Table D1 Alternative Estimates for Apparent Effects on the Vote for Party ID and All Policy-Related Preferences (Combined) Based on Two-Stage Least Squares

Social and Economic Variables Included in the Structural Equation for the Vote	Estimates for Predicted Party ID		Estimates for Predicted Policy-related Index	
	Coefficient	(Standard Error)	Coefficient	(Standard Error)
Model 1: Includes *all* social or economic variables in the vote equation	impossible	—	impossible	—
Model 2: Includes race, gender, post-New Deal, college grad, union membership, and religion (but excludes income, marital status, and home ownership)	−.031	(.383)	1.402	(.370)
Model 3: Includes race, gender, post-New Deal, and college grad (adds religion and union membership to the variables that are excluded)	.306	(.129)	.988	(.116)

Model 4: Includes only race and college grad (excludes all other variables)	.579	(.101)	.630	(.085)
Model 5: Includes only race and post-New Deal (excludes all others)	.501	(.103)	.729	(.092)
Model 6: Race alone (excludes all others)	.682	(.089)	.551	(.076)
Model 7: Includes *no* social/economic variables (all are excluded)	.804	(.077)	.536	(.079)
OLS Estimates, for Comparison:				
Model 8: OLS estimates from a single equation which includes all social or economic variables and the original (i.e., not the predicted) scores for Party ID and the 3-Category Index of Policy-related Preferences	.509	(.028)	.506	(.031)

current collection of partisan and policy-related measures. For electoral analysts who (like us) are unwilling to assume the validity of such exclusion restriction, therefore, the fundamental question concerns the (approximate) magnitude of the "feedback" effects of other causes of the vote on partisan identification and the voter's own policy-related preferences. As we argue in Chapters 11 and 12, we believe that the correct answer to that question is "relatively modest"—and all of our analyses of vote choice in recent elections are based on that assumption.

Despite that general view, we have found the differences in results between Models 2 through 8 in Table D1 to be quite informative. For example, Models 2 and 3 suggest that the exclusion of only a few of our social and economic variables from the structural equation for the vote leads to coefficients for policy-related preferences that are noticeably bigger than the corresponding coefficient for partisan identification. Indeed, the only way to produce a coefficient for partisan identification that is substantially greater than the coefficient for policy-related preferences is to exclude *all* of our social and economic factors from the vote equation—or all but the voters' race. Intermediate models, which exclude all but race and either generation or college education, yield two-stage least squares estimates that are approximately the same size for our two endogenous variables—a result which is similar to that produced by OLS for the single approach in Model 8.

In our view, the results in Table D1 underscore the decisive role played by the exclusion restrictions that are built into the structural equation for the vote in any simultaneous equation model of electoral choice—or for any other dependent variable (such as party identification) for which several of the explanatory variables are clearly "endogenous" and may therefore be correlated with other (omitted) causes of the dependent variable. If, for example, Model 2 happened to be the true causal structure, the (false) exclusion of additional exogenous variables in Models 3 through 7 would result in substantial biases in the resulting coefficients. In that (hypothetical) case, we would interpret the differences between the coefficients for Models 3 through 7 and those for Model 2 as "bias." In Model 2, however, the relatively small number of excluded variables results in substantial correlations between the explanatory variables in the second stage, so that both of our coefficients are subject to substantially larger standard errors.

On the other hand, the results in Table D1 also suggest that Model 7 cannot possibly be right. If *all* of the effects of *all* social and economic variables were (in fact) mediated by our two endogenous political variables (as assumed in Model 7), the coefficients produced by the second stage of the two-stage procedure should not be changed when we add (or include) some previously excluded exogenous variables in the vote equation—and the coefficients for those exogenous variables in the structural equation for the vote should be approximately zero. Neither of these patterns appears in our results for Models 2 through 6 (although the coefficients for exogenous variables are not shown in Table D1).

In conclusion, it may be helpful if we restate our general views concerning potential endogeneity biases in the total effect estimates we have presented in Chapters 10 through 15. We agree that each of our total effect estimates (for a specific political variable) is vulnerable to *some* association between that variable and other causes of the vote that should have been (but are not) included in the explanatory equation for that stage in our bloc recursive model. In general, however, we believe that those relationships between our explanatory variables in each stage or bloc and other (more proximate) causes of the vote that have been omitted from that stage are fairly modest.

In most instances, we are more concerned about the impact of measurement error or the omission of explanatory variables that should have been included in the current stage (and equation) but were simply unavailable. With the existing data, both of those factors are beyond our control, but they may be the source of more serious bias than "endogeneity" or "feedback" from more proximate causes of the vote. Regardless of the true size of any endogeneity bias, however, we caution electoral analysts about the major biases that can be produced by assumptions based on false exclusion restrictions in simultaneous equation models that are intended to "solve" the problem of endogeneity.

■ Alternative Analytic Procedures for Dichotomous Dependent Variables

In addition to concerns about the "endogeneity" of some explanatory variables, methodological issues within the electoral field have sometimes been defined in terms of the choice between ordinary least squares (OLS) and maximum likelihood procedures based on either the logit or probit model. In such controversies, the analytic problem is typically defined in terms of the dichotomous nature of the dependent variable, and the consequences of that constraint for the validity of key assumptions about "invariant" effects and variances for the disturbance term—

both of which are required if OLS coefficients are to be interpreted as the "best" or most appropriate estimates for the underlying "effects" and their standard errors.

In such discussions, many analysts have stated a clear preference for effect estimates based on the logit or probit analysis, because those models do not require the analyst to assume that changes in the values of the explanatory variables (of the same magnitude) produce invariant shifts in the value of the dichotomous dependent variable. Instead, such models assume that the explanatory variables that are included in a given analysis are responsible for shifts in an underlying (and unmeasured) dimension that represents a continuous form of "preference" between the two alternative choices. Voters' positions on that unmeasured preferential continuum may range from very large negative to very large positive scores, and are transformed into actual behavior by a simple sign-based rule: voters with negative scores on this continuous preferential dimension choose one candidate and those with positive scores choose the other (or opposite) candidate. For both of these alternative models, the average position of any group of voters on the continuous underlying preferential dimension is defined by the proportion who voted for the winning candidate. These differences in average score are illustrated in the following chart:

Alternative Representations for Average Scores on the Vote within Average Group (Scored on 1, 1 for the Winning Candidate) for Various Divisions of the Vote within that Group

	.00	.01	.05	.17	.50	.83	.95	.99	1.0
Proportion in Group Voting for the Winner									
Average Vote (+1/−1) Used in Chapters 10–17	−1.00	−.98	−.90	−.66	.00	+.66	+.90	+.98	+1.00
Average Position Based on Probit	$-\infty$	−3.00	−1.96	−1.00	.00	+1.0	+1.96	+3.00	$+\infty$
Average Position Based on Logit	$-\infty$	−4.60	−2.94	−1.59	.00	+1.59	+2.94	+4.60	$+\infty$

One aspect of these averages deserves special attention. In the first place, as intended, both the probit and logit models "permit" the average score for groups with very lopsided distribution on the vote (that is, groups that were mainly unanimous for or against the winner) to become even more "favorable" to that candidate because there is no limit to their average distance from the neutral point (0.0). In contrast, average scores based on the simple proportion are sharply limited by the absolute "floor" and "ceiling" of 0.0 and 1.0. For example, when the simple proportion (for the winner) in a group goes from .95 to .99 (a difference of only .04), the change in average probit is 1.04—approximately the same magnitude in the change in probit associated with a shift in proportion from .50 to .83. Both the probit and logit models represent a powerful transformation in the apparent magnitude of changes in the dependent variables that are designed to remove such restrictions on the "floor" and "ceiling."

For models which include only linear and additive terms, however, these three methods can produce very similar results, as they have for assessments of the overall (total) effects for specific variables in each of the stages in our own model. To document this apparent convergence between statistical methods in explaining vote choice in 1992, Table D2 presents parallel estimates based on OLS, probit, and logit analysis of the apparent total effects for each variable in each causal stage or bloc within our overall model. In particular, the first four columns of Table D2 give OLS estimates for the total effect and standard error for each variable, both with and without the use of the NES "sample weights" which correct for known differences in response rates between different types of voters. All of the 1992 OLS estimates represented in the rest of this book are based on this standard weight variable and are simply restated in columns 1 and 2, labeled "OLS wtd." We have introduced an unweighted set of estimates in columns 3 and 4 (labeled "not wtd.") to document the very modest consequences of the standard NES weights for OLS-based estimates and to provide a more straightforward comparison between OLS estimates and parallel results from logit and probit analyses—which appear in the fifth through eighth columns—neither of which used a weight variable of this kind.

For each stage in our model, these three statistical procedures lead to sets of total effect estimates that suggest *very* similar substantive conclusions. The three methods use different statistical metrics for describing the strength of the "connection" between each explanatory variable and the vote, but they preserve the same rank order in the relative magnitude of the apparent effects for different explanatory variables in the same causal stage. For example, our (unweighted) OLS estimates for percep-

Table D2 Apparent Total Effects on Voting for Clinton vs. Bush in 1992: Alternative Estimates for Each Explanatory Variable Based on Ordinary Least Squares (OLS), Logit Analysis, and Probit Analysis

(Coefficients in Parentheses Have P Values Greater than .1)
(All Analyses Based on an Unweighted N of 1193)

	OLS (wtd.)		OLS (not wtd.)		Logit		Probit	
	Coeff.	S.E.	Coeff.	S.E.	Coeff.	S.E.	Coeff.	S.E.
SOCIAL AND ECONOMIC CHARACTERISTICS								
Generation (Post-New Deal)	−.163	.057	−.145	.058	−.357	.147	−.213	.088
Race (Black)	.907	.082	.882	.082	3.126	.374	1.721	.183
Gender (Female)	.117	.053	.098	.053	.250	.136	.157	.082
Religion (Base = None)								
(Nominal Mainline)	−.379	.098	−.416	.099	−.979	.255	−.591	.152
(Committed Mainline)	−.614	.153	−.602	.151	−1.424	.374	−.868	.226
(Nominal Evangelical)	−.484	.101	−.488	.102	−1.135	.270	−.693	.161
(Committed Evangelical)	−.845	.105	−.806	.106	−2.101	.293	−1.246	.170
(Nominal Catholic)	(−.151)	.098	(−.162)	.099	−.424	.258	−.254	.153
(Committed Catholic)	−.446	.135	−.426	.137	−1.038	.338	−.619	.205
(Jewish)	.441	.181	.390	.186	1.266	.654	.729	.349
(Other/Non-Ascertained)	−.285	.139	−.250	.142	(−.589)	.363	(−.346)	.219
Income (Bottom Quintile)	.218	.083	.255	(.079)	.745	.224	.427	.131
Income (Top Quintile)	−.133	.063	−.136	(.065)	−.279	.162	−.170	.098
Marital Status (never married/partner)	.227	.077	.242	.077	.745	.213	.432	.126
Education (College Grad)	(−.077)	.063	(−.051)	.063	(−.157)	.160	(−.094)	.096
Home Ownership (renter)	.121	.069	(.071)	.066	(.205)	.175	(.127)	.105
Union Membership (someone in household)	.245	.067	.271	.069	.636	.179	.377	.107
PARTISAN AND POLICY-RELATED PREDISPOSITIONS								
Party Identification	.481	.029	.486	.029	1.723	.145	.972	.078
Liberal/Conservative Self-designation	.265	.044	.251	.043	1.301	.227	.723	.123
Equality	.217	.057	.238	.057	1.193	.297	.687	.163

Gov't/Individual Responsibility	.084	.031	.073	.031	(.237)	.149	(.135)	.083
Morality	.220	.056	.213	.056	1.038	.295	.544	.162
Business/Union Identification	.094	.038	.111	.038	.595	.202	.348	.111
Gays/Fundamentalists	.147	.065	.157	.064	.958	.339	.529	.186
Isolationism	.066	.024	.056	.024	.246	.124	.117	.068
Vietnam Service	.082	.021	.095	.021	.427	.104	.222	.057
POLICY PREFERENCES AND PERCEPTIONS OF CONDITIONS								
Disadvantaged	.123	.040	.099	.040	.514	.219	.281	.119
Defense	.165	.050	.158	.049	.792	.276	.429	.151
Homosexuals in the Military	.115	.028	.116	.029	.550	.154	.285	.084
Public Support for Private Schools	.055	.022	.041	.022	.267	.122	.132	.067
Tax Increase	.041	.022	.040	.022	.231	.121	.123	.066
State of the Economy	.191	.045	.181	.045	.919	.247	.519	.134
U.S. Position	.063	.026	.064	.026	.363	.139	.202	.076
Layoffs in Family	.400	.156	.415	.156	2.020	.902	1.196	.515
RETROSPECTIVE EVALUATIONS OF PRESIDENTIAL PERFORMANCE								
General Approval/Disapproval	.332	.036	.320	.036	1.057	.222	.587	.118
The Economy	.078	.636	.107	.036	.648	.253	.337	.134
Foreign Affairs	.053	.026	(.036)	.026	.328	.183	.167	.096
Deficit Blame	.215	.025	.197	.025	.846	.158	.456	.084
EVALUATIONS OF THE CANDIDATES' PERSONAL QUALITIES								
Trust	(.110)	.070	.128	.071	1.383	.584	.672	.302
Empathy	.235	.077	.182	.077	1.208	.587	.611	.312
Leadership	.192	.077	.242	.077	2.730	.692	1.315	.351
PROSPECTIVE EVALUATIONS OF CANDIDATE/PARTY PERFORMANCE								
Candidates on Economy	.303	.036	.286	.036	1.335	.310	.707	.154
Candidates on Poverty	.104	.033	.110	.033	.564	.288	.277	.145
Parties on Economy	.067	.034	.074	.034	.633	.308	.286	.152
Parties on Affordable Health Care	.100	.031	.105	.032	.752	.265	.371	.136

tions of current conditions are .191 for the economy, .063 for the U.S. position in the world, and .400 for any layoffs in the household. The parallel logit coefficients for the same condition-related variables are .919, .363, and 2.020—and the same relative magnitudes can be seen in the corresponding coefficients from probit analyses (.519, .202, and 1.196).

Likely Differences Concerning Interaction Effects. This general similarity in results produced by OLS and either logit or probit procedures arises frequently in analyses based on large samples and explanatory equations that are entirely composed of linear and additive terms. In models of that kind, most pairs of variables have apparent effects that take on the same (approximate) relative magnitudes, regardless of the analyst's choice between statistical procedures. To be sure, violation of the standard OLS assumption concerning invariant effects will almost certainly be accentuated by the dichotomous nature of the dependent variable, and the standard errors produced by OLS are not unbiased estimates of the "true" standard errors for those coefficients. (In this connection, we should also note that our estimates for the standard errors of our total effects were not appreciably changed by switching from simple OLS to generalized least squares.) Beyond those qualifications, however, OLS tells the same (approximate) story as the other two methods concerning the relative magnitudes of apparent effects within groups of variables that have been assigned to the same stage or bloc in our purely additive model—even though the logit and probit procedures were explicitly designed for analyses (like ours) with a dichotomous dependent variable.

That kind of general conclusion does *not* apply, however, to more complex electoral models which include interaction effects that can be represented by non-linear or non-additive terms in the equation used to predict the vote. As emphasized in the following section, apparent effects whose magnitudes are "conditioned" by other variables can be summarized in substantially different form by OLS and either logit or probit analysis.

▪ Differences between Voters in the Magnitude of Specific Effects

Since *The American Voter,* many analysts have suggested that substantially different explanations of electoral preference may be appropriate for different types of voters. At one extreme, media speculation about "single issue voters" suggests that electoral analysts should try to identify individuals who are primarily motivated by specific issues or topics. Similar hypotheses are involved in attempts to differentiate among "issue publics" for a given campaign, or suggestions that candidates build successful coalitions by emphasizing a family of topics that appeal to different types of voters. In this book, most of our analyses have been based on statistical procedures that ignore such differences between voters, in order to describe the "electorate as a whole." We believe that such analyses provide important information about the overall sources of voters' decisions in a given context, but we also recognize that such accounts conceal significant differences between voters concerning the factors that shaped their choices for President.

In several chapters, we have noted that survey respondents' own reports concerning their "reasons" for supporting or opposing specific candidates represent an unreliable source of information about differences between voters in the impact of specific kinds of opinions. Similar negative results (in identifying individuals for whom a particular topic has a substantially larger effect) can be obtained for voters' responses to the NES open-ended question concerning the "most important problem facing the nation." Furthermore, other efforts to directly measure individual differences in the electoral importance of specific topics or issues have not been very successful. Because of those negative results, we have concluded that the only way to assess the extent of variability among voters in the magnitude of specific effects is to test a variety of hypotheses about other characteristics that have been suggested as potential sources of "conditional" effects.

Most hypotheses about conditional or "interaction" effects in the electoral context can be classified into four broad categories, depending on whether the explanatory variables involved are assumed to be more salient for specific social groups in the society, for different generations of voters, for voters who identify with one of the major parties, or for voters with different levels of political information or sophistication. The first three of these types of conditional effects have been almost entirely ignored in this book, because of the large number of hypotheses involved—and because explanatory analyses have not produced any consistent differences in electoral effects that are defined in terms of different social groups, generations, or parties. Furthermore, many such differ-

Table D3 Average Vote for President Within Groups Defined by Policy-related Preferences, Party Identification, and Levels of Political Information

	Cell Entries are Average Scores on the Vote (Weighted Numbers of Cases Appear in Parentheses)			
	Level of Information			
	Low	Medium	High	Total
Republicans				
Conservative Policy-related	−.720	−.959	−.969	−.917
Preferences	(47)	(109)	(78)	(234)
Moderate Policy-related	−.573	−.347	—	−.411
Preferences	(34)	(40)	(11)	(85)
Liberal Policy-related	—*	—	—	—
Preferences	(2)	(2)	(0)	(4)
Independents				
Conservative Policy-related	−.273	−.698	−.880	−.626
Preferences	(39)	(61)	(35)	(135)
Moderate Policy-related	.481	.456	.575	.491
Preferences	(69)	(61)	(32)	(161)
Liberal Policy-related	.660	1.000	.938	.871
Preferences	(21)	(24)	(40)	(85)
Democrats				
Conservative Policy-related	.275	.388	—	.346
Preferences	(42)	(37)	(8)	(87)
Moderate Policy-related	.756	.926	.916	.850
Preferences	(109)	(103)	(33)	(245)
Liberal Policy-related	.933	1.000	1.000	.984
Preferences	(37)	(69)	(51)	(157)

*Means are replaced by — when N is less than 10.

ences in effect estimates based on OLS can be shown to be much smaller (or nonexistent) when the interaction effects involved are estimated with logit or probit analysis. Interaction effects based on differences in voters' political sophistication, however, deserve special attention, for there seems little doubt that some electoral effects are subject to significant differences between voters who possess different levels of information about politics.

Information-based Differences in the Role of Policy-related Preferences. Electoral analysts from many different perspectives have hypothesized that opinions about specific policy-related conflicts that are emphasized in a given campaign have a stronger influence on voters' eventual choices for President among those with higher levels of political information, and have a weaker influence among those who had not received or understood campaign-based political communications in that area.

This kind of information-related conditioning (for the influence of policy-related preferences on the vote) may be attributable to a variety of psychological processes, including differences in attention to political communications during the campaign or longstanding differences in the ability to comprehend such communications. We have no evidence concerning the relative weight of these or other explanations for interaction effects between policy-related preferences and levels of information. It is clear, however, that a variety of indicators of survey respondents' level of political information (or sophistication) can be used to identify voters with very low levels of political information whose combined policy-related preferences are only modestly linked to their vote choices, and a contrasting set with very high levels of information whose policy-related preferences are extremely closely linked to their choices— with intermediate results for the majority of voters in between. These kinds of differences can be demonstrated by using the voters' levels of formal education or one of several direct measures of the extent of voters' information about politics, including the measure of "Levels of Conceptualization" used in *The American Voter.* At the time this appendix was prepared, the 1992 coding of those "levels" from the NES open-ended questions about the parties and candidates had not been completed, so we have relied on a simple index based on interviewers' ratings of respondents' overall level of political sophistication as well as factual questions about government and politics.

Table D3 makes it possible to examine this general pattern of information-related differences in relationships between policy-related preferences and the vote in a fairly simple fashion. That table presents average scores on the vote for groups that are defined in terms of trichotomous indices for policy-related preferences and party identification, and three different levels of "political information." Table D4 then converts the mean scores in Table D3 to differences in means, to show the apparent impact (on the vote) of shifting from a moderate overall position to a conservative position—or to a liberal position—for voters with different levels of political information and partisan identifications.

Table D4 Apparent Differences in the Impact of Policy-related Preferences Between Voters with Different Levels of Information, Based on Simple Differences in Means

Cell Entries are Differences in Average Scores on the Vote (From Table D3)

	Level of Information			
	Low	Medium	High	Total
Republicans				
Conservative instead of	−.143	−.613	—	−.559
Moderate Preferences			(N < 25)	
Liberal instead of	—	—	—	—
Moderate Preferences	(N < 25)	(N < 25)	(N < 25)	(N < 25)
Independents				
Conservative instead of	−.754	−1.154	−1.456	−1.077
Moderate Preferences				
Liberal instead of	.178	.544	.363	.349
Moderate Preferences				
Democrats				
Conservative instead of	−.481	−.538	—	−.499
Moderate Preferences			(N < 25)	
Liberal instead of	.177	.074	.084	.114
Moderate Preferences				

For example, the average vote for fairly conservative Republicans with a "low" level of information is −.720 (based on a weighted N of 47), and the corresponding average for the group of (equally) low-information Republicans with "moderate" policy-related preferences is −.573. Based on these results, Table D4 presents the simple difference between these (and other) pairs of means. The difference between the above two means for low-information Republicans is −.143 (−.720 minus −.573), which we have interpreted as the apparent influence (for that group) of having conservative instead of moderate policy-related preferences.

On the basis of these differences (in Table D4) for Republicans, Independents, and Democrats, it does appear that the cumulative impact of all our policy-related preferences is somewhat greater for individuals who have more general information about politics. For example, among Republicans with "low" levels of information, the difference in average scores on the vote between respondents with "conservative" versus "moderate" policy preferences is −.143, while the same difference for Republicans with "medium" levels of information is −.613. (The corresponding difference for respondents with "high" levels of information has not been shown, because of the small number of Republicans in the base category—that is, with high levels of information and moderate policy-related preferences.) The three corresponding differences for Independents between individuals with moderate and conservative preferences show the same (increasing) pattern, starting with $-.754$ for those with low levels of information, growing to -1.154 for those with medium levels of information, and culminating with -1.456 for those with the most political information. We note, however, that the same pattern (of increasing policy-related differences based on more information) does not hold for Democrats because the average vote in 1992 was nearly unanimously pro-Democratic for all Democrats except those who were clearly conservative.

In general, Table D4 suggests that increasing information is associated with greater differences in the vote (or apparent effects) based on policy-related preferences *unless* the group involved is already overwhelmingly committed to one party's candidate, so that additional information cannot "move" the vote much further in that direction. In that connection (although such differences are not shown in Table D4), we also note that the apparent impact of partisan identification (for voters with the same overall policy-related preferences) appears to go *down* (not up) with increasing levels of political information—for there is much more "room" for party-related shifts in the vote among those with low levels of political information. Both of these patterns represent the kind of apparent interaction effect that may disappear entirely if we switch our analysis from simple differences in means (or OLS) to a probit or logit formulation.

The consequences of such a shift can be clearly seen in Table D5, which presents the results of parallel OLS and logit analyses that include multiplicative terms to estimate the *degree* to which the effects of policy-related preferences and party identification may be conditioned by voters' level of political information. The coefficients produced for the same explanatory variable by these two methods are not strictly comparable, because of the different assumptions made by OLS and logit concerning each voter's true "position" on the dependent variable. Despite those differences, however, both the similarities and differences between the results of these two procedures can be easily identified from Table D5.

On the basis of the OLS analysis in Table D5, we are tempted to

Table D5 Apparent Effects for Policy-related Preferences and Party Identification
Conditioned by Levels of Political Information: Ordinary Least Squares (OLS)
vs. Logit Analysis

(Estimated Standard Errors Appear in Parentheses)		
	OLS	Logit
Base Coefficient for Combined Policy-related Preferences (Where Information = 0.0)	.149 (.091)	.346 (.446)
Base Coefficient for Party Identification (Where Political Information = 0.0)	.571 (.080)	.955 (.391)
Change in Apparent Effect of Policy-related Preferences as Information Rises from 0.0 to 1.0 (Coefficient for Interaction Term)	+.641 (.156)	+3.150 (.856)
Change in Apparent Effect of Party Identification as Information Rises from 0.0 to 1.0 (Coefficient for Interaction Term)	−.148 (.146)	+1.758 (.788)

NOTE: Both analyses also include social and economic characteristics and perceptions of current
conditions.

conclude that the apparent (combined) influence of policy-related preferences on the vote goes up with increasing information, from a base of
.149 (for voters who scored 0.0 on political information) up to .790
(.149 + .641) for those with the most information (arbitrarily scored
1.0 for this analysis). The results of our parallel logit analysis suggest a
similar—but even greater—increase in the apparent influence of policy-
related preferences from .346 (for persons with 0.0 information) up to
3.496 (.346 + 3.150, or almost ten times as large) for those with the
most information. These two methods tell the same kind of story for
policy-related preferences, but the magnitude of the information-related
conditioning appears to be much greater when we use a logit (or probit)
formulation that is designed to remove the "ceiling effect" imposed by
the dichotomous nature of the dependent variable.

In contrast, our general conclusion concerning the "conditioning" role
of political information on the apparent impact of party identification is
substantially changed when we shift from OLS to logit (or probit)
analyses. As shown in the last row of Table D5, the apparent *reduction*
in the OLS-based impact of party identification (as we move from low

to high information) that is suggested by the negative coefficient for the interaction term in that equation ($-.148$) is entirely eliminated and is replaced by a position coefficient ($+1.758$) when we switch to logit analysis. In other words, when we remove the ceiling effect imposed by nearly unanimous preferences in some groups, the impact of partisan identification also appears to increase with greater information—although the magnitude of that increase is much smaller than for policy-related preferences.

In general, apparent (positive) interaction effects in OLS-based analyses often appear to be somewhat larger when the underlying model is changed to a logit or probit formulation. For the same reasons, which may be interpreted in terms of floor or ceiling effects, negative coefficients for interaction effects in OLS analyses may disappear when the same equations are used in a logit or probit model. In our view, much remains to be done in identifying the kinds of campaign content or issues for which any electoral effects are more (or less) conditioned by levels of political information—or by any other individual characteristics. Analytic results of that sort will provide important clues in improving our understanding of the process of political translation—or the ways in which voters' opinions about specific topics are activated in shaping their choices for President.

▪ A Final Note on Statistical "Control"

As we have emphasized, all of our survey-based estimates for the apparent influence of specific voter characteristics on vote choice are based on multivariate analyses in which we have "held constant" or "controlled for" a variety of other variables in our model. To assess the overall total effect of a given variable, we have introduced "controls" for other potential causes of the vote that could be assigned to the same or an earlier causal stage in our model. When we examine the ways in which a given variable's total effect may be mediated by alternative variables in subsequent stages in our model, we use the same kind of rationale to introduce additional controls for those variables that presumably intervene between the current explanatory variable and the vote. In both cases, we are interested in the overall strength of a given variable's apparent influence on the vote after all of the other variables in that analysis have been controlled or held constant through the simultaneous estimation of all the coefficients in a single explanatory equation—using either ordinary least squares (OLS) or the alternative procedures discussed earlier in this appendix. The preferred interpretation of the resulting coefficients (or apparent effects) is sometimes regarded as "understood" or non-controversial. Unfortunately, the statistical validity of such interpretations of regression-type coefficients cannot be defended in a straightforward fashion. The following observations are intended as a cautionary note, to offset oversimplified interpretations of such "effects."

In two kinds of ideal circumstances, the preferred interpretation *is* justified on the basis of assumptions that are easy to state—but are usually difficult to apply or defend in practice. In the first of these two ideal circumstances, the other variables in a given equation can be simultaneously held constant in the most direct or extreme form possible because the combined set of such variables does not involve very many different combinations of variables. In this approach, the coefficient being interpreted as an apparent effect is estimated by calculating the average of a series of differences in the average vote for different types of voters, each of which contains individuals that are *exactly* alike with respect to *all* of the other variables being controlled. In this procedure, the apparent effect of the given explanatory variable is a weighted average of the difference in vote choice that can be observed for individuals with different scores on the given variable who do not differ in *any* of the other variables in the analysis—or when all of those variables are literally "held constant." (In such a case, the apparent effects estimated by ordinary least squares can be seen as a kind of weighted average of coefficients for specific subpopulations that are identical with respect to all of the variables being controlled. Analysts who use that method, however, should understand that OLS uses a non-obvious set of rules for calculating the weighted average of the effect estimates across all the groups involved.)

In many respects, this kind of analysis appears to be the most appropriate or satisfactory kind of "control" for potentially confounding variables. When this method is used, we are sure that the average difference in the vote that we are attributing to the given explanatory variable cannot be confounded by one or more control variables, because that average has been calculated within subsamples for which all of those other variables do not vary *at all*. Unfortunately, this method is usually impractical or impossible, because of the number of variables to be controlled and the number of distinct values for those variables.

In most electoral explanations, therefore, the analyst cannot "hold other variables constant" by examining differences (in vote choice) between groups of voters with different scores on the given explanatory variable but identical scores on all the other variables being controlled. In such analyses, including our own, the only kind of controls that make sense require that effect estimates be produced for all the explanatory variables simultaneously. In such a case, we would like to estimate effect coefficients simultaneously for all of the variables in a given explanatory equation in such a way that each coefficient provides an unbiased assessment of the apparent influence of that variable that remains after we adjust for the influence of the other variables in that equation.

Unfortunately, neither of these ideal procedures is entirely appropriate in the electoral case. Control by physical segregation breaks down when the number of explanatory variables and their categories grows to the point where very little (or no) variation remains within groups of people who have identical scores on all of the other variables to be controlled. On the other hand, procedures which estimate the apparent effects of all explanatory variables simultaneously require that the underlying effects be invariant across the individuals involved—an assumption that most analysts are unwilling to make.

In this situation, electoral analysts who want to assess the overall influence of a specific explanatory variable should recognize the limitations of their multivariate statistical procedures. In particular, the coefficients described as "apparent effects" do *not* represent direct estimates of the average differences in vote choice that can be observed in circumstances where the (designated) explanatory characteristic varies but all other variables in the analysis do not. Furthermore, such coefficients are not guaranteed to be unbiased estimates of the average effect of a one-unit change in the (designated) explanatory variables in models where each (true) effect is assumed to vary in ways that are not incorporated in the model.

In our view, these cautionary statements about our designation of specific coefficients as "apparent effects" represent important qualifications in their substantive interpretations, as well as their methodological status. It is tempting to suggest that we have directly estimated the degree to which voters' choices have (in fact) been shaped by differences in specific explanatory variables after we have literally "held constant" all the other variables in that analysis in the sense that we have eliminated any potentially confounding variation in those variables. Unfortunately, we have so many categories to "control" that there would not be enough variation in any (given) explanatory variables left to examine after we make sure that the individuals involved have identical scores on all of the other variables.

Similarly, it is tempting to suggest that our procedures have produced unbiased estimates of the average for underlying (true) effects which are subject to unexplained variations among voters, based on equations for which all of the coefficients are estimated simultaneously. This interpretation, however, is also inappropriate as stated, because we are unwilling to assume that the unmeasured differences among voters (in their true effects) are uncorrelated with all of the explanatory variables in our model.

In this situation, we continue to interpret each of the coefficients produced by our analyses as approximate values for the average consequence of a one-unit shift in that variable (on vote choice), after we have controlled for the other variable in that analysis. We have examined the accuracy of such averages in several cases where we understand something about individual differences in apparent effects, and have found the summary coefficients produced by OLS to be reasonable approximations of the true average of the varying coefficients involved. Readers and analysts should be warned, however, that such estimates do represent imperfect approximations because they would only be unbiased estimates of true averages within the NES sample, and therefore for the population of voters, if the unmeasured variation (between voters) were uncorrelated with all of the explanatory variables in the analysis.

Notes

1. Electoral Explanation and Survey Research

1. For the origins of contemporary political surveys, see *Survey Research in the United States: Roots and Emergence, 1890–1960* (J. Converse, 1987).

2. Sections of this chapter are based on an earlier essay entitled "Unresolved Issues in Electoral Decisions: Alternative Perspectives on the Explanation of Individual Choice" (Shanks, 1994).

3. Almost every analysis of presidential elections includes a discussion of partisanship (if not party identification) and various types of "issues." See Kinder (1980) for a review of measurement objectives and strategies concerning perceptions or evaluations of presidential candidates.

4. See Berelson et al. (1954), Stokes (1966), and Shanks and Miller (1990) for earlier discussions of this pervasive distinction. For a related discussion based on the 1992 election see Donald Stokes and John Dilulio (1993).

5. Our strategy brings us full circle from *The Voter Decides,* published in 1954. One of the many methodological debates between senior figures in the Columbia Bureau of Applied Social Research and the Michigan Survey Research Center focused on the use of structured and unstructured survey questions, with Michigan championing "open" questions. Ironically, before *The Voter Decides,* responses to the permissive, open questions had never been used in any SRC work involving the creation and measurement of analytic variables. The responses were always used in lists of "reasons" given to describe or explain the respondent's attitudes, but never to measure the presence or absence, or strength or intensity of the attitude. *The Voter Decides* presumed the existence of voter "orientations" to parties, issues, and candidates. The presence or absence, partisan direction, and intensity or extremity of candidate and issue orientations were measured by literally counting the number of volunteered responses (reasons) that were "coded" as fitting each analytic category. For the first time at

the Survey Research Center, unstructured questions were used in the derivation of quantitative measures in *The Voter Decides*.

6. Between 1980 and 1988, NES made a substantial effort to identify the source of over-reporting through "validating" all respondent reports by checking them against official voting records. This entailed a prodigious effort to train field interviewers to cope with the great variety of local circumstances governing vote record-keeping. Given the expense and administrative costs involved, this effort was closely monitored and carefully evaluated. Before the 1992 NES study, the staff recommended discontinuation of the vote validation process because of their conviction that the very marginal net improvement in measurement did not warrant the expense. As an incidental consequence, we have not used any "validated" reports concerning turnout in this book but, instead, have used respondents' self-reports in order to maximize comparability of measurement across the full time span covered by our analyses.

7. The results of these and other related attempts are reported in "Attempts to Improve the Accuracy of Self-Reports of Voting" by Abelson, Loftus, and Greenwald in Chapter 7 of Tanur's *Questions About Questions* (Tanur, 1992).

8. To provide the reader with complete access to the data underlying our substantive interpretations, all of the individual-level data and documentation are available through the Inter-university Consortium for Political and Social Research (ICPSR). Detailed descriptions of derived variables and analytic procedures that are not explicitly provided in this volume will be made available on the World Wide Web. The Web-based location of those materials may change over time, but can be obtained from either author. In addition, the software used for most of the multivariate analyses in this book is developed and distributed by the Computer-assisted Survey Methods (CSM) Program at the University of California, Berkeley.

2. Political Change in the United States

1. Angus Campbell, Philip E. Converse, Warren E. Miller, and Donald E. Stokes, *The American Voter* (New York: John Wiley and Sons, 1960). Well after the fact, the NORC study of the 1944 elections provided estimates for national political parameters as of eight years before the 1952 election survey. The Erie County and Elmira studies in 1940 and 1948 had made their signal contributions to our views of American voting behavior in presidential elections. The first Michigan report, *The People Elect a President,* by Angus Campbell and Robert Kahn (Ann Arbor, Michigan: Survey Research Center, ISR, University of Michigan, 1952), depicted the Truman victory in 1948. The second, *The Voter Decides,* by Angus Campbell, Gerald Gurin, and Warren E. Miller (Evanston, Indiana: Row, Peterson and Company, 1954), chronicled the Eisenhower election of 1952. The individual level data which have been most central to the study of mass electoral

behavior in the United States have been produced by the still growing series of biennial studies associated with the University of Michigan Survey Research Center, its Center for Political Studies, and, since 1978, the American National Election Studies.

2. Anthony Lewis, "Time for a Change," *New York Times,* April 9, 1992, p. A25.

3. McWilliams (1995), p. 116.

4. As the manuscript for this book was being completed, Wilson Carey McWilliams published *The Politics of Disappointment.* With very different kinds of evidence from what we shall present in this book, McWilliams describes what we think to be the origin of generational differences which can be seen in the elections of the 1980s. However, neither he nor we can link the origins and consequences of those differences in a fashion that we would find conclusive.

5. Black registration in the South has been estimated by Wolfinger at 29% in 1960, 42% in 1964, and 59% by 1968. Personal communication with the authors.

6. The ad was a minor part of the Bush campaign. However brief, it received a great deal of media attention because it attacked Dukakis as "weak" on crime through the device of publicizing a rape and assault committed by a Black man on parole from the Massachusetts penal system following a murder conviction.

7. In an ironic side note, pre-election polls in New Hampshire, conducted by both ABC and NBC, showed that McCarthy, the only alternative to Johnson on the ballot, was indeed supported by the peace vote, but actually drew most of his support from New Hampshire hawks who were dissatisfied with Johnson's reluctance to escalate the war effort. In a state constituency in which hawks greatly outnumbered doves among those who had any commitment at all, Johnson won because of plurality, middle-of-the-road support for his "moderation" in Vietnam. However, pre-election evidence of the limited appeal of a highly intellectual "peace candidate" campaigning in a poorly educated, blue-collar constituency was dismissed by the media because it was so out of keeping with conventional expectations about the presumed nature of public support for the peace candidate. In a similar vein, the media so underestimated the protest nature of the anti-Johnson vote that on election night the TV tote boards did not carry a possible entry for the Republican Nixon. It was only after the formal counting of the votes that it became apparent that Nixon received a telltale 5% of the vote in the Democratic presidential primary (Converse et al., 1969, pp. 1083–1105).

8. Given the relative closeness of the 1980 vote decision—and its apparent dependence on last-minute decisions—it is at least mildly interesting to speculate how much the label "failed presidency" depended on electoral defeat and how much it was a hasty judgment about the accomplishments of Jimmy Carter's four years in office.

9. Dennis F. Thompson, *Ethics in Congress* (Washington, D.C.: Brookings Institute, 1995), p. 198.

3. Voting Turnout in Presidential Elections

1. The quite different question of whether differential voter turnout has affected the outcome of elections is generally answered in the negative. An excellent discussion of this possibility is provided by Teixeira (1992), pp. 87–97.

2. These summary statistics on voter turnout are taken from Rosenstone and Hansen (1993), p. 57. Unless otherwise noted, all other data pertaining to voting or non-voting are derived from our own NES analyses, based on citizens' self-reports of their own voting behavior. As noted in Chapter 1, such reports invariably result in the apparent over-reporting of turnout when compared to statistics compiled from official election returns and census estimates of the size of the eligible electorate. The problem is familiar and is well described in Rosenstone and Hansen (1993), pp. 58–59, and in Teixeira (1992), p. 27.

3. However, see Teixeira (1992 and 1987). Although not included in the Cassell-Luskin review, Teixeira's work presents the most thoroughgoing of all analyses of the problem. He anticipated most of the Cassell-Luskin critique of other works, such as noting underspecification as a consequence of uncritical emphases on parsimony in the development of the theory. He also argued that income and occupation had joined education in the upgrading of personal resources that provided an upward "push" of voter turnout—thereby exacerbating the conditions of Brody's puzzle.

4. Sociologists and social theorists following Mannheim (1952) have an established tradition of interest in "generations," an interest that has been slow to develop in political science. Subsequent to Butler and Stokes (1969) a number of political scientists—and political sociologists—have turned to cohort analysis in tackling one or another problem of understanding political change at the macro or societal level, but there is no general work in political science that complements the generic sociological analyses of generational theory or methodology. A seminal article by Paul Beck is directly relevant to our interest in electoral cohorts just entering the electorate (Beck, 1974). An excellent recent example of cohort analysis, centered on changes in party identification, is provided by Paul Abramson's article "Generations and Political Change in the United States," pp. 235–280. For an excellent discussion of the use of long-term panel data in the study of political generations, see Jennings and Niemi (1981). For an incisive discussion of the ambiguities surrounding the concepts of generational effects and period effects, see Converse (1976). Although our analysis was developed independently, the logic that governs it fits in every detail with that of Alwin et al. (1991).

5. For a similar set of generation boundaries, see Rosenstone and Hansen (1993), p. 140, note 11, but note the difference in terminology with our usage. We treat each four-year interval as defining a cohort, and we define generations as aggre-

gations of cohorts. In contrast, Rosenstone and Hansen call the aggregations "cohorts."

6. David Butler and Donald E. Stokes (1969) present an admirable treatment of our generic problem of understanding the consequences of generational replacement. Among other topics, Butler and Stokes provide an instructive treatment of the conditions necessary for a state of equilibrium and the contrasting conditions provided by an expanding electorate. See Chapters 10 and 11. Jennings and Niemi (1981) present an excellent succinct summary of models of persistence and change in individual attributes in *Generations and Politics* (Princeton: Princeton University Press, 1981), pp. 19–25.

7. After reviewing an earlier draft of this discussion, Kent Jennings noted that our reliance on presidential year data led us to miss the significance of the transitions from 1929 to 1931 and 1965 to 1967. His work on the long-term parent-child socialization study had led him to identify those two periods as particularly important in the separation of current political generations (Jennings, 1981).

8. It should also be noted that the time span of the cumulative NES data set, 1952–1992, sharply truncates our view of the first years of the first three generations in Table 3.1. More generally, as Figure 3.1 illustrates, it is impossible to observe comparable evidence of possible life cycle changes across all generations. This is troubling because we shall note some evidence of the possible effects of aging—or life cycle—influences in our most nearly complete middle generations. This evidence, even if only suggestive, reminds us that we have captured data from the oldest generations at the very end of their life cycle, and can observe the youngest generations only at the very beginning of theirs.

The forty-year time span of this analysis covers only about two-thirds of the full political life cycle of any modern generation. If the processes of aging produce only gentle slopes measuring change over a thirty-year period—giving the essential impression of temporal stability within sampling error—our comparisons of the last twenty-eight years of the pre-New Deal generations (1952–1980) with the first twenty-four years of the post-New Deal generations (1968–1992) may attribute period-based generational differences to what are, at least in small part, life-cycle differences. Nevertheless, our own conclusion is that generational differences, and generational replacement, account for most of the aggregate shifts over this time span; our conclusion agrees with Abramson's earlier more comprehensive rendering cited above (Abramson, 1989).

9. Although we include turnout data for 1992 throughout the next two chapters, we will reserve comment on 1992 for special attention. Because of a major protest against the performance of the federal government and the increase in interest aroused by the Perot candidacy, turnout increased slightly in 1992, thereby underscoring the short-term contribution of political leadership to the long-term trends.

10. Despite our clear difference with Rosenstone and Hansen concerning the inter-pretation of the turnout decline between 1960 and 1988, their book presents an extraordinary summary and synthesis of the research on mass participation in both governmental and electoral politics in the United States. For many pur-poses, it is the definitive source for access to the modern scholarly literature on electoral participation prior to 1995.

11. Some part of their increase in voting may be a consequence of socioeconomic status–related mortality, as high-status citizens lead somewhat longer if not fuller lives.

12. An algorithm for allocating "credit" for net aggregate change among the com-ponents involved in compositional change has been developed, reported, and discussed by Rapoport and Stone (1992).

13. This conclusion is scarcely a new contribution from this analysis. The point was made more than ten years ago by Abramson, Aldrich, and Rhode in their analysis of the 1980 election (Abramson, Aldrich, and Rhode, 1982). An exhaustive study of trends in turnout would follow Teixeira's suggestion and investigate changes in income and occupation, as well as education.

14. This is not to evade the issue of understanding the mechanisms involved in the enormous effects of education. In an earlier critique of this discussion, Luskin (1987) questioned the assumption that higher rates of voting among the better educated were a function of either the development of cognitive skills or the acquisition of information. He suggested, instead, the possibilities that *brighter* people tend to go further in school *and* to vote more *and* tend to be placed in milieux which provide social incentives for political participation. It is also true, of course, that education reflects family socialization, which may establish the high rates of participation noted among those exposed to college, whatever their generation. In our own view, we simply need a better understanding of the many ways in which education makes such a difference to rates of turnout on election day (Rosenstone and Hansen, 1993, chap. 5).

15. The average turnout rate was 82% among the pre-New Deal, 1952–1964; the average rate was 65% voting in 1972–1988.

16. A very small part of the difference between the pre-New Deal and post-New Deal generations is contributed by the inclusion of 18-, 19- and 20-year-olds in the latter. Their voting rates do inflate the estimates of non-voting, and their continued poor performance on election day does not augur well for a future upturn in turnout. However, given the age span of the post-New Deal genera-tions in the late 1980s (from 18 to 45 in 1992), the 18–20-year-olds make up only a very small fraction of the full generation. Removing them from the base for the estimates of non-voting reduces the figures for 1984, 1988, and 1992 by no more than one or two percentage points.

It should also be noted at this point that party changes in the South (Black and Black, 1987; Miller, 1991) had an interesting correlate in the 30-year changes in turnout. The basic pattern of increased non-voting as a consequence of generational replacement did not differ between the North and the South. There was, however, a pronounced difference in the turnout rates within the New Deal generation. In the South evidence of *increased* voting is manifest, and is directly related to levels of education. Among those with grade school education (0 to 8 years), reported turnout in the 1980s was 17 percentage points higher than in the 1950s; turnout was up 10 points for those who had one or more years in high school; and it was up 3 points for those with some college. The general increase may well be one result of increasingly lively two-party competition. Outside the South there was very limited evidence of increased voting within the continuing members of the New Deal generation. One consequence of these and related regional differences in generational patterns of turnout was a marked reduction in the magnitude of regional differences within generations, a narrowing of the historical turnout gap led by those with less formal education.

17. Evidence of a turnout "plateau" commencing in the citizen's mid-twenties was anticipated in the analysis of panel data on which *Continuities in Political Action* (Jennings, van Deth, et al., 1989) was based. Jennings and van Deth introduced their volume with an excellent discussion of cohort analysis and the important role played in population replacement as the source of social change. Their discussion calls attention to the theme of political generations as an important element in promoting political change while preserving continuity. Jennings has a particularly pertinent treatment of individual level stabilization or "crystallization" in Chapter 10, "The Crystallization of Orientations," pp. 313–348. In this discussion he emphasizes the relatively young age, the mid- to late twenties, when crystallization takes place.

4. The Three Stages in the Political Life of the Citizen

1. For the purpose of an initial testing of the scope of declining political participation, one might take the nettle—the scarcity of data—for a rose—similarity among data. One could argue that even if we had a full set of broader measures of different activities, such as petitioning public officials or joining single-issue causes, the tactic of looking first to *pre*-election modes of participation in partisan *electoral* politics would be an appropriate first step in determining whether declining turnout is a manifestation of a broader withdrawal from politics.

2. The pattern of decline in pre-election campaign activities both in the New Deal and post-New Deal generations at all levels of education may be more pertinent to normative alarms about the health of the body politic than the national voting turnout rates on election day.

3. For each time period, the difference in turnout of regular attenders and the

others can be measured by various statistics that associate church attendance with voting turnout. In Table 4.2 we relied on differences in proportion voting associated with differences in attendance. In succeeding tables we will use one or another coefficient of correlation.

4. The Methodological Appendix (Appendix D) includes a brief discussion of alternative meanings of statistical control.

5. A more extensive description and discussion of this research strategy, introduced in Chapter 1, is presented in Chapter 8.

6. Our first bloc of twelve social and economic variables includes the following: Age, Education, Gender, Marital status, Home ownership, Length of residence in current dwelling, Length of residence in the community or neighborhood, Frequency of church attendance, Subjective social class, Income, Union membership, and Urbanism of residence. In order to maximize the congruence of zero-order bivariate estimates (comparing categorical differences in percent voting with product moment correlations) to assist us in the interpreting of the "apparent total effect" coefficients produced by multiple regression analyses, we used the same categorizations for all three analyses, including the ordinary least squares estimates for the multivariate analysis.

Party Identification is treated simply as a two-category variable: Identified (Democrat or Republican) and Not Identified (Independent or No Preference). Use of the conventional seven-point measure of partisanship was rejected on the grounds that only the basic differentiation between (1) those who accept self-classification and (2) those who do not justifies classifying Party Identification as a stable long-term factor affecting political participation. In Chapter 6 we will return to a more complete discussion underlying this operational decision.

Seven of the nine remaining attitudinal measures constitute our third bloc. Some of the third bloc variables could conceivably be separated out as antecedent to others, or at least as more stable and therefore probably prior in a causal sequence. Nevertheless, we have treated these measures as a single bloc because the point of our inquiry is *not* to differentiate their ability to account for turnout, but to assess their joint power to predict turnout. To this end, the variety of patterns that might be displayed by these seven measures does not call for justifying a particular causal ordering. This is not the case for the final two variables in the fourth bloc. "Expressions of interest" in an election campaign and "caring who wins" seem likely candidates for very short-term variables—those that are likely to move one to vote after one assimilates the prior sources of influence concerning vote turnout.

7. The regular appearance of "Age" as an independent predictor in all four sets of elections also bears comment. Referring to the previous chapter and Appendix Tables A4, A5, and A6, as well as the discussion of the very broad voting plateau for New Deal cohorts, it is clear that the age-related correlations in Table 4.4 are primarily the product of the historical age of the electors, rather than their

biological aging. The regressions of time (election year by election year) on turnout for each of the nine cohorts of the New Deal generation (Tables A4, A5, and A6) did not differ from zero, in contrast to the partial regression coefficients for temporal cross-section data reported in Table 4.4. Given the middle-aged character of the New Deal generation throughout our analytic period, aging did not appear to have any impact on the generation's turnout record until 1992. However, as with the explanation for increased turnout among those disposed to vote, or decreased turnout among those less disposed to vote, the reasons behind differences in turnout rates for different political cohorts must be added to the list of phenomena that need "explaining."

5. Explanations of Generational Differences in Turnout

1. For an explication of this choice see Miller (1990, 1991). Abramson followed the same convention in his generational analysis of party identification (Abramson, 1989). The data in Tables 5.10 and 5.11, and our general line of argument, do not attempt to take account of over-time variations in the strength of partisanship among party identifiers nor the partisan ebb and flow among "leaning" independents who feel closer to one party or the other. This reflects our interest in persistent long-term factors that influence turnout as opposed to short-term election-specific influences.

2. The possibility of a *change* in the relationship between an independent variable and its dependent consequence that is not the result of a change in the sheer distribution of the independent variable is nicely argued by Teixeira (1992) in his critique of Abramson and Aldrich. In examining antecedents of voter turnout, Teixeira also identified cohort differences in the incidence of party identification. However, he stopped short of conducting a parallel cohort analysis of turnout itself. Nevertheless, pursuing his own analytic strategy, Teixeira concludes that "it is precisely in this period after the 1968 election that [my] model first suggests the presence of an unknown factor depressing turnout levels" (Teixeira, 1987, p. 124).

3. Closely related work includes that of Eulau and Siegel, Eulau and Rothenberg, and, more recently, Huckfeldt and Sprague.

4. Unfortunately, "years of residence in the community" was not collected in 1952, 1956, or 1960; "home ownership" was not ascertained in 1956 or 1960; and "years in home" was omitted in 1952, 1956, 1968, and 1972. Nonetheless, it is possible to create an index of social connectedness for each of the elections included in our study and then to separate the electorate into two groups, relatively high and relatively low, on these indicators of social contacts.

5. We think it inappropriate to attempt multivariate analyses accounting for cross-time variance in turnout until we have a better understanding of each of these generic problems.

6. The results of the Teixeira analysis differ somewhat from our conclusions. Although we both find evidence that changes related to one's sense of party identification and one's degree of social connectedness help account for declining turnout, the primary analysis reported in this discussion did not corroborate Teixeira's conclusion that the changing influence of involvement ("care" and "interest") or sense of political efficacy were relevant to the aggregate decline.

7. Many other scholars have worked in the same tradition as the present discussion, exploiting time series developed for other purposes and pursuing post-hoc analyses of cohorts or generations. Too few research projects have persisted long enough to generate data relevant to longitudinal analysis. However, for important examples of research designed for the joint assessment of period and generational effects, see Inglehart, 1977; Jennings and Niemi, 1981; Jennings, van Deth, et al., 1990.

8. Memorandum from Brian Gratton, Professor of History, Arizona State University, February 27, 1991.

6. Conceptualization and Measurement of Party Identification

1. The first portion of this chapter is based on Warren E. Miller's "Party Identification" in *Political Parties and Elections in the United States: An Encyclopedia* (1991).

2. The emphasis on an extended time horizon is properly the center of the recent Abramson and Ostrom critique of "Macropartisanship" by MacKuen, Erikson, and Stimson (1989): Paul Abramson and Charles W. Ostrom, Jr., "Question Wording and Partisanship: Change and Continuity in Party Loyalties During the 1992 Election Campaign," presented at the annual meeting of the American Political Science Association, Washington, D.C., 1993. See also Abramson and Ostrom, 1991.

3. It should be noted that the authors of *The American Voter* have, both early and late, contributed to the conventional wisdom against which this argument is directed. For example, in the *American National Election Studies Data Sourcebook* (Miller and Traugott, 1989) summary measures of the partisan balance of party preference combine partisan leaners with party identifiers, as in Table 2.32, pp. 103–104. It might also be noted, however, that the definition of party identification groups displayed in tables in *The American Voter* (1960) usually followed the orthodoxy being promoted in this discussion, and the *Data Sourcebook* treats party identification as separate and distinct from party preference, as in Table 2.34, pp. 105–106.

4. In this regard our conclusion is congruent with the analysis of Abramson and Ostrom, who demonstrate that the temporal stability of party identification can be missed—and often has been missed—when Gallup-like questions that emphasize the current moment ("In politics as of today . . .") are used as indicators

of party identification (Abramson and Ostrom, 1991). The general point is well made by Richard A. Brody and Lawrence S. Rothenberg in Table 1 of "The Instability of Partisanship: An Analysis of the 1980 Presidential Election," *British Journal of Political Science* 18 (1988): 445–465.

5. Although the literature is replete with references to "the Michigan School" emphasis on the inheritance of family traditions of party identification, it should be noted that the presumed source of the references, *The American Voter* (1960), devoted much more attention to the external, non-familial origins of party identification than to the evidence of familial transmission.

6. The most complete accounts have been produced from the three-wave Jennings panel study of parents and children. See, in particular, Jennings and Niemi (1974, chap. 10). The extended work of Jennings and his coauthors has not been widely utilized in the party identification literature, presumably because it was originally treated primarily in the context of studies of political socialization.

7. For an insightful analysis, see Philip E. Converse, *The Dynamics of Party Support* (1976).

8. See Teixeira (1992) and Knack (1992) on the role of social connectedness. See also Thad Brown (1988) on the effects of geographic migration, and Abramson (1989) on generational replacement.

9. It might be argued that the psychological impact of Kennedy's assassination was akin to that of other frustrated hopes and expectations and, therefore, that Kennedy should be included as the first of the post–World War II "failed presidencies."

10. This analysis also illustrates the difference between accounting for differences in individual vote choice and accounting for aggregate election outcomes. David Leege has noted in a letter to the authors that without probable net gains in states such as New York, New Jersey, Delaware, and Pennsylvania, the Catholic Kennedy would have lost the election.

11. Given new data from the 1980s, Converse's earlier analysis of the contribution of migration of Northern Republicans to the South should be revisited. Migrating may be a special case of "mobilization" contributing to the changing composition of the Southern electorate.

12. Our earlier comment on measurement comes into play here. If one focuses on "strength of partisanship" and takes variations in the proportions of "strong" identifiers *and* the proportions with no partisan preference into account, one sees the aggregate evidence that prompted discussions of dealignment. These variations are *not* reflected in root self-identification for non-Black voters outside the South. For an elaboration of this discussion, see Miller, 1990.

13. Further work on the responsiveness of party identification to short-term forces should also take into account the analyses by Donald P. Green and Bradley Palmquist (1990). Their analyses suggest the importance of taking measurement

error into account when looking for evidence of partisan instability in nonrecursive models.

14. We are indebted to David Leege for the observation that, given the dispersal of Black voters throughout the nation, their mobilization did not redress the potential shift in electoral votes resulting from the regional concentration of Democratic losses and Republican gains in the Southern states.

15. One consequence of our separation of voters and non-voters should be a reinvigoration of interest in citizen turnout. It is quite possible, for example, that some portion of the apparent pro-Republican swing among Southern, non-Black male voters in the 1980s may have been caused by declining turnout among Southern, non-Black *Democratic* males rather than by pro-Republican conversions within a constant, unchanging population of voters.

16. It should be noted that the Republican record of party voting is more characteristic in presidential than congressional elections.

7. Realignment and Generational Change in Party Identification

1. In a private communication, John Kessel noted that the first stage in the decline in strong partisans began in 1964 with a drop in the number of strong Republicans. This was followed in 1966 with a decrease in the proportion of strong Democrats. The two moves taken together belie the existence of a "Goldwater effect" and marked the decline in national aggregate measures of strength by 1968.

2. The discovery that partisan "leaners" often manifested partisanship similar to that of weak party identifiers led to frequent aggregate measurement of strength of partisanship derived from subtracting the proportion with no partisan predisposition (Independent-Independents) from the proportion of "strong" identifiers. This measurement combines the increase in the number of pure non-partisans (Independent-Independents) with the absolute decrease in the proportion of strong partisans. Although we shall follow this convention to document variations in the intensity of partisanship, we must keep in mind that it does not necessarily reflect changes in the incidence of party identification as measured by the root question, "In general, do you usually think of yourself as a Republican, a Democrat, an Independent, or what?"

3. At least since the time of Key's seminal article "A Theory of Critical Elections" (Key, 1955), analysts have used the concept of political alignment to describe the composition of the competing sides in electoral competition. Realignment occurs when changes take place in the competitive balance between the parties. Realignment may also be *geographic,* as regional alignments change, or *group-based,* as social or economic groups shift their party support, or simply *numerical,* as one party grows in size in relation to the other. The idea of individuals

or groups not taking sides is inherent in the concept of non-alignment, just as moving from support for one side to a middle ground between the parties is described as dealignment. For a good summary discussion, see Sorauf and Beck (1988).

4. In 1952, almost 80% of all Southern white males identified with one or the other of the two major parties: 69% Democratic, 10% Republican. The Democratic advantage was 59 percentage points.

5. An alternative formulation is offered in Chapter 9 with evidence that the partisan realignment between 1980 and 1992 centered in Evangelical protestantism. This alternative possibility is buttressed with a sensitive and detailed analysis provided by Leege (1993), among others.

6. Changing party identification during this period of the late 1980s is amenable to a different interpretation offered by Leege (1993) and elaborated by Green, Guth, Kellstedt, and Smit and by Leege and Wald in a forthcoming discussion. The argument of these scholars emphasizes the cultural roots of national politics and the political conversions that have followed from the leadership in Evangelical protestant churches.

7. The transformation of the college-educated may well have been accentuated by the migration of white-collar Northerners to the South. See Philip E. Converse (1976).

8. For a more detailed discussion of the stability of party voting through time, see Miller (1989, 1991a, 1992).

8. Multiple-Stage Explanation of Political Preferences

1. As emphasized repeatedly in this chapter, in assigning both partisan and policy-related predispositions to the same (second) stage in our model, we make no assumption about the degree to which policy-related predispositions may have played some role in the evolution of voters' partisan identifications nor the impact of partisan identifications on policy-related predispositions.

2. Indeed, comparisons between explanations that are defined in terms of "policy" versus "performance" played a central role in our previous essays on the 1980, 1984, 1988, and 1992 elections (Miller and Shanks, 1982; Shanks and Miller, 1990, 1991).

3. For a discussion of the issues involved in this shift away from self-reported "reasons" for choice, see Rahn et al., 1994.

4. See "Heterogeneity in Models of Electoral Choice" (Rivers, 1988).

5. For an early, and historically influential, statement of this concern, see Jackson (1975), and also Nisbet (1977).

6. For an influential discussion of these potential problems concerning "issue voting," see Page and Brody (1972).

7. For analyses that consider the "endogeneity" of party identification, based on reciprocal causation or correlated disturbances, see Fiorina (1981), Jackson and Franklin (1983), and Green and Palmquist (1990).

8. See Bartels (1991) for a discussion of this issue, which emphasizes the consequences of false exclusion restrictions as well as the potential for biases due to simultaneity.

9. In addition to Wattenberg (1994) and Hagen (1994), see Charles E. Smith, Jr., and John H. Kessel, "The Partisan Choice: George Bush or Bill Clinton," in Herbert F. Weisberg, ed., *Democracy's Feast: Elections in America* (Chatham, N.J.: Chatham House, 1995) for a direct extension of the alternative approach as employed in *The American Voter.*

9. The Political Importance of "Non-Political" Variables

1. "A person thinks politically, as he is socially. Social characteristics determine political preference." Lazarsfeld, Berelson, and Gaudet (1948), p. 27. See also Miller and Janowitz (1952), "The Index of Political Predisposition in the 1948 Election," pp. 710–727.

2. For an interesting perspective on this topic see Visser (1994), pp. 43–52.

3. Many of these constancies are illustrated for the four elections of the Reagan-Bush-Clinton era in the tables that make up Appendix B.

4. The preceding paragraphs are based on pages 153–154 of "Partisanship, Policy, and Performance: The Reagan Legacy in the 1988 Election" (Shanks and Miller, 1991).

5. Some of this increase is only apparent because it is the consequence of improved measurement in NES data collections. Beginning in 1990, following the 1989 NES Pilot Study, the question format was changed in a number of respects to permit more accurate characterizations of religious affiliations and behaviors. The principal consequence was to reduce slightly the numbers classified as Mainline Protestants and Catholics, thereby apparently showing an increase in the number of "seculars."

6. Black sample sizes were 187 in 1980 and 319 in 1992.

7. For slightly different estimates, see Garin (1994), "The Religious Factor: How Is It Shaping American Politics?" pp. 17–19.

10. Explanations of Group Differences in the Vote

1. In designating Row 5 entries as coefficients reflecting each variable's "apparent total effect," we are presuming that other social or economic variables are the only candidates for confounding vote relationships with given social or economic characteristics.

2. Differences in effect coefficients are sometimes colloquially spoken of as "per-

centage point" differences. This is technically incorrect, although the differences in magnitudes of effect coefficients do have a meaning analogous to percentage point differences. Given the scoring of one dependent variable ($+1$ or -1), each mean score on the vote equals 1/100 times the difference between the percent voting Democratic and the percent Republican. Differences in means are therefore directly related to differences in percentage differences.

3. Several policy-related predispositions were considered at length prior to their inclusion in National Election Studies in 1988 and 1922. They were introduced through pilot studies as multi-item measures that met statistical tests for reliability and analytic tests for validity before being included in the major NES data collections. See Pilot Study Reports to NES Board, NES, University of Michigan, 1985, 1987, 1989, 1991.

The authors and titles of the relevant NES Pilot Study Reports are as follows: Pamela Johnston Conover and Stanley Feldman, "Measuring Patriotism and Nationalism," cited in ICPSR Codebook for the 1988 American National Election Study; Stephen Craig and Richard Niemi, "Political Efficacy and Trust," September 25, 1987; Stanley Feldman, "Evaluation of New Equality Items," September 19, 1987; Stanley Feldman, "Memo to NES Board of Overseers and 1984 Planning Committee, Values and the Rolling Cross-Section," October 19, 1983; Kathleen Knight, "Comparisons of Liberal-Conservative Items in the ANES 1989 Pilot Study"; Kathleen Knight, "Measurement of Liberal/Conservative Identification," September 23, 1987; Gregory Markus, "Measuring Popular Individualism," cited in ICPSR Codebook for the 1992 American National Election Study; Richard Niemi and Herb Weisberg, "1987 Pilot Study 'First Choice' Party Identification Question Experiment," September 25, 1987; Mark Peffley and Jon Hurwitz, "Report on Foreign Policy Items, 1987 Pilot Study."

4. The complex relationship between party identification and the other predispositions is revealed among Committed Catholics: adding PI, in Row 9, to the others from Row 8 accentuates its role as a pro-Democratic suppressor that is earlier revealed in the difference between Rows 5 and 6. It may seem more important when its effect is added to that of the other eight in Row 9 than when it alone is added to the effects of the social and economic characteristics in Row 6. It should be noted that at this stage in our analysis we have set $p < .1$ as sufficient for the likelihood that an effect coefficient differs from zero.

5. This unexpected result of our analytic scheme is considered at greater length in the next chapter, in our discussion of attitudes toward race.

6. Green and Guth (1993), "Salience: The Core Concept?" chap. 8, pp. 157–174.

7. Others have noted vote differences related to marital status, and some have argued that the antithesis to the vote of the "never married" is the vote among married people who have children. This corollary to the 1992 campaign emphasis on family values certainly existed. However, in our analysis the difference in vote division between the "married with children" and the "married with no

children" disappeared once the confounding influences of other social and economic characteristics were taken into account. However, see Weisberg (1987), pp. 335–343; Kingston and Finkel (1987), pp. 57–64.

8. In other work, Verba and colleagues have translated amount of schooling into a "constant" metric by using deciles (Verba et al., 1992).

II. Continuing Conflicts within the Society

1. See Shanks and Miller (1991) for estimates of apparent effects of policy-related predispositions on the vote which include the indirect effects of such predispositions "through" voters' partisan identifications, based on the provisional (or hypothetical) assumption that such predispositions are causally prior. See Shanks and Miller (1990) for an analysis which explores the consequences of designating ideological position as causally prior to partisan identification.

2. Rows 6 and 9 are not relevant in assessing the impact of party identification, but are maintained to simplify comparisons across the many tables that are presented in this format. It will be noted that the coefficient for ideology is larger than that for party identification in the preceding table. This occurs because there is more variation between −1 and +1 when "closeness" is used to refine the self-definitions of liberals and conservatives but is not added to the three category definitions of Democrat, Independent, and Republican. Similar variations in the measures used for other variables make it inappropriate to compare directly or without qualification the effect coefficients in Row 5 for different variables.

3. See Knight (1987), Miller and Levitin (1976), and Feldman (1984) for a discussion of alternative measures concerning ideological self-designation.

4. In particular, we shall note that our statistical procedures for selecting specific policy-related measures resulted in the deletion of a very visible NES measure concerning Blacks and racial discrimination. In general, we believe that variables whose coefficients are smaller than this fairly generous threshold (a p value of .1) are not important enough to justify further discussion. The calculation of p values is, of course, partially a function of the number of cases being analyzed. Cases such as the one under discussion, where the progressive change in coefficients is "well behaved," offer no problem of interpretation. Where the coefficient drops below even our lenient standard for statistical significance, we may—as in this case—note the continuing decline in the sheer magnitude of the coefficient even though the limited number of cases involved does not sustain evidence of statistical significance.

5. For six statements, respondents were given six response alternatives: Agree Strongly, Agree Somewhat, Neither Agree nor Disagree, Disagree Somewhat, Disagree Strongly, and Don't Know. The statements were: (a) Our society should do whatever is necessary to make sure that everyone has an equal opportunity

to succeed. (b) We have gone too far in pushing equal rights in this country. (c) This country would be better off if we worried less about how equal people are. (d) It is not really that big a problem if some people have more of a chance in life than others. (e) If people were treated more equally in this country, we would have many fewer problems. (f) One of the big problems in this country is that we don't give everyone an equal chance. Although equality of opportunity is implicit in many of these items, items b, c, and d refer to equality in the results of social policy.

6. These three questions combined in this additive index were preceded by the following instructions: "Next, I am going to ask you to choose which of two statements I read comes *closest* to your opinion. You might agree to some extent with both, but we want to know which one is *closer* to your views." Response categories for all three questions included options for "both, or depends" (if volunteered) and "don't know." The three pairs of statements read to each respondent were: (a) one, the less government, the better; or two, there are more things the government should be doing; (b) one, we need a strong government to handle today's complex economic problems; or two, the free market can handle those problems without government being involved; (c) one, the main reason government has become bigger over the years is because it has gotten involved in things that people should do for themselves; or two, government has become bigger because the problems we face have become bigger.

7. From Rows 3 and 4, we note that the difference between these average scores (or vote divisions) is 1.13, and that the regression coefficient for the bivariate relationship between those variables is approximately half of that difference (.55). It may be noted that the magnitude of this bivariate coefficient is not as large as the corresponding figure for equality (1.05), but some of that difference should be attributed to the smaller number of survey questions involved—and the resulting limitation in variability at both "ends" of this measure.

8. Response options for these four agree/disagree items were the same as for equality: (a) The world is always changing and we should adjust our view of moral behavior to those changes. (b) We should be more tolerant of people who choose to live according to their own moral standards (even if they are very different from our own). (c) This country would have many fewer problems if there were more emphasis on traditional family ties. (d) The new life-styles are contributing to the breakdown of our society.

9. Jack Dennis, "Political Ideology in the 1992 Presidential Election," paper presented at the Annual Meeting of the Midwest Political Science Association, Chicago, 1995.

10. The wording of these two questions is: (1) Do you think this country would be better off if we just stayed home and did not concern ourselves with problems in other parts of the world? and (2) Do you think that most men who tried to avoid the military service during the Vietnam War should have served regardless

of their personal beliefs? Both of these questions were converted to a simple trichotomy, with isolationist sentiments and responses sympathetic to Vietnam draft avoidance scored +1 and the opposite views scored −1.

11. This index was constructed by calculating the average of voters' responses to those four questions, each of which was scored from −1 (for the response that was least sympathetic concerning discrimination against Blacks) to +1 (for the most sympathetic response). The specific statements for those agree/disagree questions are as follows: (a) Irish, Italians, Jews, and many other minorities overcame prejudice and worked their way up. Blacks should do the same without any special favors. (b) Over the past few years, Blacks have gotten less than they deserve. (c) It's really a matter of some people not trying hard enough; if Blacks would only try harder, they could be just as well off as Whites. (d) Generations of slavery and discrimination have made it difficult for Blacks to work their way out of the lower class.

12. With a quite different research strategy, Joel Bloom also failed to find a significant connection between various measures of attitudes toward racial issues and the vote in 1992. Joel D. Bloom, "The Return of Overt Racism in the 1992 National Election Studies," paper presented at the Midwest Political Science Association meeting, Chicago, 1995.

13. We did identify one way to summarize voters' attitudes toward several minority groups for which the apparent impact on the vote is significant after we control for other predispositions as well as social and economic characteristics. Like other variables in this area, the bivariate relationship between that summary and the vote had the expected sign, for voters with more negative attitudes toward ethnic minorities were more likely to vote for George Bush. The sign of that coefficient, however, was *reversed* when we controlled for our other policy-related variables. Because of its composite nature, we are very unsure of the meaning of that summary, so we have omitted it from our final model. We note, however, that this summary of attitudes toward ethnic minorities is the only variable in this area to exhibit a significant (although inexplicably negative) relationship to the vote after we control for other policy-related variables.

14. For a comprehensive critique of measures based on the NES "likes and dislikes," see "Rationalization and Derivation Processes in Survey Studies of Political Candidate Evaluation" (Rahn et al., 1994).

12. Voting and Current Policy Preferences

1. See Pomper (1993); Abramson et al. (1994); Flanigan and Zingale (1994), and Weisberg (1995) for general essays on the types of issues that may have played some role in shaping voters' choices between Clinton and Bush.

2. This battery of questions was introduced in the following fashion: "If you had your say in making up the federal budget this year, for which of the following

programs would you like to see spending *increased* and for which would you like to see spending *decreased?*" The eight items that concerned general assistance to the disadvantaged were "food stamps," "welfare programs," "financial aid to college students," "solving the problems of the homeless," "child care," "government assistance to the unemployed," "poor people," and "aid to big cities."

3. The specific questions are as follows. J3: "Some people say the U.S. should maintain its position as the world's strongest military power even if it means continuing high defense spending. Would you say you *strongly agree, agree somewhat, disagree somewhat,* or *disagree strongly?*" J5: "In the future, how willing should the United States be to use military force to solve international problems . . . *extremely willing, very willing, somewhat willing, not very willing,* or *never willing?*"

4. See Stoker (1990) and Strand (1992) for analyses of potential NES questions in this area.

5. The item used in this area was the following. H8: "Do you think homosexuals should be allowed to serve in the United States armed forces or don't you think so?" A following question then asked if the respondent felt "strongly" or "not strongly" about that preference.

6. See Welch et al. (1995).

7. This summary was constructed by calculating the simple average of each respondent's position on all thirteen of those variables, each of which was scored from -1 to $+1$. Voters' "positions" on the resulting index therefore range between a theoretical minimum of -1.0 (for respondents who had the most conservative positions on all of our policy-related variables) to a theoretical maximum of $+1.0$ (for respondents who had the most liberal positions on all of those variables).

8. See McClosky (1966) and Miller and Jennings (1986) for extended discussions of policy-related differences between leaders and followers of the two major parties in American politics.

9. For a discussion of the design and a sample size for this three-wave panel, see Miller, Rosenstone, and Kinder (1993).

13. Voters' Perceptions of Current Conditions

1. See Weisberg, ed. (1995) and Levine (1995) for extended discussions of issue voting.

2. A question about the prospective standard of living twenty years hence provided no assistance in our analysis of the 1992 vote.

3. The wording for the first two questions was: "Would you say that over the *past year* the *nation's economy has gotten better, stayed about the same, or gotten worse?*" "During the past year, would you say that the United States' position in the

world has *grown weaker, stayed about the same,* or *has it grown stronger?"* Reports of recent experience with being laid off work were combined reports for respondent and spouse that they had been temporarily laid off.
4. See Kinder and Kiewiet (1979).

14. Retrospective and Prospective Evaluations of Candidate and Party Performances

1. See Rahn, Aldrich, and Borgida (1994).
2. See Miller (1992).
3. For a discussion of the importance of conditions and retrospective evaluations in 1992, see Stokes and Dilulio (1993).
4. "Who do you think is more to blame for the federal budget deficit, the *Bush administration* or the *Democratic Congress?"*

15. Evaluations of the Candidates' Personal Qualities

1. See Hagen (1994), paper delivered at the 1994 meeting of the American Political Science Association, New York, September.
2. Rahn et al. (1990).
3. Carolyn Funk, "Understanding the Importance and Structure of Trait Inference in Candidate Images," paper presented at the Conference on Candidate Evaluation, Berkeley, sponsored by the National Election Studies, December 2–3, 1994; based in part on a chapter to be published in *Research in MicroPolitics,* edited by Robert Shapiro, Michael Delli Carpini, and Leonie Huddy.
4. The questions are as follows:
   K2a. How well does the word or phrase describe (George Bush or Bill Clinton) . . . Intelligent?
   K2b. (how about) Compassionate? . . . as a word or phrase that describes (George Bush or Bill Clinton).
   K2c. How well does the word or phrase describe (George Bush or Bill Clinton) . . . Moral?
   K2d. How well does the word or phrase describe (George Bush or Bill Clinton) . . . Inspiring?
   K2e. How well does the word or phrase describe (George Bush or Bill Clinton) . . . Provides strong leadership?
   K2f. How well does the word or phrase describe (George Bush or Bill Clinton) . . . Really cares about people like you?
   K2g. How well does the word or phrase describe (George Bush or Bill Clinton) . . . Knowledgeable?
   K2h. How well does the word or phrase describe (George Bush or Bill Clinton) . . . Honest?

K2i. How well does the word or phrase describe (George Bush or Bill Clinton) . . . Gets things done?

5. Ross Perot's interruption of his own campaign not only limited its effectiveness but, by its timing, eliminated NES questions from the pre-election survey where candidate traits would have been assessed. As a consequence, there are no NES data on public perceptions of Perot's personal attributes.

6. This is a particularly frustrating analytic result, in part because so much of the literature on political personalities stresses concepts like competence, effectiveness, efficiency, and strength.

16. Electoral Explanations for Third-Party Candidates

1. Kessel (1984), p. 441.

2. See Kessel (1984), Chapter 13, "Three-candidate Campaigns"; see also Levine (1995) and Flanigan and Zingale (1994) for an extended discussion of the Perot candidacy; Herb Asher devotes a full chapter to Perot in Wiesberg (1995).

3. Keith et al. (1992), p. 52.

4. Zaller (1994, 1995).

5. It is worth noting that, at least in 1992 with only a foreshortened NES coverage of the Perot campaign, our strategy of relying on measures of predispositions, policy preferences, and conditions with no mention or evaluation linking them to the candidates permits analysis of all but the most short-term of the factors involved in the election. Unhappily, of course, we cannot know the extent to which variables in the latter stages of the model mediated the effects in the stages we can observe, nor can we estimate the independent explanatory contributions from the latter stages.

17. The Importance of Specific Variables and General Themes in 1988 and 1992

1. For earlier discussions of this fundamental distinction see Achen (1982), pp. 68–77, and Shanks and Miller (1990).

Appendix D. Methodological Commentary

1. As this book was being edited, it was discovered that different sets of cut-points were used for the 3-category index of policy-related preferences here and in Chapter 12. This discrepancy did not affect any of the substantive conclusions from the analyses in this appendix, but it did lead to somewhat different numbers of cases and means in each of the cells.

References

★ ★ ★

Abramson, Paul R. 1979. "Developing Party Identification: A Further Examination of Life-Cycle, Generational, and Period Effects." *American Journal of Political Science* 23: 78–96.

———— 1989. "Generations and Political Change in the United States." *Research in Political Sociology* 4: 235–280.

Abramson, Paul R., and John H. Aldrich. 1982. "The Decline of Electoral Participation in America." *American Political Science Review* 76: 502–521.

Abramson, Paul R., John H. Aldrich, and David W. Rhode. 1982. *Change and Continuity in the 1980 Elections*. Washington, D.C.: Congressional Quarterly Press.

———— 1991. *Change and Continuity in the 1988 Elections*. Washington, D.C.: Congressional Quarterly Press.

———— 1994. *Change and Continuity in the 1992 Elections*. Washington, D.C.: Congressional Quarterly Press.

Abramson, Paul R., and William Claggett. 1989. "Race-Related Differences in Self-Reported and Validated Turnout in 1986." *Journal of Politics* 51: 397–410.

———— 1991. "Racial Differences in Self-Reported and Validated Turnout in the 1988 Presidential Election." *Journal of Politics* 53: 186–197.

Abramson, Paul R., and Charles W. Ostrom, Jr. 1991. "Macropartisanship: An Empirical Reassessment." *American Political Science Review* 85: 181–192.

———— 1992. "Question Wording and Macropartisanship: Response." *American Political Science Review* 86: 481–486.

———— 1994. "Question Wording and Partisanship: Change and Continuity in Party Loyalties During the 1992 Election Campaign." *Public Opinion Quarterly* 58: 21–48.

Achen, Christopher H. 1975. "Mass Political Attitudes and the Survey Response." *American Political Science Review* 69: 1218–1231.

———— 1982. *Interpreting and Using Regression*. Beverly Hills, Calif.: Sage.

———— 1992. "Social Psychology, Demographic Variables, and Linear Regression: Breaking the Iron Triangle in Voting Research." *Political Behavior* 14: 195–211.

Aldrich, John, and Richard G. Niemi. 1989. "The Sixth American Party System: The 1960s Realignment and the Candidate-Centered Parties." Manuscript.

Aldrich, John H., John L. Sullivan, and Eugene Borgida. 1989. "Foreign Affairs and Voting: Do Presidential Candidates Waltz Before a 'Blind Audience'?" *American Political Science Review* 83: 123–142.

Alford, Robert. 1963. *Party and Society.* Chicago: Rand McNally.

Allsop, Dee, and Herbert F. Weisberg. 1988. "Measuring Change in Party Identification in an Election Campaign." *American Journal of Political Science* 32: 996–1017.

Almond, Gabriel. 1988. "The Return to the State." *American Political Science Review* 82: 853–874.

Almond, Gabriel, and Sidney Verba. 1963. *The Civic Culture.* Princeton, N.J.: Princeton University Press.

Alvarez, Michael R. 1990. "The Puzzle of Party Identification." *American Politics Quarterly* 18: 476–491.

Alvarez, Michael R., and Charles H. Franklin. 1994. "Uncertainty and Political Repression." *Journal of Politics* 56: 671–688.

Alwin, Duane F., Ronald L. Cohen, and Theodore M. Newcomb. 1991. *Political Attitudes Over the Life Span: The Bennington Women After Fifty Years.* Madison, Wisc.: University of Wisconsin Press.

Apter, David E., ed. 1964. *Ideology and Discontent.* London: Collier-Macmillan Ltd.: The Free Press of Glencoe.

Asher, Herbert B. 1992. *Presidential Elections and American Politics,* 5th ed. Belmont, Calif.: Wadsworth.

Axelrod, Robert. 1972. "Where the Votes Come From: An Analysis of Electoral Coalitions." *American Political Science Review* 66: 11–20.

Bargh, John A., and Roman D. Thein. 1985. "Individual Construct Accessibility, Personal Memory, and the Recall-Judgement Link: The Case of Information Overload." *Journal of Political and Social Psychology* 49: 1129–1146.

Barnes, Samuel H., and Max Kaase, et al. 1979. *Political Action.* Beverly Hills, Calif.: Sage.

Barnes, Samuel H., M. Kent Jennings, Ronald Inglehart, and Andrew E. Smith. 1988. "Party Identification and Party Closeness in Comparative Perspective." *Political Behavior* 10: 215–231.

Bartels, Larry M. 1991. "Instrumental and 'Quasi-Instrumental' Variables." *American Journal of Political Science* 35: 777–800.

———— 1993. "Messages Received: The Political Impact of Media Exposure." *American Political Science Review* 87: 267–284.

———— 1988. *Presidential Primaries and the Dynamics of Public Choice.* Princeton, N.J.: Princeton University Press.

Baumer, Donald C., and Howard J. Gold. 1995. "Party Images and the American Electorate." *American Political Science Quarterly* 23: 33–61.

Beck, Paul Allen. 1974. "Environment and Party: The Impact of Political and Demographic County Characteristics on Party Behavior." *American Political Science Review* 68: 1229–1244.

———— 1976. "A Socialization Theory of Partisan Realignment." In *Controversies in American Voting Behavior,* ed. Richard G. Niemi and Herbert F. Weisberg. San Francisco: Freeman.

———— 1979. "The Electoral Cycle and Patterns of American Politics." *British Journal of Political Science* 9: 129–156.

———— 1988. "Incomplete Realignment: The Reagan Legacy for Parties and Elections." In *The Reagan Legacy: Promise and Performance,* edited by Charles O. Jones. Chatham, N.J.: Chatham House.

Beck, Paul Allen, and M. Kent Jennings. 1991. "Family Traditions, Political Periods, and the Development of Partisan Orientation." *Journal of Politics* 53: 742–763.

Beckwith, Karen. 1986. *American Women and Political Participation.* Westport, Conn.: Greenwood Press.

Beere, Carole A. 1990. *Sex and Gender Issues: A Handbook of Tests and Measures.* Westport, Conn.: Greenwood Press.

Bennett, Stephen. 1988. "'Know-Nothings' Revisited: The Meaning of Political Ignorance Today." *Social Science Quarterly* 69: 476–490.

———— 1989. "Trends in Americans' Political Information, 1967–1987." *American Politics Quarterly* 17: 422–435.

Berelson, Bernard. 1959. "The State of Communication Research." *Public Opinion Quarterly* 23: 1–6.

Berelson, Bernard R., Paul F. Lazarsfeld, and William N. McPhee. 1954. *Voting.* Chicago: University of Chicago Press.

Bishop, George F., Alfred J. Tuchfarber, and Andrew E. Smith. 1992. "Question Wording and Partisanship: An Experimental Test of the Hypothesis." Paper presented at the annual meeting of the American Political Science Association, Chicago, September 3–6.

Black, Earl, and Merle Black. 1987. *Politics and Society in the South.* Cambridge, Mass.: Harvard University Press.

Bloom, Joel. 1995. "The Return of Overt Racism in 1992 National Election Studies." Paper presented at the Midwest Political Science Association, Chicago.

Blumenthal, Sidney. 1990. *Pledging Allegiance: The Last Campaign of the Cold War.* New York: Harper Collins.

Borelli, Stephen, Brad Lockerbie, and Richard G. Niemi. 1987. "Why the Democrat-Republican Partisanship Gap Varies from Poll to Poll." *Public Opinion Quarterly* 51: 115–119.

Bourqe, Susan C., and Jean Grossholtz. 1974. "Politics as Unnatural Practice: Political Science Looks at Women's Participation." *Politics and Society* 4: 225–266.

Box-Steffensmeier, Janet, and Renee Smith. 1994. "The Microfoundations of Macropartisanship." Paper presented to the Annual Political Methodology Conference in Madison, Wisc.

Brady, David W. 1988. *Critical Elections and Congressional Policy Making.* Stanford, Calif.: Stanford University Press.

Brady, Henry E., and Paul M. Sniderman. 1985. "Attitude Attribution: A Group Basis for Political Reasoning." *American Political Science Review* 79: 1061–1078.

Brody, Richard A. 1978. "The Puzzle of Political Participation in America." In *The New American Political System,* edited by Anthony King. Washington, D.C.: American Enterprise Institute.

Brody, Richard A., and Benjamin I. Page. 1972. "Comment: The Assessment of Policy Voting." *American Political Science Review* 66: 450–458.

Brody, Richard A., and Lawrence S. Rothenberg. 1988. "The Instability of Partisanship: An Analysis of the 1980 Presidential Election." *British Journal of Political Science* 18: 445–465.

Brown, Thad. 1988. *Migration and Politics: The Impact of Population Mobility on American Voting Behavior.* Chapel Hill, N.C.: University of North Carolina Press.

Budge, Ian, Ivor Crewe, and Dennis Farlie, eds. 1976. *Party Identification and Beyond: Representations of Voting and Party Competition.* London and New York: Wiley.

Burnham, Walter Dean. 1970. *Critical Elections and the Mainsprings of American Politics.* New York: Norton.

——— 1975. "Insulation and Responsiveness in Congressional Elections." *Political Science Quarterly* 90: 411–435.

Butler, David, and Donald Stokes. 1969. *Political Change in Britain.* New York: St. Martin's Press.

Cacioppo, John T., and Gary G. Berson. 1994. "The Relationship Between Attitudes and Evaluative Space: A Critical Review, with Emphasis on the Separability of Positive and Negative Substrates." *Psychological Bulletin* 115: 401–423.

Campbell, Angus, Philip E. Converse, Warren E. Miller, and Donald E. Stokes. 1960. *The American Voter.* New York: John Wiley & Sons.

——— eds. 1966. *Elections and the Political Order.* New York: Wiley.

Campbell, Angus, Gerald Gurin, and Warren E. Miller. 1954. *The Voter Decides.* Evanston, Ill.: Row Peterson.

Campbell, Angus, and Robert Kahn. 1952. *The People Elect a President.* Ann Arbor, Mich.: Survey Research Center, ISR, University of Michigan.

Carmines, Edward G., and James A. Stimson. 1980. "The Two Faces of Issue Voting." *American Political Science Review* 74: 78–91.

——— 1989. *Issue Evolution: Race and the Transformation of American Politics.* Princeton, N.J.: Princeton University Press.

———— 1989. *Race and the Transformation of American Politics.* Princeton, N.J.: Princeton University Press.

Carmines, Edward G., John P. McIver, and James A. Stimson. 1987. "Unrealized Partisanship: A Theory of Realignment." *Journal of Politics* 49: 376–400.

Cartwright, Dorwin and Alvin Zander, eds. 1968. *Group Dynamics: Research and Theory,* 3rd ed. New York: Harper & Row.

Cassell, Carol A., and Robert Luskin. 1988. "Simple Explanations of Turnout Decline." *American Political Science Review* 82: 1321–1330.

Ceaser, James, and Andrew Busch. 1993. *Upside Down and Inside Out: The 1992 Elections and American Politics.* Lanham, Md.: Rowman & Littlefield.

Chaffee, Steven H., and K. H. Jamieson. 1994. "Studies of the 1992 U.S. Election Campaign: An Overview." *Communication Research* 21: 261–263.

Chaffee, Steven H., X. Zhao, and G. Leshner. 1994. "Political Knowledge and the Campaign Media of 1992." *Communication Research* 21: 305–324.

Chubb, John E., and Paul E. Peterson. 1985. *The New Direction in American Politics.* Washington, D.C.: The Brookings Institution.

Citrin, Jack, and Donald Philip Green. 1990. "The Self-Interest Motive in Public Opinion." *Research in Micropolitics* 3: 1–28.

Citrin, Jack, Beth Reingold, and Donald Green. 1990. "American Identity and the Politics of Ethnic Change." *Journal of Politics* 52: 1124–1154.

Claggett, William. 1981. "Partisan Acquisition versus Partisan Intensity: Lifecycle, Generation and Period Effects, 1952–1976." *American Journal of Political Science* 25: 193–214.

Clarke, Harold D., and Motoshi Suzuki. 1994. "Partisan Dealignment and the Dynamics of Independence in the American Electorate, 1953–88." *British Journal of Political Science* 24: 57–78.

Clubb, Jerome, William Flanigan, and Nancy Zingale. 1980. *Partisan Realignment: Voters, Parties, and Government in American History.* Beverly Hills, Calif.: Sage.

Conover, Pamela Johnston. 1981. "Political Cues and the Perception of Political Candidates." *American Politics Quarterly* 9: 427–448.

———— 1984. "The Influence of Group Identifications on Political Perception and Evaluation." *Journal of Politics* 46: 760–785.

———— 1985. "The Impact of Group Economic Interests on Political Evaluations." *American Politics Quarterly* 13: 139–166.

———— 1988a. "Feminists and the Gender Gap." *Journal of Politics* 50: 985–1010.

———— 1988b. "The Role of Social Groups in Political Thinking." *British Journal of Political Science* 18: 51–76.

Conover, Pamela Johnston, and Stanley Feldman. 1981. "The Origins and Meanings of Liberal/Conservative Self-Identification." *American Journal of Political Science* 25: 617–645.

———— 1986. "I'm as Mad as Hell and I'm Not Going to Take It Any More." *American Journal of Political Science* 30: 30–78.

———— 1986. "1985 Pilot Study Measures on Civic Obligation." NES Report.

———— 1986. "Morality Items on the 1985 Pilot Study." NES Report.

———— 1988. "Measuring Patriotism and Nationalism." NES Report.

———— 1989. "Candidate Perception in an Ambiguous World." *American Journal of Political Science* 33: 912–940.

Conover, Pamela Johnston, and Virginia Sapiro. 1992. "Gender Consciousness and Gender Politics in the 1991 Pilot Study: A Report to the ANES Board of Overseers." NES Pilot Study Report, January.

Converse, Jean M. 1987. *Survey Research in the United States: Roots and Emergence 1890–1960.* Berkeley, Calif.: University of California Press.

Converse, Philip E. 1958. "The Shifting Role of Class in Political Attitudes and Behavior." In *Readings in Social Psychology,* edited by Eleanor Maccoby, et al. New York: Henry Holt & Company.

———— 1964. "The Nature of Belief Systems in Mass Publics." In *Ideology and Discontent,* edited by David E. Apter. London: Collier-Macmillan Ltd.: The Free Press of Glencoe.

———— 1966. "The Concept of a Normal Vote." In *Elections and the Political Order,* edited by Angus Campbell, Philip E. Converse, Warren E. Miller, and Donald E. Stokes. New York: Wiley.

———— 1966. "Information Flow and the Stability of Partisan Attitudes." In *Elections and the Political Order,* edited by Angus Campbell, Philip E. Converse, Warren E. Miller, and Donald E. Stokes. New York: Wiley.

———— 1966. "On the Possibility of a Major Political Realignment in the South." In *Elections and the Political Order,* edited by Angus Campbell, Philip E. Converse, Warren E. Miller, and Donald E. Stokes. New York: Wiley.

———— 1966. "Religion and Politics: The 1960 Election." In *Elections and the Political Order,* edited by Angus Campbell, Philip E. Converse, Warren E. Miller, and Donald E. Stokes. New York: Wiley.

———— 1969. "Of Time and Partisan Stability." *Comparative Political Studies* 2: 139–171.

———— 1975. "Public Opinion and Voting Behavior." In *Handbook of Political Science,* vol. 4, edited by F. I. Greenstein and Nelson W. Polsby. Reading, Mass.: Addison-Wesley.

———— 1976. *The Dynamics of Party Support: Cohort Analyzing Party Identification.* Beverly Hills, Calif.: Sage.

———— 1979. "Rejoinder to Abramson," *American Journal of Political Science* 23: 97–100.

———— 1990. "Popular Representation and the Distribution of Information." In *Information and the Democratic Process,* edited by John Ferejohn and James Kuklinski. Urbana, Ill.: University of Illinois Press.

Converse, Philip E., and Angus Campbell. 1968. "Political Standards in Secondary Groups." In *Group Dynamics: Research and Theory,* 3rd ed., edited by Dorwin Cartwright and Alvin Zander. New York: Harper & Row.

Converse, Philip E., Angus Campbell, Warren E. Miller, and Donald E. Stokes. 1961.

"Stability and Change in 1960: A Reinstating Election." *American Political Science Review* 55: 269–280.

Converse, Philip E., Aage R. Clausen, and Warren E. Miller. 1965. "Electoral Myth and Reality: The 1964 Election." *American Political Science Review* 59: 321–336.

Converse, Philip E., and Gregory B. Markus. 1979. "Plus ça Change . . . The New CPS Election Study Panel." *American Political Science Review* 73: 32–49.

Converse, Philip E., Warren E. Miller, Jerrold G. Rusk, and Arthur C. Wolfe. 1969. "Continuity and Change in American Politics: Parties and Issues in the 1968 Election." *American Political Science Review* 63: 1083–1105.

Converse, Philip E., and Roy Pierce. 1985. "Measuring Partisanship." *Political Methodology* 11: 143–166.

———— 1986. *Political Representation in France.* Cambridge, Mass.: Harvard University Press.

Conway, M. Margaret. 1990. *Political Participation in the United States,* 2nd ed. Washington, D.C.: Congressional Quarterly Press.

Craig, Stephen, and Richard Niemi. 1987. "Political Efficacy and Trust." NES Report, September 24.

Crigler, Ann N., and Marion R. Just. 1994. "Constructing Candidate Images." Paper presented at the World Congress of the International Political Science Association, Berlin, August 21–24.

Dahl, Robert A. 1989. *Democracy and Its Critics.* New Haven, Conn.: Yale University Press.

Dalton, Russell J. 1987. "Generational Change and Elite Political Beliefs: The Growth of Ideological Polarization." *Journal of Politics* 49: 976–997.

Dalton, Russell J., Scott C. Flanagan, and Paul Allen Beck. 1984. *Electoral Change in Advanced Industrial Democracies: Realignment or Dealignment?* Princeton, N.J.: Princeton University Press.

Davis, James A. 1990. *The Logic of Causal Order.* Beverly Hills, Calif.: Sage.

de Toqueville, Alexis. 1969. *Democracy in America.* New York: Anchor. (Original work published in 1848.)

Delli Carpini, Michael X., and Scott Keeter. 1991. "Stability and Change in the U.S. Public's Knowledge of Politics." *Public Opinion Quarterly* 55: 583–612.

———— 1993. "Measuring Political Knowledge: Putting First Things First." *American Journal of Political Science* 37: 1179–1206.

Dennis, Jack. 1988. "Political Independence in America: I. On Being an Independent Partisan Supporter." *British Journal of Political Science* 18: 77–109.

———— 1994. "The Perot Constituency." Report to the Board of Overseers of the National Election Studies, March 10.

———— 1995. "Political Ideology in the 1992 Presidential Election." Paper presented at the annual meeting of the Midwest Political Science Association, Chicago.

Dinerman, Helen. 1948. "Votes in the Making: A Preview." *Public Opinion Quarterly* 12: 585–598.

Downs, Anthony. 1957. *An Economic Theory of Democracy.* New York: Harper & Row.

Eagly, Alice H., Mladinic, Antonio, and Otto, Stacey. 1994. "Cognitive and Affective Bases of Attitudes Toward Social Groups." *Journal of Experimental Social Psychology* 30: 113–137.

Easton, David, and Jack Dennis. 1969. *Children in the Political System.* New York: McGraw-Hill.

Edsall, Thomas Byrne, with Edsall, Mary D. 1992. *Chain Reaction: The Impact of Race, Rights, and Taxes on American Politics.* New York: Norton.

Einhorn, Hillel J., Don N. Kleinmutz, and Benjamin Kleinmutz. 1978. "Linear Regression and Process-Tracing Models of Judgement." *Psychological Review* 86: 465–485.

Enelow, James M., and Melvin J. Hinch. 1984. *The Spatial Theory of Voting: An Introduction.* New York: Cambridge University Press.

Eulau, Heinz. 1994. "Electoral Survey Data and the Temporal Dimension." In *Elections at Home and Abroad,* ed. M. Kent Jennings and Thomas E. Mann. Ann Arbor: University of Michigan Press.

Eysenck, Hans J. 1954. *The Psychology of Politics.* London: Routledge and Kegan Paul.

Eysenck, Hans J., and Glenn D. Wilson, eds. 1978. *The Psychological Basis of Ideology.* Baltimore, Md.: University Park Press.

Fazio, Russell H., and Carol J. Williams. 1986. "Attitude Accessibility as a Moderator of the Attitude-Perception and Attitude-Behavior Relations: An Investigation of the 1984 Presidential Election." *Journal of Political and Social Psychology* 51: 505–514.

Feldman, Stanley. 1983. "Economic Individualism and American Public Opinion." *American Politics Quarterly* 11: 3–29.

——— 1983. "Report on Values in the 1983 Pilot Study." NES Report, October 19.

——— 1984. "The Measurement and Meaning in Trust in Government." *Political Methodology* 9: 341–54.

——— 1987. "Evaluation of New Equality Items." NES Report, September 29.

——— 1987. "Values and the Rolling Cross-Section." NES Report, September 29.

——— 1988. "Structure and Consistency in Public Opinion: The Role of Core Self and Values." *American Journal of Political Science* 32: 416–440.

Ferejohn, John A., and James H. Kuklinski, eds. 1990. *Information and Democratic Processes.* Urbana, Ill.: University of Illinois Press.

Finifter, Ada, ed. 1983. *Political Science: The State of the Discipline.* Washington, D.C.: American Political Science Association.

Fiorina, Morris P. 1977. *Congress: Keystone of the Washington Establishment.* New Haven, Conn.: Yale University Press.

——— 1981. *Retrospective Voting in American National Elections.* New Haven, Conn.: Yale University Press.

Fiske, Susan T., Richard R. Lau, and Richard A. Smith. 1990. "On the Varieties and Utilities of Political Expertise." *Social Cognition* 8: 31–48.

Fiske, Susan T., and S. Taylor. 1984. *Social Cognition.* New York: Random House.

Flanigan, William H., Wendy M. Rahn, and Nancy H. Zingale. 1992. "Dynamics of

Voter Decision-Making." Paper presented at the annual meeting of the American Political Science Association, Chicago, September.

Flanigan, William H., and Nancy H. Zingale. 1994. *Political Behavior of the American Electorate,* 8th ed. Washington, D.C.: Congressional Quarterly Press.

Franklin, Charles H. 1984. "Issue Preferences, Socialization, and the Evolution of Party Identification." *American Journal of Political Science* 28: 459–478.

———— 1992. "Measurement and the Dynamics of Party Identification." *Political Behavior* 14: 297–309.

Franklin, Charles H., and John E. Jackson. 1983. "The Dynamics of Party Identification." *American Political Science Review* 77: 957–973.

Frankovic, Kathleen A. 1981. "Public Opinion Trends." In *The Election of 1980,* edited by Gerald M. Pomper, et al. Chatham, N.J.: Chatham House.

———— 1993. "Public Opinion in the 1992 Campaign." In *The Election of 1992,* edited by Gerald M. Pomper. Chatham, N.J.: Chatham House.

Gamson, William A. 1992. *Talking Politics.* Cambridge: Cambridge University Press.

Garin, Goef. 1994. "The Religious Factor: How Is It Shaping American Politics?" *The Public Perspective* 5: 17–19.

Geer, John G. 1988. "What Do Open-Ended Questions Measure?" *Public Opinion Quarterly* 52: 365–371.

———— 1991. "Do Open-Ended Questions Measure 'Salient' Issues?" *Public Opinion Quarterly* 55: 360–370.

———— 1991. "The Electorate's Partisan Evaluations: Evidence of a Continuing Democratic Edge." *Public Opinion Quarterly* 55: 218–231.

———— 1992. "New Deal Issues and the American Electorate, 1952–1988." *Political Behavior* 14: 45–65.

Gerber, Elisabeth R., and Arthur Lupia. 1993. "When Do Campaigns Matter? Informed Votes and the Responsiveness of Electoral Outcomes." California Institute of Technology and the University of California, San Diego.

Gilens, Martin. 1988. "Gender and Support for Reagan: A Comprehensive Model of Presidential Approval." *American Journal of Political Science* 32: 19–49.

Githens, Marianne. 1983. "The Elusive Paradigm: Gender, Politics, and Political Behavior: The State of the Art." In *Political Science: The State of the Discipline,* edited by Ada Finifter. Washington, D.C.: American Political Science Association.

Glock, Charles Y., and Rodney Stark. 1965. *Religion and Society in Tension.* Chicago: Rand McNally.

Gosnell, Harold F., and Charles E. Merriam. 1924. *Non-Voting.* Chicago: The University of Chicago Press.

Graber, Doris. 1988. *Processing the News: How People Tame the Information Tide,* 2nd ed. New York: Longman.

Granberg, Donald, and Soren Holmberg. 1988. *The Political System Matters.* Cambridge: Cambridge University Press.

Grant, Michael M., and Norman R. Luttberg. 1991. *American Electoral Behavior.* Itasca, Ill.: F E Peacock.

Greeley, Andrew M. 1989. *Religious Change in America.* Cambridge, Mass.: Harvard University Press.

Green, Donald Philip. 1990. "The Effects of Measurement Error on Two-Stage, Least Squares Estimates." *Political Analysis* 2: 57–74.

Green, Donald Philip, and Bradley Palmquist. 1990. "Of Artifacts and Partisan Instability." *American Journal of Political Science* 34: 872–902.

———— 1995. "How Stable Is Party Identification?" *Political Behavior,* forthcoming.

Green, Donald Philip, and Eric Schickler. 1993. "A Multiple Method Approach to the Measurement of Party Identification." *Public Opinion Quarterly* 57: 503–535.

———— 1994. "The Grim Reaper, the Stork, and Partisan Change in the North and South, 1952–1992." Paper presented at the annual meeting of the American Political Science Association, New York, September 1–4.

Green, John C., and James Guth. 1993. "Salience: The Core Concept?" In *Rediscovering the Religious Factor,* edited by David C. Leege and Lyman A. Kellstedt. Armonk, N.Y.: M. E. Sharpe.

Greenstein, F. I., and Nelson W. Polsby, eds. 1975. *Handbook of Political Science,* vol. 4. Reading, Mass.: Addison-Wesley.

Grofman, Bernard. 1985. "The Neglected Role of the Status Quo in Models of Issue Voting." *Journal of Politics* 47: 230–237.

Gurin, Patricia. 1985. "Women's Gender Consciousness." *Public Opinion Quarterly* 49: 143–163.

Guth, James L., and John C. Green. 1993. "Salience: The Core Concept?" In *Rediscovering the Religious Factor in American Politics,* edited by David C. Leege and Lyman A. Kellstedt. Armonk, N.Y.: M. E. Sharpe.

Hagen, Michael G. 1994. "Candidate Centered Politics and the Level of Attention in Presidential Elections." Unpublished paper presented at the annual meeting of the American Political Science Association, New York, September.

Hamilton, Richard. 1972. *Class and Politics in the United States.* New York: Wiley.

Hastie, Reid, and Bernadette Park. 1986. "The Relationship Between Memory and Judgement Depends on Whether the Judgement Task Is Memory-Based or On-Line." *Psychological Review* 93: 258–268.

Hastie, Reid, and Nancy Pennington. 1989. "Notes on the Distinction Between Memory-Based Versus On-Line Judgements." In *On-Line Processes in Person Perception,* edited by John N. Bassili. Hillsdale, N.J.: Lawrence Erlbaum Associates.

Hays, Samuel P. 1980. *American Political History as Social Analysis.* Knoxville, Tenn.: University of Tennessee Press.

Heath, Anthony, Geoffrey Evans, and Jean Martin. 1994. "The Measurement of Core Beliefs and Values: The Development of Balanced Socialist/Laissez Faire and

Libertarian/Authoritarian Scales." *British Journal of Political Science* 24: 115–132.

Herbst, S. 1992. "Surveys in the Public Sphere: Applying Bourdieu's Critique of Opinion Polls." *International Journal of Public Opinion Research* 4: 220–229.

——— 1993. *Numbered Voices: How Opinion Polling Has Shaped American Politics.* Chicago: University of Chicago Press.

Hess, Robert D., and Judith V. Torney. 1967. *The Development of Political Attitudes in Children.* Chicago: Aldine.

Himmelweit, Hilde T., Marianne Jager Humphreys, and Michael Katz. 1981. *How Voters Decide.* New York: Academic Press.

Hochschild, Jennifer L. 1981. *What's Fair? American Beliefs About Distributive Justice.* Cambridge, Mass.: Harvard University Press.

——— 1995. *Facing Up to the American Dream: Race, Class, and the Soul of the Nation.* Princeton, N.J.: Princeton University Press.

Hodges, Sara D., and Timothy D. Wilson. 1993. "Effects of Analyzing Reasons on Attitude Change: The Moderating Role of Attitude Accessibility." *Social Cognition* 11: 353–366.

Houston, David A., and Russel H. Fazio. 1989. "Biased Processing as a Function of Attitude Accessibility: Making Objective Judgements Subjectively." *Social Cognition* 7: 51–66.

Howe, Neil, and Bill Strauss. 1991. *Generations.* New York: William Morrow and Company.

——— 1993. *13th Gen: Abort, Retry, Ignore, Fail?* New York: Random House.

Huckfeldt, Robert. 1968. *Politics in Context.* New York: Agathon.

Huckfeldt, Robert, and John Sprague. 1987. "Networks in Context: The Social Flow of Political Information." *American Political Science Review* 81: 197–216.

Huckshorn, Robert J., and John F. Bibby. 1983. "National Party Rules and Delegate Selection in the Republican Party." *Political Science* 16: 656–666.

Inglehart, Ronald. 1977. *The Silent Revolution.* Princeton, N.J.: Princeton University Press.

——— 1990. *Culture Shift in Advanced Industrial Society.* Princeton, N.J.: Princeton University Press.

Iyengar, Shanto. 1991. *Is Anyone Responsible? How Television Frames Political Issues.* Chicago: University of Chicago Press.

Iyengar, Shanto, and Donald R. Kinder. 1987. *News That Matters.* Chicago: University of Chicago Press.

Iyengar, Shanto, and William McGuire, eds. 1993. *Explorations in Political Psychology.* Durham, N.C.: Duke University Press.

Jackson, John E. 1975. "Issues, Party Choices, and Presidential Votes." *American Journal of Political Science* 19: 161–185.

Jacobson, Gary C. 1992. *The Politics of Congressional Elections.* New York: Harper Collins.

Jacoby, William G. 1988. "The Impact of Party Identification on Issue Attitudes." *American Journal of Political Science* 32: 643–661.

Jennings, M. Kent, and Gregory B. Markus. 1984. "Partisan Orientations Over the Long Haul: Results from the Three-Wave Political Socialization Panel Study." *American Political Science Review* 78: 1000–1018.

———— 1988. "Political Involvement in the Later Years: A Longitudinal Survey." *American Journal of Political Science* 32: 302–316.

Jennings, M. Kent, and Richard G. Niemi. 1968. "The Transmission of Political Values from Parent to Child." *American Political Science Review* 62: 169–184.

———— 1971. "The Division of Political Labor Between Mothers and Fathers." *American Political Science Review* 65: 69–92.

———— 1974. *The Political Character of Adolescence: The Influence of Families and Schools.* Princeton, N.J.: Princeton University Press.

———— 1981. *Generations and Politics.* Princeton, N.J.: Princeton University Press.

Jennings, M. Kent, Jan W. van Deth, et al. 1990. *Continuities in Political Action.* Berlin: de Gruyter.

Johnston, Richard, Andre Blais, Henry E. Brady, and Jean Crete. 1992. *Letting the People Decide: Dynamics of a Canadian Election.* Stanford, Calif.: Stanford University Press.

Jones, Charles O., ed. 1988. *The Reagan Legacy: Promise and Performance.* Chatham, N.J.: Chatham House.

Judd, Charles M., and Jon A. Krosnick. 1989. "Structural Bases of Attitude Constituency." In *Attitude Structure and Function,* edited by Anthony R. Pratkanis, Steven R. Breckler, and Anthony G. Greenwald. Hillsdale, N.J.: Lawrence Erlbaum Associates.

Katz, Elihu, and Paul Lazarsfeld. 1955. *Personal Influence.* New York: Free Press.

Keith, Bruce E., David B. Magelby, Candice J. Nelson, Elizabeth A. Orr, C. Westlye, and Raymond E. Wolfinger. 1986. "Further Evidence on the Partisan Affinities of Independent 'Leaners'." *British Journal of Political Science* 16: 155–184.

———— 1992. *The Myth of the Independent Voter.* Berkeley, Calif.: University of California Press.

Kelley, Stanley, Jr. 1983. *Interpreting Elections.* Princeton, N.J.: Princeton University Press.

Kellstedt, Lyman A. 1993. "Religion, the Neglected Variable: An Agenda for Future Research on Religion and Political Behavior." In *Rediscovering the Religious Factor in American Politics,* edited by David C. Leege and Lyman A. Kellstedt. Armonk, N.Y.: M E Sharpe.

Kellstedt, Lyman A., and John C. Green. 1993. "Denominational Preferences and Political Behavior." In *Rediscovering the Religious Factor in American Politics,* edited by David C. Leege and Lyman A. Kellstedt. Armonk, N.Y.: M E Sharpe.

Kellstedt, Lyman A., and Mark A. Noll. 1990. "Religion, Voting for President, and Part Identification, 1948–1984." In *Religion and American Politics: From the Co-*

lonial Period to the 1980s, edited by Mark A. Noll. New York: Oxford University Press.

Kellstedt, Lyman A., and Corwin E. Smidt. 1993. "Doctrinal Beliefs and Political Behavior: Views of the Bible." In *Rediscovering the Religious Factor in American Politics,* edited by David C. Leege and Lyman A. Kellstedt. Armonk, N.Y.: M E Sharpe.

Kenney, Patrick J. 1993. "An Examination of How Voters Form Impressions of Candidates' Issue Positions During the Nomination Campaign." *Political Behavior* 15: 265–288.

Kenney, Patrick, and Tom Rice. 1988. "The Evaporating Independents." *Public Opinion Quarterly* 52: 231–293.

Kessel, John. 1984. *Presidential Parties.* Homewood, Ill.: Dorsey Press.

Key, V. O. 1949. *Southern Politics in State and Nation.* New York: Knopf.

——— 1952. *Politics, Parties, and Pressure Groups.* New York: Thomas Crowell.

——— 1955. "A Theory of Critical Elections." *Journal of Politics* 17: 3–18.

——— 1959. "Secular Realignment and the Party System." *Journal of Politics* 21: 198–210.

——— 1961. *Public Opinion and American Democracy.* New York: Knopf.

Key, V. O., and Milton C. Cummings, Jr. 1966. *The Responsible Electorate: Rationality in Presidential Voting, 1936–1960.* Cambridge, Mass.: Harvard University Press.

Kiesler, Sara B., James N. Morgan, and Valerie K. Oppenheimer, eds. 1981. *Aging: Social Change.* New York: Academic Press.

Kinder, Donald R. 1978. "Political Person Perception: The Asymmetrical Influence of Sentiment and Choice on Perceptions of Presidential Candidates." *Journal of Personality and Social Psychology* 36: 859–871.

——— 1981. "Presidents, Prosperity and Public Opinion." *Public Opinion Quarterly* 45: 1–21.

——— 1983. "Diversity and Complexity in American Public Opinion." In *Political Science: The State of the Discipline,* edited by Ada W. Finifter. Washington, D.C.: American Political Science Association.

——— 1986. "Presidential Character Revisited." In *Political Cognition: The 19th Annual Symposium on Cognition,* edited by Richard R. Lau and David O. Sears. Hillsdale, N.J.: Lawrence Erlbaum Associates.

——— 1994. "Reason and Emotion in American Political Life." In *Beliefs, Reasoning, and Decision Making: Psycho-Logic in Honor of Bob Abelson,* edited by R. Schank and E. Langer. Hillsdale, N.J.: Lawrence Erlbaum Associates.

Kinder, Donald R., Gordon Adams, and Paul Gronke. 1989. "Economics and Politics in the 1984 American Presidential Election." *American Journal of Political Science* 33: 491–515.

Kinder, Donald R., and D. Roderick Kiewiet. 1979. "Economic Discontent and

Political Behavior: The Role of Personal Economic Grievances in Congressional Voting." *American Journal of Political Science* 23: 495–527.

Kinder, Donald R., Mark D. Peters, Robert P. Abelson, and Susan T. Fiske. 1980. "Presidential Prototypes." *Political Behavior* 2: 315–338.

Kinder, Donald R., and Lynn M. Sanders. 1986. "Survey Questions and Political Culture: The Case of Whites' Response to Affirmative Action for Blacks." Paper prepared for the annual meeting of the American Political Science Association, Washington, D.C.

Kinder, Donald R., and David O. Sears. 1985. "Public Opinion and Political Action." In *The Handbook of Social Psychology,* vol. 2, edited by G. Linzey and E. Aronson. Reading, Mass.: Addison-Wesley.

King, Anthony, ed. 1978. *The New American Political System.* Washington, D.C.: American Enterprise Institute.

Kingston, Paul William, and Steven Finkel. 1987. "Is There a Marriage Gap in Politics?" *Journal of Marriage and Family* 49: 57–64.

Klein, Ethel. 1984. *Gender Politics.* Cambridge, Mass.: Harvard University Press.

Kleppner, Paul. 1970. *The Cross of Culture: A Social Analysis of Midwestern Politics, 1850–1900.* New York: Free Press.

——— 1982. *Who Voted: The Dynamics of Electoral Turnout, 1870–1980.* New York: Praeger.

——— 1987. *Change and Continuity in Electoral Politics, 1893–1928.* Westport, Conn.: Greenwood Press.

Knack, Stephen. 1992. "Civic Norms, Social Sanctions, and Voter Turnout." *Rationality and Society* 4: 133–156.

——— 1992. "Social Connectedness and Voter Participation: Evidence from the 1991 NES Pilot Study." NES Pilot Study Report, January.

——— 1992. "Community Cohesion and Voter Turnout in the District of Columbia." Unpublished paper (1990) cited in NES Pilot Study Report, January.

Knight, Kathleen. 1985. "Ideology in the 1980 Election: Ideological Sophistication Does Matter." *Journal of Politics* 47: 828–853.

——— 1987. "Measurement of Liberal/Conservative Identification." NES Pilot Study Report, September 23.

——— 1989. "Comparisons of Liberal-Conservative Items in the ANES 1989 Pilot Study." NES Pilot Study Report.

Koning, Hans. 1987. *Nineteen Sixty-Eight: A Personal Report.* New York: Norton.

Korchin, Sheldon. 1946. "Psychological Variables in the Behavior of Voters." Ph.D. dissertation, Harvard University.

Krosnick, Jon A. 1988. "The Role of Attitude Importance in Social Evaluation: A Study of Preferences, Presidential Candidate Evaluations, and Voting Behavior." *Journal of Personality and Social Psychology* 55: 196–210.

Krosnick, Jon A., and Matthew K. Berent. 1990. "Government Policy and Citizen

Passion: A Study of Issue Politics in Contemporary America." *Political Behavior* 12: 59–92.

———— 1990. "Americans' Perceptions of Presidential Candidates: A Test of the Projection Hypothesis." *Journal of Social Issues* 46: 159–182.

———— 1991. "The Stability of Political Preferences: Comparisons of Symbolic and Nonsymbolic Attitudes." *American Journal of Political Science* 35: 547–576.

———— 1993. "Comparisons of Party Identification and Policy Preferences: The Impact of Survey Question Format." *American Journal of Political Science* 37: 941–964.

Kuklinski, James H., ed. 1995. *Political Psychology and Public Opinion.* Cambridge, Mass.: Harvard University Press.

Kuklinski, James H., and Norman L. Hurley. 1995. "It's a Matter of Interpretation." In *Political Persuasion and Attitude Change,* edited by Diana C. Mutz, Paul Sniderman, and Richard Brody. Ann Arbor, Mich.: University of Michigan Press.

Ladd, Everett C. 1982. *Where Have All the Voters Gone?* 2nd ed. New York: Norton.

Lane, R. 1962. *Political Ideology: Why the American Common Man Believes What He Does.* New York: Free Press.

Langton, Kenneth P., and M. Kent Jennings. 1968. "Political Socialization and the High School Civics Curriculum in the United States." *American Political Science Review* 62: 852–867.

Lau, Richard R. 1994. "Information Search During an Election Campaign: Introducing a Process Tracing Methodology for Political Scientists." In *Political Judgment: Structure and Process,* edited by Milton Lodge and Kathleen McGraw. Ann Arbor, Mich.: University of Michigan Press.

Lau, Richard R., and David O. Sears. 1986. "Social Cognition and Political Cognition: The Past, the Present and the Future." In *Political Cognition,* edited by Richard R. Lau and David O. Sears. Hillsdale, N.J.: Lawrence Erlbaum Associates.

———— eds. 1986. *Political Cognition.* Hillsdale, N.J.: Lawrence Erlbaum Associates.

Lazarsfeld, Paul F., Bernard R. Berelson, and Hazel Gaudet. 1948. *The People's Choice.* New York: Columbia University Press.

Leege, David C. 1988. "Catholics and the Civic Order: Parish Participation, Politics, and Civic Participation." *The Review of Politics* 50: 704–736.

———— 1993. "The Decomposition of the Religious Vote: A Comparison of White, Non-Hispanic Catholics with Other Ethnoreligious Groups, 1960–1992." Paper presented at the annual convention of the American Political Science Association in Washington, D.C., September 2–5.

Leege, David C., and Lyman Kellstedt, eds. 1993. *Rediscovering the Religious Factor in American Politics.* Armonk, N.Y.: M E Sharpe.

Leege, David C., Joel A. Lieske, and Kenneth D. Wald. 1991. "Toward Cultural Theories of American Politics: Religion, Ethnicity, Race, and Class Outlook."

In *Political Science: Toward the Future,* edited by Cathy Williams. Evanston, Ill.: Northwestern University Press, pp. 193–238.

Leege, David C., and Michael R. Welch. 1989. "Religious Roots of Political Orientations: Variations Among American Catholic Parishioners." *Journal of Politics* 51: 137–162.

Leighley, Jan E. 1990. "Social Interaction and Contextual Influences on Political Participation." *American Politics Quarterly* 18: 459–475.

Levine, Myron A. 1995. *Presidential Campaigns and Elections,* 2nd ed. Itasca, N.Y.: F E Peacock.

Levitin, Theresa E., and Warren E. Miller. 1979. "Ideological Interpretations of Presidential Elections." *American Political Science Review* 70: 751–771.

Lippmann, Walter. 1925. *The Phantom Public.* New York: Harcourt Brace.

———— 1965. *Public Opinion.* New York: Free Press. (Original work published in 1922.)

Lipset, Seymour Martin. 1960. *Political Man.* Garden City, N.Y.: Doubleday Anchor.

Lipset, Seymour Martin, and Stein Rokkan, eds. 1967. *Party Systems and Voter Alignments: Cross-National Perspectives.* New York: Free Press.

Lodge, Milton, and R. Hammill. 1986. "A Partisan Schema for Political Information Processing." *American Political Science Review* 80: 505–519.

Lodge, Milton, and Kathleen McGraw, eds. 1994. *Political Judgment: Structure and Process.* Ann Arbor, Mich.: University of Michigan Press.

Lodge, Milton, Kathleen McGraw, and Patrick Stroh. 1989. "An Impression-Driven Model of Candidate Evaluation." *American Political Science Review* 83: 399–420.

Lodge, Milton, and Patrick Stroh. 1993. "Inside the Mental Voting Booth: An Impression-Driven Model of Candidate Evaluation." In *Explorations in Political Psychology,* edited by Shanto Iyengar and William McGuire. Durham, N.C.: Duke University Press.

Lodge, Milton, Patrick Stroh, and John Wahlke. 1990. "Black-Box Models of Candidate Evaluation." *Political Behavior* 12: 5–18.

Lupia, Arthur. 1994. "Short Cuts versus Encyclopedias: Information and Voting Behavior in California Insurance Reform Elections." *American Political Science Review* 88: 63–76.

Luskin, Robert C. 1987. "Measuring Political Sophistication." *American Journal of Political Science* 31: 856–899.

Luskin, Robert C., John P. McIver, and Edward G. Carmines. 1989. "Issues and the Transmission of Partisanship." *American Journal of Political Science* 33: 440–458.

Luttbeg, Norman R., and Michael M. Gant. 1995. *American Electoral Behavior 1952–1992,* 2nd ed. Itasca, N.Y.: Peacock.

Maccoby, Eleanor E., et al., eds. 1958. *Readings in Social Psychology.* New York: Holt.

MacDonald, Stuart Elaine, and George Rabinowitz. 1993. "Ideology and Candidate Evaluation." *Public Choice* 76: 59–78.

Mackie, Diane M., and Arlene G. Asuncion. 1990. "On-Line and Memory-Based Modification of Attitudes: Determinants of Message Recall–Attitude Change Correspondence." *Journal of Political and Social Psychology* 59: 5–16.

MacKuen, Michael B. 1984. "Exposure to Information, Belief Integration, and Individual Responsiveness to Agenda Change." *American Political Science Review* 78: 372–391.

MacKuen, Michael B., and Courtney Brown. 1987. "Political Context and Attitude Change." *American Political Science Review* 81: 471–490.

MacKuen, Michael B., Robert S. Erikson, and James A. Stimson. 1989. "Macropartisanship." *American Political Science Review* 83: 1125–1142.

——— 1992. "Peasants or Bankers? The American Electorate and the U.S. Economy." *American Political Science Review* 86: 597–611.

——— 1992. "Question Wording and Macropartisanship." *American Political Science Review* 86: 475–481.

Maisel, L. Sandy, ed. 1991. *Political Parties and Elections in the United States: An Encyclopedia.* New York: Garland.

——— 1993. *Parties and Elections in America,* 2nd ed. New York: McGraw-Hill.

Mann, Thomas E., and Raymond E. Wolfinger. 1980. "Candidates and Parties in Congressional Elections." *American Political Science Review* 74: 617–632.

Mannheim, Karl. 1936. *Ideology and Utopia: An Introduction to the Sociology of Knowledge.* London: Routledge and Kegan Paul.

——— 1952. *Essays on the Sociology of Knowledge.* New York: Oxford University Press.

Marcus, George E. 1988. "The Structure of Emotional Response: 1984 Presidential Candidates." *American Political Science Review* 82: 737–761.

——— 1991. "Emotions and Politics: Hot Cognitions and the Rediscovery of Passion." *Social Science Information* 30: 195–232.

Marcus, George E., and Michael B. MacKuen. 1993. "Anxiety, Enthusiasm and the Vote: The Emotional Underpinnings of Learning and Involvement During Presidential Campaigns." *American Political Science Review* 87: 688–701.

Marcus, George E., J. L. Sullivan, E. Theiss-Morse, and S. Wood. 1995. *Experimenting with Tolerance: How People Make Civil Liberties Judgements.* New York: Cambridge University Press.

Markus, Gregory B. 1982. "Political Attitudes During an Election Year: A Report on the 1980 NES Panel Study." *American Political Science Review* 76: 538–560.

——— 1983. "Dynamic Modeling of Cohort Change: The Case of Political Partisanship." *American Journal of Political Science* 27: 717–739.

——— 1992. "The Impact of Personal and National Economic Conditions on Presidential Voting, 1956–1988." *American Journal of Political Science* 36: 829–834.

——— 1992. "Measuring Popular Individualism." NES Report.

——— 1995. "American Individualism Reconsidered." In *Political Psychology and*

Public Opinion, edited by James Kuklinski. Cambridge, Mass.: Harvard University Press (forthcoming).

Markus, Gregory B., and Converse, Philip E. 1979. "A Dynamic Simultaneous Equation Model of Electoral Choice." *American Political Science Review* 73: 1055–1070.

Marsden, Peter V. 1987. "Core Discussion Networks of Americans." *American Sociological Review* 52: 122–131.

Mattei, Franco, and Richard G. Niemi. 1991. "Unrealized Partisans, Realized Independents, and the Intergenerational Transmission of Partisan Identification." *Journal of Politics* 53: 161–174.

McAllister, Ian, and Martin P. Wattenberg. 1995. "Measuring Levels of Party Identification: Does Question Order Matter?" *Public Opinion Quarterly* 59: 259–268.

McClosky, Herbert. 1958. "Conservatism and Personality." *American Political Science Review* 52: 27–45.

———— 1964. "Consensus and Ideology in American Politics." *American Political Science Review* 58: 361–382.

McClosky, Herbert, and Alida Brill. 1983. *Dimensions of Tolerance: What Americans Believe About Civil Liberties.* New York: Russell Sage.

McClosky, Herbert, Paul J. Hoffman, and Rosemary O'Hara. 1960. "Issue Conflict and Consensus Among Party Leaders and Followers." *American Political Science Review* 54: 406–427.

McClosky, Herbert, and John Zaller. 1984. *The American Ethos.* Cambridge, Mass.: Harvard University Press.

McGinniss, Joe. 1988. *The Selling of the President.* New York: Penguin Books.

McGraw, Kathleen M., Milton Lodge, and Patrick Stroh. 1990. "On-Line Processing in Candidate Evaluation." *Political Behavior* 12: 41–59.

McGraw, Kathleen M., and Neil Pinney. 1990. "The Effects of General and Domain-Specific Expertise on Political Memory and Judgement." *Social Cognition* 8: 9–30.

McGraw, Kathleen M., and Marco Steenburgen. 1994. "Pictures in the Head: Memory Representations of Political Candidates." In *Political Judgment: Structure and Process,* edited by Milton Lodge and Kathleen McGraw. Ann Arbor, Mich.: University of Michigan Press.

McLeod, Jack M., and Lee B. Becker. 1981. "The Uses and Gratifications Approach." In *Handbook of Political Communication,* edited by Dan Nimmo and Keith R. Sanders. Beverly Hills, Calif.: Sage.

McWilliams, Wilson Carey. 1993. "The Meaning of the Election." In *The Election of 1992,* edited by Gerald M. Pomper. Chatham, N.J.: Chatham House.

———— 1995. *The Politics of Disappointment: American Elections 1976–94.* Chatham, N.J.: Chatham House.

Medvic, Stephen K. 1994. "The Political Attitudes of Generation X: A Preliminary

Inquiry." Paper presented at the annual meeting of the Midwest Political Science Association.

Milbrath, Lester W., and M. L. Goel. 1977. *Political Participation.* Chicago: Rand McNally.

Miller, Arthur H., Patricia Gurin, Gerald Gurin, and Oksana Melanchuk. 1981. "Group Consciousness and Political Participation." *American Journal of Political Science* 25: 494–511.

Miller, Arthur H., and Warren E. Miller. 1976. "A Majority Party in Disarray." *American Political Science Review* 70: 753–778.

Miller, Arthur H., and Martin P. Wattenberg. 1983. "Measuring Party Identification: Independent or No Partisan Preference?" *American Journal of Political Science* 27: 106–121.

Miller, Arthur H., Martin P. Wattenberg, and Oksana Melanchuk. 1986. "Schematic Assessments of Presidential Candidates." *American Political Science Review* 80: 521–540.

Miller, Warren E. 1956. "One-Party Politics and the Voter." *American Political Science Review* 50: 707–725.

———— 1980. "Disinterest, Disaffection, and Participation in Presidential Elections." *Poltical Behavior* 2: 7–32.

———— 1991. "Party Identification, Realignment, and Party Voting: Back to the Basics." *American Political Science Review* 85: 557–568.

———— 1991. "Party Identification." In *Political Parties and Elections in the United States: An Encyclopedia,* edited by L. Sandy Maisel. New York: Garland.

———— 1992. "The Puzzle Transformed: Explaining Declining Turnout." *Political Behavior* 14: 1–44.

———— 1992. "Generational Changes and Party Identification." *Political Behavior* 14: 333–360.

———— 1994. "An Organizational History of the Intellectual Origins of the National Election Studies." *European Journal of Political Research* 25: 247–265.

Miller, Warren E., and Morris Janowitz. 1952. "The Index of Political Predisposition in the 1948 Election." *Journal of Politics* 14: 710–727.

Miller, Warren E., and M. Kent Jennings. 1986. *Parties in Transition.* New York: Russell Sage.

Miller, Warren E., and Teresa E. Levitin. 1976. *Leadership and Change: Presidential Elections from 1952–1976.* Cambridge, Mass.: Winthrop.

Miller, Warren E., and J. Merrill Shanks. 1982. "Policy Directions and Presidential Leadership: Alternative Interpretations of the 1980 Presidential Election." *British Journal of Political Science* 12: 299–356.

Miller, Warren E., and Santa Traugott. 1989. *The American National Election Studies Data Sourcebook, 1952–1986.* Cambridge, Mass.: Harvard University Press.

Montjoy, Robert S., William R. Shaffer, and Ronald E. Weber. 1980. "Policy Preferences of Party Elites and Masses: Conflict or Consensus?" *American Politics Quarterly* 8: 319–344.

Morton, Rebecca B. 1991. "Groups in Rational Turnout Models." *American Journal of Political Science* 35: 758–776.

Mutz, Diana C., Paul Sniderman, and Richard Brody, eds. 1995. *Political Persuasion and Attitude Change.* Ann Arbor, Mich.: University of Michigan Press.

Nardulli, Peter F. 1989. "Geo-Political Cleavages, Conflict, and the American States." In *Diversity, Conflict, and State Politics: Regionalism in Illinois,* edited by Peter F. Nardulli. Urbana, Ill.: University of Illinois Press.

———— 1994. "A Normal Vote Approach to the Study of Electoral Change: Presidential Elections, 1828–1984." *Political Behavior* 16: 467–503.

———— 1995. "The Concept of a Critical Realignment, Electoral Behavior, and Political Change." *American Political Science Review* 89: 10–22.

Natchez, Peter B. 1970. "Images of Voting: The Social Psychologists." *Public Policy* 18: 53–58.

Nelson, Michael, ed. 1993. *The Elections of 1992.* Washington, D.C.: Congressional Quarterly Press.

Neuman, W. Russell. 1986. *The Paradox of Mass Politics: Knowledge and Opinion in the American Electorate.* Cambridge, Mass.: Harvard University Press.

Neuman, W. Russell, Marion Just, and Ann Crigler. 1992. *Common Knowledge: News and the Construction of Political Meaning.* Chicago: University of Chicago Press.

Nie, Norman H., Sidney Verba, and John Petrocik. 1979. *The Changing American Voter.* Cambridge, Mass.: Harvard University Press.

Niemi, Richard, and Larry Bartels. 1985. "New Measures of Issue Salience: An Evaluation." *Journal of Politics* 47: 1212–1220.

Niemi, Richard G., and M. Kent Jennings. 1991. "Issues and Inheritance in the Formation of Party Identification." *American Journal of Political Science* 35: 970–988.

Niemi, Richard G., Richard S. Katz, and David Newman. 1980. "Reconstruction, Past Partisanship: The Failure of the Party Identification Recall Question." *American Journal of Political Science* 24: 633–651.

Niemi, Richard G., David R. Reed, and Herbert F. Weisberg. 1987. "1987 Pilot Study First Choice Party Identification Question Experiment." NES Report, September 25.

———— 1991. "Partisan Commitment: A Research Note." *Political Behavior* 13: 213–21.

Niemi, Richard G., Stephen Wright, and Lynda W. Powell. 1987. "Multiple Party Identifiers and the Measurement of Party Identification." *Journal of Politics* 49: 1093–1103.

Nimmo, Dan, and Keith R. Sanders, eds. 1981. *Handbook of Political Communication.* Beverly Hills, Calif.: Sage.

Nimmo, Dan, and Robert L. Savage. 1976. *Candidates and Their Images*. Pacific Palisades, Calif.: Goodyear.

Nisbett, Richard E., and Timothy D. Wilson. 1977. "Telling More Than We Can Know: Verbal Reports of Mental Processes." *Psychological Review* 84 (May), pp. 231–259.

Noelle-Neumann, Elizabeth. 1984. *The Spiral of Silence: Public Opinion—Our Social Skin*. Chicago: University of Chicago Press.

Noll, Mark A., ed. 1990. *Religion and American Politics: From the Colonial Period to the 1980s*. New York: Oxford University Press.

Norpoth, Helmut. 1987. "Under Way and Here to Stay: Party Realignment in the 1980s?" *Public Opinion Quarterly* 51: 376–391.

Norpoth, Helmut, and Jerrold G. Rusk. 1982. "Partisan Realignment in the American Electorate: Itemizing the Deductions Since 1964." *American Political Science Review* 76: 522–537.

Olson, James M., and Zanna, Mark P. 1993. "Attitudes and Attitude Change." *Annual Review of Psychology* 44: 117–154.

Orenstein, Norman, Andrew Kohut, and Larry McCarthy. 1988. *The People, the Press, and Politics*. Reading, Mass.: Addison-Wesley.

Ottati, Victor, M. Fishbein, and S. E. Middlestadt. 1988. "Determinants of Voters' Beliefs About the Candidates' Stands on Issues: The Role of Evaluative Bias Heuristics and the Candidates' Expressed Message." *Journal of Political and Social Psychology* 55: 517–529.

Ottati, Victor C., Marco R. Steenbergen, and Ellen Riggle. 1992. "The Cognitive and Affective Components of Political Attitudes: Measuring the Determinants of Candidate Evaluations." *Political Behavior* 14: 423–442.

Ottati, Victor C., and Robert S. Wyer, Jr. 1993. "Affect and Political Judgement." In *Explorations in Political Psychology*, edited by Shanto Iyengar and William McGuire. Durham, N.C.: Duke University Press.

Page, Benjamin I. 1978. *Choices and Echoes in Presidential Elections*. Chicago: University of Chicago Press.

Page, Benjamin I., and Richard A. Brody. 1972. "Policy Voting and the Electoral Process: The Vietnam War Issue." *American Political Science Review* 66: 979–995.

Page, Benjamin, and Calvin Jones. 1979. "Reciprocal Effects of Policy Preferences, Party Loyalties, and the Vote." *American Political Science Review* 66: 979–985.

Page, Benjamin I., and Robert Y. Shapiro. 1992. *The Rational Public: Fifty Years of Trends in Americans' Policy Preferences*. Chicago: University of Chicago Press.

Palmquist, Bradley, and Donald P. Green. 1992. "Estimation of Models with Correlated Measurement Errors from Panel Data." In *Sociological Methodology*, vol. 22, edited by Peter V. Marsden. Washington, D.C.: American Sociological Association.

Park, Bernadette. 1986. "A Method for Studying the Development of Impressions of Real People." *Journal of Political and Social Psychology* 51: 907–917.

———— 1989. "Traits Attributes as On-Line Organizers in Person Impressions." In *On-Line Processes in Person Perception*, edited by John N. Bassili. Hillsdale, N.J.: Lawrence Erlbaum Associates.

Pateman, Carole. 1970. *Participation and Democratic Theory.* London: Cambridge University Press.

Patterson, Thomas E. 1980. *The Mass Media Election.* New York: Praeger.

———— 1993. *Out of Order.* New York: Knopf.

Patterson, Thomas E., and Robert D. McClure. 1976. *The Unseeing Eye: Myth of Television Power in Politics.* New York: Putnam.

Payne, John W., James R. Bettman, and Eric J. Johnson. 1992. "Behavioral Decision Research: A Constructive Processing Perspective." *Annual Review of Psychology* 43: 87–131.

Peterson, Steven A. 1992. "Church Participation and Political Participation." *American Politics Quarterly* 20: 123–139.

Petrocik, John R. 1974. "An Analysis of Intransitivities in the Index of Party Identification." *Political Methodology* 1(3): 31–47.

———— 1981. "Voter Turnout and Electoral Oscillation." *American Politics Quarterly* 9: 161–180.

———— 1987. "Realignment: New Party Coalitions and the Nationalization of the South." *Journal of Politics* 49: 347–375.

Pierce, Patrick A. 1993. "Political Sophistication and the Use of Candidate Traits in Candidate Evaluation." *Political Psychology* 14: 21–35.

Piven, Frances Fox, and Richard Cloward. 1988. *Why Americans Don't Vote.* New York: Pantheon.

Polsby, Nelson W., and Aaron Wildavsky. 1991. *Presidential Elections: Contemporary Strategies of American Electoral Politics,* 8th ed. New York: Free Press.

Pomper, Gerald M. 1981. "The Presidential Election." In *The Election of 1980,* edited by Gerald M. Pomper, et al. Chatham, N.J.: Chatham House.

———— ed. 1981. *The Election of 1980.* Chatham, N.J.: Chatham House.

———— ed. 1993. *The Election of 1992.* Chatham, N.J.: Chatham House.

Pomper, Gerald M., and Loretta A. Sernekos. 1991. "Bake Sales and Voting." *Society* 28: 10–16.

Popkin, Samuel L. 1994. *The Reasoning Voter,* 2nd ed. Chicago: University of Chicago Press.

Price, Vincent, and John Zaller. 1993. "Who Gets the News? Alternative Measures of News Reception and Their Implications for Research." *Public Opinion Quarterly* 57: 133–164.

Quirk, Paul J., and John K. Dalager. 1993. "The Election: A 'New Democrat' and a New Kind of Presidential Campaign." *The Elections of 1992,* edited by Michael Nelson. Washington, D.C.: Congressional Quarterly Press.

Rabinowitz, George. 1978. "On the Nature of Political Issues: Insights from a Spatial Analysis." *American Journal of Political Science* 22: 793–817.

Rabinowitz, George, and Stuart Elaine MacDonald. 1989. "A Directional Theory of Issue Voting." *American Political Science Review* 83: 93–121.

Ragsdale, Lyn. 1991. "Strong Feelings: Emotional Responses to Presidents." *Political Behavior* 13: 33–65.

Rahn, Wendy M. 1994. "Candidate Evaluation in Complex Information Environments: Cognitive Organization and Comparison Processes." In *Political Judgment: Structure and Process,* edited by Milton Lodge and Kathleen McGraw. Ann Arbor, Mich.: University of Michigan Press.

—— 1994. "In Search of Unified Field Theories of Voting Behavior: Reconciling Political Psychology and Political Behavior Accounts." Paper presented at the NES conference on candidate evaluation, Berkeley, Calif., December 2–3.

Rahn, Wendy M., John H. Aldrich, and Eugene Borgida. 1994. "Individual and Contextual Variations in Political Candidate Appraisal." *American Political Science Review* 88: 193–199.

Rahn, Wendy M., John H. Aldrich, John L. Sullivan, and Eugene Borgida. 1990. "A Social-Cognitive Model of Political Candidate Appraisal." In *Information and Democratic Processes,* edited by John Ferejohn and James Kuklinski. Urbana, Ill.: University of Illinois Press.

Rahn, Wendy M., and Katherine J. Cramer. 1994. "Activation and Application of Political Party Stereotypes: The Role of Cognitive Busyness." Paper presented at the annual meeting of the Midwest Political Science Association, Chicago, April.

Rahn, Wendy M., Jon A. Krosnik, and Marjke Breuning. 1994. "Rationalization and Derivation Processes in Survey Studies of Political Candidate Evaluation." *American Journal of Political Science* 38: 582–600.

Ranney, Austin. 1983. *Channels of Power: The Impact of Television on American Politics.* New York: Basic Books.

Rapoport, Ronald, and Walter Stone. 1992. "Disaggregating Political Change: The Case of the Iowa Caucuses, 1984–1988." *Journal of Politics* 54: 1074–1097.

Rivers, Douglas. 1988. "Heterogeneity in Models of Electoral Choice." *American Journal of Political Science* 32: 737–757.

Robertson, David. 1976. "Surrogates for Party Identification in the Rational Choice Framework." In *Party Identification and Beyond: Representations of Voting and Party Competition,* edited by Ian Budge, et al. London: Wiley.

Robinson, M. 1975. "American Political Legitimacy in an Era of Electronic Journalism: Reflections on the Evening News." In *Television as a Social Force: New Approaches to TV Criticism,* edited by D. Carter and R. Alder. New York: Praeger.

Rokeach, Milton. 1973. *The Nature of Human Values.* New York: Free Press.

Roseman, I., R. Abelson, and M. Ewing. 1986. "Emotions and Political Cognition: Emotional Appeals in Political Communication." In *Political Cognition,* edited by Richard R. Lau and David O. Sears. Hillsdale, N.J.: Lawrence Erlbaum Associates.

Rosenberg, Morris. 1968. *The Logic of Survey Analysis.* New York: Basic Books.

Rosenberg, Sharon. 1988. "The Structure of Political Thinking." *American Journal of Political Science* 32: 539–566.

Rosenberg, Shawn, L. Bohan, P. McCafferty, and K. Harris. 1986. "The Image and the Vote: The Effect of Candidate Presentation on Voter Preference." *American Journal of Political Science* 30: 108–127.

Rosenstone, Steven J., Roy L. Behr, and Edward H. Lazarus. 1988. *Third Parties in America: Citizen Response to Major Party Failure.* Princeton, N.J.: Princeton University Press.

Rosenstone, Steven J., and John Mark Hansen. 1993. *Mobilization, Participation and Democracy in America.* New York: Macmillan.

Rosenstone, Steven J., John Mark Hansen, and Donald R. Kinder. 1986. "Measuring Change in Personal Economic Well-Being." *Public Opinion Quarterly* 50: 176–192.

Salisbury, Robert, John Sprague, and Gregory Weiher. 1984. "Does Religious Pluralism Make a Difference? Interactions Among Context, Attendance and Political Behavior." Presented at the annual meeting of the American Political Science Association, Washington, D.C.

Sanders, Arthur. 1989. "Ideological Symbols." *American Politics Quarterly* 17: 227–255.

——— 1990. *Making Sense of Politics.* Ames, Iowa: Iowa State University Press.

Sapiro, Virginia. 1990. "The Women's Movement and the Creation of Gender Consciousness: Social Movements as Agents of Change." In *Political Socialization, Citizenship Education and Democracy,* edited by Orit Ichlov. New York: Teacher's College Press.

——— 1991. "Feminism: A Generation Later." *Annals of the American Academy of Political and Social Sciences* 515: 10–22.

Scammon, Richard M., and Ben J. Wattenberg. 1970. *The Real Majority.* New York: Coward-McCann.

Schank, R., and E. Langer, eds. 1994. *Beliefs, Reasoning, and Decision Making: Psycho-Logic in Honor of Bob Abelson.* Hillsdale, N.J.: Lawrence Erlbaum Associates.

Schickler, Eric, and Donald P. Green. 1995. "Issue Preferences and the Dynamics of Party Identification: A Methodological Critique." *Political Analysis,* forthcoming.

Schlesinger, Arthur, Jr. 1993. "The Turn of the Cycle." *The New Yorker,* 15 November: 46–54.

Schuman, Howard, Charlotte Steeh, and Lawrence Bobo. 1985. *Racial Attitudes in America.* Cambridge, Mass.: Harvard University Press.

Sears, David V. 1981. "Life-stage effects in attitude change, especially among the elderly." In *Aging: Social Change,* edited by Sara B. Kiesler, James N. Morgan, and Valerie K. Oppenheimer. New York: Academic Press.

Shafer, Byron E., ed. 1991. *The End of Realignment? Interpreting American Electoral Eras.* Madison, Wisc.: University of Wisconsin Press.

Shafer, Byron E., and William J. M. Claggett. 1994. "The Split Two-Party System: Partisans, Independents, and Policy Preferences." Paper presented at the annual meeting of the American Political Science Association, New York, September 1–4.

Shaffer, Stephen D. 1981. "A Multivariate Explanation of Decreasing Turnout in Presidential Elections." *American Journal of Political Science* 25: 68–95.

Shanks, J. Merrill, and David P. Glass. 1988. "Conflict and Consensus in Electoral Politics." Unpublished paper presented at the American Political Science Association.

Shanks, J. Merrill, and Warren E. Miller. 1990. "Policy Direction and Performance Evaluation: Complementary Explanations of the Reagan Elections." *British Journal of Political Science* 20: 143–235.

——— 1991. "Partisanship, Policy and Performance: The Reagan Legacy in the 1988 Election." *British Journal of Political Science* 21: 129–197.

Shanks, J. Merrill, with the assistance of Douglas A. Strand. 1994. "Unresolved Issues in Electoral Decisions: Alternative Perspectives on the Explanation of Individual Choice." In *Elections at Home and Abroad,* ed. M. Kurt Jennings and Thomas E. Mann. Ann Arbor: University of Michigan Press.

Shively, W. Phillips. 1979. "The Development of Party Identification Among Adults: Explanation of Functional Model." *American Political Science Review* 73: 1039–1054.

——— 1979. "The Relationships Between Age and Party Identification: A Cohort Analysis." *Political Methodology* 6: 437–446.

Silbey, Joel H. 1991. *The American Political Nation, 1838–1893.* Stanford, Calif.: Stanford University Press.

Smith, Charles E., and John H. Kessel. 1995. "The Partisan Choice: George Bush or Bill Clinton." In *Democracy's Feast, Elections in America,* edited by Herbert F. Weisberg. Chatham, N.J.: Chatham House.

Smith, Eric R. A. N. 1989. *The Unchanging American Voter.* Berkeley, Calif.: University of California Press.

Smith, Tom W. 1990. "Liberal and Conservative Trends in the United States Since World War II." *Public Opinion Quarterly* 54: 479–507.

Sniderman, Paul M. 1993. "The New Look in Public Opinion Research." In *Political Science: The State of the Discipline II,* edited by Ada W. Finifter. Washington, D.C.: American Political Science Association.

Sniderman, Paul M., Richard A. Brody, and Philip E. Tetlock. 1991. *Reasoning and Choice: Explorations in Political Psychology.* New York: Cambridge University Press.

Sniderman, Paul M., and Michael Gray Hagen. 1985. *Race and Inequality: A Study in American Values.* Chatham, N.J.: Chatham House.

Sniderman, Paul M., Philip E. Tetlock, and Edward G. Carmines, eds. 1993. *Prejudice, Politics, and the American Dilemma.* Stanford, Calif.: Stanford University Press.

Squire, Peverill, Raymond E. Wolfinger, and David P. Glass. 1987. "Residential Mobility and Voter Turnout." *American Political Science Review* 81: 45–65.

Stanley, Howard M. 1988. "Southern Partisan Changes: Dealignment, Realignment, or Both." *Journal of Politics* 50: 64–88.

Stark, Rodney, and Charles Y. Glock. 1968. *American Piety: The Nature of Religious Commitment.* Berkeley, Calif.: University of California Press.

Stewart, Marianne C., and Harold D. Clarke. 1992. "The (Un)Importance of Party Leaders: Leader Images and Party Choice in the 1987 British Elections." *Journal of Politics* 54: 447–470.

Stimson, James A. 1991. *Public Opinion in America.* Boulder, Colo.: Westview.

Stockton, Ronald R., and Frank W. Wayman. 1983. *A Time of Turmoil: Values and Voting in the 1970's.* East Lansing, Mich.: Michigan State University Press.

Stoker, Laura. 1993. "Judging Presidential Character: The Demise of Gary Hart." *Political Behavior* 15: 193–223.

———— 1994 "Race, Group-Interest, and American Public Opinion." Paper prepared for the annual meeting of the American Political Science Association, New York, September 1–4.

Stoker, Laura, and M. Kent Jennings. 1992. "Life-Cycle Transitions and Political Participation: The Case of Marriage." Revised version of a paper prepared for the annual meeting of the American Political Science Association, Chicago, September.

Stokes, Donald E. 1963. "Spatial Models of Party Competition." *American Political Science Review* 57: 368–377.

———— 1966. "Some Dynamic Elements of Contests for the President." *American Political Science Review* 60: 19–28.

Stokes, Donald E., and John J. Dilulio, Jr. 1993. "The Setting: Valence Politics in Modern Elections." In *The Elections of 1992,* edited by Michael Nelson. Washington, D.C.: Congressional Quarterly Press.

Stokes, Donald E., and Warren E. Miller. 1962. "Party Government and the Saliency of Congress." *Public Opinion Quarterly* 26: 531–546.

Stouffer, Samuel A. 1955. *Communism, Conformity, and Civil Liberties.* New York: Doubleday.

Straits, Bruce C. 1990. "The Social Context of Voter Turnout." *Public Opinion Quarterly* 54: 64–73.

———— 1991. "Bringing Strong Ties Back In: Interpersonal Gateways to Political Information and Influence." *Public Opinion Quarterly* 55: 432–488.

Sundquist, James L. 1973. *Dynamics of the Party System: Alignment and Realignment of Political Parties in the United States.* Washington, D.C.: Brookings Institution.

Swierenga, Robert P. 1990. "Ethnoreligious Political Behavior in the Mid-Nineteenth Century: Voting, Values, Cultures." In *Religion and American Politics,* edited by Mark A. Noll. New York: Oxford University Press.

Tanur, Judith M. 1992. *Questions about Questions.* New York: Russell Sage Foundation.

Tate, Katharine. 1992. *From Protest to Politics: The New Black Voters in American Elections.* Cambridge, Mass., and New York: Harvard University Press and Russell Sage Foundation.

Teixeira, Ruy A. 1987. *Why Americans Don't Vote: Turnout Decline in the United States, 1960–1984.* New York: Greenwood Press.

—— 1992. *The Disappearing American Voter.* Washington, D.C.: The Brookings Institution.

Thomassen, Jacques. 1976. "Party Identification as a Cross-National Concept: Its Meaning in the Netherlands." In *Party Identification and Beyond,* edited by Ian Budge, Ivor Crewe, and Dennis Farlie. London: Wiley.

Times-Mirror. 1994. *The People, the Press, and Politics: The New Political Landscape.* Washington, D.C.: Times-Mirror Organization.

Truman, David B. 1971. *The Governmental Process.* New York: Knopf.

Uhlaner, Carole J. 1986. "Political Participation, Rational Actors, and Rationality: A New Approach." *Political Psychology* 7: 551–573.

—— 1989. "Rational Turnout: The Neglected Role of Groups." *American Journal of Political Science* 33: 390–422.

Verba, Sidney, and Norman H. Nie. 1972. *Participation in America.* New York: Harper & Row.

Verba, Sidney, and Gary Orren. 1985. *Equality in America: The View from the Top.* Cambridge, Mass.: Harvard University Press.

Verba, Sidney, Kay Lehman Schlozman, Henry Brady, and Norman Nie. 1992. "Race/Ethnicity and Political Participation: The Role of Religion." Paper presented at the annual meeting of the American Political Science Association, Chicago.

Visser, Max. 1994. "The Psychology of the Voting Act." *Journal of the History of the Behavioral Sciences* 30: 43–52.

Wald, Kenneth D. 1990. "Political Cohesion in Churches." *Journal of Politics* 52: 197–215.

—— 1992. *Religion and Politics in the United States,* 2nd ed. Washington, D.C.: Congressional Quarterly.

Wald, Kenneth D., Lyman A. Kellstedt, and David C. Leege. 1993. "Church Involvement and Political Behavior." In *Rediscovering the Religious Factor in American Politics,* edited by David C. Leege and Lyman A. Kellstedt. Armonk, N.Y.: M E. Sharpe.

Wald, Kenneth D., Dennis E. Owen, and Samuel S. Hill. 1988. "Churches as Political Communities." *American Political Science Review* 82: 531–548.

Wald, Kenneth D., and Corwin E. Smidt. 1993. "Measurement Strategies in the Study of Religion and Politics." In *Rediscovering the Religious Factor in American Politics,* edited by David C. Leege and Lyman A. Kellstedt. Armonk, N.Y.: M E Sharpe.

Wattenberg, Martin P. 1984, 1990. *The Decline of American Political Parties, 1952–1992.* Cambridge, Mass.: Harvard University Press.

————— 1991. *The Rise of Candidate-Centered Politics.* Cambridge, Mass.: Harvard University Press.

Weber, M. 1978. *Economy and Society,* edited by G. Roth and C. Wittich. Berkeley, Calif.: University of California Press. (Original work published in 1922.)

Weisberg, Herbert F. 1980. "A Multidimensional Conceptualization of Party Identification." *Political Behavior* 2: 33–60.

————— 1987. "The Demographics of the New Voting Gap: Marital Differences in American Voting." *Public Opinion Quarterly* 51: 335–343.

————— ed. 1995. *Democracy's Feast: Elections in America.* Chatham, N.J.: Chatham House.

Weisberg, Herbert F., and Charles E. Smith, Jr. 1991. "The Influence of the Economy on Party Identification in the Reagan Years." *Journal of Politics* 53: 1077–1092.

Welch, Michael R., and David C. Leege. 1991. "Dual Reference Group and Political Orientations: An Examination of Evangelically Oriented Catholics." *American Journal of Political Science* 32: 28–56.

————— 1992. "Abortion Attitudes and the Potential for Political Mobilization Among American Catholics: Symbolic Politics, Boundary Maintenance, and Power of a Galvanizing Issue." Paper presented at the annual meeting of the American Political Science Association, Chicago.

Welch, Michael R., David C. Leege, and James C. Cavendish. 1995. "Attitudes toward Abortion among U.S. Catholics." *Social Science Quarterly* 76: 142–157.

Welch, Michael R., David C. Leege, Kenneth S. Wald, and Lyman A. Kellstedt. 1993. "Are the Sheep Hearing the Shepherd? Cue Perceptions, Congregational Responses, and Political Communication Processes." In *Rediscovering the Religious Factor in American Politics,* edited by David C. Leege and Lyman A. Kellstedt. Armonk, N.Y.: M E Sharpe.

Whiteley, Paul F. 1988. "The Causal Relationship Between Issues, Candidate Evaluations, Party Identification, and Vote Choice—The View From 'Rolling Thunder.'" *Journal of Politics* 50: 961–984.

Wilcox, Clyde, Ted G. Jelen, and David C. Leege. 1993. "Religious Group Identifications: Toward a Cognitive Theory of Religious Mobilization." In *Rediscovering the Religious Factor in American Politics,* edited by David C. Leege and Lyman A. Kellstedt. Armonk, N.Y.: M E Sharpe.

Wildavsky, Aaron. 1987. "Choosing Preferences by Constructing Institutions: A Cultural Theory of Preference Formation." *American Political Science Review* 81: 3–21.

Wilson, Timothy D., Delores Kraft, and Dana S. Dunn. 1989. "The Disruptive Effects of Explaining Attitudes: The Moderating Effect of Knowledge about the Attitude Object." *Journal of Experimental Social Psychology* 25: 379–400.

Wirls, Daniel. 1986. "Reinterpreting the Gender Gap." *Public Opinion Quarterly* 50: 316–330.

Wolfinger, Raymond E., and Steven J. Rosenstone. 1980. *Who Votes?* New Haven, Conn.: Yale University Press.

Wright, Gerald C. 1993. "Errors in Measuring Vote Choice in the National Election Studies, 1952–88." *American Journal of Political Science* 37: 291–316.

Zaller, John R. 1991. "Information, Values and Opinion." *American Political Science Review* 85: 1215–1237.

——— 1992. *The Nature and Origins of Mass Opinions.* Cambridge: Cambridge University Press.

Zaller, John R., and Stanley Feldman. 1992. "A Simple Theory of the Survey Response: Answering Questions versus Revealing Preferences." *American Journal of Political Science* 36: 579–616.

Zaller, John R., and Mark Hunt. 1994. "The Rise and Fall of Candidate Perot: Unmediated versus Mediated Politics—Part I." *Political Communication* 11: 357–390.

——— 1995. "The Rise and Fall of Candidate Perot: The Outsider versus the Political System—Part II." *Political Communication* 12: 97–123.

Index